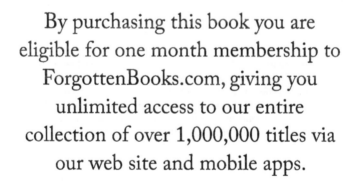

ISBN 978-0-428-19056-9
PIBN 10144591

# Livingstone's History
## of the
# Republican Party.

---

A HISTORY OF THE REPUBLICAN PARTY FROM ITS FOUNDATION TO THE CLOSE OF THE CAMPAIGN OF 1900, INCLUDING INCIDENTS OF MICHIGAN CAMPAIGNS AND BIOGRAPHICAL SKETCHES.

---

VOL. II.

---

DETROIT, MICHIGAN:
Wm. Livingstone, Publisher.

P
Winn
Detr

# TABLE OF CONTENTS.

## TABIE OF CONTENTS.

TABIE OF CONTENTS.

## TABIE OF CONTENTS.

TABLE OF CONTENTS.

## TABLE OF CONTENTS.

TABIE OF CONTENTS.

TABIE OF CONTENTS.

TABLE OF CONTENTS.

# INDEX TO PORTRAITS.

## INDEX TO PORTRAITS.

## INDEX TO PORTRAITS.

## INDEX TO PORTRAITS.

## INDEX TO PORTRAITS.

## INDEX TO PORTRAITS.

## NOTED SENATORIAL CONTESTS.

**Men Who Have Been Sent to the Upper House of Congress from Michigan Since the State Was Admitted—The List of Republican Senators Unbroken Since the Party Was Organized—A Roll of Distinguished Names From Chandler to Burrows—Two Cases in Which the Caucus Failed to Bind—A Few Other Close and Sharp Contests—Detailed Account of Ballots in the Various Contests—Senators Who Did Not Fill Out Their Terms—The Rare Case of an Appointee Who Declined the Honor—Out of Twelve Republican Senators Six Were Elected a Second Time.**

The United States Senators from Michigan elected since the first State Constitution was adopted, with their terms of service, have been as follows:

| Name. | Year. |
|---|---|
| Lucius Lyon | 1836-1840 |
| John Norvell | 1835-1841 |
| Augustus S. Porter | 1840-1845 |
| William Woodbridge | 1841-1847 |
| Lewis Cass | 1845-1848 |
| Alpheus Felch | 1847-1853 |
| Thomas Fitzgerald | 1848-1849 |
| Lewis Cass | 1849-1857 |
| Charles E. Stuart | 1853-1859 |
| Zachariah Chandler | 1857-1875 |
| Kinsley S. Bingham | 1859-1861 |
| Jacob M. Howard | 1862-1871 |
| Thomas W. Ferry | 1871-1883 |
| Isaac P. Christiancy | 1875-1879 |
| Zachariah Chandler | 1879-1879 |
| Henry P. Baldwin | 1879-1881 |
| Omar D. Conger | 1881-1887 |
| Thomas W. Palmer | 1883-1889 |
| Francis B. Stockbridge | 1887-1894 |
| James McMillan | 1889-1901 |
| John Patton, Jr | 1894-1895 |
| Julius C. Burrows | 1895-1905 |

From the time of its organization till 1854, the State was Democratic at every election except that of 1840, but the Whigs by carrying the Legislature at that time secured two United States Senators, Porter and Woodbridge. The Democrats had a chance to elect one in 1839, to succeed Lucius Lyon, but could not agree among themselves, and a vacancy remained for the Whigs to fill after their triumph the next year. Since the Republicans came into power in 1854 the Senators elected have all been of that party faith, though one of them, Mr. Christiancy, was elected mainly by Democratic votes. In a number of cases the result of the election has been practically determined beforehand, but in four cases, those of 1871, 1875, 1881 and 1883 the contest was close and exciting. In 1875 and 1883 bolts from the regular party nominations made the contests not only exciting but acrimonious.

Persons elected to the Senate did not always fill our their terms. Lewis Cass was elected for the term from 1845 to 1851, but resigned in 1848, after he was nominated for President, and Thomas Fitzgerald was appointed in his place. Failing of the Presidential election Cass was again elected to the Senate to fill out his own unexpired term, and then was elected for another full term. Zachariah Chandler died November 1, 1879. Fernando C. Beaman was appointed in his place, but declined the honor, and Henry P. Baldwin was then appointed. Mr. Baldwin was also elected in January, 1881, for the remainder of the term, but could not win the full term that followed. Francis B. Stockbridge died April 30, 1894, and five days later John Patton, Jr., of Grand Rapids, was appointed to fill the vacancy. Mr. Patton, however, was no more fortunate than Senators previously appointed, and only served from the time he received his appointment till the next Legislature had opportunity to elect.

The first opportunity the Republicans had to choose a United States Senator in Michigan was in 1857, when the term of General Cass expired. There was at first no decided concentration upon any one candidate, and after waiting until the 9th of January for holding a caucus, there were eight different names presented, all of them men who had shared in the organization of the party. The two in the lead were Zachariah Chandler, who was the last Whig candidate for Governor in 1852, and Isaac P. Christiancy, who was the Free Democratic candidate for Governor at the same election. Three informal ballots were had on the first night of the caucus, and adjournment was then taken until the next day. After the fourth ballot Christiancy's name was withdrawn and Chandler was nominated on the fifth. The ballots in detail were as follows, the first being informal:

| | 1 | 2 | 3 | 4 | 5 |
|---|---|---|---|---|---|
| Zachariah Chandler | 37 | 45 | 49 | 54 | 80 |
| Isaac P. Christiancy | 17 | 21 | 22 | 33 | 1 |
| Moses Wisner | 12 | 9 | 10 | .. | .. |
| Jacob M. Howard | 6 | 6 | 3 | 3 | 4 |
| Austin Blair | 11 | 7 | 6 | .. | .. |
| Kinsley S. Bingham | 3 | 4 | 1 | .. | .. |
| George A. Coe | 4 | .. | .. | .. | .. |
| James V. Campbell | 1 | .. | .. | .. | .. |
| Blank | .. | .. | 1 | .. | .. |
| H. H. Emmons | .. | .. | .. | 1 | 1 |

In 1859 some members of the Republican majority in the Legislature refused to go into caucus at all, unless the proceedings should be kept secret. Accordingly a conference was held with closed doors, lasting through the whole evening of January 6. An adjournment was then had until the next day, when the pledge of secrecy was removed and the doors were thrown open. The first ballot, informal, resulted in 48 votes for Kinsley S. Bingham; Fernando C. Beaman, 18; Austin Blair, 12; Hezekiah G. Wells, 1; David S. Walbridge, 2; blank, 1. The second ballot gave Bingham 74, to 6 scattering.

Senator Bingham died October 5, 1861, when his term was about half completed, and this precipitated an election to fill the vacancy at a special session of the Legislature in January, 1862. The candidates in the lead were Austin Blair and Jacob M. Howard. Six informal ballots and one formal ballot were taken for the nomination for Senator with the following result:

| | 1 | 2 | 3 | 4 | 5 | 6 | 7 |
|---|---|---|---|---|---|---|---|
| Jacob M. Howard | 21 | 33 | 38 | 39 | 39 | 44 | 49 |
| Austin Blair | 20 | 16 | 15 | 13 | 13 | 11 | 9 |
| H. G. Wells | 16 | 17 | 15 | 14 | 13 | 12 | 14 |
| I. P. Christiancy | 2 | 6 | 12 | 16 | 16 | 16 | 12 |
| Henry Waldron | 11 | 9 | 9 | 10 | 11 | 9 | 5 |
| Scattering | 22 | 12 | 4 | 2 | 1 | 1 | 2 |

Mr. Howard's nomination was then made unanimous.

In the campaign of 1862 the Fusion opposition to the Republicans made their hostility to the re-election of Senator Chandler an issue. The Republicans accepted the issue, and when the Legislature met in August, 1863, Mr. Chandler was unanimously renominated by acclamation. The Fusionists nominated James F. Joy in the hope of drawing Republican votes away from Chandler, but did not succeed, as the latter in the election received every Republican vote in both Houses.

In 1865, when Mr. Howard's term expired, only one candidate appeared against him, Ex-Governor Blair. One ballot settled the matter, Mr. Howard having 56 votes and Mr. Blair 42.

There was not, upon the surface, anything exciting nor even anything especially interesting in the canvass for the Senatorial nomination in 1869, but it was the occasion of a great deal of bitterness in the contest that came two years later. Governor Blair afterwards claimed that there was an understanding between himself and Thomas W. Ferry that they should use their combined strength to defeat Mr. Chandler, who had already served two terms, and to throw the nomination to the interior of the State. But, much to Mr. Blair's disappointment Mr. Ferry did not appear at Lansing at all while the vote was pending. In the caucus, out of 96 votes Chandler had 73, Blair and Ferry 3 each, 6 were blank, and the other 11 were distributed among six different candidates. Six weeks after that George W. Fish, of Flint, a friend of Blair's, wrote to the latter that he had learned the reason of Ferry's failure to carry out the agreement against Chandler. In a conversation on a railroad train Randolph Strickland had told him that an agreement had been reached by which Ferry was to receive the aid of the Chandler forces two years later, when Jacob M. Howard's term expired; that it was supposed Howard could not be renominated anyway, and that Ferry was toenter the field against Blair. Chagrined at the miscarriage of his plans, and angered at this information, Mr. Blair wrote to Mr. Fish, under date of Washington, February 28, 1869, a very bitter letter, attacking Jacob M. Howard, Chandler, Ferry and other Republicans.

Within the next two years Dr. Fish vacated his Federal office at Flint, leaving this letter either among his official papers, or, as he said, locked in his private desk. Wherever it was left a copy of it got away, and it cut quite a figure in the Senatorial canvass of 1871. For the nomination at that time there were four candidates; Jacob M. Howard, whose term was about to expire; William A. Howard, Austin Blair and Thomas W. Ferry. Detroit then had the Governor, and had for many years had both the Senators. The feeling was aroused that the Senatorship, this time, should go to the interior or Western part of the State. This feeling was so strong that it seemed to render certain the defeat of Jacob M. Howard. It operated also against William A. Howard, for though that gentleman was then a resident of Grand Rapids, he had lived for many years in Detroit. It was even said that he moved from Detroit to the Second City in order to be eligible for the nomination.

The Detroit Advertiser and Tribune, which had been troubled with Chandlerophobia for several years before this, had bitterly attacked him in 1869, and now supported Blair, because Chandler was opposed to him, if for no other reason. The Detroit Post, in accordance with its usual policy, kept hands off until the nomination was made, although it was well known that it was not friendly to Blair. Ferry was younger than either of the others, both in years and in political service. But he was very popular in his own Congressional district, which he had repeatedly carried by very large majorities, and he was supported by a large and hustling delegation of young men from the Western part of the State. When it came to a contest of lung power and claim-making they were winners. What, with this delegation and the friends of other candidates, there was the largest lobby in Lansing that had ever, up to that time, visited the Capital. It was generally thought beforehand that Ferry's chances were the best, although Blair's friends were confident. When the balloting came in caucus the two leading candidates started even. Then Ferry led slightly for two ballots, and after that Blair was ahead for two. The contest through these five ballots was so close that the excitement in the crowd that thronged Representatives Hall was intense. The sixth ballot was decisive in Ferry's favor, though by only one vote more than was required to nominate. The ballots in detail were as follows:

| | 1 | 2 | 3 | 4 | 5 | 6 |
|---|---|---|---|---|---|---|
| Thomas W. Ferry | 30 | 32 | 37 | 37 | 41 | 50 |
| Austin Blair | 30 | 31 | 35 | 40 | 43 | 43 |
| Jacob M. Howard | 20 | 18 | 16 | 15 | 9 | 4 |
| William A. Howard | 17 | 16 | 9 | 5 | 4 | .. |
| Whole number of votes | 97 | 97 | 97 | 97 | 97 | 97 |
| Necessary to a choice | 49 | 49 | 49 | 49 | 49 | 49 |

The Legislature and lobbying friends of the different candidates kept in reasonably good nature during the contest and accepted the result as final, though the Blair and Anti-Blair newspapers in Detroit continued to fight over it for some days thereafter.

There was some dispute afterwards as to how much Senator Chandler had to do with the result. He was not at Lansing any time during the contest, and his hand did not appear. But he was doubtless interested in the outcome. He said to the writer, four or five years later: "I could not, at that time, have elected either of the Howards if I had tried to. I might have elected Mr. Blair, but I did not choose to."

The sweeping Republican victory of 1872 was followed two years later by a turning of the tide in almost every state in the Union. This was chiefly due to the panic of 1873 and the financial and business depression that followed, though the Whisky Ring and Star Route scandals, and the irregularities that led to the impeachment trial of Secretary of War Belknap also had much to do with it. The tidal wave in Michigan not only cost the party three members of Congress but reduced the majority in the legislature much below the usual figure. In the House there were 53 Republicans to 47 Democrats, and in the Senate there were 18 Republicans to 14 Opposition. Among the latter was the Dr. George W. Fish, whose correspondence with Mr. Blair occasioned so much stir four years earlier. He was elected as an Independent, but acted with the Democrats throughout the session. The division of the two parties, so nearly equal, early gave the Democrats hope of defeating Senator Chandler for re-election, and they studiously fostered the discontent that existed in the minds of a few Republicans in the legislature. They were assisted by the influence of the Detroit Advertiser and Tribune, which had been bitterly and unreasonably hostile to Mr. Chandler for ten years previous, and by a few malcontents outside the legislature. The first step was to induce Republicans to stay out of the senatorial caucus, and in this they were successful beyond expectations, as of the 71 men elected as Republicans, only 57 attended the caucus. The vote there was fifty-two for Chandler, three for J. Webster Childs and one each for John J. Bagley and James V. Campbell.

The fourteen who were not in the caucus were the subjects of incessant attention during the few days between that and the election. Personal solicitation met them everywhere, and letters and dispatches from their constituents came in showers. About half of them were brought over to the support of Chandler, but the other half remained obdurate. They agreed among themselves not to vote for any Democrat, but to vote for any Republican upon whom the Democrats could unite. But here came another difficulty. Although Mr. Chandler was a strong partisan in political matters, he had looked after the interests of the State and the claims of its citizens, without reference to party, and several of the Democratic members said they would prefer Chandler to any other Republican. But the strongest party pressure was brought to bear upon these men, and in some cases threats were made that none of the bills in which they were interested should be allowed to pass unless they went with the party. They all surrendered, one by one, and in the end the Democratic vote was solid. The attempt was made first to unite on J. Webster Childs, of Washtenaw County, himself one of the malcontent Republicans, but his mental equipment was such that the suggestion of his succeeding Chandler in the Senate excited only ridicule. Justice Thomas M. Cooley was then tried, but without success. It was difficult then, and is now, to understand why an agreement could not be reached on Judge Cooley, for he was one of the ablest and clearest headed men in the State, and although twice elected to the Supreme Bench as a Republican, he was not a partisan. In fact party obligations rested very lightly upon him.

The caucus was held January 7, and when the time for the election came, January 19, no agreement had yet been reached. The Democrats and bolters had a conference the night before, and it was afterwards reported that all the Democrats and all the bolters except three, had agreed to vote for Judge Christiancy, but this was denied by some members who attended. A few Democrats still held out in their purpose not to vote for any Republican. A conference of about sixty Republicans was held the same evening, and figured out seventeen sure votes for Chandler in the Senate and forty-five or forty-six in the House. When the vote was taken in the Legislature on the 19th, Chandler had seventeen in the Senate and forty-six in the House, a total of sixty-three, or four less than the number required to elect. The opposition vote was scattered among nine different candidates in the Senate and thirteen in the House. The disaffected Republicans voted, four for J. Webster Childs, three for Isaac P. Christiancy, and one for John J. Bagley.

A long conference was held that evening between seven of the disaffected Republicans and a committee of the regular Republicans. All of the former except E. I. Briggs, of Kent, pledged themselves not to vote for any Democrat. They refused to vote for Chandler, but offered to compromise on John J. Bagley, Henry Waldron or Omar D. Conger. This the Chandler Republicans refused to do, and the conference was fruitless of results. In joint convention the next day

Chandler had 64 votes, G. V. N. Lothrop 60, Isaac P. Christiancy 5 and J. Webster Childs 2. The result was a disappointment to the opposition, who had expected a break in the Chandler forces, but it was not sufficiently encouraging to the latter to make them desire another trial that day. An adjournment was had, therefore, by vote of more than two to one. The Democrats spent the evening in their utmost efforts to combine on Christiancy. Five of their number had repeatedly said that they would not under any circumstances vote for him, but that if the Democrats took up him or any Republican they should vote for Chandler. They doubtless thought so then, but party pressure proved too much for them. Three of the Republican bolters promised that if Christiancy was not elected on the first roll call the next day, they would fall into line for Chandler, but they were not called upon to redeem their promise.

When the joint convention met on the 21st, Representatives Hall was, as on the previous day, crowded, and the responses of the first few Senators were awaited with breathless interest. In the Senate there were only two votes regarding which there was any question, those of Senator Jones, of Branch County, who was one of the bolting Republicans, and Senator White, of Marquette, who was personally friendly to Chandler, and who had been opposed to the combination on Christiancy. Jones voted for Christiancy, and when White did the same such whispered remarks as "that settles the matter," "that fixes it," etc., were heard in various directions. The votes of three or four Republican Representatives, who it was claimed, would desert Mr. Chandler were awaited with curiosity, and those of two or three Democrats, who it was supposed would hold out against Christiancy were also watched with interest. But the regular Republicans all held firm except one and the Democrats stood together to a man. The end of the roll call gave Christiancy 68, Chandler 63, John J. Bagley 1. Mr. Briggs then changed his vote from Christiancy to J. Webster Childs, leaving the former with barely enough to elect. Desperate efforts were made to induce the Branch County Representatives to change from Christiancy to some one else, so as to put the election over one day and give opportunity to unite on some other Republican than Chandler. But it was too late, and Christiancy was declared elected. The Republicans who voted for him were Senator John H. Jones and Representatives Robinson and Van Aken, of Branch County; LeRoy Parker, of Genesee; E. L. Briggs, of Kent; Lorison J. Taylor, of Shiawassee, and Cady Neff, of Wayne. Of these Parker had given his most solemn promise, after he reached Lansing, that he would vote for Chandler, and confirmed the promise by shaking hands with the members to whom he made it. The Branch County Convention, at which one of the Representatives from that County was nominated, and in which the other was a delegate, declared in favor of Senator Chandler. Without questioning the motives of the other four, these three were the special objects of Republican wrath. None of the seven cut much of a figure in politics after that, except Taylor, who was in the State Senate two years later and who had a transitory prominence in the Greenback party. The hostilities engendered during this contest were bitter and enduring, and even had a determining effect on the Senatorial contest six years later.

In an authorized interview the day after his election to the Senate, Mr. Christiancy dispelled some of the illusions under which the bolters and Democrats had voted for him. He said that he was as good a Republican as ever; that he did not support Greeley for President, nor seek a nomination for Congress on the Greeley ticket. On the contrary, though he received several letters urging him to run on such a ticket, he refused. He heartily supported the Constitutional Amendments, and always had. He had always advocated free trade doctrines when there was an opportunity to adopt them. But there would not be such opportunity in this country during the lifetime of the present generation. As long as we had a large public debt we must have a large revenue, and part of it must come from the tariff, and as long as we had a tariff it should furnish incidental protection. One of the Democrats, whose first personal choice was Mr. Chandler, and who intended to yield that choice only in favor of a pronounced Democrat, was boasting, after the election, of the victory and quoted the statements which had been made to him in proof of Mr. Christiancy's Democracy. He was induced to call on the Senator-elect, and after hearing his views, came out and remarked: "I have been lied to or I never would have voted for him."

When in the Senate Mr. Christiancy acted uniformly with the Republicans. But the duties of the position were distasteful to him. He had been long on the bench and his habits were those of the scholar, rather than of the practical legislator. On the 8th of February, 1879, he sent to Governor Croswell his resignation as Senator to take effect February 10th. The Legislature being then in session, a new election became necessary, and Republican opinion as well as popular expectation pointed to Zachariah Chandler as the man to fill out the term to which a large majority of Republicans in the Legislature had sought to elect him in 1875. The only other person mentioned in connection with the position was ex-Governor John J. Bagley. At first Mr. Bagley's candidacy was spoken of seriously, but the current set so strongly in favor of Chandler that the Governor's friends finally announced that they desired to give him as large a complimentary vote as possible on the first ballot, and then withdraw his name. The caucus was held February 13, Chandler receiving 69 votes, Bagley 19, and Thomas W. Palmer 1. Representative George H. Hopkins, in behalf of Governor Bagley's friends, and at his request, moved to make the nomination unanimous. This was done. In the election on the 20th Mr. Chandler received the vote of every Republican present, 88 in all, to 22 for Orlando M. Barnes, Democrat, and 18 for Henry Chamberlain, National.

The Senatorial election in 1881 was, in the final caucus vote, the closest of any in the whole history of the party. There were three candidates in the field, with chances at the outset appearing somewhat nearly even. They were Ex-Governor John J. Bagley, Senator Henry P. Baldwin and Congressman Omar D. Conger. There were 116 Republicans in the Legislature and of these the friends of Bagley and Baldwin each claimed in the neighborhood of fifty on the first ballot, some of the claims going much higher than that. Conger's friends made no definite claims, but gave reasons for expecting a favorable conclusion to the contest. The Legislature did not meet until the 5th of January, and the Senatorial caucus was called for the same evening. There was an exceedingly large lobby present consisting of friends of all of the candidates from all parts of the State. The nominating speeches were of a high order, and the result of the first ballot was awaited with intense interest. It was a disappointment to two of the candidates. Governor Baldwin's friends had, that afternoon, raised their claims to fifty-one votes, and some of Bagley's friends went as high as sixty-two for him. The Conger men were very well satisfied, as he had received more votes than the others had, at any time, conceded him. On subsequent votes Conger and Bagley made slight gains, while Baldwin lost, until at the end of the fifth ballot Senator Farr, of Ottawa, stepped on a chair and said: "At the request of the friends of Senator Baldwin I withdraw his name and substitute in its place the name of the great Commoner, Omar D. Conger." This bold attempt to stampede the caucus for Conger was promptly checked by Senator Patterson, of Calhoun, who stood upon a seat and said excitedly: "I have the right to control my own vote. I have voted for Henry P. Baldwin for my first choice; now I vote for John J. Bagley as my second choice." Representative Adam E. Bloom, of Detroit, followed with: "I have voted for Henry P. Baldwin for my first choice; now I vote for Omar D. Conger." Then Senator James Caplis jumped upon a chair and sought to make himself heard amid loud cries of "ballot," "ballot," "Conger," "Conger." In the confusion Caplis was heard to say: "I shall stay here all night before I will relinquish my right to the floor." Order was finally restored and then Senator Caplis said: "I appeal to the members of this caucus, the friends of Senator Baldwin, not to be carried over bodily by the Senator from Grand Haven and the distinguished gentleman from Wayne." Another ballot was taken and stood 59 for Conger to 58 for Bagley. As this was one more vote than there were members present it was not announced, but it soon became known. There was then a great hustling of the Bagley men to break the Conger lines, but without avail, and the next ballot showed Conger two ahead, giving him the nomination. Jonathan J. Woodman had one vote on the first ballot. The votes for the others, by ballots, were as follows, 59 being in each case necessary to a choice:

| | 1 | 2 | 3 | 4 | 5 | 6 | 7 |
|---|---|---|---|---|---|---|---|
| Omar D. Conger........ | 32 | 33 | 34 | 36 | 36 | 38 | 59 |
| John J. Bagley.......... | 43 | 45 | 44 | 44 | 45 | 48 | 57 |
| Henry P. Baldwin....... | 40 | 38 | 38 | 36 | 35 | 30 | .. |

The disappointment of Governor Bagley and his friends was embittered by the fact that in Detroit they had practically controlled the City Convention, and for the most part dictated the Legislative nominations. Adam E. Bloom, who was at the time non-committal on the Senatorial nomination, might, they thought, have been kept off the ticket, and a staunch Bagley man nominated in his place. But they learned his attitude too late.

The Senatorial election of 1883 was long and bitter, and left animosities that lasted for years. Senator Ferry was a candidate for re-election, but long before the Legislature met opposition to him was organized by a number of Republicans who met at the Russell House in Detroit. The occasion was favorable for the sowing of disaffection. The party had just, for the first time, been defeated on the head of its ticket, and there was much of ill-feeling and discontent in its ranks.

Mr. Ferry was in no wise responsible for the misfortunes of the last election, but he happened to be the convenient victim. The opposition to him was so well fostered and organized that before the Legislature met nearly twenty members had decided not to go into a Senatorial caucus conducted after the usual manner. Their purpose finally took definite form in the adoption of a resolution signed by nineteen members and having this wording; "That we will attend any caucus of the Republican members of the Legislature wherein 67 Republican votes are necessary to nominate a candidate for the United States Senate, and it is so stated in the call for such caucus." One of the men who signed the stipulation said, and he represented the sentiment of others, that he was not a bolter. He called attention to the number of Federal officeholders that were working for Ferry, and said that he declined to submit to their dictation. He was trying to vindicate and sustain the integrity of the Republican party. This paper was signed on Wednesday, January 3. The next evening a caucus was held which none of the nineteen attended. On an informal ballot it gave Ferry 46 votes, to 10 divided among eight different candidates. On a formal ballot Ferry had 50 votes to 6 scattering. There were 81 Republican members of the Legislature, so that 25 did not vote at this caucus, although some of them afterwards voted for Ferry.

On Tuesday, January 16, the vote was taken in the Legislature when Ferry had 59, Bryan G. Stout, Democrat, 50, and the rest were scattered among fifteen different candidates. The balloting continued at intervals till the 1st of March, the feeling growing more and more embittered all the time. Ferry's vote never exceeded that on the first ballot, and he dropped out of the race about the middle of February. The highest vote reached by any other Republicans until the last day of the balloting, was 33 each for Thomas W. Palmer and Francis B. Stockbridge. The Democrats tried, at different times, concentrating their votes on Byron G. Stout, William Newton, George V. N. Lothrop, Henry Chamberlain, O. M. Barnes and Charles S. May, but did not, with any of these except Stout, reach as high as 50 votes. On the 28th of February the Republican State Convention met at East Saginaw, and there was such an expression of impatience there at the prolonged contest that the Republicans in the Legislature were spurred to an effort to terminate it. They had been gradually approaching an agreement that whenever, in joint convention, any one received a clear majority of all the Republican votes cast, enough others would go to him to give him the nomination. That point was reached on the eighty-first ballot, which was as follows:

| | |
|---|---|
| Byron G. Stout | 42 |
| Thomas W. Palmer | 40 |
| Moreau S. Crosby | 20 |
| Charles Upson | 8 |
| Thomas W. Ferry | 6 |
| James B. Angell | 1 |
| Perry Hannah | 1 |
| Edwin Willits | 1 |
| Marsden C. Burch | 1 |
| J. W. Champlin | 1 |
| Whole number of votes | 121 |
| Necessary to a choice | 61 |

There were 78 Republican votes cast, so that Mr. Palmer's 40 gave him the required majority. Changes were speedily made, enough to give him 75 votes and the election. His election was acceptable to all Republicans except a few of those who first put up the fight against Ferry. But the effects of the long and bitter contest were disastrous to the party, for in the spring election which came a month later, both the Republican candidates for Supreme Court Judge, and those for Regents of the University were defeated.

The Senatorial contest of 1887 was short, and without any elements of bitterness. The first ballot in the Republican caucus was as follows:

| | |
|---|---|
| Francis B. Stockbridge | 34 |
| Omar D. Conger | 23 |
| Edward S. Iacey | 10 |
| J. C. Fitzgerald | 7 |
| Jay A. Hubbell | 4 |
| John K. Boies | 3 |
| E. B. Fairfield | 2 |

And one each for six other candidates.

The tenth and decisive ballot gave Stockbridge 46, Conger 23, Iacey 16, Fitzgerald 2, Hubbell and Henry W. Seymour one each.

In the Senatorial elections of 1889 and 1895 there was a refreshing unanimity after the contests that had preceded. At the first date James McMillan was nominated by acclamation, no other name being mentioned. In 1895 Mr. McMillan was not only renominated by acclamation, but was re-elected by unanimous vote. From the clean sweep which the Republicans made at the previous election only one solitary Democrat escaped to sit in the Legislature, "John Donovan, of Bay." When it came to the Senatorial election Mr. Donovan thought it not best to disturb the harmony of the occasion, and voted for McMillan with the rest.

In 1893 there was a warm, and what at one time promised to be a close, contest between Senator Stockbridge and Ex-Governor Luce. There were several days of active canvassing, in which the question arose whether the vote in caucus should be secret or viva voce. The Stockbridge men were at first inclined to insist upon the former, but finally yielded that point. When the caucus was held the Luce men introduced a resolution that it should require a majority of all the Republicans elected to nominate, but this proposition was lost by a vote of 38 to 47, which was considered nearly a test of the Stockbridge and Anti-Stockbridge strength. The only ballot taken was as follows.

| | |
|---|---|
| Francis B. Stockbridge | 46 |
| Cyrus G. Luce | 20 |
| Jay A. Hubbell | 10 |
| William Hartsuff | 3 |
| Jonathan G. Ramsdell | 2 |
| Oliver L. Spaulding | 2 |
| J. C. Fitzgerald | 1 |
| James O'Donnell | 1 |
| Byron M. Cutcheon | 1 |
| Total | 86 |
| Necessary to a choice | 44 |

The nomination was then made unanimous.

The death of Mr. Stockbridge in 1894 left a vacancy which was filled temporarily by the appointment of John Patton, Jr., but which required another election when the Legislature met in 1895. There were three candidates in the field, all with confident claims, but the matter was settled by two ballots as follows:

| | 1 | 2 |
|---|---|---|
| Julius C. Burrows | 64 | 70 |
| Schuyler S. Olds | 32 | 32 |
| John Patton, Jr. | 23 | 25 |
| Samuel M. Stephenson | 7 | .. |
| Jay A. Hubbell | 5 | 4 |
| Total number of votes | 131 | 131 |
| Necessary to a choice | 66 | 66 |

In 1899 when the term, of which Mr. Burrows had served a part, was completed, efforts were made to induce three or four different candidates to take the field against him. Albert Pack finally consented to make the run, and for a time with a fair show of strength, but as the time for the caucus approached he became convinced that he could not win and withdrew. Mr. Burrows was then renominated by acclamation, and was elected by the full Republican vote.

The first Senatorial nomination of the present century was made with unanimity and under unusually brilliant circumstances. It occurred on the afternoon of January 1, 1901, in Representative Hall, Lansing. In addition to the Republican members of the Legislature, there were some of the State officers and many prominent politicians present, while the galleries were occupied by ladies who took advantage of a pleasant holiday to witness a political ceremony. James McMillan was placed in nomination for a third term as United States Senator, the nomination was supported in half a dozen graceful and complimentary speeches, and was then made unanimous by acclamation.

Of the twelve Republican Senators elected in this State six were so honored more than once, two died before their terms expired and one resigned. To the practice of giving a second term to those whose services are acceptable, and who are in the field for that honor, is due in part, the commanding position which the State has held in that body.

## II.

## THE STATE INSTITUTIONS.

**The Educational, Elemosynary, Reformatory and Penal Institutions of Michigan—Nearly All Established Since the Republican Party Came into Power—They Rank with the Best in the Country—Iiberal Provision Made for All the Needs of the State.**

The right of the Republican party to rule could have no better demonstration than the manner in which it has adapted itself to the changing needs of a rapidly growing State. It has been obliged, in Michigan, to meet the wants, coming not only from a natural growth under established conditions, but those coming from newly created conditions of business and of industrial and economic life. When the Constitution of 1850 was adopted the State had just recovered from the blighting effects of a period of inflation and of wild speculation, and that Constitution was framed with certain narrow limitations intended to prevent similar disastrous results in the future. The State had a population of less than 400,000, and their business wants were largely those of an agricultural people. Four years later, when the Republican party was organized, the population had increased to 511,720, but business conditions remained very much the same. Wayne County had then 65,778 people and Kent 17,809, and the modern problems in municipal government were yet to be worked out to meet the needs of the populous cities that have since grown up within her borders. Saginaw County then had 1,653 people, two saw mills, with a capital investment of $8,000, and a cut of 1,500,000 feet of lumber annually, while Bay County was not yet organized. The law makers of that day had not dreamed of the legislation necessary for the regulation of an industry that, less than thirty years later, cut over a thousand million feet of lumber in the Saginaw Valley alone in a single season, and three times as much as that in other parts of Michigan; that involved the control of scores of logging streams and many logging railroads; that covered two thirds of the State with lumber camps; that made the enactment of boom and scaling laws necessary; that required, in short, an entirely new body of legislation. The manufacture of salt, an attendant industry to lumber, had not then been taken into account, and there were no laws for its inspection. There was in 1854 only one coal mine in the State, which took out a product valued at $180 the year before. There were only three organized Counties in the Upper Peninsula, Michilimackinac, Houghton and Ontonagon. There was only one developed iron mine, whose product the year before was valued at $32,750. The whole body of legislation regulating this immense industry has been enacted since then. The whole copper product for the census year 1854 was 3,447,881 pounds, equal to about a fortnight's production of the largest mine of the present day. The laws covering this industry were also a creation of the next thirty years. The more numerous and vastly more important railroad laws were enacted during the period of Republican supremacy. So of the Banking Law, the Law for the Incorporation of Manufacturing Companies, the laws creating the present system of courts, the laws controlling the fisheries and regulating the taking of fish and game—in fact all the laws that distinguish the needs of nearly two and a half million people, with diversified industries, from the needs of one-fifth that number depending mainly on one industry.

In nothing has greater progress been made under Republican Administrations in Michigan than in the matter of institutions for promoting the higher education, and for taking care of the unfortunate, the dependent and the criminal. In 1854, there were only three State institutions—the Prison at Jackson, the University at Ann Arbor, and the Normal School, then only two years old, at Ypsilanti. The care of criminals, and the neglect of the unfortunate classes were both of a character that is shocking to the humane spirit of the present age. Criminals of both sexes, and of all degrees of crime, except for misdemeanors involving a comparatively slight penalty, were confined in the same prison, under unwholesome sanitary conditions and without adequate employment. In the County jails boys and girls, under accusation or penalty for minor offenses, were brought in contact with criminals of the worst classes, from whom they could hardly fail to receive a moral taint, even when they did not learn lessons in actual crime. Legislation and supervision since then have brought wonderful changes in these institutions. The severe discipline at the State Prison has been relaxed, regular employment is furnished to nearly all the convicts, opportunities for instruction have been increased and the sanitary condition of the prison has been improved. This institution has been supplemented by the construction of a branch prison in the Upper Peninsula. By the construction of the State House of Correction at Ionia, opportunity has been made for the separation of different grades of criminals, and the whole system has been so modified as to give less of cruel punishment and more hope of reformation. But the best work in this direction is in the changes of the methods of treating the youth of both sexes who are viciously inclined. The Industrial School for Boys at Lansing, formerly called the Reform School, was built as a sort of sub-prison, for the discipline of boys caught in petty crimes. It had, at the outset, the advantage of taking them away from the contaminating influences of the County jails, but it still put the stamp of crime upon them. The aim of the school now is educational and reformatory, rather than penal. Although high walls and prison bars have been removed there are few escapes or runaways, nor have the boys been spoiled by kind treatment. The 650 inmates of the institution have four and one-half hours a day of instruction in the studies that make up a common school education, and are taught besides the industrial trades of carpentry, printing, baking, shoemaking, tailoring and farming. The proportion of those who graduate into good citizenship is very large, while that of those who fall back into crime is small. The Industrial School for Girls, established in 1879 for the reformation of juvenile female offenders, does similar work for its 350 inmates, teaching them cooking, sewing, knitting, dressmaking and all useful duties of the household.

Half a century ago the insane who were not cared for in their own homes were locked up in cells and in the poor houses, with little regard for their comfort and no care suited to their maladies. Now four large asylums, located respectively at Kalamazoo, Pontiac, Traverse City and Newberry, and one for the homicidal and criminal insane at Ionia, give the best of care that medical skill and the most careful studies of maladies of the mind can devise.

A school at Lansing for the blind, one at Flint for the deaf, one at Coldwater for dependent children, one at Lapeer for the epileptic and feeble minded, and a home for veteran soldiers at Grand Rapids, are other institutions which an enlightened humanity has established under Republican rule.

There is no other State in the West that has provided so amply for the higher education as Michigan. Its University goes back in its foundations to Territorial days, although its real growth as an educational institution of the higher order has been mostly within the past half century. It has met with some discouragements, and has sometimes been cramped for funds, but all recent Legislatures have been reasonably liberal with appropriations for its support. In speaking of the Universities of the country it is always mentioned in the same class with Harvard and Yale among the older institutions, and with Cornell among the younger, while the general appreciation of its excellent work is shown by the number of students, ranging in recent years from 3,000 to 3,450.

Next to the University in point of age, among the State educational institutions, is the Normal College at Ypsilanti, originally called the State Normal School. It is one of numerous evidences of the progressive character of the people of Michigan that this State was the fourth in the Union to establish such an institution, only Massachusetts, New York and Connecticut preceding it. As early as 1848 Bills were introduced into the Legislature for establishing a separate department of the University for the instruction of teachers, and for the establishment of temporary normal schools, or teachers' institutes. The Senate passed a Bill providing that one of the branches of the University should be organized as a Normal School, but this did not pass the House. None of the Bills became laws, but the agitation of the subject at this time produced results the next year, when a Bill passed providing for the establishment of a separate Normal School, and providing also for a State Board of Education, to have charge, among other duties, of this institution. That and a supplementary Act were consolidated in 1850, and it was under this legislation that the State Normal School began its existence. It is among the best equipped schools in the country, as well as among the largest in the number of its students. During some portion of the year 1899 there were 1,029 students in attendance in the Normal Department, and 294 in the Training School, with 271 graduates for the year. The success of this institution in supplying the schools of the State with competent teachers led to the establishment, in 1895, of a second Normal School at Mount Pleasant, which in its third year had 314 students.

Among the educational institutions that have shown rapid growth within the past few years is the State Agricultural College. The Constitution of 1850 required the Legislature to provide, "as soon as practicable, for the establishment of an Agricultural School," but it was not until 1855 that an Act in conformity with this provision was passed. This Act provided for the selection of a site which was to be within ten miles of Lansing, and on not less than five hundred acres, nor more than one thousand acres in one body, at a cost not to exceed fifteen dollars per acre. On the 16th of June, 1855, the location for the college was fixed upon a tract of 676.57 acres, and the conveyance was made to the State of Michigan. About three acres of the land only was cleared at the time of the purchase, the conditions prescribed by law, as to price and nearness to Lansing, very much restricting the choice of a site. The College was put under the supervision of a State Board of Education, where it remained until the close of the year 1860. This Board having erected a College Hall, a boarding-hall, a brick barn, and purchased some farm implements, stock, etc., opened the college to students the 13th of May, 1857. The students worked three hours daily, and within a year sixty acres were brought under cultivation. The next year four brick dwellinghouses were erected, and a small wooden dwelling house purchased and repaired, for the occupancy of the foreman of the farm.

This was not a very encouraging start for a great educational institution and the Board of Education gladly relinquished the care of it. In 1861 a State Board of Agriculture was created, among its prescribed duties being the control of the College. It was many years before the College came into great favor with the class for whom it was especially intended. There was some jealousy between its supporters and those of the University, and there was complaint that the studies were too little in the direction of the industrial and the practical. There has, however, been a great change in this respect, within the past few years. The college is now one of the leading institutions in the country and its students count up among the largest in number of any industrial institution in the country, and the change has been brought about largely through the genius of one man.

JONATHAN LE MOYNE SNYDER, to whom the College owes much of its present prosperity, was born on a farm in Butler County, Pennsylvania, October 29th, 1859, his parents being Hiram Snyder, a farmer, and Eliza Patton Snyder. His father's family, several generations back, came from Holland and his mother's family was Scotch Irish. He was educated in Westminster College, Pennsylvania, graduated from the classical course in 1886; received the degree of A. M. in 1889, and completed a post graduate course in 1891, receiving the

*J. L. Snyder.*

degree of Ph. D. He was brought up on a farm and made his way through college by teaching country school. After graduating he was principal of a Village school for one year, then was elected Superintendent of Schools of Butler County, Pennsylvania; was elected for a term of three years and resigned at the end of the second year to accept the principalship of the Fifth Ward Schools in Allegheny, Pa. He remained in this position seven years, and resigned to accept the Presidency of the Michigan Agricultural College. While Superintendent of the Butler County schools he assisted in the establishment of the Slippery Rock Normal School, which is now one of the best schools in the country. He also introduced into the common schools a graded course of study which has been largely accepted by the schools of Pennsylvania and other states. The City school of which he had charge was one of the largest in the country, having an enrollment of fifteen hundred pupils and thirty-three teachers. During his administration, in connection with this school a very fine manual training department was established. A building was erected for this special purpose and to the boys were given wood and iron work, mechanical drawing, etc., and to the girls cooking and sewing. This is considered one of the finest manual training departments in connection with a grammar school in the whole country. Mr. Snyder was married to Clare Maude Mifflin, June 15th, 1892, and has three boys: Robert Mifflin, Le Moyne, and Halderman Patton. He has had charge of the Agricultural College since March 20th, 1896. During these four years the attendance has rapidly increased. Special courses have been added in agriculture, a five-year course in mechanical engineering, and the women's department. Many improvements have been made in the way of building. The street car and railroad have been brought upon the campus; the women's building, dairy and barns have been erected and rapid progress made along all lines of work. The improved methods have not only largely increased the number of students, but have infused a new spirit, enthusiasm and zest into their work.

The latest addition to the educational institutions of the State is the College of Mines at Houghton. It was established under an Act passed in 1885, but did not receive funds for its proper equipment and successful working till three years later. It has already taken rank as one of the largest and foremost schools of mining engineering in the country, and the only one which has a full and free electric system. This institution fairly rounds out an educational system fully adapted to the wants of this modern era.

## III.

## BIOGRAPHICAL SKETCHES OF LEADING MICHIGAN REPUBLICANS.

GENERAL RUSSELL ALEXANDER ALGER, who has attained high distinction in military, political and business life, comes of New England and patriotic stock, his great grandfather having fought in numerous battles in the War of the Revolution. His father, as a boy, with his widowed mother, moved from the old family home in Connecticut to Richfield, Ohio, in 1832, and when grown to manhood started the life of a pioneer in the wilderness in Lafayette, Medina County, Ohio, where, in a log cabin, the subject of this sketch was born, February 27th, 1836. His father soon afterwards lost his farm, through the foreclosure of a mortgage, and in 1848 died, leaving four children penniless, his wife having died the same year, previous to his death. The oldest child soon afterwards died, leaving Russell, the second child, to care for his younger brother and sister.

The boy went to work with the same energy that marked his after life. He secured homes for the other children in the families of neighbors, and himself went to live with an uncle, who gave him lodging, board and clothes, and three months schooling a year, in return for his work upon the farm. Two years later he took the work of a farm hand, commencing at $3 a month, and continuing such work until he was 20 years old, when he was getting $15 a month. Meantime he had attended the Richfield Academy for five winters, and had taught school for two winters. He had also contributed toward the support and education of his brother and sister.

In 1857 Mr. Alger went to Akron, Ohio, began studying law in the office of Wolcott & Upson, and two years later was admitted to the bar of the Supreme Court of that State. A year more was spent in legal study and hard work at Cleveland, when his health broke down and he was obliged to seek some other occupation. On the last day of December, 1859, he set out for Michigan, stopped at Grand Rapids and went into the lumber business with a friend. But although this business has since been the making of his fortune, as it has that of a great many other men in Michigan, it has its reverses, as it had in this case. The failure of a firm in Chicago destroyed his business and left him heavily in debt.

The War of the Rebellion called Mr. Alger into new fields of action. He enlisted August 19th, 1861, in the Second Michigan Cavalry, and went to the front as Captain, his commission dating from

September 2d, of that year. At the Battle of Boonville, July 1st, 1862, his company was in a desperate attack upon the rear of General Chalmers. In this engagement he was taken prisoner, but almost immediately escaped, and the next day he was promoted to be major. He was with this regiment through numerous battles and skirmishes until October 16th, 1862, when he was commissioned Lieutenant Colonel of the Sixth Michigan Cavalry, and was subsequently made Colonel of the Fifth Michigan Cavalry, the commission to date from February 28th, 1863. His regiment was under General Custer in the Army of the Potomac, and did splendid work, at and after Gettysburg. He was wounded at Boonsboro, Maryland, July 8th, 1863, served with Sheridan in the Shenandoah in 1864, won especial distinction at Trevilian Station, on June 11th, 1864, and was recommended for promotion to Brigadier General by Generals Custer, Kilpatrick, Sheridan, Meade and Grant. He was honorably mustered out in September, 1864. On October 10th, 1865, he was brevetted Brigadier General for gallant and meritorious services, to rank from the Battle of Trevilian Station, June 11th, 1864. In June, 1866, he was brevetted Major General of United States Volunteers "for gallant and meritorious services during the war." He had participated in sixty-six battles and skirmishes during his term of service.

When General Alger returned from the war he did not have a cent of capital, but he had plenty of energy and some knowledge of the lumber business. Into the latter he went as a partner of the firm of Moore, Alger & Co. The business prospered and in time General Alger became the head of the firm of R. A. Alger & Co. In 1881 the business was incorporated under the name of Alger, Smith & Co., and the company has since established a branch known as the Manistique Lumbering Co., of both of which General Alger is President. They operated largely in the Northern part of the Lower Peninsula, and later in the Upper Peninsula and Minnesota, their lumber business being one of the largest in the world, the annual product of the companies being 150,000,000 feet. Although General Alger started without capital, he never had a note go to protest, and in the immense business that has grown up since, he never had a law suit, and never had a strike. The companies organized and controlled by him in Michigan have paid, for labor and supplies alone, since 1866, over $20,000,000. General Alger is a stockholder and director of the State Savings Bank of Detroit, is the chief owner of the Volunteer mine in Marquette County, a director of the United States Express Co., and the owner of extensive timber lands on the Pacific Coast, and the Southern States.

General Alger has long been earnest and conspicuous in Republican politics. in fact has been heard to say, that Republicanism was part of his religion. His is a familiar figure at the Michigan Club gatherings on Washington's birthday, and at other large meetings of Republicans. He was a delegate to the National Republican Convention in 1884, and the same year was nominated for Governor of

Michigan. He put up a successful fight, both for the National and State tickets, in that contest, which was one of the warmest in the history of Michigan politics. At the end of his term he broke the traditional, two-term rule of the party in the State, by declining a re-nomination. In 1888 he was a candidate in the Chicago Convention for the Presidential nomination, and on the ballots from the fourth to the eighth inclusive, stood third in the list of candidates for whom votes were cast, there being altogether thirteen candidates. Throughout the contest he had a most loyal and flattering support from the City and State of his residence. He was, the same year, one of the Presidential Electors-at-large from Michigan. It was in the Chicago Convention that the cry, "What's the matter with Alger?" and the response, "He's all right" were first heard; a call and response that have since been echoed on many public occasions when he was present, or his name mentioned. Indeed, as the General says, all candidates have adopted it.

On March 4th, 1897, General Alger entered President McKinley's Cabinet as Secretary of War. In that office he organized, equipped and transported to the field, the great volunteer army in the Spanish War, with a celerity of movement and a completeness in equipment and armament that have never been equaled in the history of warfare. He resigned his office, August 1st, 1899, reopened his elegant residence in Detroit, and has since devoted his attention to his private interests.

General Alger was married on April 2d, 1861, to Miss Annette H. Henry, daughter of William Gilmore and Huldana Squier Henry. Nine children have been born to them, of whom five are living, as follows: Caroline, wife of Henry Dusenburg Shelden, of Detroit; Fay, wife of William Elder Bailey, of Thorndale, Penn.; Francis, wife of Charles Burrall Pike, of Chicago; Russell Alexander, Jr., who married Miss Marion Jarves, daughter of Deming Jarves, of Detroit, and Frederick Moulton, who graduated at Harvard University in the class of 1899.

General Alger's charities have been abundant and widely distributed. His hospitable mansion in Detroit has been often open for receptions on the occasion of political and military gatherings in the City. He is well known in business and social circles in New York, and in that City belongs to the Union League Club and to the Ohio Society. He is an active member of the Grand Army of the Republic, and in 1889 was elected its Commander-in-Chief for one year. He is also a member of the military order of the Loyal Legion and a Son of the American Revolution.

General Alger has carried into public life the same practical spirit and direct methods that have characterized his business career. When Governor he employed, at his own expense, a capable legal adviser, to whom all bills which had passed the Legislature, were submitted, in order that he might pass judgment upon their constitutionality and their relations to existing statutes, thereby probably

Sincerely yours

 Geo. L. Adams

saving much litigation and some adverse Supreme Court decisions. It was during his time also, and at his request, that an Act was passed, establishing the Board of Pardons, thus introducing some system into the examination of appeals for executive clemency.

There was one incident of his executive career that has not found its way into any previous biographies. In the summer of 1886 there was a strike of mill hands throughout the Saginaw Valley. It was so complete as to tie up every mill, most of them not being allowed by the strikers to carry sufficient steam even to run their pumps. The lumber cut of the valley had then passed its maximum cut of over 1,000,000,000 feet in a single season, but it was still larger than that of any other district in the world. There was almost a continuous line of mills and lumber piles along the river from Saginaw to Essexville, below Bay City. The season was dry, and there were grave apprehensions of a fire that would spread through the valley, as the strikers were in almost complete control. Governor Alger went to Saginaw, where he met a number of the business men. They were in a state of grave alarm, but begged him as also did the sheriff, not to send troops there, lest the act should irritate the men, and lead them to violence or incendiarism. He then went to Bay City, where the same condition of things existed. While at the latter point a large company of the strikers approached, with a band of music, cheered the Governor, for whom many of them had worked at different times, and wanted him to address them from the balcony of the Frazer House. Instead of speaking from that place he mounted a table out in the street and told the men that they had a perfect right to work or not, as they liked, but they had no right to use violence toward others who wanted to work, nor to injure property. If they did use violence the whole force of the State would be called out if necessary, and if through their acts a single life was lost, there was not a man of them who would not seriously regret it. They again cheered him and marched away. The Governor returned to Detroit, without communicating his purpose to any one, but early next morning a brigade of the State Militia stacked arms in the main street in Bay City, and a regiment was found stationed at Saginaw. The men quieted down and the strike gradually faded away, without a cartridge being exploded by the military, and without the loss of a life or the destruction of a dollar's worth of property.

JOHN QUINCY ADAMS, of Negaunee, one of the leading lawyers and Republicans of the Upper Peninsula, was born in Cornwall, Connecticut, November 2d, 1837. He is a descendant of one of five brothers who came from England, and settled in Massachusetts, his father's name being Samuel Adams and his mother's Lorilla Adams. His early education was that of the common school, and he worked on the farm until 18 years of age. He was then in the drug business or teaching school for four years, and was engaged in making shears and scissors for two years after that. He afterwards took a thorough course of study in law and was admitted to the bar in 1867. He formed a co-partnership with George Wheaton, continuing the business alone after the death of the latter. In 1872 he removed to Negaunee, Marquette County, where he has enjoyed, for many years, a large and lucrative practice, and where he is now the leading attorney.

Politicians are pretty thick in the Upper Peninsula and Mr. Adams is one of them. He has always been a Republican; was a delegate to the Minneapolis Convention of 1892, which renominated Harrison for President, and has been a delegate to all the important Michigan Republican State Conventions for the past twenty years. His tall form, long smooth beard, quick movements, and readiness in debate have made him a conspicuous figure at these political gatherings.

Mr. Adams was elected Circuit Court Commissioner in 1874, and Prosecuting Attorney in 1876 and for two subsequent terms. He was a member of the Legislature of 1883, and was one of the "Immortal 19" who prevented the re-election of Senator Thomas W. Ferry, and secured the election of Thomas W. Palmer to the Senate. He is now Collector of Customs for the District of Superior.

Aside from his law practice Mr. Adams has business interests in the Negaunee Street Railway Company and the First National Bank of Escanaba. He is connected with all Masonic Societies, Knights Templar, Scottish Rite, Shrine, etc., and with the Business Men's Club of Negaunee. He was married at Cornwall, Conn., January 20th, 1858, to Sophronia A. Owen, of Sharon, Conn., and has one son, Eugene Warner Adams.

DAVID DEMOREST AITKEN, one of the best known citizens of Flint, Mich., was born in Flint Township, Genesee County, September 5th, 1854. His parents were Robert P. Aitken and Sarah J. Aitken, the former a member of the Michigan Legislature. Both father and mother were from New York, settling in Michigan in 1841. David D. Aitken worked on the farm, attended District school winters, and later attended High School at Flint and taught school two winters. After leaving school he sold goods as a drummer and kept books until 1877, then commenced the study of law and was admitted to the bar in 1879, and has been in constant practice ever since. He was never a candidate for office until 1892, when he was elected to Congress. He was re-elected in 1894 and refused to be a candidate for another term, one of the rare instances where Congressional life had no charms. Mr. Aitken differed from the average Congressman and politician in another respect. Upon certain financial questions he did not agree with the majority of his party, nor with the utterances of some of its platforms, yet he had the courage to express his views plainly and to give warnings openly, without leaving the party with whose history

D. D. Aitken

he had been identified, and with whose essential principles he agreed He continued to vote the Republican ticket, as he had done since he cast his first vote for Hayes for President.

Besides having his law business Mr. Aitken is President of the People's Electric Light Co. at Flint; Director in the Citizens' Commercial and Savings Bank; Director in the McCormick Harness Co.; principal owner of the Flint Woolen Mills Co.; owns and operates a farm of 700 acres in Genesee County, raises fine stock and always drives a good span of standard-bred trotters. He is a Knight Templar, a Shriner, a Knight of Pythias, General Counsel for the Order of Maccabees, and member of many fraternal benefit societies. He was married at Milburn, N. J., to Miss Ada Elizabeth Long, in 1878, and has no children.

EDWARD P. ALLEN, of Ypsilanti, ex-member of the Legislature, ex-member of Congress and a campaigner who is in great demand whenever an election comes in sight, was born in Sharon, Washtenaw County, October 28th, 1839. His father, a farmer, was Lewis Allen, and his mother Eliza Marvin Allen. Up to the time he was twenty years old he went through the experience very common with farmers' boys who desire an education, working on the farm in summer and attending school and teaching during the winter. He graduated from the State Normal School in March, 1864; taught the Union School in Vassar, Mich., for the three months following, when he enlisted and helped to raise a company for the Twenty-ninth Michigan Infantry; was commissioned First Lieutenant in that Regiment in the following September, and went with it southwest, where the regiment was engaged in active campaigning until the 1st of April; in September, 1865, was mustered out of the service with his regiment as Captain; entered the Law School at Ann Arbor, graduating in March, 1867, and formed a partnership with Hon. S. M. Cutcheon. Upon the removal of Mr. Cutcheon to Detroit, in 1875, he continued the practice alone at Ypsilanti; was elected Alderman in 1872 and 1874, and Mayor in 1880; was Prosecuting Attorney of Washtenaw County in 1872; was elected to the Lower House of the Legislature in 1876, serving as Chairman of the Committee on Education; was again elected in 1878, at which time he was elected Speaker pro tempore; was appointed Assistant Assessor of Internal Revenue in 1879; was United States Indian Agent for Michigan in August, 1882, which office he held until December, 1885. He was elected to the Fiftieth and Fifty-first Congresses, in 1886 and 1888 respectively, from the Second District of Michigan, which is always close and usually deemed doubtful. Upon his return from Congress, he resumed the practice of law at Ypsilanti which he has continued ever since. He was married May 12th, 1869, at Sharon, to Clara E. Cushman. Their children now living are Elmer C. and Louise Allen.

Captain Allen has been a Republican and an active one since the time the party was organized. He cast his first vote for President

Lincoln, and has not only often been a delegate to local and District Conventions, but has attended as a delegate many State Conventions as well as the National Convention in St. Louis, in 1896. He was permanent President of the State Conventions held in the spring of 1880 and 1892 to elect delegates to the National gatherings of the party. He first suggested the phrase, "which we pledge ourselves to promote" in the monetary plank of the platform of 1896, a promise which did much to restore the Republican party to power in that year. His familiarity with the affairs of the State and Nation and his readiness of speech, have made him a prudent and useful adviser at conventions, and an effective speaker in campaigns, where the committees have highly valued his services.

In the Legislature of 1877 Washtenaw County was the most conspicuous in its representation of any County in the State. Captain Allen represented the Ypsilanti District and Andrew J. Sawyer the Ann Arbor District. They made themselves heard on many occasions, and with such resonance of voice as to give to the portion of the House in which they sat the name of "fog horn corner." Both exerted an important influence in legislation, and Captain Allen, as Chairman of the Committee on Education, had opportunity to render the State especially great service in connection with the educational appropriations. There was in that Legislature, a conservative reaction against the University, the State Normal School and the Agricultural College, whose appropriations were seriously threatened, and Captain Allen's support of the committees on those institutions in their appeals for needed funds, was both earnest and effective. A pronounced temperance man himself, he did much toward securing strong legislation, restrictive of the liquor traffic, at a time when a considerable section of the party were in favor of a laxity of action in the Legislature and of a timidity of utterance in Convention that would have alienated thousands of staunch Republicans.

Captain Allen's Congressional career was in keeping, on a larger scale, with that in the Legislature. In the Fiftieth Congress, which was Democratic, he was appointed by Speaker Carlisle a member of the Committee on Indian Affairs. In the Fifty-first Congress he was appointed by Speaker Reed a member of the Committee on Agriculture. He was Chairman of the sub-committee that reported a Bill, which afterwards passed, transferring the weather bureau from the War Department to that of Agriculture, and putting it on essentially the same basis as it is at present, a measure which has been of immense value to the agricultural interests of the country. In this Congress he was called upon, as often as anyone else, to preside in Committee of the Whole, a duty for which he has excellent qualifications. He also took part in the discussion of the Lodge Bill, which was the last attempt made in Congress, to secure to every man in the South the right to vote once and to have his vote counted. The Bill passed the House, but was defeated in the Senate.

M50L

Respectfully

AUSTIN WHITE ALVORD, a prominent Battle Creek physician, was born at Chester, Mass., February 3d, 1838, son of Rev. Alanson Alvord, a Congregational Minister, and Adaline Barrows Alvord. His ancestors on his father's side lived in Massachusetts 200 years and were originally English. On his mother's side the family came from England and settled in Salem, Massachusetts, in 1640.

Austin W. Alvord was educated at Chester Academy, Vermont, Oberlin College and Michigan University, filling some intervals with teaching. and afterwards studying medicine. He went into the army as Captain in the line, then attended more medical lectures and began practice in Clinton, Mich., in 1865. He remained there until 1882 when he moved to Battle Creek, his present home. He obtained his literary and medical education without assistance, working his own way through, and much of the time boarding himself. He has been interested in manufacturing institutions, and several public enterprises; was last year President of the Michigan State Medical Society; is a member of the State Medical Board; was active in securing the passage of our State Medical Law, which has disposed of a large amount of ignorance and quackery in medical practitioners.

In politics Dr. Alvord has always been a Republican and cast his first vote for Lincoln, in 1860. He has held no political offices, only such positions as are in line with his profession, as Health Officer, member of the Pension Board of Examiners, State Board of Registration and Examination in Medicine. He has been President of the State Medical Society and is a member of the Battle Creek Academy of Medicine, the Calhoun County Medical Society, the Michigan State Medical Society, the American Medical Association, the Tri-State Medical Association and the American Public Health Association. He is also a member of Lodge, Chapter, Council and Commandery in Masonry, and of the G. A. R. and Loyal Legion. He was married to Eliza Barnes, of Ann Arbor, in 1861. She died in 1877, leaving two children, Mary Grace Alvord Kelleher and William Roy Alvord, now a student at Ann Arbor. His second marriage was to Fannie R. Little, of Grinnell, Iowa, in 1878, and he had two children by her, Louise Alvord and Max Barrows Alvord.

TOM SEAL APPLEGATE was born at Blandford, Dorsetshire, England, June 8th, 1839, his father's name being William Applegate and his mother's Eliza Seal. His father's occupation was that of baker and confectioner. The family moved to this country in 1851, living first in Utica and then in Rome, N. Y., where the father became a successful merchant. Tom received his early education in England and at Utica, N. Y. Academy. After three or four removals Mr. Applegate settled in Adrian, Mich., where, on the 6th of April, 1870, he married Harriett M. Sinclair, and where he died December 27th, 1891. He had no children.

Mr. Applegate was, from the time he left school till his death, a printer or an editor, and through most of his adult life, a prudent and successful politician. He was apprenticed to the printer's trade in the office of the Rome Sentinel, and on completing his apprenticeship went to New York where he held cases in various offices, and also on the Brooklyn News. In November, 1863, in company with George W. Larwill, he went to Adrian, where they purchased an interest in the Adrian Watchtower. From this time till his death Mr. Applegate was almost continuously connected with the leading newspaper in Lenawee County. After various changes of name and partnership control, it finally became the Adrian Times and Expositor, with Mr. Applegate as sole proprietor.

Early in his connection with the paper he began introducing new ideas in news gathering and publishing, and did much to shake the interior weeklies out of their routine and often dull methods. He established the first daily in Southeastern Michigan. He was a member of the Chicago Press Club, and the Inland Press Association, and was one of the most popular members and officers of the Michigan State Press Association.

Mr. Applegate's newspaper associations naturally led him into politics, for which he had a natural taste. He attended almost every Republican State Convention from 1864 to 1890, often as a delegate. He served eight years as a member of the Republican State Central Committee, and was Chairman of the Executive Committee six years. He was also Chairman of the Congressional Committee for the Second District, where he exerted great influence. United States Senators, Congressmen, and many State Officers, from Governor down, had occasion to thank Mr. Applegate for his powerful influence in helping them to success, but he showed a remarkable indifference to official position for himself. He might have been Representative in the Legislature, State Senator, Congressman, or on the State ticket almost any time for the asking, but he always declined to be a candidate for any of these places. The only official positions he ever held were the non-salaried appointive ones of member of the board to locate the State School for the Blind, and member, for ten years, of the Board of Control of that Institution. He preferred to help others rather than to seek honors for himself.

He had a number of business interests outside of the newspaper and at the time of his death was President of the Adrian Petroleum Light and Heat Company, and Secretary of the Adrian National Paving and Construction Company.

WILLIAM HENRY ARTHUR, of Marshall, was born in Palmyra, N. Y., July 26, 1862, of an old Scotch family on the side of his father, whose name was John F. Arthur. Young Arthur attended the common school at Coldwater, and after leaving school commenced an active newspaper career which he has continued ever since. At

W. H. Arthur

THE MARSHALL STATESMAN.

the age of fifteen he commenced an apprenticeship in the office of the Marshall Statesman. This paper was one of the oldest in Michigan, having been established in 1839. For many years it ranked among the three or four most influential papers in the State, and has always held a high position among the interior weeklies. Mr. Arthur has been connected with it in every department. After serving his apprenticeship he was foreman of the printing department for four years, and then local editor. He left Marshall in 1888 but returned in 1892, and took the management of the Statesman Printing Company. In 1894 he bought a half interest in the business and became editor of the paper, which position he still holds. In the interval between 1888 and 1892 he was at first city editor of the Jackson Morning Patriot. Then finding that, on account of his health, he could not follow morning newspaper work, he accepted a similar position on the Jackson Evening Courier. After remaining in Jackson about a year he went to Albion, Michigan, and took the foremanship of the Recorder mechanical department, and in 1891 went on the road for the Chicago Newspaper Union, the well-known ready-print newspaper establishment. He continued in that work until his return to Marshall. In June, 1898, he was appointed postmaster at Marshall on the recommendation of Senator J. C. Burrows.

Mr. Arthur has always been a Republican, and cast his first vote for Blaine. He was a member of the Republican County Committee in 1896, and is at present a member of the advisory board of the Republican State League. He is Captain of Uniform Rank, Knights of Pythias; Member of Marshall Commandery, 17, Knights Templar; Member of Benevolent and Protective Order of Elks; Member of the Modern Woodmen; Secretary of Calhoun County Agricultural Society. He was married to Miss Hattie M. Amlar in September, 1887.

THERON W. ATWOOD, Senator from the Twenty-first District, composed of the counties of Lapeer and Tuscola, was born at White Oak, Ingham County, Michigan, January 3, 1854, but has been a resident of Tuscola County since infancy. He received his early education in the schools of that County, graduated from the Law Department of Michigan University in 1875, and has been in the active practice of law for twenty-three years. He was Prosecuting Attorney of Tuscola County during the years 1886, 1888, 1892 and 1894, and was elected to the Senate of 1899-1900 by a vote of 6,313 to 4,732 for James S McArthur, Democratic People's Union Silver candidate. He was renominated for the Senate in the campaign of 1900, and was re-elected by a large majority.

ALEXANDER R. AVERY, of Port Huron, was born November 14, 1846, in the Township of Pickering, County and Province of Ontario. His father was Anthony R. Avery, a farmer, and his mother was Sarah Hilborn Avery. Although born in Canada Mr. Avery comes of good old New England stock. The original ancestor arrived from England at Plymouth Colony on the "good ship Arabella" with Governor John Winthrop in 1630. His great grandfather and other members of his family were soldiers in the War of the Revolution, being then residents of Connecticut. A number of them who were in the garrison, were slain in the massacre at Fort Griswold on Groton Heights, which followed the invasion of the Connecticut coast by Benedict Arnold's force of British and their Indian allies. Mr. Avery's grandfather removed from Pennsylvania to the Province of Ontario immediately preceding the war of 1812 (while Mr. Avery's father was an infant) and during that war was pressed into the British service though always remaining strongly American in sentiment.

Mr. Avery's ancestors on his mother's side were also Americans. They were Quakers and therefore non-combatants, but that did not prevent the death of a portion of them in the massacre at Wyoming by Butler's Rangers. This branch of the Avery family also moved to Ontario, and it was there that the parents of the subject of the present sketch were united in marriage. The family moved to St. Clair County, Michigan, in 1862, when Alexander R. was sixteen years of age.

Mr. Avery received his education in the primary schools except two terms at the State Normal School at Ypsilanti, and one year in the Law Department of Michigan University. At intervals during the period when he was pursuing these studies he taught in the primary schools of St. Clair and Sanilac counties. He began the study of law under the direction of Nims & Beach, of Lexington, Sanilac County, about 1869, using his spare moments when teaching school and going into their law office between terms. During the holiday vacation 1871-2 he was examined and admitted to the bar at Port Huron, but continued his studies at the law school at Ann Arbor till the spring of 1872, when he opened a law office in Port Huron. He has been since that time in the practice of law at that place.

Mr. Avery took naturally to politics. He has always been a Republican and cast his first vote for Grant and Colfax in 1868. He has attended, as a delegate, nearly every Republican State Convention held in Michigan since 1874. He was elected Circuit Court Commissioner in St. Clair County in 1872, Prosecuting Attorney of the County in 1874, and re-elected in 1876. He has held no other elective offices. He was postmaster of the City of Port Huron under the Harrison Administration and is, at present, Collector of Customs for the District of Huron.

Mr. Avery has a fancy for clubs, societies and political organizations. He is a member of the Michigan Club, Blaine Club, and local Republican Clubs of Port Huron. Of social organizations he belongs to the Port Huron Club and the Rainbow Trout Club, whose headquarters are located on the Au Sable River, twelve miles from Grayling. He belongs to Lodge No. 58, F. & A. M.; Huron Chapter No. 27,

of Port Huron; Port Huron Commandery No. 7, Knights Templar; both orders of the Maccabees; both orders of the Woodmen and the A. O. U. W. He was married July 22d, 1866, at Jeddo, Mich., to Miss Martha Locke of that place. They have three children, Henry, Minnie and Kittie.

LINCOLN AVERY, a prominent attorney and business man of Port Huron, was born October 24th, 1860, in the township of Pickering, Province of Ontario, Canada. His parents were Anthony R. Avery, a farmer, and Sarah Hilborn Avery. He is a younger brother of Alexander R. Avery, whose sketch, preceding this, gives a brief account of their common patriotic ancestry.

The elder Avery moved from Canada to St. Clair County, Michigan, in 1862, when the subject of this sketch was less than a year and a half old, and the training of the son, as well as his ancestry, was, therefore, thoroughly American. He studied in the district schools of Grant Township, St. Clair County, the State Normal School, Michigan Agricultural College, where he took the degree of B. S. in 1882, and Michigan University, where he took the degree of LL. B. in 1886. In July of the latter year he commenced the practice of law in Port Huron in partnership with A. R. Avery under the firm name of Avery Brothers. He was a close student while in the law school, and has since given equally close attention to his law business, which has become satisfactorily large and remunerative.

Mr. Avery has a commendable taste for public life, and has been a very active politician in a county where political campaigns are generally quite lively. His convictions have always been with the Republican Party, and his first Presidential vote was cast for Benjamin Harrison. He has attended all Republican State Conventions since 1892, and was a member of the State Central Committee in the campaigns of 1896 and 1900. He was elected County Superintendent of Schools in 1882, while yet a student at the Agricultural College, and after graduation assumed the duties of the office, which he held for three years. In 1890 he made the run for Prosecuting Attorney, the County being Democratic by about 1,500, and came within 433 of being elected. Associated with others he then went to work to organize the County for the entire party, and in 1892 they elected a Republican ticket, with the exception of two officers, and he was himself elected Prosecuting Attorney, by 600 majority. In 1894 he was again nominated and was elected by 2,500 majority, each time leading his ticket. He is at present City Attorney of Port Huron. Among other acts of local importance in which he has been interested he drafted the bills, which afterwards became law, requiring each township and City within St. Clair County to look after their own contagious diseases, which resulted in a saving to the County of about $12,000 a year. Mr. Avery has business interests aside from his law practice, especially in the St. Clair County Savings Bank of Port

Huron, and the Yale National Bank of Yale, Michigan, and is a member of the Port Huron Club. He was married in Port Huron, August 23d, 1892, to Elizabeth Northup, and has three children: Florence Hilborn, Elizabeth Northup, and Lincoln, Jr.

SAMUEL SHORT BABCOCK, of Detroit, is a son of Abelino Babcock, a pioneer farmer, and of Emeline Short Babcock, and was born February 2d, 1842, in Genesee County, Michigan. He was named for his maternal grandfather, Samuel Short, a soldier of the War of the Revolution. Both his parents were born in the State of New York, and both his father's father and grandfather were Revolutionary soldiers. His father's family are Scotch-Irish, originally from Bristol, and his mother's family are English-Dutch. The log school house of Michigan furnished his education until he was twelve years old, attending school winters and doing the work of a pioneer's boy during the summer. This was supplemented by study at the Academy at Flint, Michigan, also Cooperstown, N. Y., and two years at Oberlin, Ohio. At the age of fourteen young Babcock started out to get an education, doing the usual work of a man on the farm in the spring, summer and autumn, going to school in the winter. He has done about every kind of hard work, including chopping cord-wood and feeding a threshing machine. He taught his first school in the winter of 1857-8, in the Township of Davison, this State, his next in the Village of Atlas and the next two winters he was at Novi Corners, Oakland County. Mr. Babcock enlisted in the Third New York Volunteer Infantry in May, 1861; went to the front with the regiment; was present at the Battle of Big Bethel and followed the fortune of his regiment during the term of his enlistment, except during the fall and winter of 1861-2, when he was detailed as Provost Sergeant of Fort McHenry, about as important a position as a lad of nineteen years could be called upon to fill; was First Sergeant of his company for over eighteen months, and was listed for First Lieutenant when he was mustered out. There were three of the Babcock brothers who enlisted in the War of the Rebellion; one died in the service. His brother who, with him, survived that war, sent his only son to Cuba. He commanded his company in the fight in which General Duffield commanded, but died soon after of yellow fever. Had his father been engaged in any war for the United States, there would have been five generations of them who have fought for "Our Country." On both his father's and mother's side they have been loyal even to the offering of the best they had to give, their lives for the flag.

Returning from the Army in 1863 Mr. Babcock taught, in the winter of 1863-4, in the Webster District, Washtenaw County, graduated from the State Normal School in 1865; had charge of the schools at Howell for two years and the schools at Greenville three years; filled the chair of mathematics and Natural Sciences in the Old Ypsilanti

Seminary for two years and a half, then filled the chair of mathematics in the Kansas State Normal School at Emporia for one year, and had charge of the schools of Mt. Clemens two years. During this time he also delivered courses of lectures on the Science of Government, wrote many articles on educational topics for various Educational publications; commenced the study of law in 1872 as leisure was found; was admitted to the bar in the spring of 1876, came to Detroit in July of 1876, and has continued to reside and practice here ever since. He was elected member of the State Board of Education in 1886, and served for six years, declining a renomination when his term expired, and served two years as member of the Board of Geological Survey. The work which he did for the State while serving it speaks for itself. He has been twice elected Estimator from the Fourth Ward of Detroit. Every political office he has held has come to him unsought.

Mr. Babcock's business life has been filled with a good measure of success, due to intelligence and upright endeavor. In politics he has been a Republican ever since there was such a party, having cast his first vote for Lincoln. He has been delegate to four State Conventions and has had much to do with educational legislation in this State, while the present law relative to the Michigan State Normal School was very nearly all drafted and rearranged by him. He has been a member and director of the Michigan Club since its organization; was one of its directors up to the spring of 1900, when he resigned from the board on account of business engagements which required all his time and strength. He was its President in 1897. He has always been a member of his Ward Club, as a matter of course. He is a member of the American Historical Society, a member of the Grand Army of the Republic, is a member of the Royal Arcanum, and has been honored by his comrades and brethren with trusts of importance. He was married in 1865 to Olive Perkins, who died in 1870, and he married Frances E. Everts in 1872. They have three daughters, Margaret H., Myrtle E., and Myra E.

JOHN JUDSON BAGLEY would be characterized by those who knew him most intimately as emphatically the large-hearted Governor of Michigan, for there was none that had a warmer side toward the unfortunate, the dependent and even the criminal wards of the State. He was a descendant of the Bagley family who came from England early in the Seventeenth Century. His grandmother, Olive Judson, was a daughter of Captain Timothy Judson, a soldier of the Revolution. The Judsons were a prominent family in Connecticut, descended from an old English family in Yorkshire, who came to America in 1634 and first settled in Concord, Mass. There were many ministers in the family, among them the Rev. Adoniram Judson, the noted foreign missionary. Through the Judsons he was also a descendant of Rev. Thomas Hooker, who came from Hertfordshire, England, and established the first church in Connecticut.

John Bagley, the father of Governor Bagley, was born in Durham, Greene County, New York. He established himself in business in Medina, but afterwards moved to Lockport. His wife was a native of Connecticut, a woman of education and refinement, with great strength and force of character, and the son always spoke with great respect and affection of her and of her influence in moulding his own character. He was one of a family of eight children, and was born at Medina, Orleans County, New York, July 24th, 1832. Both parents were devout and active members of the Episcopal Church, and his mother intended to educate him for the ministry; but financial reverses came to the family, and they found what in those days was considered a fortune suddenly swept away. Michigan had recently been admitted as a State, and Mr. Bagley, hoping to regain what he had lost, moved from Lockport to St. Joseph County, in this State, stopping a few months at Mottville, and then going to Constantine, and from there to Owosso, in Shiawassee County.

John J. Bagley attended school at Constantine, White Pigeon and Owosso. He began his business life in a country store in Constantine, and after the family moved to Owosso he was engaged as clerk in the firm of Dewey & Goodhue and there he received his early business training. The hours of work were early and late, but a little time could always be found for reading and study. When fourteen years of age he left Owosso and found employment in the tobacco store and factory of Isaac S. Miller, in Detroit.

In 1853, when twenty-one years of age, he established a tobacco manufactory of his own on Woodward avenue, below Jefferson. From a moderate beginning the business, afterwards incorporated under the firm name of John J. Bagley & Co., grew to be one of the largest of its kind in the country, and the source of an ample income to its founder. Although he had passed through pinching times in his youth, Mr. Bagley was both liberal and enterprising with the profits that came from this business in after years. He was not only generous toward his own employes, who were very much attached to him, but made other investments in concerns that gave employment to labor, particularly in the Detroit Safe Company, of which he was one of the original stockholders and for several years President. He was one of the incorporators of the Michigan Mutual Life Insurance Company, and served as its President for several years. He was also one of the first stockholders in the Wayne County Savings Bank and the American National Bank, and helped organize the Merchants' and Manufacturers' Exchange.

Mr. Bagley took early to political life, and was always interested in municipal and other public affairs. He was at first a Whig, but joined in the movement to organize the Republican Party, to which he was always afterwards attached. He was a member of the Board of Education soon after he became a voter, and of the Common Coun-

Jno. J. Bagley

cil eight years later. He drafted the Act under which the Metropolitan Police Force of Detroit was organized; was one of the first Commissioners, and after he became Governor was especially careful in his selection of members of that body. He also helped to establish the Detroit House of Correction, and was one of its first inspectors.

In 1872 Mr. Bagley, who had previously done good service on the Republican State Central and local committees, was elected Governor, by over 56,000 plurality and was re elected in 1874. His first message as Governor was a breezy, bristling document, full of original suggestions and altogether out of the usual stereotyped run of official communications. During his Administration the State Board of Health, and the State Board having general supervision of the charitable and penal institutions were permanently established, though the latter had been recommended by his predecessor. An Act had been passed in 1871, looking toward the establishment of a school for dependent children. Governor Bagley was a member of the first Board of Control, of which he afterwards remained, as Governor, an ex-officio member. He ever took a great interest in this institution, remembered it annually at Christmas time with presents for the scholars, and left a fund of $1,000, the income of which is devoted to the same purpose. He also gave to the school a fountain to ornament the grounds. Through his efforts some of the prison features of the State Reform School were relaxed and that was made more of an educational institution than before, while the harsh discipline of the State Prison and House of Correction was modified. He was a strenuous advocate of the taxing system of regulating the liquor traffic, in place of the inoperative prohibitory system, and it was during his second term that the prohibitory clause was stricken from the Constitution. He also urged the reorganization of the militia, and aided in establishing that service on its present foundation. During his Administration also a general railroad law was passed, and the office of State Railroad Commissioner was created. All of these and many other important measures were promoted by Governor Bagley, either through his messages or by his direct personal influence.

Governor Bagley was twice a candidate for the Republican nomination for the United States Senate, once in 1879, after Senator Christiancy's resignation, and again in 1881 after Senator Chandler's death. The last time he came within one vote of the nomination, which finally went to Omar D. Conger. In September, 1880, he had a slight stroke of paralysis, from which he never recovered, and he died July 27th, 1881, at the age of 49. His will contained bequests for a number of local charities. He also made generous gifts to all who had been in his employ for five years or more, and left the sum of $5,000 with which to erect a public drinking fountain in Detroit. His heirs increased this amount to about $10,000 and the fountain was erected on the open square at the head of Fort Street West, and was unveiled on May 30th, 1887.

In 1855 Mr. Bagley married Miss Frances E. Newbury, of Dubuque, Iowa, whose father, Rev. Samuel Newbury, a Presbyterian clergyman, was one of the pioneers in the establishment of the educational institutions of the State, helping to do in Michigan what his friend and correspondent, Horace Mann, did in Massachusetts. Mr. and Mrs. Bagley had eight children, of whom are living: Mrs. Florence B. Sherman, John N. Bagley, Mrs. Frances B. Brown, Mrs. Olive Bagley Buttrick, of Concord, Mass.; Paul Frederick and Mrs. Helen Bagley Anderson, of Colorado Springs, Colorado. The two sons are in the business which their father established in 1853.

DR. HENRY BROOKS BAKER, of Lansing, for nearly three decades the zealous and efficient Secretary of the Michigan State Board of Health, was born in Brattleboro, Vermont, December 29th, 1837, the son of Ezra Baker, a fulling mill proprietor, and Deborah K. Baker. Dr. Baker's ancestors came from England, but lived several generations in New England. His great grandfather was an officer in the Revolutionary War, his grandfather was a member of the Vermont Legislature, and his grandmother was a member of the Brooks family in Massachusetts. His mother was from the Bigelow family in the same State, and her ancestry is from the same stock as Senator Hoar and General Garfield. There were the same number of generations from a common ancestor to President Garfield as to Dr. Baker's sons.

Dr. Baker received his elementary education in the common schools of Vermont, Massachusetts and Michigan, and studied medicine in the University of Michigan, and in Bellevue Hospital Medical College, New York City. From the latter he received the degree of M. D. in 1866, and from the former the honorary degree of A. M. in 1890. From the time he was 14 years of age young Baker maintained himself, being clerk in stores and hotel, and later a school teacher. With his brother he was proprietor of the old "Lansing House" in Lansing, Mich., for a few years, including the legislative session of 1857. Among the guests at the Lansing House that session, were Governor Kinsley S. Bingham, Hon. Jacob M. Howard, Hon. S. M. Holmes, Hon. Francis W. Kellogg, and Hon. Perry Hannah. He enlisted as a private in the War of the Rebellion, served for about a year as hospital steward, about one year as acting-assistant surgeon, and one year as assistant surgeon; the first two years of his army service he being on duty at the operating table at division hospital whenever his division was engaged in battle.

Dr. Baker cast his first ballot for Abraham Lincoln in 1864, and has worked with the Republican party ever since, though he has never held any political office, except that of Village Treasurer of Wenona, Bay County, in 1870. An interesting political reminiscence is of meeting Kinsley S. Bingham in Jackson at the time of the meeting "Under the Oaks;" he having then been a clerk in a store, the "cost

Ntou

REED CITY CLARION.

mark" in which was "R-e-p-u-b-l-i-c-a-n," the letters representing the numerals in their regular order. This cost mark was adopted previous to the meeting under the oaks, but immediately after a visit, by the proprietor, to New York City, indicating that the name of the new party was known to a few before the meeting under the oaks.

But it is in connection with his efforts for the promotion of the public health that Dr. Baker's enduring fame rests. The Michigan State Board of Health was created by Act of the Legislature of 1873, and in July of that year it was organized with Dr. Baker as Secretary, a position which he has held continuously until the present time. He entered zealously upon this work, and has carried it on with discriminating judgment, with methodical habit, and with the courage that has often been required to combat old prejudices. It might also be said that he created the Board, for he started the movement that resulted in the law establishing it, and originated a very large proportion of the plans which it has since carried out. In the course of his long service he has acquired an immense fund of knowledge, and is recognized as one of the best authorities in the country in sanitarian lines. He has attended a great many conventions, made many addresses, and contributed much to the literature of sanitation. He is a member of many associations, among them the State Medical Society, the American Medical Society and American Public Health Association, of which he has been President. He is also an honorary member of the French Society of Hygiene. Aside from public health and medical associations, he is a member of the Loyal Legion, the G. A. R., and the Sons of the American Revolution.

He was married in Lansing, September 9th, 1867, to Miss Fannie H. Howard, daughter of Hon. Sanford Howard. Their children are Dr. Howard B. Baker, of Detroit; Henry B., Jr., student in the Agricultural College; Burton A., student in the Lansing High School, and Helen F., in the primary school.

LORENZO ABEL BARKER, familiarly known as "Ren." Barker, editor of the Reed City Clarion, was born at Naples, Ontario County, New York, August 16th, 1839. His father, George W. Barker, was born in Deerfield, Mass., March 1st, 1815, and learned the carpenter and joiners' trade in that State, but moved to New York, where he engaged in mercantile pursuits. Again he moved, in 1853, this time to Battle Creek, and engaged in the picture business until he died in Kalamazoo, in March, 1895. Lorenzo's mother's name was Weltha Tyler Barker, born in Deerfield, Mass., June 21st, 1816. She was married to George W. Barker in Naples, N. Y., in 1837, and died in Italy Hollow, N. Y., November 14th, 1852. Five children were born to them, of whom two are now living, Lorenzo and a sister, Mrs. Eugenia Dickinson, of Alba, Antrim County, Mich.

"Ren" attended the district school in the town of Italy, Yates County, N. Y., until 1853, when he attended one term of the Battle

Creek High School. At the death of his mother, and the marriage of his father to a second wife on their arrival in Battle Creek, he was turned from his home, and, though only 14 years of age, was thrown upon his own resources. For a year he worked upon a farm, for Albert Cummings, of Goguac Prairie. In the fall of 1854 he entered the Battle Creek Journal office, under the tuition of Hon. W. W. Woolnough, founder and at that time editor of that paper, to learn the printer's art, Mr. and Mrs. Woolnough making for him a home. He remained there until the great civil war broke out, when he enlisted, serving four years. Mr. Barker's military career was not only long but active. All through the earlier months of the war while his fingers recorded the dispatches of the opening campaign, and also the varied literature which arose from the exigencies of the times, he was awakened to the fact that men with the true fire of patriotism blazing in their breasts were surely needed at the front. Consequently, on the 28th of September, 1861, he enlisted under Captain John Piper, in Company E, Thirteenth Missouri, or Berge's Sharpshooters. The style of the organization was afterwards changed to Company "D," of the same regiment, which was known as the Sixty-sixth Illinois Western Sharp Shooters. In October of the same year, the company left Battle Creek for St. Louis, Mo., where it remained in camp of instruction until, in December of 1861, it was sent into Northern Missouri. Mr. Barker was first under fire at Mt. Zion, Mo., December 23d, 1861; next at Fort Donelson, Tenn., February 13-16, 1862; Shiloh, April 6 and 7, 1862; Siege of Corinth, from April 20 to May 30, 1862; Iuka, September 19th; Corinth, October 3 and 4, 1862. After this with his regiment he was occupied in camp duty, guerrilla warfare, and in building a large stockade on the Tuscumbia River, six miles south of Corinth. While here the regiment, at its own expense, armed itself with the celebrated Henry Repeating Rifle, or seventeen-shooter. In 1863 it marched from Camp Davis to Pulaski, Tenn., where Barker, with the rest of the regiment, was discharged on the 23d of December, 1863. He immediately re-enlisted in the same command, and went home on a veteran's furlough for thirty days. He was afterwards with General Sherman in the Atlanta campaign, was wounded in the foot at Rowe Cross Roads, and was assigned with 10,000 other wounded men, to the Provisional Division of the Army of the Tennessee. In the first part of 1865 the Division was sent to North Carolina to join Sherman's Army and "Ren" was in active service till the end of the war. He was mustered out in July, 1865.

Since the war ended Mr. Barker has been about as active in newspaper life as he was before in the military service. He has founded three papers, and has been connected with eight different papers in Michigan and Iowa. He is best known in this State from his connection ever since May 30th, 1884, with the Reed City Clarion. He is a wide-awake member of the State Press Association and in some years he, and a half dozen others, editors of interior weeklies, have been

George W. Bates.

the life of the annual meetings, the staid and serious editors of the city dailies being nowhere by the side of them.

When a lad of fifteen "Ren" attended, with Mr. Woolnough, the Convention "Under the Oaks" at Jackson, and he has been a Republican of the stalwart kind ever since. He has been a delegate to numerous County, District and State Conventions, was Presidential Elector in 1884 and 1896 and was chosen by acclamation a delegate to the Philadelphia National Convention in 1900. He was Postmaster at Reed City under the Harrison Administration, and was from 1892 to 1896 a member of the Republican State Central Committee. He has held a number of positions in the local Post and at State Encampments of the G. A. R., and has been four times delegate to the National Encampments. He is also a member of the Michigan Club, and the State and National Leagues of Republican Clubs and of the Knights of Pythias. When anything is going on in these organizations "Ren" is on hand. He is in attendance at all Grand Army gatherings, State and National Encampments and all political conventions, whether a delegate or not.

Mr. Barker was married, April 16, 1876, to Mrs. Eliza Reagan Grant, at Shenandoah, Iowa. They have no children. Mrs. Barker is an active worker in the Grand Army and Woman's Relief Corps; has been President of the Relief Corps of Reed City, twice delegate to the National Convention and has held other positions in connection with the organization.

GEORGE WILLIAMS BATES was born in Detroit, Mich., November 4th, 1848. His father was Samuel Gershom Bates, a merchant, and his mother was Rebecca Williams. His ancestors came from England and were a part of the Puritan Settlement in Massachusetts Bay Colony, many of whom rendered public service in the Colony, either as soldiers in King Philip's War or as deputies to the General Court. They permanently settled at Charlestown, Mass., Stamford and Saybrook, Conn.

The original ancestor was Robert Bates, of Wethersfield, Conn., whither he had gone in 1640 with the Connecticut contingent from the Massachusetts Bay Colony, and in 1641 settled at Stamford, where he lived and died. Mr. Bates is also a descendant from the Bucknam family, of Malden, Mass., and through them related to Nicholas Stowers, Captain John Sprague, and Lieutenant Ralph Sprague, among the original settlers of Newtown or Charlestown in 1628. On the maternal side, he is a descendant of Roger Williams and of Carey Latham, two of the earliest settlers of Connecticut and whose descendants lived respectively at Saybrook and New London. He was educated in the public schools of Detroit and the University of Michigan, where he graduated in the Classical course in 1870 and now holds the degree of M. A.

Mr. Bates' first occupation was that of representative in 1870 and 1871 at Detroit, of the publishing house of James R. Osgood & Co., of Boston. This occupation continued for one year, and in the fall of 1871 he entered the law offices of Newberry, Pond and Brown and later that of Meddaugh and Driggs, two of the leading law firms of Detroit at that time. He was admitted to the bar in December, 1874, and has since continued to practice law in Detroit. He has been actively concerned in politics and in social, moral and educational matters, and while he has never held political office, except that of Estimator-at-large for Detroit, he has been a delegate to several State Conventions and taken an active part in the politics of his City and County. He was candidate for Attorney General of the State at the Grand Rapids Convention in 1894. He has always been a Republican, and cast his first vote for Grant and Wilson in the Presidential election of 1872.

He is identified with many of the leading social, Masonic and educational organizations of Detroit; among others he is a member of the Oriental Masonic Lodge, also of King Cyrus Chapter of Royal Arch Masons and of the Michigan Sovereign Consistory; is Secretary and Treasurer of the Detroit Archaeological Society, a councillor of the American Institute of Archaeology; is Registrar and Treasurer of the Michigan Society of the Sons of the American Revolution and has been a delegate to many Congresses of the National Society of that organization. He is also a member of the New England Society and the University Club of Detroit, the University Alumni Association, the Detroit, Michigan State and American Bar Associations.

He married Miss Jennie Marie Fowler, April 26th, 1887, and his children are Stanley Fowler Bates and Virginia Williams Bates.

THOMAS TOMLINSON BATES, of Traverse City, Michigan, was born December 13th, 1841, at Keeseville, Essex County, New York. His father was Rev. Merritt Bates, and his mother Eliza A. Tomlinson. The father and mother were both of English ancestry His father was a Methodist Episcopal clergyman, an active and uncompromising Anti-Slavery man through all the thirty-five years preceding the civil war. A man of strong convictions and great ability, he occupied a prominent place in his church, and lived to see the triumph of the cause to which he had given the best years of his life. His mother was of the old New York family of Tomlinsons, prominent in New York City in Revolutionary times and the years immediately following.

Thomas T. Bates was educated in the public schools. At sixteen he began life for himself, clerking at one dollar a week and boarding himself. A year later he was general helper in a bank at Glens Falls, N. Y. At eighteen he occupied an important position in a banking house in Memphis, Tenn., but came North at the outbreak of the war. He removed to Traverse City in 1863, was cashier for

Thos. T. Bates

GRAND TRAVERSE HERALD.

Hannah, Lay & Co. two years, and resigned to open a real estate office with Hon. D. C. Leach, whose interest in the business he bought in 1871.

In 1858 his uncle, Hon. Morgan Bates, established the Grand Traverse Herald and sold the paper in 1867 to Hon. D. C. Leach. Thomas T. Bates, who had had the business management since 1865 bought the Herald of Mr. Leach in 1876 and has since that time been editor and proprietor. His wife, Mrs. M. E. C. Bates, is associate editor, and his daughter, Miss Mabel, local and society editor and associate business manager. Mr. Bates has always been active in politics. He was prominent in Eastern New York in 1856, when only 15 years old, in the youths' organization of "The Rocky Mountain Boys," in the Fremont campaign. His first Presidential vote was for Lincoln, in 1864, and he has never missed voting a straight Republican ticket since. He has never been a political officeholder, with the exception of that of postmaster at Traverse City 1881-83, resigning the position on account of the increasing business of the Herald, which demanded all his time. He was for several years Chairman of the Township and County Committees. In 1880 he was chosen a member of the State Central Committee of his party, and served ten consecutive years, the longest consecutive service ever given by any member of the party. He represented his District as delegate in the Republican National Convention of 1892, and was made secretary of the delegation.

In 1885 Mr. Bates was appointed a member of the Board of Trustees of the Northern Michigan Asylum, located at Traverse City, and opened to patients that year. He was re-appointed in 1889, and again in 1895, and is still acting on the Board. For seven years he was President of the Board. In the fall of 1885 he was also appointed a member of the Board of Building Commissioners for the same institution, to fill the vacancy caused by the resignation of Hon. Perry Hannah, and was at once chosen Chairman of the Board, serving in this capacity until the completion of the work of the Commission in the fall of 1886. He was elected Secretary of the Traverse City Railroad Company upon its organization in 1871, and served in that capacity until the road was leased to the Grand Rapids & Indiana Company; was then placed on the Board of Directors of the Traverse City Railroad Company, which organization has been continued, and for several years past has been President of the Company. He is a member of the F. & A. M. and R. A. M., the K. P. and K. O. T. M. organizations, and has been for a number of years past President of the Traverse City Business Men's Association, which has been instrumental in locating at that point nearly all the important manufacturing establishments of Traverse City. In 1897 he established with J. W. Hannen, the Morning Record, the only morning daily in Northern Michigan, and the enterprise has been very successful. Both that and the Herald are aggressively Republican in politics.

He was married in 1867 to Miss Martha E. Cram, daughter of Jesse Cram, who for many years was identified with the early history of Wayne and Genesee Counties, and who was also one of the pioneers of Grand Traverse County. The family consists of two daughters, Miss Mabel and Miss Clara, and a son, George G. Bates, who is in the publishing business in Chicago.

WILLIAM RUFUS BATES was born in Cazenovia, Madison County, N. Y., June 28th, 1845. His father was Emilius A. Bates, a farmer and Methodist Episcopal Minister, and his mother was Marie L. Bates. His father's ancestry was English, and his mother's French and English. His education was received at Cazenovia Seminary and in a partial course at the University of Michigan.

Mr. Bates has had an extensive newspaper, as well as political experience. He commenced editorial work on the Addison, N. Y., Advertiser, and also acted as Albany Correspondent during a session of the New York Legislature. After he came to Michigan he was local editor of the Wolverine Citizen at Flint, editor of the Saginaw Enterprise, and after that managing editor of the Chicago Republican, now the Inter Ocean. His health failing he made a radical change, becoming superintendent of the Enterprise Boom Co., at Au Gres, Bay County, now in Arenac County.

While at Au Gres, Mr. Bates served as Justice of the Peace and Supervisor in 1869 and 1870, and in the latter year was elected to the Legislature from Bay County. He resigned in the spring of 1871, and was appointed Register of the U. S. Land Office at East Saginaw. He resigned this position in 1876, and was appointed Special Agent of the United States Pension Bureau the same year by Secretary Chandler. He resigned this place in 1879, and became Secretary to U. S. Senator, Henry P. Baldwin. In 1881 he was appointed Special Agent for the United States Treasury, and was removed by President Cleveland in 1885 for "offensive partisanship," being the first Republican in Michigan to be so honored. He practiced law in Flint and Detroit from 1885 to 1888, and then became political secretary to United States Senator James McMillan, a position from which he resigned in 1895. He was elected to the Legislature of 1897 and appointed United States Marshal for the Eastern District of Michigan in 1898, a position which he still holds.

Mr. Bates is a good organizer and was the efficient Secretary of the Republican State Central Committee in the campaigns of 1880, 1882, 1886, 1888, 1890, 1892 and 1894. He has been delegate to State Conventions quite regularly since 1868. His Republicanism might be said to be inherited from his father who was an original Abolitionist. His first Presidential vote was for Grant in '68. He is a member of the Michigan Club, Fellowcraft Club, Detroit Club; Cosmos Club, Washington, D. C.; Union Club, Flint; American Historical Association,

Junius E. Beal

THE ANN ARBOR COURIER-HERALD.

Zeta Psi Fraternity of Ann Arbor; is a thirty-second degree Mason and a member of the Shrine; is Past Grand Chancellor and Past Supreme Representative of the Knights of Pythias. At Flint, January 11, 1866, he married Gertrude A. Belcher. Their children are: Irving Belcher Bates and Mrs. Eusebia F. Hardy.

JUNIUS EMERY BEAL was born at Port Huron, Mich., February 23, 1860. His parents were James E. Field, a druggist, and Loretta Beal Field. On the Field side he is the seventh descendant of Zachariah Field who came to this country about 1630 or 1632. He was the grandson of the celebrated astronomer, John Field, who was granted a crest over his family arms in 1558, in England. David Dudley, Henry M., Cyrus W. and Judge Stephen J. Field are from this American ancestor. The name originally was de la Feld, from Alsace. On the Beal side he is number nine from John Beal who landed at Hingham, Mass., in 1638, coming from England. His grandfather, Emery Beal, was contractor of the Michigan Central construction, from Dexter to Chelsea, and Postmaster of Plainfield for many years. The mother of the infant Field dying when he was eleven months old, he was adopted by Rice Aner Beal and his wife, Phoebe B. Beal, whose name he assumed. He was educated in the Ann Arbor Schools and at the University of Michigan, where he graduated with the B. L. degree in 1882. His first occupation was to learn to set type in the Courier office. On leaving College in 1882 he took up the editorial management of the Ann Arbor Courier for a year and until the death of his father, Rice Aner Beal, when he assumed direction of his business affairs and the management of his estate. He has continued the printing and newspaper business, adding on by purchase the Weekly Register and the Daily Times. He has been a Republican since beginning to vote in 1881, has been delegate to several State Conventions, was Presidential Elector in 1888, and was President of the Michigan League of Republican Clubs, in 1889-90.

Mr. Beal's business interests are very numerous. He is President of the Ann Arbor Printing Company, Secretary-Treasurer of the Ann Arbor Electric Company, Vice-President of the Peninsular Paper Mills at Ypsilanti, Vice-President of the Iron Mountain Water Company at Iron Mountain, Mich., Director of the Detroit Fire and Marine Insurance Company, Director of the Michigan Club in Detroit, Director of the Farmers' and Mechanics' Bank in Ann Arbor, Treasurer of the Ann Arbor School District, Treasurer of the Wesleyan Guild Corporation at the University of Michigan, Treasurer of the Beta Theta Pi Club of Michigan, Director of the Students' Christian Association, Newberry Hall, Assignee of the Ann Arbor Agricultural Works, and Trustee of the South Carolina Cypress Company. In the Masonic Order he is a member of the Scottish Rite, and Shrine, and is a Knight Templar. He is also connected with the Beta Theta Pi College Fraternity; the Ann Arbor Golf Club, and the Michigan Press

Association. He was married November 28, 1889, at Cooper, Kalamazoo County, to Miss Ella Louise Travis. Their children are: Travis Field Beal, born September 3, 1894, and Loretta Beal, born April 16, 1897.

Mr. Beal was President of the Michigan Press Association in 1893. In 1889 he rode over 2,000 miles on a bicycle over European roads, across Ireland, England, France, Switzerland, Germany, Belgium, Norway and Sweden.

GEORGE BECK, for many years prominent in Detroit business and political circles, was the son of William B. and Anna Lee Beck, and was born in Tivorton, Devon, England, August 27, 1843. His parents came to this country in 1850, and settled first in Memphis, Tenn., afterwards moving to Detroit. His early education was given him by his parents, and he commenced earning his own living at a very early age. When only ten years old he was employed by Smith & Coles, butchers, on Woodbridge street, Detroit, and in April, 1857, he took a position with William Wreford in the Central Market. Five years later, being then nineteen, he started in business for himself, buying and selling country produce. In 1863 he entered the Chicago live stock market, and purchased cattle for the Detroit, Buffalo and Albany markets. Eleven years later he changed his purchasing point to St. Louis, continuing in this business until 1892. During this long period he made his purchases with good judgment, carried on a large business, and accumulated a comfortable fortune. In 1890 he organized the Michigan Beef and Provision Company, of which he has been President and active manager ever since. He was elected Treasurer of the National Protective Butchers' Association in 1888, and again in 1889.

In addition to being prominent and successful in the business world, Mr. Beck has attained distinction in municipal affairs. He was the first Republican Alderman elected in the Eighth ward, which he carrried in 1892, 1894 and 1896. He was elected President of the Board in 1894, and again in 1897, the latter after a prolonged contest, in which ninety-seven ballots were taken. He was an excellent presiding officer. When not holding that position he was on important committees, and during his whole three terms of service was one of the most influential members of the Council. In 1898 he was a prominent candidate for the Republican nomination for County Treasurer, and in 1900 for that of Sheriff. He has frequently been a delegate to County conventions and, in the same capacity, attended the State conventions of 1892, 1894 and 1896.

Mr. Beck is a member of the Michigan Sovereign Consistory; Damascus Commandery, Knights Templar; Royal Arcanum and the Michigan and Fellowcraft and Detroit Bowling Club, the German Salesmen, the Detroit Wheelmen. In 1863 he married Miss Minnie

Very Truly Yours

J. R. Bennett

A. Miller, of Detroit. She died in 1893, leaving two daughters, Mrs. H. B. West and Mrs. Charles G. Wynn. In 1895 he was married a second time to Miss Jennie M. Smith.

JOSEPH R. BENNETT, of Adrian, has been for many years a sturdy figure among the Republicans of Michigan. He stood with them "Under the Oaks at Jackson," when the party came to its baptism and began its career. There were none more enthusiastic and active in the campaign of 1856 when Fremont held the banner and inspired the march, nor none more devoted in the cause of Lincoln in 1860. The Union held none more faithful and patriotic than "Uncle Joe" in the stirring days of '61 to '65. And so of every campaign since, National, State or County; this consistent and enthusiastic Republican has inspired the earnest work and helped direct the triumphant march of the party cohorts in Southern Michigan.

In the early days, when his County of Lenawee was hopelessly Democratic, he sounded the slogan and led an aggressive fight. He was for "Tippecanoe and Tyler, too," in 1840 and steadily in array on the side of Free Soil. The Whigs nominated him for Sheriff of Lenawee in 1848, but Bennett fell that time. In 1850 he came in again and this time conquered, being the only Whig elected. He held the office of Sheriff for four terms, with an intermission between as the law prescribes.

In 1861 he was appointed a Deputy United States Marshal. In 1862 Abraham Lincoln commissioned Mr. Bennett Assessor of Internal Revenue for the First District. Toward the last of his term in this office the Administration of Andrew Johnson undertook to use Mr. Bennett to advance their political schemes. Finding him incorruptible Uncle Joe was removed from office. Senator Howard remarked on this occasion that Uncle Joe's head would fall. "Let it fall," said Bennett, "the President may cut it off but he can't turn it Andy's way." In 1869 President Grant appointed Mr. Bennett United States Marshal of the Eastern District of Michigan. This office he held for eight years. During that time he had experiences with counterfeiters, smugglers, and other law breakers and had occasion to use all his skill, craft, tact, presence of mind and courage, but Uncle Joe boasts not of his work in the line of duty. In 1870 he was Supervisor of the Census for Michigan. For the rest he has been a progressive and successful farmer. For years an officer of the Lenawee County Agricultural Society, he was instrumental in securing the fine fair grounds in Adrian in 1884. Mr. Bennett has been successful in other lines of business. He began first as a manufacturer of potash in the days when the pioneers burned up the timber to clear their farms and sold nothing but the ashes. Then he engaged in the drug trade, and followed it for years. He became President of the Lenawee

County Savings Bank, which he helped to organize, succeeding the late Governor Croswell, and still holds this position.

Joseph R. Bennett was born in Shelby, Orleans County, New York, May 18th, 1819. Six years later the family moved to Genesee County, New York, and there, in the town of Alabama, the youthful Bennett attended the district school. When he was 15 years old the Bennett family removed to Michigan, and settled in Rollin, Lenawee County. The father built the third house in that Township. In 1839, being then 20 years old, Joseph R. Bennett married Miss Nancy J. Rowley, born in Onondaga, N. Y., in 1824. The young couple moved at once to a log house in a clearing on a newly acquired Government "80." The house at first lacked doors and windows. Blankets closed the openings at night. The distant howling of wolves disheartened not the brave young people. Industry soon made a comfortable, as love made a happy, home in the wilderness that then was in 1840. April 18th, 1880, Mrs. Bennett passed away, having been a loving partner and faithful helpmate to Uncle Joe for 41 years. Their children are Helen M., wife of Major S. E. Graves, of the Twelfth Michigan Infantry. Mrs. Graves, dying in 1883, left one child, Walter J. Graves, now civil engineer in the U. S. Survey of the Lakes. Mr. Bennett's second daughter, Dora E., lives at home, caring for the fireside and guarding the domestic welfare of the family home.

Let the sketch close with a picture of Mr. Bennett in every day life as his friends and neighbors know him. The poem is by Will Carleton, and it reveals an amiable phase of the character of one who may justly be styled "a war horse of the Republican party." The "me" of the poem is J. R. B. Adair, son of Mr. and Mrs. Ed. Adair, formerly of Adrian:

Of all the peoples in this town,
  So far as I can see,
The best two fellows, up and down,
  Is Uncle Joe an' me.
We found each other long ago—
How much it is I can't quite know—
I guess a thousan' years or so—
  An' never didn't agree.

We know where all the bluejays nest,
  Does Uncle Joe an' me,
An' when the robins sing the best,
  An' where the squirrels be;
An' when the rabbits romp an' play,
An' where the biggest woodchucks stay,
An' where the owl sleeps every day,
  An' where the thrushes be.

When we drive out he lets me drive,
  An' then we both agree.
There ain't two bigger sports alive,
  Than Uncle Joe an' me.
He says he' just as lives as not
Lend me the fastest horse he's got,
He wouldn't let no other "tot"
  Take hold the reins, you see!

We know the biggest stories, too,
  Does Uncle Joe an' me,
An' some of 'em is partly true,
  An' some is goin' to be;
'Bout Injuns, full of scalps an' noise,
An' giants that had trees fur toys,
An' how things was wh n we was boys —
  Some years ago, you see!

My mommer says we've got to die,
  An' angels live an' be,
An' go and live up in the sky,
  From sin forever free;
But that's what I don't mean to do,
'Till Uncle Joe gets started, too.
For Heaven would be ten times as blue,
  'Thout Uncle Joe an' me!

THOMAS BERRY, son of John and Catharina (Hooper) Berry, was born in Horsham, England, February 7th, 1829. His father, John Berry, was engaged in the tanning business, and with his family removed to America in 1835, locating at Elizabeth, N. J., where he resumed his former occupation. Thomas, the subject of this sketch, received his education in a private school at Elizabeth, and at an early age entered his father's employ. Upon gaining a thorough knowledge of the business, he was placed in charge of a branch of his father's affairs in the State of Virginia, where he remained five years. In 1856 he removed to Detroit, Mich., where his parents had preceded him, and after a short time spent in search of a location, with his brother Joseph he formed the firm of Berry Brothers, and established a factory for the manufacture of varnish. The original location of their plant was in Springwells, but after a few months their business was removed to its present quarters at the foot of Leib street.

Owing to the untiring energy, sterling integrity and correct business methods of this firm, the name of Berry Bros. has become the most widely known of any varnish manufacturing concern in the world. Their business, ranking first of its kind, requires eight branch establishments, scattered throughout the principal cities of the United States, and affords constant employment to about three hundred persons. Politically Mr. Berry is a Republican, and although taking an active part in the councils of his party, he has been adverse to holding public office, other than that of a local nature. He was appointed President of the Board of Poor Commissioners by Mayor Thompson, being the first to serve in that capacity; in 1876 was elected a member of the Board of Estimates, serving one term; in 1881 he was elected a member of the Council for a term of three years, and was re-elected in 1884, serving until that board was legislated out of office. He was subsequently elected a member of the School Board, serving four years. He was one of the earliest members of the Michigan Club, served on its Board of Directors for several years, and has been President and Vice-President of the Club.

Mr. Berry has been prominently identified with the growth and development of the manufacturing interests of Detroit, and aside from his interest in the firm of Berry Brothers he is a large stockholder in the Detroit Linseed Oil Co., a joint partner with his brother, Joseph H. Berry, in the Combination Gas Machine Company, is a director in the Citizens' Savings Bank and a Trustee of the Michigan College of Medicine. He is prominent in Masonic circles, being a member of Detroit Commandery No. 1, Knights Templar; Monroe Chapter, R. A. M., and Zion Lodge, F. & A. M. He is also a member of the Jefferson Avenue Presbyterian Church, of which his family are regular attendants. Mr. Berry was married on December 21st, 1860, to Miss Janet Lowe, daughter of John Lowe, of Niagara, Ontario, who died in August, 1893, leaving four daughters.

CHARLES FREDERICK BIELMAN, of Detroit, was born in the same City, April 20th, 1859. His father, Frederick Bielman, came to this country from Prussia, and was, at different times, school teacher, farmer and officer in the Federal Army. His mother, Ellen Daily Bielman, was from Ireland.

Charles F. was educated in the public schools of Casco, St. Clair County, Mich. He helped do chores on a farm till he was fourteen years of age, then went to work in a general store, which was also postoffice, telegraph office, steamboat landing, etc., at Marine City. He has been on wharf or boat ever since, and knows the passenger traffic business of these waters about as well as any one along the docks. He remained in Marine City till he was 21, when he returned to Detroit and went to work for the Detroit & Cleveland Steam Navigation Co., as purser of the Steamer Evening Star. When the original Steamer City of Mackinac was put in commission he was transferred to her, and remained there as chief purser for six successive seasons. He then became Treasurer and Traffic Manager of the combined Star-Cole lines of steamers. In 1886, he, with Captain Darius Cole, purchased controlling interest in the Star Line of steam-

ers, and he has ever since been connected with the different combinations of Star Line, Red Star Line, and White Star Line steamers, as Director, Treasurer, Secretary or Traffic Manager. He is at present Secretary and Traffic Manager of the White Star Line, Secretary and Treasurer of the Stewart Transportation Co., and he is also a director in the Detroit River Savings Bank, and is connected with the Harmonie Society.

Mr. Bielman has been a Republican all his life, and cast his first Presidential vote for Garfield. He has never been delegate to a Convention, and has never held or sought any office. His name was mentioned as a possible and popular candidate for Mayor on the Republican ticket in 1899, but without any encouragement or countenance from himself.

Mr. Bielman was married January 22d, 1890 to Miss Katherine Barlum. They have two children, Florence C., aged 9, and C. Frederich, aged 6.

ARTHUR CRANSON BIRD was born in Highland, Oakland County, Mich., May 22d, 1864, his father being Joseph Johnson Bird, a farmer, and his mother, Elizabeth Cranson Bird. The ancestry was English on both sides. The Bird and Cranson families were in the first company of settlers in Livingston County, Mich., Gardner Bird and Job Cranson being the heads. Job Cranson was the well known banker at Fenton, Genesee County, during the last twenty years of his life. Joseph Johnson Bird was the first white child born in Livingston County.

Arthur Cranson Bird received his education at the Michigan Agricultural College, graduating and receiving the degree of Bachelor of Science in 1883. He was granted the degree of Master of Agriculture in 1884. From 1883 to 1898 he combined the business of farming with those of loaning money for Eastern capitalists and conducting a real estate business. He began on a farm of 110 acres in Highland, Oakland County, and soon enlarged it to 260 acres. He also has farms in other parts of the State, and is the heaviest stockholder in the West Michigan Nurseries at Benton Harbor. In addition to paying attention to these extensive interests he was, for five years, associate editor of the Michigan Farmer. He was member of the State Board of Agriculture from 1897 to 1899, and is now its Secretary. He was one of the founders of the State Association of Farmers' Clubs, and has served as its Secretary and President.

In politics Mr. Bird was always a Republican. He cast his first Presidential vote for Harrison, and was delegate to the Republican State Conventions of 1890 and 1896. His only society connections are with the Masonic order. He was married August 16th, 1889, to Josephine St. John, of Highland, Mich., and has two sons, Harold S. and Clarence S.

JEROME HOLLAND BISHOP, son of William Bishop, is a direct descendant of the Bishops who landed in Salem, Mass., in 1628, coming from Ipswich, England, with Governor Endicott. His mother's name was Betsy Jerome Stearns. She was own cousin to Leonard and Lawrence Jerome, of New York City, making the subject of this sketch second cousin to Lady Randolph Churchill, who was the daughter of Leonard Jerome, of New York. As both the Bishops and the Jeromes served in the Revolutionary War, Jerome Holland Bishop is a Son of the American Revolution from both ancestors. He was born in Oxbow, Jefferson County, N. Y., September 3rd, 1846, and was educated at a private academy at Redwood, N. Y., which was his home from the age of four till he was twenty-one. After leaving the academy he had an extensive experience as school teacher. He taught at Chippewa Bay, St. Lawrence County, when fifteen years of age; was principal of the school at Redwood at the age of eighteen; was teacher in Dyrenfurth College, Chicago, in 1869; came to Michigan as principal of the Decatur public schools in January, 1870, and went to Wyandotte as principal of the Public Schools, in August, 1871, remaining in the position four years.

An interval of two years in other business occurred in this round of school teaching. From 1861 to 1863 he was with Sterling & Mosher as clerk in a book store in Watertown, N. Y. But it was after he reached Wyandotte that he made the venture which has given him fame in the commercial world. He established the business now carried on by the J. H. Bishop Company, that of manufacturing skin rugs, sleigh robes and fur overcoats. In the fall of 1898 he established a branch in Sandwich, Ontario, for Canadian business. The company has the largest manufacturing plant in that line in the world, does the largest business and makes the finest goods in the world. The business grew up from a very small beginning and required a good many years of hard work and study. Mr. Bishop is President of the Company and gives so much attention to its affairs that he has never taken time to form any other business connections.

During his school teaching period he also had a little militia experience. He was too young for the service when the war broke out, but in the latter part of 1864 and the first part of 1865 he was bookkeeper for a firm in Memphis, Tennessee, and being then 17 years of age, he served as Fourth Sergeant of Company D, First Tennessee Militia.

Mr. Bishop came of an Abolition family and has been a Republican ever since the party was organized. He cast his first vote for Grant. He was Mayor of Wyandotte two terms, 1885-6; President of the Board of Education two terms; member of the Board of Control of Ionia House of Correction, from which he resigned in 1898. He was a candidate for Congress from the Second Congressional District, in 1898, when he had the unanimous support of Wayne County, but after the forty-fifth ballot, withdrew and finally the nomination went

to Henry C. Smith, of Adrian. His political life has been more in the nature of contributing to the support of the party and working for its best interests rather than of holding office.

Mr. Bishop is a Congregationalist in religious belief, is a Trustee of Olivet College and has been, for many years, Superintendent of the Congregational Sunday School in Wyandotte. He is a member of the Detroit Club, Fellowcraft Club, St. Clair Fishing and Shooting Club and North Anderdon Shooting Club. He is a 32d Degree Mason and a Knight Templar.

Mr. Bishop has been married twice. His first wife, Jennie Gray, of Redwood, N. Y., who died in 1873, left one daughter, Maud, now the wife of William J. Burns, of Windsor, Ontario. In 1876 he married Ella M. Clark, daughter of Isaac and Lydia Clark. Their children are Jerome Holland, who was married June 4th, 1900, to Miss Helen F. Chapin, of Chicago, and is now in Berlin; daughters, Della and Mabel, and youngest son, Wallace Clark.

HON. ROSWELL P. BISHOP, of Ludington, Mich., was born at Sidney, Delaware County, N. Y., January 6th, 1843. He is a direct descendant of the Bishop family which came from Old England in the early days of Colonial American history and settled in the State of Connecticut. His grandfather, Joseph Bishop, was born in Westchester County, N. Y., and served as a soldier in the War of 1812, and afterwards settled in Delaware County, N. Y., where Edward Bishop, father of Roswell P. Bishop, was born. At the age of sixteen, Edward Bishop became a Methodist local preacher and so continued for upwards of fifty years. Edward Bishop married Anna Andrews, a native of Delaware County, a descendant of the Andrews family of Massachusetts, and from this union, seven children were born, one of whom was Roswell P. Bishop. Owing to the financial condition of his family, he was called upon at a tender age to shift for himself, and when ten years old, went out from his home to earn a livelihood and hew for himself his own pathway for advancement. His first experience was that of a farm hand near the town of Otego, N. Y., where he worked for six months for the magnificent salary of $1.50 per month. He was afterwards employed for a number of years by Henry Wickham, at Oneonta, N. Y., and when the Civil War broke out, he was earning $13 per month. He was one of the first to offer his services, and enlisted July 28, 1861, in Company C, Forty-third New York Infantry Volunteers. He participated in the Battles of Yorktown, Williamsburgh, Antietam, first Battle of Fredericksburg, and was with McClellan during the ever memorable Peninsular campaign. At the Battle of Lee's Mill, Va., April 28th, 1862, his right arm was shattered, which necessitated its amputation near the shoulder. He took a short furlough of only four weeks, and then returned to his regiment, actively engaging in the various contests and duties of his regiment, until the last of December, 1862, when he accepted his discharge and went home to prepare himself, thus handicapped, for the contest of life. He at once entered district school, later Unadilla Academy, Cooperstown Seminary and Walton Academy, from which institution he graduated in his preparatory course for a collegiate education. He earned his money by teaching school to thus educate himself. In 1868 he entered Michigan University and remained there, with the intermission of one year, until 1872, when he obtained a position as one of the Police Force at the United States Capitol, at Washington, D. C., upon the recommendation of all the professors of the University, Judge Claudius B. Grant, of our Supreme Court, and other well known politicians of that date, and especially through the efforts of Hon. Thomas W. Ferry, then acting as Vice-President of the United States.

Mr. Bishop remained in Washington for three years, and while there married Louise Gaunt, of Ann Arbor, Michigan, one of the teachers in the public schools of that city. He returned to Ann Arbor in 1875, was admitted to the bar, and in June of that year, settled in Mason County, Michigan, where he took up a homestead of 160 acres. After proving up on his homestead, he actively entered the practice of law at Ludington in the summer of 1876, and in the fall of that year, was elected Prosecuting Attorney. He was re-elected in 1878, and declined a renomination in 1880. In 1882, he was elected to the Legislature, and participated in that ever memorable Senatorial contest, in which Senator Ferry was defeated for re-election as United States Senator. He entered that contest for the express purpose of paying back to Senator Ferry a debt of gratitude which he owed to the Senator for his appointment to a position in Washington, and stood by Mr. Ferry until the very end of the contest. He was again elected Prosecuting Attorney for Mason County in 1884, and again declined a renomination. He was again elected to the Legislature in 1893. He was elected to the Fifty-fourth Congress in the election of 1894, was elected to the Fifty-fifth and Fifty-sixth Congresses. He was renominated for the Fifty-seventh Congress by acclamation, and was re-elected by 9,211 plurality, carrying every County in the District.

In politics, Mr. Bishop has always been an active Republican, his first vote having been cast for Abraham Lincoln in 1864. His valuable services have been recognized in Congress, first by his appointment as a member of the Committee on Military Affairs, and in the Fifty-fifth Congress he was appointed to a leading position on the Rivers and Harbors Committee. He is still a member of this Committee.

In his home life, Mr. Bishop has been singularly fortunate. His union has resulted in a family of one son, Roswell F. Bishop, who graduated in the class of 1899 from the University of Michigan. He is a member of the Grand Army of the Republic, Independent Order of Odd Fellows, Knights of Pythias, and Elks.

*F. A. Blades.*

Mr. Bishop's Congressional career was marked by a very large measure of success. His usefulness to his District was very apparent and his place in the Committee on Rivers and Harbors made him valuable to the whole State, as well as to the Ninth Congressional District. Many of the river and harbor appropriation bills which finally passed Congress for the benefit and improvement of Michigan interests can be directly traced to his influence upon the Committee of which he is such a hard-working member. Not only upon the Committee of Rivers and Harbors did he serve well and faithfully, but in his careful watchfulness of the other interests of his District was he as efficient. No worthy member of the grand old army in blue ever appealed to Roswell P. Bishop unsuccessfully, and through his endeavors many a worthy old soldier has obtained his just deserts from a grateful and never-forgetting Republic.

FRANCIS ASBURY BLADES, at present Controller of the City of Detroit, was born in Newtown, Worcester County, Md., August 7th, 1821, his parents being William Blades, a clergyman, and Charlotte Furness. The family were English, but came to this country in the early settlement of the colony in Maryland. William Blades left Maryland in 1828 on account of the institution of slavery. He was then a hatter by trade, went to Newark, N. J., thence to Batavia, N. Y., thence to East Avon, N. Y., and from East Avon to Grand Blanc, Mich., in May, 1835. He was a member of the Legislature of Michigan in 1848.

Francis A. Blades was educated at his father's fireside by the light of hickory bark torches and bears' oil tapers; spent his spare time evenings in reading everything he could get hold of; went through Dayboll's Arithmetic alone; worked two days to buy a Brown's Grammar, and in the fall of 1840 walked three miles and back every day for six weeks to attend a grammar school. He commenced teaching in the winter of 1840 at $12 per month and board around; taught school four winters, and one summer; when not teaching, worked for J. K. Abbott in his general store in Grand Blanc, assisting in looking after a large farm and ashery, making black salts for market in Detroit. In September, 1844, he entered the ministry of the Methodist Episcopal Church. His first appointment was to Shiawassee Circuit, including Shiawassee County and part of Genesee, Livingston, Clinton and Saginaw Counties; preached twenty-eight times every four weeks, and rode about three hundred miles on horseback to reach the several appointments. He received less than $50 for the whole year's work, and not ten per cent of that in money. His second appointment was to Lyons Circuit, including Portland, Lyons, Ionia and the country round about for two years. His subsequent appointments from 1847 to 1850 were to the Clinton and Bennington circuits. In 1850 he was appointed to the Grand Rapids Station, and successively to Albion,

Ypsilanti, Woodward Avenue and Congress Street Churches, Detroit, and Ann Arbor and Adrian Churches. He was Presiding Elder of Adrian District from 1865 to 1868, and was appointed Presiding Elder of Detroit District in the latter year and served four years. His health breaking down, he took a superannuated relation at the Conference in 1872, went home and did not leave the house again until March, 1873.

When he recovered sufficiently to go out his money was all gone and prospects dark, but, as he says, "Henry C. Hodges was a friend indeed and his kindness will never be forgotten by me. He gave me the use of a desk and chair in his office, and on April 1st, 1873, I opened a real estate office, and made more money that year than in any ten years of my life; had just got nicely a-going when the panic of 1873 struck us and the profits made melted away like a snow bank in an April sun." In 1874 Mr. Blades was appointed Appraiser of Merchandise for the Port of Detroit, through the influence of Senators Z. Chandler and T. W. Ferry, and he remained in office until removed by President Cleveland in 1886. In March, 1894, he was appointed Deputy Controller of Detroit, and July 2nd, 1895, was by Mayor Pingree, appointed Controller for a term of three years. In 1898 he was reappointed by Maybury for another term of three years. Though never in the field Mr. Blades had an exceedingly useful and creditable war record. While pastor of the Church in Ann Arbor, he recruited over 1,500 men, and raised a large amount of money as bounty for the soldiers, and in 1862, with Professor Cooley, afterwards Judge Cooley, he went to Detroit to offer his services to Governor Blair for active service in the field. Mr. Blades was gazetted for Colonel and Cooley for Lieutenant Colonel, but at the special request of Governor Blair, Alanson Sheeley, Jacob S. Farrand, John Owen and Senator Chandler, they remained at home, and continued their work, Cooley in the University and Blades in the pulpit and on the stump, raising money and soldiers.

William Blades was a Henry Clay Whig and the first Whig elected Sheriff of Genesee County, in 1844, and a member of the Legislature for Genesee County in 1848. F. A. Blades came under the influence of Daniel B. Wakefield of Genesee County, a personal friend of General Cass, often met General Cass at Wakefield's house, and a friendship sprung up between the boy Blades and the General. His last work in the Democratic party in 1850, was to go to Lansing at the request of General Cass, Lieutenant Governor William M. Fenton and Honorable E. H. Thomson, of Flint, to aid in nominating the General for the United States Senate. The Democratic party of Michigan was at that time strongly "Free Soil," and General Cass was at one time in great danger of being left out on account of his "Nicholson Letter," written in 1847. After the nomination of the General, Mr. Blades, on bidding him good-bye, said: "General, if you people down there in Washington stand by the principles of the Democratic party as held and expressed by the Democracy of Michigan for Free Soil, all right, but, should you be misled by the sophistry of the South, and be led away and pledge the Democratic party in favor of carrying slavery into free territory, you will be the last Democratic Senator from Michigan for the next twenty-five years, if not forever." General Cass arose from his chair and still holding Mr. Blades' hand, said: "My friend Blades, I think the wisdom of the Democratic party can be safely trusted on that question, and the Democratic party will be the ruling political power in this country for the next twenty-five years, if not forever;" and, with a cordial shake of the hand they parted, not to meet again until General Cass had resigned from the Cabinet of James Buchanan, and had come home to Detroit to be received by his fellow citizens with open arms.

In 1852 Mr. Blades left the Democratic party on the question of carrying slavery into free territory, and for two years he had no political affiliations, having no more confidence in the old Whig party than in the Democratic party. It was in the late summer of this year, 1852, that he made the acquaintance of Zachariah Chandler, who was then the Whig candidate for Governor, and a friendship sprang up between them that lasted until severed by the death of Mr. Chandler. Mr. Blades took part in the conferences and preparation for a new party that took place in 1852 and 1853 and was present in Jackson on the evening of the organization of the Republican party. From that time until now he has been an earnest advocate of the principles of that party. He has personally known every Governor of Michigan, from Stevens T. Mason in 1835 to the present time. In Republican politics Mr. Blades has been classed as a "Stalwart," with not a drop of "Mugwump" blood in his veins. He was intimately associated with Senator Chandler in all of his campaigns after 1854, and no man enjoyed Mr. Chandler's confidence more than he. He took a very active part in the election of T. W. Ferry and of T. W. Palmer to the United States Senate. He was also very earnest in advocating the first election of Senator McMillan. His admiration of Senator Palmer led to very close relations and a warm friendship that has continued until now. He was the first man to propose Hazen S. Pingree for the Republican nomination for Mayor in 1889, and he has since then been a warm friend and earnest supporter of Mayor and Governor Pingree. The last campaign of Mr. Blades was that for the nomination and election of Governor Pingree in 1896, making over sixty speeches in different parts of the State, commencing in March and ending in November.

Mr. Blades was first married September 6, 1845, to Helen Brown, of Grand Blanc, Michigan, daughter of Chauncey and Rebecca Brown. She died October 1st, 1849. His second wife was Eliza Jane Ament, nee Eliza Jane Hartwell, daughter of Jonathan and Eliza Hartwell, of Bennington, Shiawassee County, Michigan, and widow of Edward L. Ament, of Owosso, Michigan. They were married in 1850, and she died January 8th, 1898, at Detroit. He has two sons living, William H. Blades, born in 1852, and Harry H. Blades, born in 1864.

Mr. Blades was made a Master Mason in June, 1850; a Royal Arch Mason in 1852; a Knight Templar, Detroit Commandery, in 1856; received the several grades of the A. and A. Rite in 1862, and the thirty-third Degree in 1863. He has been active in all departments of the work since 1850.

AUSTIN BLAIR, one of the great War Governors in whom the exigencies of the times gave development and play to the highest qualities, came of a sturdy ancestry, and proved worthy of his parentage and early training. The first of the race in this country was James Blair, who came from Scotland in 1756, and settled on a piece of land near Worcester, Massachusetts. His grandson, George Blair, felled the first tree, built the first log cabin and burned the first log heap in Tompkins County, New York, in 1809, and lived there until his death sixty years later. He married Rhoda Blackman, an energetic, thrifty, warm-hearted woman of Dutch descent, and to them the subject of this sketch was born February 8th, 1818. During his early years he had the usual routine of a farm boy, working on the farm two-thirds of the year, and attending school the other third. The father was an educated man and the mother was ambitious for her family, and means were furnished Austin to aid in securing a better education. He took mathematical and classical studies in Cazenovia Seminary; spent one year in Hamilton College and then went to Union College, which was under the Presidency of the eminent Dr. Nott, graduating from there in 1839. He immediately began the study of law in the office of Sweet & Davis, at Owego, was admitted to the bar in 1841, and the same year moved to Jackson, Michigan. In 1842 he located in Eaton Rapids and was elected Clerk of Eaton County. In 1844 he returned to Jackson, which was his home for the next half century.

Mr. Blair was, from the outset, deeply interested in public affairs and always took an active part in politics. He was in demand as a speaker, as early as the Henry Clay campaign of 1844, and then laid the foundation for his enduring reputation as a campaign orator. In 1845 he saw his first Legislative experience as a member of the Lower House of the Michigan Legislature, in which he rendered valuable service in the work of revising the Statutes. He was also largely instrumental in securing the abolition of capital punishment in Michigan. For this he was denounced as an infidel, in a sermon preached by Rev. Dr. George Duffield, of Detroit. He also reported from the Judiciary Committee a proposition to strike the word "white" from the clause of the Constitution which related to the suffrage. In this matter he was away in advance of the sentiments of the Whig party, and his advocacy of the measure caused his defeat in the next election.

In 1848 he was a member of the Free Soil Convention at Buffalo, and was one of the Committee of Conference, representing different party interests, that nominated Van Buren and Adams. Six years later he was among those who hailed with acclaim the movement for uniting in one organization the anti-slavery sentiment of all the old parties. He attended the Convention at Jackson, was one of the Committee on Resolutions, and reported to the Convention a minority platform, because he thought the one prepared by the majority of the committee was not strong enough in its utterances. Any one who has read the platform as adopted, and as given in the third chapter of Volume I. of this publication, will see that Mr. Blair's views on the slavery question must have been very pronounced if that was too mild for his liking. In that campaign he was elected to the State Senate, where he assisted in drafting the "Personal Liberty Bill," designed for the protection of fugitive slaves. He supported Fremont for President in 1856, and in 1860 he was Chairman of the Michigan Delegation in the Convention at Chicago which nominated Lincoln for President. He was, with the rest of the delegation, a strong Seward partisan, but when Lincoln's nomination was made he pledged support to the nominee in one of the most graceful speeches of the occasion.

In the State Convention that followed Mr. Lincoln's nomination. Mr. Blair was named as the Republican candidate for Governor, was elected by over 20,000 majority over the Democratic candidate, the popular Ex-Governor Barry. Two years later, when the Union arms had met with reverses, and the dissatisfied elements in the North were consolidated into the Union party, he was re-elected by 6,614 majority over Byron G. Stout. For the four years of his incumbency of this office Governor Blair's biography is an important part of the war history of the State. He was not only patriotic to the core, but was energetic in recommending and pushing all war measures, in equipping Michigan troops, who were second to none in the volunteer army, and was solicitous in looking after the comfort and welfare of these troops. During this period he not only expended the meager salary which the State paid its Governors, but depleted his private means, in paying the extraordinary expenses which attended the position.

Governor Blair was elected a member of Congress in 1866, re-elected in 1868, and again in 1870. His most conspicuous service in the House of Representatives was as a member of the Committee on Foreign Affairs and the Committee of Ways and Means. He supported vigorously the principle of protection, as embraced in the bill for the revision of the tariff in the Forty-first Congress. He was also a member of the Committee on Revision of the Laws. His integrity under great temptations was recognized by Speaker Blaine in his appointment to the Chairmanship of the Committee on Claims in the Forty-second Congress, a committee whose firmness and honesty are often subjected to the severest test by the methods of men having large claims of questionable character. Governor Blair was a man who could be trusted under any circumstances. Whatever interest enlisted his support must first secure the approval of his conscience; after that he was earnest and persistent in its advocacy. A great question involving principle aroused him and occasioned the display of rare powers of oratory.

Of his Congressional career James G. Blaine said in his "Twenty Years in Congress:" "Austin Blair, who had won great praise as Governor of Michigan during the war, now entered as Representative of the Jackson District. He exhibited talent in debate, was distinguished for industry in the work of the House and for inflexible integrity in all his duties. He was not a party man in the ordinary sense of the word, but was inclined rather to independence in thought and action. This habit separated him from his friends who had wished to promote his political ambition, and estranged him for a time from the Republican party. But it never lost him the confidence of his neighbors and friends and did not impair the good reputation he had earned in his public career."

Governor Blair had senatorial aspirations, but they were never realized, although in the caucus in 1871 he seemed to be very near the prize. There were many things in President Grant's first administration that he did not approve, and he went into the Liberal Republican movement in 1872, heading that ticket as the candidate for Governor. His subsequent welcome back to the Republican party, in spite of this defection, showed how strong a hold he had upon the affections of the people. In 1881 he was elected Regent of the University of Michigan and in 1885 he was chosen Prosecuting Attorney of Jackson County. He was nominated by the Republicans for Justice of the Supreme Court in the spring of 1883, but that was a year when the whole Republican ticket was defeated.

In the intervals of his official life Governor Blair practiced the profession in which he had a high standing. He was admitted to the bar in the Circuit and Supreme Courts of the United States, and received the degree of LL. D. both from Hillsdale College and from Michigan University. He continued in practice almost up to the time of his death, August 6th, 1894. The Legislature of 1895 passed an appropriation for a memorial statue, which now stands in the Capitol grounds at Lansing.

Governor Blair was married, February 16th, 1849, to Sarah L. Ford, nee Horton. Four sons, George H.; Charles A.; Fred J. and Austin T. Blair, survive them.

CHARLES A. BLAIR, of Jackson, is a member of one of the very large number of families that moved originally from the British Isles to New England, thence, after two or three generations to "York State," and after another generation or two to Michigan or Wisconsin. Robert Blair, Sr., and his wife, Elizabeth Rankin, were both of Scotch ancestry, though Mr. Blair was born in Londonderry, Ireland. They emigrated to New England in 1718. Two generations of their descendants spent their lives in Massachusetts and the third moved to Caroline, Tompkins County, N. Y. The fourth, Austin Blair, afterwards the distinguished war Governor of his State, moved from Caroline to Jackson, Mich., in 1841. February 16th 1849, he married Sarah Louise Ford. Of their five children, Charles A. Blair, born at Jackson, April 10th, 1854, was the third.

Mr. Blair graduated from the Jackson High School in June, 1872, and from the classical course, literary department, University of Michigan in June, 1876. While in the University he was elected Class Seer by the Seniors and was chosen by the Faculty one of the ten commencement orators. At graduation he received not only the regular diploma, but a special diploma for proficiency in Greek and Latin.

After graduation he studied law with his father, and was admitted to the bar of Jackson County, September 5th, 1878. He was subsequently admitted to practice in the Supreme Court of the State, and on February 1st, 1897, to practice in the Supreme Court of the United States. His chief aspirations, efforts and studies have been in the line of his chosen profession in which he has a large growing practice in the courts of the State. The offices which Mr. Blair has held, or to which he has aspired, have all been closely connected with that profession. He was appointed City Attorney of Jackson for the year 1882, was appointed Assistant Prosecuting Attorney for Jackson County for the years 1885 and 1886, and was appointed by Governor Rich, Prosecuting Attorney from September, 1895, to December 31st, 1896. At one time when a candidate for the office of United States District Attorney for the Eastern District of Michigan, he received letters from a majority of the Justices of the Supreme Court, and many other eminent men of the State, testifying to his knowledge of the law, and his competency for the position. In the spring of 1899 he was nominated for Judge in the Jackson Circuit Court. The party in that campaign had very little organization while the opposition had the best organization it ever had, and the opposing candidate had made a remarkably efficient and popular judge, yet Mr. Blair ran 800 votes ahead of his ticket. He has never made a business of politics, but has always taken a keen interest in public affairs, and believing that the business interests of the country and the welfare of the people would be best served by perpetuating the rule of the Republican party, he has labored earnestly in its cause. He has been sent as a delegate to party conventions without any solicitation on his part for the past ten years. His first vote was cast for Tilden for President, but since that campaign he has acted with the Republicans.

Mr. Blair was married October 8th, 1879, to Effie C. North. They have had four children, of whom two are now living, George Fred Blair, born July 18th, 1880, now a cadet in the first class at the U. S. Naval Academy, and Helen Marie Blair, born May 28th, 1898.

a
e
a
o
e
o
p
o
a
lo
ag
es
as
m
fo
an
se
ar
Co
ma
sm
Th
die

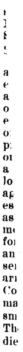

were afraid that officers would plot and lead the men, so I came out and told my rank and they removed me to Macon, Ga. Here we formed a plan to tunnel out, and worked away for a long time, carrying out the dirt in small bags and sprinkling it around so that it would not be noticed. Our plan was to get outside, seize the guard, grab the guns in an adjoining arsenal and free every man in the prison, but at the last moment we were betrayed and had to give the scheme up.

"From this place, with 600 other officers, I was taken to Charleston, S. C. The Union batteries were shelling the City, and we were under fire for about a day, when a singular thing happened. A stranger was seen to enter the building where we were, and inquire for General Stoneman. The two went up in the tower and that night rockets were fired from the roof. The stranger made his escape. We didn't know what it meant until the next day, when we found that no more shells were sent our way. The stranger was a Northern spy, who had been sent on this desperate piece of business, so that our gunners could be warned and not fire our way. I never learned his name, but it certainly was one of the most desperate deeds of personal service in the history of the great Rebellion.

"I was taken sick with yellow fever, and was sent to the Colored Men's Home, outside the prison bounds, and as soon as I was convalescent, I made arrangements with George Hauffman, a colored man, to help me escape. He made his plans, and we got as far as the river, but the man he had engaged to meet me there did not come, and the affair ended in my recapture. I was placed in a dungeon on a diet of bread and water, and in the dungeon opposite me Hauffman was locked up. They refused to give him anything to eat or drink, saying they would starve him to death as a warning to the negroes not to help Union prisoners. I was there three days, and I will never forget his awful groans and calls for help.

"When I was taken out I was sent to Columbia. It was from here that finally I managed to escape. This is the way it was done. They would send twenty men out to cut and carry wood, and one day, when I was one of the twenty, while the guard was playing cards, just before coming to pick us up, I said: 'Now,' and a fellow threw brush over me, and I lay there waiting for night to come to escape. Pretty soon they missed me, and a couple of others, and the alarm went out. They came back, and I could see them poking with their bayonets in the underbrush to see if they could wing any of us, but they missed me. As soon as I could, I ran back and hid under a scrub pine, and saw them pass and repass, and as they had no hounds, I felt that I might possibly have a chance. For eighteen days and nineteen nights I traveled through the woods, heading as near as I could, in the direction of Sherman's Army, which was now on its march to the sea. I came to the huts of negroes in the fields, who gave me sweet potatoes and salt, an act I will never forget, for I was half starved in prison. The colored men helped me on my way the next night. In this manner I reached the line of Sherman's march opposite Augusta, Georgia, only to find that the army had passed and that the Rebels were following close behind picking up stragglers. I fell in with some negroes, who gave me some food, and I started on my way, rafting over rivers, and sleeping in the swamps. I finally reached General Sherman's Army near Savannah."

Captain Bliss was sent to his command near Petersburg, where he proved unfit for service on account of ill health. He was given a thirty days' furlough, but was too much run down as the result of his prison trials to recuperate soon enough for active work, and was discharged February 27th, 1865, having been in service three years and three months, of which six months were spent in Rebel prisons. After his discharge he went home to recuperate and thence to Saginaw where he entered on the business which laid the foundations for his large fortune. During the fall and winter of 1865 he worked in logging camps on Pine River, and the following summer in a shingle mill. In the fall of 1866 he formed a partnership with his brother, Lyman W. Bliss, and J. H. Jerome, under the firm name of A. T. Bliss & Co., and took a contract for the cutting and skidding of a quantity of logs upon land adjacent to the Tobacco River, a tributary of the Tirtabawassee. The next year the brothers operated the Jerome Mill at Zilwaukee, and the year following, being joined by another brother, Joseph H. Bliss, they bought the mill, chiefly on credit. From this start, by shrewdness and industry A. T. Bliss went on, step by step, into the large lumber business and large fortune which he has since acquired. His estimable wife, who, as Miss Allaseba M. Phelps, of Solsville, Madison County, N. Y., he married in 1868, shared in the labors and hardships of this early period, overseeing the mill boarding house, and looking after the economical use of supplies. Mr. Bliss figured out that her help saved him at least $3,000 in the next five years, and this amount was put into a home which he built in Saginaw in 1873, and which they have occupied as a residence for many years.

Among Colonel Bliss' present possessions are 46,000 acres of hardwood lands in Arkansas, the Coleman farm, 1,000 acres, near Saginaw; farm at Carrollton, 500 acres, improved; Central Lumber Company, corporation at Zilwaukee, sawmill and salt works, employing 130 men and assessed for $60,000; pine stump lands in Gladwin, Arenac, Midland and in Roscommon Counties; immense timber limits on the Pacific coast; timber limits on Blind River, Ontario, where he has taken off 50,000,000 feet of pine and still has 20,000,000 feet left; Thomas Jackson Company, corporation, composed of Thomas Jackson, A. T. Bliss and A. F. Cook, employing 150 men and shipping doors to Europe; stockholder in the Bank of Saginaw, one of the strongest financial institutions in the Valley; also a stockholder and director in the Saginaw County Savings Bank. He also raises shorthorn cattle, and has taken an interest in the newly developed beet sugar business of the Valley.

Mr. Bliss has always been an active Republican in politics. In addition to holding a number of local offices he was elected to the State Senate in 1882, and was on Governor Alger's staff in 1885-6, this giving him the title of Colonel. He was elected to Congress from the Saginaw District in 1888 and served one term. He was five years a member of the Board of Managers of the Michigan Soldiers' Home and has been Treasurer of the National League of Republican Clubs. In 1896 he was a candidate for the Republican nomination for Governor, and came near winning. In the Convention in Grand Rapids in June, 1900, he was more fortunate, receiving the nomination on the nineteenth ballot. Colonel Bliss was not widely known as a talker, but, as one of the party papers put it, he "showed up strong as a campaigner." He not only made many political speeches and good ones, too, but made a number of very happy speeches on occasions not political. The campaign closed by his election by about 80,000 plurality over Mayor William C. Maybury, of Detroit, the Democratic candidate.

Governor Bliss has taken the various degrees in Masonry up to the 32d, and is prominent in G. A. R. circles. He was for three years Commander of Pennoyer Post. In 1897 he was Commander of the Department of Michigan, has served several years on the staff of various national Commanders-in-Chief, and in 1899-1900 was a member of the National Council of Administration and a member of the Executive Committee. He is a Maccabee and a Forester.

DELOS ABIEL BLODGETT, son of Abiel D. and Susan (Richmond) Blodgett, was born in Otsego County, N. Y., on the 3rd day of March, 1825. He is of New England parentage and ancestry. When the subject of this sketch was four years of age the family removed from Otsego County, to Erie County, in the same State. From that time until he was 20 years of age, a period not marked by any special event, he resided with his parents, and assisted in the farm work and attended district and select schools. This comprised his opportunity for education.

Shortly before he became of age he persuaded his parents to permit him to take a journey through the South. This was in the year 1845, when the South was not well known to Northern people. nor even yet very well developed. Young Blodgett worked his way, as a flatboatsman and raftsman, down the Allegheny River; thence down the Ohio River and down the Mississippi, as far as New Orleans.

This trip was one of rare educational value to the young man, who was then observant enough to see something of the extent of the natural resources of the country through which he traveled, and to shape his life plans on a resultant wider basis. At New Orleans he was attacked with malarial fever, and obliged to retrace his steps to the North. Accordingly he started for McHenry County, Illinois, to which point his parents had, in the meantime, removed from New

York State. He joined his family in Illinois in 1847 so reduced in health that he was compelled to remain in idleness for the greater part of the year. He did, however, attend a term at a select school at Geneva, Wis., during this time. The following spring his ambitious spirit again started him out in the world. He walked into Chicago, and there secured a position to work in a saw mill for Reed & McKegg at their mill on Little Bay-de-Noquet, near the point where the Village of Masonville, Mich., is now situated.

The season's work in the mill created such an interest in lumber in his mind, that he resolved to make it his occupation. Returning to Chicago at the close of the season he found that the west shore of the State of Michigan was then sending the choicest pine lumber to market, and to that territory young Blodgett repaired without delay. In October, 1848, he entered the employ of Henry Knickerbocker, then a prominent logger of Muskegon, in whose camp he spent the winter. The following winter he was made foreman of the Knickerbocker camp, and so continued until July, 1850.

In the autumn of 1850 he formed a partnership with the late Thomas D. Stimson, for logging on their own account. This was his first business venture. Together with Mr. Stimson he explored the then unbroken pine wilderness along the Muskegon River, and finally located a tract in what is now Clare County, on a stream tributary to the Muskegon River. This stream was afterwards called "Doc and Tom" Creek, in honor of the partners, who were familiarly known as "Doc." Blodgett and "Tom" Stimson. Here they built a camp and operated as partners under a verbal contract. During this first winter they lumbered 600,000 feet, a quantity that would barely have run the Blodgett saw mills in 1880 for a period of twenty-four hours. At that time there were no wagon roads in the territory where they were operating, and all supplies and provisions were taken up the Muskegon River in canoes, a distance of 100 and 150 miles. After the winter set in communication with the outer world was entirely closed. In 1854 he closed his partnership with Mr. Stimson, and each continued along the same line, in their individual interests.

From this time Mr. Blodgett's career forms a prominent part of the development of Northern Michigan, in which the lumber industry was the most important feature. His foresight early showed him the future value of the pine forests of Michigan. His tremendous energy and pioneering tendencies fitted him for his chosen profession as a lumberman, and in that career his chief commercial successes have been made. After the dissolution of his partnership with Mr. Stimson, he continued buying pine lands and logging the timber therefrom, gradually expanding his operations until he became one of the largest pine timber owners in the State. Until 1878 he either sold his logs or hired the lumber manufactured, but in that year he bought mills at Muskegon, Mich., which he continued to operate until 1893, when his timber tributary to that point was exhausted. During this time

D. A. Blodgett

he was also interested with the late Thomas Byrne, of Grand Rapids, under the firm name of Blodgett & Byrne, who were extensive pine land owners and lumber manufacturers, owning large mills at Muskegon. During this period Mr. Blodgett, with his various interests, was one of the most extensive lumber manufacturers in the North west. He has since been interested extensively in the manufacture of lumber at Cadillac, Mich.

Following his early predilection for timber investment, Mr. Blodgett has invested extensively in Southern pine lands and also in the heavily timbered lands in the Pacific Coast States. Incidental to, and connected with his lumber enterprises, Mr. Blodgett has founded several Northern Michigan towns, among which is the Village of Hersey, where he lived from 1854 until he removed to Grand Rapids in 1881. He has always been actively interested in the agricultural development of this State, and was for many years one of the directors of the Michigan State Agricultural Society, and also of the Western Michigan Agricultural & Industrial Society. He owns several large farms which he cleared from the natural forest himself. Upon these he has raised extensively French draft horses, as well as other kinds of finely bred stock.

As was natural, in the course of such an extensive and active commercial career, Mr. Blodgett has become interested in various other enterprises. He owns several large business blocks in Grand Rapids and Chicago, and is a stockholder in several banks and manufacturing companies. He was President of the Fourth National Bank of Grand Rapids for many years, but in 1898 he retired from official connection with that, and all the other enterprises in which he is interested. At this date, 1900, he is living in comparative freedom from business cares, beloved and respected by all who know him, and a striking example of what ability and strict integrity can accomplish, when backed by never ending perseverance.

Mr. Blodgett was married in September, 1859, to Miss Jennie S. Wood, of Woodstock, Illinois. She died in October, 1890, leaving a son and daughter. In 1893 Mr. Blodgett was married the second time, to his present wife, who was Miss Daisy A. Peck, of Atlanta, Ga. There are three children, two daughters and a son, born of this marriage.

In religious belief, Mr. Blodgett is an agnostic, but of such a broad-minded and liberal type, that churches and religious societies of all denominations have been generously aided by him. Indeed, next to his strict sense of honesty and justice, his generosity is, perhaps, his most prominent characteristic. He is ever ready to listen to the most humble, and to aid those that are deserving.

The qualities that gave Mr. Blodgett his prominence in the commercial and industrial development of his State, naturally made him an equally important factor in its political history. He espoused the cause of the Republican party at its organization, and has always continued to be one of its most ardent adherents. His executive ability and wide influence made him a valuable member of his party from a very early date. He has always given freely of his time and means to promote his party's success, and has many times served on campaign committees in various capacities. His efforts in the party's behalf have been unceasing, and its continued success in Michigan is due, in no small part, to his influence and exertion. He has always steadfastly declined to become a candidate for any political office. In spite of this fact, however, his party has made recognition of his services, and of the esteem in which he was held, by twice electing him a delegate-at-large to National Conventions, and also selecting him a delegate from his Congressional District. In all of these instances, it has been stated that these honors were conferred without any expression of desire from Mr. Blodgett, and sometimes during his absence from the State. These facts testify in a most convincing manner to the obligations which the Republicans of Michigan feel toward him, and are a magnificent recognition of his party services.

JOHN WOOD BLODGETT, of Grand Rapids, was born July 26th, 1860, in Osceola County, Mich., where the village of Hersey now stands. His father was Delos A. Blodgett, the noted lumberman, whose biography precedes this, and his mother was Jennie S. (Wood) Blodgett. His father was of New England stock, coming originally from England, and his mother was a native of Pennsylvania and of North of Ireland ancestry. He received his education in village and district schools, Todd's Seminary for boys at Woodstock, Ill., and the Highland Military Academy at Worcester, Mass. He went to Muskegon in 1878 and took charge of his father's saw mills and lumber manufacturing at that point, and of the extensive logging operations connected with same. He also had charge of the large lumber business and operations of Blodgett & Byrne after the death of Thomas Byrne, of that firm, in 1882. He remained in Muskegon until all the timber tributary to that place, owned by his father and the firm of Blodgett & Byrne, had been cut, and then removed to Grand Rapids, where he has since resided, dealing in pine lands. He is now largely interested in local enterprises and in timber lands in the South and on the Pacific Coast.

Mr. Blodgett has always been a Republican of the stalwart kind and cast his first National ballot for Blaine and Logan in 1884. Of social organizations he belongs to the Peninsular Club, the Kent Country Club, Lakeside Club of Grand Rapids, and the Chicago Club of Chicago. Of political organizations he is a member of the Lincoln Club of Grand Rapids and the Michigan Club of Detroit. He was married January 16th, 1895, at Lowell, Mass., to Miss Minnie Cumnock. They have one child, Katherine C. Blodgett.

BENJAMIN BOUTELL, of Bay City, is one of the stalwart Republicans who contributes liberally to the party campaign funds, but who never found time to run for office nor to do much party work. He has always been a Republican, cast his first vote for Grant in 1868, and has attended a number of State and local Conventions, but has had too many other things on hand to warrant giving much time to politics. He was born for business at Deerfield, Livingston County, Mich., August 17th, 1844. His father was Daniel Boutell, of Huguenot descent, but a native of New Hampshire. He was a miller in his early days, then owned and ran boats on the Erie Canal, and drifted to Michigan in 1827. He was one of the first settlers in Deerfield, where he took up and cleared a large tract of land. Benjamin's mother was Betsy Adams, a native of New York State, but of New England ancestry, and a niece of President John Quincy Adams. She died in 1861, outliving her husband 16 years.

Benjamin had only a common school education, working summers on the farm and going to school winters. Nearly all of the summer when he was seven years old he drove four yoke of cattle to plow, breaking up land on the farm. The summer in which he was ten years old he went to the County fair at Howell and took a premium for plowing. In 1859 the family moved to Bay City which then had a population of about 700, of whom half were Indians. He assisted his father in the hotel business until 1864, when the hotel burned down, and he took to the water as wheelsman on one of the river boats. The next year he went as mate of the same boat, and sailed different boats till 1867, when he bought an interest in the tug Union and the tug Annie Moiler, with Captain Win Mitchell, the firm being Mitchell & Boutell. They bought and owned several boats and did a large business. In 1888 they dissolved partnership. Mr. Boutell retained the tugs and the log towing business, and went into partnership with P. C. Smith. The firm engaged extensively in log towing. They owned and operated twenty tugs, and never brought down less than 100,000,000 feet of timber in a season, and one year towed the enormous amount of 366,000,000 feet, operating on Lakes Superior, Michigan and Huron, Georgian Bay and Saginaw Bay. With the prohibition now in force of the exportation of logs from Canada and the consequent decline of the lumber interest on the east shore, their business has fallen off, but they still own and operate ten tugs. Captain Boutell has also been interested in a number of freighting boats, and for twenty years was master of different vessels, sailing all of the Great Lakes. He is now President of the Saginaw Bay Towing Co., the Boutell Towing & Wrecking Co., the Boutell Transportation Co., and the Hampton Transportation Co.: Vice-President of the Boutell Towing & Transit Co., which is located down the coast, with the head office in Boston. This sums up his marine interests, but he has others on land. He is President of the Marine Iron Co., and the Excelsior Foundry Co., both of Bay City; Vice-President of the Craig Foundry Co. of Toledo; Director and one of the largest stockholders in the Commercial Bank and stockholder in the Second National Bank, both of Bay City; Vice-President of the State Chickory Co.

He was also a pioneer in another direction. He had previously given much study to the beet sugar industry, as conducted in other countries, and after the Michigan Legislature passed the sugar bounty act, he, in association with others, organized the Michigan Sugar Co. and built the first sugar factory in the State at Bay City. In the following year, 1899, he organized the Bay City Sugar Co., which has the largest sugar plant in the State, of which he is Vice-President. He is also a large stockholder in the West Bay City Sugar Co. and a stockholder and director in the Marine City Sugar Co. In connection with this line of business he has gone into farming again, having purchased near Bay City a tract of 1,100 acres, of which 50 acres was in sugar-beet last season. He is also incidentally connected with a number of other companies aside from those mentioned.

Captain Boutell has been a Mason for twenty years, and a Trustee in the Methodist Church for a still longer period. He was married in December, 1869, to Amelia C. Dudlinger. They have had three children of whom two survive, Frederick and William. They both had good educations, but were brought up to work, as their father was before them, and are now valuable associates with him in his various enterprises.

MAJOR NATHAN SMITH BOYNTON, of Port Huron, is one of the few men of the day who can point to a great organization as an enduring monument to his life's work. This work he did not take up until he was past 40, having previously obtained prominence in business, military and political paths. He was born in Port Huron, June 23rd, 1837, son of Granville F. and Frances Rendt Boynton, his father being descended from Sir Mathew Boynton, an Englishman who was knighted in the Seventeenth Century for being the first to bring sheep and goats to America. His mother was a daughter of Captain Lewis Rendt, who was born in Bremen, served several years in the German army, and was afterwards in the British Army in the War of 1812.

Nathan S. Boynton's elementary education was obtained chiefly in the public schools of Marine City and Port Huron, supplemented by a term in the High School at Waukegan, Ill., but he was always a great reader, and acquired a fund of wide and accurate information. While he was in school he worked on the farm summers, and after leaving school he entered at once upon an active and restless business life, the details of which must be briefly summed up. First he was clerk in a grocery store in Port Huron, then learned the trade of manufacturing whips by hand; started in the grocery business on his own account; made some money, which he invested in pine lands

MroU

and lost after the panic of 1857; spent a few months in Ohio and then went to New Orleans, which he found too hot for a Northern man with Anti-Slavery convictions and a strong inclination to speak them out; returned North to St. Louis, Mo., thence to O'Fallon, Ill., and went to work clearing land for a farmer; taught singing school and also worked at the carpenter's trade; in July, 1858, had saved over $200; returned to Cincinnati, commenced the study of medicine, and also engaged in selling electrical apparatus for curative purposes. He did not take kindly to the medical profession and did not pursue that study.

Although he had a wife and one child when the war broke out, his patriotism impelled him to break away from these domestic ties, and he enlisted as a private in the Eighth Michigan Cavalry, in which he was soon promoted to First Lieutenant of Company L. In this capacity, at the head of a detachment of 100 men, he cut off the retreat of General John Morgan, in his celebrated raid through Kentucky, Indiana and Ohio, and under Lieutenant Boynton's Company flag Morgan surrendered the last of his forces. Major Boynton served under Burnside in the campaign in East Tennessee. At Athens, in that State, he took possession of a printing office, the proprietor of which fled with the Rebel troops, and he printed the first Union paper in that section after Parson Brownlow was driven out. But only one number of this was issued. The second was ready for the press when the perniciously active rebel, General Forrest, came suddenly on the Union forces, drove them out, captured the printing office and all the printers who were occupying the building, and sent them to Andersonville prison. Lieutenant Boynton, who was at Brigade headquarters, fell back with the troops and escaped capture, which was lucky for him, for the Rebels, after reading the Union paper, began a hunt for the Yankee editor, threatening to make quick work of him if they could once lay hands on him. Subsequent to this Lieutenant Boynton was at Knoxville, during the siege of that place by General Longstreet; was with General Sherman's forces during the Atlanta campaign; led the column of cavalry that entered Atlanta as General Hood's forces retreated; was in the unfortunate Stoneman raid at Atlanta, and was with General Thomas during the Hood campaign in Tennessee.

Returning to Port Huron, after three years' service in the army, Major Boynton entered again into active business, being successively editor and publisher of the Port Huron Press; conducting a real estate and insurance business, and acting as general manager for Michigan of the business of the publishing house of Sheldon & Co., of New York. He was also the inventor of the Boynton fire escape and hook and ladder truck, and the Boynton system of fire rope trussing for fire ladders. He is now President of the firm of Boynton & Son; the Tunnel City Regalia Company; Home Protectors' Building and Loan Association; the Auditorium Co.; and the Masonic Building Association. He owns and controls over five hundred acres of rich garden lands on the east coast of Southern Florida, with a mile of ocean front, and has a winter hotel on the beach. For the past five years he has spent his winters there, with personal friends. He is now interested in promoting an electric line of railway from Port Huron to Bay City.

Major Boynton has not only had a military and business career, but has been active in politics, in which he commenced taking an interest when he was ten years old. He was radical and positive in his views then, as he has been ever since. His father was an Anti-Slavery Democrat, and the son, with literature of that class before him, became an Abolitionist before he was of age. He was never inclined to keep his opinions to himself, and when he was twenty-two years of age he wrote very radical articles for the Nation, an Anti-Slavery paper published by Rev. Charles Boynton of Cincinnati. Three years later, when President Lincoln revoked General Fremont's proclamation freeing the slaves in Missouri, he shared and expressed the disappointment which many Anti-Slavery men felt. He wrote several articles taking the position that the time would come before the war closed when Lincoln would issue a proclamation of emancipation covering all the Slave States; further that he would put into their hands arms to assist in securing their own freedom, and that the war would not close until slavery was wiped out. These utterances, which proved to be prophetic, were, at the time very distasteful to people on the border, who were inclined to handle the slavery question very tenderly, and he was threatened with expulsion from the city. He was for nearly twenty years in full sympathy with the most radical wing of the Republican party; was a great admirer of Horace Greeley, whose Tribune was to him a political Bible, and followed him into the Liberal Republican ranks in 1872. Six years later he joined the National Greenback party, and was very active in that organization up to the first election of Cleveland, when, deeming the tariff issue of paramount importance, he rejoined the Republican ranks. In the course of his long career he has held official positions a number of times. On his return from the army in 1865 he was appointed Deputy Assessor of Internal Revenue and Postmaster of Marine City, where he also held the positions of Village Clerk and President. In 1868 he was elected to the State Legislature. At a later period he took rank among the best and most energetic of the reform Mayors with which Michigan cities have occasionally been blessed. He was elected Mayor of Port Huron in 1874, and again in 1875 by an increased majority. In 1894 he was again elected Mayor of that City by a vote so large as to show that there was no politics in it, receiving 2,353 votes to 1,020 for his opponent, the largest majority ever given a Mayor of the city. The next year he was again elected by a majority so large as to make it a grand testimonial to the esteem of his fellow citizens, and to his efficiency in the public service. An earnest effort to make unimproved city property, held for speculative purposes, pay its just share of taxation; a rejuvenated City Hall; an era of cement sidewalks in place of plank; and other splendid public improvements, with a reduced tax rate, are the lasting tributes to his business-like and non-partisan administration. He was also a member of the Port Huron Board of Education for six years and its President for four.

But Major Boynton is best known for his prominence and zeal in connection with the Knights of the Maccabees, an order of which, in its prosperous modern phase he is the founder. Into the work of this Order he has put immense enthusiasm, great executive ability and remarkable skill as an organizer. He became a charter member of Diamond Tent, K. O. T. M., of Port Huron, in 1878. In the spring following he attended, as a delegate, the general review of the order at Buffalo. A warfare between the factions, which had been going on for some time, then culminated in a division, one faction withdrawing, while the other adopted a new Constitution and elected Sir Knight Boynton Supreme Lieutenant Commander of the First Supreme Tent of the Order. Soon afterwards, by the resignation of the Supreme Commander, Lieutenant Commander Boynton was required to take up the burdens of the chief executive office. He succeeded in bringing the two factions together in joint review at Port Huron in 1881, and then retired from the position of Supreme Commander. The management, after his retirement, was not good, and the Order seemed on the eve of dissolution, when in order to save the membership in Michigan, a separate endowment jurisdiction was obtained for the State. The Great Camp of Michigan was organized with Sir Knight Boynton as Great Record Keeper, and from that time on the history of the Maccabees has been one of constant growth. In 1883 the Supreme Tent was reorganized, with Sir Knight Boynton as Supreme Record Keeper, and he retained both of the offices named up to 1894, when he withdrew from the office of Great Record Keeper and was elected Great Commander. He attended the first National Fraternal Congress in 1886, has attended every Congress since then, and to him belongs the credit of securing for the K. O. T. M. national recognition among the fraternities. He was unanimously elected Vice President of the Congress in 1892, and President in 1893, and is now a life member of that organization.

Major Boynton is familiarly and affectionately termed the Father of the Maccabees, and no greater testimonial to his popularity in the Order could be given than that furnished by the election in June, 1900, for Great Commander of the Great Camp of Maccabees for Michigan, a position which he had held since 1894. On this occasion another candidate was in the field, but Great Commander Boynton was re-elected by the decisive vote of 1,520 to 561. The newspaper congratulations on this personal triumph, and the reception that awaited him on his return to Port Huron were of the most flattering nature. These testimonials were doubtless very gratifying, but the growth of the Order from the small beginning in 1881 to a membership of nearly half a million at the present time, and the magnificent

Maccabee Temple which has been erected at Port Huron, largely through his efforts, are a more enduring monument.

Aside from the Maccabees Major Boynton belongs to the following clubs and societies: F. & A. M., Knights of Pythias, A. O. U. W., Independent Order of Foresters, Ancient Order of Foresters, Modern Woodmen of America, Woodmen of the World, National Fraternal Congress, Ben Hur, Order of Elks, Korassan, Port Huron Club, Fellowcraft Club, Michigan Club, Home Protectors' Fraternity, Grand Army of the Republic, the Military Order of the Loyal Legion, and several other societies. He was married in Cincinnati, Ohio, June 20th, 1859, to Annie Fields. Their children are Charles Lincoln, who was Colonel of the Thirty-third Michigan Infantry during the Spanish-American war; and appointed November 10, 1900, to the chief command of the Michigan National Guard; Granville, who died in infancy; Anna L.; George H., manager of Boynton & Son Company, and Tunnel City Regalia Company; Frankie, now Mrs. J. H. Patterson; and Edith, now Mrs. H. H. Wright, all living in Port Huron.

NATHAN BALL BRADLEY, of Bay City, was one of the pioneers in what was for a long time the greatest lumber manufacturing district in the world. He was the son of William and Lucy Bradley, and was born in Berkshire County, Massachusetts, May 28, 1831. The Bradleys in this country go back in their ancestry to Plymouth Rock, and one branch of the family has resided in Berkshire County, Massachusetts, more than a century and a half. One of those in direct line of descent, William Bradley, helped organize the first Protestant Episcopal Church in Berkshire County, at Lanesborough, in 1767.

In 1835 the parents of N. B. Bradley removed to New Connecticut, as the Western Reserve, in Northern Ohio, was then called, and settled in the town of Wellington. Here the son lived until he was sixteen years old, working on the farm and attending the district school when he could be spared from the farm work. At the age of sixteen he apprenticed himself to a trade, serving his time thereat. He then foresaw that greater opportunities offered in other branches of industry and decided to make a trip to the Western country. He located at Oshkosh, Wis., which place was then in its infancy. Saw milling and lumbering had just begun to develop in this young town of the West, and here Mr. Bradley acquired his first experience in sawing pine lumber, which proved to be his principal business in after life. He afterwards returned to Ohio where, in connection with a brother, he built a small saw mill for the manufacture of hardwood lumber; this, however, he found to be slow work in comparison with sawing pine, and in 1852 he made his first venture in Michigan, locating near Lexington on Lake Huron's shore. Here he became part owner in and manager of a saw-mill having a daily capacity of 16,000 to 18,000 feet, a fair sized mill for that time, but

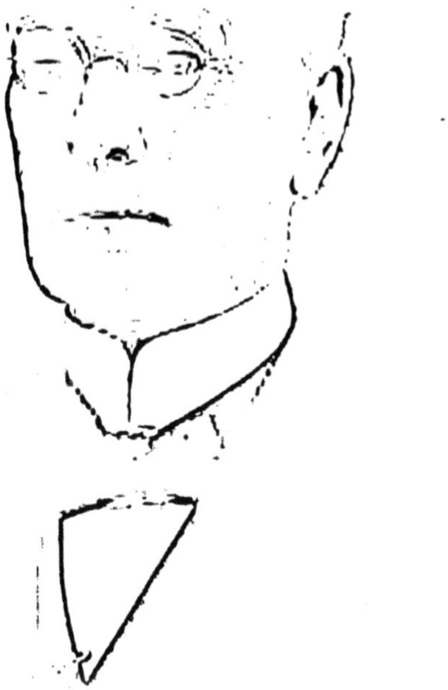

N. B. Bradley

oU

small as compared with mills of later years. Having exhausted the stock of timber available for this mill, which was limited, he removed to the Saginaw Valley, the center of lumbering operations in Michigan. He took charge of a saw-mill and lumbering operations of Frost & Bradley at St. Charles, the Bradley mentioned being a brother. He afterwards became owner in this mill, and associated with him Mr. Lewis Penoyer, under the name of L. Penoyer & Co. In 1858 he removed to Bay City, taking charge of the mill afterwards known as the N. B. Bradley & Sons mill, which he subsequently enlarged and gave it a capacity of 20,000,000 feet per season. This mill he operated for thirty-two years under the firm names of N. B. Bradley & Co., N. B. Bradley, Trustee, and N. B. Bradley & Sons. It went out of commission in 1891, after cutting the supply of timber which had been provided for it. In addition to the Bay City operation, Mr. Bradley was interested in other lumbering plants, one at Deer Park, Mich., and one at Lake Charles, La. At the latter the yellow pine of the South is being handled, and recently he has, in connection with his sons, invested in a lumbering plant in East Tennessee.

Saginaw Valley reached its greatest output of lumber about the year 1882, when it exceeded one thousand millions, nearly all of which was shipped by water as raw material to the yards at various lake ports, where it was manipulated and resold to the consumer. Mr. Bradley was among the earliest ones to perceive the possibility of handling lumber in the Saginaw Valley and shipping it by cars direct to the retailers through the country, dressing and finishing it ready for the builders' use. In furtherance of this purpose he called to his assistance Mr. D. A. Ross, of Detroit, an experienced man in the car load trade, and the corporation of Ross, Bradley & Co. was formed. Later the name was changed to Bradley, Miller & Co., which company is still carrying on the yard and planing mill business. Since the organization of this company over four hundred millions feet of lumber has been purchased, manipulated, sold and shipped by it. Mr. Bradley was among the first to build and operate a steam salt block in connection with the saw mill in the Valley, burning up the mill refuse, and using the exhaust steam to evaporate the brine. His steam block was patterned after for years by other mill men.

He was an active member of the Bay County Salt Company, afterwards the Saginaw Bay Salt Co., a company organized for the purpose of taking the salt from the manufacturer and marketing it and dividing the proceeds pro rata among the manufacturers. He was a Director, a member of its Executive Committee, and Treasurer of the company for several years. He was the active man in the organization of the Bay City Street Railway Co., one of its managers, a Director and Secretary of the company. He also took an active part in the promotion and organization of the first beet sugar factory company, that of the Michigan Sugar Co., organized January, 1898, being a Director, member of its Executive Committee and Vice-President of the company.

In politics Mr. Bradley has been a Republican ever since the party was organized, casting his first Presidential vote for Fremont in 1856. He was the first Mayor of Bay City after its incorporation as a City in 1865; was elected, in 1866, a member of the State Senate, declining a renomination two years later. He represented the Eighth Congressional District of Michigan in Congress from 1873 to 1877, his increasing business requiring him to withdraw from politics.

In church connection Mr. Bradley is a Presbyterian, has been for more than thirty years a member of the Board of Trustees, and for several years an Elder in the First Presbyterian Church of Bay City. He was a charter member of Bay City Lodge and of Joppa Lodge of F. & A. M., and for several years presiding officer of the former. He was a charter member of Blanchard Chapter of R. A. M., and presiding officer thereof, and a member of Bay City Commandery No. 26, Knights Templar.

November 12th, 1853, Mr. Bradley was married at Sparta, Morrow County, Ohio, to Miss Huldah L. Chase, by whom he had two sons, Elemer E. and Fred W. His wife died in March, 1881. He was again married in 1882 to Mrs. Emeline E. Gaylord, widow of the late Hon. A. S. Gaylord, of Saginaw.

MARK SPENCER BREWER, of Pontiac, was born in the township of Addison, Oakland County, Mich., October 22d, 1837, and worked upon his father's farm until he was twenty years of age; received an academic education, and began the study of law with Hon. William L. Webber, of Saginaw, in 1861, but was compelled to teach a district school in the winters of 1861-2 and 1862-3, in order to earn sufficient means for him to complete his law study. In the spring of 1862 he entered the law office of Ex-Governor Moses Wisner, at Pontiac, and remained with him until the Governor entered the Civil War as Colonel of the Twenty-second Michigan Infantry. Thereupon Mr. Brewer became a student in the office of Hon. M. E. Crofoot, at Pontiac, and remained such until he was admitted to the bar in 1864. Soon after this he entered into partnership with Judge Crofoot, his preceptor, which partnership existed until 1875. Mr. Brewer was admitted to the bar of the Supreme Court of the United States in 1880, and has been engaged in the practice of his profession at Pontiac, since his admission to the bar in 1864, except when engaged in the public service. He was Circuit Court Commissioner for his County from 1866 to 1870, inclusive, and at the same time was City Attorney of Pontiac. He was State Senator in 1873 and 1874. He represented his District in the Forty-fifth, Forty-sixth, Fiftieth and Fifty-first Congresses, and declined a renomination in 1890. He was appointed by President Garfield Consul-General at Berlin, Germany, and served in that position from 1881 to 1885, inclusive, when he returned to his home in Michigan, and again entered upon the practice of his profession, continuing in such practice, except while serving in the Fiftieth and Fifty-first Congresses, until February, 1898, when he was appointed by President McKinley a member of the U. S. Civil Service Commission, which position he occupies at the present time. Mr. Brewer was a Delegate-at-Large from the State of Michigan to the Republican National Convention at St. Louis in 1896, and represented his State upon the Committee on Resolutions and platform at that Convention.

Peter Brewer, the father of Mark S. Brewer, was born in Duchess County, New York. The father of Peter was born in Holland, and emigrated to America previous to the Revolutionary War, in which he served as a private. His name also was Peter Brewer. The mother of Mark S. Brewer was Miss Mary Turnes; she was born in the north of Ireland near Enniskillen, and was brought to America by her parents when three years of age. Both the parents of Mark S. Brewer died at their home in the township of Addison aforesaid on the 23rd day of September, 1866, at a ripe old age, leaving a family composed of five sons and four daughters, all of whom are living at the present time, Mark S. being the youngest of the sons. His first wife was Miss Lizzie Simonson, a daughter of the late James B. Simonson, of Holly, Mich. She died in 1886. His second wife, whom he married in 1889, was Miss Louise B. Parker, daughter of Abiram Parker, of Pontiac, Mich. Mr. Brewer has no children living. The parents of Mr. Brewer settled in the township of Addison in 1833. His father was among the few Whigs who settled in that township, the most of the earlier settlers in the township being followers of Andrew Jackson. Peter Brewer remained a Whig until the Republican party was formed, in 1854, whereupon he became a member of that party.

Mark S. Brewer, the subject of this sketch, has always been an active member of the Republican party, and as such has taken an active part in every political campaign since 1862, with one exception, when he was abroad in an official capacity. He has not only taken an active part in such campaigns in Michigan, but also in Ohio, Indiana and other states. His judgment on political matters has been often solicited by National, State and local political committees. The demand for his services in many campaigns has been beyond his ability to supply.

There were a number of interesting events in Mr. Brewer's long and useful Congressional career. When he entered Congress on the 4th of March, 1877, William McKinley, Jr., now President, entered Congress at the same time. The two were sworn in together, and soon after, in drawing seats, became seatmates, which positions they occupied during the Forty-fifth Congress. Like the President, when Mr. Brewer entered the Forty-fifth Congress, he was a Republican and a strong protectionist, and during that Congress both desired to present their views upon that subject. They were both new members and were unable during the daytime to get the floor for the purpose of making speeches, and were compelled to make them at an evening session. Many thousands of both speeches were published by the Republican Congressional Committee and circulated by that Committee and the National Committee as well, as campaign documents. The last term that Mr. Brewer served in Congress he was a member of the Committee on Appropriations and Chairman of the sub-Committee on Fortifications, and gave much attention to this subject; and many of the large guns in the fortifications around our coasts, as well as the fortifications themselves, were started and constructed under a measure which he succeeded in having passed in the Fifty-first Congress. Mr. Brewer was an active participant in opposition to the passage of the free coinage of silver measure at the ratio of 16 to 1 during the pendency of that measure in the Forty-sixth, Fiftieth, and Fifty-first Congresses. A bill of this kind passed the House in 1878 with only 32 votes in opposition, and his name will be found among the 32 in the Congressional Record. He also strenuously opposed the passage of a free coinage bill in 1890. He is now and has been constantly opposed to any such measure, as he was opposed to the old Greenback party of 1878 and the views which it held and advanced. His familiarity with the whole scope of the free coinage question, and the probable results of the adoption of such a measure made him an especially effective speaker in the exciting campaign of 1896.

FLAVIUS LIONEL BROOKE, Supervisor of Census for the First District of Michigan, was born October 7th, 1858, in Simcoe, Norfolk County, Province of Ontario. His father, John Brooke, came from Devonshire, England to Canada, when about 25 years of age and became a farmer. His mother, Sarah Brooke, was born in Norfolk County, Ontario, her mother, Sarah Dunham, being born in Long Island, and her father, John Mann, in Pennsylvania.

Flavius Brooke was educated in the Canadian common schools, in Albert University, Belleville, Ont., and Osgood Hall, Toronto, Ont. He worked on a farm in the summer time, going to school winters until sixteen years of age, when he commenced to teach school, continuing this for three years. At nineteen he matriculated into the University and took two years of arts course, at twenty he matriculated in law and spent one year in Belleville and four years in Toronto as student-at-law, the four years in Toronto being spent in the offices of Mowat, MacLennan & Downey, Mr. Mowat being then Attorney General for Ontario and leader of the Liberal Party. After being called to the bar in Toronto in 1884, he removed to Detroit in 1885, entering the office of Colonel John Atkinson and Judge Isaac Marston. About the year 1887 Judge Marston retired from his association with Colonel Atkinson and the law firm of Atkinson, Carpenter & Brooke was formed, which continued for several years and until Judge Carpenter went on the bench. The law firm of Brooke & Spalding was

Will H. Munson.

then formed, continuing from 1892 to 1896, since which time Mr. Brooke has practiced law alone.

Mr. Brooke has been a Republican since 1885, casting his first vote for Harrison in 1888. He attended four successive State Conventions, commencing with 1888. He was appointed by President McKinley in 1900, Supervisor of the Census for the First District of Michigan, the District including the whole of Wayne County. At the November election, 1900, he was elected Circuit Judge, for the Third Judicial Circuit, to hold office during the ensuing five years.

Mr. Brooke is a member of the Michigan Club, of which he has been Director and Secretary. He was married to Miss B. Reidy, at Stratford, Ont., November 27th, 1884, and has four children: John, Kathleen, Josephine and Frank.

WILLIAM HENRY BRUNSON, of St. Johns, was born March 8th, 1858, at Victor, Clinton County, Mich. His father was William Brunson, a farmer until middle life, and after that lawyer, and his mother was Mary A. Pierce. His father and mother were born in East Bloomfield, Ontario County, New York. They were married and went to Victor in September, 1843, and began farming. In 1860 William Brunson was elected Sheriff of Clinton County and served during the war. He served as Deputy Collector of Internal Revenue under Grant. It has been said a great many times that he made the best Sheriff Clinton County ever had. He removed to St. Johns, Mich., in 1861, and after serving his two terms as Sheriff, he was admitted to practice law, and after that he followed that profession until his death in February, 1893. His ancestors were English, coming from Massachusetts and Connecticut.

The son, William Henry, was educated at St. Johns High School and at the University of Michigan. At sixteen he began to support himself, first working as a laboring man and on the farm. At eighteen he taught district school and boarded round. He then taught in the St. Johns Schools for four years and after that was principal of the Dewitt schools for one year. He was elected and served as County School Examiner and County Commissioner of Schools of Clinton County. In 1884 he had saved enough money to take him through the Law Department at the University of Michigan, and graduated there in 1886. He immediately began the practice of law at St. Johns and has practiced there ever since. He is regarded as a safe counsellor and a good lawyer. He has a good practice with important cases in the Circuit and Supreme Courts of Michigan; has been City Attorney of St. Johns for ten years, and has never lost but one of the many cases he tried for that municipality.

At 20 years of age Mr. Brunson began stumping Clinton County for the Republicans, and in 1880 cast his first vote for Garfield. He was elected Secretary of the Republican County Committee in 1886, and held that position during the campaigns of 1886-8, 1892-4-6-8.

During those campaigns he was in charge of the work in the County, and has been credited with winning several of the victories in that County, notably that of 1896, when a perfect fusion of four parties against the Republicans was overcome and every man but one of the County ticket was elected, the one Democrat being the only one elected during the six campaigns which Mr. Brunson conducted in that county.

In 1899 he was appointed Postmaster of St. Johns by President McKinley, being the only candidate presented for the place, all the others withdrawing and signing his petition when he announced himself as a candidate. The Detroit Journal, in announcing his appointment, said that he was one of the most popular young Republicans in Michigan. Many politicians have said that they believe him to be the best political organizer in the State. This is evidenced by the organization in Clinton County which is said to be the best in Michigan. He has been a delegate to most of the State Conventions of his party for the last 15 years. He belongs to the Phi Delta Phi, the best and largest of the legal fraternities. He is also a Knight of Pythias. He was married June 14th, 1888 to Elizabeth Finch. His only child is Lawrence W. Brunson, born March 25th, 1894.

The Clinton County Republican Convention in 1897 indorsed Mr. Brunson unanimously for the position of District Attorney for the Eastern District of Michigan, and he had very strong indorsements for this place from lawyers and politicians of the best class in various parts of the State. He has been for years Chairman of the City, Township, Senatorial and Judicial Committees and a member of the Congressional Committee.

CHRISTIAN H. BUHL, was, in the course of his long and active life, interested in many industrial, financial and mercantile enterprises in Detroit, but it is doubtful if any of his later undertakings were of greater benefit to the City than that in which he first engaged, over sixty years ago, the fur trade; for it was upon the foundations which he and his brother laid in 1835, that a business was built up which has made Detroit, ever since, one of the leading fur marts in the country. Mr. Buhl was started in life with a good common school education, and a trade, and he made the best use of both. His father, Christian Buhl, was a German, who came to this country in 1802, and settled in Butler County, Pennsylvania, where the subject of this sketch was born, May 9th, 1810. At the age of 21, having completed his school education, and his apprenticeship in the hatter's trade, he started westward, settled in Detroit, and with his brother, Frederick, opened a hat and cap store, manufacturing to some extent, their own goods. To this they soon afterwards added the fur trade, which came chiefly under the supervision of Christian H. Buhl, his brother attending to the hat and cap department. There were then many fur-bearing animals in the woods, lakes and streams of Michigan and

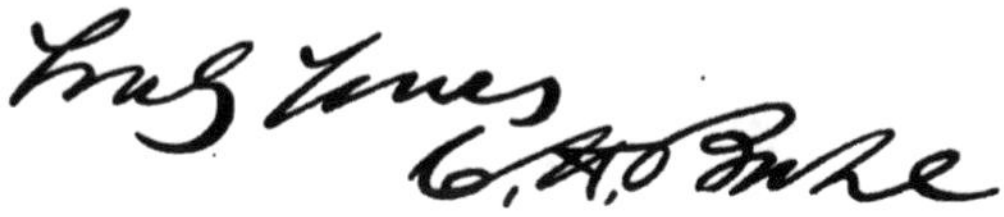
Truly Yours

Wisconsin, and Detroit was a natural market for the peltry. The business was pushed with energy and soon assumed very large proportions. In 1843, after the failure of the American Fur Co., their trading posts fell into the hands of P. Chouteau & Co., and the Messrs. Buhl arranged with them for the purchase, on joint account, of furs in the States of Ohio, Indiana, Northern Illinois, Wisconsin, Michigan and the Province of Ontario, or Upper Canada, as it was then called. They carried on a very large fur trade until 1853, when the firm dissolved, F. Buhl taking the hat and cap department, and C. H. Buhl continuing to deal in furs, upon his own account, for two years. He then turned this over to his brother, and formed a partnership with Charles Ducharme, under the firm name of Buhl & Ducharme, for the purpose of engaging extensively in the hardware and iron business. They purchased the large wholesale houses of Alexander H. Newbold and Ducharme & Bartholomew, and consolidated the two, thus forming one of the largest hardware establishments in the West. After the death of the junior partner, Charles Ducharme, in 1873, Mr. Buhl purchased his interest, and then admitted his oldest son, Theodore D. Buhl, to the firm, which has continued to be one of the most prosperous of its kind in the West. A second son, Frank H., was subsequently admitted, and the firm took the name of Buhl, Sons & Co. In 1863, Mr. Buhl, with other gentlemen, purchased the works and effects of the Westerman Iron Company, at Sharon, Penn., changing the name to the Sharon Iron Works. He afterwards became the controlling owner of this very large and prosperous concern, which employed over a thousand men, turning out one hundred tons of finished product daily.

In 1864 Mr. Buhl purchased a controlling interest in the Detroit Locomotive Works, and put not only more capital but renewed vitality into the concern, and for fifteen years it was largely profitable to the stockholders and of much advantage to the City. In 1880 these works were incorporated as the Buhl Iron Works, with Mr. Buhl as President. At a still later date this plant was taken by the Buhl Stamping Co., manufacturers of tin plate and its products, and still doing a large and prosperous business. Mr. Buhl also, in 1881, organized the Detroit Copper & Brass Rolling Mill Company, whose works on McKinstry avenue have been repeatedly enlarged, until they comprise one of the largest manufacturing establishments in the City. Among numerous other undertakings of magnitude, and of importance to Detroit that shared the benefits of Mr. Buhl's capital and enterprise were the Detroit, Hillsdale & Indiana and the Detroit, Eel River & Illinois Railroads, of both of which he was President; the Second National Bank, now the Detroit National, of which he was one of the original incorporators, and of which he was President after Governor Baldwin's retirement in 1887, and the Union Railroad Depot and Station Company. He had smaller investments in other enterprises, and also constructed a number of blocks and stores for business purposes.

The first decade of Mr. Buhl's business career in Detroit covered a period of intellectual and social life that has certainly not been improved upon at any time since then, a period in which the old Fire Department flourished; in which the Young Men's Society was the center of forensic practice; in which social life was frank and hearty; in which the best business men were willing to serve the public in the Common Council, and in which the same class of men aspired to the office of Mayor. Mr. Buhl was on even terms with the best of his fellow citizens in sharing the duties and enjoying the benefits of this social and public life. In politics during this period he was active. In 1851 he was elected Alderman from the Second Ward and in 1860 was elected Mayor. He held no political offices after that, but took a deep interest in the success of the Republican party. He was one of the founders of the Michigan Club, one of its first incorporators, was for several years on its board of directors, was President one term, and was always a liberal giver to the party campaign funds. He was liberal also in response to the demands of charity, and in contributing to the needs of public institutions. He gave a valuable law library to the University of Michigan. He was one of the original promoters of the Art Museum, a Trustee of the original Detroit Medical College, and was prominently identified with the Fort Street Presbyterian Church.

He was married in 1843 to Miss Caroline DeLong, of Utica, N. Y. They had five children, of whom two are living, Theodore D., who has charge of the firm's interests in Detroit, and Frank H., who lived for some years at Sharon, Penn., to look after the branch of their business located in that place. Mr. Buhl died in 1894, January 23rd.

CHARLES AUGUST BUHRER, of Detroit, is one of the men who have held public positions with credit to themselves and with benefit to the public. He was born in Detroit, August 5th, 1855. His father, Christian Frederick Carl Buhrer, was born in Ludwigsburg, Germany, on the 6th day of October, 1820. He learned the trade of nail-maker, emigrated to America in 1846, and died in Wayne, Mich., on the 6th day of January, 1866. His mother, Eva Buhrer, was born in Nierstein, Germany, the 23rd day of June, 1820, and died August 5th, 1895, in Detroit. The son's education was obtained in the public schools. Early thrown upon his own resources he was, at the age of 14, apprenticed to Conrad Marxhausen, publisher of the Michigan Journal, which publication went out of existence within a year, and with it went Buhrer's first job. He completed his trade in the Post Job printing office and became a full-fledged typo, joining Typographical Union No. 18, of which organization he was a member in good standing until he severed his connection with the craft to embark in the hardware business with his brother, William F. Buhrer, in 1883. Persistent application to business, unfailing courtesy to customers and square dealing with everybody had the effect of building up for the firm a flattering patronage. The business is still conducted under the firm name of Buhrer Bros.

Mr. Buhrer's political experience commenced in 1889, at the same time that Hazen S. Pingree was first elected Mayor. The Common Council had been getting into a bad way before then, or at least had gained a bad reputation. With a view of bringing about reforms in the City Government, a large number of voters in the Tenth Ward, having the greatest confidence in Mr. Buhrer's integrity, signed a petition to him to run for Alderman. He accepted, and though the ward had been strongly Democratic, he was elected by a handsome majority. He was of great service in the Common Council, where he served three terms, in breaking up the old sewer and paving rings, and was a staunch supporter of Mayor Pingree in carrying through the many reforms which he instituted.

Ald. Buhrer has ever been the consistent friend of organized labor and laboring men. City laborers still talk of a characteristic act of his in their behalf. In 1891 the two elements in the council became deadlocked. Certain Aldermen successfully defeated all efforts to obtain a quorum of the Council, and many a laborer was put to distress because of the failure of the Council to pass the weekly budget. After trying ineffectually to get the budget allowed, Alderman Buhrer gave the City Treasurer his personal check for something over $1,500, out of which the laborers were paid, and as a result the deadlock was broken.

In 1895, at the solicitation of Treasurer McLeod, Mr. Buhrer became Deputy County Treasurer. When it was determined to inaugurate sweeping reforms in the office and to facilitate the work of carrying through the vast number of transactions that are required in the business of the office, particularly during the tax-paying month, Mr. Buhrer became an active spirit in the work, in which his long experience in business made him a valuable aid. It required many months to devise and elaborate the system, which has since been in vogue, and which has added greatly to the satisfaction and convenience of the public. In view of his valuable service as deputy, Mr. Buhrer was naturally the successor of Mr. McLeod as Treasurer, to which office he was elected by a handsome majority in November, 1898. Mr. Buhrer, throughout his whole business and political career, has made his way through his individual efforts without the aid either of inherited means or of outside political influence.

Mr. Buhrer is a member of the Michigan Club, Harmonie and Concordia Singing Societies, American Tent of Maccabees, U. and I. Social Club and Huragari Society. He was married to Julia Kengott, August 28th, 1883, in Detroit. Their children are Louise Eva Buhrer, Russell Alger Buhrer, and Carl Rudolph Buhrer.

ORRIN BUMP, who has been a resident of Bay City for thirty-four years, was born in Flushing, Genesee County, August 13th, 1843, son of David Bump, a farmer. He graduated from Flint, Mich. High School; enlisted as a private in the Eighth Michigan Infantry when he was about 18 years old; participated in all the campaigns and battles of that regiment, and was adjutant of the regiment when discharged. He was wounded slightly three times. Immediately after the war he took a commercial course in a Business College in Detroit and then accepted a position in a bank in Flint. In 1866 he removed to Bay City and was bookkeeper and teller in the First National Bank. In 1870 he organized the State Bank and was its cashier, and when this was merged into the Second National Bank in 1877, he was made cashier of that. When its charter expired in 1894, the bank was reorganized under the title of the Old Second National Bank of Bay City, and he was made its President, which position he now occupies.

Mr. Bump has always devoted his time and energies to the bank, and has no aspirations for political honors, but he has always been a staunch Republican and cast his first vote in Virginia, while in the Army in 1864, for Abraham Lincoln. He is a Trustee of the Bay City Library, President of the Belgian Chicory mills, and Treasurer of the Valley Telephone Co. In 1868 he married Ella Fray, daughter of George C. Fray, lumberman, who died the same year. In 1875 he married Hattie L. Crosthwaite, of Buffalo, daughter of William Crosthwaite, the ship-builder. A daughter by this wife died when about seven years old, and the wife died in 1893. He married his present wife, the widow of Henry C. Chapin, in 1895.

JULIUS C. BURROWS was born January 5, 1837, at Northeast, Erie County, Pennsylvania, of New England ancestry. When but a mere lad his parents removed to Ashtabula County, Ohio, where he attended district school, and afterwards Kingsville academy. It was while attending the latter school that he determined upon the profession of the law, but, his parents being poor, he was thrown entirely upon his own resources and turned toward teaching as the most natural stepping stone to his chosen profession. During the winter of 1853-54 he taught school, and was thereby enabled to attend Grand River Institute, at Austinburg, Ashtabula County, the following year. At 19 years of age he was principal of Madison Seminary, Lake County, Ohio, and during these school days he kept the law books so familiar to every student of the law, under the light of the evening lamp, and would pore over them until late in the night. In 1858-59 he was principal of the Union School at Jefferson, and while occupying this position read law in the office of a firm well-known at the time in the famous Western Reserve, Cadwell & Simonds, and was admitted to the bar. Young Burrows acquired a taste for politics early in life, and his first campaigning was in 1856, before he was

twenty years of age, when he took the stump for Fremont and the young Republican party.

In 1860 he removed to Michigan and took charge of Richland Seminary, in Kalamazoo County, and in the spring of 1861 was admitted to practice before the Supreme Court of the State. In the fall of the same year he moved into the then Village of Kalamazoo, and began the practice of his chosen profession. Soon the war broke out and young Burrows threw himself into the contest for National union and supremacy with all the ardor of his vigorous young manhood. He spoke for the Union cause and his powers as an orator and organizer were readily recognized, and, upon raising a company for service, he was chosen its captain. This company became a part of the Seventeenth Michigan Infantry, the "stonewall regiment," that won for itself a proud fame and name. Captain Burrows served with this regiment and company until the fall of 1863, and participated in the battles of South Mountain, Antietam, Fredericksburg, Vicksburg, Jackson and Knoxville, and for gallant service won the hearts of the commanders over him, as well as the men under him.

In 1864 he took part in his first political campaign, being elected Circuit Court Commissioner for Kalamazoo County, and has been engaged in every political contest since that date. In 1866 he was elected Prosecuting Attorney, and was re-elected in 1868. The year following he was tendered the position of Supervisor of Internal Revenue for Michigan and Wisconsin by General Grant, but declined. In 1872 he was elected to the Forty-third Congress, as a Republican; served upon the Committee on Claims and Expenditures in the War Department, and made his first speech, December 17, 1873, in favor of the repeal of the Silver Act. This speech brought him at once into National prominence. Since that day Mr. Burrows has made many illustrious speeches in Congressional halls, which have stamped him as a leading debater and orator. In 1874 he was defeated in a contest for re-election, but was elected to the Forty-sixth, Forty-seventh, Forty-ninth, Fiftieth, Fifty-first, Fifty-second, Fifty-third and Fifty-fourth Congresses. During the latter years of his career in the House of Representatives he was always nominated by acclamation and in his election to the Fifty-fourth Congress received upwards of 13,000 plurality.

In the House of Representatives Mr. Burrows won a commanding position, and was a prominent member of the Ways and Means Committee, standing next in line for the Chairmanship at the time of his election to the Senate. His speech upon the McKinley Tariff Bill in the Fifty-first Congress placed him readily in the forefront of defenders of the policy of protection. In the same Congress he was Chairman of the Committee on Levees and Improvements in the Mississippi River. He was more than once pressed for Speaker of the House, and was twice elected Speaker pro tempore of the body. In January, 1895, he was elected United States Senator as successor to the Hon. Francis B. Stockbridge, deceased, and at once assumed the office. He was re-elected by a unanimous vote of the Republican members of the Legislature in January, 1899, and his term of service will expire on March 3, 1905. He has been honored with splendid recognition upon important committees in the Senate, being Chairman of the Committee on Revision of the Laws of the United States, and member of the Committees of Finance, Military Affairs and Privileges and Elections. He has taken an active and conspicuous part in the Senate debates and is recognized as one of the leaders upon the Republican side.

He has been twice married—in 1856 to Miss Jennie S. Hubbard, of Ashtabula County, Ohio, by whom he has one daughter; and in 1865 to Miss Frances S. Peck, of Kalamazoo.

When in practice Mr. Burrows was a successful lawyer. From 1867 to 1886 he was associated in partnership with Hon. Henry F. Severens, now United States Judge for the Sixth Federal Circuit.

The Washington home of Senator and Mrs. Burrows is at 1404 Massachusetts avenue, in the midst of a number of Senatorial residences, and is modest, and yet comfortable, in its appointments.

COL. LOU BURT, who has cut quite a figure in Wayne County political and official life, was born April 18th, 1852, at Cardington, Ohio. His father was M. Burt, by occupation a jeweler, whose ancestors had come from England to Springfield, Mass. The son completed his education at Hiram College, Ohio, learned the trade of watchmaker and jeweler, and was in business for some years in Detroit as a wholesale jeweler. In politics he has been a Republican from the start, cast his first vote for Hayes and Wheeler, and during the past ten years he has been a delegate to most of the State Conventions. He was Alderman from the Fourth Ward four years. While in the Common Council he introduced and put through the measure which provided for the collection and incineration of garbage. He was Chairman of the Republican City and County Committee eight years, and Colonel and Aide-de-Camp on the staff of Governor Rich for two years.

Colonel Burt is very socially inclined and is a member of the following organizations: Rushmere Club, St. Clair Flats; Detroit Yacht Club; Riverside Lodge, Odd Fellows; Erie Lodge, K. P.; Detroit Lodge of Elks; A. O. U. W.; Union Lodge, S. O. No. 3; King Cyrus Chapter; Monroe Council; Michigan Sovereign Consistory; Past Commander of Detroit Commandery No. 1, K. T., and Past Potentate Moslem Temple, N. M. S. He was married in 1873 in Cleveland, to Mary S. Ingersoll and has two children, Elizabeth C. and Lou, Jr.

When Colonel Burt went into politics he put energy and system into his work. He was in charge of the campaign in Wayne County for eight years, and during that time but three Democrats were

# [illegible] PARTY.

[illegible] Republic [illegible]

[illegible] with Hon. [illegible]

[illegible] Wayne Co[illegible]

[illegible] Conventions. [illegible]

[illegible] member of the [illegible] Lodge [illegible] K. P. [illegible] Chapter [illegible] Michigan [illegible] Past Commander [illegible] No. [illegible] K. T., and Past Potentate [illegible] He was married in 1873 in Cleveland to [illegible] Ingersoll [illegible] Elizabeth C. and [illegible], Jr.

[illegible] energy and system [illegible] in Wayne County [illegible] Democrats were [illegible]

J. A. RUFF, ENG.

J. C. Burrows

Butterfield

elected to any County office. One of his first moves was to bring about a consolidation of the City and County Committees, the best thing that was ever done for the party in the County, as it concentrated the work, prevented duplicating, and made a saving of funds. He made it a point before opening a campaign to have money enough collected or pledged to carry him through, with a little left over to help elect Supervisors in the spring. He was the first to inaugurate a thorough literary campaign, keeping up a fire of folders, circulars and cartoons from house to house. Before he was through he had the most complete list of voters, with their political preferences, and of good party workers that was ever made out in the County. Colonel Burt was very active in all the Pingree campaigns, except the first Mayoralty canvass. He is now serving his third term as County Auditor, in the duties of which he has also been very systematic and thorough. The last time he was before the people for that office he had a majority of 12,562, leading the ticket.

ORA ELMER BUTTERFIELD, of Ann Arbor, was born November 9th, 1870, at Brattleboro, Vt., his father's name being Oscar Holland Butterfield, his mother's name Rosalia Elmer. His father was a contractor and builder, a carpenter by trade, descended from English ancestors. Ora Elmer was educated in the Brattleboro schools, from which he graduated in the Latin English Course in 1886. He worked at the carpenter's trade for some time and then went to Child's Business College in Springfield, Mass., graduating in 1888. He went thence to Colorado, remaining a year employed in the office of the Register of Deeds of Weld County at Greeley, and while there determined to study law. He entered the University of Michigan in 1889, graduated in 1891, and was admitted to the bar in June, 1891, before he was yet twenty-one. He has been engaged continuously in the practice of law at Ann Arbor ever since. He has always been a Republican. His father was a Republican, but when he reached majority, he read the history of the parties for himself and decided independently that this party was his proper place, although at that time the County in which he lived was overwhelmingly Democratic. His first vote was cast for Harrison in 1892, and he has voted the Republican ticket at every election since. He was a delegate to the National Convention of the League of Republican Clubs at Omaha in 1898, and was elected Michigan Member of the Executive Committee. He is Chairman of the Washtenaw Republican County Committee and has been since 1896. He was Circuit Court Commissioner four years, City Attorney of Ann Arbor one term and is at present, with his associate, local attorney for the Michigan Central Railroad Company and also counsel for the Ann Arbor Water Company.

Mr. Butterfield was married September 14th, 1893, to Amy Iola Dunklee and has one child named Helen Iola Butterfield.

BURT DUWARD CADY was born in Port Huron, St. Clair County, Mich., July 25th, 1874. His father was Elwin Marvin Cady, a lumber and grain merchant, and his mother was Mehitable E. Cady. His ancestors on his father's side were early settlers in the Eastern States, mostly Connecticut, and on his mother s side in Vermont and New Hampshire. He was educated in the public schools of Port Huron and his first occupations on his own account were peddling newspapers and working in a grocery store. Mr. Cady entered a law office when eighteen years of age, was admitted to the bar on his twenty-first birthday, commenced practice October 4th, 1897, and continued in practice alone until May, 1900, when he formed a partnership with Clifford W. Crandall, under the firm name of Cady & Crandall. He was elected Assistant Police Justice when twenty-two years of age, at the fall election of 1896, carrying the City of Port Huron by eight hundred majority; was elected Circuit Court Commissioner in November, 1898, by over twenty-three hundred majority, leading the County ticket; was appointed member of the Advisory Council of the Republican State League in 1898 to represent the Seventh Congressional District; was elected Secretary of the League in February, 1899, and in February, 1900, was elected Vice-President. He organized the Municipal League of Republican Clubs in Port Huron in the fall of 1898. He is President of this League, which embraces eleven active working clubs with a membership of over 1,000, and Secretary and Treasurer of the Blaine Club of the Seventh Congressional District. He cast his first Presidential vote for McKinley in 1896.

Mr. Cady is at present Assistant Police Justice at Port Huron, and Circuit Court Commissioner for the County. He is a director of the McCormick Harness Co., and of the Port Huron Driving Park Association. He is a member of Pine Grove Lodge, F. & A. M.; Port Huron Lodge, B. P. O. E.; Charter Lodge, K. of P., No. 18; member of Temple No. 56, D. O. K. K.; also a member of the Society of Sons of the American Revolution.

EDWARD CAHILL was born at Kalamazoo, Mich., August 3rd, 1843, being the eldest son of Abram and Frances Maria Marsh Cahill. He had one sister older than himself and one brother and three sisters younger. His father, Abram, was born in Westmoreland County, Pennsylvania, in 1808, and was one of thirteen children born to Abram Cahill and Nancy Wallace Cahill. His grandfather, Edward Cahill, the great-grandfather of the subject of the present sketch, was born in Ireland and emigrated to this country before the Revolution, settling in Philadelphia. Both Edward and his son Abram served in the Revolutionary Army. Abram the elder was accidentally drowned while his son Abram was a lad, and the necessities of a large family led to Abram being early apprenticed to the trade of a tanner. After serving his apprenticeship he removed, in 1830, to Kalamazoo,

Burt D. Cady

where he established himself in that business. In 1841 he married Frances Maria Marsh, daughter of John Pitt and Fanny Ransom Marsh, who had come from Vermont and settled in Kalamazoo in 1832. John Pitt Marsh was one of the early Abolitionists and was at one time a candidate for Congress on the Free Soil ticket. Both he and his wife, who was a sister of Governor Epaphroditus Ransom, came of Revolutionary stock. In 1854 Abram removed to Holland, Ottawa County where, in partnership with Hon. Manley D. Howard, he engaged in lumbering. He lived only a few months after his removal, dying there August 31st, 1854. His widow, left with six children and only a small estate, returned the next year to Kalamazoo, undertook with courage and cheerfulness, the burden of rearing and educating her children, and lived to see her labors rewarded. She died in 1894 at her son's house in Lansing, where she had made her home for many years.

In 1856, at the age of thirteen, Edward, the subject of this sketch, entered the preparatory department of Kalamazoo College, and remained in that institution until the spring of 1860, when necessity compelled him to seek some employment that would aid his mother in the support of her family. He therefore entered the office of the Kalamazoo Gazette, then the leading Democratic paper of Western Michigan. He followed the occupation of a printer two years, during which time he did duty also as a reporter, it being his practice to make brief notes of local events that came under his notice, and from these notes to set up the items of news at his case without being at the trouble of writing them out. His taste for writing led him also to furnish a variety of articles for the Kalamazoo papers and as correspondent for the Detroit and Chicago papers.

In the fall of 1861 he went to Illinois and taught school at Metamora for a few months. In 1862 he enlisted as a private in Company A, Eighty-ninth Illinois Infantry, and went at once to Kentucky, where his regiment became a part of Buell's army, then being concentrated at Louisville to confront the advance of General Bragg. The hardships and exposure, however, were too much for him in an enfeebled condition occasioned by being overcome by heat while at Louisville, and in December, 1862, he was discharged for disability. Returning to his old home in Kalamazoo he speedily regained his health and began the study of law in the office of Miller & Burns, where he remained until the fall of 1863, when he learned that the President had given authority to Colonel Henry Barns, of Detroit, to raise a regiment of colored troops in Michigan. He applied for and received authority to raise a company, which was in camp in a few weeks, and Cahill was commissioned first lieutenant. With this regiment he served in South Carolina, Georgia and Florida, until October, 1865, when he was mustered out as captain of Company D. During these years of military service he was on staff duty for brief periods at various times, and in the summer and fall of 1865, was Provost Marshal of the Western District of South Carolina, a position which involved civil as well as military administration. On his return he resumed the study of the law at St. Johns, Clinton County, and was admitted to the bar in that County in June, 1866. He removed at once to Ionia County and opened an office at Hubbardston, then a prosperous lumbering town, where he remained four years. In 1870 he was elected Circuit Court Commissioner of Ionia County and removed to Ionia. He remained there for only a few months, and in June, 1871, he removed to Chicago and opened an office at the corner of Clark and Madison streets. A few months later came the great fire of October 9th, and his office being in the heart of the great conflagration, was burned with all its contents. He remained in Chicago until the summer of 1873, when he returned to Michigan and settled in Lansing, where he has since resided.

Mr. Cahill has always been a Republican. He cast his first vote for Lincoln while in the army in 1864. Always taking a deep interest in politics he has never sought or held any office not in the line of his profession. His advice to young lawyers has always been never to seek political office, but to stick strictly to business. In 1876 and 1878 he was elected Prosecuting Attorney of Ingham County. In 1887 he was appointed by Governor Luce a member of the Advisory Board of Pardons. On the death of Justice James V. Campbell, in 1890, he was appointed a Justice of the Supreme Court to fill the vacancy. At the election held the following autumn he was the nominee of his party for the same office, but for the first time in thirty years the entire Republican State ticket was defeated. During his short service on the bench many important decisions were rendered by the Court. His opinions are to be found in the 80th to 85th of the Michigan Reports.

On his retirement from the bench he resumed the practice of his profession in Lansing. In the course of his long and varied practice he has been engaged in some cases of great public interest: In the litigation between the State and certain land grant railroads, over the swamp lands, in 1888 and 1889, he was associated with the Attorney General as counsel for the State. In 1894 he was one of the counsel for the State in the cases brought by Governor Rich against the Secretary of State, State Treasurer and Commissioner of the State Land Office, as the members of the Board of Canvassers, to remove them from office for gross neglect of duty in connection with the canvass of votes upon the Amendment to the Constitution, relative to the salaries of State officers. He was also employed by the State to assist the Prosecuting Attorney of Ingham County in the criminal prosecution of the same officers and the Attorney General for corrupt conduct in relation to the same matter.

In the more recent cases growing out of the indictments found by the Grand Jury of Ingham County in the fall of 1899, he was engaged as counsel for the State to assist the Prosecuting Attorney and took part in all the trials. That he was the only counsel employed by the State to contend with numerous and able counsel employed by the persons indicted, made his duties and responsibilities very great. As counsel for Governor Pingree and the Attorney General in the long controversy relating to the taxation of corporations and the repeal of the Special Railroad Charters he took an important part.

In 1867 he was married to Lucy A. Crawford, a daughter of Henderson Crawford, of Milford, Oakland County. They have had three sons who died in infancy, and two daughters, both of whom are married, the eldest, Clara, to Robert E. Park, a well known newspaper man, and the youngest, Margaret, to Henry S. Bartholomew, of Lansing.

HENRY MUNROE CAMPBELL was born in Detroit, April 18th, 1854. His father was the eminent jurist, James V. Campbell, for thirty-two years a justice of the Supreme Court of the State, and for twenty-five years a lecturer in the law school of Michigan University. His mother was Cornelia Hotchkiss. He was educated in the public schools, graduated at the Detroit High School in 1872; graduated from the literary department, University of Michigan, in 1876, with the degree of Ph. B.; graduated from the law department, University of Michigan, in 1878, with the degree of LL. B. He studied law in the office of Alfred Russel and was admitted to the bar in October, 1877. In 1878 the firm of Russel & Campbell was organized, consisting of Henry Russel and Henry M. Campbell, and he has continued a member of the firm since that time. In 1880 he was appointed Master in Chancery of the United States Circuit Court, which position he still holds. He is a member of the American Bar Association and of the State and Detroit Bar Associations. November 22d, 1881, he was married to Caroline B. Burtenshaw and they have two children, Henry M., Jr., and Douglas.

Mr. Campbell never held a political office and has never sought one. His business is largely railroad and corporation business, representing the Michigan Central Railroad, Pere Marquette Railroad, Pontiac, Oxford and Northern Railroad; counsel for the Union Trust Company, Parke, Davis & Co., Michigan Carbon Works, American Radiator Co. and other corporations. He is also a Vestryman of Christ Church, a Director of the State Savings Bank, Director and Treasurer of the River Rouge Improvement Co. and of the Cass Farm Co.; Chairman of the Executive Committee of the Woodward Lawn Cemetery; Director of the Detroit Bar Library; Director and President for three years of the Detroit Club, and was one of the organizers and at one time President of the Detroit Naval Reserves. He is a member of the Country Club, Detroit Boat Club, Prismatic Club, Huron Mountain Hunting & Fishing Club and Fontinalis Club.

JAMES VALENTINE CAMPBELL was born in Buffalo, N. Y., February 25th, 1823. His father, Henry Munroe Campbell, was a merchant and banker in Buffalo and in Detroit, and also held an appointment as "side judge" for many years. His position was one not known at the present time, but it was customary in the early days to call in lay judges to sit with the regular judges in the trial of causes. His mother, Lois Bushnell, was a member of the well known Bushnell family of Connecticut, and was a descendant of Colonial Governor Sedgwick. His grandfather, Thomas Campbell, was a son of Duncan Campbell, who came to this country prior to the Revolutionary War from Scotland, as an officer in a Highland regiment. Thomas Campbell settled on the banks of the Hudson River near Plattsburg and served in the American Army in the Revolutionary War.

James V. Campbell had his education at St. Paul's College, Flushing, Long Island, an Episcopal institution of high rank, presided over at that time by Dr. Muhlenberg. He came to Detroit as a child in 1826 and lived in the city from that time until his death. He studied law in the office of Walker & Douglas, was admitted to the bar in 1844 and became a member of the firm. In 1845 he was Secretary of the Board of Regents of Michigan University, and in 1857 was elected Justice of the Supreme Court, being one of the first judges of the court, which was organized at that time on its present basis. He remained a member of the bench until his death, March 26th, 1890. In 1859 he became one of the founders of the law school of Michigan University, and held the Marshall Professorship in that institution until 1885, at which time he was compelled to resign because of increased work on the bench. He was the first man to receive the honorary degree of LL. D. from Michigan University. He was always particularly interested in educational affairs and served for many years on the Board of Education, and was also a member and the first President of the Public Library Commission. He was the author of numerous pamphlets, and of a history of the State entitled "Outlines of the Political History of Michigan."

Judge Campbell was a deeply religious man without ostentation or bigotry, and was for a long time a member of the standing committee of the Diocese of Michigan and Vestryman of St. Paul's, the mother church of the diocese. He was married November 17th, 1849, to Cornelia Hotchkiss and left six children: Cornelia L., Henry M., James V., Jr., Charles H., Douglas H., and Edward D., all of whom except James V., Jr., are now living.

When Mr. Campbell was first nominated for Justice of the Supreme Court, some objected to him as being too young for that high office, he being then only 34, but he soon demonstrated his fitness for the position and his subsequent re-elections were practically without opposition. While he and his illustrious associates, Christiancy, Cooley and Graves were on the bench the demand for Michigan

*Jas. V. Campbell.*

Supreme Court reports was greater than for those of any other State in the country except Massachusetts and New York.

Gentle and kindly in manner, Judge Campbell was nevertheless firm and inflexible in what he deemed correct judicial opinions. Of this trait, Hon. Hugh McCurdy, of Corunna, gave this illustration at the Supreme Court memorial services after Judge Campbell's death. "The case of Twitchell vs. Blodgett, 13 Mich. 127, probably put the severest test of partisanship to this Court which has ever been presented for adjudication. The question involved was the constitutionality of the Soldiers' Voting Law, passed by a Republican Legislature in 1864. Upon the decision of the case depended the unseating of Republican members of the Legislature, and many County officers all over the State. The case was brought on for argument in this City, January 26th, 1865, before a full bench, all the members of which had been elected on the Republican ticket. The City was crowded with the leading politicians of the State, and the excitement ran high on the fate of the issue involved, and everything was done that could be to induce the Supreme Court to sustain the law and save the party. At this time I was State Senator and boarded at the American Hotel, where nearly all the Judges also stopped while here holding Court. On the morning of the 28th of January it was well understood that the Court would decide the case. Judge Campbell's room was across from me, and as he started for the Court I met him in the hall with a bundle of papers, and remarked to him jocosely, 'Now Judge, comes the tug of war,' and he replied: 'Yes, Senator, and I am going to do what I believe is right, and let the consequences take care of themselves.' Judges Campbell, Christiancy and Cooley rendered decision declaring the law unconstitutional. In closing his opinion Judge Campbell uses this clear and emphatic language: 'And I am, therefore, compelled to declare that in my opinion the act of the Legislature authorizing voting on a different basis is invalid. Public duty will not permit me, as a magistrate, to offer excuses for performing an unavoidable office. If our Constitution deprives of the privilege of voting a class of men to whom we are largely indebted for having the right preserved to ourselves, the only remedy is to invoke the people to amend a restriction which has become too narrow for complete justice.' It would have been as easy to swerve the sun in its diurnal course as to move him from the faithful discharge of the trust confided in him. No taint or suspicion ever attached to his name while living—no stain can ever disfigure the bright escutcheon of his memory now that he is gone."

MILO DEWITT CAMPBELL was born in the township of Quincy, Branch County, Mich., October 25th, 1851. His father was Rollin Madison Campbell, a farmer, and his mother was Susan Ann Campbell. His ancestors on his father's side came from Scotland about four generations back, and some time between 1700 and 1750.

His great-great-grandfather was in the Revolutionary War. His mother's ancestors were of English descent. Both father and mother were born in Western New York, and came to Michigan in 1848. He was educated at a country school until fourteen years of age; graduated from the Coldwater High School in 1871, and from the State Normal School at Ypsilanti in 1875.

His first occupation in life was that of farming. His father owned a small farm of thirty acres, and the son when not occupied with him in tilling that, worked out by the day and month doing farm work. At fourteen years of age, desiring better schooling than he could get at the country school, his father gave him his time, and during the summer he worked out to earn money, and in winter attended school at Coldwater, Mich., keeping up with his class until at the age of 17 years, be began teaching country schools winters and attended school during the balance of the year, except during the vacation when he worked upon the farm. After arriving at the age of fourteen he never received a penny of support or assistance from others. In 1877 he was admitted to the bar and for ten years practiced his profession at the Village of Quincy. His practice became one of the largest in the County, and along with the best in the southern part of the State. In 1886 he moved to Coldwater, where he has since resided, and formed a partnership with Clayton C. Johnson, who had been a student in his office. The partnership has continued uninterruptedly since. The offices he has held have been, first, Superintendent of Schools of Branch County, to which office he was elected at the age of twenty-one. He was afterwards elected Circuit Court Commissioner of Branch County and in 1885 was elected a member of the Legislature. In January, 1887, he became Governor Luce's Private Secretary, which office he held for four years. In 1891 he was appointed by Governor Winans, as the Republican member of the State Board of Inspectors, having charge of all the penal and reformatory institutions of the State, together with the Pardon Board. He was made President of this Board and held the office for two years and until the law creating the Board was changed. By Governor John T. Rich, he was appointed a member of the Railroad and Street Crossing Board in 1893, and served upon this Board one term. In 1897 he was appointed Commissioner of Insurance by Governor Hazen S. Pingree, and held the office two years when, at the solicitation of the Governor, he was appointed a member of the Board of State Tax Commissioners, which office he now holds, and was made President of the same.

Mr. Campbell has attended many State Conventions as a delegate and has been four times Chairman of the delegation from Branch County. He has attended as delegate many International and National conferences of the Board of Corrections and Charities, and also as delegate to the National Conference at New York to prepare extradition agreements between the States, together with several other conferences of like character. He has always been a Republican

Milo D. Campbell

His first ballot was cast for Grant in 1872. He is owner of stock in several corporations and companies, principally local in their character. He is a stockholder in the First National Bank at Quincy and Director of the Coldwater National Bank. He belongs to the Presbyterian Church of Coldwater; the Patrons of Husbandry, the Commandery, the Chapter and other orders of Masonry, and the Order of Elks. He was married October 18th, 1876, at Quincy, to Marion Florence Sears and has no children except an adopted daughter, Jessie May Campbell, now seventeen years of age, adopted when she was three years old.

During the two years that Mr. Campbell was Commissioner of Insurance he completely renovated the insurance business of the State. He closed up and put into the hands of receivers thirty or more insolvent and worthless companies, and drove more than fifty other fraudulent and fake concerns from the State. He secured a reduction in fire insurance rates from the stock companies, which resulted in a saving of more than $800,000 annually to the people of the State. The Tax Commission, of which he was made President, in its first year of work, increased the assessed valuation of property in the State by more than $360,000,000, or more than 35 per cent.

WILLIAM LELAND CARPENTER was born November 9th, 1854, at Orion, Oakland County, Mich. His father was Charles Ketcham Carpenter, a farmer, and his mother was Jennette Coryell. His father's ancestors were of English birth. He was a lineal descendant of William Carpenter, who came from Amesbury, England, and in 1637 settled at Providence, in Rhode Island. His mother's ancestors, viz. the Coryells, were French Huguenots, driven from France in 1685 by the revocation of the Edict of Nantes.

He graduated at the Michigan Agricultural College in 1875 and at the Law Department of Michigan University in 1878. The first money he ever earned was by teaching school in a country district, and in this way he earned nearly all the money expended in getting through college. He commenced the practice of law in 1879 at Detroit, and had no other business until he went on the bench in January, 1894. During the period of his active practice he was associated at different times with J. R. McLaughlin, under the firm name of Carpenter & McLaughlin, with Ovid N. Case, under the style of Case & Carpenter, and with Colonel John Atkinson.

Mr. Carpenter has been a Republican ever since he could vote, his first Presidential vote being for Hayes in 1876. He was a delegate to the Republican State Conventions in the spring of 1883 and 1889, and in the fall of 1886, 1890 and 1892. He was elected Judge of the Wayne Circuit Court in the spring of 1893 and again in 1899. The Judge is a member of the Detroit Club, Fellowcraft Club, Union Lodge of S. O., F. & A. M., and Michigan Lodge, I. O. O. F. He was married in Detroit, October 15th, 1885, to Miss Elizabeth C. Ferguson. They have two children, Lela and Rolla Louis.

At the polls Judge Carpenter is a great favorite with the voters, and on the bench he is popular, both with litigants and jurors. He gives the impression of entire independence of outside influence and absolute impartiality, and is very prompt and clear in his decisions. The Wayne Circuit Court has had many important civil cases, but very few that were more important or more hotly contested, than that brought by the heirs of the late Captain E. B. Ward against the trustees of the estate, charging fraud, and involving property valued at several million dollars. Several of the leading attorneys of Detroit and Chicago were engaged in the trial, which lasted six weeks, with voluminous evidence, and with complicated questions involved, yet the morning after the arguments were ended Judge Carpenter gave his decision, going into many details of the case, showing a quick comprehension of all its complications and intricacies, and the law applying to them, which was a marvel to many of the attorneys present.

J. HENRY CARSTENS, M. D., was born June 9th, 1848, in Kiel, Province of Schleswig-Holstein, Germany. His father, John H. Carstens, a merchant tailor, was an ardent Revolutionist, and had been captured and was in prison when his son was born. Later on he was released, and almost immediately emigrated, with his family, to America, settling in Detroit, where he has since remained. J. Henry Carstens was educated in the public schools of Detroit and in the German-American Seminary, where he spent six years. He early evinced an eager desire for intellectual work, excelling in his studies and taking high rank, especially in things pertaining to natural sciences and mathematics. He became proficient in all the details of the drug business. He began the study of medicine and graduated in 1870. He was appointed lecturer on minor surgery in the Detroit Medical College in 1871, and afterwards lectured on nearly every branch of medical science. He was the professor of materia medica and therapeutics in the Detroit College of Medicine for some years, and in 1881 he accepted the professorship of obstetrics and clinical gynecology and has held that position ever since.

In 1876 he entered politics, was a member of the County Committee and was elected Chairman of the Republican City Committee. These positions he held for three years. He was elected to the Board of Education in 1875, and re-elected in 1879. In 1877 he was elected President of the Board of Health. It was through his efforts, while in that position that the law was passed requiring death certificates from physicians and coroners, and making the change in the Board of Health from the Aldermen and City Physicians to a separate board, as at present.

Dr. Carstens has been a delegate to innumerable Conventions, and Chairman of City and County Conventions a number of times. In 1892 he was elected Presidential elector for the First District, and ran ahead of his ticket several hundred votes. He was an alternate at the National Convention at Philadelphia in 1900.

He made his first political speech before he was of age for U. S. Grant, in 1868; helped to organize a Tanner Company and was active in every direction. He was selected to nominate John S. Newberry for Congress. He has been in demand to make nominating speeches, and has stumped the State from one end to the other in different campaigns. He never had a political office except, as mentioned above, in that case, overcoming in the Third Ward an adverse majority of 150 in the vote of 700. In two different campaigns he might have had the Republican nomination for Mayor without any effort on his part, but declined to have his name used.

Dr. Carstens holds the position of gynecologist to Harper Hospital, being chief of the medical staff. He is attending physician to the Women's Hospital, and is obstetrician to the House of Providence. He is a member of the American and Michigan State Medical and Library Society, of the Detroit Academy of Medicine and of the British Gynecological Society, and is Ex-President of the American Association of Obstetricians and Gynecologists. He is also prominent in many other societies, and has gained almost world-wide renown through the papers and books he has written on the different modern discoveries and treatments in medical science. He has long since given up "general practice," and devotes himself exclusively to abdominal surgery and diseases of women.

He is one of the Trustees of the Detroit College of Medicine, is Chief of Staff of the Harper Hospital and as such member of the Board of Trustees of that Institution. He is also a member of the Detroit Club, Harmonie Society, Rushmere Club, and many other social and fraternal societies. Dr. Carstens was married on October 18th, 1870, to Miss Hattie Rohnert of Detroit.

DAVID CARTER is associated in the minds of everyone with the oldest and best passenger navigation company on the lakes, and has been longer with one company than any other man that looks out on the docks, anywhere between Buffalo and Chicago. He was born February 27th, 1832, at Ohio City, now West Cleveland, Ohio. His father, who was a school teacher, was also named David, and his mother's maiden name was Mary Louisa Davis. His father was descended from Rev. Thomas Carter, who emigrated from England in 1636, and was ordained the first Minister of the Congregational Church in the town of Woburn, Mass., in 1642.

The son David had his education principally in the High School in Sandusky, Ohio. He early commenced working on a farm, but left home at the age of 13, with all his belongings tied up in a bundle, and became a clerk in a small lumber yard in Sandusky, Ohio. He followed this business until 1851, when he became cashier and bookkeeper of a large forwarding and commission house, where he stayed until April, 1852. Then on account of too much confinement he engaged to go as purser of the new steamer "Forest City," owned by the predecessors of "The Detroit & Cleveland Steam Navigation Co." He has remained in the employ of that company and that of its successor, "The Detroit & Cleveland Navigation Co.," ever since, a period of nearly forty-nine years, and has been its Secretary and General Manager for the past 32 years. Through the whole of this long period Mr. Carter has, by strict attention to business, and his accommodating disposition, gained high esteem, not only from the company, but from the traveling public.

Mr. Carter has been a Republican all his life, and voted first for Fremont. He is one of the oldest members of the First Presbyterian Church of Detroit. He was married in Cleveland, Ohio, on Christmas Day, 1856, to Fannie J. Leonard. The names of their children are: Harry L., Jessie June, David S. and Raymond L. Carter.

JOHN JAY CARTON, a leading lawyer and Republican in Central Michigan, is the son ot John and Ann Maguire Carton, and was born on his father's farm in the Township of Clayton, Genesee County, Michigan, November 8th, 1856. His father and mother both came from Ireland, his father from Wexford County and his mother from County Monaghan. They were married in the City of Flint, June 2d, 1851, lived on and cleared up the farm which was their home from the date of their marriage until 1891, when they removed to the City, during which time thirteen children were born to them, of whom nine are now living. John Jay was the fourth oldest in the family. His father died in the City of Flint, November 24th, 1892, and his mother died September 30th, 1895, also in the same City.

The subject of this sketch worked on a farm, except when in school, until he was fourteen years old, helping to clear the farm. After he left the district school he worked and paid the expense of all the schooling he had, sometimes by working night and morning for his board and at other times by getting trusted for his board, and then either working or teaching to get the money with which to pay it. When fourteen years of age he entered the drug store of Heard & Coope, in the Village of Flushing as a clerk and remained one year. After leaving the store he attended the High Schools in the Village of Flushing and in the City of Flint until he was seventeen years of age. He then commenced teaching in the district schools and taught five terms, four winters and one summer. In the intervals between the terms he attended school at Flushing High School a portion of the time, and the remainder of the time he worked at whatever he could get to do. At the conclusion of the fifth term of teaching, which was in the spring of 1877, he entered

John J Carton

the employ of Brunson Turner in the Village of Flushing, as a clerk in his drug store, the agreement being that he was to work for $12.50 per month and his board, and to open the store at five o'clock every morning. He was anxious to get into business and accepted the offer, thinking it might be a stepping-stone to something better. He remained in Mr. Turner's store until August 11th, 1877, at which time he was offered and accepted the position of bookkeeper for Niles & Cotcher, general merchants in the village of Flushing, where he remained until December 1st, 1880. . In the fall of that year he was nominated and elected County Clerk of Genesee County, took the office on January 1st, 1881, and went to Flint to reside. He was re-elected County Clerk in 1882, serving in all four years; was City Attorney of Flint during the years of 1890 and 1891; served as member of the Board of Health of Flint during the years 1893 and 1894; was elected to the House of Representatives in November, 1898, and was renominated for the same place in 1900. While he was County Clerk Mr. Carton studied law during all his spare time, including evenings, and was admitted to the bar on August 21st, 1884. He at once formed a co-partnership with Hon. George H. Durand and has been in partnership with him ever since, under the firm name of Durand & Carton, with the exception of about three months when Judge Durand was on the bench of the State Supreme Court. The partnership has been pleasant and successful. In the Legislature of 1899 Mr. Carton was a candidate for the Republican nomination for the speakership, and although he did not secure the prize he received a surprisingly large vote for a new member. Among other measures he introduced and had charge of the Bill to Provide for the Establishment of Day Schools for the Deaf, in the State of Michigan. He was identified with the bill creating the Tax Commission in the House of Representatives. He was re-elected to the Legislature in November, 1900, and was easily elected Speaker.

Mr. Carton has been a Republican ever since he was of age. His first ballot, a straight Republican ticket, was cast in 1878, and his first presidential vote was for Garfield in 1880. Since 1884 he has generally been a delegate to the Republican State Conventions, but has never attended a National Convention. He has had some business relations of importance, aside from his law practice. He has been a member of the Board of Directors of the First National Bank of the City of Flint during the last five years, and has been President of the bank since January, 1899. He is Chairman of the Board of Managers of the Flint Factory Improvement Company, which has for its purpose the locating of manufacturing industries in the City of Flint.

He is a member of the Genesee Lodge No. 174, F. & A. M.; Washington Chapter No. 15, R. A. M.; Flint Council No. 56; Genesee Valley Commandery No. 15, Knights Templar; Michigan Sovereign Consistory, Scottish Rite; Moslem Temple, Nobles of the Mystic Shrine; Venus Tent No. 275, Knights of the Maccabees; Subordinate

Division No. 1, Knights of the Loyal Guard; Court Kearsley No. 3108, Independent Order of Foresters; Flint Lodge No. 222, B. P. O. E.; was Worshipful Master of Genesee Lodge No. 174 in 1890 and 1891, and Grand Master of the Grand Lodge of Michigan, F. & A. M., in 1896; has been Commander of Venus Tent No. 275, two years, and is at the present time General Counsel of the Great Camp of the K. O. T. M. for Michigan. He was elected Exalted Ruler of Flint Lodge No. 222, B. P. O. E., in the spring of 1893, and served one year, was again elected Exalted Ruler in the spring of 1900 and is the present Exalted Ruler. He was married to Addie C. Pierson at Ukiah, in the State of California, on November 22d, 1898, but has no children.

ZACHARIAH CHANDLER was, for nearly a quarter of a century, the most conspicuous figure in Michigan politics, and was among the most distinguished Republicans in the whole country. Many events of his career have fallen naturally into the recital of the general history of the time. But the history would not be complete without, in addition, at least a brief personal sketch. Mr. Chandler belonged to the New England family of that name, descendants of William Chandler, who came from England in the days of the Puritan immigration, about 1637, and settled in Roxbury, Massachusetts. A century later Zechariah Chandler received a grant of land in Sauhegan-East in the right of his wife, who was the daughter of a soldier in the King Phillip war. The land thus granted was situated in what is now the town of Bedford, New Hampshire, and is the only farm in the town that has remained continuously in the ownership of descendants of the original grantees. It was upon this farm that Zachariah Chandler, or as he was christened Zacharias Chandler, was born, December 10th, 1813. His parents were Samuel Chandler and Margaret Orr, daughter of General Stark's most trusted officer, Colonel John Orr. Their children were seven in number, Zachariah being the sixth. The father, Samuel, died in 1870 at the age of 95 and the mother in 1855 at the age of 81. Both the Chandler and Orr families had generally been long lived, and though his two brothers died when comparatively young, Zachariah seems to have inherited the robust qualities of his ancestors.

As a boy Zachariah was described as being healthy, strong, quick-tempered and self-reliant, "as good a farm hand as there was," fond of athletic sports and the best wrestler in town, a good leader but an unruly subordinate. He was enrolled one year in the local militia, but at the first general muster was arrested for disobedience to the orders of his captain, who was younger than himself and whom he could easily outmow and outwrestle. His rudimentary education was obtained in a little brick school house in Bedford that was still standing at the time of his death, fifty years later. He also attended the academies at Pembroke and Derry, and taught school one winter in a neighboring district. That same winter a Dartmouth Sophomore taught in the little brick school house, "boarded around," and was a welcome visitor at the Chandler farm. This was James F. Joy, between whom and young Chandler there sprang up an intimacy which lasted a life time, and which was one of the influences that subsequently turned Mr. Joy's attention to Detroit.

In 1833 Mr. Chandler commenced his long mercantile life, first as clerk in a store in Nashua, and later in the same year, in company with his brother-in-law, Franklin Moore, he moved to Detroit, where they opened a small general store, under the firm name of Moore & Chandler. Three years later Mr. Chandler bought out his partner and continued, on his own account, a business which laid the foundations of a large fortune. He was prudent and economical, worked early and late, and slept in the store. He kept a good stock, bought with judgment, and was not surpassed as a salesman by any one in the city. As the interior of the State was developed, he added jobbing to his retail trade, cultivated this branch with assiduity, frequently visiting the interior towns, and commenced the wide acquaintance that, in after years, was an important factor in his political success. He was a good judge of character, and numbered the best men in the State among his friends.

Mr. Chandler, during his earlier residence in Detroit, took but little time away from business, except to keep up an active connection with the Presbyterian Church and the Young Men's Society, but when his mercantile success became assured he began to take an active part in municipal and political affairs. His first appearance in politics was as one of the Wayne County Delegates to the Whig State Convention in 1850. A year later he was nominated for Mayor against General John R. Williams, who had held that office for six terms and who was considered invincible. Mr. Chandler organized his first political battle with characteristic vigor and thoroughness, visited every ward and made a strong personal canvass. In the election he carried every precinct and was elected by 350 majority, though the Democrats elected at the same time a large portion of their ticket. In the Whig State Convention of 1852 on an informal ballot for Governor Mr. Chandler had seventy-six votes against thirteen for all others and on a formal ballot received every vote but three. The nomination was made against his wish, but having been made, he accepted it and went into the canvass with a will. He visited all the leading towns in the State, and spoke almost constantly for six weeks before election. He was defeated, but in the campaign developed a strength that placed him at the head of the Whig party in the State, for he received 800 more votes than were given to the party candidate for the Presidency, and led the rest of his ticket from 500 to 4,000 votes. The Democrats had a large majority in the Legislature chosen at that time, and elected Charles E. Stuart to the United States Senate, but Mr. Chandler received a complimentary vote from the entire Whig membership.

Mr. Chandler's party, as well as personal attachments, were very strong, and he was reluctant to give up the Whig organization when that step was first proposed in order to form a union of all the Anti-Democratic forces. But he soon saw that that was the only way to give effect to Anti-Slavery sentiment, which he greatly desired, or to beat the Democrats, for which his desire was still stronger. He therefore joined in the movements which led to the Jackson Convention, attended that gathering, made one of the best short speeches that was there uttered, and afterwards took the stump for the ticket. When the Senatorial term of General Cass expired in 1857 Mr. Chandler was naturally among those thought of for the succession, and after a short contest received the nomination. He at once took rank among the radical leaders in the Senate, a position which he maintained during the whole of the stormy period that followed. He was courageous and outspoken in opposition to the aggressions of the Pro-Slavery element in the Democracy, a staunch supporter afterward of President Lincoln in all his war measures, an advocate of the Constitutional Amendments and of the radical reconstruction measures that followed. No better indication of his inherent strength of character could be given than the fact that he was one of the most trusted advisers of the two greatest men of the time, Lincoln and Grant.

Aside from his important contributions to the general legislation of the period Senator Chandler was, more than any other single individual, entitled to the credit of three great measures. He was one of the first advocates, and certainly the most strenuous of any, of Government improvement of the harbors and great waterways of the country, and as Chairman, for many years, of the Senate Committee on Commerce he was able to give effect to his views, and crystallize them into a fixed policy. He was the principal mover of the Committee on the Conduct of the War, and was its leading spirit throughout its whole service, and it was this committee that first put into definite statement the vague popular impression of defects in our military system, and of shortcomings in some of our leading generals. The committee not only pointed out defects, but proposed remedies, and was probably the most useful civil commission organized for war purposes, that ever existed in any country. If it had done nothing more than to rid the Army of the Potomac of General McClellan and to give Grant a chance, it would have been entitled to the thanks of the Nation. Senator Chandler was the first very prominent man in the West to take a stand against the soft money ideas that became current in that section in the seventies. And he took his position then, knowing well that it might endanger his political future. When it was announced that he was to lead the honest money forces in the Republican State Convention of 1878 one of his friends remonstrated with him, saying that the Republicans were going to be defeated, and defeat under Chandler's leadership would injure his future prospects. Mr. Chandler's reply was: "You're a coward in politics. I'm going to preside at that Convention, and I'm going to be Chairman of the Committee. And I think we shall win. But if Michigan Republicanism goes down, I will go with it." The reply was characteristic, for there never was a time when Mr. Chandler would not have suffered defeat rather than to yield his convictions.

Mr. Chandler's appointment as Secretary of the Interior by President Grant afforded him a new opportunity. He proved to be the best practical reformer of the decade. The department was filled with incompetents and honeycombed with corruption. In less than six months he made it one of the best organized and freest from scandals of any department.

During the last year of Mr. Chandler's life he stood higher in public esteem than ever before. The stalwart character of his politics and his abrupt way of stating opinions did not strike the fancy of some of the Eastern Republicans who had leanings toward Mugwumpism. But when those in Massachusetts saw defeat staring them in the face in 1879, they besought Mr. Chandler to come to their State, and make a few of his hard money speeches, and nothing in the whole campaign pleased him more than this.

At the time of his father's death Mr. Chandler told a fellow Senator that he was going to attend the funeral of his father who died at the age of 95, when the Senator replied, "Zack, you'll live to be a hundred and then you'll die in a fight." He did not live to be a hundred, but he did die in the thick of a fight, for he had just concluded a remarkably successful stumping tour in Wisconsin and had made one excellent hard money speech in Chicago, when during the night of October 31st, 1879, he died at his rooms in the Pacific Hotel, leaving a reputation as one of the strongest of the great men whom the war period produced.

THOMAS HAWLEY CHRISTIAN has had a varied business experience in Wayne County, and a political experience of some note as well. He is the son of Dr. Edmund P. Christian, one of the best known physicians and druggists in the County, and was born in Detroit, June 30, 1856. He was educated mainly in the common schools, completing his education in the Wyandotte High School. After graduation he commenced work for himself in the Wyandotte Silver Smelting Works. He stayed there two years, and in the few following years was successively employed in the Pharmaceutical laboratory of Farrand, Williams & Co., of Detroit; proprietor of a drug store in Farwell, Mich.; an employe in the laboratory of John J. Dodds & Co.; traveling salesman for Perrin & Snow, of Detroit, and afterwards of a Cleveland firm; assistant bookkeeper for the Eureka Iron & Steel Works; teller and bookkeeper of the Wyandotte Savings Bank, and finally in the employ of the extensive rug manufacturing firm of J. H. Bishop & Co.

Amidst all his multifarious occupations Mr. Christian has taken an active interest in politics, doing a fair share of committee work, and often appearing as delegate to Conventions. He was appointed Deputy Sheriff in 1893, and Deputy County Clerk the next year. The insight into public affairs which the latter position gave him added to his qualifications for the County Auditorship, and he was elected as the County member of that Board in 1897. He has proved a careful and faithful member of the Board, looking zealously after the interests of the taxpayers.

Mr. Christian is a stockholder in the two banks at Wyandotte; is a member of Wyandotte Lodge, F. & A. M.; Wyandotte Chapter, R. A. M.; Monroe Council, R. & S. M.; E. B. Ward Lodge, I. O. O. F., and Wyandotte Tent, K. O. T. M. He was married June 10, 1879, to Miss Anna M. Bloodgood, of Wyandotte, and they have two children, M. Evelyn and George E. Christian.

JAMES CHYNOWETH, of Calumet, Mich., was born January 31st, 1846, in Cornwall, England. His father was John Chynoweth, a miner, and his mother was Elizabeth Chynoweth. He attended school in Cornwall until ten years of age and then began work in the mines of that district. He continued in the occupation of a miner at that place, and in the North of England for the next fifteen years. He emigrated to America in 1871; was engaged in the same occupation in New Jersey and Pennsylvania for the next seven years, and in 1878 removed to the copper district in the Upper Peninsula of Michigan. He was employed in the copper mines of Ontonagon County until 1881, and was appointed mining captain at the Mass mine in that year. Since that time he has held the position of mining captain at various mines in Houghton and Ontonagon Counties. In 1897 he was appointed superintendent of the Centennial mine, and in 1899 superintendent of the mining properties known as the Fay group, comprising the holdings of the following companies: Centennial Copper Mining Company, Tri-Mountain Mining Company, Elm River Copper Company, Old Colony Copper Company, Mayflower Mining Company, Allouez Mining Company, Washington Copper Mining Company and the Tecumseh Copper Company.

Mr. Chynoweth has been for the last fifteen years connected with matters of education, both in Houghton and Ontonagon Counties. He is at present a member of the School Board in School District No. 2, Calumet Township, Houghton County, holding the office of Director. In politics he has been Republican ever since he began to study the principles of American politics, and he first voted for Hayes in 1876. He was for two years Treasurer and Supervisor of Greenland Township, Ontonagon County. He was married at Plymouth, England, March 5th, 1866, to Elizabeth Milford.

James Chynoweth

FREDERICK O. CLARK, of Marquette, has been, for nearly four decades, associated with the interests of the thriving centers of Michigan's mining industries. He was born December 18th, 1843, in Girard, Erie County, Pennsylvania, where his father, John B. Clark, a native of Vermont, manufactured leather and harness. His grandfather was Major Clark, of Vermont, who with other members of the family served in the Revolutionary War. His mother, Charlotte M. Woodruff, was a native of Connecticut, and a lineal descendant of John Alden, of Miles Standish courtship fame. Her father, Rev. Ephraim T. Woodruff, was a minister of the Congregational Church, first in his native State, Connecticut, and afterwards on the Western Reserve, Ohio.

The subject of this sketch passed his boyhood in assisting in his father's tannery, and in attending school, taking an academic course. He was prepared to enter the Sophomore class in Hamilton College, New York, when failing health caused a change in his plans. In 1862 he went to the Lake Superior region. He was employed first as a civil engineer, and aided in locating and in the construction of the Upper Peninsula branch of the Chicago & Northwestern Railroad. Having fully recovered his health in this out-door occupation, he followed his first inclination, the study of law, and was admitted to the bar in 1871. Law and politics went together after that, for Mr. Clark was always active in public affairs. He practiced his profession in Escanaba for five years, and during that time filled a number of official positions. In 1872 he was elected President of the Village and in 1873 he was Prosecuting Attorney for Delta County. In 1874 he was elected to the Legislature without opposition, was Chairman of the Committee on the State Library and a member of the Committees on the Judiciary, Agriculture, and Religious and Benevolent Societies; and was, in general legislation, a useful member. In 1876 he moved to Marquette, where he has since maintained a leading position at the bar; and where he has been Supervisor, twice Mayor of the City, and for nine years a member of the Board of Education. He is now a member of the State Prison Board for the Upper Peninsula.

Aside from his law business Mr. Clark has had other material interests. He is a stockholder and Director in the Baraga Mining Company and President of the Marquette City Electric Street Railway Company. He was married in 1877 to Miss Ellen J. Harlow, only daughter of Amos R. Harlow, founder of the City of Marquette. They have a son and daughter, Harlow A. and Martha B. Clark. Both Mr. and Mrs. Clark are members of the Presbyterian Church, in which he is both elder and trustee.

GEORGE HENRY CLIPPERT, of Detroit and Springwells, was one of the hustling Republicans of Wayne County before he approached middle age; was an active member of the Alger Club, and is still a favorite with the younger members of the party. He came very near being nominated for Sheriff in 1896, and undoubtedly would have been if a Heathen Chinee game had not been played against him by men who had the cards up their sleeves for another candidate. As it is, he has held no elective office of importance, though he has been twice delegate to State Conventions, and many times delegate to local conventions, and has been Chairman of the Wayne County Republican Committee. He was always a Republican and cast his first Presidential vote for Blaine in 1884.

George was born March 24th, 1860, in Springwells, son of Ex-Sheriff Conrad Clippert, a brick manufacturer, deceased, and his mother's maiden name was Frederika Pfeifle. Both were from Germany. George had his education at St. John's German School, the private school of Philo M. Patterson, and Goldsmith's Business College. He commenced work as a clerk in a grocery store, worked in a machine shop when 16 years old; started on the M. C. R. R. as fireman, and was promoted to engineer at 19, and in 1884 went into the brick business with his father. He has kept at that ever since and is now President of the George H. Clippert & Bro. Brick Co., and Secretary of the Exposition Brewing Company. He is a member of Union Lodge of Masons, the Elks, Harmonie, D. Y. C. and Michigan Club. He was married September 28th, 1886 to Flora A. Lyon, of Detroit. Their children are Edna H., Harrison F., Phyllis M., Helen C. and George F. Clippert.

WILLIAM JOHNSON COCKER was born in Almondbury, Yorkshire, England. His father was Benjamin F. Cocker, professor of psychology, speculative philosophy, and philosophy of religion in the University of Michigan, who died at Ann Arbor, April 8th, 1883. His mother was Mary Cocker, who died at Adrian, December 9th, 1885. The family sailed from Europe to Australia in 1850, and came to the United States in 1857. Mr. Cocker graduated from Ann Arbor High School in 1864, and entered the University the same year. He was a member of Alpha Delta Phi Fraternity; Captain of the University Baseball Club in 1867; Assistant Librarian in 1867-1868; President of the University Baseball Club in 1869; associate editor of the Michigan University Magazine 1868-69, and graduated in 1869. He was principal of the Adrian High School, 1869-1879; Superintendent of Schools in Adrian, 1879-1885; member of the School Board, 1885-1888. Aside from his work in connection with the Adrian schools he has been active in other directions. He has been President of the Commercial Savings Bank since 1888; was member of the Executive Council of the American Bankers' Association, 1896-1899, and is now a Director of the Adrian Brick and Tile Machine Company, and a Trustee of the Oakwood Cemetery Association. He is also a member of the Detroit Club and the Michigan Club, President of the Alumni Association of the University of Michigan, President of the Adrian

Republican Club, Director of the Young Men's Christian Association, and Vestryman of Christ's Church, Adrian.

Mr. Cocker has always been a Republican, casting his first vote for Grant. He was Chairman of the Republican State Convention, February 22d, 1895, and his address on "The History of American Money," delivered at Grand Rapids, September 3rd, 1896, was circulated as a campaign document in the Presidential election of that year.

He has been Regent of the University of Michigan since January 1st, 1890, with five years yet to serve in that capacity. He was nominated Regent by acclamation at the State Convention, February 22d, 1889, and was renominated by acclamation, February 24th, 1897. In his official capacity as Regent his business experience has been of great service to the University. Though the funds of that institution were always carefully husbanded the method of their distribution which had prevailed for some time was neither systematic nor satisfactory. At each meeting of the Board the immediate needs of each department, as presented at the time, were considered, and appropriations made accordingly. The departments whose heads were most persistent in their applications, were apt to get more than fair proportion, and the appropriations were sometimes exhausted before the end of the year. For this haphazard method Regent Cocker, as Chairman of the Finance Committee, introduced a much more systematic mode of procedure. He first visited a number of the eastern universities, reported upon their methods and proposed the plan since adopted. Under it the Regents, at the beginning of the year, make a careful estimate of their total resources, and careful inquiry into the needs of each department. They then make an apportionment of funds to each department to be drawn only as needed, and not in any case to be exceeded. If any balance remains at the end of the year it is returned to the general fund, and reapportioned. Under this method, which must commend itself to every business man, neither the University nor any of its departments has in any year gone beyond its income. He has also introduced other changes in the financial methods of the University. In the general concerns of the University Regent Cocker has taken an active and intelligent interest. During his first eight years' service he never missed a meeting of the Board, except when he was out of the State, and has usually gone to Ann Arbor a day or two in advance of the meetings in order to inform himself thoroughly in reference to the business in hand.

Mr. Cocker has also been a versatile writer. He is the author of a "Hand-Book of Punctuation," published by A. S. Barnes & Co., New York; "The Civil Government of Michigan," published by the Richmond, Backus Co., Detroit, which has already reached its fifteenth edition; "The Government of the United States," published by Harper & Bros., New York. This has been translated in Spanish by Juan Rice Chandler, and published by the Government Press of Guatemala.

The translation is accompanied by an introduction by Valero Pujol, now a member of the Spanish Royal Academy, who was at one time a colleague of Emilio Castelar, and one of the most distinguished citizens of Guatemala. Mr. Cocker's published addresses are: An Address at the Quarter-Centennial Celebration of the Presidency of Dr. James B. Angell; "Practical Thoughts on Education," delivered at the opening of the Hackley Manual Training School; "The History of American Money," before the State Bankers' Association; "The Present Monetary System of the United States," before the Bankers' Club of Detroit.

Mr. Cocker was married March 28th, 1870, to Isabella M. Clark, only daughter of E. L. Clark, of Adrian. They have one son, Benjamin Clark Cocker.

J. HERBERT COLE, an active young Republican, was born April 10th, 1868, on a farm in the township of Pontiac, Oakland County, his father being Porter C. Cole, a farmer, and his mother, Dorlesca Burdick Cole. His father and mother both came from New York and the earlier ancestors from New England. He was educated in common country schools, and at High School at Brooklyn, Jackson County, Mich., graduating therefrom in 1885. He also took a business course at the Cleary Business College in Ypsilanti. He lived and worked on a farm until twenty years of age, having removed with his parents to Jackson County when a child. He began the study of law in the office of Geer & Williams, at Lapeer, Mich., in 1888, and was admitted to the bar in 1890 by Judge Joseph B. Moore.

Mr. Cole has been a Republican all his life, casting his first vote for Harrison for President in 1892. He has been a delegate to nearly every State Convention since 1889, his first one being the one held in Detroit in the spring of that year, which nominated Judge C. B. Grant. He was alternate delegate from the Seventh District to the Republican National Convention at St. Louis in 1896. He was the author of the "Parole Law" as it stands upon the statute books of Michigan today, a law which was drafted after a careful study of the prison and parole systems of the several states. He was instrumental in getting the same passed by the Legislature of 1895. He was Circuit Court Commissioner of Lapeer County in 1891-92 and was re-elected in 1892, but did not qualify; was Executive Clerk to Governor John T. Rich, and Secretary of the Advisory Board in the Matter of Pardons, 1893-96; removed to Detroit in January, 1897, and has since been engaged in the practice of law. Mr. Cole is a Director of the Michigan Club; member of the Advisory Council of the State League of Republican Clubs, and member of the Republican State Central Committee, and was a member of the Committee on Resolutions in the Republican State Convention of 1900 at Grand Rapids. He is also a member of the Detroit Boat Club, the Michigan

Geo. H. M. Collier

[illegible]

from her husband in a Michigan court. She was a member of the titled family, Salvini, in Italy, and had inherited, prior to her marriage, large estates in that country. As she belonged to the Catholic Church, and the estates were situated in a Catholic country, she was unable to control the property unless the decree of divorce obtained in Michigan should be affirmed by the Courts of Italy. Up to that time neither the Roman Catholic Church nor the Italian Government had ever recognized the law of divorce in the States. Mr. Collier succeeded in securing an affirmation by the Courts of Italy of the decree obtained in Michigan for his client, securing to her all property rights, real and personal. This case established a precedent, and affirmed the supremacy of Civil Law over Ecclesiastical authority in Catholic countries.

CHARLES BARNARD COLLINGWOOD, one of Ingham County's attorneys, was born at Plymouth, Mass., May 1st, 1860. His parents were Joseph W. Collingwood, a cooper, and Rebecca W. Collingwood. The Collingwood family came from England in the early part of this century. Joseph W. Collingwood enlisted as Captain of Company H, Eighteenth Massachusetts Volunteers, and was killed at the Battle of Fredericksburg. The son, Charles B., was educated at the Boston public schools and at the Michigan Agricultural College. His first employment was as office boy in Boston in 1876 and 1878, and he was on a Colorado ranch in 1878 and 1879, earning enough money to pay his way through college. He taught school at Howard City in 1885-6, and was adjunct professor of chemistry in the Arkansas University from 1886 to 1887, and professor of chemistry in the University of Arizona from 1887 to 1892. He then took up his residence in Lansing, where he has since practiced law. He was City Attorney in that City from 1897 to 1900. He was elected State Senator from the Fourteenth District for the term of 1898-1900. In addition to his law business he is a Director of the Consolidated M. & M. Co. He was married to Harriet Thomas, of Middleville, Mich., August 18th, 1887, and has three children, Harris, Rebecca and Laura.

CHARLES PARKER COLLINS was born on Christmas Day, 1848, in Detroit, his father being Thomas Collins, a stone and brick mason, and his mother Mary Hosie. His grandfather was from England, but moved to Ireland shortly before the birth of his father, who came to America in 1840. His mother's family were from Scotland. His father died when he was about two years of age and his mother died in 1856, during the cholera epidemic in Detroit. She left a family of five children, of whom Charles was the youngest. He was then sent to the Protestant Orphan Asylum on Jefferson avenue. From there he was adopted by Mr. and Mrs. J. W. Kimball, of Port Austin, Mich., and while with them worked on the farm and in the

Charles B. Collingwood.

saw-mill, and drove a mail route between Port Austin and Sebewaing, a distance of forty miles. He returned to Detroit in 1864; worked in a grocery store until the spring of 1865, and then shipped as a cabin boy on the steamer Huron, running between Saginaw and Goderich, Ontario. In July of the same year he shipped before the mast and sailed from Buffalo to Chicago, where he spent the winter of 1865-6. He again shipped before the mast, made one trip, and returned to Detroit. For a time he was unable to secure employment of any kind, but finally secured a position with William Beyer in the Michigan Exchange Barber Shop, where he had charge of the bath rooms. He remained there but a short time, and was then employed by Hoffner & Mayes to learn the sail-making and rigging trade. He served his time with them, then engaged with a cigar manufacturing firm as a traveling salesman, and later purchased an interest in the firm, and has continued the cigar business ever since. The cigar firm of which he is the head is now C. P. Collins Co.

His first experience in political life was as a member of the Fifth Ward Republican Committee in this City in 1870. He was afterwards Chairman of the Ward Committee and member of the City Committee, and has been delegate to nearly all the Republican State Conventions for the past twenty years. He was Secretary of the County Committee from 1886 to 1888, during the memorable Littlefield Sheriff campaign. At the meeting of the Board of Wayne County Supervisors, held in October, 1887, he was elected County Auditor to succeed Charles G. Moran. In 1890 he was nominated for Sheriff of Wayne County. While he ran over 5,000 ahead of his ticket he was defeated by a small majority, but was renominated in 1892 and elected by 3,426 majority. He was again nominated in 1894 and re-elected by nearly 9,000 majority.

Since retiring from the Sheriff's office he has devoted his attention chiefly to his business affairs, although he has been repeatedly asked to permit the use of his name as candidate for Mayor and other positions. His services on political committees have been renewed from time to time, and he is recognized as one of the shrewdest and most successful campaigners that the Republicans of Wayne County ever had. He was one of the first promoters of the Detroit Telephone Company, of which he was Director for three years and Treasurer for one year. He is now Director and Vice-President of the Central Savings Bank. In the State Convention held in Detroit, May 3rd, 1890, he was named as Presidential Elector of the First Congressional District, and also a member of the State Central Committee from the First District. His first vote was cast for U. S. Grant for President, and he never voted a mixed ticket.

Mr. Collins is a member of all the Masonic bodies: Detroit Commandery; Wayne Lodge, K. P.; Michigan Lodge No. 1, Odd Fellows; Star Council, Royal Arcanum; Detroit Lodge of Elks; President of the Marshland Yachting and Fishing Club, and member of the Citizens' Yacht Club. He was married to Ida L. Cotton, December 12th, 1878, and has had two children, Charles P. Collins, Jr., aged 21, and Irene B. Collins, aged 10.

HUTSON BENEDICT COLMAN, of Kalamazoo, was born June 8th, 1855, on a farm in Oakland County, Michigan. His father, Francis Colman, was a farmer, Government surveyor, lumberman and druggist. His mother was Mary Benedict Colman. Both his parental and maternal grandfathers came to Michigan from New York; were pioneers and frontier Baptist preachers in Oakland and adjacent counties in an early day. Both cleared up good farms and reared good families. Their ancestors came from England. Hutson's education was obtained in country district schools till he was eleven years old, when the family moved to Kalamazoo to educate their children in public schools and Kalamazoo College, from which last he graduated in June, 1877, with the degree of A. B. His first occupation was teaching, being Superintendent of Schools at Hastings, Barry County, Mich., one year, 1877 to 1878. He spent the summer of 1878 in France and England visiting the Exposition and writing a few letters which appeared in the Lansing Republican. He became principal of the Kalamazoo High School in the fall of 1878 and taught there two years, resigning in 1880 to go into business. Since 1880 he has been actively engaged in business, mainly manufacturing and mercantile. In December, 1892, with others, he organized the Home Savings Bank of Kalamazoo, of which he was the first President, resigning in 1895, to give personal attention to other important business interests. He is now a stockholder and Director of that bank.

Mr. Colman was elected member of the City Council in 1893, for a term of two years, but declined renomination. He was elected to the State Senate in 1896, serving one term, but business and other plans rendered it impractical for him to be a candidate for renomination. At the Congressional Convention of the Third District in 1898 his name was placed in nomination with many others. In this long contest 333 ballots were taken before the nomination of the successful candidate, and the eleven votes from Kalamazoo were cast continuously and on the last ballot for him. He was appointed Postmaster in July, 1899, to succeed Hon. James Monroe, deceased. He has been a delegate to several State Conventions. He was an active and watchful worker in the State Senate, giving close detailed attention to all Bills presented and gaining from his colleagues the kindly title of "Watch-Dog" of the Senate. He has been a Republican all his life and cast his first vote for Hayes and Wheeler, in 1876.

Mr. Colman is at present a stockholder in three banks and a Director in one; stockholder in two corset companies and Director in one; stockholder in a local paper company, several land companies and many other business corporations. He is a member of the Kala-

GRAND RAPIDS HERALD.

mazoo Club, of all the Masonic bodies, Commander of Kalamazoo Commandery No. 8, K. T.; Master of Robinson Chapter of Rose Croix; DeWitt Clinton Consistory, Scottish Rite, of Grand Rapids, and has been President of the Young Men's Republican Club of Kalamazoo since 1892. He was married January 17th, 1883, at Climax, to Fannie Z. Lovell, daughter of Hon. L. W. Lovell. She died December 16th, 1884. His only child, Lovell Colman, was born December 14th, 1884, and died May 2d, 1897. He again married September 28th, 1897, at Kalamazoo, to Kathren Fletcher, daughter of Hon. Calvin Fletcher, deceased, of South Haven.

During his Senior year he represented Kalamazoo College in the Inter-Collegiate Oratorical Contest and was awarded the medal, having also won several prizes during his college course, and was valedictorian of his class. For years he has been a member of the Board of Trustees of Kalamazoo College and Secretary of the Board. He was elected in June, 1900, a member of the Kalamazoo Board of Education. His tastes are strongly for study, literature and language, and are gratified as fully as a very active and exacting business and official life will permit. He is also very fond of travel, and has visited nearly every portion of the United States. He has been an active worker and speaker in the last three political campaigns.

EUGENE D. CONGER was born November 4th, 1861, in Litchfield, Hillsdale County, Mich., his father, a farmer, being Albert G. Conger, and his mother, Mary Riblet Conger. Eugene D. Conger is the oldest son of a family of five children, two sons and three daughters. His grandfather on his mother's side, Samuel Riblet, was of German ancestry, and came to Michigan from Pennsylvania, one of the Pennsylvania Dutch, as they are styled. His father, Albert Conger, and his grandfather, Jacob Conger, came to Michigan from New York State, their ancestors being American born for several generations. The family came to New York from New Jersey, where nearly two centuries ago three brothers located. They were French Huguenots. Eugene D. Conger received his education in the Litchfield High School, and one year in Hillsdale College. He worked on a farm summers and taught school winters, until twenty-two years of age. He went to Grand Rapids in May, 1884, and in December of that year entered the office of the Grand Rapids Morning Telegram at a salary of $5 a week. Promotions to various positions in the business office came rapidly until, in April, 1886, he was made business manager, having in the meantime acquired a small stock interest. In August, 1888, he acquired with C. C. Swensburg, now deceased, a controlling interest in the Telegram Publishing Co., and the name of the paper was soon changed to the Grand Rapids Herald. In December, 1897, after Mr. Swensburg's death, his interest was purchased and Mr. Conger now owns more than 85 per cent. of the stock of the company. The paper is prosperous and whatever he has, has been made out of the business. Mr. Conger has kept his paper abreast of the times and has made a good reputation in the editorial fraternity. He is a Republican and has been active in politics since attaining his majority. He is a member of the Republican State Committee and Chairman of the Executive Committee of that organization. He was Chairman of the Republican Congressional Committee of the Fifth District in the campaign of 1898 and served again in 1900. He has been delegate to probably two-thirds of the Republican State Conventions during the past ten years, but has only once been a candidate for an elective office. He was nominated and elected Alderman from the Second Ward of Grand Rapids in the spring of 1891, carrying the ward by the largest majority ever received by any Republican up to that time. In September, 1898, he was appointed by President McKinley a member of the U. S. Industrial Commission, which office he now holds. The term will expire December 31st, 1901.

Mr. Conger is a director of the Grand Rapids Board of Trade, member of the Peninsular Club, a Mason and belongs to De Molai Commandery, K. T.; a Knight of Pythias, a K. O. T. M., and a member of the Modern Woodmen. He was married in Milwaukee, April 18th, 1888, to Bertha Wilhelmina Bretzman, but has no children.

MARSHALL L. COOK, one of the leading business men of Barry County, was born in Prairieville Township, in that County, August 12th, 1858. His father, David R. Cook, was then a farmer. Afterward he moved to Hastings, and became a real estate dealer, abstracter and money loaner, and retired from active business about five years ago. His mother is Martha M. Cook. His father's family came from Western New York State, Steuben County. He came to Michigan in 1852, located on a farm, and lived there until 1863, when he moved to Hastings. He has always been a Republican, voted for Fremont in 1856, and for every Republican candidate since; was State Senator from his district twice; was Mayor of Hastings two terms; was Presidential Elector and delegate to the Convention when Garfield was nominated, and was Chairman of the Republican County Committee from 1868 to 1878.

Mrs. Cook's maiden name was Martha M. Marshall. Her father's family came from Maryland, and was related to Chief Justice Marshall's family. Her mother's people were Scotch-Irish.

Marshall Cook graduated in the first class from the Hastings High School after it was organized in 1877; went to Albion College in 1878; took two years of study there, and was obliged to quit in 1880 on account of ill health. In that year, in company with George E. Bowers, he bought the Hastings Banner. It was not then the leading paper, having a paid circulation of less than 700. In 1882 he bought Mr. Bowers' interest, put the Banner on a profit paying business, with a circulation of 2,000, and it has more than held its

M. L. Cook

own. In 1889 his brother, W. R. Cook, became associated with him as an equal partner and they own the Banner together now. Having become associated with others in two manufacturing institutions, it was the judgment of Marshall Cook's associates that he should relinquish his work on the Banner, which he did in 1893, and he has since given his entire time to factory supervision. He has been manager of the Hastings Wool Boot Co. since January, 1894, and a Director of it since its foundation in 1891; is Secretary of the Hastings Table Co.; the International Seal & Lock Co., all of Hastings. He is a director of all three, also of the Hastings City Bank.

Mr. Cook has always been a Republican and cast his first Presidential vote for Garfield. He never attended any National Conventions but has been a delegate to several State Conventions. He never filled any political offices, and never would allow his name to be mentioned as a candidate, or be considered as such. He has, however, done active political work. He was Chairman of the Barry County Republican Committee from 1886 to 1892; is now a member of the Republican State Central Committee; was Secretary of the Republican State Press Association when it was first formed, and is now a member of the Advisory Council of the State League of Republican Clubs. He belongs to no social clubs, but is a member of the Masons and Knights of Pythias. He was married May 7th, 1884, to Belle W. Youngs, and has two sons, Robert, aged 15, and Hubert, aged 12.

WILLIAM R. COOK was born January 28th, 1866, in Hastings, Mich., his parents being David R. Cook, a railroad solicitor, and Martha M. Cook. His parents both came from New York, where his ancestors settled in an early day, taking part in the Revolutionary War. His father represented the Eaton and Barry District in the State Senate several terms. William R. Cook graduated from the Hastings High School and spent two years in the Literary Department at Ann Arbor. He purchased a half interest in the Hastings Banner in 1888, and has been connected with it ever since, for the past eight years having entire management. He was "born a Republican and hopes to die in the faith." He has attended every State Convention since he was a voter, generally as a delegate. He is at present Postmaster, the only political position he ever held or sought. He is connected with the Hastings Wool Boot Co., the Hastings Table Co. and the International Seal and Lock Co., all of Hastings. He is Chancellor Commander of Barry Lodge No. 13, Knights of Pythias; member of Masonic Lodge, and Maccabee Lodge and D. O. K. K.; has been President of the Michigan State Press Association, and Secretary of the Michigan Republican Newspaper Association. He was married in Hastings, September 1st, 1891, to Miss Sarah E. Roberts of that City, and has one child, Miss Dorothy, aged two and one-half years.

ALEXANDER BENNETT COPLEY, long an honored resident of Van Buren County, was of English descent, his ancestor on the paternal side, four generations back, having emigrated from England to Boston in the beginning of the eighteenth century, and afterwards settled in Suffield, Hartford County, Connecticut. Alexander B. was born in Champion, Jefferson County, New York, March 11th, 1822. He subsequently resided with his parents at the manufacturing villages of Whitesboro, New York Mills, Walden and Mattawan, in that state, until September 12th, 1829, when the family removed to Dayton, Ohio, from which place his family moved to Michigan Territory, arriving at Little Prairie Ronde July 1st, 1833. This move was mostly with ox teams. On the fiftieth anniversary of his leaving Dayton he went back and crossed the old bridge at the same time of day just fifty years from the time he left there a barefooted boy. The last camping place of the family was on the banks of Stone Lake, on the place where the village of Cassopolis now stands. They finally settled in Volinia Township, where the village of Nicholsville now is. Their first log house was roofed with shakes, and the bed was often covered with snow in the morning. Indians would cross the ford near the house every morning sober, glum and silent, going to the town of Charleston after whiskey. At 8 or 9 o'clock at night they would return gloriously drunk, and cross the ford again, giving war whoops and all kinds of Indian yells and gestures.

Young Copley's education was limited to the meager facilities afforded at that early day by the common schools of the Territory, having been a pupil in the first school taught in Van Buren County, in the winter of 1834-5. He was left at the age of twenty with a widowed mother, a brother and five sisters younger than himself, to help care for. This, added to the illness of his father several years previous to his death, did not leave much time to cultivate the intellect, had there been opportunity to do so, but his life was one of continuous study and advancement so that he was ever well abreast of the times on all questions of general interest.

By occupation Mr. Copley was a farmer, taking a just pride in agricultural experiments and improvements. He had on his farm over a mile of the finest Osage hedge in Western Michigan. In 1874 he moved to the Village of Decatur, where he resided for a quarter of a century. He was President of the First National Bank of Decatur, of which he was one of the original stockholders, and after its charter expired he reorganized it as the First State Bank, and was continued as its President.

He was married March 26th, 1850, to Jane Helen Hathaway, who was his beloved companion till her death, September 20, 1890. She was a sister of Benjamin Hathaway, the Farmer Poet of Michigan. March 20, 1892, he was married to Mrs. Emma Pritchard, who was with him at the time of his death at Havana, Cuba, March 27, 1899, at which time his family consisted of wife and two sons by his first

A. B. Copley

wife. The elder, Edwin B., is married and manages the farm, and the younger, A. Ward, practices law at Detroit.

Mr. Copley was always a consistent Republican and was frequently honored by his fellow citizens with places of trust and responsibility, having served as Supervisor of Volinia Township, Cass County, for six terms, and having represented the First District of that County in the Legislatures of 1865 and 1871, and the First District of Van Buren County in 1875 and 1881. The magnificent road built across the swamp southerly from Decatur was projected and brought into successful operation largely through his individual efforts, and it was also through his efforts that the big ditch which drains the swamp tract south of Decatur was made: this brought into tillable condition several thousand acres of swamp land, in some years furnishing employment to two or three hundred men from the vicinity of Decatur alone. He sought to enlist in the war for the preservation of the Union; but, being prevented by disability, he made patriotic addresses, and used his means and influence in taking care of those who did go; and even after their return he continued to do so wisely until his death, even delivering an address for the G. A. R. of his town, when he was scarcely able. It was his loyalty and patriotism that led him to Cuba. Wintering in Florida he desired to visit Cuba and see for himself how matters stood, and while there he met his death by a fall from his carriage.

While a man of deep religious convictions, Mr. Copley never tried to force his views on others, yet his implicit faith in the revelations and teachings of Emanuel Swedenborg could scarcely fail to command the respect of any inquirer. His regard for this great writer was notably attested a few years since when he caused a family monument to be erected, the handsome shaft for which was specially imported from his revered teacher's native land, Sweden.

HON. JOHN BLAISDELL CORLISS, of Detroit, was born in Richford, Franklin County, Vermont, June 7th, 1851, of old New England stock. For years before his advent into the world his parents and grand parents, on both sides of the house, were of that hardy, Green Mountain pioneer heritage that betokened sterling integrity and worth. His immediate paternal ancestor was Hezekiah Corliss, who is still living and resides on the old farm.

Mr. Corliss began his education in the public school, that species of common school for which New England is famous, and from which the boy student comes out well equipped for the more stern battle of life. As a farmer's boy he was not unaccustomed to toil. He early knew what it was to arise with the lark, to labor all day until sundown with the farm hands and then to well employ the short evening in study. When John B. Corliss was but 14 years old his father sent him to the French Academy, over across the line into the Province of Quebec, to study the French language. Returning he continued his studies in the graded school at Richford, and then spent the required time in the preparatory schools at Fairfax, Vermont. Closing his career there he was matriculated in the Vermont Methodist Seminary at Montpelier and graduated from that institution in 1871.

Choosing the study of the law for his avocation in life he entered the law office of Noble & Smith in St. Albans, Vermont. The head of the legal firm, at which he began his law study, was then the general attorney for the Vermont Central Railroad, and Mr. Corliss' three years spent there gave him a general acquaintance with railroad law which afterwards proved of great value to him. The proficiency which he attained in his reading enabled him to pass the examination and enter the Senior class of the Columbian Law School in Washington, D. C., from which he graduated in the spring of 1875 and was admitted to practice before the Supreme Court of the District of Columbia.

A bit of romance crept into his life on his return to his native State. He was engaged to Elizabeth N. Danforth, the daughter of Judge William C. Danforth, and proposed on her account to settle in his native State. With this intent in mind he opened an office in Burlington, but at the end of six weeks decided that Horace Greeley's advice to young men was a good thing to follow, but before doing so he visited his sweetheart. Upon announcing his intention to go West her mother declared, "You can go, but if you do you cannot have my daughter." Miss Danforth, however, agreed with her lover and said to the future Congressman, "You go, and when you want me I will be ready."

Hardly needing this, but much strengthened by her womanly reply, he went to his home and informed his parents that he was about to go West. They all wanted him to remain, but his father, sturdy old New Englander that he was, said, "I have done all I could to secure an education for you; and you know what is best, and if you think it wise to go West you have my approval."

His family was then in unfortunate financial circumstances, but raising a hundred dollars through the kindness of his father's friend, he started for the West with no objective point in view, except that an esteemed friend, the Hon. Levi Underwood of Burlington, Vermont, had advised him to locate either in Detroit or Minneapolis. On reaching Detroit he was so favorably impressed that he decided to go no further, and on September 23d, 1875, he drove his professional stake within the confines of Detroit, and nailed to it his humble shingle as an attorney. He was a stranger in a strange land, with a total capital of $35 and without any acquaintance in the State. He first entered the law office of Hon. E. Y. Swift, a native of his own State, and he labored so well that at the end of less than a year and a half he was able to return to Vermont to repay the borrowed money and to claim the fulfillment of the promise which his sweetheart had made to him on his departure. They were married in 1876, and he

Jno B. Corliss

brought his young wife to Detroit. By dint of hard work and constant application he rose very rapidly at the bar of Detroit, and five years later was elected City Attorney and was re-elected in 1883. As City Attorney he prepared the charter of the city which, with but slight modifications, has remained in effect ever since. In 1886 he formed the law partnership of Corliss, Andrus & Leete, naturally taking the first place in the name, and since that time the firm has become recognized as one of the leading ones of the State. Venturing outside the law for investment he became interested in railroad construction and street railway lines. So successful was he in this that when the new Detroit Electric Railway company was formed, he was selected as its general counsel. His speculative interests also prospered, and by the time he was chosen to enter the field of national politics, he was interested in several street railway companies, in the Michigan Lubricator Company, the Shipman Koal Company, and large tracts of unimproved land about Detroit.

His entrance into national politics was in 1894, when he was selected to lead the forlorn hope in the Democratic Congressional District of Detroit, a district which had not sent a Republi an to Congress in years. He made a gallant fight and was elected, the first Republican to be sent from Detroit since 1880. Even in his first term he engrafted upon National legislation his personality, and became known as an active, aggressive worker. He fought for a measure to restrict indiscriminate immigration, and was so largely successful that he became known as a persistent and forceful legislator. Another measure which he espoused with all his heart was that for the election of Senators by the direct vote of the people. Speaker Reed, recognizing the fighting ability of the member from the First Michigan District, placed him upon the Committee on Interstate and Foreign Commerce, and there, too, he shortly became known as one of the strongest members.

In the heat of the campaign of 1896 he returned to his constituents, and they unanimously asked him to stand for a re-election. He adopted no middle course, but standing solidly upon the rock of a sound currency, he achieved even a greater success at the polls, than on his first candidacy. During the Fifty-fifth Congress he successfully opposed the monopolistic grant of an exclusive franchise to the Pacific Cable Company for a cable to Hawaii. He delved deep into the subject, and very largely through his personal efforts the Cable King was defeated, and the subsidy measure went over.

He again returned to his constituents in 1898 basing his campaign entirely upon his record. After a most bitter personal fight he was re-elected for a third term, and in his third term became known as the leader of the Michigan delegation. He continued his work in the Fifty-sixth Congress for the election of Senators by the people, was vigorous in his opposition to the Pacific Cable subsidy, and by his personal influence alone was able to fight through, at the closing hour of the first session of the Fifty-sixth Congress, a Bill which the railroad labor unions had unsuccessfully endeavored to engraft on National legislation for many years. By this one Act alone he endeared himself to the labor unions all over the country.

He also fought the Anti-Scalping Bill, and introduced and pushed to successful issue the bill to recognize and reward the bravery of the revenue cutter officers at Manila and Cardenas during the war against Spain. He made one of the strongest speeches heard in Congress in favor of the ownership and control of the proposed Nicaraguan Canal and against any alliance with Great Britain in the control thereof.

One of the most important, at the same time least heralded battles of his career against monopolistic control, was his contention against one of his own party colleagues. The Bill proposed to give to a certain influential company the right to use the United States mail for its own exclusive benefit. In ordinary parlance there was a "snake" in the Bill and Congressman Corliss was the first to discover it. The devious ways by which such a Bill may be brought up for consideration required the utmost vigilance on the part of Congressman Corliss to prevent its passage. Week in and week out, he watched and waited his chance. He knew very well that the Bill would be sprung at some apparently opportune moment. When it was announced that he had been obliged to seek a rest the advocates of the Bill brought it up. They had reckoned without their host, for the Congressman from the First Michigan District was still on guard and when they tried to hustle the bill through the House, he suddenly appeared in opposition and in a very short address to his conferees, he ruined every chance the monopoly ever had of winning and saved the U. S. Postoffice Department thousands of dollars. In November, 1900, Mr. Corliss was again elected to Congress by a majority of 4,490.

His domestic life was most happy, as he was always a devoted family man. In January, 1886, he lost the partner of his selection, and was left with a family of four children, the youngest only two weeks old. He has entrusted the care of that family to no stranger, and remained single that he might devote all his energies and thoughtfulness to the comfort of the little ones left to his care. The four children are John B., Jr., Elizabeth D., Margery M. and Cullen D. Corliss.

EBER WARD COTTRELL, of Detroit, was born February 17th, 1841, in the Township of Cottrellville, St. Clair County, Mich. About the year 1753 his great grandfather, Henry Hoofer, was born in Schenectady County, New York, and when only seven years old was captured by the Indians, together with a younger sister. The Indians tomahawked and scalped the rest of the family, five in number, one an infant in its cradle. No tidings were ever heard of the sister, but, a few years later, Henry's captors took him to Montreal, where

Eber W. Cottrell

he was ransomed, adopted and educated by an English Army officer, named Cottrell, whose name was given to young Hoofer. In 1774, when he became of age, he went to his native place in search of his family, but soon returned to Montreal, his quest having been in vain. He came to Detroit in 1779, traded with the Indians along the river to the north, and married Anne Curtis, a French lady of Detroit, in 1781. They had nine children, of whom the eldest, George, lived and died on the banks of the St. Clair River, and was the father of thirteen children, the eldest of whom, George H. Cottrell, was a very popular and well known pioneer lake captain, more particularly identified with the Detroit, St. Clair River and Saginaw commerce and travel. He was married to Submit Ward, daughter of the Hon. Zael Ward, at Buffalo, N. Y., in May, 1838. They had five children.

Eber W. Cottrell, the eldest of these children, was educated at Newport, now Marine City, Academy, and at an early age commenced a maritime life upon the Great Lakes, where he became proficient in all branches of that pursuit. He also made several sea voyages, and spent some time upon the Mississippi and other Southern rivers. His career as a sailor was marked by many thrilling and interesting incidents. In 1866-7 he made a tour of the West Indies, visiting all the islands, and spending six months in Jamaica. While there he wrote a series of letters upon those islands for the Detroit Tribune. In 1868 he married Miss Ellen Smith, and removed to Greenfield, Wayne County, Mich. Entering upon agricultural pursuits, he became interested in and successfully managed one of the finest stock farms in the State. He also engaged in the growing of small fruit, owning a fine vineyard and fruit farm within two miles of Detroit. He is a prominent member of the State Horticultural Society, and has written extensively upon agricultural topics for the press.

Mr. Cottrell early entered politics, and his strong character and rare powers of organization soon raised him to the leadership of the agricultural element of the Republican party in Wayne County. He has filled the offices of Justice of the Peace, Supervisor and Superintendent of Schools for the Township of Greenfield, and was a member of the Republican State Central Committee for two terms, 1882 and 1886. He was appointed by President Grant, Receiver of Public Moneys for the Detroit District of the U. S. Land Office, but declined the position. In 1879 he was elected Representative to the State Legislature from the Third District of Wayne County, and so well did he fulfill the duties of his office that on his return home at the close of the session he was tendered a public reception, and was presented with an elegant gold watch and chain by his constituents, "for faithful and efficient services in the Legislature." At the end of his term he was re-elected by an increased majority. While a member of the Legislature he introduced and secured the passage in the House, of the Bill that secured to Detroit the Grand Boulevard that encircles the City.

Mr. Cottrell was a trusted friend of the late Senator Zach Chandler during the latter part of his life, and was also a friend and adviser of Ex-Governor H. P. Baldwin during his political career. While in the Legislature of 1879, a warm and lasting friendship grew up between him and Thomas W. Palmer, then State Senator, and later United States Senator, and United States Minister to Spain, and the most confidential relations have ever since existed between them. Mr. Cottrell was an active leader in Mr. Palmer's contest for the gubernatorial nomination in 1882, and after the defeat of United States Senator T. W. Ferry, he bent his energies towards securing Mr. Palmer's election to the United States Senate. After this achievement had been accomplished, he accompanied Senator and Mrs. Palmer upon an extended tour through Europe. During this trip they selected many of the fine and valuable Percheron horses and Jersey cattle that for a long time formed the chief attractions of the celebrated Log Cabin Stock Farm. In 1887 he again visited Europe, extending his travels to Africa and Asia, bringing with him on his return home some valuable animals for the stock farm.

In 1881, when the northern part of the Lower Peninsula was desolated by forest fires, over two millions of dollars were contributed to relieve the homeless and destitute people, and the Michigan Fire Relief Commission was constituted to take charge of the distribution of this fund, with Governor Jerome as Chairman. Upon Mr. Cottrell, who was the general manager and confidential agent of the Commission, devolved the active work of distributing aid, and under his careful direction three thousand families were succored and relieved from distress. He received much credit for the prompt and efficient manner in which he conducted the work of the Commission.

In the winter of 1888-89 Mr. Cottrell conceived the idea of a permanent exposition for Detroit. Upon him fell the mass of detail incident to this great undertaking, the laying out of ground, the supervision of plans, the arrangement of buildings, machinery, approaches, docks, etc. The able manner in which he carried out the work was testified by Senator McMillan, President of the Association, who, in his address at the opening of the Exposition, paid the following tribute to Mr. Cottrell: "In all such enterprises there must be one man to take the lead, and that man was Eber W. Cottrell, who, believing that the time had arrived for Detroit to have a permanent exposition, induced others to join him, and to his untiring energy and large experience we are largely indebted not only for the Exposition itself, but for the admirable arrangement both of the grounds and buildings." At the close of the second year's Exposition he resigned his position as Secretary to accept the office of Land Commissioner for the Detroit, Mackinaw & Marquette Railroad, which position he still holds. When the National G. A. R. Encampment was in Detroit in 1892, Mr. Cottrell, as Chairman of the Accommodations Committee, planned and successfully carried out the details of all the camps, a work of great magnitude. The next year he was appointed chief of the stock department of the World's Fair at Chicago, and the appointment was confirmed by the Commissioners, but he declined the place for business reasons. He was manager of the street car interests of Detroit at the time the electric cars were first put on Jefferson avenue.

Mr. Cottrell is a member of the Detroit Club, the Michigan Club, the Fellowcraft Club, the Country Club, Rainbow Fishing Club, North Channel Fishing and Shooting Club, the Detroit Commandery of Knights Templar, Michigan Sovereign Consistory, Moslem Temple and other organizations. He has one son living, George William, aged 24 years.

ARTHUR STANLEY COUTANT, of Mt. Pleasant, was born December 11th, 1854, on the Western Reserve, Greenwich, Ohio, his father being Isaac Newton Coutant and his mother, Anne Oglevee Coutant. His father was a railroad man in the employ of the Cleveland, Columbus & Cincinnati Railway, now known as the Big Four. He died in March, 1864. He was time and bookkeeper at the round house, Columbus, and prior to this was a school teacher. The father's ancestors came from France at some period of the Huguenot persecution. His mother was born in Fayette County, Pennsylvania. Her father was Scotch-Irish and her mother pure German. A. S. Coutant was educated in the City schools of Columbus, Ohio, and the country schools of Pennsylvania and Ohio. In 1875 he entered Greenville, Mich., High School, graduated in 1879, entered Oberlin, O., College, completed Freshman year and resumed work as foreman of the Greenville Independent. From ten to eighteen he was on four farms working for board, clothes and schooling in winters, except one year when he received $8 a month and board. At eighteen he commenced learning the printing business, with E. F. Grabill, of the Greenville Independent, completed three years' apprenticeship, and then spent five years attending school and working for board, clothes and books. He was foreman of the Greenville Independent from 1881 to 1887. In April, 1886, he was elected City Collector for the City of Greenville, but refused renomination to move to Mount Pleasant, where he purchased the Isabella County Enterprise, May 1st, 1887, and has been successful financially with the paper. In 1892 he bought the Northwestern Tribune of George McConnelly and has continued its publication since in his name, and at his request. In 1896 he was elected a member of the Republican State Central Committee, faithfully performing all duties connected therewith for four years. In 1897 he was appointed Postmaster of Mt. Pleasant, and under his administration it was raised from a third-class office to second-class.

Mr. Coutant was a delegate to the National Convention of Republican Clubs at Cleveland in 1896, Detroit in 1898, and St. Paul in 1900. He has been delegate to every State Convention held by the Republicans since 1887, except two. He was identified very closely with the passage of the Act establishing the Central State Normal School at Mt. Pleasant by the Legislature of 1895. He "was born a Republican" and cast his first vote for Rutherford B. Hayes for President and C. C. Ellsworth for Congress. He is President and Director of the Central Michigan Building & Loan Association and the Mt. Pleasant Improvement Company; is a member of Wabon Lodge, F. & A. M. No. 305; Mt. Pleasant Chapter 111, R. A. M.; Mt. Pleasant Chapter No. 55, O. E. S.; Ithaca Council, R. & S. M.; Mt. Pleasant Lodge No. 217. I. O. O. F.; Tipsico Council No. 1099, Royal Arcanum; Mt Pleasant Tent No. 129, K. O. T. M., and Slagle Trout Club. He was married December 29th, 1881, to Anna M. Satterlee and has two children, Florence Ruth Coutant, and Benjamin Wallace Coutant, aged 13 and 11 years respectively.

GEORGE GARY COVELL was born, October 16, 1860, at Dundee, Monroe County, Mich. His father's name was Daniel H. Covell, and his mother's name, Corlin Dustin Covell. His father was a Justice of the Peace and U. S. Pension Attorney. The Covell's from whom he is a descendant, originally came from England. His grandmother Covell was of Holland Dutch descent, and her father was a grandson of General Schuyler, of Revolutionary fame. His mother's ancestors came from Pennsylvania, though she was born in Michigan. George Covell had his education at Dundee Union School, and was junior in the 1885 law class of the University of Michigan. He first worked upon the farm and in factories, but was admitted to the bar at Monroe, Mich., on the 25th of May, 1887, and in August of the same year, located at Benzonia, Benzie County. He spent the winter of 1887 and 1888 working in the lumber woods doing whatever law business he could get, and in November, 1888, was elected Prosecuting Attorney of the County, being re-elected in 1890, holding the office until the summer of 1892, when he resigned and moved to Traverse City. During his career as a lawyer, he has been interested in some noted cases, two of the most important being the Wright murder case, which he prosecuted, and which will be found in Volume 89 of the Michigan Reports on Page 70, and the Thacker murder case, which is reported in Volume 108, Michigan Reports, page 652. In the fall of 1892 he was elected a member of the Legislature on the Republican ticket, being re-elected in 1894. In 1896 he was elected a member of the State Senate from the Twenty-seventh District. While in the Legislature in 1893 he was Chairman of the Committee on Private Corporations and a member of the Judiciary Committee. In 1895 he was Chairman of the Judiciary Committee of the House, and in 1897 was Chairman of the Judiciary Committee of the Senate. He resigned the Senatorship in April, 1898, to accept the office which he now holds that of United States Attorney for the Western District of Michigan. It was his Bill that provided for the

George G. Covell,

Thomas Cranage

compilation of the laws recently completed by Lewis M. Miller. He was the author of the bill that disorganized the only Democratic County in Michigan in 1895, namely the County of Manitou. He was the author of a great many bills of more or less importance which became enacted into laws. He has always been a Republican, cast his first Presidential vote for James G. Blaine in 1884, and has attended every Republican State Convention since 1888. Mr. Covell is a Mason, being a member of the Traverse City Commandery, and Saladin Temple, Shrine, Grand Rapids, Mich.; belongs to the Odd Fellows' organization, Traverse City; also Elks and Loyal Guards of the same place. He was married to Alice J. Kyle at Corunna, Mich., May 21st, 1885. Their only child is Beulah Land Covell, aged fourteen.

THOMAS CRANAGE, of Bay City, has achieved social and business distinction in two cities, and easily ranks among Michigan's most successful business men. He was born at Ludlow, Shropshire, England, July 2d, 1833. His father, Thomas Cranage, Sr., came to America in 1835, but returned to his native country five years later, and did not finally settle in this country till 1845, when he made his home in the beautiful and growing City of Detroit. He was a stirring, prudent and successful business man, and took an active interest in the affairs of the City of his adoption. He amassed a comfortable fortune, which, at his death, was inherited by a family of three daughters and one son, the latter the subject of this sketch.

The son, Thomas, had the advantages of a good literary and business education, attending the best schools in the City of Detroit, and afterwards acquiring a thorough knowledge of the drug business, in which he was engaged for several years. But the lumber industry, which was then rapidly assuming large proportions in Eastern Michigan, offered greater attractions and better promise of profit, and he engaged in this, going, after some experience in Detroit, to what soon became the center of that industry in Michigan, the Saginaw Valley. He removed to Bay City, taking a position as resident manager and junior partner of the firm of Samuel Pitts & Co., one of the leading lumber manufacturing firms in the Valley. The head of the firm, Samuel Pitts, was not only successful in that line of business, but was one of the pioneers in the salt manufacture, which has since then assumed such large proportions in Michigan. Upon his death in 1868, the firm name became Pitts & Cranage, and to the conduct of its prosperous affairs Mr. Cranage applied himself with industry, ability and skill for more than three decades.

But he has not limited his business activities to a single field. The lake carrying trade is intimately associated with the lumber industry, and Mr. Cranage is largely interested in that, being President of the McGraw Transportation Co., having an investment of over

$300,000. He is also President of the Bay County Savings Bank and is interested in numerous other local enterprises. With the falling off in the lumber business the Valley cities have turned attention to other industries, and Bay City took the lead in the manufacture of beet sugar, which is destined to become of great importance to the State. The Michigan Sugar Co. of that City was the pioneer, was incorporated in 1897, and its mill was built in 1898. With Mr. Cranage as President and Manager, it achieved a success that has not only been gratifying in itself, but far-reaching in its results, for several other corporations have followed its lead, thus creating a new business of great magnitude, and contributing to the prosperity of the farmers in several large districts of Eastern Michigan. The Michigan Sugar Co. received a gold medal for the exhibition of its product at the Paris Exposition in 1900, where it came into comparison with the great sugar growing countries of Europe, France and Germany.

Mr. Cranage has traveled much, having visited, with his family, most of the European countries, and in 1890 he made the tour of the Nile Valley and the Holy Land. He was married in October, 1863, to Julia, oldest daughter of his partner, Samuel Pitts, of Detroit. They have had three children, a daughter, who died in 1875, Samuel Pitts Cranage, Secretary of the McGraw Transportation Company, and interested with his father in other branches of business; and a younger daughter, Mary H. Cranage.

In politics Mr. Cranage has always been a staunch Republican and a liberal contributor to the party funds, as well as to numerous religious and social institutions that make for the good of the community.

HON. ROSSEAU O. CRUMP, of West Bay City, was born at Pittsford, Monroe County, N. Y., May 20th, 1843. His parents, Samuel Crump and Sarah Crump, nee Cutting, were born respectively in Kent and Suffolk Counties, England. They lived for a short time after their marriage in 1841, in London, where Samuel Crump, Sr., was a contractor on the London & Greenwich Railroad, one of the first steam railroads in the British possessions. Samuel Crump's politics, which were decidedly liberal, led him to look to the New World for his future, and in 1842, he immigrated to America and went to Rochester, N. Y., where many Kent County families had settled. Shortly after arriving at Rochester he moved to Pittsford, a small town six miles east of Rochester, where Congressman Crump was born.

The father of R. O. Crump was so intensely liberty-loving that he had not been in the country six months before he declared his intention of becoming a citizen, and allied himself with the Whig party. In the atmosphere of liberty the subject of this sketch was born. His earliest political training was received from his father, who was

M. C.

in turn an ardent Whig, Free Soiler and Abolitionist. Under this tuition it is no wonder that Congressman Crump had early instilled into his mind the principles for which his father stood. He also inherited from his father a love of literature and a tendency to the life of a student, but showing an aptitude for mechanical pursuits he was apprenticed to a carriage-making firm, and afterward took up the building and millwright occupation, finally drifting into the lumber business. He followed Horace Greeley's advice and went West, grew up with the country, and after serving in various capacities of trust, he settled in 1868, in Winona, Minn., where he found occupation as a millwright and became interested in lumber and timber land. He remained there a year and settled in Plainwell, Mich., in July, 1869, where he remained until December, 1872, when illness compelled him to return to his birthplace, where he operated a lumber yard and planing mill until 1879. He then closed his interests and formed a partnership with his uncle in Simcoe, Ont., and engaged in a general lumber, stave and shingle business. There he continued until the fall of 1881, when he started upon a tour of the Great Lakes.

Congressman Crump was not impressed particularly with the enterprise of Canada and on this visit to the Eastern shore of the State of Michigan, found in the then growing communities of Bay City and West Bay City a place much more to his liking. So favorably did the condition impress him that he prevailed upon his uncle to move, and in October, 1881, they built a new mill at West Bay City. About two years later he purchased his partner's interest, and about four months later formed the corporation known as the Crump Manufacturing Company, of which he was the majority stockholder. This industry grew to be one of the largest box and package manufacturing plants in the United States. In addition to this industry, which proved to be very successful, he established the saw mill and lumbering plant of R. O. Crump & Son, at Roscommon, and became known through all Northern Michigan as one of the fairest dealers with labor in that portion of the country. It is a somewhat remarkable fact that in his entire life as a manufacturer, extending over thirty years, he never had a strike or any difficulty with the workingmen he employed.

In politics Mr. Crump has always been a Republican of the stalwart type. His first Presidential vote was cast for Abraham Lincoln in 1864. His first appearance in official life was when elected alderman from his ward in West Bay City, and he served the people four years in that capacity. In 1892 he was elected mayor and re-elected by an increased majority. As the leader of a forlorn hope he was nominated by the Republicans of the Tenth District for a seat in the Fifty-fourth Congress. The District had been represented in the Forty-ninth, Fiftieth, Fifty-second and Fifty-third Congresses by Democrats, each of whom was elected by a large majority. Mr. Crump made a practical, earnest campaign and the result surprised the electors of the Tenth District, as he defeated his opponent, one of the most popular and wealthy lumbermen in the State, by a majority of nearly 4,000. He was renominated in 1896 and, upon the record he made, was re-elected, although by a decreased majority. The reason for this falling off in his vote is not hard to find. Even early in the campaign he was advised by his medical friends to submit to a dangerous operation. He put it off as long as he could, but right in the heat of the campaign he was ordered to a Chicago hospital, where the operation was performed, and on the day of election it was a question in the District whether the electors were voting for a live man or one who might be dead before the votes were canvassed. Despite this handicap he won out against a fusionist, lacking one vote of 2,000 majority, and on his record he increased his majority by over 1,200 in 1898. For his seat in the Fifty-seventh Congress he eclipsed all his previous political work and carried the district by 8,231 plurality.

Congressman Crump's home life has been most happy. He was married in 1868 to Phoebe A. Tucker, of Craigsville, N. Y., who came from Revolutionary stock. Of that union were born six children, Shelley C., Mildred S., Mabel A., Ada B., Enid A. and Susie M., all of whom are now living except Ada B. Crump, the only one of his children born on foreign soil.

Despite Mr. Crump's busy mercantile life and the time he has devoted to his family he has found time to ally himself with the various social societies of the day. He was early made a Mason and worked himself upward through the branches of the York Rite, the Chapter and Commandery, and through the Scottish Rite, to the 32d degree, and in every one has become prominent. At the present time he is a member of Winona Lodge, F. & A. M.; Blanchard Chapter, R. A. M.; Bay City Commandery; Michigan Sovereign Consistory of the A. A. S. Rite; Moslem Temple of the A. A. O. N. M. S.; Ancient Order of United Workmen, Royal Arcanum, the Knights of Pythias and the Independent Order of Foresters. He was one of the first Trustees of the Masonic Temple Association of Detroit, and has achieved as much of honor in the secret societies as he has in his political and social life.

Mr. Crump's position in the Michigan delegation in Congress during the Fifty-fifth, Fifty-sixth and Fifty-seventh Congresses is best attested by the regard in which he is held by his associates. While there are older members in the delegation, yet his associates always address him as "Pa," and look to him with the same amount of respect and esteem that a son pays in filial obedience to his parent.

GENERAL BYRON M. CUTCHEON, distinguished both as a soldier and in civil life, comes of a family whose original name was McCutcheon, the M standing for Mac, and was born May 11th, 1836, at Pembroke, Merrimac County, New Hampshire, his parents being James M. (or Mc) Cutcheon, and Hannah Tripp. James McCutcheon

was the son of Frederick McCutcheon, who served four enlistments in the American Revolution. He was born at Pembroke, N. H., 1791, and died at the same place in 1855. Frederick McCutcheon, grandfather of Byron, was born at Barrington, N. H., in 1751, and died at Bridgewater, N. H., in 1844. Hannah Tripp (McCutcheon) was granddaughter of Richard Tripp, of Epsom, N. H., who served several enlistments in the War of the American Revolution, under General John Stark, of that State, and was with him at the Battle of Bennington. The family is largely Scotch-Irish on both sides, being descended from the McCutcheons and the McClarys, the latter of Epsom, N. H., distinguished both as soldiers and civilians.

Byron M. Cutcheon commenced his education at Pembroke Academy, Pembroke, N. H.; prepared for the University of Michigan at Ypsilanti, 1855-57, graduated from the University, June, 1861, with degree of B. A. in the full classical course, and from the University Law School in 1866, with the degree of LL. B. He received the degree of A. M. the same year. His first occupation, outside of work on a farm at home, was as "bobbin boy" in a cotton factory at Suncock, a Village in his native town, and the next as "spinner boy" in the same factory. He worked at this twelve hours a day between one and two years. He began teaching district school at 17, at Pembroke, and taught two winters in Washtenaw County, Mich., while preparing for college; was principal of Birmingham, Oakland County, Academy in 1857-58, and of "Oak Grove" Academy, at Medina, Lenawee County, in the winter of 1859. After graduation from the law school in 1866 he was for six months the agent of the Michigan Soldiers' Monument Association, and raised $12,000 for the Soldiers' Monument, now standing on the "Campus Martius," Detroit. In the fall of 1866 he removed to Ionia, and commenced the practice of law, as a member of the firm of Bennett & Cutcheon. In September, 1867, he removed to Manistee, became member of the law firm of Bullis & Cutcheon, and continued in active practice there until he entered Congress in 1883.

In the interval between his graduation from the University and his entering the law school, Mr. Cutcheon made a splendid war record. He entered service July 15th, 1862, as Second Lieutenant, the first man to enlist in Michigan's quota under the 300,000 call of the President. He recruited Company B, Twentieth Michigan, at Ypsilanti; was commissioned Captain in the regiment July 29th, 1862; Major October 14, 1862; Lieutenant Colonel November 16th, 1863, and Colonel November 21st, 1863. He was wounded twice at the Battle of Spottsylvania, Va., May 10th, 1864, and was in the hospital until July 5th, 1864. After rejoining the regiment he was assigned to the command of the Second Brigade of General O. B. Willcox's Division, Ninth Army Corps, October 16th, 1864, and commanded the same until March 6th, 1865. He participated actively in the following campaigns: Army of the Potomac, Antietam campaign, September 2d, 1862; Fredericksburg, Va.; campaign, November, 1862, to January, 1863; Army of the Ohio, Kentucky campaign, April to June, 1863; Vicksburg, Miss., campaign and Jackson, Miss., campaign, summer of 1863; East Tennessee campaign, September, 1863, to March, 1864; Army of the Potomac, the Wilderness, Spottsylvania and Petersburg campaigns, 1864 and 1865. He was in twenty-five battles and engagements; was promoted Brevet Colonel United States Volunteers, August 18th, 1864, "for gallant service at the Battle of the Wilderness, Va., and Spottsylvania, and during the present operations before Petersburg, Va." He was Colonel of the Twenty-seventh Michigan Volunteers, November 12th, 1864, to March 6th, 1865, and Brevet Brigadier General United States Volunteers, March 13th, 1865, "for conspicuous gallantry at the Battle of the Wilderness." He received the U. S. "Congressional Medal of Honor" "for distinguished bravery in leading a charge of his regiment on a block-house occupied by the enemy" at Horse Shoe Bend, Ky., May 10th, 1863. He is a member of the following Military Societies: Sons of the American Revolution, Grand Army of the Republic, Military Order of the Loyal Legion and Medal of Honor Legion.

Mr. Cutcheon was young when he commenced his political activity. He was President of the "Young Men's Fremont Club," at Ypsilanti in 1856; was Captain of the Ann Arbor "Wide Awakes" in 1860; was first President and Permanent Vice-President and State Organizer of the Boys in Blue in 1866. In that campaign he stumped the Fifth Congressional District under the auspices of the State Central Committee, making more than forty speeches in Livingston, Oakland, St. Clair and Macomb Counties, and he has been on the list of speakers in different parts of the State in many campaigns since. He was also political writer for the Detroit Tribune in 1895 and part of 1896, until that paper took its free silver shoot in May of the latter year, when he transferred his services to the Detroit Journal, where they were continued through the rest of 1896 and 1897. He was a delegate to every biennial Republican State Convention from 1870 to 1884; was Temporary Chairman in 1874; was the author of the platforms in 1880, 1882 and 1884 and was Chairman of the Committee on Resolutions in the Conventions of 1882, 1884 and 1896. He was also Chairman of the Manistee County Committee from 1868 to 1876, inclusive.

General Cutcheon has often had expressions of confidence from the citizens of his locality in Convention and at the polls, and has also filled with honor, positions conferred by appointment. He was a Presidential Elector in 1868, for Grant and Colfax, and was Secretary of the Michigan Electoral College; was Alderman in the new City of Manistee in 1869; City Attorney, 1870-1872; Prosecuting Attorney for the County, elected in 1872, and declined re-election; Regent of the University from January 1st, 1876, to March, 1883; Postmaster at Manistee, 1877 to 1883; being first appointed by President Grant, and was a member of the United States Board of Ordnance and Fortifications, by appointment of President Harrison, from July, 1891, to March, 1895.

But his most notable public service was in the House in Congress, to which he was four times elected, commencing with 1882. His work there was largely of a military character, he being assigned to the Committee on Military Affairs, and related to the old soldiers of the Civil War, their pensions, their back pay and bounty; their rank and pay; and to reforms in the regular army; in regard to enlistments and desertions; in regard to promotions on examinations; for the relief of the retired list, and the establishment of a retired list for enlisted men; to improve discipline; to provide for sea-coast defenses, and to increase the artillery arm of the service and for the protection of the new sea-coast defenses. He also took a deep interest in Indian affairs, and secured the passage of several acts for the better protection of Indian rights and the promotion of education and civilization among them. His speeches were largely on the tariff, on river and harbor improvements; on pensions, and perhaps his most widely known speeches were those on the Bill for the restoration of General Fitzjohn Porter to the Army.

After this sketch it is hardly necessary to say that General Cutcheon has been a Republican ever since there have been any Republicans. He cast his first Presidential vote for Abraham Lincoln in 1860, and voted for him again in the Army in 1864; for Grant in 1868, and wrote every ballot cast for Grant and Colfax in the Michigan Electoral College; for Grant in 1872; for Hayes in 1876; for Garfield in 1880, for Blaine in 1884, for Harrison in 1888 and 1892, and for McKinley in 1896 and 1900.

General Cutcheon has not accumulated much of this world's goods, but is connected in a modest way with the Manistee National Bank, the Manistee Manufacturing Company, the State Bank of Michigan, Grand Rapids, and the Citizens' Telephone Company. Besides the military orders before given he belongs to the following: Corporate member of the American Board of Foreign Missions; Park Congregational Church, Grand Rapids; Hesperus Club of Grand Rapids; Lincoln Republican Club of Grand Rapids; State Bar Association and numerous other legal, military, educational and religious organizations. He has been President, Orator and Poet of the Michigan University Alumni Association. He was married to Miss Marie Amnie Warner, of Dexter, Mich., June 22d, 1863. Their children are Frank Warner, born 1864; Charles Tripp, born 1867; Max Hartranft, born 1872; Frederick Richard, born 1874, and Marie Louise, born 1880.

SULLIVAN M. CUTCHEON was a contribution from the Granite State to the list of able men who became prominent in law, political and business circles in Michigan. He was the son of Rev. James and Hannah M. (Tripp) Cutcheon, and was born in Pembroke, N. H., October 4th, 1833. He received the advantages of a liberal education, first in the common schools, then in the Gymnasium and Blanchard Academies, and then in Dartmouth College, from which he graduated in 1856, and from which he received the degree of M. A. in 1859. After graduation he came West, was principal of the High School at Ypsilanti, Mich., and then from the fall of 1858 to the summer of 1860, he was Superintendent of the Public Schools at Springfield, Ill. Completing a course of law studies in the latter City, he was admitted to the bar in July, 1860, returned to Ypsilanti and entered upon the practice of his profession, which he continued there until 1875. Then, desiring a larger field, he removed to Detroit, where he continued in practice until his death, April 18th, 1900. He was first in partnership with Judge Hiram J. Beakes and after that the head of the firms successively of Cutcheon & Stellwagen, Cutcheon, Crane & Stellwagen, Cutcheon, Stellwagen & Fleming and Cutcheon, Stellwagen & MacKay. Mr. Cutcheon was a thorough student of the principles and application of the law, and had a large and lucrative practice, including the care of a number of large estates. He was also interested in banking, being President of the Dime Savings Bank of Detroit from the time of its organization in 1884 till his death, and of the Ypsilanti Savings Bank from 1892. He was also President of the Michigan Banking Association in 1894 and 1895.

Mr. Cutcheon was an ardent Republican and took an active part in political campaigns, particularly the Grant campaign of 1872 and the fight against the 16 to 1 theory in 1896, when his sound money arguments in numerous meetings were effective. He was a member of the Legislatures of 1861 and 1863, and was Speaker of the latter. He was Chairman of the Michigan delegation at the Chicago Convention in 1868 which first nominated Grant. In 1865 he was appointed National Bank Examiner for Michigan and held that position for seven years. In 1868 he was appointed by Governor Baldwin a member of the State Military Board and served four years. In 1873 he was appointed by Governor Bagley one of the eighteen Commissioners to revise the State Constitution, and was elected President of the Commission. From March, 1877, till May, 1885, he served as United States Attorney for the Eastern District of Michigan. In 1892 he was appointed by Governor Winans one of the Commissioners for Michigan for securing uniformity in the laws of the different States, was chosen President of that Board and held the position for a number of years. In this capacity he attended several meetings of the Commissioners from the several States, and at the meeting in Detroit in 1897 he was made President of the National Conference.

Mr. Cutcheon was a zealous member and an elder in the Presbyterian Church both in Ypsilanti and in Detroit, was a Commissioner to the General Assembly which met in Brooklyn in 1876 and to that held in Washington in 1893. He was also a member of the Pan-Presbyterian Council at Toronto in 1892. But his religious and philanthropic zeal was not confined to his own denomination. He took a deep interest in the Young Men's Christian Association of

Lemuel J. Dafoe

Detroit, was its President for many years, and was largely instrumental in securing for it the building at the corner of Griswold street and Grand River avenue, which is one of the finest association buildings in the country, costing about one hundred and twenty thousand dollars. He was also President of Harper Hospital for several years, secured additions to its buildings, and was mainly instrumental in raising two hundred thousand dollars for its endowment. He was one of the men who helped organize the New England Society of Detroit, and was its President in 1897. He was a man of dignified manner and imposing presence, a fine parliamentarian and a model presiding officer.

Mr. Cutcheon was married December 8th, 1859, to Josephine Louise Moore, of Ypsilanti. Their children were Adeline L., wife of Edwin E. Armstrong, of Detroit, and Sullivan M., who died in 1877, at the age of five years.

LEMUEL GRANT DAFOE, one of the most prominent attorneys of the Lake Huron Shore, was the son of Samuel I. and Catherine Dafoe, and was born in Dunville, Ontario, October 1st, 1857. His ancestors on his father's side were French Huguenots, whose property was confiscated, and who were obliged to leave France on account of their religion. His father was born in New York State, and his grandfather fought under the Count de Rochambeau in the War of the Revolution. His mother was born in the north of Ireland, and was of the Protestant faith.

The son was educated in the public schools of Alpena, the State Normal School, and the law department of the University of Michigan. He paid his way through the latter institutions, earning his first money by packing shingles, and subsequently working in shingle and lumber mills and in camps in the woods. He also inspected lumber. In those days nearly every employment about Alpena turned upon lumber, but Mr. Dafoe also, for three years, taught school. He was admitted to the bar in 1883, and in July of the same year formed a partnership with Hon. J. D. Turnbull, of Alpena, under the firm name of Turnbull & Dafoe. January 1st, 1885, Hon. John C. Shields became associated with the firm, and remained in it until 1886, when he was appointed Supreme Court Justice of Arizona. The firm of Turnbull & Dafoe continued till 1892. Since then Mr. Dafoe has continued in practice, part of the time alone, and part of the time in partnership with Hon. Henry K. Gustin, under the firm name of Dafoe & Gustin. His practice has been very extensive and he has conducted some of the most important trials, both civil and criminal, in Alpena and adjoining counties. He conducted the defence for Stephen Reiger in the famous Molitor trial, Reiger being the only defendant tried that was acquitted. There have been terms of court where no case, either civil or criminal, has been tried but that he has been engaged therein.

Mr. Dafoe and his law partners have all been active in politics. He has always been a Republican, and cast his first Presidential vote for Garfield. His first run for office was for a position in the line of his profession, that of Prosecuting Attorney, for which he was nominated in 1884. Alpena County was then Democratic by four to five hundred majority, but he beat his Democratic opponent and old law partner, by 78 votes. One of the arguments used against him was that he was young and inexperienced, and it was said that crime would run rampant if he was elected. But at the first term of Circuit Court after entering upon the discharge of his duties as Prosecuting Attorney, seven cases were tried, all important cases, and convictions were obtained in each case. Four of the defendants were men who had lived in the community for years, and had been arrested many times, but always escaped. It was such an event that when the Sheriff took the prisoners, seven of them chained together, to Detroit, almost the entire population of the City covered the docks and lumber piles on both sides of the river. Mr. Dafoe was again nominated in the fall of 1886 and was defeated by Hon. James McNamara. He was tendered the nomination by acclamation for the same office in 1888 and 1890, and refused, but served another term in 1893-4. He was also City Attorney from April, 1890 to April, 1891.

Mr. Dafoe's Legislative experience covers one term in the House, to which he was elected from the Alpena District in 1890, and in which he served on the Committees on the Liquor Traffic, Railroads and State House of Correction. That year was the only one since the Republican party was organized, in which the Democrats carried the State, but Mr. Dafoe run 800 ahead of his ticket, and was elected in a District which was then Democratic by 500. In 1894 and 1896 he was the candidate of his section for the Congressional nomination, but missed it by three votes. Mr. Dafoe has done good service at different times in committee, convention and campaign work. He was Chairman of the Republican County Committee during the years from 1894 to 1898, and was Chairman of the City Committee in the years 1895-6. He has been a delegate to every State Convention since 1890, except the Conventions that nominated Pingree for Governor and the last State Convention held in Grand Rapids in 1900. He was a Delegate-at-Large from Michigan to the National Convention of Republican Clubs, in the year 1896, at Detroit, and at St. Paul in 1900. He was a member of the Advisory Council of the State League for the years 1896-7-8 and 1900, and was elected Vice-President of the National Republican League Clubs from Michigan, at the National Convention at St. Paul in 1900. He was appointed Postmaster at Alpena by President McKinley, March 16, 1898.

Mr. Dafoe is a member of the Detroit Club, is a Pythian, Elk, Odd Fellow and Maccabee. He was married January 4th, 1888, at Fenton, Mich., to Marie M. Gallagher, daughter of the late David Gallagher, of Detroit, and has one child eight years old, Naomi Dafoe.

ARCHIBALD BARD DARRAGH, son of Benjamin F. and Catherine Bard Darragh, was born on a farm in LaSalle Township, Monroe County, Mich., December 23rd, 1840. The Darragh and Bard families are of Irish and Scotch descent and settled in this country long before the Revolution. In that war they took an active part, many of their names being found on the Colonial Army register. Mr. Darragh's parents settled in Michigan in 1834 and engaged in farming. The subject of this sketch was kept in the country schools until his twelfth year, varying school work with the various duties of a farmer's boy. At the age of twelve his parents moved to Monroe, where, at the old Monroe Academy, he prepared for the University, which he entered in 1857. In 1859 he left college and went to Mississippi, where he taught for two years. That State was then the hot-bed of secession and as the Yankee schoolmaster was somewhat outspoken in his opinions it became necessary for him to take his departure, and only the friendship of two college chums, members of the same college fraternity, enabled him to get out of that locality alive.

On arriving home he re-entered college, but found it difficult to settle down to the old time student life. The nation was grappling in a life and death struggle with a giant Rebellion. The need of men was great. Already thousands had gone from Michigan and thousands more were needed. The students in the old University town were restless, uneasy and excited, and at last, after standing it for a year, young Darragh volunteered in Co. H., Eighteenth Michigan Volunteer Infantry on August 14th, 1862, and on September 1st went to the front with his regiment, which was assigned to General Q. A. Gilmore's Brigade of the United States forces opposing Kirby Smith in Kentucky. On September 25th, he was captured, and when exchanged in January, 1863, he was transferred to Company D, Ninth Michigan Cavalry, and was afterwards commissioned as Second Lieutenant. His regiment first met the enemy in the spring of 1863, when it routed a portion of Buckner's command at Triplets Bridge, Kentucky. It took a prominent part in the chase after John Morgan in the final round up of that raider. In August the regiment marched into East Tennessee and under Burnside participated in the hot fighting in that State. In July, 1864, the regiment picked its way through Kentucky and Tennessee into Georgia, where it joined Sherman's victorious regiments at Marietta. Until the close of the War the Ninth Cavalry was in Kilpatrick's Division of the Army, and was in one continued skirmish with Rebel cavalry. On July 21st, 1865, Mr. Darragh was mustered out as Captain of his company, having been in the service three years.

After leaving the Army he entered the law office of Ex-Governor Blair. The training of three years in the service had apparently unfitted him for the legal profession, and after practically fulfilling all the requirements for admission to the bar, he decided not to apply, and again sought another field, this time as teacher in the Jackson City

Schools, from which position he was called to act as Superintendent of Schools of Jackson County. This office he filled for two years, and then went north to Gratiot County, where, in 1870, he opened at St. Louis, the first Bank in North Central Michigan. Since that time Mr. Darragh has been identified with the growth of his Town and County. He has taken an active interest in politics and always on the Republican side, having cast his first vote for Lincoln. He has attended State Conventions regularly since 1870. In 1872 he was elected County Treasurer by a large majority. In 1882 he was urged by his party to accept the nomination for Representative in the State Legislature. The situation was regarded as hopeless by the Republican managers. His opponent was also a resident of St. Louis, an able man in every respect and regarded as the strongest man on that side. When the vote was counted Mr. Darragh was elected by 62 majority, the rest of the Republican ticket being defeated except one Circuit Court Commissioner. In 1884 he refused a renomination. Since then Mr. Darragh has at different times taken control of the Republican County campaign and always with success, and in the campaign of 1900 he was nominated for Congress in the Eleventh District.

In his business life Mr. Darragh has the warm esteem of every honest man with whom he is thrown in contact. Scrupulously honest he demands and expects the same from others. The institution of which he is the head, is known far and wide as a safe one with which to do business. In the financial crisis of 1893 it stood firm as a rock, and was able not only to aid the business men of its own town, but to extend aid to some of the suffering institutions of other towns.

Mr. Darragh has served his home town in various official capacities, has also served on the Board of Control of some of the State Institutions, and is now a member of the Board of Control of the Ionia Asylum. His ability as a financier was recognized last year by Controller Dawes, who selected him to settle up the affairs of the defunct Citizens' National Bank of Niles. Since leaving the Army in 1865 Mr. Darragh has taken an active interest in the welfare of the veterans and in the work of the G. A. R. He was organizer and first Commander of the local Post of St. Louis. He is a member of the Masonic Order, Odd Fellows and G. A. R. He was married June 8th, 1875, to Miss Annie P. Culberson, of Monongahela City, Penn., but has no children. In the campaign of 1900 he was nominated for Congressman from the Eleventh District, and carried every County in the District, his total plurality being 14,456.

C. HOWARD DASKAM was born in Bridgeport, Conn., April 2d, 1854, his father being Charles S. Daskam, a carpenter, and his mother, Lucretia H. Daskam. The great-grandfather of the subject of this sketch, was born in England, but early in life an admiration for the institutions of the United States, combined with a spirit of

C. Howard Gaskarn.

adventure, caused him to remove to this country, permanently locating in Connecticut. His grandfather was born in Stratton, Conn., and his father at Bridgeport, but removed to Michigan a few years previous to the War of the Rebellion, upon the breaking out of which he promptly enlisted in the Third Michigan Cavalry and faithfully served his country until the end of the war, receiving his final discharge only after the last enemy had surrendered. C. Howard Daskam was educated at Albion. His first occupation in life was that of a moulder, learning his trade with the Gale Manufacturing Company of Albion, and continuing in their employ for a period of seven years, when he engaged for himself in the wood and coal business, and so continued until December, 1898, when he removed to Marshall to assume the duties of the office of Register of Deeds, to which he had been elected. He has been a Republican ever since he became a voter, and a stalwart one, casting his first vote for Rutherford B. Hayes, and has attended several State Conventions. He was elected Supervisor of Albion for 1895, Village Treasurer in 1886; again Supervisor in 1887, and City Treasurer for one year, holding various City offices until 1895, when he was elected Supervisor from the First Ward of the City of Albion and served until elected to the office of Register of Deeds, which office he still holds. He is a member of the Leisure Hour Club of Albion; Murat Lodge No. 14, F. & A. M.; Lodge 919, Modern Woodmen of America; Albion Lodge No. 60; I. O. O. F.; Tent No. 180, K. O. T. M.; Albion Lodge No. 36, A. O. U. W., all of Albion.

GEORGE BURLINGHAM DAVIS, of Utica, Macomb County, is one of the pushing business men and active Republicans of Eastern Michigan. He was born in Detroit, June 23rd, 1858. His father, J. E. Davis, was a physician and during the war was surgeon in the Twenty-seventh Michigan Infantry. His mother was Margaret S. Davis. His grandfather was Judge Calvin Davis, who came to Michigan at an early day from the State of New York and who was a member of the State Legislature in 1845, just fifty years before the subject of this sketch was a member of the same body.

Mr. Davis was educated in the public schools, which he left at the age of 16 to accept a position as shipping clerk in the wholesale oil house of M. V. Bentley, at Grand Rapids. He stayed here and spent an equal length of time in the real estate and insurance business at Oxford, Mich. He then accepted a position as city salesman for Perrin & Bentley, wholesale oil dealers in Detroit. For two years he acted as city salesman and traveling man for this firm, leaving them at the expiration of this period to travel for the music firm of R. D. Bullock, of Detroit. While engaged in this business Mr. Davis traded a second-hand piano for some oak timber land in Macomb County, which deal eventually resulted in taking him into the manufacture of hardwood lumber. He has now an excellent business in this line, his office and residence being at Utica, Macomb County. For the past fifteen years he has made a specialty of piles, bridge, car and ship timber. His largest and oldest patrons are the Michigan Central Railroad Company, the Detroit Shipbuilding Company, and the Michigan-Peninsular Car Company. In 1890 he organized the Utica Hoop & Lumber Company, at Utica. He also organized the Detroit Sand & Gravel Company, and bought one of the largest standard sand and gravel pits in the State, being arranged to load forty cars a day. Mr. Davis is now its sole owner. In 1898 he organized the Detroit, Utica & Romeo Railway Company, of which he is President, and which has an electric railway under construction between the points named.

Mr. Davis has been a Republican all his life and cast his first vote for Garfield. He has attended nearly all State Conventions for the past fifteen years. He was elected Representative in the State Legislature from the Second District of Macomb County in 1894, re-elected in 1896, and was elected State Senator from the Macomb-Oakland District in 1898. While in the Legislature he aided in securing the passage of several important local measures, and in defeating the Single Tax measure. In the Legislature of 1897 he was Chairman of the Committee on Fisheries and Game, and conducted the fight, against a strong lobby, for a closed season for fishing. This was the first fish legislation of any consequence that was enacted for twenty years. Mr. Davis also framed, introduced and pushed to its passage the Act reducing the legal rate of interest in Michigan to five per cent. and had much to do with other important matters of general legislation. He married Miss Marion St. John, daughter of S. P. St. John, and has one child, Lucille, eight years of age.

HARLOW PALMER DAVOCK, of Detroit, was born in Buffalo, N. Y., March 11th, 1848. His father, John W. Davock, a dealer in hardware and lock supplies, was of Irish descent; was born in Dublin, Ireland, but came to this country from Manchester, England, in 1832. His mother, Maria Davock, was of New England descent, but was born in New York State. Harlow P. mixed self-support and education from the time he was fourteen years of age until he had graduated from the Buffalo High School and the literary course of the University of Michigan, working vacations and saving money to enable him to carry on his studies. At the age of fourteen he was office boy for the Buffalo & Erie Railroad, and afterwards traveling agent for the same road. Immediately after his graduation in 1870, he commenced to practice as a civil engineer; was engaged as such upon different railroads through the United States, being U. S. Assistant Civil Engineer in the construction of the Government locks at Sault Ste. Marie, Michigan, and the Cascade Locks, Oregon. Meantime he had studied law; was admitted to the bar in 1878, and resigned from the Government service in 1882. He has made the prac-

tice of law his chief occupation since that time, taking a hand, however, in politics in each campaign. He has always been a Republican; cast his first ballot for Hayes for President; was delegate to the State Conventions in the spring of 1891, fall of 1894, and spring of 1897. He was a member of the Michigan Legislature in 1893 and 1894; was appointed member of the Detroit Board of Health by Governor Rich, in March, 1895; reappointed March 1st, 1896, and held the position for five years, being President of that body for two years. He was United States Chief Supervisor of Elections in the Eastern District of Michigan in 1893; was appointed United States Referee in Bankruptcy for the Eastern District of Michigan, Southern Division, August 1st, 1898, and reappointed August 1st, 1900. During the session of the Legislature of 1893, the proposition of the Log Cabin, or Palmer Park, so called, had been defeated, and after several weeks hard work, Mr. Davock secured unanimous consent to have the same question called up in the House, and secured its passage.

Mr. Davock is a member of the Detroit Boat Club, Detroit Golf Club, and Michigan Club. He is a member of the Society of the Sons of the American Revolution, and a Trustee of the Westminster Presbyterian Church, Detroit. He was married January 4th, 1883, to Sarah Whiting Peabody and has had three children, Clarence W. Davock, age 16; Harlow Noble Davock, age 14, and Henry Whiting Davock died February 19th, 1894, age 6 years and 6 months.

HENRY STUART DEAN, of Ann Arbor, has had an exceedingly varied business, military and political career. He was born at Lima, Livingston County, New York, June 14th, 1830. His father, William Whitten Dean, was a miller and merchant, and his mother was Eliza Hand Dean. His ancestors on his father's side emigrated from England to America, and on his grandmother's side they came from Holland. On both sides they took an active part in securing the independence of the Thirteen Colonies, his grandfather, Captain Stuart Dean, having commanded the Sloop Beaver, six guns and twelve swivels, under commission of the State of New York, capturing several British vessels during the Revolutionary War.

Henry S. Dean received his education in the district schools of Michigan, Professor Nutting's Academy at Lodi Plains and West Bloomfield Academy, New York. His first occupation in life was that of clerk in a general store, from 1846 to 1850. From 1850 to 1852 was spent in school. In March, 1852, he went around Cape Horn to California, where he remained until March, 1857, engaged in mining operations and general business. He was President and Manager of the Union Tunnel Company which conceived and executed successfully the plan of draining Stockton Hill in Calaveras County, by means of a tunnel, the first one ever attempted in that county. The tunnel was four and one-half feet wide and six feet high, and ran 2,000 feet into the mountain at a depth of from 125 to 250 feet from the surface through solid granite, every foot of which had to be blasted. It was one year and nine months in construction, gangs working night and day. In 1857 he returned to Michigan, purchased flouring and saw mills in Livingston County, and continued to operate them until 1866. In the latter year he disposed of his milling and farming interests and went to Ann Arbor to give his personal attention to the business conducted under the firm name of Dean & Co., in partnership with his brother Sedgwick, which business was established in 1861. The firm still remains the same, and is the only firm in Ann Arbor that has not changed in its personal membership since its formation.

Colonel Dean's military service continued from June 17th, 1862, when he was commissioned by Governor Blair as Second Lieutenant, and mustered in as recruiting officer, till July 11th, 1865, when he received his final discharge as Lieutenant Colonel. His first service was to raise a company for the Twenty-second Michigan Infantry commanded by ex-Governor Moses Wisner. As Captain of this company from July 31st, 1862, he participated in the marches and skirmishes of the Regiment in Kentucky till February 5th, 1863, when he was promoted to be Major of the regiment. His subsequent varied and active service may thus be briefly summarized: With his regiment until May, 1863; on duty as Inspector General on the Staff of Brigadier General R. S. Granger, and member of a commission to try cotton speculators till September 24th, 1863; in command of his regiment from September 27th, 1863, till June 26th, 1865. In February, 1864, he was appointed a member of a Board to examine candidates for commission as officers of colored troops; on June 7th, 1864, he was commissioned Lieutenant Colonel of his Regiment. He took part in the operations in and about Chattanooga and mention is made of him on the Monument erected by the State of Michigan on the Battlefield of Chickamauga in honor of the Twenty-second Michigan Infantry in the following words: "In the Chattanooga campaign it performed important engineer service, Major Henry S. Dean, Commanding." He participated in the Battle of Missionary Ridge, having been assigned to the important and difficult duty of moving the pontoon train, over which General Sherman crossed the Tennessee River from Chattanooga to the point of crossing, four miles above the latter place, without letting the enemy see it from their position on Lookout Mountain, from which they could see all that was going on during the daytime. He participated in the Atlanta Campaign up to and including the Battle of Jonesboro. After the close of the Atlanta campaign his regiment was ordered back to Chattanooga, where it remained until the close of the war. He took part in the Battle of Nashville, serving as aid on the Staff of Major General James B. Steedman.

Colonel Dean has been a Republican since the party was organized. He cast his first Presidential vote for Fremont in California in 1856, and has been delegate to six State Conventions. He was elected

*E. O. Dewey.*

**OWOSSO TIMES.**

Justice of the Peace in 1858 and again in 1862, but resigned when he went into the Army. He was Postmaster at Ann Arbor from 1870 to 1874, was appointed a member of the State Prison Board by Governor Luce and remained on the board until it was legislated out of existence in 1891; was elected Supervisor from the First Ward in Ann Arbor in 1898; was appointed Regent of the University of Michigan by Governor Rich to fill the vacancy occasioned by the death of Henry Howard, served five years under this appointment, and in 1899 was elected to the same position for eight years. July 31st, 1900, he was nominated for Judge of Probate for Washtenaw County on the Republican ticket.

Mr. Dean is a member of the firm of Dean & Co.; President of the Michigan Milling Company, President of Forest Hill Cemetery Company, Director of the Owosso Gas Light Company, Director of the University School of Music and has been President of the Business Men's Association of the city of Ann Arbor, and President and Director of the Washtenaw County Fair Association. He is a member of the Grand Army of the Republic, in which he was elected Commander of the Department of Michigan in 1893; Military Order of the Loyal Legion of the United States and was elected Commander of the Michigan Commandery in 1896; American Historical Society; Sons of the American Revolution, and Michigan Club.

He was married August 24th, 1865, at Detroit, to Miss Delia Brown Cook, and has one daughter, Elizabeth Whitten Dean.

EDMUND OTIS DEWEY, of Owosso, came by inherited right into the newspaper business and into Republican politics. He was the son of George M. Dewey, a sketch of whom follows this, and of Emma Bingham Dewey, and was born at Niles, Michigan, August 24th, 1861. He received a common school education, supplemented by a course at the Hastings High school. Before graduation he learned the printer's trade in his father's office and in November, 1881, he became Local Editor of the Owosso Times, which has been his business home ever since. He leased the plant in 1887, purchased a half interest in 1890, purchased the balance in 1892, and has conducted the business on his own account ever since. When asked about his war record Mr. Dewey said it consisted in "Gunning for delinquent subscribers." If he has had as good success in that as he has in politics he ought to be getting rich. His first vote was cast for D. H. Jerome for Governor in 1882, and he has never swerved from the Republican faith since. He has been a delegate to nearly every Republican State Convention since 1886. He was School Inspector in Owosso city, 1883-86; City Clerk, 1886 and 1887; Supervisor-at-Large, 1887-88; Deputy Oil Inspector, Twelfth district, 1893-97 and was appointed Postmaster at Owosso April 15th, 1900. He is Secretary and Treasurer of the Owosso Telephone Company; stockholder in the Owosso Savings Bank. Of fraternal societies he is a member of the Knights of Pythias, Maccabees, Modern Woodmen, A. O. U. W., and Loyal Guards. He has long been active in the State Press Association and the Michigan Republican Newspaper Association and has held official positions in both. He was married in Owosso September 21st, 1887, to May C. Williams, daughter of Hon. A. L. Williams, the first settler and founder of that place. He has a daughter, Harriet Emma Dewey, and has had two sons, who died in infancy.

GEORGE M. DEWEY, who was for forty years connected with Michigan newspapers, and who was for a still longer period active in politics, was born in Lebanon, Grafton County, New Hampshire, February 14, 1827, the son of Granville and Harriett Freeman Dewey, both natives of the same place, where their son first saw light. The mother was born in the same room which afterwards was the birthplace of her son. The grandfather was Martin Dewey, who was a revolutionary soldier, and the great grandfather, Elijah Dewey, who settled in Lebanon at a very early day, was of English parentage. The mother of George M. Dewey was a descendant of the Plymouth Pilgrims, and in the direct line of that branch of the Standish family which settled in Connecticut. Granville, father of George M. Dewey, was a soldier in the war of 1812 and was a farmer by occupation, residing on the old homestead which had been handed down for generations, from father to son.

The subject of this sketch received a common school education, then graduated from the High School at Lowell, Massachusetts, and entered Harvard College, but in his sophomore year was employed by Charles E. Smith on an astronomical expedition in South America, which consumed about eighteen months. Returning to Lowell he undertook teaching, which profession he pursued for over three years in the east, after which he came west in 1852, taught for another year and was then appointed Deputy Superintendent of Public Instruction. He had moved to Michigan just in time to come into the spirit of the movement which was then culminating in the fusion of all Anti-Slavery elements in the Republican party. He went heart and soul into this movement, and was one of the delegates to the Convention at Jackson, July 6th, 1854. About the same time he hit upon his true vocation, that of editing a newspaper. He took charge of the Niles Enquirer, afterwards the Niles Republican, which he conducted for nine years. After that he edited the Hastings Banner for a number of years, and still later the Owosso Times and the Odd Fellow, continuing in charge of the latter till his death in June, 1897.

Mr. Dewey was a clear thinker and a forcible and convincing speaker, and during almost this whole period his services were in demand on the stump, not only in Michigan, but in Central New York and in two or three of the New England States, where he was

Geo. M. Dewey.

well known. He also did his share of political committee work, and in the Legislature of 1873 represented his district in the State Senate. He was Alderman of the City of Hastings for four years and a member of the Board of Education for six years.

Mr. Dewey was prominent in the Royal Templars and Oddfellows, and reached high rank in both orders. In 1887 he was Supreme Councillor of the Grand Council of Royal Templars, and in 1888-9 he was Grand Master of the Grand Lodge of Michigan I. O. O. F. He was married May 28th, 1857, to Miss Emma Bingham, of Niles, and five children survived him—Edmund O., editor of the Owosso Times; Henry B., of Tacoma, Washington; Emma G., of Gambier, Ohio; George M., and Mary Hannah, of Owosso.

FREEMAN BENJAMIN DICKERSON, for three years Postmaster of Detroit, was born at Mecca, Trumbull County, Ohio, July 14th, 1850, his parents being Jacob M., a builder and farmer, and Teresa Dickerson. The family moved from Ohio to Montcalm County, Michigan, in 1863. The father was a prominent citizen, and was for a number of years Judge of Probate of that County, and also Chairman of the Board of Supervisors.

Freeman B. Dickerson worked first in clearing up a new farm, working with his father at the carpenter trade and teaching country school winters. He attended the country schools, afterwards studied at the Agricultural College in Michigan and at the Normal School at Valparaiso, Indiana. After finally leaving school, he started out as canvassing agent for the Western Publishing House, Chicago; soon after became general agent and manager of their publications for Michigan; afterwards started an establishment of his own, began publishing books, and the result is the present firm of F. B. Dickerson Company, of which he is President, and which sends its publications not only to every part of this country, but to many other parts of the world.

In politics Mr. Dickerson has always been a Republican. He has never sought an elective office, but was once, against his protest, nominated for Senator in a district nearly 2,000 Democratic, and came within seven votes of being elected. He was appointed by the Mayor of Detroit in 1892 City Poor Commissioner, and was afterwards elected President of the Commission. In 1894 he was appointed by the Governor of the State member of the State Board of Fish Commissioners, and is still a member of this Commission, and President of the Board. He has taken great interest and pride in the work of this Commission, and the value of his work has been recognized beyond the limits of the State. At last summer's meeting of the American Fisheries Society, at Woods Hole, Massachusetts, he was chosen President of the Society, which is composed of members of Boards of Fish Commissioners and scientific men who are interested in the subject.

Mr. Dickerson has been Chairman of the Republican Congressional Committee for the First District four terms, and has shown the same thoroughness in organizing the canvass and campaign work of the district, that he had before shown in the canvass for a new publication. He was a delegate to the National Convention in 1896, and has been several times a delegate to State, County and Congressional Conventions.

In 1897 Mr. Dickerson was appointed Postmaster of Detroit by President McKinley, and he has since made many improvements in the office, which, in respect to mail matter handled, is one of the largest, for a city of the size of Detroit, in the country. During his administration new buildings have been erected for the sole use of sub-stations A, C and D, and each is a completely equipped postoffice of itself. The Detroit postoffice, under his administration was the first office in the country to establish a night registry, where money orders can be handled and letters registered till 11:30 p. m. He has also improved the marine mail service, established mail carrier service to St. Clair Flats, and added an information bureau to the central office. He was the originator of the National Association of First Class Postmasters, and was recently, for the third time, elected its President.

Mr. Dickerson is a Knight Templar, an Elk, a member of the Detroit Club and of the North Channel Club, and the Rainbow Fishing Club. He was married in 1877 to Mary M. Marshall of Valparaiso, Indiana, and the name of their only child is Eloise.

JULIAN GEORGE DICKINSON, one of the leading attorneys in Detroit, was born in Hamburg, Erie County, New York, November 20th, 1843, the son of William Dickinson and Lois Sturtevant Dickinson. His father was a carriage manufacturer until 1856 when he was appointed keeper in Jackson State Prison, holding the position there until 1864. His father's family lived near Auburn, New York, where William Dickinson was born. The father of William was of Welsh ancestry and his mother English (Quaker). They both died when he was a child. Julian's mother's people were early settlers in Boston, Massachusetts. The first known ancestor, Samuel Sturtevant, came over from Holland with the Puritans.

Julian was educated in the public schools of Jonesville and Jackson, Michigan, and at the Michigan University. His first occupation in civil life was as a law student and clerk in the law office of Moore & Griffin at Detroit, in March, 1866, until the year 1867. He was admitted to the bar on examination before the Supreme Court of Michigan, in October, 1866, and commenced the practice of law in Detroit in October, 1867, in the firm of Dickinson & Burt, which continued until 1869, when he became partner of Don M. Dickinson, under the firm name of Dickinson & Dickinson, continuing until 1873. From that time he has maintained independent offices in this city and has

had his share of legal business at Detroit, devoting his principal time to that.

Mr. Dickinson has a good record in the Civil War, 1862-65. He enlisted July 10th, 1862, in the Fourth Michigan Cavalry and served constantly with that regiment three years. In 1862, he was with his regiment in the Army of the Cumberland, pursuing Bragg's army through Kentucky to Nashville, Tenn. In 1863, he was in the Murfreesboro campaign and the Battle of Stone River and numerous engagements with Wheeler's Cavalry; with the advance of the army against Bragg's forces through Tennessee to Chattanooga; at the Battle of Chickamauga, and the pursuit of Wheeler's Cavalry in the raid against the communications and supplies of Rosecrans' army in September and October, 1863; in the Battle of Chattanooga and relief of the Army of the Ohio at Knoxville; in 1864 in General Sherman's command in the Atlanta campaign and through all the battles of that campaign; in 1865 in General James H. Wilson's Cavalry command in the memorable campaign through Alabama and Georgia striking Selma and Montgomery, Ala., Columbus and Macon, Georgia; and lastly with the detachment of the Fourth Michigan Cavalry under Pritchard, that captured Jefferson Davis and escort at Irwinville, Ga., May 10th 1865, and personally arrested and placed him under guard. He was promoted to Sergeant in Company I, Ordnance Sergeant and Sergeant Major of the regiment, First Lieutenant and Adjutant of the regiment, Brevet Captain U. S. Volunteers for meritorious service in the capture of Jefferson Davis, commissioned Captain in the Second Michigan Cavalry in July, 1865, and remained in service after the muster out of his regiment, being appointed to the command of Company I of a detachment awaiting muster till August, 1865. He is a member of Detroit Post, G. A. R., and of the Loyal Legion.

Mr. Dickinson has always been a Republican and cast his first vote for General Grant. He has not sought a political career, but was a delegate to the two State Conventions which nominated D. H. Jerome for Governor. He is President of the Detroit Vapor Stove Company, and is connected with several other business companies as a stockholder and director. He is a member of the Detroit Club, Detroit Boat Club and Masonic fraternities, W. L. S. O., King Cyrus Chapter; Detroit Commandery and the Consistory, S. R. He was married June 25th, 1878, to Clara Matilda Johnson, daughter of Hiram Johnson, at Detroit. His children are Alfred Thornton Julian, Philip Sheridan, Stanley and Clara.

FRED ARDEN DIGGINS, a successful lumber manufacturer in Osceola and Wexford Counties, was born July 8th, 1862, near Harvard, McHenry County, Ill., son of Franklin and Ellen Blodgett Diggins. His father was born in Vermont and his mother in Cattaraugus County, New York. He was educated in the district and High Schools at Harvard, and Swensberg's Commercial College in Grand

Rapids, Mich. He left home and parents in Illinois in 1878, went to Hersey, Osceola County and worked as bookkeeper for his brother, Delos F. He began handling and manufacturing lumber on his own account in a small way at Hersey in 1884; went to Cadillac in 1886, and entered the bank of D. A. Blodgett & Co. as assistant cashier and bookkeeper. In 1888 the firm of F. A. Diggins & Co. began the manufacture of lumber in Cadillac, with Mr. Diggins at its head as manager. This firm was succeeded by Murphy & Diggins, composed of Joseph Murphy and F. A. Diggins, in 1897, and is still in existence, handling about 12,000,000 feet per annum. The father of Mr. Diggins voted for James G. Birney, Free Soil, and for John C. Fremont, the first Republican candidate for President, and all subsequent candidates of that faith, so the son never knew any other than Anti-Slavery and Republican precepts. His first vote was cast for the Blaine Electors in 1884. He is a member of the Michigan Club, has attended nearly all the State Conventions for the past twelve years, and was delegate to the National Convention at Minneapolis in 1892. He has been elected Mayor of Cadillac six times at the spring elections of 1892-3-6-7-8-9; was elected twice, 1894-1900 as member of the Board of Education of Cadillac, served eight years as member and ex-officio member of the Board, and is still a member.

Mr. Diggins was married in Cadillac in 1890 to Carrie E. Cummer, only daughter of Jacob Cummer, of that City, and has two children, Helen and Dorothy.

EDWARD NELSON DINGLEY, of Kalamazoo, is one of the most prominent figures at meetings of the Michigan State Press Association, the League of Republican Clubs, the State Association of Republican Newspapers and other gatherings where working Republicans or newspaper men convene. He was born at Auburn, Maine, August 21st, 1862. His mother was Salome McKenney Dingley and his father was Nelson Dingley, Jr., who was a journalist, before he was sent to Congress, where he reached the culmination of his fame as the framer of the Dingley Tariff Act. His father's ancestors came from England about 1630, and settled in Lynn, Mass. They then moved to Duxbury, Mass. Mary Dingley, a daughter, married a son of Miles Standish. About 1780 the descendants moved to Maine and settled first at Cape Elizabeth, near Portland, and then at Durham. The grandfather of Edward N. moved from Durham to Unity, then to Auburn, Maine, and his father moved to Lewiston, in the same State, in 1863.

The subject of the present sketch was educated in the High School at Lewiston, Maine; was in Bates College, Lewiston, one year; then in Yale University, graduating in 1883, and Columbia, Washington, D. C., University Law School in 1885. His work, however, has been mostly that of a journalist; for two years as a reporter on the Lewiston Journal, and the Boston Advertiser and Record and was

Edward N. Dingley



KALAMAZOO TELEGRAPH.

made political writer on the latter papers. In 1888, with others of the family, he purchased the Kalamazoo Telegraph and has been its editor ever since. In 1897 he was elected President of the Michigan League of Republican Clubs. In 1898 he was Michigan's candidate for President of the National League of Republicans at the Convention in Omaha. In June, 1898, he was appointed clerk of the Committee on Ways and Means of the National House of Representatives, but resigned from this position January 1st, 1900. In August, 1898, he was nominated for Representative to the Michigan Legislature by the Republicans of the First Kalamazoo District, and was elected by a large majority. While in the Legislature he assisted in framing and passing several tax measures, including the inheritance tax law. His political affiliations have always been with the Republicans. He cast his first vote in September, 1884, for his father for Congress, and his first Presidential vote was for James G. Blaine in November of the same year. He was delegate to the Republican National Convention at Philadelphia in 1900 and was Michigan's member of the Committee on Resolutions in that Convention; was delegate to the State Republican Conventions in 1890, 1892, 1896 and 1898, and assisted in framing the Republican State platforms in 1896, 1898 and 1900. In addition to his active political work, Mr. Dingley has contributed articles to magazines on political and social topics. He was married to Miriam Gardner Robinson, of Boston, Mass., December 20th, 1888, and has had four children, Irene, Nelson Third, Miriam, deceased, and Madalen.

GEORGE DINGWALL would be taken by a stranger who glanced at his commanding stature, broad forehead and keen eye, as a man robust, both physically and intellectually, and as one alert in his perceptions, and ready in resource. The stranger on further acquaintance would find that he was not mistaken. Mr. Dingwall was the second son of Alexander and Jeanette (Jack) Dingwall, and was born in Fayetteville, New York State, July 22d, 1843. He is a descendant from a Highland Scotch family, and can trace his family ancestry back as far as the year 783, on their arrival in Scotland, they having come from Norway, and locating in Ross Shire, County of Ross, Scotland. From this settlement sprang the City of Dingwall, now a thriving City of several thousand people, the same being named in honor of one of the Dingwalls. Dingwall was enacted a Royal Burgh by Alexander the Second, and its charter was renewed by James the Fourth. The parents of George Dingwall came to America and settled in Fayetteville about 1839, and ten years later moved to Detroit, where the son received an elementary education in the public schools, and where he had to commence, at a very early age, taking care of himself. When nineteen years old, August 13th, 1862, he gave up his business pursuits, and with an older brother enlisted as private in Company A, Twenty-fourth Michigan Volunteer Infantry, which saw active service and plenty of it. The brother, John, was killed at the Battle of Gettysburg, July 1st, 1863, and George continued his service with the regiment, in the "Iron Brigade" of the Army of the Potomac in Virginia, being promoted successively to Corporal, Sergeant and Lieutenant. At the Battle of the Wilderness, May 5th, 1864, he was badly wounded and taken prisoner, and thereafter, for over seven months, languished in the Andersonville, Ga., and Florence, S. C., prisons. He was finally exchanged at Annapolis, Md., on December 20th, 1864, and, after partially recovering from the effects of his prison life, returned to his regiment at Springfield, Ill., and was mustered out of service in June, 1865.

At the close of the war he became a member of the Detroit Police force, then was appointed a letter carrier, and after a brief experience in the grocery business for himself, was made United States Gauger under General L. S. Trowbridge, then Collector of Internal Revenue.

In 1884 Mr. Dingwall, who had already done some real estate business in Detroit, went into partnership with Collins B. Hubbard, under the firm name of Hubbard & Dingwall, who soon ranked among the largest real estate operators in the city. They handled large amounts of high class residence property, and purchased and subdivided several large tracts in or near the city. They were largely instrumental in getting Warren avenue opened west of the railroad tracks, and were always staunch promoters of the Boulevard and other improvements. They also, some years ago, purchased several thousand acres of land on the line of the Flint & Pere Marquette railroad, subdivided and improved it, thus establishing the town of Hubbard, Mich.

Mr. Dingwall has taken a hand in politics, among other things, having frequently attended Republican Conventions and served on Republican Committees. In 1889 he was elected Alderman from the First Ward, and served as Chairman of the important Committees on Ways and Means and Street Openings, besides being a member of several other committees. In 1897 he was again elected Alderman, this time from the Second Ward, and was made Chairman of the Committee on Charter and City Legislation and the Committee on Rules, and a member of the Committee on Taxes. He is a good debater, and always ranked among the leaders of the Council. Mr. Dingwall was married in 1865 to Miss Phoebe Renz. They have had three children, two of whom survive: Edward A. and Harrie R. Dingwall.

ROSCOE D. DIX, of Berrien Springs, who has served with credit in two important administrative departments in the State Government, was born in Jefferson County, New York, June 11th, 1839, and moved, with his parents, to Bainbridge Township, Berrien County, Mich., in 1852. Both in his earliest home, and in his second place of abode, he worked on his father's farm, attending the district schools in which he afterwards taught, and later attended Albion College. Before he had settled into any regular business the war broke out and he was among the first to go from Michigan, enlisting in Company K, Second Michigan Infantry, April 26th, 1861. The Second Regiment saw hard and almost constant service for many months in the Western campaigns. Mr. Dix was with his regiment and company in everyone of its engagements as private, corporal and sergeant, until he was severely wounded at Knoxville, November 24th, 1863. He was in hospital until May 25th, 1864, when he was honorably discharged, being permanently disabled for active military duty. His interest in the war and his participation in active service led him afterwards to take great interest in G. A. R. organizations. He was one of the founders and organizers of Kilpatrick Post No. 39, and was for twelve years its commander. He is very popular with the order outside of his own post, as well as in, and has been Inspector General of the Department of Michigan, Judge Advocate General, delegate to the National encampment, and a member of the Executive Committee of the National Council of Administration.

It is hardly necessary to say that Mr. Dix was a Republican before he entered the army and has been no less a Republican since he left it. He has attended many Conventions as a delegate, and has been several times honored by the suffrages of his fellow citizens. In 1864 he was elected Register of Deeds of Berrien County, and re-elected in 1866-68, and in 1874. In 1869 he engaged in the abstract and real estate business and has since been connected with the firm of Dix & Wilkinson in that business, at Berrien Springs and St. Joseph. He is a member of the Berrien County bar, was a member of the School Board of Berrien Springs twelve years, Village Trustee eight, and Village President two terms. Mr. Dix was elected Commissioner of the State Land Office in 1886, and re-elected in 1888; and gave the same painstaking care to that as he has done in all other positions. He was elected Auditor General in 1896, and soon greatly improved the condition and discipline of that very important office, to which he was re-elected in 1898, by nearly 66,000 plurality. When he first took possession of the office of Auditor General he had an opportunity to show his capacity for meeting an emergency. At the time he assumed its duties, the State Treasury was short $21,993. His predecessor advised him to make a loan of $200,000, to meet the immediate demands on the Treasurer for vouchers in support of State institutions and other purposes. Instead of creating an expense and humiliating the State by contracting a loan he wrote every County Treasurer in the State, stating the financial condition and asking each to forward to the State Treasurer all moneys held by them as State money. This request was promptly complied with, and March 31st, 1897, there was on hand after paying the deficiency, $538,225. About May 15th, there was paid the primary school fund $376,000, and on June 30th, the end of the fiscal year, six months after General Dix took charge of the Auditor's office, there was in the Treasury of the State $783,888, with every voucher due up to that date paid, without borrowing a cent.

Auditor General Dix has from the day of his first installation into that office persisted in the most vigilant scrutiny of all disbursements for which he has drawn his warrants upon the State Treasurer, and he has insisted upon the most rigid practicable economy, and. applying the same careful rules and principles to the management of State affairs that he would give to his own private business. He has saved the State many times the amount of his salary over that which would result from a careless and extravagant direction of the office.

JUDGE JOSEPH W. DONOVAN, for fifteen years a strong and effective Republican campaigner, who has won distinction at the bar, on the bench and in literary work, and has more than met his life's ambition, was born near Toledo, Ohio, March 2d, 1846, on his father's farm, where he lived but two years. He removed to Southern Michigan; attended district Union School and later graduated from Jonesville Academy, paying his way with a builder in vacations; took lectures from Hillsdale College professors; taught school one term; took a course of law lectures in Ohio Law School; was admitted to practice law in the Michigan Supreme Court in April, 1870.

Mr. Donovan's career at the bar was greatly aided by his strong, robust body, genial manner and unusual gift of memory. He inherited an eloquent voice from his father, who was from Syracuse, a strong Seward Republican, and his gift of writing from his mother's side, who was of the Chambers Cyclopedia family. His first vote was for Lincoln and all other votes Republican.

Before 1893 he had built up a large practice, even going into Western and Southern States in commercial transactions. and was very successful both before a jury and in the Supreme Court, his client never having to pay costs in a higher court—a record that few can ever claim. He had many cases well known in the State Courts and his struggle in life was largely at the bar. He is a Mason, Maccabee, member of the Elks, Loyal Guard and Michigan Club, and likes them all.

He married Nettie L. Brainard, of Waterville, Ohio, just before admission to the bar and is strongly devoted to his home life. He keeps a vigorous body, attends all lectures, is a diligent student, speaks often and is in demand at Decoration days, school exercises, jury days and farmers' picnics, where he was a strong favorite before his election as Wayne Circuit Judge in April, 1893 and 1899, which he carried by decided majorities. He has published four widely read legal works and has prepared a Boys' Reader, of which 100,000 copies will soon issue in an illustrated edition of fine finish. His life work will end with the bench in which he is at home, original, courageous and deservedly popular. It is difficult to find a man who carries a boy heart up into manhood any more than does the subject of this sketch, or to find one more readily listened to in the counsels of his party. His fund of stories and illustrations is unique, and his speeches are pictures and paintings that enforce attention and command belief. He is perfectly satisfied in his ambition and ever ready to help deserving boy lawyers and newsboys over the same rugged pathway that he has traveled to a deserved success.

HENRY MARTYN DUFFIELD, who has been prominent in politics, in the law and in military service in two wars, was born in Detroit, May 15th, 1842. He comes of distinguished families, both on his father's and mother's side. His paternal great grandfather, Rev. George Duffield, was, on the 6th of July, 1776, appointed by Governor Morton, Chaplain to the Pennsylvania forces in the Revolutionary Army. On the Sunday following he dismissed his congregation with these words: "I hope the women will worship here in silence on the next Sabbath, and the men will be with me in Washington's Army." He was called "the fighting parson," and a price of fifty pounds sterling was put upon his head. He was subsequently associated with Bishop White as joint chaplain of the Continental Congress.

The parson's son got out of the clerical line, was well known in Philadelphia commercial circles, and was also, for nine years, Comptroller General of Pennsylvania. The next in line, Rev. George Duffield, was a native of Strasburg, Pennsylvania, born July 4th, 1794. He came to Detroit in 1838, and from then until his sudden death in 1868, he was pastor of the First Presbyterian Church. His wife, Isabella Graham (Bethune) Duffield, was a daughter of Divie Bethune, a prominent New York merchant, and granddaughter of Isabella Graham, a woman whose memory is revered in the Presbyterian churches of Scotland and America. Dr. Duffield was, for many years, the most prominent Presbyterian clergyman in Michigan. His wife was a woman of superior education and refinement, and their hospitable mansion was not only a center of religious activity, but of the best social life that the City afforded. Their children all received the benefits, not only of liberal education in the schools, but the refining and broadening influences of a cultured home.

The subject of this sketch attended the public schools of Detroit, graduating from the Old Capitol School in 1856. He spent one year in Michigan University, but the personal warfare made upon Chancellor Tappan, of that institution, was so offensive to Dr. Duffield that he transferred the son to Williams College, Mass., where he graduated in 1861.

Soon after graduation young Duffield commenced his first military experience, enlisting in August, 1861, as a private in the Ninth Regiment, Michigan Volunteers. He was made First Lieutenant and Adjutant of the regiment October 12th of the same year. He participated in the engagement with the Rebel forces under General N. B. Forrest at Murfreesboro, Tenn., in July, 1862. In this engagement his brother, General W. W. Duffield, then Colonel of the regiment, was twice wounded. The fighting was so severe that the wounded could not be removed from the field, and after the engagement Adj. Duffield, together with his wounded brother, was captured, but was exchanged two months later. In the spring of 1862 he was detailed Assistant Adjutant General of the Twenty-third Brigade, Army of the Cumberland. In the campaign from Nashville to Chattanooga, 1863, he was attached to the headquarters of General George H. Thomas, and given command of the mounted Provost Guard of the Eleventh Army Corps, the members of which he was allowed to select, and took an active part in all the important battles of that campaign, including Stone River and Chickamauga, where he was wounded. During the siege of Chattanooga, October 23rd, 1863, by the Confederate forces under General Braxton Bragg, he was promoted Post Adjutant. In this office, by order of Major General Thomas, he issued the orders for the establishment of Chattanooga United States cemetery, giving particular attention and direction to its purpose, and to the plan for carrying out that purpose. The plan was subsequently adopted by General Thomas, and from it grew the system of National cemeteries which are enduring evidences of the devotion to their country of the brave soldiers, and of the gratitude of their fellow countrymen. When Major General Thomas was assigned to the command of the Department of the Cumberland, Colonel Duffield was appointed on his staff as Assistant Provost Marshal General of the department, in which capacity he served for the remainder of the war. During the memorable campaign of Gen. Thomas from Chattanooga to Atlanta, Colonel Duffield was acting Provost Marshal General of the Army of the Cumberland, participating in all the hard fought battles of this gallant Union commander, among them being Resaca, Missionary Ridge, Peach Tree Creek and Jonesboro. This campaign terminated at Atlanta, where, on October 14th, 1864, he was mustered out by reason of expiration of service.

On returning from the army Colonel Duffield began the study of law, and in April, 1865, he was admitted to the bar, and formed a partnership with his brother, D. Bethune Duffield, which continued until 1876. He was attorney for the Board of Education from 1867 to 1871. While in this position he carried to a successful termination suits brought to recover from the County Treasurer, moneys received from fines in the municipal courts. Under provision of the State Constitution these funds were required to be applied to the support of a public library, but had been diverted to the payment of expenses of the courts and to other uses. Their recovery to the Board laid the foundation for the present magnificent public library system of Detroit. Commencing with 1881 Colonel Duffield served two terms as City Counselor, and represented the municipality in all its litigation during that period. Both in his official capacity, and in private practice, he has had very many important cases, including, in the latter, the famous Reeder farm escheat cases, and the Stroh-Winsor-Hudson crooked paper case, in which he defeated the holders of the paper. He argued the case against the validity of the Miner Electoral Law, both in the State and United States Supreme Courts, and was also engaged in the Detroit Street Railway cases in the higher United States Courts. With the exception of the time spent in service during the Spanish American War, General Duffield has continued in practice, in which he has been very successful. He has a keen appreciation of the underlying principles of the law, goes into court with his cases well prepared, and is convincing in argument.

General Duffield has a taste for politics in which he has been active, and is always on the Republican side. He has been a conspicuous figure in many of the City and County Conventions, and for a period of about fifteen years attended every State Convention. He was Permanent Chairman of the spring State Convention in 1877 and of the fall Convention at Jackson in 1880. In 1888 he was Chairman of the State Central Committee and was delegate both to the State and National Conventions. He was also Chairman of Michigan's delegation in the Minneapolis Convention in 1892, when he cast the vote of nineteen of the delegates for William McKinley. Though a delegate only twice he has attended every National Convention since 1876. He was candidate for Congress in the First District in that year, but that was not a good year nor a good district for Republican candidates, and he was defeated, though running ahead of the party Electoral ticket. He has since been importuned to take the nomination for Mayor and other important offices, but has steadily refused.

During the long interval of peace between the close of the War of the Rebellion and the opening of the Spanish-American War, Colonel Duffield never lost his military tastes nor associations. He was on the staffs successively of Governors Bagley, Croswell, Jerome and Alger, and kept up a lively interest in the Detroit Light Guard with which he had long been connected. When the call came for volunteers in the war against Spain, although the general officers were taken mostly from the Regular Army, it was determined to select some from among the men who had already seen service in the volunteer army, account being taken of their age, condition of health and record in the Civil War. It was in carrying out this purpose that a commission as Brigadier General was offered to Colonel Duffield, and accepted, dating from May 27th, 1898. On the 14th of June following he assumed command of a separate Brigade of the Second Army Corps, composed of the Thirty-third and Thirty-fourth Michigan and Ninth Massachusetts Volunteers. It was the desire of the Government to reinforce General Shafter's army which had just landed in Cuba, but only one vessel, the transport Yale, was then available, and that could carry only one brigade. There were two brigades in Camp Alger, and it was determined to take the one which should first report in readiness to move. General Duffield's brigade was then on a practice march to the Potomac, but it returned to camp, won in the test and was forthwith dispatched to Santiago. In the Battle of July 1st, General Duffield was assigned to the duty of making a demonstration on the extreme left, at Aguadores, without any means of crossing the stream, and thus coming into the general engagement. The task was performed in a manner of which General Shafter afterwards said, in an interview in Detroit: "As for General Duffield, of your City, he is a soldier, every inch of him. He had a thankless job at the Battle of Aguadores, but he acquitted himself nobly." A few days afterwards at Siboney, Major General Young was taken ill, and the command of the Division was turned over to General Duffield, but he was himself attacked with yellow fever, went into hospital, and later in the month was sent north as a convalescent. He joined his family and spent several weeks with them on the coast of Maine, regaining his health. His last act in connection with the war was as one of the speakers at the Peace Jubilee in Chicago, October 18th, 1898.

General Duffield has associations with a number of the best political, military and social organizations. He is a member of the Union League Club of New York; the University Club of New York; the Army and Navy Club of Washington; the Society of the Army of the Cumberland; the Society of the Army of Santiago de Cuba; the Society of the Spanish-American War; the Loyal Legion; Detroit Post, G. A. R.; Sons of the American Revolution; the Yondotega, Detroit and Country Clubs of Detroit; the Chi Psi College Fraternity, and of the Michigan Club. Of the latter he has been President and is now a Director.

In 1863, while yet in the Union Army, he was married to Miss Frances Pitts, daughter of Samuel and Sarah Merrill Pitts. They have six children, Henry M., now with the Detroit White Lead Works; Divie Bethune, a law partner with his father; Pitts, with Charles Scribner's Sons. New York; Francis, physician in Bellevue Hospital, New York; Morse Stewart, in the mining business in Dawson City, Col., and Graham, with the Commonwealth Electric Co. of Chicago.

JOHN DUNCAN is one of the best known men in the Upper Peninsula and there is no one in the whole mining region who is held in higher esteem. He was born in Canada in 1836, and went to Lake Superior in 1859. The whole copper product of the Lake Superior mines that year was only 4,463 tons, or less than the present output for a single month, of the mine with which he is now connected. He has not only seen the development of the copper country from that small beginning, but has aided materially in the marvelous growth of its industries. He commenced work in that district as foreman carpenter for the Quincy Mining Company, and subsequently became general surface superintendent. He remained with that company

John Duncan

nine years, and then transferred his services to the Calumet & Hecla, where he is now assistant manager and general superintendent of field and surface operations. He is an energetic, shrewd, farseeing business man, familiar with all practical mining operations, and has been largely instrumental in building up the immense industry which has made the Calumet & Hecla mine famous the world over, and which has created the City of Calumet. He is greatly beloved by the hundreds of men working under him, who all look upon him as a personal friend. There is no one in the Upper Peninsula who is more highly regarded for business ability and sterling integrity, nor one who has more personal friends.

Mr. Duncan has always been active in local political and in social, as well as business affairs. He is one of the little circle of staunch, discreet and untiring workers who have made the Northern Peninsula Republican. He has never sought office for himself, and has never held any office of which the remuneration was worth considering, but he has helped send other men to the State Senate and House, and to Congress. He has been Supervisor of Calumet Township for twenty-nine years, has been Chairman of the Board for twenty-seven years, and has looked after the interests of the people so closely that no one ever thinks of being a candidate against him. He has been on the Board of Commissioners for the State House of Correction and Branch Prison in the Upper Peninsula since its organization, was a Presidential Elector in 1884, and was a Delegate-at-Large to the Convention that nominated McKinley in 1896. Mr. Duncan is a prominent member of the Masonic fraternity, and is known all over the United States among Masons of high degree.

THOMAS BREE DUNSTAN, of Hancock, is one of the Cornishmen who came from the old country to the Upper Peninsula of Michigan, and engaged in some other industry than that of mining. He was born January 4th, 1850, in Camborne, Cornwall County, England, his parents being James Dunstan, a miner, and Emma Dunstan. His parents emigrated to America in the spring of 1854, and settled in Ontonagon County, Michigan.

The subject of this sketch first attended the public schools of the Upper Peninsula, and in June, 1871, graduated from Lawrence University, Appleton, Wis. He attended the law department of the Michigan University during the winter of 1871-2, and was admitted to the bar in the Keweenaw Circuit in the fall of the same year. He practiced in the Circuit till July, 1879, then in Pontiac, Mich., for three years, then removed to his old home in Central Mine, Keweenaw County, and finally, in 1883, to Hancock, Houghton County, where he has since resided. The twin Cities of Hancock and Houghton are the business centers of the whole copper country, and here Mr. Dunstan has not only built up a lucrative law practice, but has become associated with a number of industrial and financial enterprises of that section. He is a stockholder and Director in the Adventure Consolidated Company, the Victoria Copper Mining Company and the Rhode Island Mining Company. He is also President of the Ontonagon County National Bank at Rockland, a director of the First National Bank at Hancock, and counsel for the Quincy Mining Company.

Mr. Dunstan has not limited his activities to his law practice and general business, but has also participated in the political work of his section. He has been a Republican ever since he reached his majority, having cast his first Presidential vote for Grant, and has helped to keep Houghton among the strongest Republican counties in the State. He has attended numerous conventions, including the National Convention of 1888, at which he was one of the Delegates-at-Large, and has a number of times received nominations from his party and the suffrages of the people. His first official positions were in the line of his profession. In his old County of Keweenaw, as in some others of the least populous counties of the State, two offices are frequently combined, and he was both Judge of Probate and Prosecuting Attorney from January, 1873, to January, 1879, when he resigned on his removal to Pontiac. From January, 1885 to 1889, he was Prosecuting Attorney of Houghton County, his nomination the second time being endorsed by the Democrats as well as by the Republicans. He has also had Legislative experience, having represented the Keweenaw District in the House in the session of 1883, and the Houghton District in the Senate in the session of 1889. When in the House he was one of the nineteen Republicans who held out persistently against the re-election of the caucus nominee, Thomas W. Ferry, to the United States Senate. In both House and Senate he served on important committees, and was an influential member. In 1896 he was elected Lieutenant Governor by one of the sweeping majorities that went with the Republican ticket along in that period, and presided over the Senate with dignity, and with acceptance to the members. He also served one term on the Board of Control of the Michigan College of Mines.

Mr. Dunstan is prominent in society and social circles and is a Knight Templar in the Masonic Order. He was married in 1875 to Miss Mary A. McDonald, of Hancock, and has four children, Robert P., James S., Helen B. and Emma H. Dunstan.

EDGAR O. DURFEE is probably acquainted with more persons living, and knows about the affairs of more persons deceased, than any other man in Wayne County. It is said that almost the entire property of any given locality passes through the Probate Court, about once in a generation of thirty-five years, and if that is the case four-fifths of the tangible property of the wealthiest and most populous County in Michigan has passed under Judge Durfee's review, during his twenty-eight years in that Court.

He was born in Livonia Township, Wayne County, October 28th, 1842. He has always lived in the County and was a student in the State Normal School at the age of nineteen, when his patriotism impelled him to enlist as a private in the Twenty-fourth Michigan Infantry. On July 1st, 1863, on the field of Gettysburg, he lost his right arm. When he recovered he went back to his studies at the Normal School. He taught one year in the Ypsilanti High School and in 1869 came to Detroit and studied law. In 1872 he was appointed Register of Probate, under Judge Wilkinson. Four years later he was elected Judge of Probate, although in that election the Democrats gave more than 2,000 majority for some of their candidates on the County ticket. Public confidence in his integrity, and the public appreciation of the methodical manner and discriminating judgment with which he has conducted the affairs of his office, have been shown by his re-election at every quadrennial period since then. He has been seven times a candidate for the position, and no matter what the drift of party movements might be at the time, or how strong a candidate might be nominated against him, he has always received a substantial, and sometimes a very large majority. He is quiet and unassuming in manner, but prompt and positive in giving his opinions, whether personal or judicial. He has endeared himself to thousands of persons of limited means, by settling up estates without the intervention of attorneys, himself acting as adviser and counselor, without monetary reward.

Judge Durfee is an exceedingly industrious official, and has handled more estates than all his predecessors combined. When he first entered upon the duties of Probate Judge, January 1st, 1877, the total number of estates which had been administered upon by all the probate judges of Wayne County, from 1794 to that date, was 8,233. From January 1st, 1877, to October 31st, 1900, Judge Durfee administered 19,321 estates. The average number of new estates which were annually entered for probate during Judge Durfee's first term of office, was 450. At the present time the annual number is over 1,600. The first year Judge Durfee held office he heard 1,320 cases. During the first nine months of the year 1900 he heard and decided 6,282 cases.

From the beginning of the present century up to August 1st, 1887, it required 135 volumes to record the work of the probate office. From August 1st, 1887, to October 31st, 1900, a period of only about thirteen years, it has required the same number. The total number of estates which were entered for probate, from the beginning of the century to August 1st, 1887, was 13,725. The total number entered from August 1st, 1887, to October 31st, 1900, was 13,725; so that one-half of the entire work of the office has been performed by Judge Durfee, in the last thirteen years. Yet, notwithstanding the large increase of business, he has only increased his office force by the addition of four clerks, while in other courts of the City and County the number of judges and clerks has been doubled within the past fifteen years.

Judge Durfee has been a Republican ever since he became a voter, has canvassed the County in a number of campaigns and has always been accounted a shrewd adviser in political matters. He has three or four times been urged to run for Congress in the belief that his popularity would render surely Republican a district that has sometimes been doubtful, but he has always refused the honor. He is ex-officio Chairman of the Election Commission, which has to do with the arrangement and printing of the official ballots for the County and is also Chairman of the Board of Canvassers of Wayne County.

HENRY ELDRED EDWARDS is one of the talented attorneys of Central Michigan, and one of the stirring Republicans who have occasionally succeeded in turning Jackson County away from its natural Democratic leanings. He was the son of Randolph D. M. Edwards, a farmer, and Harriett M. Edwards, formerly Harriett M. Powers, and was born in Albion, Calhoun County, Michigan, October 3d, 1863, and moved to Liberty, Jackson County, in the spring of 1868. His father's people came at an early date from New York State to Michigan and settled in Lenawee County. His mother's people came from New Hampshire and were among the first settlers in the same County, his maternal grandfather, Isaac Powers, being a farmer and country lawyer.

The subject of this sketch obtained his education as many farmers' boys have done, working on the farm while he was receiving such instruction as the country schools of Jackson County afforded. He cut corn for the neighbors, nights, in order to get the money necessary for buying books, and later, while in the Jackson High School he worked nights and did chores for Judge Gridley, thus supporting himself and paying his way. He graduated from the High School in 1884, as valedictorian of his class, and at once entered the law office of Gibson & Parkinson of Jackson.

Mr. Edwards was admitted to the bar in September, 1886, and the same day was nominated by the Republican County Convention for Circuit Court Commissioner. He was elected, and filled the office so acceptably that he was elected for two more terms in succession. He was nominated for Prosecuting Attorney in 1892, but was defeated by a small majority, the County going generally Democratic. Two years later he was appointed Assistant Prosecuting Attorney under Charles A. Blair. In the first year of his incumbency of this office he prepared and assisted in trying seventeen jury cases in the Circuit Court, securing convictions in fifteen of them. He was again nominated for Prosecuting Attorney in 1896, but was swept away by the silver tide in the County. February 14th, 1898, he was appointed Postmaster at Jackson and still holds that office.

Mr. Edwards was born a Republican and has never changed. He "was rocked in a Republican cradle by a Republican mother and spanked with a Republican shingle by a Republican father." Since reaching maturity he has not only voted the Republican ticket but has done his share of political work. He has been Chairman of the City Committee and belongs to the Republican County organization and the Lincoln Club. Of societies not political he is a member of the Jackson City Club; is Chancellor Commander of Rowena Lodge, No. 29 K. P.; member of Michigan Lodge No. 50, F. & A. M.; Jackson Council No. 32, R. & S. M.; Jackson Chapter No. 3, R. A. M., and Jackson Lodge No. 113, B. P. O. Elks. He is also, outside of his law practice, interested in a number of business enterprises, being Vice-President of the Foote & Jenks Manufacturing Company, perfumers; Secretary and Treasurer of the Jackson Starch Company; Treasurer of the Jackson Cushion Spring Company; Director in the Boulder County Gold Mining Company, and Director of the Peninsular Building and Loan Association.

Mr. Edwards was married January 1st, 1890, at Rockland, Maine, to Mabel J. Abbott. Their children are Harriet, Emily and Joseph Abbott Edwards.

WILLIAM HERBERT ELLIOTT, one of Detroit's leading merchants and active in politics as well, was born near Amherstburg, Ontario, October 13th, 1844. His father was James Elliott, a farmer and country merchant, and his mother was Elizabeth Pastorius Elliott. He is a descendant of Andrew Elliott, who came from Somersetshire, England, and settled in Beverly, Massachusetts, in 1670. His great grandfather and his brother were at the Battle of Bunker Hill. One of his ancestors was on the jury that hung the witches at Salem. In justice to him, it may be said that he and his fellow jurors publicly expressed their regret therefor. His mother was a descendant of Pastorius, one of the early settlers of Pennsylvania, and said to have been one of the best learned men of his day.

Young Elliott received his education in the common schools in Canada, and his first occupation was as clerk in a country store at the age of fifteen, with a salary of three dollars a month. He remained in that position four years, his salary in the meantime being advanced to $100 a year. He came to Detroit in 1864, with seven dollars in money, absolutely a stranger, not knowing a soul, and took the first position offered, which happened to be in a small dry goods store on Jefferson avenue. Early in 1866 he went to work for George Peck in one of the stores, afterwards occupied by himself, where the Majestic Building now stands. Peck's was then the most aggressive dry goods house in Detroit. After being there five years on a salary Mr. Elliott was admitted to the firm and for several years had a position rather too good to throw away, but not quite good enough to keep. His ambition had always been to have a business that was absolutely his own, and in accordance with this ambition he, in 1880, started in business at 139 Woodward avenue. All that it is necessary to say is that the business was a success from the start. He has had flattering propositions to leave Detroit, but was never willing to consider them.

Mr. Elliott was always a Republican, and has been quite an active one. He cast his first vote for Grant; was one of the first members of the Michigan Club, was once its President during the days of its most useful service to the party. He has been urged to permit the use of his name as candidate for Mayor of Detroit, but has always refused, and has never been a candidate for any elective office. He was a member of the Prison Board of Jackson Prison for two years and is at present a member of the Republican National Committee.

Outside of his dry goods business Mr. Elliott is a Director and member of the Executive Committee of the Union Trust Company; director in the State Savings Bank and Preston National Bank and a trustee of Harper Hospital. He is a member of the Country Club. Detroit Club, Fellowcraft Club, Lake St. Clair Fishing and Shooting Club and the Detroit Boat Club. He was married in 1870 to Miss Helena Caverly, who died in 1871, and was married again in 1875 to Miss Susan Fidelia Hogarth, daughter of the late Dr. William Hogarth, formerly of this city, and for fifteen years Pastor of Jefferson Avenue Presbyterian Church. They have no children.

JOHN S. ESTABROOK, of Saginaw, has been in the lumber business in Michigan almost as long as any other man now living. He was born in Alden, Erie County, New York, in 1826, and came by natural training into the lumber industry, for his father, Seth Estabrook, was a farmer, merchant and lumberman, and was connected with other enterprises of his day. The mother of John S. was Hannah Alden Hebard, a lineal descendant of John Alden and Priscilla Mullen. His oldest paternal ancestor, Rev. Joseph Estabrook, was born in Enfield, Middlesex County, England, in 1640, came to America in 1660, graduated from Harvard College in 1664, and in 1667 was ordained as colleague to the celebrated pastor at Concord, Mass., Rev. Edward Bulkley. He succeeded Mr. Bulkley in the pastorate, which he retained till his death, in 1711.

The subject of this sketch received his education in the Alden Village schools, with one winter's course in a select school added in his fifteenth year. He remained at the homestead until 1844, when he took a situation in a grocery store in Buffalo. In June, 1845, he went on the schooner Cambria, of which his brother, Moses Hebard Estabrook was captain, to St. Clair, Mich., which had shared with Port Huron the name of being the largest lumber manufacturing points west of Buffalo. He worked in St. Clair County, off and on, until 1852, attending school as he could find opportunity, making one winter visit to his old home in New York State, and spending the month of October, 1849, in work on a Government coast survey of a part of the Upper Peninsula, including part of the Manistique Lake region.

In 1852 Mr. Estabrook came by accident to the locality which was to be the scene of his labors for the next half century. In June of that year he was sent to Sand Beach and the Huron Shore to ship a lot of lumber for his employer, Willard Parker. The weather was too rough to admit of landing on that shore and he was driven into Saginaw Bay and River. At Carrolltown he noticed a pile of lumber which his experienced eye showed at a glance to be of unusually high grade, which he took the risk of purchasing at what he thought a very moderate figure. He then proceeded to Saginaw and purchased 200,000 feet more of equally high grade at the same price, subject to the approval of Mr. Parker. The deal was closed out at a profit of $10,000 and Mr. Parker was so pleased with the young man's discretion that he gave him a thousand dollars out of the profit and instructed him to return to the valley and pick up some more bargains on joint account. Following these instructions he made large purchases of lumber in Saginaw and along the Cass, Flint and Shiawassee Rivers, which were tributary to the Saginaw. He paid $4, $8 and $15 per M. respectively for the different grades and before navigation opened in the spring sold out at $8, $15 and $22. With the profits of these ventures Mr. Estabrook began to invest in pine lands and to lumber on his own account. The pine lumber business has always alternated large profits with seasons of shrinkage and disaster, and Mr. Estabrook soon came upon one of the latter. In 1856 he put in several million feet of logs on the Shiawassee River, which on account of the dry seasons and low water were hung up till the summer of 1858. Meantime prices had fallen and the run resulted in a heavy financial loss. In the spring of 1858 Mr. Estabrook was given charge, by the Lee Bank of Massachusetts, of a mill property owned by the bank at St. Charles, in the Southern part of Saginaw County, and in the fall of that year he opened a general commission and inspection business, in which he established a high reputation for fair dealing and for skill in the judgment of quality and value of all lumber products. From that time to this Mr. Estabrook has been intimately associated with the interests of the valley. From 1862, for several years, he was associated with L. P. Mason in the commission and inspection business under the firm name of Estabrook & Mason. In 1871, in company with Alexander Gebhard, he purchased a saw mill at South Saginaw, rebuilt and modernized it, and entered upon the milling branch of the business, and for nearly thirty years, till its dissolution in 1899, the firm of Gebhard & Estabrook was considered one of the soundest and most reliable in the valley.

Mr. Estabrook was married in 1854 to Miss Ellen R. Burt, of Ypsilanti, who died in 1863, leaving a daughter, Winifred. In 1865 he was married to Miss Helen C. Morris, of Ypsilanti, who died April

17th, 1887, leaving two children, Justus Norris and Mary Elizabeth. In 1889 he married Miss Harriet E. Sharp, of Jackson, Mich.

Mr. Estabrook stands high in Masonry, being active in lodge, chapter and commandery. In politics he was a Democrat till the forming of the Republican party in 1854; cast his first ballot for Kinsley S. Bingham in November, 1854, and first vote for President for J. C. Fremont in 1856. He was never a seeker after office, but has been delegate to numerous Congressional and State Conventions and has held the offices of Alderman, School Inspector, Mayor, Water Commissioner, Police Commissioner, and member of the Board of Public Works, all in East Saginaw or the consolidated Saginaws. In the forty-eight years of his residence in Saginaw he has most of the time held some public office, either appointed or elected, but says he never held one that paid its own expenses. He has always been an active member of the Saginaw Board of Trade and was, for five years, its President. He represented the East Saginaw District two terms in the Legislature, where he was not much given to discussion, but was recognized by everyone as a level-headed legislator and a prudent adviser. He was especially watchful of the navigation and lumber interests of the State.

Since the firm of Gebhart & Estabrook was dissolved in the spr ng of 1899, Mr. Estabrook has not been in active business. Commencing life under adverse circumstances he has conquered obstacles which lay in his path, and in the ripeness of his old age he enjoys the love and respect of all classes of the community which he has done so much to mold, and which in no small degree exhibits in its growth and prosperity the effects of the influence of a man of brains coupled with integrity.

PROFESSOR DELOS FALL, an educator of more than State reputation, was born January 29th, 1848, in an humble farm house about a mile north of the present City limits of Ann Arbor. His father was Benjamin F. Fall, a blacksmith, and his mother Ann Bassett Fall. On his mother's side he traces his ancestry in a direct line back to the Percys of England, who with his father's ancestors were among the British soldiers who came to fight for the mother country in the War of the Revolution, but finally remained to make their home in America. His father very early stated that the greatest ambition of his life was to see his boy an educated man and a successful teacher. The boy learned his letters and his "a, b, abs" standing with other children about the feet of Mrs. Mudge, a forceful teacher and afterward the accomplished wife of the present President of the University of Wisconsin. His education was continued through the primary and grammar grades of the "lower town" school, but in 1861, the family having removed to a farm in Livingston County, for six successive winters he attended the district school, where he imbibed a sympathy for the cause of rural education which

*Prof. Delos Fall.*

has not been lost during all his subsequent career. Afterward the family removed to Ann Arbor and his education was resumed at the High School. His father died without even seeing his boy adequately prepared for college, and the same winter he engaged to teach his first country school in the district where he was born. It was a large and unruly school, having thrown successive teachers out of doors. One such attempt was made on young Fall, but the embryo teacher conquered and his reputation as an organizer and disciplinarian was established. His entrance into the University was delayed one year for the sake of better preparation, and during this year a second term was taught in Webster, Washtenaw County. At the close of his Freshman year he received the unanimous invitation from the Board of Education of Ann Arbor to take charge of the newly established science department in the High School. He was urged to remain permanently in the position, but decided to return to the University and finish his course. During the spring of his Senior year the Superintendent of the Flint Schools invited him to fill a vacancy as principal of the High School in that City. His conduct of this school for three and one-half years was most signally characterized by the fact that the number of pupils who finished the entire course and graduated was increased by nearly eight fold.

In 1878 he was elected to the chair of Natural Sciences at Albion College, where he has taught continuously since that time. In 1893 Senator James McMillan erected for him a chemical laboratory, which in size and equipment is scarcely equalled in schools of its grade in all the West, in which the most modern and advanced methods of laboratory instruction are carried on.

Through all these years of activity, Professor Fall has found time to do much for the cause of education, aside from his own college work. He has been active in the State Teachers' Association, serving one term as its President. He is at present Vice-President for Michigan of the North Central Association of Colleges and Secondary Schools and an active member of the National Educational Association. He has also had continued and emphatic success as an institute conductor, a public lecturer and a writer for various papers and magazines.

As a conductor of Teachers' Institutes there are few men in Michigan who have served for a longer time and none more acceptably. His earnestness and enthusiasm have been felt in every section of the State and his high ideals of the teachers' calling have done much to elevate the profession and to improve our common schools. In this important work and in his long years of college teaching he has touched and inspired the lives of thousands of young men and women who are now in active life.

In addition to his work as teacher Professor Fall has, as an expert chemist, paid particular attention to the manufacture of Portland cement and has aided in the formation of several large companies.

He has also been active in politics, and has had considerable experience in official life. He has always been a Republican, cast his first vote for Grant, and has been an active worker for his party both in local and National campaigns. In the heated campaign of 1896 especially, he showed marked power as a political speaker. He was a member of the State Board of Health appointed by Governor Luce in 1889 and reappointed for six years in 1895 by Governor Rich; served two years as Alderman at Albion; nine years as member of the Board of Education and four years as President of the local Board of Health. At Flint, July 25th, 1877, he married Ida Andrews. Their children are Frank A., Fellow in comparative literature, Columbia University, New York City; A. Percy, student in Albion College; Mark H.; Florence and Donald Mac, pupils in the public schools of Albion.

COLONEL FREDERICK EUGENE FARNSWORTH is the eldest son of Leander L. Farnsworth, who came to Detroit in 1836. Fred E. was born in the same City, December 2d, 1852, and was educated in the public and private schools. In 1867, at the age of fifteen, he was given an interest in the shoe business of his father, a house established in 1848, and at this time took active control, which he retained until 1883. During this time the concern was built up from a comparatively small business to the largest retail shoe trade in Detroit. Shortly after Mr. Farnsworth took hold of this business he went to the Eastern markets, and was considered the youngest shoe buyer who ever visited New England. In 1883 he retired on account of ill-health. In March of that year the Detroit Art Loan Association was organized, and Mr. Farnsworth was elected General Secretary, and devoted all his time to this enterprise as its executive officer until the business was closed up. The Detroit Museum of Art was then organized, and he is one of the forty corporators and was its first Secretary, in which position he served for two years, during the preliminary organization of that institution. In February, 1887, he was elected Secretary of the Michigan Club, which position he held for five years, and during this period the Club was prominent in all matters political pertaining to the City, State and Nation. He was again elected Secretary of the Club June 1st, 1895, holding the position until February 28th, 1898, when he resigned on account of his duties as bank cashier. Having been a close personal friend of Hazen S. Pingree, dating from the time Mr. Pingree started in business in 1866, and having had close relations with him, he was appointed to the position of City Assessor on July 1st, 1891, and was appointed for a second term by the Common Council and held the office until November 4th, 1897.

Mr. Farnsworth has been actively and closely identified with the public enterprises of the City of Detroit for many years, and among them was Secretary of one of the committees of the Army of the Potomac reunion; Secretary of the Executive Committee of the Army of the Tennessee; National Editorial Association and Michigan Press Association, when these organizations met in this City. He was Assistant Treasurer of the first meeting of the Detroit Fair and Exposition Association; was one of the Secretaries of the famous World's Peace Jubilee, held in Boston in 1872, and Secretary of the Convention held in New York City in 1887, which organized the National League of Republican Clubs. Mr. Farnsworth has been prominently identified with the Masonic fraternity, having joined Union Lodge of Strict Observance, May, 1878; is a member of Detroit Commandery, Knights Templar; Michigan Sovereign Consistory and Mystic Shrine, and has joined in many of the pilgrimages of these bodies to other States. He has also been prominently identified with the National Guard of the City and State.

His early military training was in the "Brother Jonathan Zouaves," a company of boys which existed in 1863 and 1864. He joined the Detroit Light Guard in March, 1876, was elected Second Lieutenant January 1st, 1878, and was promoted to First Lieutenant. In January, 1885, he was appointed by General I. C. Smith to be Aide-de-Camp with rank of Captain, First Brigade, Michigan State Troops. This position he held until appointed a member of the State Military Board, with rank of Colonel, in October, 1887, on the staff of Governor Cyrus G. Luce, and held for nearly four years this position, and Treasurer of the State Military Board. He was one of the active members of the Excelsior Boat Club during the life of that organization.

Mr. Farnsworth has traveled quite extensively throughout the United States, east of the Mississippi, and Canada and West Indies; in 1890 he visited Great Britain and the Continent. He was married on December 2d, 1891, to Henrietta B. Clarkson, of Jackson, Mich., and by the union has two sons, Frederick Clarkson, born October 22d, 1892, and Clarkson Lewis, born September 22d, 1896. He is very domestic in his habits, has a comfortable home at No. 70 Frederick avenue, and being interested in art matters and curios, has a fine collection of these articles picked up on his various trips. He has quite a complete library, his particular fad being scrap books, and has upwards of 100,000 clippings. He is a member of the Detroit Club, Michigan Club, and Harmonie Society, also the Knights of Pythias, as well as his Masonic affiliations. On leaving political life he was appointed Cashier of the Union National Bank January 1st, 1898 which position he now holds. He is Secretary of the Michigan Bankers' Association, Secretary of Group 7, Michigan Bankers' Association; Secretary of the Executive Committee of the Bankers' Clearing House Conference of the United States; Secretary of the Detroit Museum of Art; Secretary of the National Guard Association of the United States, and Vice-President of the Veteran Corps of the Detroit Light Guard. Mr. Farnsworth has always been a Republican. His father voted for the first Republican ticket in 1856, and the junior cast his first vote for the Republican ticket in 1874.

GEORGE ALEXANDER FARR, of Grand Haven, is among the best of the ready and eloquent speakers that have enlivened Republican Conventions and done good work for the party on the stump during the past twenty years. He was born in Niagara County, New York, July 27th, 1842, his parents being Sylvester A. Farr, a farmer, and Julia Farr. His father's ancestors came from Wales, or on the border between England and Wales, and his mother's people from Scotland. Both his father's and mother's ancestors settled in Massachusetts, the first about 1670, the latter somewhat later. His grandfather on his father's side was a surgeon in the Army of 1812, and was at Queenstown Heights. The son, George A. Farr, attended common schools till about nine years of age; entered Michigan Agricultural College in 1866 and graduated in 1870. He worked on a farm until 1861, having moved from New York in 1851 upon a farm in the Township of Whiteford, Monroe County, Mich., where he shared all the privations of that early period, hard work, want of schooling and annual ague fits. North of the house in which the family lived for nine miles there was not a clearing nor a settler.

April 17th, 1861, he enlisted in the Hardee Cadets at Adrian, Mich.; entered the First Michigan Infantry three months' men, and was in the first Battle of Bull Run; was discharged at Detroit, then enlisted in the Lancers, so called, and was mustered out with the regiment. On the 10th of April, 1862, he enlisted in the Regular Army and was assigned to Battery M, Fourth U. S. Artillery; served in this battery during the war; was in the Army of the Cumberland: participated in the battles of that army and was mustered out April 10th, 1865, as First Sergeant of the battery; returned to Blissfield, Mich.; worked on a farm and in other occupations until February, 1866, when he entered the Agricultural College. After leaving college, Mr. Farr taught school for three years, then studied law, and was admitted to the bar in Monroe, Mich., March 30th, 1873, and has also been admitted to the Circuit and Supreme Courts of the United States. He went to Ottawa County in 1873 and has practiced law there ever since.

Mr. Farr has been a Republican, as boy and man, ever since the party was organized. His first vote for President was cast for Grant in 1868. He could not vote for Lincoln, as he was at that time in the Regular Army. He attended the National Republican Convention of 1880 as a delegate and voted for James G. Blaine till the last ballot, when, with the other Michigan delegates, except Wm. G. Thompson, he voted for Garfield. He has attended nearly every Michigan Republican Convention for the past twenty years; was Permanent Chairman of the State Convention of 1888 at Detroit; was Temporary Chairman of the Judicial Convention that nominated Judge Montgomery in 1891. Mr. Farr was State Senator from 1878 to 1882, and had charge of the liquor tax and restrictive legislation in the session of 1881. He was a member of the Board of Trustees for Northern Michigan Asylum for the Insane, at Traverse City from 1885 to 1891,

MroU

*rand*

appointed by Governor Alger; was appointed Regent of the State University by Governor Rich in 1886 to fill the vacancy caused by the resignation of Charles Hackley, and still holds that office. Governor Pingree claimed that his appointment only extended to the next election and that there was a vacancy in the office of Regent, both in his case and in that of Colonel Dean, of Ann Arbor. Nominations were made by the Republicans to fill both supposed vacancies at the State Convention of 1898. The Democrats made no nominations for those offices. J. Byron Judkins and Eli R. Sutton were elected, but made no contest and did not take their seats. It was claimed that an appointment by the governor was for the full unexpired term by the provisions of the Constitution. His associates on this Board speak of Mr. Farr as an exceedingly industrious and useful member. He was appointed Collector of Customs for the District of Michigan on the 24th day of May, 1897, and still holds the office. Mr. Farr is a Director in the National Bank of Grand Haven and is an Odd Fellow, Knight Templar and member of the G. A. R. He was married at Stowe, Vt., September 24th, 1879, to Sue C. Slayton and has seven children, as follows: Frances Indiana Farr, George A. Farr, Jr., Natalia S. Farr, Millison Farr, Leslie S. Farr, Carrie E. Farr and Sue S. Farr, all girls but one. His two eldest children are now students at the University of Michigan.

JACOB SHAW FARRAND was, for more than three score years, associated with the business and religious life of Detroit, and for most of that time was interested also in its political and municipal affairs. He was the son of Bethuel and Marilla Shaw Farrand, and was born in Mentz, Cayuga County, N. Y., May 7th, 1815. In 1825 his parents moved to a farm near Ann Arbor, and when he was thirteen years old he carried the mail from that Town to Detroit on horseback. He received only a common school education, and when fifteen years old he entered the drug store of Rice & Bingham, of Detroit, as a clerk. Five years later the firm was dissolved and a new one formed, under the name of Edward Bingham & Co., with Mr. Farrand as the junior partner. In 1842 the establishment suffered the fate which is not uncommon with drug stores, that of being burned out, but Mr. Farrand started again and conducted the business as sole proprietor till 1855, when William W. Wheaton was admitted to partnership, the firm name being Farrand & Wheaton. In 1858 the name was again changed to Farrand & Sheley, the second partner being Alanson Sheley, between whom and Mr. Farrand the closest personal and business relations existed for more than thirty years. The style of the firm was subsequently changed to Farrand, Williams & Co., and later the firm of Farrand, Williams & Clark was organized and still continues. During this long period of business life, from 1835 till his death, in 1891, Mr. Farrand was eminently successful, building up a house which was among the largest in its line in the country. He also had numerous other material interests. Among other business positions which he held were those of President of the First National Bank and the Michigan Mutual Life Insurance Company of Detroit, Treasurer of the Detroit Gas Light Company, Director in the Wayne County Savings Bank, and Director of the Detroit Fire & Marine Insurance Company.

In the early days of controversy over the slavery question Mr. Farrand was in full sympathy with the opponents of the peculiar institution. His name was signed to the call for the Jackson Convention, and he was a member of the Republican party from its inception. He was very active also in municipal affairs, was Deputy Collector of the port from 1841 to 1845, President of the Board of Police Commissioners, and for many years President of the Board of Water Commissioners. He was also a Trustee of the Eastern Asylum for the Insane at Pontiac.

Mr. Farrand was as sedulous in his attention to religious duties as he was faithful in business and political life. He was a ruling Elder in the First Presbyterian Church from 1856 till his death, was three times Commissioner of the General Assemblies of the denomination, and in 1877 was a delegate to the Presbyterian Alliance held in Edinburgh, Scotland. He was a liberal giver to missionary and philanthropic work, was a Trustee of the Northwestern Theological Seminary and President of the Board of Trustees of Harper Hospital, a member of the Young Men's State Temperance Society and Secretary of the Detroit City Temperance Society. He was recognized everywhere as a man of earnest, but unassuming piety, and of sincere devotion to the good of his fellow men.

Mr. Farrand was married August 12th, 1841, to Olive M. Coe, of Hudson, Ohio. Their children were: Mary Coe, wife of Rev. James Lewis, who died in Joliet, December 3, 1889; Martha E., who died in infancy; William Reynolds, now Treasurer and Manager of the Farrand & Votey Organ Co.; Jacob S., Jr., of the firm of Farrand, Williams & Clark, and Olive Curtis, wife of Richard P. Williams, of the same firm.

DEXTER MASON FERRY, who today stands in the front ranks of Detroit's business men, and who, for the past four years has been much under the public gaze in his political relations, belongs to one of the very many Michigan families which represent, in their ancestry, the combined influences of New England and New York.

The name indicates that the family was of French origin, but the removal to America was from England, probably after generations of English residence. Its founder in the American line was Charles Ferry, who swore allegiance at Springfield, Mass., in 1678. His son, Charles Ferry, married a descendant of Richard Montague, whose family trace their lineage, through noble channels, from royal sources. Dexter Mason, maternal grandfather of the subject of this sketch, represented for several terms the District of Berkshire in the Massachusetts Legislature, and was a cousin of the late Governor George N. Briggs of that State.

The paternal grandparents of Dexter M. Ferry removed from Massachusetts to Lowville, Lewis County, N. Y., where his father Joseph N. Ferry, was born and reared. The latter married Lucy D. Mason, of Berkshire County, Massachusetts, and lived at Lowville, pursuing his trade as a wagon-maker, until his death. It was at that place, on the 8th day of August, 1833, that D. M. Ferry was born.

In 1836 his father died, and shortly after that the family removed to the Township of Penfield, in the garden of the Genesee, eight miles from Rochester. There D. M. Ferry passed his boyhood, attended the country schools, and, at the age of sixteen years, permanently assumed his own independence, engaging to work for a neighboring farmer at ten dollars a month. This he continued through two summers, attending the district schools in winter, and then, having advanced as far in his education as the teachers of the neighborhood could lead him, he found employment near Rochester, in order to attend the higher schools of that City.

In 1852 he removed to Detroit, Mich., and obtained, through the influence of his Rochester employer, a position in a wholesale and retail book and stationery house in that City, where he was first errand boy, then salesman, and at last bookkeeper.

Mr. Ferry was content to be an employe only until he had gained experience and accumulated capital sufficient to warrant an independent venture. In 1856 he deemed himself justified in making the experiment, and was one of the organizers and junior partner of the firm of M. T. Gardner & Company, seedsmen. The partnership so formed continued only until 1865, when Mr. Gardner's interest in the business was purchased, and it was continued with Mr. Ferry at its head. The style of the firm, after several minor changes, became, in 1867, D. M. Ferry & Company, and has so continued. Mr. Ferry from the day of Mr. Gardner's retirement assumed direction and control of the business, placed it upon a sound financial basis, and is today the only person connected with it who had such connection in its earliest days of struggle and doubt.

The firm of D. M. Ferry & Company was originally composed of D. M. Ferry, H. K. White, C. C. Bowen and A. E. F. White. From that time to the present year, through the existence of the establishment under the control of the firm and its later experience as a corporation, these gentlemen were constantly associated with its management, and side by side with Mr. Ferry worked for its success. The death of C. C. Bowen in the summer of 1900 was the first break in the long-continued association.

In 1879 the business had reached such dimensions that it was thought best to incorporate it under the laws of the State, and a charter for thirty years was obtained, under the official style of D. M. Ferry & Company, with a paid up capital of $750,000. The Detroit

Seed Company, a young concern, was then absorbed, and its principal owners have since been represented upon the directorate of the company. From the time of the incorporation, as before, Mr. Ferry retained a principal interest, and has been the President and General Manager of the company. This is a mere outline of the history of one of the largest and most successful seed establishments in the world, but it gives no hint of the immense labor of mind and hand required to build so splendid a structure from the small beginnings of 1856, of the ceaseless watchfulness, the tireless energy and the consummate business ability, which has enabled one person in the thirty years from boyhood to maturity, to win and hold a place of unquestioned leadership in a field closely contested by many able men. Mr. Ferry's early experience as a worker on a farm, and the familiarity which he has constantly maintained with the details of the business, are among the secrets of his success. Another important factor, and one which has vitally contributed to the advantage of the corporation, is his judgment in the selection of assistants and associates, his skill in attaching them permanently to his service, and the tact with which he excites in every one an emulous interest in the welfare of the business.

The firm of M. T. Gardner & Co., began business on a very small scale in a Monroe avenue store. Its entire sales for the first year were about six thousand dollars, and its market was confined mainly to the Western States. By way of contrast, it may be said that the sales of D. M. Ferry & Company, in a single year, have exceeded $1,-500,000. Their importations are among the heaviest in Michigan, including dealings amounting to tens of thousands of dollars annually with English, French, Dutch, German and other European concerns. In a single winter the firm has supplied more than one hundred thousand merchants with complete assortments of seeds for retailing, besides heavy sales to jobbers and dealers in bulk. More than 200,000 boxes of different sizes, some of elaborate design, have been used in filling these orders, and these boxes, when empty, represent an outlay of over $100,000. Upon an average, more than three car loads of seeds pass through the doors of the warehouse every day in the year. In its sales the company reaches almost every township in the United States, covers Canada with equal thoroughness, and has a large foreign connection and correspondence.

Mr. Ferry has invested a considerable part of his large fortune in real estate of the best class, and in various financial and manufacturing enterprises in the city. His most prominent real estate investment is the magnificent five-story iron building on Woodward avenue, which he erected in 1879, and which is occupied by the firm of Newcomb, Endicott & Co., of which he is also a special partner. This property is considered to be worth over $300,000, and the building is architecturally a model. He owns a controlling interest in the National Pin Company, which he established in 1875, and has been

D. M. Ferry

its President from the first. His principal object in founding this company was to introduce and develop a new industry in the West. Mr. Ferry is President of the First National Bank of Detroit, and of the Union Trust Company; was one of the organizers and from the outset has been a Trustee and is now Vice-President of the Wayne County Savings Bank. He is also one of the directors of the Detroit City Gas Company, and Michigan Mutual Life Insurance Company. He aided in organizing the Standard Life and Accident Insurance Company of Detroit, of which he is President. He is also President of the American Harrow Company, Vice-President of the Michigan Fire and Marine Insurance Company, and one of the Directors of the Detroit Copper & Brass Rolling Mills. He is also officially connected with the Santa Fe, Prescott & Phoenix Railway Company, the Prescott National Bank, and Phoenix National Bank of Arizona. His money and his personal countenance and aid have been freely given to every project and enterprise, social or charitable, that promises to be of public benefit, and his private charities are large, discriminating and entirely lacking in ostentation. He is one of the Trustees of Grace Hospital, Detroit, and also of Olivet College, Olivet, Mich. He has manifested much interest in the growing art movement in Detroit, and was one of the original contributors to the building fund, by which has been insured to the City as a permanent institution, the Detroit Museum of Art, of which he is also one of the Trustees.

Mr. Ferry was reared a Baptist, and early united with that church. In later years, however, he became associated with Congregationalists, and is now one of the Trustees of the Woodward Avenue Congregational Church of Detroit.

He married, October 1st, 1867, Miss Addie E. Miller, of Unadilla, Otsego County, N. Y. Mr. and Mrs. Ferry have one son and two daughters living—Dexter M. Ferry, Jr., and Misses Blanche and Queene Ferry.

Politically, Mr. Ferry is known as a loyal supporter of the Republican party, and a staunch believer in its principles. He has been a Republican since the organization of the party, and cast his first Presidential vote for John C. Fremont in 1856. He was a Delegate-at-Large from Michigan to the Republican National Convention held at Minneapolis, Minn., in 1892. He has also at times served the people and party well in positions of trust to which he has been called, but has rarely been a candidate for an elective office, and has held public positions only when they have come to him unsolicited. In 1877 and 1878 he was a member of Detroit's Board of Estimators from the First Ward. In 1884 and 1885 he was one of the Commissioners of Parks and Boulevards. He also advanced the interests of the party by services rendered as Chairman of the Republican State Central Committee of Michigan from 1896 to 1898, including the memorable Presidential campaign of 1896. In 1900, at the request of his friends, he consented to become a candidate for the

Republican nomination to the Governorship of Michigan, and at the Grand Rapids Convention, held in June of that year, after leading in the race among the six candidates who contested for that nomination, he was defeated on the nineteenth ballot.

While domestic in his tastes, and inclined to prefer, in his leisure hours, home pursuits and pleasures rather than club life, yet Mr. Ferry encourages many of the leading clubs and societies of Detroit, and is a sustaining member of the Michigan Club, Detroit Club, Fellowcraft Club, Detroit Fishing and Hunting Association (Rushmere), Country Club, Detroit Golf Club, Detroit Light Guard and Detroit Grays.

Mr. Ferry is a man to whom the most envious can scarcely grudge success, so well has he earned it, so well does he use it, so entirely does he lack pride of purse. He is kind, unaffected, approachable, unspoiled. Every comer has a claim upon his courteous attention, and the irascibility so common among busy men is entirely foreign to his character. His history, like of that of thousands of others who have begun life poor, and by industry, energy and economy, risen to places of trust and honor, proves conclusively how false is the view now advanced by so many "agitators" and demagogues, that there is a natural and impassible barrier between labor and capital.

THOMAS WHITE FERRY, for many years one of the most prominent men in public life in the country, was one of the comparatively few Michigan men of his generation who were natives to the State which they served. His father, William Montague Ferry, was of a family originating in France, then living several generations in England, and emigrating to New England in the Seventeenth Century. He graduated at Union College in 1817, completed a theological course in 1821, and then went as missionary of the Presbyterian Church to the Island of Mackinac, in Lake Huron. Here Thomas W. was born, June 1st, 1826, his mother being Amanda White Ferry. His father remained at Mackinac in missionary work, largely among the Indians, for twelve years, when his health failing, he moved to the Western coast of Michigan, established, with others, a settlement at Grand Haven, and soon afterwards commenced a lumber business that laid the foundations of a very comfortable fortune.

The son, Thomas W. Ferry, had a common school education, and when quite young commenced business pursuits. He was clerk for two years in a store at Elgin, Ill., and then returned to Grand Haven, where he was employed by his father and his brothers in the firm of Ferry & Sons, lumber manufacturers and dealers. After the death of his father, in 1867, the business was conducted mainly by his two brothers, William W. and Edward P. Ferry, though he still retained an interest in it.

Mr. Ferry had a natural aptitude for politics and public life, and this found opportunity for its manifestation when he was quite young. The same year that he became a voter he was elected County Clerk, and two years later represented his District in the State Legislature. Originally a Whig, he went heartily into the movement for the organization of the Republican party, and was elected as a Republican to the State Senate in 1856. In both House and Senate he served on important committees, and his quickness of perception and readiness in debate soon gave him a leading position. For eight years, about this time, he was a member of the Republican State Central Committee, besides serving on local committees and attending numerous local and State Conventions. In 1860 he was Delegate-at-Large and one of the Vice-Presidents at the National Convention at Chicago which nominated Lincoln and Hamlin. In 1863 he was appointed Commissioner for Michigan of the Soldiers' National Cemetery at Gettysburg, and the next year he was elected to the Thirty-ninth Congress from a district which was giving, in those days, the largest Republican majority of any district in the State.

Mr. Ferry's election to Congress put him in the way to National distinction, and his services were so satisfactory that he was thrice re-elected, his majority on one occasion approaching 10,000. His first committee memberships were on the Committee on Postoffices and Post Roads, in which he was useful to the State in securing increased postal facilities; the Committee on the State Militia and that on the war debts of the United States. He commenced, where new members have the best opportunity to gain favor with the older ones, with industrious committee work, and was soon advanced to more important positions, including the Committee on Finance. His district had a long stretch of coast line, as did other districts in the State, and he was a valuable aid in the House, to the work which Zachariah Chandler was doing in the Senate, to secure the improvement of rivers and harbors, not only in their own State, but on the other Great Lakes and connecting rivers.

Mr. Ferry's efficient service in the House, and especially his close attention to the needs of his own district, gave him a strong support for higher honors. In 1871, after a sharp contest, in which he was supported by delegations from Western Michigan of which any man might be proud, he was elected to the United States Senate, and was re-elected without opposition in 1877. Among his first appointments in the Senate was that of Chairman of the Committee on the Revision of the Rules, a position for which his long legislative experience and knowledge of parliamentary law peculiarly fitted him. The rules then adopted, in accordance with his revision, are still in force in the Senate. He was afterwards repeatedly elected President pro tem. of that body. Upon the death of Vice President Wilson, in November, 1873, he was chosen acting Vice-President of the United States, and held the office with dignity and ability throughout the stormy period of the Hayes-Tilden Electoral contest, gaining great reputation as a tactician and practical parliamentarian. In the absence of President Grant he further discharged the duties of his temporary office by formally opening the Centennial Exposition at Philadelphia, July 4th, 1876. Grant's term expiring on Sunday, March 4th, at noon, and Hayes being inaugurated on March 5th, at noon, he was President of the United States for the twenty-four hours intervening. He was a candidate for a third term in the Senate in 1883, but met with a strenuous opposition which culminated in his defeat. In the excitement of this campaign his business interests in the firm of Ferry Bros., lumbermen and proprietors of the Ottawa Iron Works at Ferrysburg suffered so greatly that the hitherto prosperous concern was placed in the hands of a trustee. After this double calamity, Senator Ferry spent three years in travel through Europe, Egypt and the Holy Land, and upon his return resumed business. Although he never recovered his former prosperity, he continued to be prominent in local and State affairs. By appointment of Governor Rich he became President of the Mackinac Park Commission, and it was largely through his efforts in Congress that the most attractive portion of that island was preserved for the use of the public.

Almost from the beginning of his public career to the end, Senator Ferry took part as a speaker, in political campaigns, and his ready and convincing speech was heard, at one time or another, in almost every County in the State. Among his special characteristics were untiring industry and a never faltering loyalty to his friends and his party. He was of fine presence, and of genial manner. He was in religious faith, a Presbyterian, and a consistent adherent to its standards. He was never married, and resided with his aunt, Mary A. White, until his death at Grand Haven, Michigan, October 14th, 1896.

HENRY OTIS FIFIELD is one of the Michigan editors who have been intimately associated with Republican politics for many years. He was born at Corinna, Maine, August 7th, 1841, his father being Samuel S. Fifield, a merchant, and his mother Naomi Pease Fifield. Samuel S. Fifield was born in Goffstown, New Hampshire, and emigrated to Maine with his father in 1801, settling in Garland, Penobscot County. At an early manhood he engaged in the mercantile business at Corinna, where he married Miss Naomi Pease, daughter of Albana Pease, a prominent citizen and farmer. The Fifields were originally from England, as were also the Peases.

Henry Otis Fifield was educated partly in the schools of Prescott, Wisconsin, where he lived from 1856 to 1861, but most of his education has been obtained in the printing office. He entered a printing office at Prescott, Wisconsin, in 1858, and upon the outbreak of the civil war, was the first man in the city to enlist, joining the First Minnesota Infantry, April 29th, 1861. He served three years and six days in that regiment, participating in all the important battles from first Bull Run to Gettysburg, where the "Old First" immortalized itself. On the second of July, 1863, it stopped the advance of Barks-

H. O. Fifield

MENOMINEE HERALD.

DETROIT JOURNAL.

dale and Wilcox' brigades, that were following up the defeated Third Corps under Sickles, and out of the 262 men who charged the enemy's lines, only forty-seven reported for duty after the fight. Seventy-five were dead and the balance wounded. Every man was accounted for and there was not a skulker in the command. The loss in this charge was eighty-three per cent., the largest recorded in history. After returning from the war Mr. Fifield resumed the printing business in which he has always worked hard, and in which he has prospered in a moderate degree. In 1869 he and Sam S. Fifield, an older brother, began the publication of the Bayfield, Wisconsin, Press, with H. O. Fifield editor. After two years he removed the Press to Ashland, where it is still published. It was the first paper there and he set the first type and printed the first issue on a hand press in June, 1871. After four years' connection with the Press he sold to Sam S. Fifield, who continued its publication for a dozen years, when he sold it to its present proprietor, Joe M. Chapple. Mr. Fifield's early experience in the print shop would fill a large volume. He had a hard struggle, but succeeded finally in making a paying business out of his present paper, "The Menominee Herald."

Mr. Fifield has been a Republican since the party had its birth, voted for Abraham Lincoln for his second term, and has ever since been faithful to the party of protection and prosperity. He has attended numerous State Conventions as a delegate during the past sixteen years and has always been active in political matters, but has never held a political office. He is a member of the Michigan Club and all Masonic bodies from Blue Lodge to Commandery. He is a Shriner and belongs to the Maccabees, A. O. U. W. and National Union. He was married to Emma L. Walker at Osceola Mills, Wis., in 1866, and had one son, Henry Dana, who died in 1897 at the age of 29 years.

ALBERT HENRY FINN, who has been conspicuous in Michigan newspaper circles for nearly twenty years, was born in St. Clair, Mich., June 15th, 1862. His father was Rev. Silas Finn, one of the pioneer Baptist ministers of the State, and his mother was Cynthia Eaton. On his father's side, two ancestors, James Finn and James Wells, saw service in the Revolutionary War, and both families have been prominent in the Wyoming Valley for over a century. The ancestors on the Finn side came from Ireland and the Wells family were Welch. His mother was descended from the Dedham, Mass., Eatons, from whom also came General William Eaton, the late professor D. C. Eaton, of Yale, and brilliant men of the pulpit and bar.

Albert H. Finn had a common school education, supplemented with a short period of study at Kalamazoo College. At the age of thirteen he became clerk in his brother's store. From early childhood he had a strong penchant for printing, and had dreams of doing newspaper work, and even owning a newspaper of his own when he should come to man's estate. This idea took a firm hold upon him and from that day his energies have been bent upon realizing it. His country store experience was simply a means to that end, as the little amateur printing outfit which he bought when yet a small boy, continued to grow into a complete job printing office.

At seventeen, as associate of J. E. Soults, he started the Royal Oak Midget, a three-column four-page weekly paper. This was continued for four or five months, when a larger field was sought, and the Capac Argus was started as a five column four-page paper. With this as a starting point young Finn soon became one of the best known newspaper men in the Seventh Congressional District. He was always ready to take hold of a new enterprise or to let go of an old one when he could do so to advantage. His newspaper connections for the next few years included part ownership and editorship of the Fort Gratiot Sun, in which he conducted a successful fight against a gang of toughs who infested the border; a position on the Port Huron Times; one on the Michigan Christian Herald at Detroit, and finally the ownership and editorship of the Port Huron Tribune, which he successfully published for eight years. Upon the consolidation of the latter with the Commercial he accepted the editorship of the Patron's Guide, the organ of the then flourishing order of the Patrons of Industry. This paper grew to have a circulation under his direction of over 75,000 copies. Later its publisher started another paper for general circulation—The Farm and Home—which Mr. Finn also edited with ability. In addition to this work he was appointed Manager of the Port Huron Fair and Exposition, which proved a great success, being the largest and best exhibition in Eastern Michigan. In the summer of 1890 Mr. Finn accepted the advertising management of the Detroit Journal. For over ten years now he has given his best efforts to The Journal. First as Advertising Manager, then Business Manager, afterward Manager of Foreign Advertising, and since December, 1895, as Assistant Manager.

Mr. Finn has been a Republican from early boyhood. Old citizens recall how in the old Greenback campaign that Finn, then but a mere boy, was conspicuous at town meetings and during campaigns, earnest in his advocacy of honest money and the success of the Republican party. He has attended scores of conventions, but generally in his capacity of a newspaper man.

He is a member of the Sons of the American Revolution, Palestine Lodge, F. & A. M.; the Fellowcraft Club, the Republican Press Association, Y. M. C. A., and is a trustee of the North Baptist church. Mr. Finn was married to Katherine Scott, in Detroit, June 30th, 1886, and has four children, Juliette Irene, aged 12 years; Eaton Scott, aged 9; James Crampton, aged 3, and Silas Munger, an infant.

CHARLES FLOWERS, who has been conspicuous in public affairs in Detroit for some years past, is the son of Joseph Flowers, a farmer, and Sarah Pickering Flowers, and was born December 14th, 1845, in Bucks County, Pennsylvania. His father was descended from English and Dutch families; on the Dutch side from the Van Horn family. His mother was English, from the Quimby and Pickering families, the latter descendants of General Timothy Pickering, of Revolutionary fame, and Secretary of State under Washington. Both parents were Quakers.

Charles Flowers' education commenced in the common schools of Bucks County, Pennsylvania, and was continued in academy, and in Fort Edward Collegiate Institute, N. Y. His first occupation was farming. He then studied shorthand and took the position of stenographer in the office of the Grand Trunk Railway in New York. At the close of the war he was engaged by the United States Government to report the proceedings of a military commission, at Raleigh, N. C. He studied law in New York City for one year, 1867, then came to Detroit in April, 1868; drew the Act for the appointment of a stenographer for the Wayne Circuit Court, which was passed in 1869, and the same year was appointed first official stenographer in Michigan by Governor Baldwin and held the position until 1881. He was one of the official stenographers of the Illinois Constitutional Convention in 1869; of the Pennsylvania Constitutional Convention in 1872, and the Ohio Constitutional Convention in 1873. While actively engaged in this work Mr. Flowers had the reputation of being the fastest and most accurate stenographer in the United States, and his services were in great demand.

At intervals during his stenographic practice Mr. Flowers continued the study of law, and was admitted to the bar in 1879. He was elected Circuit Court Commissioner in 1880, re-elected in 1882 and was Corporation Counsel of Detroit from July, 1886, to July, 1900.

In politics Mr. Flowers has always been a Republican, casting his first vote for Grant. He has frequently been a delegate to local Conventions, and was delegate to the Conventions of 1894, 1896, 1898 and 1899; placed Governor Pingree in nomination for his third and fourth terms as Mayor and as Governor for both terms. His Convention oratory is of the most polished and ornate character, and is always listened to with pleasure, even by those who do not favor the candidate whose claims he advocates.

Mr. Flowers is interested in the Detroit and New State Telephone Companies, and is a member of the Michigan Club and the Harmonie Societies. He was married June 30th, 1868, to Mary E. DeNormandie, and has three children, Norman, Mary and Herbert.

HON. JOSEPH W. FORDNEY is the product of an American farm. Born November 5th, 1853, in Blackford County, Indiana, upon the farm of his father, John Fordney, he passed through that rigorous and most excellent training that comes only to the farmer's boy.

The stock from which he came was of revolutionary fame, as Grandfather Fordney came from Alsace-Lorraine, on the River Rhine, during the years of the patriot struggle for freedom and fought with Lafayette in the war which brought the present American nation into birth. When the war was over Grandfather Fordney settled in Lancaster County, Pennsylvania, and there married a daughter of France, who had somewhat earlier settled in Pennsylvania. There the father of Joseph W. Fordney was born. There was a queer admixture in the ancestral antecedents of Congressman Fordney His grandfather from Alsace-Lorraine, his grandmother, whose maiden name was Cotton, was of English-Irish extraction.

Joseph W. Fordney obtained his early education in the common schools of Indiana working between the terms on his father's farm. When sixteen years old his parents moved from Indiana to Saginaw and in June, 1869, young Joe Fordney became an inhabitant of Michigan. When he started to shift for himself he found employment in the then plentifully wooded district around Saginaw Bay. This avocation he followed, growing in occupation from workman to land-looker, until 1872, when his proficiency became so well known that he was given more important positions and for the next ten years was sent out to estimate the value on timber land. Then he became associated with the late Wilhelm Boeing, of Detroit, and shortly became a partner with him in the ownership of pine land. In this he continued until 1890, when the partnership was dissolved by the death of Mr. Boeing. Then he organized the firm of Ring, Merrill & Fordney and continued in the firm two years in the lumber business. At the conclusion of the second year he organized a new firm under the name of Merrill, Ring & Company, which operated in Michigan and at Byng Inlet, Canada, for two years. He sold out his interest in the firm to his partners in 1894, since which time he has been engaged principally in lumbering and dealing in pine lands on his own account.

His political career began in the spring of 1894, when he was elected a member of the Common Council of Saginaw. His work in that body was such that he was re-elected in 1896 and he carried out many important reforms in the City of Saginaw. His fellow citizens, appreciating his worth, nominated him for many positions and on every nomination he achieved a greater success than had previously attended his appearance in the political arena. He was nominated for Congress in 1898 against a Democratic candidate supposed to be invincible, but his personal popularity and his record of public service were such that he not only defeated his Democratic opponent but was given a very substantial majority. In minor political affairs he has been equally successful. He has represented his district in several State Conventions, has never been anything but a Republican and when his opportunity came to cast his first presidential vote he gave it to Rutherford B. Hayes, of Ohio.

His business interests outside of lumbering, have been many, and at the end of the Nineteenth Century he not only held his lumber

J. W. Fordney

interests, but also was an active partner in the firm of Charles H. Davis, of Saginaw, in the Chappell & Fordney Coal Company, of Saginaw, and a silent partner in an artificial ice manufacturing company at Hartford City, Indiana. His social affiliations have been many, as he is a member of the Saginaw Club, the B. P. O. E., the Maccabees and the Michigan Royal Arcanum.

Mr. Fordney filled an unique position in the Fifty-sixth Congress. As a new member he won his way into the affections of his fellow Republicans by his inexhaustible fund of good humor, good stories and good fellowship. There never was a time that Congressman Fordney was not a most welcome member of any Congressional group. He did not appear as a public speaker in the House until that rabid anti-pension member, Jasper Talbert, attacked the integrity of the old soldiers. Blazing with indignation and furious in anger against the attacks of the ex-Rebel, he took the floor, and in a five-minute speech not only electrified the House but completely annihilated the Union soldier hater, Talbert. After that he was a marked man on the Republican side of the chamber and ex-Rebel Talbert was very chary of crossing swords with the member from the Eighth Michigan. His committee work was even more important than his defense of the soldiers, as he formed the combination by which he allied Stevens, of Minnesota; Miner, of Wisconsin, and Jones, of Washington, against the Payne-Hanna Subsidy Bill, and defeated that veteran soldier-statesman, General Grosvenor, the chairman of the Committee. Congressman Fordney's other work as a member of the Fifty-sixth Congress raised him far above the ordinary level of first termers. In November, 1900, he was re-elected to Congress by 4,209 majority.

In his private life he has been most happy. He was married in Saginaw, Michigan, in 1873, to Catherine Harren, whose parents were both of Irish extraction. Of that union came nine children—Bregetta, Josephine, Ernest, Agnes, Joseph, Chester, Mary, Grace and Theodota. Being a devoted family man he takes more pleasure in an evening devoted to his wife and little ones than in celebrating the greatest political victory he ever won.

ALLAN HOWARD FRAZER, who has had the most brilliant and useful career of any of Wayne County's prosecuting officers, and some of the others have been excellent public servants, is the son of Thomas and Cecilia C. Frazer, and was born in Detroit, January 26th, 1859. His father, whose occupation was that of civil engineer, is still living at the age of eighty-six. His parents were both Scotch-Irish.

Allan H. Frazer was educated at the Detroit Public Schools, including the High School, and afterwards graduated from the Literary Department of Michigan University in 1881, with the degree of Ph. B. He was admitted to the bar in 1882, and from 1884 to 1900 practiced law by himself. In the latter year he joined with two others in the law firm of Foster, Frazer & Aldrich. He was Assistant Prosecuting Attorney in 1889 and 1890. In 1892 he was elected Prosecuting Attorney and was thrice re-elected, leading the county ticket each of the four times that he ran. His nomination for the fifth time by the County Convention in October, 1900, was considered a certainty, until he positively withdrew, in order to devote his whole attention to law practice.

In politics Mr. Frazer was always a Republican, casting his first Presidential vote for Garfield in 1880. He was the youngest delegate in the State Convention of 1884, which nominated General Alger for Governor, and was President of the Alger Club in 1888. He is a Mason, Odd Fellow, and a Fellowcrafter and a Knight of Khorassan and Pythian, and is a member of the Harmonie Society, St. Andrew's Society, the Michigan Club and the Detroit Boat Club. He was married December 9th, 1890, to Jennie Palmer, of Detroit, and has one son.

The first year of Mr. Frazer's incumbency of the office of Prosecuting Attorney showed that its duties had fallen into the hands of a man of determination, energy and impartiality. When he entered upon the duties of his office in January, 1893, the docket was flooded with criminal cases in various stages of delay. There were 566 cases in the Recorder's Court for the Prosecutor to dispose of. Besides handling the current business of the office, Prosecutor Frazer in less than two years reduced the number of cases of the docket to 200. He made it a rule upon entering the office that law only should govern, and that no man or set of men should rule. After two years the police reported that the city was freer from crime than ever before. He had sent eight murderers to prison, and there was then no person in jail awaiting trial for murder. The expose of the pilfering of some of the County Justices should be mentioned. The expose had hardly been made when Prosecutor Frazer began a rigid investigation. Justice after Justice was called into his office, directed to fetch his books and accounts and compelled to go over them, showing up case after case where unemployed workingmen had been sent to the House of Correction without trial or without a charge being brought against them, while the Justices pocketed fees from the County. The workingmen, many of them were unknown and friendless. Within a week Prosecutor Frazer secured their release from unjust imprisonment. The lax methods in keeping accounts in the various offices of the Justices were laid bare to the County officers through Prosecutor Frazer. Week after week the investigation continued, culminating in the Prosecutor preferring charges against Justice McCoy to the Governor, forcing his dismissal from office. The Prosecutor also forced Justice Riopelle to resign. The system of justices' accounts has been overhauled. There are no more fees on trumped-up charges, and the saving from this source alone to the County through Prosecuting Attorney Frazer has been large.

Within two years after coming into office Mr. Frazer had broken up the notorious Considine gang of criminals, who, for fifteen years had been operating in Detroit, defying the officers of the law, when arrested getting out on straw bail, or by some other device escaping punishment. Mr. Frazer in spite of powerful influences against him, and threats upon his life, succeeded in breaking up the gang, and sending their leader to State Prison. Mr. Frazer also broke up the boodle ring in the Board of Education and sent one of the members to the penitentiary, while another attempted suicide and a third fled the country. He also enforced the law vigorously against the saloon keepers, in respect to whom great favoritism had before his time been shown. In one year he diminished the number of saloons in the County by 150, and at the same time the receipts from liquor taxes were $108,000 more than in the first year of his predecessor's administration. He also rendered a service to the community by showing that the saloon interest is not all-powerful at the polls. The second time he was a candidate that element was bitterly opposed to him, yet he led the County ticket in the number of votes received, giving a wholesome lesson to candidates who, before that, had allowed their fears of this class to overcome their desire to enforce the laws.

HON. ROBERT EMMETT FRAZER, Circuit Judge in Wayne County, was the son of Thomas and Sarah Wells Frazer, and was born in Adrian, Michigan, October 2d. 1840. He is of Scotch-Irish ancestry, descended from Andrew Frazer, who removed from Scotland to Ireland about 1730 and settled in County Down. Thomas Frazer was born in that country in 1814, was a civil engineer by profession, and served seven years with the Royal Engineers in the survey of Ireland. In 1835 he was married to Sarah Wells, and in 1837 came to this country, and located in Monroe, Michigan. He subsequently removed to Adrian, then to Galesburg and finally to Detroit.

Robert E. Frazer was educated in the boarding school of Rev. Moses H. Hunter, where he was placed shortly after the death of his mother in 1849, and in Gregory's Select School at Detroit, where he remained until he entered the University of Michigan in 1855. He graduated from the Literary Department of that institution at the age of eighteen. In the fall of 1859 he entered the Law Department of the University, and graduated with the degree of B. A. in March, 1861, his case presenting the unusual feature of one not yet having attained his majority holding two degrees from a recognized University. Subsequent to the completion of his education he began the practice of his profession at Ann Arbor, where he remained until he removed to Jackson, Michigan, in August, 1882. While in Ann Arbor he was associated with Daniel S. Twitchell, the firm being Twitchell & Frazer; then with Judge Edwin Lawrence, as Lawrence & Frazer;

then with Judge Harriman and A. W. Hamilton, as the firm of Frazer, Harriman & Hamilton. On his removal to Jackson he formed with Mr. A. E. Hewitt the firm of Frazer & Hewitt, a copartnership which existed until his removal to Detroit in May, 1885. Shortly after his arrival in Detroit he became associated with Levi L. Barbour and Dwight Rexford, they forming the firm of Frazer, Barbour & Rexford, among the most prominent law firms of the city.

In April, 1893, he was nominated for the position of Circuit Judge, but was defeated by twenty-four votes. June 5th, 1893, he was appointed, by Governor Rich, Judge of the Circuit Court of Wayne County, in conformity with an act of the Legislature passed the preceding winter, giving a fifth Judge to the County. In 1894 he was again nominated and elected by a plurality of 10,091, the highest number of votes received by any candidate at that election. In April, 1899, he was re-elected. At the time of his appointment by Governor Rich, Judge Frazer found that the business of the Court, owing to lack of a proper system of assignment among the different Judges, was accumulating beyond their power of disposition and he originated the system now in use. It has been so thoroughly successful as to cause its permanent adoption, and it has been highly commended by members of the bar throughout the country.

Possibly the most important case in which Judge Frazer has been retained as counsel was in the defense of Daniel Holcomb at Jackson, Michigan, in 1884; the case was known throughout the country as the Crouch murder trial, in which he secured the acquittal of the prisoner. Up to the time of the nomination of General Garfield for the Presidency Judge Frazer was a Democrat, but since that date he has affiliated with the Republican party. In 1864 he was appointed the City Attorney of Ann Arbor for a term of one year, and was twice reappointed. In 1865 he was elected Circuit Court Commissioner of Washtenaw County for a term of two years; in 1867 he became Prosecuting Attorney of that County, being re-elected for the terms beginning in 1869 and 1874. In 1880 he was elected a delegate to the National Republican Convention, and in a masterly and eloquent manner presented the qualities of his friend and placed in nomination for the Presidency, General Russell A. Alger. August 3d, 1863, he married Abbie M. Saunders, daughter of Thorndyke P. Saunders, of Ann Arbor, Mich., and they had three children: Carrie W., wife of Walter W. Ruan, of Chicago; Frances A. and William Robert.

GEORGE EDWARD FROST, a successful attorney at Cheboygan, was born March 24th, 1851, at Pontiac, Mich. His father's name was Alonzo P. Frost, whose principal occupation was farming, but in his earlier days he learned the trade of harnessmaking and also did something in the mercantile line. His father was born in Marcellus, Onondaga County, New York, came to Michigan in 1836, and in 1838 married Nelly Voorheis, then of Bloomfield near Pontiac. His ances-

Geo. E. Frost.

tors were among the early comers from Great Britain and afterwards settled in Massachusetts. Several of them took an active part in the War of the Revolution. A. P. Frost died February 21st, 1898, at Cheboygan, Mich., where his widow is still living. She was born at Fayette, Seneca Co., New York, March 3d, 1819, and came to Michigan with her parents when a girl. On her mother's side she is one of the 80,000 heirs to the celebrated Anneke Jans estate and so possesses rich Holland blood.

George Edward Frost was educated in the public schools of Pontiac. His first occupation was assisting in the farm work. He was called upon to do as so many farmer boys have done, attend school in winter and work a farm in summer. The farm was small and the family large, and his time was often taken up in hiring out to neighbors. He commenced handling a plow when twelve years old. In the fall and winter of 1872 he taught a district school and boarded around. The following summer he entered the law office of Judge A. C. Baldwin, where he remained two summers, teaching schools winters. He entered the office of Alfred Russell, of Detroit, in August, 1874, was admitted to the bar in 1875, and for the next four years had an office in Detroit, his principal business being collecting. He thought it advisable to seek a newer field and in May, 1879, went to Cheboygan, Mich., where he has built up a very successful business, ranking among the leading lawyers in the North country. He is annually retained as attorney for the Pfister Vogel Leather Co. of Milwaukee; the Cheboygan River Boom Co.; First National Bank; Thompson Smith's Sons; Pelton & Reid, and Swift & Clark, the last three named being large lumber manufacturers. He is also retained annually by several smaller institutions, and is proprietor of the Central dry goods store in Cheboygan. He is also interested in City property and in wild lands, and owns three good farms near Cheboygan.

In politics Mr. Frost has always been a Republican and a working one. He cast his first vote for Grant in 1872. He has been delegate to several State Conventions, and was alternate delegate to the National Convention at Minneapolis in 1892. The first time he voted he entered upon the work of trying to get votes for the ticket, and has done the same ever since. When he went to Cheboygan the County was strongly Democratic and the Republicans seldom had a party ticket in the field. He at once advocated putting up one every time, and making the best showing possible and from that time it was done. To-day the City and County are Republican. His first political speech was made in 1880, when with others, he stumped the County for Garfield and the Republican ticket generally.

Mr. Frost was elected Circuit Court Commissioner in 1880 and 1882. In 1881 he was appointed United States Commissioner for Eastern Michigan, a position which he still holds. In 1883, and for two terms after that, he was elected President of the Village of Cheboygan, although it was considered a strong Democratic Village. He was elected Prosecuting Attorney in 1884, 1888 and 1898 and has several times been tendered the nomination for Representative or Senator in the State Legislature, but has declined for business reasons.

Mr. Frost is a member of the First Congregational Church and has been Chairman of its Board of Trustees for several years. He is a member of the Blue Lodge, Chapter and Council in the Masonic order, a K. of P. and an Elk. He was first married to Mollie L. Bailey, daughter of John R. Bailey, of Mackinac Island, September 22d, 1881. She died with that dreaded disease, consumption, November 14th, 1882. On April 30th, 1885, he married Mrs. Emma C. Freeman, of Middleport, N. Y., daughter of John H. Waterman, then of Cheboygan. They have three sons, George Edward, Jr., Stanley Howard and Russell Waterman.

OTIS FULLER, a well known newspaper publisher, and also somewhat familiar to the public in official life, was born at Elba, Genesee County, N. Y., July 14th, 1853. The ancestors of his father, who was named James Fuller, a farmer, were English, and those of his mother were Scotch-Irish. Both branches settled in New England about 1640. The son attended district school until ten years old, and then Fuller Academy, near Mason, Ingham County. He went to school and worked on the farm until he was nineteen, and meanwhile earned his first $500 by bee-keeping. He taught school winters, grafting fruit trees in the spring and working on farm summers, until he was twenty-three. He purchased the Ingham County News at Mason in 1876; sold it in 1880; purchased the St. Johns Republican; sold that paper in 1889, and was engaged in the United States Internal Revenue Service from 1889 to 1894. In the latter year he was appointed Warden of the State House of Correction and Reformatory, a position which he still holds. His first political office was that of Township Superintendent of the Vevay and Mason City schools, to which he was elected at the age of 21, and was soon after elected Secretary of the County Association of Superintendents, compiling the questions for teachers' examinations for Ingham County. He was nominated for State Senator from the Ingham and Clinton District in 1884, on the Republican ticket, but defeated by a fusion of the Democratic and Greenback parties. His war record consists of "making war on the Democrats and Greenbackers while editing a Republican newspaper." He was elected delegate to the first State Convention after he became a voter, and was elected a delegate to nearly all of the Republican State and Congressional Conventions for twenty years thereafter. He cast his first Presidential ballot for Hayes, and never voted anything but a Republican ticket. He was a member of the Sixth District Republican Congressional Committee for ten years, was Chairman of the Committee several years and a member of the Republican State Central Committee from 1888 to

1890. In September, 1900, he was elected President of the National Warden's Association.

Mr. Fuller is President of the Pulaski Heights Land Co., of Little Rock, Ark., and of the Michigan Lumber Co. of Arkansas. He has never been married and so has time to attend to his duties as a member of the Town Club, Ionia, and St. Johns Commandery No. 24, K. T., of the latter place.

DEWITT CLINTON GAGE, for over thirty years a leading attorney and citizen of the Saginaw Valley, was born at Bellona, Yates County, New York, August 28th, 1820. His remote ancestors were from England, but several generations of them lived in New England. His father, Martin Gage, was born in Massachusetts, while his mother was the daughter of Nathan Rockwell, of Catskill, New York. His father, in addition to cultivating a farm, conducted a general store and the spare time of DeWitt was spent in farm work and in making himself useful at his father's store. His winters he devoted to acquiring an education in the district school, and supplemented the instruction there received by a year's study in the academy at Lima. He was now nineteen years of age and the oldest child among seven brothers and one sister. His father died a year later and the responsibility of caring for and closing up the decedent's estate fell largely on his shoulders. His father had been quite prosperous in business, and aside from his store had made considerable investments in farming lands. The duties thus unexpectedly thrown upon him were carefully and successfully attended to, and after handling his trust for about four years the estate was settled and divided among the heirs. The portion of the property received by DeWitt embraced a farm at Italy Hill, Yates County, New York. He married in 1844, Catherine A., daughter of Judge James Glover, of Auburn, New York, and settled on his farm at Italy Hill, where he remained for two years, leaving it then and removing to Gorham, Ontario County. Here he associated himself with his brother-in-law, Stephen M. Whittaker, in a general merchandise business, bringing to it the experience he had acquired in his father's store. Although success rewarded his efforts in his business pursuits, neither the life of a farmer nor that of a merchant was congenial to his nature, and after remaining with Mr. Whittaker for three years, he withdrew from the firm and determined to make the practice of law his life work. The late Judge Folger, a lawyer of eminence and keen judgment, received him into his office as a student and directed his studies, discerning in him those qualities that were destined to bring him honor and substantial success in after life. At the age of thirty-one he was admitted to the bar, and for the next three years was associated with Judge Folger in the general practice of law.

He had for some time displayed military tastes, and it was while with Mr. Folger that these came to the attention of Governor William

H. Seward and he appointed Mr. Gage Colonel of a militia regiment, giving him a title that clung to him through life. Although enjoying a marked success in his profession at Geneva, and among the most successful of its legal fraternity, a feeling of unrest or a desire to enter larger fields of usefulness, presenting opportunities for greater advancement, induced him to make a journey westward. He visited many points, particularly in Iowa, Illinois and Michigan, and was especially impressed by the possibilities of development in the Saginaw Valley. He, therefore, closed up his affairs in New York State, and in 1855 commenced the practice of law in East Saginaw. His forecast of the growth of the Saginaw Valley was not wide of the mark, for he lived to see that section of the State increase many fold in population and wealth. In that development he aided, and from it derived a share of the personal benefits. He soon built up a large practice, and invested his earnings with such good judgment as to lay the foundation of an ample fortune.

Col. Gage was active in Republican politics and in public affairs, as well as in law and business, and filled a number of positions of trust. He was Private Secretary to Governor Bingham, during his second term, 1857 to 1859. He was Postmaster of East Saginaw by appointment of President Lincoln, and in 1880, Governor Croswell appointed him Judge of the Saginaw Circuit, to fill the vacancy caused by the resignation of Judge William S. Tennant. He accepted this position with some misgivings, feeling that his method of conducting the business of the court might not be acceptable to the attorneys having business there. He was, by nature, bold and impetuous, and prompt in the transaction of business. The dilatory methods that often prevail in court were distasteful to him, and he knew that the innovations which he felt impelled to introduce, in order to dispatch business more rapidly, would not find favor with attorneys and perhaps not even with litigants. He finally accepted the position, however, and carried out his views in such a way as to shorten the terms of court, and make a great saving of expense to the County, and his methods outlasted his term of office.

Col. Gage's devoted wife died in 1882, and the sad event affected his own health, already somewhat impaired. He failed gradually and died July 31st, 1887, from a bilious attack that came on two days earlier. He left the memory of a useful citizen, a man of generous hospitality, of strong personality; a clear and vigorous speaker, and a good organizer, whether in business or political affairs.

WILLIAM GLOVER GAGE, a leading lawyer in Saginaw County, is a son of DeWitt C. Gage, a sketch of whom precedes this, and of Abigail Rockwell Gage, and was born in Italy Hill, Yates County, N. Y., April 11th, 1847. He began his education in the common schools of Seneca County, N. Y., and continued his studies in the public schools of Saginaw, on the location of his parents there

 Wm G. Gage

in 1855. Seven years later he dropped his books, at the call for volunteers, and although not yet sixteen years of age, he enlisted in 1862, in Company C, Seventh Michigan Cavalry, and served in General Custer's brigade, Army of the Potomac, in the campaign of 1863. He participated in the Battle of Gettysburg, where he had his horse shot under him and was captured. After remaining a prisoner at Richmond something over a month, he was exchanged, returned to his regiment, and took part in the fall and winter operations on the Rapidan. In 1864 he was honorably discharged, having shown the marked military tastes and adaptability that were afterwards exceedingly serviceable to the State of Michigan.

Mr. Gage, after his discharge, returned to his studies, completed his course at the Saginaw High School, and took one year in the literary department of Michigan University, and then entered the law office of his father, Judge DeWitt C. Gage. He was appointed Assistant Postmaster at East Saginaw, and held the position four years. Meantime he continued his law studies, and was admitted to the bar in 1873. He then went into partnership with his father, under the firm name of Gage & Gage, the partnership continuing until the senior member took his seat upon the bench in 1880. Since that time William G. Gage has been alone in his practice, and has built up a large and remunerative business.

Aside from the law Mr. Gage has been active in both political and military affairs. Politically, he has always been a working Republican and there has not been a time in twenty years until the past fall, when he has not taken an active part on the City, County or Congressional Committees.

Two years ago last fall there was a very strong pressure brought to bear by many Republicans in all the counties of the Eight Congressional District to induce him to accept the nomination for Congress, but he absolutely refused to accept it. A year ago last spring he was unanimously nominated as one of the candidates for Circuit Judge of the Tenth Circuit, but the district proving at that time strongly Democratic, both nominees of the Republican party were defeated. Two years ago last fall he was Chairman of the Republican Congressional Committee, and organized the district. Mr. Brucker, the Democratic candidate, who had defeated Mr. Linton by a large majority, was himself defeated by Mr. Fordney by nearly 1,800 plurality.

Last spring the President sent Mr. Gage's name to the Senate as a member of the United States and Chilean Claims Commission. He was confirmed in May and entered upon his duties June 5th, last. There are three commissioners, Mr. Gage, the Minister from Chile to the United States, with the Minister from the Swiss Republic as the third member and President and umpire.

Mr. Gage was, for eight years, identified with the State troops. In 1880 he was appointed Inspector General on the staff of Governor Jerome, with the rank of Brigadier General. While filling this office he originated a system of "company inspections," visiting in person every portion of the State in the discharge of his duty. His influence on the militia system of the State, in molding it into a more nearly perfect and more efficient organization, was of great and far-reaching influence. The system then established has continued and the efficiency, high organization and fine equipment of our State troops today may be traced to the zealous and intelligent effort and military zeal that he exercised while filling that office. In 1883 he was appointed by President Arthur, Postmaster of East Saginaw, and served until 1884 when he was superseded by the appointee of President Cleveland. In 1894 he was appointed City Attorney of Saginaw.

He is an attendant of the First Congregational Church, and prominent in social and fraternal affairs. He is a member of Saginaw Lodge No. 10, K. of P.; Brigadier General of Uniformed Rank, K. of P. of Michigan; a member of Gordon Granger Post No. 38, G. A. R., in which he takes an active interest, and of Ancient Landmarks Lodge No. 303, F. & A. M. Mr. Gage married Alice B. Sanborn, of Madison County, New York, in 1873, and to the esteemed couple have been born six children, Kate A., DeWitt, George S., Walter H., Alice A. and Louise R.

In addition to his law practice Mr. Gage has extensive real estate interests in Saginaw, and in other parts of the valley.

HON. WASHINGTON GARDNER was born in Lincoln Township, Morrow County, Ohio, February 16, 1845, his father, John L. Gardner, was also born in Ohio, the paternal grandfather having come to America during the War of the Revolution. The grandfather's birthplace was Glasgow, Scotland, and after the War of Independence and he had settled in Loudon County, Virginia, he met a Holland lassie who was afterwards his wife and the paternal grandmother of the subject of this sketch. His mother's maiden name was Sarah Goodin, whose paternal ancestors came from old New England stock, her great grandfather having been born in Rhode Island in 1740. On the grandmother's side of the family was a strain of German extraction, now referred to as Pennsylvania Dutch.

As a child young Gardner's life was saddened by the death of his mother, which left him somewhat alone in the world. Indeed, he went to live with his uncle very shortly after and resided with him until sixteen years old. From eleven to sixteen years of age he supported himself, doing chores and working on a farm for his board and schooling. When he was but little beyond sixteen years of age the news came that Sumter had been fired upon. Young Gardner was working on a farm when he first heard the news. He immediately hurried to his uncle and asked to be permitted to go to the war, but his uncle refused his consent and tried to discourage young Gardner's

Washington Gardner

notion. But, a few weeks later, Gardner's elder brother came home from college and enlisted and Washington Gardner was then allowed to enlist. He at once wrote to his father, then in Iowa, informing him of the move. His father answered the letter by writing: "I am glad of it. If it were not for my rheumatism I would go too."

Young Gardner was the second of the five brothers to enter the service of the common country. He enlisted in Company D, Sixty-fifth Ohio Volunteer Infantry, in 1861, and was one of the three youngest men in that regiment which had on its rolls over 1,200 men. The regiment in which he served was a noted one as it was part of the brigade organized by Hon. John Sherman and known by his name, and was commanded by such famous generals as Thomas J. Wood, James A. Garfield and General Harker. Especially under Harker's command was it known as a fighting brigade.

Young Gardner shared with his regiment in all the hardships of the campaign, siege and battle in which the Army of the Cumberland participated clear up to May, 1864. He was at Shiloh, Corinth, Stone River and Chickamauga; was one of the besieged garrison at Chattanooga and charged with the gallant boys in blue up the heights of Missionary Ridge. At the Battle of Resaca, Ga., he was badly wounded in the right knee and sent to the hospital at Chattanooga and afterwards to Nashville. It was six months before he was able to be about, and just before New Year's Day, 1865, he was discharged by reason of expiration of term of service.

It was of a fighting stock that this young soldier came. His father's oldest brother fought in the War of 1812-14, and his youngest in the War of the Rebellion. Of his immediate family in the war of 1861-65 were three uncles, two of whom were commissioned, and five brothers, four of whom were commissioned and four wounded in battle. His four brothers and himself served an aggregate of fifteen years, nine months and twenty-nine days. His own issue was no less patriotic as, when the call came for troops in the Spanish War, two of his sons enlisted and went to the front.

In December, 1864, Washington Gardner limped back to his Ohio home, aided by a cane and crutch, having served thirty-eight months before he was twenty years old. While still on crutches he started to renew his search for an education. A man in experience and a veteran of the war, he was compelled to take up his studies along with mere boys in the early days of his scholastic training. So well did he apply himself to his studies that in 1865 he entered the preparatory class at Berea, Ohio, and in the fall of 1866 entered the Freshman class in Hillsdale College. He studied three years at Hillsdale and in the fall of 1869 he entered the Ohio Wesleyan University, from which he graduated in 1870. His frugality while in the army, serving as private, Corporal and Sergeant, had enabled him to save up quite a little sum, which he entrusted to his uncle while in the service. This money, and what he earned during vacations, was his sole reliance during the years of his student life.

In the summer of 1870 he entered the Methodist Episcopal Theological Seminary in Boston. Under the strain of years of hard study and hard work his health broke down, and for three years he was unable to resume mental labor. Then his old ambition to enter the law reasserted itself, and he matriculated at the Albany Law School, where he graduated in 1876, as the valedictorian of his class. One year's practice of the law in Grand Rapids convinced him that it was not his greatest field of usefulness, and he in 1877, entered the Michigan Conference of the Methodist Church on trial. He was ordained in 1881 and filled pulpits at Rockford, Ionia, Kalamazoo, Jackson, Albion and one year at Cincinnati. In the latter City his old wound became unusually troublesome, causing him great suffering and finally compelled his resignation and retirement from the ministry. Shortly after he accepted a professorship in Albion College.

In politics Washington Gardner has never been anything else but a Republican. His fellow churchmen and fellow citizens have called upon him to fill many of the most important offices in their gift and in succession he has been Regent of the Grand Council of the Royal Arcanum, Chaplain of the Supreme body, many times re-elected, has been twice President of the Michigan State Sunday School Association, Department Commander of the Michigan Grand Army of the Republic, a delegate to the General Conference of his Church and was elected Secretary of State of Michigan, March 20, 1894, and twice re-elected to that important position.

In the National Congressional contest in 1898 he was selected by the Republicans of the Third District to carry their banner against the combined opposition of Democrats, Populists and Union Silver men, all united with perfect fusion. In that campaign the candidate of the opposition was a prominent fusionist who was at the time a member of Congress. Mr. Gardner carried the District by nearly 1,400 majority. The distinction which had come to him by reason of his magnificent presence and oratorical powers stood him well in hand during his first Congressional term and his first speech in the House of Representatives attracted so favorable attention that he was sought after during his entire term to make public addresses. In 1900 he was reelected by 4,704 plurality.

In November, 1871, Mr. Gardner was married to Anna Lee Powers, of Abington, Mass., a descendant of Mayflower stock. Of this union seven children, Grace Bartlett, Mary Theo, Carleton Frederick, Elton Goldthwait, Raymond Bigelow, Lucy Reed and Helen Louise, were born and all are now living except the first named.

J. WIGHT GIDDINGS, of Cadillac, has been known throughout Michigan as newspaper publisher and editor, legislator, Lieutenant Governor and campaign orator, and throughout the West as a scholarly and eloquent public lecturer. He was born at Romeo, Mich., September 27th, 1858, his parents being Moses A. Giddings, a

merchant, now retired, and Caroline A. Beekman. His father's branch of the family came from England, John Alden being the most prominent among the ancestors. The name Alden which runs all through the family, was the early family name. His mother's ancestors came from Holland stock and the name was originally Von Beekman.

The subject of this sketch graduated at Romeo High School; took one year at Oberlin College and was then at Amherst College, Amherst, Mass., and studied law in the law department of the Chicago and Northwestern Railroad in Chicago. He purchased the Cadillac News, Cadillac, Mich., in February, 1882, and published the same until February, 1887. He was elected to the State Senate in 1886, and again in 1888 as a Republican and was President pro tem. of the Senate in the session of 1889. He was elected Lieutenant Governor in 1892, and served in the session of 1893. He practiced law from 1887 to 1896, and in the spring of the latter year was elected Judge of the Recorder's Court of Cadillac for a term of six years. He has been a member of the Board of Education in Cadillac for seven years and is still on the Board. He was a candidate for Congress in 1894 and was defeated for the nomination by R. P. Bishop after 136 ballots. He has been a Republican from birth; cast his first vote for Garfield; has attended nearly every State Convention since 1882, and has been heard as an effective speaker in every campaign since 1884.

When in the State Senate Mr. Giddings was recognized as one of the clearest thinkers and most convincing debaters in that body. He made it a point to get the full grasp of a subject before he began to talk about it, and his speeches bore the mark of being made to convince rather than for display. But it was in the session of 1893, when he was Lieutenant Governor, that his abilities were put to the severest test. A Democratic tidal wave had swept the country in the preceding election, and had left the Republicans with but a small majority in the Michigan State Senate. There has probably not been a session of the Senate since Michigan became a State, when there were so many parliamentary battles as the one in 1893, and there were able men on both sides to contest disputed points. The ability with which Lieutenant Governor Giddings presided over this body, and the promptness with which his decisions were given, established his reputation as one of the best presiding officers in the country. This reputation was further enhanced by his conduct of affairs at the Republican State Convention in 1896 at Grand Rapids, of which he was Permanent Chairman. The Pingree and Anti-Pingree forces made this a very warm, not to say turbulent, Convention, in which more technical parliamentary questions than usual were raised, and Mr. Giddings received hundreds of compliments for the skill with which he kept the tumultuous body within parliamentary control.

Mr. Giddings has for several years past been in the lecture field, part of the time under the auspices of the Central

Lyceum Bureau, and has met with success in that field also. A fair example of the press comments upon his platform speaking is the following from the Chicago Inter Ocean, referring to his lecture on "Uncle Sam's People." "Mr. Giddings' lecture was received with marked attention, and proved clearly that he is the possessor of rare natural gifts as a speaker. His diction is cultured, his enunciation clear and distinct, while his gestures are easy and graceful. The pith of his lecture was the pointing out of the various traits and characteristics of the American, which was illustrated with the relation of many pleasing incidents, skillfully interwoven, and having a bearing upon the methods, habits and distinctive vagaries of American life."

Mr. Giddings is not much devoted to fraternal societies, but is a member of the Knights of Pythias, and D. K. E. College fraternity. He was married at Pontiac in January, 1883, to Fidele E. Fitch and has had one child, Harold, who died in January, 1886.

THERON FRANCIS GIDDINGS, who has been a good worker in Michigan Republican politics, was born December 25th, 1843, in Charlestown, Kalamazoo County, Mich. His father was Orrin N. Giddings, an attorney and real estate dealer, and his mother was Harriet A. Giddings, nee Harriet A. Cook. His ancestors on his father's side emigrated from England on the ship Planter, locating at Ipswich, Mass., in 1635. His ancestors on his mother's side emigrated from England about the year 1700, locating in New York. His mother's ancestry and immediate family were members of the Society of Friends or Quakers.

The subject of this sketch was educated at Kalamazoo College. He began in life as a clerk in the mercantile business, struggled for an existence for a few years in Kansas during the late sixties; returned to Michigan and began a mercantile business, in which he was interested for fifteen years, during which time he held some minor political offices. In 1879 he was elected Clerk of Kalamazoo County, and held that office for twelve successive years, during which time he studied law and was admitted to practice. In 1891 he was appointed Receiver of the National City Bank of Marshall, and from a very bad lot of assets succeeded in paying all claims in full. In 1893 he was appointed by Governor John T. Rich, Commissioner of Insurance, held the office for four years, and in August, 1897, joined the Michigan Mutual Life Insurance Company as General Superintendent of Agencies, which position he now holds.

Mr. Giddings cast his first vote for Lincoln in 1864, and has been a working Republican ever since. He was Chairman of the Kalamazoo County Republican Committee for eight years, a member of the State Central Committee for six years, during four of which he was a member of the Executive Committee, and has been a delegate to State Conventions on numerous occasions since 1875.

The only corporation Mr. Giddings is connected with is the Michigan Mutual Life Insurance Company, in which he is a Director and one of its officers. He resides now in Detroit. He is a Mason in Lodge, Chapter and Commandery of K. T.; is a past High Priest of Chapter and Past Commander of Commandery Knights Templar and Past Grand Priest of the Grand Chapter of Royal Arch Masons of Michigan. He was married in 1869 to Julia E. d'Arcambal, of Kalamazoo, and has one daughter, Bessie E. Giddings.

O. N. Giddings, the father of Theron F., was one of the pioneers of Kalamazoo County, coming from Duchess County, New York State, and locating in Kalamazoo County in 1836. He was a member of the Legislature in 1847-8, County Treasurer of Kalamazoo County from 1853 to 1861, and Quartermaster General of the State during a portion of the Civil War. He was one of the original delegates who met at Jackson and formed the Republican party, being previous to that time a Whig. He was very active in raising troops in Western Michigan during the Civil War, and was a prominent Republican in that section of the State up to the time of his death which occurred in 1898 at the age of 85. He came from Revolutionary ancestors, his grandfather having been a Captain of Connecticut Troops at that period. He was a grand old man, ever respected and honored in the community in which he lived for 60 years.

FRANK W. GILCHRIST, of Alpena, has been active in lumbering and navigation interests for more than thirty years. He was born in Concord, N. H., in 1845, but at the age of three years was taken by his parents to Marine City, St. Clair County, Mich., where the father, Albert Gilchrist, bought the mill formerly owned by Rust Bros., which had a capacity of 20,000 feet per day, the logs being obtained from the region of Pine River. He had had previous experience in a lumber mill in New Hampshire, and had also conducted a mercantile business there, but he met with reverses after engaging in the former business in Michigan, for his mill caught fire and burned down in 1856. He then removed to Sand Beach and bought a water mill, owned by a Mr. Whitcomb, which he soon remodeled and changed to a steam mill and fitted it up with such modern machinery as could be procured at that time, among which were two circular saws, by which the capacity was increased to 40,000 feet per day. In 1863 he disposed of his plant and moved to Oberlin, Ohio, where he lived in retirement till past the age of 80.

Frank W. Gilchrist went to Alpena in 1867, and erected a large saw mill, having previously located ten or twelve thousand acres of pine lands upon adjacent streams. The mill was fitted up in modern style, has a capacity of 150,000 feet per day, and still gives employment to about one hundred men. He is also interested in the Rust-Owen Lumber Co., incorporated, with head offices at Eau Claire, Wis., also the Three States Lumber Co., with offices at Eau Claire, the latter company owning large timber claims in Missouri. Besides this Mr. Gilchrist has large interests in steam barges, tugs, etc., and the Gilchrist fleet is famous as one of the largest on the lakes. With others he owns large tracts of redwood land in California, in fact his interests are many and varied, as well as highly important. As a Republican Mr. Gilchrist was elected Mayor of Alpena, and he has also been supervisor several terms. He is a member of the Masonic body, in which he has taken all the degrees with the exception of the 33rd. He was married to Miss Mary E. Rust, of Saginaw, and they have a family of three sons and one daughter.

FRANK RINDGE GILSON, editor and proprietor of the Benton Harbor Palladium, was born December 30th, 1848, in Charlestown, now a part of Boston, Mass. His father, Edmund L. Gilson, was for many years engaged in the freight transfer business in Boston. His mother's maiden name was Eloiza Charlotte Butters. Her grandfather came over from France with Lafayette and belonged to the nobility of France, escaping death in the reign of terror by flight. F. R. Gilson traces his ancestry back to France, Germany and England. He was educated in the public schools and in Grand Prairie Seminary at Onarga, Ill.; was reared on a farm in Central Illinois, entering a country printing office at twenty and continuing since in the newspaper business. He has always been a Republican, voting first in a national campaign for U. S. Grant in 1872. The only public office he ever held was that of City Clerk of Clinton, Iowa, for four years. He was twice elected President of the Michigan Republican Newspaper Association, and was one term Chairman of the Republican Congressional Committee of the Fourth Michigan District. He is married and has two children, both grown to maturity.

WILLIAM DONALD GORDON, everywhere recognized as one of the strongest Republican leaders in Northern Central Michigan, was born in Bayfield, Ontario, June 7th, 1858. His father, Donald Gordon, a merchant, was Scotch, and his mother, Susan McCann Gordon, was Scotch-Irish. William D. was educated in the common schools and the law department of the University of Michigan, graduating from the latter in 1879. He located at Midland, Mich., soon after graduating, opened a law office in June, 1879, and has continued in business at Midland since. In addition to law business he has bought and sold farms and farming lands extensively; also has been interested in lumbering operations and manufacturing lumber and shingles. He has been very successful in all his business and professional undertakings. His legal business has extended for years beyond the limits of Midland County and he has been retained in many important suits in that and other counties. His law business is now shared with a partner under the firm name of Gordon & Kimmis.

In politics Mr. Gordon has been a Republican from his youth up, having cast his first vote for James A. Garfield. He has been a delegate to a majority of the Republican State Conventions held in Michigan for the past sixteen years, and was Chairman of the Midland Republican County Committee about ten years from 1884 to 1894. He has been honored by his fellow citizens with numerous offices, having been elected to the folllowing positions: Circuit Court Commissioner, 1880; Prosecuting Attorney, 1882 and 1884; City Attorney, 1887, 1888, 1889 and 1890; Judge of Probate, 1888, for four years; Representative in the State Legislature, 1892, 1894 and 1896. He was nominated for the Legislature each time by acclamation, and each time ran ahead of his ticket, leading even the large Pingree vote in 1896. In the sessions of 1895 and 1897, he was Speaker of the House. He is now United States District Attorney for the Eastern District of Michigan, having been appointed in 1898.

His legislative service was especially fruitful. He introduced a "General Tax Law" Bill at the session of 1893, and was Chairman of the Committee to which the taxation bills were referred for final action in the House. The Bill reported was a Senate Bill with a multitude of amendments, the amendments being the salient features of his bill, so that he claims to have taken an important part in the drafting and passage of the present tax law. He had charge of the Bill on the floor of the House also.

During the sessions of 1895, 1897 and 1898, being Speaker of the House, he introduced no bills in his own name and took no part in the debates, but his name was permanently connected with a proposed amendment to the Constitution providing "Home Rule for Cities." The measure passed the House in 1895, but failed to pass the Senate. He also took a prominent part in the passage of bills providing for the payment of franchise fees by corporations, and in the passage of the Merriman Bill, which materially increased the specific tax on railroads. At the opening of the session of 1897, in an address to the House, he advised the abandonment of the annual "Junket" so-called. The House adopted his suggestion and did not adjourn to allow the committees to visit the State Institutions, the committees visiting the institutions at different times without any apparent interference with business. He was commended much by the press and letters from prominent citizens for such action. He was first elected Speaker in 1895, nominated in caucus by acclamation and elected by the House unanimously, and although the sessions of 1895-97-98 were noted for many exciting and acrimonious debates, and the Republicans were many times divided upon important questions, not one appeal was taken during the three sessions, two regular and one special, from his decisions.

Mr. Gordon is a member of the F. & A. M.; R. A. M.; Knights of Pythias; Uniformed Rank K. of P.; K. O. T. M.; Independent Order of Foresters; Modern Woodmen and Michigan Club. He was married March 8th, 1882, at Bay City, Mich., to Miss Lizzie Ferguson, but has no children.

VICTOR MICHAEL GORE, a leading attorney of Southwestern Michigan, is the son of David Gore, a farmer, and Cinderella Keller Gore, and was born September 29th, 1858, at Plainview, Macoupin County Ill. His father's ancestry came from England in the eighteenth century, and his mother's ancestors came from Germany in the same century. His father was and is one of the prominent men in Illinois; was a member of the State Senate for some years and was President of the State Board of Agriculture for years, and for four years Auditor General of the State. The son, Victor, commenced his education in the public schools, graduated at Blackburn University, Carlinville, Illinois, in 1880, and two years later from the law department of Michigan University. He commenced a successful practice of law at Minneapolis, Minn., in 1882, and in 1890 removed to Benton Harbor, Mich., where he has ever since practiced with marked success, his profession.

Mr. Gore has been a Republican ever since he became a voter, and cast his first Presidential ballot for James G. Blaine. He has spoken for the Republican ticket since 1884. In the two days' Convention in Grand Rapids in 1896, when Hazen S. Pingree was first nominated for Governor, Mr. Gore was Temporary Chairman, and his address on that occasion, which was afterwards widely printed, was considered a model of Convention oratory.

Mr. Gore's social and family relations are exceedingly pleasant. He was married August 17th, 1882, at Carlinville, Ill., to Miss Clara S. Whitaker. Their children are Clara Louise, Helen Virginia, Thaddeus Fletcher and Charles Whitaker.

CHARLES T. GORHAM, of Marshall, is one of the oldest of the surviving Anti-Slavery and Republican veterans in Michigan, and one of the best examples of a well-preserved and serene old age. He was born in Danbury, Fairfield County, Connecticut, May 29th, 1812, one of a family of four sons and a daughter, whose parents were William and Polly Weed Gorham. They all received the advantages of a good education, and all became prominent in professional, business or literary circles. Charles T. Gorham first intended to take a complete college course, for which he made ample preparation. But he had already shown marked business qualifications, and was induced to accept a position in a mercantile house in Oneonta, Otsego County, N. Y., whither his parents had moved from Danbury, when he was quite young. The house into which he thus entered was owned by Mr. Ford, who was one of the most successful men in Central New York, and Mr. Gorham's stay there served to give him a valuable business training. He remained with Mr. Ford till 1835, when he removed to Marshall, Mich., and, in company with C. M. Brewer, opened a general store. Marshall was then, and for many years afterwards, one of the most important towns in interior Michigan, and the new house soon built up a large and lucrative trade. In 1840

Mr. Gorham sold his interest to his partner, and opened a private bank, which for a quarter of a century was one of the best known and soundest institutions of the kind in the State. In 1865 the business was incorporated as a National bank, of which Mr. Gorham was for thirty years President. The care of his banking interests constituted, through most of his active business life, his main occupation, though he was associated with other enterprises in the vicinity. He was a prudent and sagacious business man, of an integrity that was never questioned, and was almost uniformly successful.

Mr. Gorham has always taken an active interest in politics. He was a Democrat until 1848, but the management of the party in that campaign showed, as he thought, dangerous tendencies, and he withdrew from it. He was strongly Anti-Slavery in his sentiments, and in 1847 was one of a party against whom suit was brought for recovering the value of certain slaves which he and other Marshall people had aided to escape to Canada. Judgment was rendered against the defendants for $1,926 and costs, but they were reimbursed for part of their expenses by citizens of Marshall, Battle Creek and Detroit. Zachariah Chandler took great interest in these cases and made a liberal contribution toward the expenses. It was in connection with this matter that he first made the acquaintance of Mr. Gorham, an acquaintance that became intimate and life-long.

Mr. Gorham was a conspicuous participant in the first Republican Convention at Jackson, and has ever since co-operated with the party there organized. In addition to the committee and Convention work that he did in his own locality, he has been delegate to three National Conventions, being Vice-President for Michigan of the Convention in 1864 that nominated Lincoln the second time. His commanding figure has also been seen at numerous State Conventions. In 1870 he was offered the mission to Chili, but refused the proffer. The same year he accepted the position of Minister to the Hague, which came to him without solicitation, and his conduct of this mission was the occasion of many complimentary notices from the Holland press. While holding this position he traveled extensively on the continent and made a fine collection of art works for the adornment of his home. Soon after his return he was appointed Assistant Secretary of the Interior, and remained in that position during Secretary Chandler's term of office.

Mr. Gorham has retained, till long past 80 years of age, his interest in public affairs, and did not retire from the Presidency of the bank which he founded till he was past 85. He was one of the few survivors of the Jackson Convention who was present at the unveiling of the statue of Governor Blair at the State Capitol in 1898.

CORNELIUS ALBERT GOWER, for many years prominent in educational matters in Michigan, was born at Abbott, Maine, July 3, 1845. He was the son of Cornelius N. Gower, whose occupation was milling and lumbering, and Abigail Hawes, and was descended from

Puritan stock. He entered Colby University, Waterville, Maine, in 1863, but coming to Michigan before graduation, he entered the senior class of the University in 1867. Graduating from the classical course in that year, he received the degree of A. B. and three years later that of A. M. He entered the law department in 1868. His tastes, however, inclined him to the profession of teacher, and he taught four seasons in Maine and one year in Ann Arbor. He was Superintendent of Schools at Fenton three years; was County Superintendent of Schools in Genesee County three and a half years; was Superintendent of Schools in Saginaw City four years; and was President of the Michigan City School Superintendent's Association in 1878. He was appointed Superintendent of Public Instruction, September 1st, 1878, to fill the vacancy caused by the resignation of Hon. H. S. Tarbell. He was also nominated to fill the vacancy on the Republican State ticket for that office, caused by Mr. Tarbell's declination. He was elected, with the rest of the ticket, and was re-elected in 1880. While holding this position he was especially watchful of legislation affecting the educational interests of the State, and was deemed by members of the Legislature a discreet and prudent adviser. In February, 1881, he tendered his resignation, which did not take effect until the next June. He then took charge of the State Reform School, now known as the Industrial School for Boys. Under his superintendency, the humanitarian work which had been inaugurated by Mr. F. M. Howe, was carried to a successful completion, changing the school from a prison-like institution, with high fence and iron doors, to a cheerful, busy place which well merits its new name. The Superintendent's report for 1883-4 gives in a few pages a large amount of interesting information concerning the school as it once had been and then was. Mr. Gower filled the position acceptably for eleven years, when he retired to engage in manufacturing pursuits. He very readily adapted himself to this new line of work, and is now Vice-President of the manufacturing company of E. Bement's Sons, Lansing.

Mr. Gower was married at Fenton, Mich., September 12, 1871, to Dora L. Walton, and has three children, Helen D., Charles A. and Clara A.

CLAUDIUS B. GRANT, Justice of the Supreme Court, comes of a sturdy New England ancestry and was born in Lebanon, York County, Maine, October 25th, 1835. His parents, Joseph and Mary Grant, were descendants of the early settlers of Maine, and were of Scotch-English extraction. They were not able to give him more than a common school education, but by his own efforts he was able to work his way through the higher branches. After passing through the elementary grades of scholarship in the district school, academic education was begun at the Lebanon Academy, where he took the regular classical course. In 1855 he came to Michigan, and, entering

the University at Ann Arbor, graduated in the class of 1859. After leaving the University he engaged in the Ann Arbor High School, first as a teacher of classics, and the succeeding two years as principal of the school.

Unable to longer restrain the ardor of patriotism, he, on July 29th, 1862, dropped his books and entered the service of the United States, in the War of the Rebellion, as Captain of Company D, Twentieth Michigan Infantry, of which, passing through the grade of Major, he was Lieutenant Colonel at the time of his discharge and the senior officer of his regiment. In 1864 he received a commission as Colonel, but the regiment had become so reduced in members by losses in battle and from disease that the law would not permit him to be mustered as Colonel. He was at Fredericksburg with Burnside; served in the Army of the Potomac until February, 1863; was with his great namesake at Vicksburg; campaigned with Burnside against Longstreet in East Tennessee, was with General Grant in the campaign against Lee, which closed the war, and the day following General Lee's surrender, Colonel Grant closed his career as a soldier by resigning his position in the army.

Returning to Ann Arbor, he again entered the University of Michigan, this time as a student of law. Admitted to the bar in June, 1866, he at once engaged in the practice of law as a partner of Ex Governor Alpheus Felch, of Ann Arbor, who had already served the State as Governor, United States Senator, and a Justice of the Supreme Court, and whose daughter Colonel Grant had married in 1863, while yet an officer in the army.

During his residence in Ann Arbor, he was, in 1866, elected Recorder of the City; appointed postmaster in 1867; elected to two consecutive terms in the Legislature, 1871-2-3-4, and was in 1871 a Regent of the University of Michigan. His two terms in the Legislature served to give wider range to a reputation which had been hitherto chiefly local. He was quick, nervous, but energetic in manner, a ready talker, decided in his opinions and was soon recognized as one of the leading men in the House. He was a sturdy defender of the educational institutions of the State, an advocate of stringent laws for restricting the liquor traffic, and an intelligent debater upon matters of general legislation. After the close of the session of 1873 he removed to Houghton, in the Upper Peninsula, where, in 1876, he was Prosecuting Attorney of Houghton County. In 1881, although at the time not a resident of the District, he was elevated to the bench by an election which made him judge of the Twenty-fifth Judicial Circuit, and was re-elected in 1887.

Soon after taking his seat on the Circuit bench, Judge Grant became famous for his determined enforcement of the law, holding to the sound principles, that just so long as the people elect Legislatures to express their will in making law, it becomes incumbent upon judges, also elected by the people, to enforce those laws as they are found on the statute books, without either fear, favor or malice. This he did until the District over which he presided was entirely rid of the once notorious dens of infamy for which it had long been known, and the keepers of saloons concluded to conduct their business in accordance with the provisions of the law governing such traffic. It required a high degree of courage to pursue the course he did in bringing law breakers to account. Occasional threats were made against him; Prosecuting Attorneys were in some cases timid, indifferent and hostile and there was occasionally a Sheriff who showed signs of being in sympathy with the law breakers, but the Judge was courageous and persistent and gave the territory under his jurisdiction such a cleaning out as no lumbering or mining section of Michigan had ever had before. The fame which he gained by the vigorous course in these matters, led afterwards to frequent invitations from the law and order elements in other parts of the State to speak upon the best methods of suppressing existing evils. He has not been an adviser of extreme legislation, but has continuously urged the vigorous enforcement of such restrictive laws as we have.

In the spring of 1889 Judge Grant was nominated for Justice of the Supreme Court. He was naturally opposed by the liquor trade and allied interests, but ran well with the ticket and was elected by a plurality of 33,471 over Justice Thomas R. Sherwood, the Democratic candidate. He was re-elected in 1899 by a plurality of 50,346 over the combination candidate of the Democratic, People's Union Silver parties. His course upon the supreme bench has fully met the expectations of his friends. He is a thorough student of law, careful in his investigations, and though naturally a partisan has never been accused of partiality in his judicial decisions.

FRED WARREN GREEN, one of the most prominent of the younger citizens of Ypsilanti, was born October 21st, 1871. His father was Holden N. Green, a lawyer and afterwards a lumberman, and his mother's maiden name was Adeline Clark. The family are of revolutionary stock on both sides, and have long lived in New York State.

Fred W. Green graduated from the Cadillac High School; the Michigan State Normal School at Ypsilanti, and the law department of the University of Michigan. In his young manhood he was an engineer, and for two years was employed on a Republican weekly, the Ypsilantian. He early became interested in politics, a game for which he at once manifested great aptitude. Although a comparatively young man he is one of the most influential Republicans of the City in which he lives; is a recognized factor in County politics, and has an extensive acquaintance about the State. He is regularly elected a delegate to all the County and State Conventions.

He enlisted early in the Spanish-American War and went out as First Lieutenant and Company Commander of Company G., Thirty-first Michigan Volunteers, serving with great credit throughout the war.

Fred W. Green.

After his return he was appointed by Governor Pingree Assistant Inspector General of State Troops, and in 1899, upon the resignation of his superior, he was promoted to be Inspector General, with the rank of Brigadier General. This is a position for which his close attention to duty, while in service in the field, admirably fitted him. He has been very industrious and zealous in the work of this office and takes great pride in having the State troops present the best possible appearance.

General Green is a Mason and a Knight of Pythias, and is President of the Washtenaw Telephone Company, a local organization.

EBENEZER OLIVER GROSVENOR, of Jonesville, was sixteen years old when he commenced taking care of himself in 1836, has lived sixty-three years in Michigan and over sixty in the same village, and looks as if he might add twenty years more to the four score that have already passed over his head. He was born January 26th, 1820, at Stillwater, Saratoga County, N. Y. He was a son of E. O. Grosvenor, Sr., and grandson of Rev. Daniel Grosvenor, a man of sound learning and ability, who gave his children all the advantages of a liberal education. Several of them were graduates of Eastern colleges, and occupied prominent positions in the professional world. The father of the subject of this sketch was born and reared in Worcester, Mass., and there married Mary Ann Livermore, a native of Massachusetts, and an accomplished lady of true culture, who was educated at Leicester Academy, near Worcester. They had nine children, of whom the son and two sisters still survive. Having experienced some reverses, they removed from Worcester to Stillwater, N. Y., where the husband was engaged for a number of years on the public works of the State. In 1825 they removed to Schenectady, and in 1826, to Chittenango, N. Y. Young Mr. Grosvenor attended the Lancastrian Academy, in Schenectady, and afterwards the common school in Chittenango. At the age of thirteen he entered the Polytechnic Academy, at that place, where he spent two years and gained a high reputation for accurate scholarship. At the age of sixteen, he entered, as a clerk, a store in Chittenango, where he remained for two years. He then went to Albion, Mich., and was employed by an older brother, in one of the first stores of the place. Here he remained until the winter of 1839, when he went to Monroe, and was employed for one year as clerk in the State Commissioner's office, during the construction of the Michigan Southern Railroad, which was then in the hands of the State. In the summer of 1840, he removed to Jonesville, and entered a dry goods store as clerk, in which capacity he remained until April, 1844. The same year he was married to Miss Sally Ann Champlin, daughter of Hon. Elisha P. Champlin, one of the first settlers of Lenawee County. They have one daughter, who was married in 1873 to Charles E. White, of Jonesville.

It was in 1844 that Mr. Grosvenor made the real start in his long and successful business career. In connection with Mr. Varnum, he entered into a general mercantile business, in which he continued on the same site for fifty-two years. This was conducted for three years in connection with Mr. Varnum, then for four years with Mr. Champlin, who purchased Mr. Varnum's interest. From 1851 to 1864 Mr. Grosvenor conducted it alone, and then associated himself with several young men who had been in his employ. He remained connected with the business, most of the time in its active management, till 1896, when he relinquished it to one of his partners, who is still carrying it on in the same store. During the period that he was managing this business he was also engaged in buying and selling the general produce of his section, making it a feature of his business to always pay cash. In 1854 he established the banking firm of Grosvenor & Co., and afterwards started the Exchange Bank of Grosvenor & Co., of which for thirty-seven years he was President and largest stockholder. In 1891 he organized the Grosvenor Savings Bank, incorporated under the State Law. Although past 80 he is daily at the bank, and, as President, he is the active manager of its affairs. He has also been connected with other business affairs. He contributed generously both to the cotton and woolen mills of the place. He was the first Treasurer of the Jonesville Cotton Manufacturing Company, and for some time its President. In the latter part of 1868, when the Fort Wayne, Jackson & Saginaw Railroad was being located, he was largely instrumental in directing its route. He was one of the organizers of the Michigan Mutual Life Insurance Company of Detroit; the Michigan State Fire & Marine Insurance Company of Adrian, and of the Detroit Fire & Marine Insurance Co., of which he is still a Director. He has been uniformly successful in business, and is well-known throughout Southern Michigan as a man of the strictest integrity and of marked business ability and sound judgment.

Aside from his business career Mr. Grosvenor was for more than forty years in public life, and in at least two of his official positions he rendered the State conspicuous service. The first of these was in connection with the construction of the present State Capitol. When this structure was first projected, he, with James Shearer and Alexander Chapoton were appointed a Board of State Building Commissioners to superintend its construction. The Governor was ex-officio President of the Board, and at the first meeting Mr. Grosvenor was chosen Vice-President. In his remarks accepting the trust, he gave as a text and rallying cry for the Board, the proposal that at the close of every meeting the records should be completely written up and certified, so that if they should never attend another meeting their successors could take up the work without fear of doing injustice to any contractor or bringing loss to the State. This was done, and on two or three occasions, at the close of a meeting, Mr. Chapoton remarked: "Well, if lightning should strike us they'll find everything

Uo

[illegible] and [illegible] connection with Mr. [illegible] was [illegible] for four years with [illegible] interest. [illegible] and [illegible] associated [illegible] of his partners [illegible] the period that [illegible] buying and [illegible] of his [illegible] building [illegible] Mr. [illegible] in business [illegible] in the [illegible] Michigan State [illegible] business [illegible]

[illegible] Senator [illegible] Grosvenor [illegible] two of his [illegible] The first of these [illegible] and [illegible] Mr. Grosvenor [illegible] in the State [illegible] he would never attend another meeting [illegible] State. This was done, [illegible] meeting. Mr. [illegible] they'll [illegible]

E. O. Grosvenor

closed up." It was arranged that at least one member of the Board should visit the building every week, and the regular meetings were held once in four weeks. During the period of its existence 147 meetings were held, of which 103 were regular and 44 special, occupying in all 258 days. The Commission never failed to have a quorum in attendance and in no case, during the whole progress of the work, was any contractor or other person having a claim against the State on account of the construction of the capitol, obliged to wait a single day by reason of the neglect or failure of the Board to meet and act on the claim. The Commissioners not only saw that the work was well done, but, what is very unusual with a large structure, public or private, they kept the cost within the estimates and appropriations. In each one of five different funds there was a small balance when the building was turned over to the State. Out of appropriations aggregating $1,430,000 there was a total balance of about $4,000 thus remaining. The whole work of the Commission was a notable instance of systematic and faithful attention to official duty.

At the time of the dedication Mr. Grosvenor closed his official report as follows: "During all these years of watching and waiting, of toil and anxiety, the Commission has been greatly cheered, encouraged and gratified by the many evidences of confidence and approbation that have come to them from time to time from all portions of the State, and find their highest reward in the consciousness that they have been faithful to their trust and in having given to the discharge of every duty devolving upon them their earnest and persistent efforts and best thought."

Then turning to Governor Croswell, the other Commissioners rising meantime, Mr. Grosvenor said: "The Board of State Building Commissioners were appointed and commissioned to erect and complete a building suitable for a State Capitol. Having accomplished the task assigned to them, they have the honor to present this edifice, with all its appointments, complete from foundation to pinnacle of dome, trusting it will be found fitting, convenient and secure, for the proper administration of the government of this great and growing State."

The sentiments here uttered were received with prolonged and appreciative applause. It might be added that since the papers relating to the Capitol were sealed up and filed with the Secretary of State in May, 1879, it has never been necessary to open them in order to settle any question or claim.

Mr. Grosvenor soon had another opportunity to do the State good service. At the Spring election in 1879 he was chosen a Regent of the University. The Rose-Douglas controversy was then at its height, and the quarrel was injuring the University, both in the Legislature and with the public. Mr. Grosvenor was earnestly importuned by both sides of the controversy to commit himself to their views, but he could not be manipulated. He investigated for himself and concluded that the interest of the State would be best served by bringing the whole matter to a termination. His old associate, Mr. Shearer, who had been elected at the same time, accepted his conclusions, and the two carried through the Board a resolution which stopped the wasteful expenditures for litigation and soon put the matter at rest. During the last four years of his Regency, Mr. Grosvenor was Chairman of the Finance Committee, where his fine business training was of great use to the Institution.

Space will not permit of a detailed account of his other public service. He was elected to the State Senate in 1858 and 1862, being, in his second term, Chairman of the Committee on Finance, the most important then of all committees. He was President of the Military Contract Board in 1861, with the title of Colonel, and was afterwards President of the State Military Board. He was elected Lieutenant Governor in 1864, and this made him President of the State Board of Equalization. He was also elected State Treasurer in 1866 and again in 1868.

Mr. Grosvenor has also held local offices, having been Supervisor of the old Township in which both Jonesville and Hillsdale were situated, and the first Supervisor of the Township of Fayette, after they were divided. But perhaps no greater tribute has been paid to his public spirit and the esteem in which he is held by his fellow citizens, than his frequent elections to the Presidency of the Jonesville School Board. He has already held this position for thirty-three years, and in September, 1899, was elected for yet another three-year term.

OTTO E. C. GUELICH, a son of Carl L. and Henrietta Eleanora (Ravenclow) Guelich, was born on his father's estate near Holsterbro, Denmark, October 18th, 1834, and is descended from a prominent German family. He received his education under his father's tutorship until the age of 14, when he was called upon to assist in the management of the estate, owing to the political confinement of the older Mr. Guelich because of his sympathy with the rebellion of 1848-52. His uncle, Guido Guelich, held the office of President of the Republic of Schleswig-Holstein during the period. With the close of the war the family were exiled and came to America, settling at Utica, N. Y.

For several years after his arrival in America Mr. Guelich engaged in farming near Utica, and in 1861 embarked in the retail meat business at that place. During the oil excitement in Pennsylvania Mr. Guelich removed to Titusville, in that State, and for one year was active as a speculator in that line. In 1866 he returned to Utica and resumed his former business, to which he added in 1876 a line of agricultural implements. In 1884 he was offered and accepted the agency for the dressed beef firm of George H. Hammond & Co., remaining as their representative at Utica until 1887, when he disposed of his interests there and removed to Detroit, Mich.,

*O. E. C. Guelich.*

where he formed the Northwestern Stone and Marble Co., receiving the position of general manager. In 1892 he formed the Detroit & Bermudez Asphalt Co., of which he was elected first President and General Manager. This company was succeeded by the Western Bermudez Co., of which Mr. Guelich was made Vice-President and General Manager. He has the distinction of being the first person to lay Bermudez Asphalt in competition with the trust. Owing to the absorption of the Western Bermudez Company by the Barber Asphalt Company, in December, 1894, Mr. Guelich became associated with the Alcatraz Co., of which he was the Western Manager until that company too became a member of the trust. He is now President of the Illinois & California Asphalt Paving Co., of Chicago, and of the California Paving Co. for Michigan and Wisconsin. In connection with these various companies Mr. Guelich has rendered the City great service not only by keeping down the price and setting an example of high quality and superior workmanship in artificial stone sidewalks, but by doing the same thing on a larger scale with asphalt paving.

Mr. Guelich has been a Republican ever since the party was organized, and has been an active worker in politics since he came to Detroit. He has been a delegate to numerous local Conventions and two State gatherings, and is accounted a shrewd adviser in campaign matters.

Mr. Guelich is an exceedingly companionable man in social life, and is a member of Yah Num-Dah-Sis Lodge, Valley of Utica, Free and Accepted Masons. Mr. Guelich has been married twice, first to Lydia A. Cooley, of Utica, N. Y., who died in 1865, leaving a son, Charles E. Guelich. In 1867 he married as his second wife, Elizabeth D. Cooley, of Utica, N. Y. They are the parents of two children, Lillian A. and Amelia H.

CHARLES HENRY HACKLEY, of Muskegon, furnishes the best illustration in the State of the liberal traits that have been developed in men engaged in the lumber business. That industry is one that deals in large figures and in bold enterprises, and the men who engage in it are very rarely stingy or narrow. They often make money easily and give or spend it freely, and if a bad condition of the logging streams or a depression in the market brings financial disaster, they take it as cheerfully and philosophically as possible. It has been frequently remarked in the Legislature that the lumber districts are not often represented by men who are mean, or over economical, but by men who believe in liberal expenditures by the State and who are public spirited at home.

The most liberal of all Michigan lumbermen, Charles H. Hackley, was born in Michigan City, Ind., January 3rd, 1837, and is the sole survivor of the five children of Joseph H. and Selina Fuller Hackley. When he was yet in infancy his parents moved to Kenosha,

Wis., where he attended the common schools until he was fifteen years old. He then left school to assist his father who, as a contractor, was at that time engaged in railroad and plank road building, and, at the age of seventeen, was given a foreman's position, in charge of a gang of men engaged in repairing twenty miles of plank road. April 17th, 1856, Mr. Hackley came into Michigan and began the building of his fortune as a common laborer, in the employ of Durkee, Truesdell & Co., lumber manufacturers, by whom he was soon promoted to the important position of scaler, and as such spending the following winter in the pine forests of Michigan, coming out in the spring to assume the position of foreman in charge of all lumber on the outside of the mill. In the fall of 1857, being then twenty years of age, he returned to Kenosha, where he gave the winter to a course of assiduous study in a business college, preparing for the eventful business life he has since followed. In the spring of 1858 he returned to Muskegon and again entered the employ of Gideon Truesdell, successor to Durkee, Truesdell & Co., but this time instead of being employed as a common laborer, he was engaged as the firm's bookkeeper. In the spring of 1859, the firm of J. H. Hackley & Co. was organized, which comprised his father, J. H. Hackley, his former employer, Gideon Truesdell, and Charles H. Hackley. They purchased the plant of Pomeroy & Holmes, of Muskegon and engaged in the manufacture of lumber. From the day on which J. H. Hackley & Co. started in business until the present time, the ventures of Charles H. Hackley have been crowned with success. In 1860 the firm purchased the Wing mill property, and operated it in connection with their manufacturing interests, in all of which the firm was rapidly building a reputation for honorable dealing, and accumulating wealth.

In 1864, Charles H. Hackley was united in marriage to Miss Julia E. Moore, of Centerville, Allegheny County, N. Y., who now shares not only the good fortune of her husband, but also enjoys with him its beneficent disposal. The death of his father occurred in 1874, and was followed a few years later by the demise of two sons who had also been associated in the lumber business with Charles H. The last bereavement caused a reorganization of the firm, which was then changed to read C. H. Hackley & Co. In 1880, James McGordon, who was fourteen years a member of the firm of C. H. Hackley & Co., died. His interest in the business was purchased by Thomas Hume, and the present firm of Hackley & Hume, organized, a firm which has been known as one of the most extensive and reliable dealers in lumber in the country. They own extensive tracts of land in Michigan, Wisconsin and Minnesota and in four of the southern States, and are largely interested in manufacturing plants in Michigan and Minnesota, including that of the H. C. Akely Lumber Company at Minneapolis, with a capacity of 100,000,000 feet a year. They are also interested in the Gardner & Lacey Mill at Georgetown, S. C., with a yearly cut of 15,000,000 feet of cypress. Mr. Hackley is also

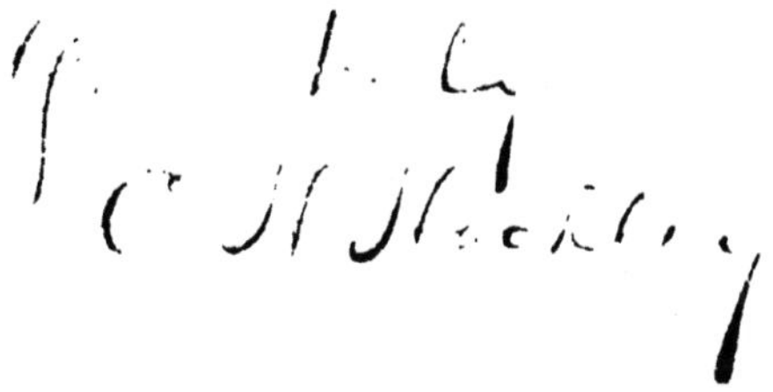

President of the Hackley National Bank, and director of the Oceana County Savings Bank, at Hart; the Michigan Trust Co. of Grand Rapids, and a number of other institutions. He was for many years a director in the Muskegon Boom Co. and is a stockholder in a number of private business corporations or firms.

In politics Mr. Hackley is a Republican and has held a number of local offices of honor and trust. He has been County Treasurer of Muskegon County; Alderman for two terms; member of the Muskegon Board of Public Works; a member of the Board of Education fifteen years, and its President for six. He was delegate from the Ninth Congressional District to the Republican National Convention at Minneapolis in 1892, when he voted for James G. Blaine, and to the St. Louis Convention in 1896, which nominated McKinley.

In 1893 he was elected Regent of the University, but finding his business engagements would not permit of his giving that attention to the duties of this position that they deserved he resigned on the day that his term of office commenced.

But it is through his munificent gifts to the City of Muskegon that Mr. Hackley was most widely known. The first of these was a gift of $100,000 for the site and cost of building a structure for use as a Public Library, and $75,000 more as an endowment fund, the income to be devoted to the purchase of books. Subsequently he added $25,000 more to be used in furnishing the library and the purchase of books.

In 1890, the Central School building, which cost the City $60,000, but which carried only $30,000 insurance, was destroyed by fire. This fire occurred at a time when the citizens of Muskegon were discussing the ways and means for the building of a new high school to cost about $45,000. This problem was now more involved, because the sum obtained from the insurance on the Central School was not enough by one-half to meet the expense of erecting such a building to take the place of the one burned, as the needs of the City required. At this juncture, Charles H. Hackley, on April 15th, 1892, came forward with a most beneficent and liberal proposal to the citizens of Muskegon, through their board of education, viz., That if the electors would vote an issue of $75,000 worth of bonds of the district, to run fifty years, bearing five per cent interest, to be expended with other funds provided by the board in the erection of a new and suitable building on the site of the one burned, with a new High School building to cost $45,000, he would cash the bonds and then donate them to the district as a trust fund, the interest of which would go to defraying the current expenses of the Hackley Public Library forever. The acceptance of this most generous offer resulted in the building of the Hackley School, one of the most beautiful school structures in the State, at a cost of about $80,000, and a new High School building which, when complete, cost nearly $60,000. Other gifts by Mr. Hackley to the City have been a square in the Hackley Park valued at $75,000; a soldiers' and sailors' monument, $27,000; endowed the same with $10,000; the Hackley Manual Training School, costing, with equipment, $100,000, with an endowment of $100,000; and finally statues of Lincoln, Grant, Sherman and Farragut, to adorn the Hackley Park. These were completed at a cost of over $28,000, and were unveiled during the summer of 1900. Mr. Hackley's total gifts for these various public purposes have aggregated about $540,000.

NORMAN WASHINGTON HAIRE, a successful attorney and capable Judge in the Upper Peninsula, was born in Columbia, Jackson County, Michigan, February 24th, 1855. His father was Frederick H. Haire, a farmer, and his mother, Lucy Jane Haire, nee Smith. His father's ancestors were Scotch-Irish Presbyterians and came to the State of New York in the Eighteenth Century. His grandfather, Robert Haire, was a scholar of more than ordinary ability for the time in which he lived, the latter part of the eighteenth and the first half of the nineteenth centuries. He had a stalwart family of ten sons and four daughters who grew to maturity. Mr. Frederick H. Haire was born in the Township of Italy, Yates County, New York, June 8th, 1824, and came to Michigan and settled in Jackson County early in the forties. He was a giant in strength, and altogether a man of wonderful endurance and energy. With but a limited education himself his great desire was to give his children the best education that the State of Michigan could afford. Norman W. Haire's mother's ancestors were Vermont Yankees named Smith. His mother was born in Albion Township, Onondaga County, New York, October 19th, 1831, and came to Michigan with her parents when she was eight years of age and settled in the wilderness in the township of Henrietta, Jackson County. His grandfather, Norman Smith, was a tall, six foot six inch, rawboned, typical Eastern Yankee. He was also a scholar whose library in the wilderness was a wonder for those days.

Norman W. Haire was educated at the country schools in the Township of Somerset, Hillsdale County; at the Butts and Annis school houses in Onondaga, Ingham County, and then in the Leslie High School, and the Ann Arbor High School, where he graduated in June, 1876, at the age of twenty-one. He then entered the University of Michigan, classical course, and graduated with the degree of A. B. on July 1st, 1880. He re-entered the University of Michigan law department, and special studies in the literary department in 1883, and graduated with the degree of LL. B. in 1885.

During the first part of the period that Mr. Haire was thus obtaining an education he worked on the farm summers and part of the winter, attending school the rest of the winter. He kept up his summer work on the farm till he graduated from the University of Michigan, being then 25 years old. At intervals, also, he taught school in the winter, near Eaton Rapids and at Leslie, Ingham

Norman W. Haire

County, and Rockland, Ontonagon County. He was admitted to the bar in 1885, settled at Rockland; was elected Prosecuting Attorney in 1886, and held the office until May, 1891, when he was appointed by Governor Winans, Judge of the new Thirty-second Circuit. In the fall of 1892 he was elected to fill out the term and was re-elected in 1893 and 1899, each time without opposition. He has also held court in Wayne and several other Counties, and on account of the serious illness of Judge Williams, and afterwards of Judge Hubbell, he held court nearly six years in all in the Twelfth Circuit. Mr. Haire moved, in 1887, from Rockland to Ontonagon, where he built up a fine practice. He removed from Ontonagon to Ironwood, Gogebic County, in May, 1892. At present he spends part of his time as counsel in the law firm of Gray, Haire & Rice, of Houghton, Mich., whose business is one of the largest in the Northwest.

Mr. Haire cast his first vote for Samuel J. Tilden in 1876, and remained a Democrat until 1892, but since that time has been a Republican. He made Republican speeches in the Upper Peninsula in the campaign of 1896, and did the same there and in other parts of the State in 1900. He was a delegate from Gogebic County to the Republican State Convention in the fall of 1898 and the spring of 1899. He is a Knight Templar and also belongs to the Mystic Shrine. He was married to Miss Lydia Moore, of Leslie, July 3rd, 1880, two days after graduating from the University of Michigan. They have two daughters, Mildred M., born at Ann Arbor, August 6th, 1884, and Paula L., born at Ontonagon, June 25th, 1890.

BRINTON FLOWER HALL, one of the enterprising and successful manufacturers of Central Michigan, is the son of Joshua and Electa Edson Hall and was born on his father's farm at Ashfield, Mass., December 15th, 1865. He is a descendant of John Hall the II., who came from Warwickshire, England, about 1630 with Governor Winthrop, and landed at Charlestown, Mass. The son was educated in the district schools of Ashfield and the Sanderson Academy in the same place. His first occupation was teaching district school in Ashfield. He then spent seven years in traveling on the road in New England, Northwestern New York and Canada selling refrigerators, and in 1891 came to Michigan, where he has since lived. He is Vice-President of the Belding-Hall Manufacturing Company of Belding, Mich., large manufacturers of refrigerators, lumber, folding tables, etc., with branch houses in Chicago, New York and Philadelphia. He is also a Director of the People's Savings Bank, of Belding.

In politics Mr. Hall has always been a Republican and cast his first Presidential vote for Harrison in 1888. He has never held any political office, but has found time, in spite of his business activity, to do some good campaign work. He attended one State Convention in Massachusetts and four or five in Michigan; was President of the Young Men's Republican Club in Belding in 1896, and was a delegate from the Fifth Congressional District to the National Convention in Philadelphia, in June, 1900. He does not belong to any fraternal society, but is a member of the Peninsular Club of Grand Rapids. He was married in Belding, October 19th, 1892, to Florence Edna Wilson, but has no children.

DEVERE HALL, of Bay City, who, as an attorney, has had an extensive practice in Eastern Michigan, and who has also shown a commendable activity in Republican politics, was born August 26, 1854, in Bedford, Monroe County, Mich. His father died two years later and the lad was obliged, when quite young, to commence the customary routine of working on the farm summers, and attending district school winters. He afterwards entered the Union School at Holly, having earned enough at teaching to pay his way through. In 1874, when only twenty years old, he became principal of the Union School at Goodrich and later held the same position at Gaines, Genesee County; at Byron, Shiawassee County, and at Caseville, Huron County, remaining at the latter place five years. The last two years of his stay at the latter place he was a member of the Board of School Examiners of the County, and for two years was Secretary of the same Board. During this period also he took what time he could after attending to the duties of his position, to study law, under the guidance of Thomas B. Woodworth, of Caseville.

Mr. Hall was admitted to the bar in the spring of 1883 and removed to West Branch, Ogemaw County, where he entered into partnership with Hon. D. P. Markey, ex-Speaker of the House of Representatives in the State Legislature, and one of the best known attorneys in that section. This association was continued under the firm name of Markey & Hall until 1891, when Mr. Markey moved to Port Huron, and Mr. Hall to Bay City. During his stay at West Branch Mr. Hall was elected Prosecuting Attorney in 1884, 1886 and 1888; in 1890 he was elected to the Legislature to represent the District comprising the Counties of Ogemaw, Crawford, Oscoda and Roscommon. He has held no other political office, although he has been a delegate to a number of political conventions.

At Bay City Mr. Hall formed a partnership with Archibald McDonell, under the firm name of McDonell & Hall, who are attorneys for many prominent firms, and who enjoy a large and lucrative practice. Mr. Hall is a Maccabee, and has for some years been special and general counsel of various orders of the Maccabees, and has had charge of nearly all the litigation in which these orders have been involved in this State. Some of these cases have brought up entirely new issues, and the decisions upon them have established a standard for the interpretation of law for fraternal societies. In addition to his position as general counsel, Mr. Hall has been Great Lieutenant Commander of the K. O. T. M. of Michigan. In his church relations he is a Methodist and is a Trustee of the Madi-

E. L. Hamilton

son Avenue M. E. Church of Bay City. He was married May 19th, 1877, to Augusta O. Brown, of Byron, and has six children: Sidney D., Vera M., Ray A., Irving J., Cecil M. and John C.

HON. EDWARD LARUE HAMILTON was born in Niles Township, Berrien County, Mich., December 9, 1857. His father, Edward L. Hamilton was of Scotch stock, and his mother, nee Jameson, was of Scotch-Irish and New England Puritan parentage. The future Congressman received the start of his education in the common schools of his vicinity. He graduated from the Niles High School in 1876 and was prevented from entering the University of Michigan for which he had been prepared, by the sudden death of his father and the consequent necessity of his assuming the responsibilities arising therefrom. In 1881 he entered the law office of Judge H. H. Coolidge, of Niles, and was admitted to the bar in 1884.

Always a Republican he threw all the influence of voice and vote to that party and was first known in the public mind as a successful and ready debater and campaign orator. He was not a seeker of public office, simply a successful lawyer with a growing practice. This was his condition when the great silver campaign of 1896 was at hand and he was selected by the delegates of his district to make the fight for Congress in that year when things looked far from roseate for a hard money man in the Fourth District of Michigan. His campaign was strong and sharply fought, and the voters, by a plurality of over 3,500, sent him to Congress as their representative.

Mr. Hamilton's very first speech on the floor of the House attracted attention. It was a tribute to a deceased member, but so different from the ordinary run that it commanded attention at once. The next speech and the one which gave him still greater standing among the members of Congress and, indeed, brought his name before the country at large, was his remarks on the silver question. It was a new handling of the subject and epigrammatic in its terseness and crispness. The telling points of it were so strongly presented that the Republicans of Oregon, then engaged in a campaign, took hold of it and scattered copies broadcast through the two Congressional districts in the state. They asserted that it was the most powerful argument they had. Then the National committee took hold of it and it has been standard ever since.

It was this speech and the following one on the question of trusts that gave Congressman Hamilton the title of "the student of the delegation." His speeches were always prepared with the greatest care and after inexhaustible study and condensation of fact. When he talked the House listened with pleasure, and the surety of getting something worth listening to. His speech upon the trusts was like that on the money question, a new presentation of the case, and the Republican National Committee saw its benefit as a campaign document, and wherever there was a controversy and doubt of the results, Mr. Hamilton's speech was shipped to the doubters. Hundreds of thousands, if indeed not millions of copies, were used by the National Committee.

Mr. Hamilton's Congressional career was prolific of much besides these oratorical successes. He was a sturdy committeeman and by his peculiar merit, for the position, was first placed upon the Committee on Territories, which had the handling of the questions arising out of the newly acquired territories. During the first session of the Fifty-sixth Congress this committee, among other things, formulated the organic law for the Territory of Hawaii, the first of our insular possessions. Mr. Hamilton's speech on our making Hawaii a territory was a condensation of Hawaiian history, a complete outline of the proposed government, and a discussion of suffrage and the public land system of Hawaii. So thorough and exhaustive was it that it at once attracted attention and was recognized as valuable. It was printed by order of the National Republican Committee at the opening of the campaign and used as reference throughout the campaign of 1900.

In the second session of the same Congress he was appointed as a member of the Committee on Insular Affairs, which is made up from carefully selected, strong men of the House.

Not alone as campaign matters, but as literary efforts have his speeches been placed before the public. The newspapers of the metropolis got in the habit of printing columns of his speeches. Rand & McNally's magazine reprinted his trusts speech entire, as did the Conservative, J. Sterling Morton's paper, and the Brooklyn Union used that speech as a serial. This speech was copied in the newspapers all over the United States, and was as familiar to readers on the Pacific Coast as in the State of Michigan.

Mr. Hamilton was married to Miss Cora V. Eddy, the daughter of Rev. Alfred Eddy, at Niles, Mich., October 8, 1883. In addition to his studious home habits and political work, he has found time to pass through the various secret society grades of Knights of Pythias, Master Mason, Royal Arch Mason, Knights Templar and Nobles of the Mystic Shrine.

He was re-elected by a majority of nearly 6,500 in the 1900 campaign.

WILLIAM W. HANNAN, for a number of years past one of Detroit's leading real estate men, was born in Rochester, N. Y., July 4th, 1854. His father is Peter Hannan, a farmer, manufacturer and real estate dealer. His father's ancestors were Scotch and Irish, and his mother's were French.

William W. Hannan graduated in 1873 from the High School at Dowagiac, Mich.; took the preparatory course at Oberlin College, Ohio, in 1874 and 1875, and entered that college, but then preferred to enter Michigan University, which he did in 1876, and took the degree of A. B. in 1880. He graduated from the law department in 1883. His early life was occupied, out of school hours, in doing anything by which he could lay aside money for educating himself. He followed the various occupations young men do in small towns. From the early age of thirteen years, he worked Saturdays and vacations in his father's basket factory, and became very proficient in the different branches of that business. When he started to college he had $2,000 saved up, which accumulations in small amounts from time to time, let out at interest, came in very conveniently in his further pursuit of educating himself for his future work in life.

He taught a district school during the winters of 1873 and 1874 in Cass County, Mich., and boarded around as the custom was. One winter he spent in canvassing in Connecticut, which familiarized him with business affairs.

During his college course he managed large railroad and steamboat excursions through Michigan, making his headquarters at Detroit. He became infatuated with Detroit and decided to make it his permanent home. He was also during two sessions of the Michigan Legislature Engrossing and Enrolling Clerk of the House of Representatives.

On finishing the law school course at Michigan University, Mr. Hannan was invited by Judge Wm. L. Carpenter to unite with him as partner, and he practiced a short time, though it was not his desire permanently to follow any profession. However, this step proved a stepping stone to his future vocation, for real estate opened up to him a very promising field and he at once took advantage of it. It was at this time that the oldest real estate man in Michigan died. The real estate business of Detroit had been in the hands of Mr. W. J. Waterman upwards of twenty-five years, and at his death business seemed to naturally drift to Mr. Hannan, who rapidly came into an extensive business. This he has since continued in all its branches, together with the allied branches of insurance and of loaning money on real estate. He has conducted many large subdivision sales; has handled some of the best pieces of business property in the city; is connected with a great many land companies, and represents large property interests in Detroit and elsewhere, both as principal and agent. He is also a stockholder in several banks and has acquired a considerable fortune as a result of his business acumen, industry and energy.

Mr. Hannan is very sociable and is fond of athletic sports. He is a member of the Detroit Club, the Rushmere Shooting and Fishing Club, Corinthian Lodge No. 241, F. & A. M., and Peninsular Chapter No. 16 of Royal Arch Masons. He was married May 18th, 1881, at Ann Arbor, to Luella Beaman, but has no children.

WALTER S. HARSHA, son of William and Mary Ann (Cook) Harsha, was born in Detroit, Mich., June 15, 1849. He received all his early education in the Detroit public schools and graduated A. B. from the literary department of the University of Michigan in 1871, and in 1875 had conferred upon him the degree of A. M. While a student at the University of Michigan he also read law in the office of C. I. Walker of Detroit, and following his graduation was made Deputy Clerk of the Recorder's Court at Detroit, retaining that position for about two years. Upon the establishment of the Superior Court of Detroit, on June 3, 1873, the County Clerk being ex officio clerk of said court, Mr. Harsha was appointed Deputy Clerk and vested with the full power of organization of the court. While clerk of this court he was admitted to the practice of law January 5, 1878. On January 1, 1879, he was appointed as deputy in charge of the Wayne County Clerk's office, which position he held until June 6, 1882, when he was appointed to his present position as clerk of the Circuit Court of the United States for the Eastern District of Michigan.

Early in 1891 Mr. Harsha elaborated a scheme of practice and rules for the United States Circuit Court of Appeals just established, which were submitted to and approved by the United States Supreme Court and, upon their recommendation, duly adopted by all of said Courts of Appeals throughout the country, and a uniform system of practice thus established, which up to this time remains substantially unchanged. In recognition of these valuable services, while still clerk of the United States Circuit Court of Detroit, he was appointed, June 16, 1891, Clerk of the United States Circuit Court of Appeals for the Sixth Circuit with clerk's office at Cincinnati, Ohio, and continued to hold both offices until he resigned from the Court of Appeals, October 2, 1894, retaining the Detroit office.

During his service in the Recorder's Court Mr. Harsha reorganized the office and was instrumental in the adoption of the system now in vogue in that court. He also reorganized the Wayne Circuit Court and inaugurated the present system with several judges.

For a number of years he gave a large portion of his time to the drafting and revision of the legal forms used in Michigan, the permanent value of which is inestimable; and to the annotating of some volumes of Michigan Supreme Court Reports, which work was subsequently completed by others. In 1886 he published "Annotated Federal Court Rules," which are in general use throughout the United States.

Mr. Harsha is a member of Delta Kappa Epsilon College Fraternity; Order of Free and Accepted Masons; Detroit Club, Country Club, Detroit Boat Club, etc. He is also a member of the Society of the Sons of the American Revolution.

January 18, 1881, Mr. Harsha married Isabella Mott, of Detroit.

GENERAL WM. HARTSUFF, one of the foremost citizens of St. Clair County, is a native of New York State, and was born January 16th, 1835. His parents, Henry and Rachell Hartsuff, came to Michigan in 1842 when he was only seven years of age. He received his education in the common schools, and at Leona College, now Adrian College. In the spring of 1857 he went to Port Huron and engaged in teaching. Upon the breaking out of the rebellion he had charge of the schools there, but with patriotic purpose resigned his position, and raised a company of volunteers, which was mustered into the service as Company E, Tenth Michigan Infantry, in command of Mr. Hartsuff as Captain. The following spring the regiment landed at Shiloh, just after the battle at that place. Capt Hartsuff was in the Battles of Franklin and Nashville, in which his command took an active part. He was promoted to Lieutenant Colonel, and was made Inspector General of the Twenty-third Army Corps, and afterwards promoted to the rank of Colonel, and appointed Inspector General of the Army of the Ohio, remaining in the service until the close of the war. Every male member of his father's family served in the war, his father being in command at Fort Gratiot. One brother, Major General George L. Hartsuff, a graduate of West Point, achieved great distinction in the service, and another brother, Dr. Albert Hartsuff, was a surgeon in the Regular Army. Dr. Duncan, of Saginaw, a brother-in-law, was surgeon of a Michigan regiment.

At the close of the war, while still in the field, Gen. Hartsuff was appointed Postmaster at Port Huron, and he has, ever since that time, been closely identified with the political and business interests of that City, and of the counties adjacent to it. He is a man of commanding presence, a forcible and effective speaker, and has done good work on the stump in numerous campaigns. He has been a delegate to several State Conventions. He has held a number of local offices, including that of Mayor of Port Huron, and in 1888 was the Republican candidate for Congress in the Seventh District. In those days the District was considered safely Democratic, but he was defeated by only a very small majority by the most popular Democrat within its borders. General Hartsuff has always been accounted a shrewd political manager. He was a leader in a County that produced many strong politicians. He was the leader of the close campaign that ended in the election of Omar D. Conger to the senatorship and is credited with doing much to bring about that result.

General Hartsuff has been among Port Huron's most active business men. He was one of the incorporators of the Port Huron and North Western Narrow Gauge Railway, which ran north to Port Austin, and which greatly increased Port Huron's trade with the counties in the Thumb. It has since been changed to a broad gauge, and is part of the Pere Marquette system. He was also one of the original stockholders of the Port Huron Times, and at a later date helped organize the Business Men's Association of Port Huron, which was a great aid in bringing business to that City. He is now President of the Commercial Bank.

General Hartsuff was married in 1858 to Miss Albenah Larned, daughter of Asa Larned. Two daughters survive the mother, Nora and Georgiana.

DAVID EMIL HEINEMAN was born at Detroit, October 17th, 1865, at the family residence on Woodward avenue, where he has since resided. His father, Emil S. Heineman, a resident of Detroit from the early '50's until his decease in 1896, was a prominent citizen, senior member of the firm of Heineman, Butzel & Co., and connected with many influential enterprises. Well equipped for the Land of Liberty, with a thorough knowledge of the English language and an education acquired in a home of culture and affluence, he came to America after the reaction of the Revolution of 1848 had dashed the hopes of the best youth of Germany, and had made liberty a byword. He was an unswerving Republican from the date of the foundation of the party until his death. The direct ancestors of the Heineman family prior to 1756, when the Seven Years' War swept away their possessions and home, were residents for many generations near the City of Bamberg in Bavaria. His mother was Miss Fanny Butzel, of a family long established in the section of Bavaria already mentioned. Both branches of the family have in past times contributed men who have rendered stalwart and unselfish service to their fellow-men and country.

David E. Heineman had the advantage of private tutoring until about twelve years of age, when he entered the public schools, completing the graded course, and entering the Detroit High School, whence he graduated as President of his class in 1883. After a year's continual travel in Europe, he entered the University of Michigan, completing the four years' course in three years, and graduating in 1887 with the Philosophical Degree. This was the semi-centennial of the University, and the exercises of commencement week were the most interesting ever held in Ann Arbor. For the evening celebration, which brought together the largest number of students, alumni and guests which the campus ever contained, Mr. Heineman was selected as orator. He was actively interested during his college years in the University Republican Club. He returned to the University for a year's work in the law department, where politics are known to consume all the energy that jurisprudence spares.

His first vote in 1886 helped elect Governor Luce, his first Presidential vote being for Harrison. He was one of the organizers of the Young Men's Republican League of Detroit, the pioneer in this State of many similar organizations, and was a delegate from the First Congressional District to the great National Convention of Republican Clubs at Cincinnati. He has also been a member of the Michigan and Alger Clubs, of Detroit, and other local Republican organizations. Since becoming a voter he has frequently been a delegate to State and local Conventions. For many years he was a member of the First Ward Republican Committee and as such effected reforms in the outrageous methods of conducting the primary elections. In 1893 he was appointed Chief Assistant City Attorney of Detroit, having charge of the entire court work of the office. During his incumbency he compiled the Revised Ordinances of the City, a volume of 700 pages, in the preparation of which, the enactment and repeal of many of the city laws were necessitated. He also gave personal attention during his term to the trial of over five thousand city ordinance cases, a task requiring a quick as well as a discriminating sense of justice.

On retiring from this office in 1896 and before entering private practice. Mr. Heineman took a foreign trip, visiting Africa and Italy. On his return he devoted his attention to practice, and to the various business interests entrusted to his care. He was at this time a Managing Director of the Fort Wayne & Belle Isle Railway Co., a Director of the Detroit Fire & Marine Insurance Co., a Director and Secretary of the Merz Capsule Co., and interested in other corporations and enterprises.

In the fall of 1899 he was elected Representative in the Legislature, receiving the highest vote of all the ten Republican candidates. As a member of the House of 1899 he took leading rank as a debater and exercised great personal influence in both Houses. He fought sturdily in behalf of the measure to establish a primary election system for Detroit, a measure which passed the House by one vote and only after a prolonged series of skirmishes and set battles. His efforts were uniform on the side of the reasonable and just legislation which the labor interests requested at that session. He had enacted into law, a long cherished plan of his for the establishment of a great aquarium and horticultural building for Belle Isle Park in his native City, a plan overwhelmingly endorsed by popular vote and now in course of realization. He interested himself in the educational polity of the State and introduced and saw enacted into law, a measure to enable the University to acquire gifts contingent upon life interests, with the result that the institution has already come into possession of properties of great value. Similarly he succeeded in passing through five committees and both Houses the Bill for a State Library Commission, which had always failed at previous sessions. This commission is more than justifying its existence by encouraging and fostering old and new libraries throughout the State. Along the same lines was the bill legalizing City aid for the Detroit Art Museum. Among others of his measures enacted into law were the Side Path Bill, the only Wheelmen's Measure that became a law that session, the St. Clair Flats Settlement Bill and the resolution to bring back from the Antilles the bodies of Michigan soldiers. He was allied with neither faction of his party as it was then divided, but consistently supported Governor Pingree on equal taxation measures at both the regular and special sessions of the Legislature.

Mr. Heineman, after the close of the session, and during the preconvention campaign was favorably spoken of in connection with the Lieutenant Governorship, but he did not enter the race. More recently strong pressure was brought to bear on him to make the run in his Senatorial District, but he publicly announced that as far as being a candidate for any office was concerned, he was not in politics.

Mr. Heineman is an Oddfellow, a Mason and an Elk, and, being a bachelor, is able to do justice to membership in many social, athletic and academic societies in Detroit and other cities. His acquaintance in all sections of his City is exceedingly large and he has friends throughout the entire State.

ALBERT McKEE HENRY, a prominent attorney, business man and Republican of Detroit, was born at Grand Rapids, Mich., September 20th, 1845, his father being William Gilmore Henry, a merchant and his mother, Huldana Squier Henry. John Henry, the great grandfather of William G. Henry, was Scotch-Irish, and emigrated from Coleraine, Ireland, to Coleraine, Mass., in 1738, when William Henry, the grandfather of William G., was four years old. William G. Henry was born at Bennington, Vt., in 1807, and died in Detroit in 1898. George Squier, the great grandfather of Huldana Squier Henry, was living in Concord, Mass., in 1642, doubtless of Welsh extraction. Her father, Wait Squier, born in 1767, at Lanesboro, Mass., was of great physical power and force of character. He was six feet, five inches in height. He moved to New Haven, Vt., in 1792, and was 92 years old at the time of his death in 1859. Huldana Squier Henry was born in New Haven, Vt., in 1811, and died in Detroit in 1880.

Albert McKee Henry graduated at the Grand Rapids High School in 1862: at the Michigan University in 1867, and the law school of Michigan University in 1869. While at the University he took up life insurance as an avocation during his vacations, and during his junior year at college and earned enough to pay his way through college. While in the University, he was a member of the Adelphi Debating Society, and during his Freshman year, a member of the Beta Theta Pi Fraternity. In his Sophomore year he became one of the charter members of the Psi Upsilon Fraternity. He is now one of the Board of Governors of the Psi Upsilon Guild. At the close of his college course, he took up life insurance again and earned enough to pay his law school expenses, and to take him to Omaha, Neb., where he was admitted to the bar in 1869. He practiced law in Omaha until the fall of 1875, when he removed to Detroit. While in Omaha, he bought a considerable tract of land with Nathan Shelton, in Omaha, and laid out Henry & Shelton's addition to the City of Omaha, which interest he owned when he removed to Detroit, and

*A. McKee Henry.*

upon which he has since realized a considerable amount. While in Omaha, he organized the Omaha Library Association, and succeeded in building it up until it had one of the largest libraries in the West. He was also one of the prime movers in organizing the Omaha Law Library, which has since become so large an institution. Starting with nothing in Omaha in 1869, in seven years he had accumulated a considerable fortune when he removed to Detroit. After removing to the latter City he practiced law until 1890, when he was appointed assignee of the R. G. Peters Salt & Lumber Co., and receiver of the R. G. Peters estate, which he closed up in 1893-4. This receivership and the attorneyship of the Detroit, Bay City & Alpena Railroad Co. occupied his entire time, and he gave up the practice of law. Since 1894, his time has been fully occupied in taking care of estates and his own property. Among other estates of which he has been administrator were those of James Burns and Aurilla A. Burns.

Albert M. Henry has been a Republican since he became of age. He cast his first ballot at a National election for General Grant, and has voted for every Republican nominee for the Presidency since then. Was a member of the City Council of Detroit, when it was first organized; was a member of the Pardon Board during the administration of Governor R. A. Alger; helped to organize the Dime Savings Bank: was its first Temporary President and was a member of its first board of directors. He has been a member of the Michigan Club, the Detroit Club and the Country Club, since their organization; belongs to the Ashlar Lodge of Masons, the Michigan Sovereign Consistory and the Mystic Shrine. He also belongs to the Sons of the American Revolution. He was married in January, 1875, to Frances M. Burns, at Detroit, Mich., and has two children, Burns Henry, who has just graduated from Yale College. and Edith Frances Henry, who graduated from Miss Porter's School at Farmington, Conn.

THOMAS HISLOP, one of Detroit's active attorneys, was born at Rodgerville, Huron County, Ontario, March 5th, 1852. His father was Thomas Hislop, a blacksmith, and his mother's maiden name was Elizabeth Clarkson. His father was a native of Peebles, Scotland, and his mother a native of Lanark, Scotland. They came to Canada about 1845, and settled on a farm on London Road between London and Goderich, Ontario.

The subject of the present sketch was educated at common school and Normal School, Toronto, and the University of Michigan. He was a school teacher in Ottawa, and St. Catherines Collegiate Institutes, for several years, and stood at the head of the profession, but took up the study of law, passed examinations at Osgoode Hall, Toronto, then completed the course, and graduated from the University of Michigan, and was admitted to the bar in 1880. He has practiced law in Detroit since that time. He was nominated and ran for

Circuit Judge on the Republican ticket in 1899, but was defeated by a small majority. He has been a Republican since 1880, first voted for Garfield, and has been a delegate to several State Conventions, the first time being when General R. A. Alger was nominated for Governor.

Mr. Hislop is a member of the Michigan Club, and other Republican Clubs; of all Masonic bodies including the Michigan Sovereign Consistory, Damascus Commandery, Moslem Temple; the Ancient Order of United Workmen, Knights of Loyal Guard, American Insurance Union and others of similar character. He was married to Janet H. Muir in 1874 and has one daughter, Miss Jennie Hislop.

FRANK A. HOOKER, Justice of the Supreme Court, is a descendant of one of the most famous families in Connecticut history. The first of the family in this country was the Reverend Thomas Hooker, one of the non-conformists, who, in the latter part of the sixteenth century, left England and, after a few years spent in the Dutch Republic of Holland, came to America in company with John Cotton and others, zealous for religious and civil liberty, and who, sailing in the good ship Griffin, landed at the town of Boston in 1633. First locating his congregation at Newton, about ten miles inland from Boston, and not finding that civil liberty for which they came to Plymouth colony, the congregation in 1663 removed to Connecticut, where at Hartford, a colony was founded and the first written constitution of the New World was adopted January 24th, 1637. At the foundation of this instrument rested the doctrine of the Declaration of Independence that "governments derive their just powers from the consent of the governed," a doctrine which Mr. Hooker had previously proclaimed in his sermons, and of which he might be said to be the founder.

Reverend Samuel Hooker, of West Hartford, a son of Reverend Thomas Hooker, and also a native of England, married a daughter of Thomas Willet, another Englishman, who had spent some time in the Dutch Republic, and who, coming to Plymouth Colony, succeeded Miles Standish in the command of the military of that colony, and, afterwards going to New York, was appointed to be the first Mayor of that City. From this union comes Justice Frank A. Hooker down through a long line of ancestry, of which he is lineal in the eighth descent from and including the Rev. Thomas Hooker, seven of whom, like himself, have been men following professional avocations; and all of whom, except the two named as born in England, were natives of Hartford, Conn., where, on January 16th, 1844, Justice Frank A. Hooker had his birth. His father, who was the only one in the line of descent who passed by the professions to engage in business pursuits, met with financial reverses which caused him to seek a retrievement of his fortunes in what then was called the Western States, coming as far west as the Town of Maumee, Ohio, remaining there about three years when, going some few miles farther West, he located with his family at Defiance, Ohio.

Justice Hooker's mother was Camilla Porter, a native of the State of New York, whose ancestors lived in Connecticut and who was related by descent to the Grants and the Fields, as well as the Porters, all prominent families in New England.

The elementary education of Justice Hooker was received in the schools of Connecticut and Ohio, and from the teaching of an older sister, who, herself, possessed of a superior education had, also, the faculty of imparting knowledge to others. After a course in the business college at Defiance, he, at 19 years of age, began the study of law, finishing in the law department of the University of Michigan, from which he graduated with the class of 1865 and, on receiving his diploma on graduation day, was at once admitted to the bar at Ann Arbor. He then went to Bryan, Ohio, where he was also admitted to practice. After practicing law for about a year in that place, he removed to Charlotte, Mich., which was his home until 1893, when the Legislature passed an act requiring Justices of the Supreme Court to reside at Lansing. When engaged in law practice in Charlotte he associated with him in partnership E. C. Hickock, and prepared abstract records of the County and subsequently he was head of the firm of Hooker & DeGraff. He was very successful in his practice and was highly regarded both as a trial lawyer and counselor.

Judge Hooker was always a Republican in politics and as such first came into public notice in matters outside of his profession. He was a member of the County Committee when Eaton was one of the best organized counties in the State and one of the surest in its Republican majorities. He was Superintendent of Schools of the County, was Prosecuting Attorney for two terms from 1873 to 1877, and was often a delegate to District and State Conventions. In 1878 Governor Croswell appointed him Judge of the Fifth Judicial Circuit, as reorganized, and he was afterwards elected and re-elected to the same position. In the fall of 1892 he was elected Justice of the Supreme Court to succeed Chief Justice Morse, resigned, and in the spring of 1893 he was elected to the same position for the full term of ten years. Of his characteristics on the bench, a discriminating writer in Bench and Bar says: "In the Circuit Court his influence over juries was unusual, and while able to conceal his opinions of the merits of the case he was able to impress them with the nature and importance of their duty to the parties litigant and the public, so that they rarely wandered from the questions at issue, or failed to reach just verdicts. The circuit in which he presided is the most populous in the State of any having a single Judge, but his industry and executive ability enabled him to dispose of the business with promptness and satisfaction, both to attorneys and litigants. He possesses certain mental traits that are most admirable in a judge—equability of temper, acute perception and a disposition to be perfectly fair; a mind trained to habits of thought; large powers of concentration and penetration; exceptional capacity for hard work. These characteristics, sustained by incorruptible integrity and supplemented by that indefinable quality which passes current under the name of judicial temper, gave him high reputation as a Circuit Judge. His breadth of view, vigor of intellect, discriminating discernment of the res gesta and the res adjudicata in a case are among his important qualifitions for the duties of a Justice of the Supreme Court. His general competency, his power of endurance in the investigation of the abstract questions of law, or reviewing the procedure of a lower court, and his sound judgment, complete the symmetry and give him rank as one of the very ablest jurists of the State." Judge Hooker was married August 5th, 1868, to Miss Emma E. Carter, daughter of Hon. William Carter, of Defiance. Their family consists of two sons, Harry E. Hooker, a lawyer, of Lansing, and Dr. Charles E. Hooker, of Grand Rapids.

CHARLES CLARK HOPKINS, who, as Clerk of the Supreme Court, has been a familiar figure to the leading attorneys of the State for nearly two decades, was born at White Lake, Oakland County, Mich., April 4th, 1849. His father was Erastus Hopkins, a farmer, born in Paris, Oneida County, N. Y., August 16th, 1804, and his mother, Climene (Clark) Hopkins, was born in Easthampton, Hampshire County, Mass., July 2d, 1810. His ancestors were among the earliest settlers in New England, coming from Coventry, Warwick County, England. The family was of established antiquity and for a long series of years enjoyed parliamentary rank and served a succession of monarchs, acquiring civil and military distinction. They were prominent in the affairs of Coventry in the sixteenth century, one William Hopkins having been Mayor of that City in 1564. Two brothers of William, Richard and Nicholas, were sheriffs in 1554 and 1561, respectively. Sampson, son of Richard, was also Mayor of Coventry in 1640. Another son, Richard, became eminent at the bar, was knighted and represented the City of Coventry in Parliament at the Restoration. John Hopkins, the progenitor of the Connecticut line of that name, came to this country in 1634 and helped to found the Hartford colony. President Mark Hopkins, of Williams College, and the eminent divine, Samuel Hopkins, founder of the Hopkinsian School of Theology, were both members of that family. Consider Hopkins, a great grandfather of Charles C., served in the Continental Army, and was Captain of a Trainband in Colonial times in Connecticut. Erastus Hopkins, father of Charles C., was one of the pioneers of Oakland County, coming West in the fall of 1834 in an emigrant wagon. He cleared a farm in the wilderness and lived there until his death in 1876, his wife having died in 1864. A brother, Dan G., was in the Civil War, being a member of the Seventeenth

(Stonewall regiment) Infantry, and died September 14, 1862, of wounds received in the Battle of South Mountain.

Charles C. Hopkins remained on the farm attending district school until the fall of 1867, entering the Normal School at Ypsilanti. He spent a portion of the time for the next few years at school, teaching district school and working on the farm, graduating at the Normal in the class of 1872. He was at once offered and accepted the position of principal of the Union School at Rockland, Ontonagon County, where he remained two years, spending the summer vacation in 1873 in surveying a section of a U. S. Military Road running from Rockland to Lac Vieux desert on the Wisconsin State line. Desiring to study law he resigned the principalship of the school and in the fall of 1874 entered the law department of Michigan University, graduating in the law class of 1876.

In the legislative session of 1875 Mr. Hopkins was clerk of the House Judiciary Committee, keeping up his studies at the University at the same time. In 1877 he was clerk of the Senate Judiciary Committee, and in 1879 and 1881 was Assistant Secretary of the State Senate. He was admitted to the bar in 1876 and practiced his profession in Detroit, becoming largely interested in real estate, until in January, 1882, when the Supreme Court, having been empowered by the adoption of a Constitutional Amendment, to appoint its own Clerk, he was appointed to that position which he has occupied to the present time. His father was a Whig, an Abolitionist and afterwards a Republican. He has always been a Republican, cast his first ballot on his twenty-first birthday, and has voted at every election since. In the campaign of 1880, he was Secretary of the Wayne County Republican Committee, and was active in politics until appointed Clerk of the Supreme Court. Since then, the court, not considering the office in any sense a political one, he has refrained from active work, but has always been an outspoken Republican and a liberal contributor to campaign funds. He is a member of the Michigan Club, Detroit Club, and Sons of the American Revolution. He was married at Enfield, Massachusetts, July 29th, 1880, to Clara J. Potter, daughter of a prominent family in Central Massachusetts. Their children are Edward Potter, born September 21st, 1881, a sophomore in Michigan University; George Hayes, born September 11th, 1884, a senior in Lansing High School; Charles C., Jr., born October 18th, 1889, who died August 2, 1891, and Carroll Lyman, born December 23rd, 1892.

GEORGE HIRAM HOPKINS, of Detroit, comes of a family that were not only among the earliest settlers in Connecticut, but had a long line of English ancestry before that. They were, according to Burke's Commoners, a family of established antiquity and eminence, long residents of Coventry, County of Warwick, and active in the York and Lancaster wars. One of them was Mayor of Coventry in 1554, and two others were sheriffs of the same place in 1554 and 1561 respectively. The first of the Connecticut line in this country was John Hopkins, who came over in 1632, and was one of the founders of Hartford Colony. One of the ancestors in this country, Consider Hopkins, was captain of a Trainband in 1767, and subsequently private in the Eighteenth Regiment of Connecticut militia in the Revolutionary War.

George H. Hopkins was the son of Erastus and Climena Clark Hopkins, and was born at White Lake, Oakland County, Michigan, November 7th, 1842, his father having moved from Steuben County, New York, to that point in 1834. George worked on his father's farm and attended school winters till 1860, when he commenced teaching and took a course in the Pontiac High School, and entered the State Normal School in 1862. In August of that year, with a number of other students of the Normal and the University of Michigan, at Ann Arbor, he caught the war fever and found the only cure for his patriotic ardor to be the carrying of a musket in the Seventeenth Michigan Infantry, serving in Company E of that regiment, which was largely composed of students from the two institutions named. The Seventeenth Michigan Infantry was noted for the valor of its men and took part in many of the most important campaigns in the War of the Rebellion, among which were those of the Maryland campaign in 1862; the Fredericksburg campaign in the winter of 1862-3; siege of Vicksburg, Mississippi, in 1863; East Tennessee campaign and siege of Knoxville, autumn and winter of 1863-4; the Wilderness; Spottsylvania; Cold Harbor; North Anna, in summer of 1864; followed by the siege of Petersburg and surrender of Lee at Appomattox. At the Battle of South Mountain, Md., his brother, Dan, was mortally wounded in the engagement which gave to the Seventeenth Michigan the name of "Stonewall Regiment," which it maintained with pride till the close of the war. When the war closed, and his country no longer needed her sons to carry the musket in her defense, Mr. Hopkins returned to his native State and took up the pursuits of peace, where he left them in August, 1862, by again becoming a student in the State Normal School, graduating in the class of 1867. He spent some time in post graduate studies there, then entered the literary department of the University at Ann Arbor, and going from there into the law school of the University, graduated in the class of 1871.

During the pursuit of his law studies, he was appointed Assistant United States Marshal for the Eastern District of Michigan, as such, taking the census of 1870 in one District of Washtenaw County and a portion of Lapeer County. He was admitted to the bar in the same year in which he graduated from the University, and coming immediately to Detroit, he entered the law offices of Newberry, Pond & Brown, and was soon thereafter made Assistant Attorney for the Detroit & Milwaukee Railroad, which he served for a period of eight years.

John J. Bagley, when he was elected Governor, induced George to lay aside other interests and serve the State in the capacity of Executive Secretary. At the expiration of Governor Bagley's second term, Governor Croswell induced him to remain as Secretary until the end of the Legislative session.

After this service Mr. Hopkins returned to the practice of his profession in Detroit. He was one of the few Republican candidates in Wayne County elected to the Legislature of 1879, where he served as Chairman of the Committee on Military Affairs, and as a member of the Committee on Railroads. He was elected to the Legislature of 1881-2 by an increased majority, and in that body served as Chairman of the Committee on the University of Michigan, and during the session secured the passage of a bill providing for the present library building of the University. He was also a member of the Committee on Railroads and of the Committee on the apportionment of the State into Congressional, Senatorial and Legislative districts. Mr. Hopkins served his third consecutive term in the Legislature of 1883-4. In this session he was elected Speaker pro tem., was Chairman of the Judiciary Committee, and member of other important committees of that session. During his legislative service, among other important measures he introduced and championed the passage of the bill providing for the purchase of Belle Isle for park purposes by the City of Detroit, and for the maintenance of the State militia, also the bill under which the Wayne County jury system was established.

The death of Governor Bagley in 1881 brought Major Hopkins into the world of general business. He was made a trustee and executor of the Governor's estate, and from that time to the present has given his chief attention to the large interests, which were there involved. He is at present a Director and Treasurer of John J. Bagley & Co., President of the Detroit Tobacco Dealer's Exchange, a Director in the Union Trust Co., Chairman of the Board of Managers of the Union Trust Building Co., Limited; Director of the American Exchange National Bank, Trustee and Treasurer of the Woodmere Cemetery Association, a Director in the Michigan Wire Cloth Co., Director and Vice-President of the Standard Life and Accident Insurance Co., also a Director in the Mutual Mercantile Agency of New York City.

Notwithstanding Mr. Hopkins' activity in business affairs he has always been active in Republican politics. He has attended as delegate, many State as well as local Conventions, was an alternate delegate at the National Convention in 1888, has served as Chairman of the Wayne County Committee, was Chairman of the State Central Committee in 1878, and again in the campaigns of 1888 and 1889. He served four years as Collector of the Port of Detroit, by President Harrison's appointment of January 20th, 1890. He has taken much interest in the welfare of the National Guard organizations and was Lieutenant Colonel and Assistant Inspector General on the staff of Governor Alger.

Major Hopkins not only saw service in the War of the Rebellion, but also occupied a responsible position in the Spanish War. May 12th, 1898, he was appointed by President McKinley, Assistant Adjutant General of Volunteers, with the rank of Major, and May 27th received an order from the War Department directing him to report in person to the Secretary of War for duty in his office. He occupied a position of confidential agent similar to that of Charles A. Dana in the Civil War. He continued there till July 31st, 1899, when, on the resignation of Secretary Alger, he sent in his own resignation. June 2d, 1898, he served on a Board, with Colonel Charles R. Greenleaf, Assistant Surgeon General, and Colonel Moore, of the Quartermaster General's Department, to examine into the condition of Camp Alger near Washington. A week later he was on a Military Board, of which the other members were Colonel Greenleaf, Major F. G. Hodgson, of the Quartermaster General's Department, and Lieutenant Edgar O. Jadwin, of the Engineer Corps, with instructions to report on the various sites proposed for army camps. There were many cities in the South that wanted camps located near them, for the money there was in it, and some of them were bringing a good deal of influence to bear in support of their claims. The Board visited Columbia, Charleston and Summerville, S. C.; Fernandina, Jacksonville, and Miami, Fla.; and Savannah, Brunswick and Augusta, Ga. A great pressure had been brought to bear, especially by General Miles, in favor of establishing a camp at Miami, Fla. Major Hopkins' report was strongly against this, both for sanitary reasons and on account of inadequate water supply, as well as lack of transportation facilities, and this scheme for the time was relinquished. At a later period, through the persistence of General Miles, a division of about 5,000 men were sent to this place, but the necessity which soon arose for the hasty abandonment of the camp vindicated the wisdom of Major Hopkins' judgment. Major Hopkins' subsequent duties involved the inspection of army hospitals and camps, and of the transport vessels. He visited Chickamauga and Montauk Point, where camps and hospitals were located, several times, made two trips to Cuba and accompanied the Secretary of War on his visits of inspection to Montauk Point, Chickamauga, Jacksonville and other points, including a trip to Cuba and Porto Rico. It was in accordance with his suggestions in a report to the Secretary that the camp at Chickamauga was abandoned after typhoid fever broke out there; that the arrangement of berths on the army transports was changed; and that, in face of the opposition of the surgeon in charge, female nurses were first employed, in a time of great need, in the hospitals at Montauk Point.

Having remained single, with no wife to make him stay in nights, Mr. Hopkins has indulged his social tastes by a liberal club membership. He is a Mason up to the 32d degree, though not par-

ticularly active in that order. He is a member of the following clubs: The Michigan, Country, Detroit, Yondotega, Bankers', Fellowcraft, Audobon, Detroit Boat, all of Detroit, and the Lake St. Clair Fishing and Shooting Club; also of the Metropolitan Club of Washington, the Union League Club of New York City, and the Sons of the American Revolution and has been an active member of the G. A. R. almost from the beginning of that organization. Has been Commander of Detroit Post, for several years a member of the Executive Committee of the National Council of Administration, and one year Adjutant General, Grand Army of the Republic.

GEORGE BYRON HORTON, a prominent farmer and cheese manufacturer in Southern Michigan, was born in La Fayette Township, Medina County, O., April 17th, 1845. His father was Samuel Horton, a farmer, and his mother was Lucina A. Horton. Samuel Horton was born in Lincolnshire, England, and came to America alone in 1820, then a lad of 16 years. He was 104 days by sail, on the ocean. The vessel was storm-tossed, lost her rigging, was out of food, and of those on board seventeen starved to death. Mr. Horton, Sr., married Lucina A. Perkins in Herkimer County, New York, and started without money and only the education received in England prior to his sixteenth year. He made his first start in Medina County, Ohio; sold and bought land in Niagara County, N. Y.; came to Michigan in 1853, settled in the Township of Fairfield, Lenawee County, and commenced the manufacture of cheese for the general market. He was considered the pioneer cheese manufacturer of the State, and was very successful, and died in 1873, leaving a farm of 400 acres of choice land, two cheese factories and other proportionate wealth.

George B. Horton, the only son, received a common school education, with one year at Adrian College. He always worked and lived on the farm where he now resides. He took up the business of his father in 1873; paid off the other heirs, and increased his land to 800 acres of the best in Southern Michigan. He owns and manages eight cheese factories, with an output of over 1,000,000 pounds of cheese annually.

Mr. Horton always worked with the Republican party, cast his first Presidential vote for Grant in 1868, and has always been active for the success of the party. He is one of those who believe in encouraging the essentials to a Republican form of government, i. e., the general intelligence of the masses of the people, so that they may intelligently lead and not blindly follow. He was appointed to the State Board of Agriculture by Governor Luce, but resigned for business reasons. He was elected to the State Senate of 1890-1, served 60 days and was unseated by the celebrated Squaw Buck Senate, without a hearing, on the charge made against him of ineligibility because of holding a commission as Postmaster at Fruit Ridge, though his resignation was sent in before election. He never asked for nor received compensation for his services in the Senate.

He is closely attached to his chosen profession, agriculture. Progressive, generous and alert in assisting all movements calculated for the improvement and extended opportunities of people and community. Mr. Horton joined the Grange movement at the first, became a charter member of Weston, now Fruit Ridge Grange, and served as its Master twenty years. From the first he gave the movement the best thought and contributed liberally in time, labor and money, to building and furnishing Fruit Ridge Grange Hall, which is one of the best planned and equipped of any in the United States. Its large library, museum, stage equipment and general program work make it one of the strongest educational forces in Fairfield and surrounding townships. He assisted in organizing Lenawee County Grange, and was its Master for six years. He considers his Grange work as his life's work, for in it is seen an opportunity to do good for others and to influence aright the affairs of the State as in no other way. He was always prominent in the State Grange work, served on the Executive Committee six years, and was elected Master of the State Grange in 1892. He is now commencing his fifth term of two years each. The order in Michigan has doubled under his administration, and several lines of practical effort have been established, calculated the better to carry out the principles of the order, i. e., the improvement of the farm people of the State, socially, educationally, morally, financially and influentially.

Mr. Horton assisted in organizing the Lenawee County Agricultural Society, and has been its only President, serving twenty-three consecutve years. The society is now one of the strongest and best in the State. As Master of the State Grange and President of the Michigan State Dairymen's Association, he was a prime mover in the demand for pure food regulations in Michigan. It was his original idea to so concentrate and crystallize the general complaints of the people regarding the inequality of State and local taxation as to give the matter such prominence as a public question, as would force its recognition and consideration by political parties and the Legislature of the State. In the furtherance of this plan, in his first annual address to the State Grange, he urged the appointment of a Tax Statistician by authority of the State, to collect and compile such data regarding the assessment and collection of taxes as might form a basis for laws compelling justice in the matter. The State Grange, of which he is the official head, was the chief promoter of equal taxation, and the prominence of the question, the tenacity with which it has been kept prominently before people and Legislature, are due largely to the influence of Mr. Horton, reflected through the State Grange of Michigan and its allied organizations. He is a close student of State and local affairs and his influence is for the good of the greatest number of people. Mr. Horton has been the Michigan delegate to the National Grange for eight years and is still a

Henry Howard

member of that body. Has always acted as Chairman of important committees and is now Priest Annalist of the Seventh, or highest degree of the order.

He has been solicited many times to stand for high offices of State, even to the highest, but has never encouraged the use of his name for these honorable and high places. Mr. Horton is associated with no persons or companies in business. If the business paid he could always manage it himself. He is a member of the Knights of Pythias and the Elks' organization. He was married in 1877 to M. Amanda Bradish, of Madison Township, Lenawee County. They have four children: Alice L., Norman B., Samuel W. and Carrie L. They are at this time living at the parental home or attending school. The ambition of their parents is to make for them a truly farm home, surrounded by all the refining influences and enjoyments of country life.

HENRY HOWARD, for many years one of the leading lumbermen of St. Clair County and vicinity, was born in Detroit, March 8th, 1833, and was less than a year old when his parents moved to Port Huron, where he received his education. He was the son of John and Nancy Hubbard Howard. His father was born at Red Stone, Pennsylvania in 1799, and early in his manhood went to Detroit, where he engaged in the grocery and hotel business. He was among the first to offer accommodations to the fast increasing army of immigrants to Michigan and the West, and he was also among the first to erect business blocks in the young City, the low row in the rear of the former site of the Michigan Exchange being a landmark for many years. Owing to the outbreak of the cholera epidemic in 1833-4 he moved his family to Port Huron, where he engaged in lumber business, and during his career as lumberman Mr. Howard built three saw mills in that City.

Henry Howard became associated with his father in the lumber business at the age of twenty-one years. The partnership existed twenty-six years, when his father retired, and he continued the business alone until his death. Since his decease in 1894, the business has been carried on under the name of the Henry Howard Estate, by his son-in-law, Albert D. Bennett, as Trustee.

Mr. Howard was identified with many Port Huron business interests. He was one of the organizers of the Port Huron Times Company in 1869, and for several years was its President, holding this office at the time of the sale of the paper to its present proprietors. He was prominently identified with the organization of the First National Bank and held the office of President of that institution up to his death. He was President of the Port Huron Gas Light Co., Vice-President of the Michigan Sulphite Fibre Co., and the Michigan Director of the Grand Trunk lines west of St. Clair River. Up to a few months before his death he held the position of Vice-

President of the Port Huron Engine & Thresher Co. He was also prominent in the Port Huron & Northwestern Railway, being elected President of the Company in 1880, and holding the office for two years. He was interested in marine matters, and owned several vessels and steamers. At one time he was a stockholder in the Star Line steamers. He was President of the Northern Transit Company of Sarnia, which owned the steambarge Tecumseh and other vessels. He formed the Howard Towing Association, which operated a line of tugs till the depression in marine business rendered the line unremunerative. He gradually disposed of his marine interests, having sold his last vessel, the schooner Wm. Shupe, to Captain Nelson Little, in 1894. One of his last acts was a generous one and was characteristic of the man. When the Shupe was lost in that year, he directed that the notes which Captain Little had given in payment for the vessel should be returned, thus saving the Captain the loss of his farm.

In politics Mr. Howard was always a staunch Republican, took a lively interest in all the actions of the party and contributed liberally to the funds necessary to party organization. He was elected Alderman from the Second Ward and held the office for fourteen years, and served as Chairman of the Committee on Ways and Means in the Council. He was also a member of the Board of Estimates and the Board of Education. In 1882 he was elected Mayor of the City, holding the office for one year. In 1870 he was elected to the State Legislature and held the office two terms. During his second term he was prominently mentioned for Speaker of the House, but declined to allow his name to be presented. He ran once for State Senator, but was defeated by William M. Cline, a surprise as great to Mr. Cline as to Mr. Howard. For several years he was mentioned in connection with the Congressional nomination, and on one or two occasions it has seemed as though he would be the candidate on the Republican ticket. While acknowledging that he would not be adverse to receiving the nomination, he would never make any effort to secure it. In 1891 he was elected Regent of the University of Michigan, which position he held at the time of his death. He was an active member of the Michigan Club and was one of its delegates to New York to organize the National League in 1887.

The mere enumeration of the positions that Mr. Howard held, numerous as they were, do not furnish a complete indication of his prominence in the party councils. Though not a frequent nor a voluble talker in the Legislature, what he said had weight on account of its clear and concise statement. He was faithful in committee work, and during his second term in the House he was at the head of the most important committee in that body, that of Ways and Means. The Convention that nominated him for Regent gave him the nomination by acclamation, a high honor in view of the fact that the applicants for that office are generally numerous.

*Jay A. Hubbell.*

In 1855 Mr. Howard was married to Miss Elizabeth E. Spalding, of New York State, who survived him. There have been six children born to them, only two of whom are living, a daughter, Mrs. A. D. Bennett, and a son, John Henry. Mr. Howard was a member of Port Huron Lodge, F. & A. M., and of Huron Chapter, R. A. M., and of Port Huron Commandery No. 7, Knights Templar. He was also a member of the Port Huron Club, and was its second President. He was a director of the Club at the time of his death. He belonged to the Lake St. Clair Shooting and Fishing Club, and the Michigan Club of Detroit. He was a prominent member of the Baptist church and always contributed liberally to its support.

In business Mr. Howard was always successful and he had accumulated a fortune. He was of a happy and contented disposition, and was always genial and good tempered, spreading a pleasant influence over those around him. He was extremely generous and charitable. No deserving person ever left him without receiving help. In almost every movement in the City, for the betterment of mankind, Mr. Howard was prominent. He was a progressive man and always worked for the best interests of his City, State and Country.

JAY A. HUBBELL, of Houghton, for more than a generation one of the foremost citizens of the Upper Peninsula, was born in Avon, Oakland County, Mich., on September 15th, 1829. His father, Samuel Hubbell, was a native of the State of New York, who removed to Oakland County about 1820, being one of the earliest settlers in that section, where he lived on a farm until his death, which occurred in 1870. Jay A. Hubbell attended the common schools and worked on his father's farm until he was eighteen years of age. After two years of preparatory study at Romeo and Rochester, at times interrupted by a painful disease of the eyes, he entered the Sophomore class of the University of Michigan, at Ann Arbor, and graduated in 1853. He then read law for two years at Pontiac and Detroit, and, in 1855, was admitted to practice by the Supreme Court, at Adrian. Immediately after his admission to the bar he removed to Ontonagon, where he formed a law partnership with Hon. A. H. Hanscom. This partnership was continued for one year, after which Mr. Hubbell became associated with George C. Jones. He continued in active practice, taking a prominent part in all the public affairs of the County, and forming an extensive acquaintance with the citizens and business interests of the copper district until 1860, when he removed to Houghton, where mining was then developing rapidly. About 1863 he formed a partnership with the late Hon. Clarence E. Eddy, who was afterwards Judge of the Circuit Court for the Upper Peninsula. He was subsequently in partnership with Hon. James O'Grady, who also became Judge of the same Circuit; with Justice Claudius B. Grant, of the Michigan Supreme bench, and with Judge

J. W. Stone, of the Marquette Circuit. He was also at one time in partnership with Thomas L. Chadbourne. In 1858 he was elected Prosecuting Attorney of Ontonagon County and was appointed District Attorney of the Upper Peninsula. He was again made District Attorney of the Upper Peninsula in 1870, and Prosecuting Attorney of Houghton County for three successive terms. He took an active part in politics, and, during the Presidential campaign of 1868, made political speeches in several counties. In the same year he was sent to Washington, by the people of the copper mining district, to aid in securing a higher tariff upon copper, imperatively required by the industry, which was then languishing, and in this mission was signally successful.

Mr. Hubbell's part in National affairs, however, may be said to date from 1872. Upon the formation of the Ninth Congressional District, comprising the Upper Peninsula counties and nineteen of those in the Lower Peninsula, he was nominated at a Convention held in Ludington in the fall of 1872, and in the exciting Grant and Greeley campaign that followed addressed political meetings in nearly every County in the Ninth District. Mr. Hubbell was elected over S. P. Ely, of Marquette, the Democratic candidate, by a majority of 6,405 votes. He was four times re-elected, serving in the 43rd, 44th, 45th, 46th and 47th Congresses, where he speedily took rank among the leading Republicans in the House, serving upon the Committees on Mines and Mining, Commerce, Banking and Currency, and other less important committees. He was a strong debater and an industrious worker, very tenacious of purpose and especially watchful of all legislation affecting the interests of Michigan. As Chairman of the Republican Congressional Committee, in the Garfield-Hancock campaign of 1880, Judge Hubbell was directly charged with the duty of raising funds for the party needs from the clerks of the various departments in Washington. The levy was made systematically, and every clerk in every department was assessed 2 per cent of his annual salary. Many of the clerks demurred and the matter speedily got into the press and became a National affair. Mr. Hubbell, as the signatory of the assessment circular, was roundly denounced by a majority of the newspapers of the country, and from half the political rostrums. Feeling the injustice of being held solely responsible for the assessments, which were decided on by the entire committee, Judge Hubbell went to Zachariah Chandler and other leaders of the party, who told him he was in for it anyway, and that it would do no good to drag them in also. Thus appealed to, he kept silence, and shouldered the entire responsibility. The incident was used against him at home, and his political enemies succeeded in making a coalition by which he was deprived of a renomination.

In 1884 and again in 1886 he was elected to the State Senate, where he took an active part in all general legislation, and where, by sheer persistence and force of character, he carried through an unwilling Legislature the first appropriation for the Michigan College of Mines at Houghton, an institution which has since abundantly demonstrated its usefulness, not only to the mining interests of the Upper Peninsula, but to those of the entire State and the country at large. Mr. Hubbell donated the site upon which the college was built, and was styled the father of the college. He was, for some years, President of its Board of Control. In 1890 Mr. Hubbell was elected Judge of the Twelfth Circuit, comprising the Counties of Baraga, Houghton and Keweenaw, and was re-elected, serving until January 1st, 1900.

Mr. Hubbell was at one time a very wealthy man. Unusual grasp of affairs and the courage to follow the deductions of a rarely logical mind enabled him to amass a large fortune, from shrewd mining investments, in addition to the large income derived from a highly successful law practice. In the middle eighties Mr. Hubbell was a heavy loser, through investment in the Santa Fe copper mine. At that time this loss was considered by his critics an evidence of lack of business judgment, but in view of recent happenings it is seen that Mr. Hubbell was merely fifteen years ahead of the development of the territory in which the Santa Fe is located. The mine is in the arid region of New Mexico, and lack of transportation facilities was solely responsible for the failure of the venture. Mr. Hubbell paid his losses without a murmur, and returned to the practice of the law. This practice was interrupted by his election to the State Senate for two terms. To descend from the position of a National lawgiver of the first eminence to the comparatively obscure place of State Senator, would not be to the taste of most strong and ambitious men, and it was not Judge Hubbell's desire to be a candidate for the office. That he took the nomination and served two terms, declining a third, is ascribed to pure patriotism and a desire to benefit his fellow citizens of the copper district. It was felt, and with reason, that Judge Hubbell, and he alone, could secure needed legislation at Lansing, and disabuse the minds of certain hostile elements of the impression that the Upper Peninsula was asking for unreasonable things. The foundation of the Michigan College of Mines, the building of the branch prison at Marquette and a considerable number of important acts passed during his two terms as State Senator, directly through his influence, bear witness to his efficiency in the minor, though honorable position, which he had accepted solely from a feeling of duty and a broad-minded desire to be of service to his fellow citizens of the copper district, who had watched his career with pride, and who, not only remaining loyal to his fortunes through prosperity, had never wavered in their faith in his honor and honesty during the dark days when he was held up to unmerited scorn throughout the breadth of the land.

The story has crept into print that Judge Hubbell was practically penniless in his latter days. Nothing could be further from the truth. In his beautiful home, "The Highlands," surrounded by his library and many varied and costly mementos of a long and eventful career, there were no evidences of the biting poverty so untruthfully ascribed. The facts of the matter are that Judge Hubbell was a money-maker and a money spender from his earliest days. To the cry of necessity he never learned to turn an unheeding ear. For public improvements he was ever the first to subscribe, and the sum was always a substantial one. Although hard hit by the failure of a trusted friend, early in 1897, Judge Hubbell long foresaw the unparalleled "copper boom" of 1898 and 1899, and by judicious investments at that time realized a fortune within a few months after his mistaken friends had begun pitying his financial distress.

In 1899 Mrs. Hubbell died, her demise proving a great shock to her companion of years. In July, 1900, his eldest daughter, Mrs. Lessing Karger, died after a very brief illness, and this grief, coming so soon after the loss of his wife, led to a paralytic stroke which deprived its victim of speech, though without impairing his mental faculties. Judge Hubbell's death was not long delayed after the passing of his wife and child, and on October 15, 1900, he breathed his last. His bier was followed to the grave by thousands, and there were few among the number to whom his death did not come as in some sense a personal bereavement. He was a man of generous mold, a born leader and as loyal as a friend as he was dangerous as an opponent. For his good deeds and great public services on earth, his memory will long be kept green.

WATTS SHERMAN HUMPHREY, one of the leading lawyers of the Saginaw Valley, was born January 3rd, 1844, at Perry, Wyoming County, N. Y. His father, Thomas Humphrey, was a native of Yorkshire County, England, who came to America in 1824, at the age ot nineteen, and settled in Canandaigua, N. Y., where he built up a considerable business as a merchant and man of affairs. He subsequently resided in Newark, N. J., and Richmond, Va., and took up his residence in Michigan, in 1844. He came to the State as agent of Henry Cleveland, a wealthy resident of Batavia, N. Y., who had large landed interests in Ingham County. The last twenty-five years of his life he spent on a farm near Okemos, Ingham County, where he died in 1872. His wife, Sarah Sherman, was a sister of the late Watts Sherman, of the firm of Duncan, Sherman & Co., for a number of years prominent bankers and brokers of New York, and she belonged to a branch of the Sherman family whose ancestors came from England in colonial times.

Watts S Humphrey was educated in the common schools, with one term at Taylor's Private School in the City of Lansing, one term at the State Normal School in Ypsilanti, and two years at the Agricultural College, and after the war he took the law course in the Michigan University, graduating in the spring of 1869.

In his earlier years he worked on the farm near Okemos, and in the interval between his elementary education and that in the more

advanced schools, he rendered his country service in the army. He enlisted in the fall of 1863 in the First Michigan Cavalry, and served in Custer's Brigade until June 13th, 1864, when he had a horse shot under him at the Crossing of South Ann River on the return from the fight at Trevilian Station. The regiment was part of the rear guard on the march back, and had pretty steady fighting all the way. He had a horse killed under him at the Wilderness by a shell, but this was of no particular consequence, as he wasn't badly hurt, but the horse killed at South Ann was on a corduroy hill, and fell on his rider's right leg, smashing it and he had to swim the river to get away. He laid in the woods all night and caught cold, and had a close shave to pull through. He was in Mt. Pleasant Hospital, Washington, until December, 1864, when he was transferred to Harper Hospital, Detroit, and discharged from the hospital in the spring of 1865, while still on crutches.

After the war Mr. Humphrey studied law in the office of Samuel L. Kilbourne, at Lansing, then took the law course at Michigan University, graduated, and was admitted to the bar in the spring of 1869. In the fall of the same year he located at Cheboygan, where he remained in practice and in the real estate business for twenty-one years. In 1891 he removed to Saginaw, where he still resides, being now the senior member of the law firm of Humphrey & Grant.

Mr. Humphrey has been a Republican since the Fremont Campaign of 1856 when, as a boy, he raised a Fremont and Dayton pole. He cast his first vote for Lincoln in 1864, when home on a furlough from the hospital in Washington. He went to the polls on crutches, and although he lacked over two months of being old enough to vote, and several copperheads stood around who knew it, they thought it best not to challenge him. After settling in Cheboygan he was active in politics, attending several State Conventions as delegate, and was also at the Convention in Saginaw in 1894, and that at Grand Rapids in 1900. He was Prosecuting Attorney of Cheboygan County two years; County Treasurer five years, and a member of the Common Council three terms. In 1890 he was nominated for Congress from the Tenth District, but that was not a good year for the Republicans and he was defeated by T. A. E. Weadock, of Bay City.

Mr. Humphrey has been attorney for the Michigan Central Railroad since 1882, and a stockholder and Director in the Saginaw Lumber Company, whose business is at Williams, Arizona Territory, since 1894. The company was reorganized in 1899, as a Michigan corporation with the name of The Saginaw & Manistee Lumber Company, of which he is a stockholder and Director. He is a member of the East Saginaw Club, Detroit Club, Fontinalis Club, Pere Marquette Club, Forest and Stream Club, Game and Forestry Protection Association and St. Bernard Commandery. He was married in April, 1870, to Emma C. Fisher, at Lansing, Mich., by whom he had three children, Mina Augusta, now Mrs. T. S. Varnum; Arthur T. and Effie Gertrude. In July, 1884, he was married again to Millie W. Smart, who died in 1885, leaving no children. In January, 1888, he was married to Carrie M. Magoffin, by whom he has four children: George M., Margaret Gladys, Winifred Sherman and Watts Sherman, Jr.

WALTER J. HUNSAKER, for several years past Managing Editor of the Detroit Journal, has been in the newspaper business ever since he engaged in any business at all. His ancestors on the paternal side were Swiss, and on his mother's side English, one of the maternal ancestors being William Coddington, the founder and first Governor of the Colony of Rhode Island. Walter J. Hunsaker was born in Keokuk, Iowa, September 19, 1857. He was educated in the common and high schools of Carthage, Ill., and in Carthage College. After leaving college he turned his attention at once to newspaper work, and was one of the founders of the Creston, Ia., Gazette, in 1874. In 1878 he became business manager of the Hannibal, Mo., Daily Clipper, and a year later he was owner and editor of the Creston, Ia., Republic. Two years later he was one of the owners and editor of the Creston Daily Gazette, and afterwards founded the Creston Every Sunday Morning, which he conducted from 1882 to 1884. During the latter part of 1884 and 1885 he was connected with the St. Paul Pioneer Press, and then went to Minneapolis, where he became editorial and special writer on the Minneapolis Evening Journal. Coming to Detroit when the Nimocks Bros. bought the Tribune, he was, at first, night editor and afterwards Managing Editor under the general management of James H. Stone and James E. Scripps. In 1892 he went to the Detroit Journal as Managing Editor, and has remained in that position ever since. Mr. Hunsaker was one of the founders of the Michigan Republican Newspaper Men's Association, and was its Treasurer one term. He was also Treasurer, for two terms, of the Michigan State Press Association.

Having had such a long connection with political newspapers it was perfectly natural that he should have other political connections. He has always been a Republican, was for four years City Clerk of Creston, and was delegate from the Eighth Iowa District to the National Republican Convention in 1884 that nominated Blaine.

He was married, October 21, 1885, to Alma Lyle Clarke, of Creston, and they have one child, Jerome Clarke Hunsaker.

WILLIAM A. HURST is one of the hustling young Republicans that have given animation to political campaign and club life in Wayne County for the past few years. He is the son of William and Margaret (Storey) Hurst, and was born in Lambton County, Ontario, April 8th, 1862. His father was born in Ireland and came to this country when very young. His mother was the daughter of an English army officer, who on account of his wounds and long service,

DETROIT JOURNAL.

received a grant of land near Courtright, Canada, opposite St. Clair, Mich. The son attended the public schools of Canada until ten years of age, when he removed with his parents to St. Clair, Michigan, where he attended school until 1879. During the ensuing seven years he was with the firm of N. & B. Mills, as lumber inspector at Marysville, and while there he took a full course of instruction at Bryant & Stratton's College, graduating in 1884. In 1886 he removed to Detroit and after a service of one year with the Delta Lumber Company, he entered the employ of J. H. Thompson & Co., wholesale tea and coffee merchants, as bookkeeper, later acting as traveling salesman, and remained with that firm until 1890, at which time they closed out their business. For two years following he engaged in real estate and insurance at Detroit, and in 1892 was appointed Clerk of the Circuit Court Commissioners. While occupying that position he attended the Detroit College of Law and was admitted to the bar in July, 1896. In the autumn of the same year he was elected Circuit Court Commissioner by a handsome majority, and filled the position so acceptably to the public and litigants, that he was re-elected in 1898. In the campaign of 1900 he was one of the Republican nominees on the City Legislative ticket and was among the highest of the ten in the number of votes received.

Mr. Hurst is a staunch Republican, cast his first vote for Blaine, was Secretary of the City and County Committee in 1895-6, and was one of the organizers of the Alger Club, of which he was President in 1896. He was a delegate to the State Convention in Grand Rapids in 1894. He has represented the Alger Club in the State League of Republican Clubs, of which he was Vice-President in 1898 and President in 1899. He is also Director of the Michigan Club, a member of the Fellowcraft Club of Detroit, the Bar Association of Detroit, and holds high rank in the Masonic fraternity. Since July, 1896, he has been a member of the law firm of Fales, Hurst & Fenton. September 16th, 1889, he married Ida E. R. Clark, of Detroit, and they have one daughter, Helen Claire.

OSCAR A. JANES, the present Pension Agent for Michigan, is the son of John E. and Esther Bagley Janes. His father was born in Grand Isle, Vt., and moved with his parents to Wayne County, New York, and from there to Johnstown, Rock County, Wis., in 1838, where he engaged in farming and for many years was prominently identified with the growth and development of that section of the State. He was a strong Abolitionist, and during the days of slavery his house was a station on the "Underground Railroad" for the harboring of runaway slaves, and the subject of this sketch in his boyhood days has driven a carriage containing runaway slaves from his father's house to other points on the road and delivered them to others who were to take them on their journey to Canada; and at the same time hand bills were posted up in the neighborhood, offering $1,000 reward for the detection of anyone harboring such slaves.

Colonel Janes is of English ancestry, being descended from William Janes, who emigrated from England to America in 1637, and was a member of the colony of Rev. John Davenport. The voyage was made in the ship Hector, and after a short stay in Boston, they journeyed south and founded the present City of New Haven, Conn. Elijah Janes, the great, great grandfather of Colonel Janes, was one of the minute men of the Colonial War, and also served as Lieutenant of Dragoons in the War of the Revolution.

Oscar A. Janes, for a long time a resident of Hillsdale, was the recipient of the first appointment made by President McKinley in his first term. Immediately following the adjournment of the first cabinet meeting, March 8th, 1897, the President sent the nomination to the Senate, where it was at once referred to committee in executive session. Within five minutes and six seconds from the time it was received a messenger was dispatched to the President to inform him that the nomination of Oscar A. Janes, of Hillsdale, to be United States Pension Agent at Detroit agency, had been confirmed by the Senate. The deserving recipient of this recognition was born in Johnstown, Rock County, Wis., July 6, 1843. During his boyhood he devoted himself to farm work in the summer and in attendance at the district school during the winter months. After preparing for college at Milton Academy, Wisconsin, he entered the college at Hillsdale, Mich., in the class of 1863.

When but two months in college he laid aside his books, and at a time when it was known that there was danger at the front and the services of every loyal son were needed, he was mustered into the United States service on November 15th, 1863, as a private in the Fourth Michigan Infantry. His army record shows that in battle he was always in the forefront, taking part in numerous engagements, among which were the Battles of the Wilderness, Spottsylvania, North Anna, Cold Harbor, Petersburg and Jerusalem Plank Road, Va., where just as day was merging into night on June 22d, 1864, he received a wound which lost him his arm and left him as dead on the field of battle. Indeed, after the orderly sergeant and Sergeant Dickerson of his company went on the next morning to seek him among the slain of the previous day and as they believed, had found and buried his body and had erected a headboard to the memory of Oscar A. Janes, he was recorded on the muster roll of his regiment as "Killed in Battle." A letter was forwarded to his parents in Wisconsin, informing them of their supposed bereavement. In the meantime he had been rescued by the ambulance corps. Of this, however, nothing was known at the front until several days after, when it was announced in the New York papers that he was then in Haddington Hospital, Philadelphia. An incident connected with the supposed burial of Comrade Janes took place at a reunion of the veterans of the Fourth Michigan, held in Hudson five years after the close of the war, when Colonel Janes met Sergeant Dickerson and, extending to him his only remaining hand,

O. A. Janes.

said: "How are you, Dick?" The Sergeant replied: "I am all right, but I don't seem to know you; who are you, anyway?" "Why, I am Janes, of your Company; don't you know me?" To this astounding statement Sergeant Dickerson answered, saying: "My God, I buried you at Petersburg."

After being mustered out of the service Colonel Janes returned to Hillsdale College, from which he graduated in 1868. He at once began the study of law and was admitted to practice in 1871. In 1873 he was married to Miss Vinnie E. Hill, of Hillsdale, whose departure from this life occurred two years later. In 1878 he was married to Miss Julia M. Mead, of Hillsdale, this last union being blessed with three children, Marie E., Henry M. and John E.

In private life Colonel Janes is recognized as a cultured, courteous gentleman, who cherishes friends and enjoys their companionship. In public affairs he is a man of marked influence, endowed with rare gifts of native courtesy and oratory. His title as Colonel was received in 1885 while on the staff of Governor Alger. He served the Union Veterans' Union as its Department Commander and was Department Commander of the G. A. R. of Michigan in 1883, and Inspector General of the National G. A. R. in 1887. He was for four years Secretary and Treasurer of Hillsdale College, of which he also has been Trustee and Auditor. He has held high rank in the orders of the Knights of Pythias and the Independent Order of Oddfellows, the last of which he served as Grand Master in the Grand Lodge of Michigan and also as Grand Representative to the Sovereign Grand Lodge of the United States. He is also a member of the Knights of the Maccabees; Detroit Lodge No. 34, B. P. O. Elks; the Fellowcraft Club of Detroit, and Michigan Society of the Sons of the American Revolution.

The citizens of Hillsdale, of which City and County he has been for most of his life a resident, have often honored him with positions of public trust, including that of City Attorney, City Clerk, Alderman, Circuit Court Commissioner, Judge of Probate for eight years, and State Senator. In politics Colonel Janes has always been a Republican, casting his first vote for President for General Grant, giving to that party the advantage of his fine oratorical gifts in the exposition of its principles, and he enjoys the distinction of having been Chairman of the Republican State Convention which selected Michigan delegates to the Convention at St. Louis, where McKinley was nominated for the Presidency. He has been many times delegate to State Conventions.

In the Michigan Legislature of 1895-6 Colonel Janes represented the Counties of Hillsdale, Branch and St. Joseph in the Senate, serving on a number of its most important committees, including the committees on Judiciary, School of Mines, Constitutional Amendments and Soldiers' Home. As Chairman of this last he made a report which caused a special investigation of the management to be made by the succeeding Legislature. In that session he was the author of the Flag Act, which provides that during school hours the flag of our country shall float over every public school building in the State, and the joint resolution appropriating $10,000 for a statue of Michigan's War Governor, Austin Blair. He also made masterly efforts in opposition to the Capital Punishment Bill, which was finally defeated by a narrow margin of votes. For his earnest and successful championship of the pure food law he received the thanks of the farmers of his district in a set of resolutions adopted by Pomona Grange of Hillsdale County.

The office of the United States Pension Agent at Detroit, for which Colonel James is so admirably qualified, is one of the most important Federal positions in Michigan, and is conducted under the rules laid down by the civil service commission. On June 30, 1900, the books of the agency showed an enrollment of 44,195 pensioners and an annual disbursement of $6,655,281.89, for every dollar of which the agent is accountable, though under the civil service rules he is not allowed to name the subordinates upon whom he must necessarily rely for a correct handling of this vast amount of money.

Since taking charge of the office, the duties have been ministered with signal ability, making quarterly payments in less than one-half of the time heretofore made, and has a record with the Bureau of Pensions of being one of the best agencies in promptness, accuracy and neatness of reports.

WILLIAM L. JANUARY was born in Greene County, O., July 9, 1853, the youngest of three sons of George Wadman January and Mary S., nee Garnett, January. His father's family was from Kentucky. His mother was the daughter of Colonel Armsted Garnett, a planter and slave owner in Buckingham County, Va. His father was opposed to slavery and as a pioneer of Southern Ohio, was known as a "Black Abolitionist." The homestead once owned by him formed a part of what was known as the "under-ground railway," between Kentucky and Canada, for the purpose of transporting negroes.

Mr. January's mother, a woman of rare common sense and noble impulses, was educated by private teachers at her father's home in Virginia, known as Oak Row. She early became convinced that slavery was wrong. She frequently "violated the law," by teaching the little negro children to read and write. At the outbreak of the war, when the news came to her in Ohio, she declared to one of her colored servants then with her, that the time had come for the negroes to be free. This was long before Lincoln had conceived his proclamation possible.

William L. January was reared on his father's farm, educated in the common and high schools of his native State; entered the University of Michigan, took an elective course, class of '80; entered the law department and graduated with the class of '83. Refusing flattering inducements to begin his law practice in Old Virginia, he at once located in Detroit with Henry M. Cheever. Two years later he opened an office for himself. He has since practiced in Detroit and Michigan. The interests of his clients, who can be numbered among the best business firms and influential men of the City, frequently take him beyond his own State and into other courts.

Republican by birth and choice, always interested in the affairs of State and Nation, he has taken a quiet, but active, part in each campaign, rendering valuable services to his party on the stump and by his writing through the press and otherwise. His services in the hard money campaign of 1896 were especially conspicuous, his clear comprehension of the issues at stake making him a valuable adviser.

In 1896 he was nominated for the legislature on the Republican ticket, and elected by a good majority. During this campaign, aside from his other work, he edited a paper in the interest of his party. As a member of the House of '97 and '98, Mr. January made himself felt, and was a conscientious, useful and forceful member of the Wayne delegation. The only Wayne member of the Committee on City Corporations; Chairman of the Committee on State Public Schools, and member of the Committee on Appropriations, he performed his work well and to the entire satisfaction of his constituents.

All bills affecting the Charter of the City of Detroit, with few exceptions, were introduced by him, the majority of which became laws. He introduced and passed the bill protecting the Belle Isle Bridge approach, making it a part of the City's parks. He introduced a bill to allow the Board of Public Works to contract direct for paving and repairing streets, in order to give employment to thousands of laborers, then out of work. This bill passed the House, but failed in the Senate. He introduced a bill to abolish caucuses and conventions, but this movement was hardly ripe at that time, is still a question agitated before the Legislature, and will probably soon become a law.

He also introduced and passed what is known as the "January Law," for the commencement of suits by and against voluntary unincorporated clubs and societies, and for the service of process in such cases. This law excited the labor element, created discussion and was declared to be a means to "end boycotts;" but, after the labor unions understood its legal effect, they endorsed the law as beneficial to the labor unions.

Mr. January also introduced a plan which, he claimed, would in a measure, do away with the objectionable lobbyist and get at the pulse of the people. His plan was to have all the bills affecting City corporations, printed, and, before reporting out, have the Committee on City Corporations, after due notice, visit the respective cities, and there before the Common Council and the people interested, present the bills for public discussion. He claims by this means more information was, and can always be, obtained as to what the people want, than from all the lobbyists at the Capital, who invariably have "axes to grind."

Believing in the principles of the Republican party, Mr. January believes that most, if not quite, all good measures, in both State and National affairs, have either originated or been completed by that party.

DAVID HOWELL JEROME, for many years one of the leading men in the Saginaw Valley, and the Eighth Republican Governor of Michigan, was the son of Horace and Elizabeth Hart Jerome, and was born in Detroit, November 17th, 1829. Several generations of the Jerome family lived in Massachusetts, and two generations of them served in the Revolutionary War; Timothy Jerome, grandfather, and Samuel Jerome, great grandfather of David. The latter enlisted four different times between July, 1777, and the close of the war, and the former saw service at three different periods. On the death of his father, which occurred when David was an infant, his mother removed to Central New York. In 1834 she returned to Michigan and settled in St. Clair County, where David received his education. In 1853 he went to California, and while there, located a claim for the Live Yankee Tunnel & Mine, at Forest City, which has since proved to be worth millions of dollars. He projected the tunnel and constructed it for 600 feet into the mountain toward the mine. The next year he returned to Michigan and settled in Saginaw, which was his home for the rest of his life. He went into business first in general merchandise, but afterwards founded the hardware and mill supply store of D. H. Jerome & Co., which became one of the largest and strongest of any in the lumber districts of the State.

In 1862 he was authorized by Governor Blair to raise the regiment apportioned to the Sixth Congressional District, and was commissioned commandant of camp with rank of Colonel, to prepare the regiment for the field. This was the Twenty-third Regiment, which afterward made a splendid record in the war. In the same year he was elected Senator in the State Legislature, and was re-elected in 1864 and 1866, serving the whole six years as Chairman of the Committee on State Affairs. He was prominent in opposition to the railroad-aid legislation of that time, and supported Governor Crapo in his veto of the same. He also assisted materially in shaping the policy of the important legislation growing out of the war. He introduced and secured the passage of the Bill creating the Soldiers' Home at Harper Hospital in Detroit. He also urged the policy of saving the proceeds of swamp lands to secure local improvements in the new counties. His whole legislative career was characterized by sound judgment, untiring industry and unquestioned integrity. During 1865-6, he was Military Aid to Governor Crapo, and was also appointed a member of the State Military Board, of which he continued a member and President until 1873. His fine record as a legislator led to his appointment as a member of the Constitutional Commission of 1873. In that body he was Chairman of the Committee on Finance. Here he took the same prominence in debate and exercised the same influence in shaping Constitutional provisions that characterized his Senatorial career.

In 1875 he was commissioned by President Grant as a member of the Board of United States Indian Commissioners. In his new field of labor he visited nearly all the uncivilized Indians of the Western territories. As Chairman of a Commission to visit Joseph, the Nez Perce Chief, in Idaho, he held a seven days' conference with that warrior and his band. He also visited the Utes in 1879, at Uncompahgre, and there, in a conference with Ouray, laid the foundation of the settlement of the land difficulties in Colorado.

Mr. Jerome was nominated for Governor by a Convention held at Jackson, twenty-six years after the famous mass gathering "under the Oaks," which organized the Republican Party. There were in the Convention five rival candidates, each one having, at the outset sufficient strength to give him some hope of success, but the prize finally went to Mr. Jerome, who was subsequently elected by a plurality of 41,273 over the Democratic candidate. Mr. Jerome, who was the first native born Governor of the State, brought to the executive office the same energy and industry that had made his fortune in business. He was a broad-minded, liberal man, kept close watch of legislation, and favored liberal support of all public institutions. It was during his administration that measures were taken, by building the School for the Blind at Lansing, to separate the education of that class of unfortunates from the deaf and dumb, with whom they had formerly been associated in the institution at Flint.

Aside from the extensive hardware trade which Mr. Jerome established, his business activities extended to other lines. He had banking interests of some magnitude, was President of the Saginaw Valley and St. Louis Railroad Company, a prominent member of the Saginaw Board of Trade, and a promoter and President of the First Saginaw Street Railway Co. He was one of the most prominent laymen in the State in the Episcopal Church, and was for over thirty years a Vestryman in the leading church at Saginaw. He was married June 15th, 1859, to Miss Lucy Peck, daughter of E. W. Peck, of Pontiac. A son, Thomas S. Jerome, is at present Consular Agent of the United States at Sorrento, Italy.

THOMAS SPENCER JEROME, son of Ex-Governor David H. Jerome and Lucy P. Jerome, was born January 24th, 1864, at Saginaw, Mich. The Jerome family came from the Isle of Wight, England, about 1715, and settled in Meriden, Conn. Their descendants moved to Stockbridge, Mass., then to Onondaga County, New York in 1796. The grandfather of Thomas S. came to Detroit in 1826 and died there in 1831. His father moved to Saginaw in 1854.

Thomas S. Jerome was educated in the Saginaw public schools, the University of Michigan, with degree of Ph. B. in 1884, and Harvard University with degree of M. A. in 1887. He commenced the practice of law in Detroit in 1887, and continued in the practice of that profession till the early summer of 1900, when he was appointed Consular Agent of the United States at Sorrento, Italy, and later at Capri. After the Spanish War he served a short time as counsel to the United States Transportation Commission at Havana. Mr. Jerome was brought up a Republican, and remained steadfast in the faith, casting his first vote for Harrison in 1888.

He is unmarried and is a member of the Alpha Delta Phi Society, Yondotega Club, Detroit Club, Michigan Club, Witenagemote of the Club Internazionale of Capri.

Of his present life on the Island of Capri a friend who visited him there last summer, writes: "The Bay of Naples is reputedly the most beautiful spot in the world, and Mr. Jerome is situated where he can enjoy it to the utmost. The island is about three miles in length and two in breadth, and is populated, so far as the native residents are concerned, by descendants of the Greeks. Mr. Jerome owns a large estate on the island, and has a handsome villa, the construction of which was begun about 200 years ago. He has a beautiful garden, and devotes his time to it and the study of Roman history and antiquities. He has entirely given up the cares of business life and has settled down on the island to remain."

ELIAS FINLEY JOHNSON, of Ann Arbor, a man active in all educational affairs, was born at Van Wert, Ohio, June 24th, 1861, his father being Abel Johnson, a lawyer, and his mother, Margaret Gillespie. His father's people came from Wales and were Quakers. They settled in Ohio in a very early day, moving there from Eastern Pennsylvania. His father was for years on the Common Pleas Bench in Ohio, and his grandfather was the first Treasurer of Van Wert County, Ohio, which office he held for years. His uncle, Davis Johnson, was also County Treasurer of the same County for a long period. He received his education at the National Normal University and Ohio State University, paying his expenses by whatever work he could find to do. He commenced to teach in the fall of 1878 in the rural schools and taught several terms in these schools.

Mr. Johnson, in 1880, was elected Superintendent of Schools in Van Wert. In 1882 he was appointed County Surveyor of Van Wert County. In 1883 he was elected to the Legislature of Ohio, and again in 1885. He came to Michigan in 1888 and ever since then has been connected with the department of law of the State University. In the spring of 1898 he was appointed by the Governor to fill a

Yours Respectfully
E. Finley Johnson.

vacancy upon the State Board of Education of Michigan, and in the fall of the same year, was nominated by acclamation by the Republican State Convention for the same position, receiving more votes than any other candidate on the ticket except Governor Pingree. He has always been a Republican and cast his first vote for Joseph B. Foraker for Governor of Ohio, and was a member of every State Convention in Ohio from 1882 to 1888. He is a member of the Knights of Pythias, Knights Templar and Shrine. In 1884 he married Clara A. Smith. They have two children, Eva and Cecil.

WILLIAM H. JOHNSTON, of Ishpeming, is one of the stirring men that have given the mining districts of the Upper Peninsula the prominence which they have in the business and political world. He is of Scotch and Irish descent, and was born in Manheim, Herkimer County, N. Y., December 1st, 1847. His parents were afterwards among the early settlers in Wisconsin, and his father built the first house in Appleton in that State. He was at one time President of the Village, was an active Republican, and was a delegate to the National Convention that nominated Lincoln.

It was at Appleton that the son received his education, which he completed at Lawrence University in that City. He went to Lake Superior in 1876, became interested in mining, and in 1880 was appointed Superintendent of the Lake Superior Iron Co., with whose prosperous business he was for many years identified. He was appointed local Manager or Agent of the company in 1898, and when the controlling interest was purchased by the Oliver Iron Mining Co., he was retained, and was also appointed Agent of the Regent Iron Co., and District Superintendent of the Oliver Iron Mining Co. for the Marquette district.

Mr. Johnston has always been a staunch Republican and an active worker in the ranks, doing his share of committee and Convention duty. He was a member of the Ishpeming City Council for several years, and served as Mayor two terms. He was married May 4th, 1870, to Miss Eva G. Rich, of Horicon, Wis. They have two daughters, Mrs. S. F. White, of Evanston, Ill., Mrs. H. S. Thompson, of Ishpeming, and one son, Henry Theodore Johnston.

JOHN JONES, of Ishpeming, is one of the pioneers of the "Up Country," having lived in the Upper Peninsula more than half a century, and having seen its mineral operations grow from almost nothing up to their present magnitude. He was born in Detroit, June 20th, 1839. His parents moved to Sault Ste. Marie in 1845, when he was only six years old, and the following spring moved to Eagle River, Keweenaw County. Two years later they moved to Ontonagon, where they remained until 1871, and where the son John received his education in the common schools. In the year last named they moved to Ishpeming, Marquette County, where the son has lived ever since. He has been, throughout almost the whole period, agent for the American Express Company, and has also had a large omnibus and express business of his own, besides doing a large retail business in coal and wood.

In politics Mr. Jones is a Republican. He has held a number of local offices, including those of City Marshal, Alderman and Mayor of Ishpeming. He represented the Second District of Marquette County in the Legislature of 1893-4, and was re-elected to that of 1895-6, receiving handsome majorities in each case. July 1, 1898, he was appointed Receiver of the United States Land office, a position which he still holds.

CHARLES DURANT JOSLYN, one of the busiest attorneys in Detroit, was born June 20th, 1846, at Waitsfield, Vt. His father, Ezra O. Joslyn, was a farmer and descended from John Josselyn, who was one of the Connecticut settlers in 1637. His mother was Eliza A. Joslyn, nee Durant, and his grandmother on his mother's side was Susanna Leland, and a direct lineal descendant of Henry Leland, who came over in the Mayflower. The Joslyn name is an ancient one and is probably of Welsh origin, but became prominent in England as early as the fourteenth century. A Josselyn was Lord Mayor of London in 1435. The great grandfather of Charles D. was in the Revolutionary Army, and was with it during the terrible winter at Valley Forge. His grandmother on his father's side, was Scotch-Irish.

Charles D had his first education in a New England red schoolhouse; graduated from the Vermont Normal School and Barre Academy, and entered Dartmouth College, but did not graduate. He taught school to obtain the means to get his own education. His father bought a large farm when the lad was thirteen years old, and from that time until he was twenty he did a "man's work" on the farm. The next three years he worked three months on the farm in each year, taught school three months, and obtained what liberal education he got in the other six months in each year. In 1870 he became Assistant Superintendent of the Reform School at Waterbury, Vt., and began studying law at the same time in the office of Governor Paul Dillingham. This was unusually hard work as his duty hours at the Reform School were from 2 o'clock to 10 p. m.. and from 8:30 a. m. to 1:30 p. m. He was admitted to the bar in due time, located in Detroit in 1874, and began practicing law, where he has since remained. He was Deputy Clerk of the Superior Court of Detroit two years, U. S. Consul at Windsor three years, and Assistant Corporation Counsel of Detroit between six and seven years. The last named position gave Mr. Joslyn opportunity for the development and use of his best talents. He has handled many large cases for the City, and has brought to the work excellent legal skill and untiring industry, making a record creditable to himself, and valuable to the municipality which employed him.

Mr. Joslyn has been a working Republican ever since he attained his majority; cast his first vote for Grant, and has voted for every Republican candidate for President since; went on the stump first in 1872, and has spoken in every campaign from that time to this. He has been delegate to nine Republican State Conventions, commencing with 1878, and ending with 1898. He has never been a member of the Legislature, but many of the most important political and Detroit municipal measures were framed by him.

Politics and law business have so absorbed Mr. Joslyn's attention, that he has not been much given to society affairs. He has retired from the political arena and is now devoting his entire time to his law practice, which is a large one. He is married and has three children, Max A., Alice E. and Louise D.

JAMES FREDERICK JOY was one of three distinguished men furnished by the Southeastern part of New Hampshire to promote the growth of Michigan and the Northwest. Lewis Cass, the first of the three, belonged to the formative period of this region, the era of exploration and of post roads, and he did more than anyone else to give Michigan Territory a system of local self government, and such road improvements as were at the time possible. Zachariah Chandler, in addition to his other illustrious services to the State and Nation, was the earliest and most efficient promoter of the system of river and harbor improvements that have made possible the mighty fleets that now traverse the Great Lakes. To Mr. Joy's efforts the West is indebted for the construction of several of the great arteries of land carriage, for he was one of the pioneers of railroad building in the West, and one of the most zealous and far seeing promoters of this modern method of transportation. The three were born in New Hampshire towns within ten, twenty and thirty-one miles of each other respectively, and they were for many years close neighbors in Detroit, the City of their adoption.

Mr. Joy was born in Durham, New Hampshire, December 20th, 1810, the son of James and Sarah Pickering Joy, his father and mother both being descended from historic families in that State. His father was Calvinist in religious faith, and brought up his family under rigid rules of conduct, with high ideals of business and political integrity, and with an eye always to a liberal education. The son attended the public schools of his vicinity, paid his way through College, in part by teaching, and graduated from Dartmouth as valedictorian of his class, in 1835. He then entered the Cambridge Law School, which was in charge of the famous Professor Greenleaf and Judge Story. He was an especial favorite with Judge Story, who predicted for him a brilliant career as a lawyer. In September, 1836, he entered the law office of Augustus S. Porter, of Detroit, and a year later was admitted to the bar and entered into partnership with George S. Porter. The two were well calculated to work together. Mr. Porter had been a banker, had a useful knowledge of financial affairs, was a good bookkeeper, and was methodical and thorough in the gathering of material bearing upon a case, while Mr. Joy had hardly a superior in the West in the conduct of cases in court. The firm soon entered upon a lucrative practice, and for many years there was hardly an important case in Michigan or Illinois in which Mr. Joy did not appear. He was counsel for the old Bank of Michigan, for a number of Eastern parties having large interests in the West, and for the Illinois Railroad, which was then laying the foundation for what is now the Illinois Central System. Railroad law was not then as well established as it is now, and the litigation connected with it led Mr. Joy into fields not before that time explored.

In 1847, after the State of Michigan had tired of its ambitious railroad and canal projects, and was nearly bankrupt, it offered the Michigan Central and Michigan Southern Railroads for sale. Mr. Joy and John W. Brooks, of Boston, used their influence to induce Boston capitalists to purchase the first named road. Mr. Brooks became President of the new company, and Mr. Joy was attorney and general counsel for the road. This connection continued until 1865, when Mr. Joy succeeded Mr. Brooks as President.

The connection thus formed brought Mr. Joy into the great work of his life, the development of the railroad system of the West. It was during his early connection with it that the Michigan Central was completed to Chicago. He had the foresight to discern the fact that the future success of the road would depend much upon the promptness with which it put out feeders into sections that were then new, but were growing. It was due almost entirely to his efforts that a new road was built from Jackson to Grand Rapids, another from Detroit to Bay City, and a third, the Air Line, from Jackson to Niles, and that the old road from Jackson to Owosso was acquired and extended through Saginaw to the Straits of Mackinac. These have since all proved valuable feeders to the main line of the Michigan Central. He was also the main promoter and builder of the Detroit, Lansing & Northern, the Chicago & West Michigan and the Kalamazoo & South Haven.

Mr. Joy also organized the Chicago, Burlington & Quincy, connecting the Imperial City of the Lakes with the Mississippi at two points, and established a connection between it and the Hannibal & St. Joseph road. He built two magnificent iron bridges over the Mississippi and then pushed the Burlington road across the Missouri at Plattsmouth, and made its Western terminus at Fort Kearney in Nebraska. He also extended a line Southwest into the Indian Territory. Mr. Joy put a tremendous amount of energy into the task of pushing the construction of these great railroad systems, and had the satisfaction of knowing that under his management the

Michigan Central and the Burlington were among the best dividend paying roads in the country.

At a later period Mr. Joy was the most active and influential of the parties interested in bringing the Wabash Railroad to Detroit, and he was the prime mover in establishing the Union Depot at the corner of Third and Fort. Though past seventy years of age when this was undertaken, he showed all his old time energy, courage and resourcefulness in overcoming the numerous obstacles that were interposed by hostile parties. The Union Depot and the viaduct which gives approach to it are a splendid monument to his public spirit and his tenacity of purpose.

Mr. Joy was a Whig in his early days and a Republican from the time the party was organized. He was a member of the Legislature of 1861, distinguished for the strength of its membership, and for the efficiency of its war measures. He was a candidate for the United States Senate in 1862, when Jacob M. Howard was chosen. He was elected a Regent of the University in 1881, but resigned after six years of service, when two years of his term yet remained. These were the only occasions on which he was a candidate for office, but he was always a liberal giver to campaign funds. In 1880 he was a delegate to the National Convention at Chicago, and made the speech nominating Blaine. In 1881 he was one of seven Detroit Republicans who bought the Post and Tribune, till then the leading Republican paper of the State. He was President of the company, and directed the tone of the paper, himself writing or dictating many of its editorials, until it was resold in 1885.

Mr. Joy retained his mental and bodily vigor to a remarkable degree. When he was long past 80 he almost always walked, and with a very brisk step, from his home to his office and did much of his work standing at a high desk. He was always approachable on business. When a visitor entered Mr. Joy would turn from his desk with a sharp and quick, "Well, sir," would hear any business proposition that the visitor had to make, give a prompt decision or make an appointment for a future conference, and turn to his work again. But after the day's work was disposed of, he was always ready for a social chat with a friend, when he was full of interesting reminiscence, and showed a fine appreciation of humor. He found time to gratify a cultured literary taste and was one of the comparatively few men of the day who could read Greek as well as the more modern languages. He was at his office almost daily up to within a very short time of his death, which occurred September 24th, 1896, at the age of 86. He was twice married, and three sons and a daughter survive him.

WILLIAM JUDSON, of Ann Arbor, whom everybody knows as a hustler, and who says he has probably spent more time and money in the interests of the Republican party than any other man of his means in Michigan, was born October 13th, 1842, in the Township of

Sylvan, Washtenaw County. His father's name was William Judson and his mother's Jane Judson. His father, whose occupation was that of a farmer, came from Lincolnshire, England, and his mother from Ireland. What little education he ever had was that which he got from going to the district school for two or three winters. He left home when he was seventeen years old and went to clerk for John C. Winans, of Chelsea, Mich.; received $5 per month the first year; $7 per month the second, and $12 per month the third. He then went to work for Whedon & Hatch, of Chelsea, receiving $300 the first year, $400 the second and $600 the third. He then took up the occupation of a drover and followed this occupation until 1894. He cast his first Republican vote for Abraham Lincoln and has voted for every Republican nominee for President from Lincoln to Wm. McKinley. He has been a delegate to every County and State Convention for the last twenty or twenty-five years. Mr. Judson was elected Township Treasurer of the Town of Sylvan for two terms; was elected a Trustee of the Village of Chelsea and served two terms; was appointed Postmaster at Chelsea by President Harrison, served three years and nine months, and was turned out by Grover Cleveland on the charge of being an "offensive partisan," which was true. He was elected Sheriff of the County of Washtenaw in November, 1894, and re-elected in 1896, being the first Republican Sheriff elected in that County since 1866. He was appointed State Inspector of Illuminating Oils by Governor Pingree in 1899. Mr. Judson was married in 1866 to Miss Fannie I. Morton. Their three children are Gertie May, William Morton and Arthur Garfield.

In the contests that have taken place within the past eight years between different sections of the Republican party, Mr. Judson has been a staunch adherent of Candidate and Governor Pingree, and has been one of the most efficient men in Central Michigan, in promoting the Governor's interests.

WILLIAM M. KILPATRICK, who for over 20 years, has been among the working Republicans of Shiawasee County, was the son of Jesse Kilpatrick, a mechanic, farmer and dealer in grain, and Catherine Seamann Kilpatrick, and was born December 25th, 1840, in Middlesex, Yates County, N. Y. His father's people came from the North of Ireland and settled in the State of New Jersey some time in the seventeenth century. His grandfather Kilpatrick and one of his brothers, of whom there were two, were in the War of 1812. His grandfather left New Jersey and went to the State of New York, Seneca County. His brothers remained in New Jersey. His father died in 1897, aged ninety-two years. His mother was born on a plantation in Maryland and came North at the age of eight years, with her parents. She died in July, 1899, aged 94 years and 6 months. His father and mother were married in 1827 and lived together until his father's death in 1897, a period of seventy years.

William Judson

William M. Kilpatrick received his first education in the district school and Genesee Seminary at Lima, N. Y. He worked summers on the farm until 1860, when he went to Lima for a year, and afterwards taught school two years in the State of New York. He went to Tazewell County, Ill., in 1863, and taught school there one year, came to Ann Arbor, Mich., from Illinois, in 1865, and entered the law department of the University. He graduated in 1866 and the same year went to Owosso, where he has practiced law ever since. Mr. Kilpatrick was appointed City Attorney in 1870, and was elected Supervisor-at-Large for the City from 1873 to 1875; Mayor of Owosso in 1875; Prosecuting Attorney for Shiawassee County from 1876 to November, 1880, but resigned the office before the November election in 1880, when he was elected State Senator. He was Chairman of the Republican County Committee from 1872 to 1894, with the exception of 1884, 1885 and 1892. He was again elected State Senator in 1895 and was President of the Owosso School Board thirteen years.

Mr. Kilpatrick began voting the Republican ticket early and he has voted it often. He cast his first vote for Lincoln in 1860, seven weeks before he was twenty-one years old, and has voted the Republican ticket ever since. He was a member of the Republican State Central Committee for six years; was delegate to all Republican State Conventions for nomination of Governor from 1872 to 1898; was alternate delegate to the National Republican Convention at Chicago in 1888, and delegate to the Minneapolis Convention in 1892.

Mr. Kilpatrick has been attorney for the Shiawassee Savings Society, for the past twelve years, and is now attorney for and one of the directors of the Owosso Savings Bank. He was married to Miss Mary Williams, of Owosso, in 1869. His wife dying in 1870, he married Miss Emma Williams, of Owosso, cousin of his first wife, in 1873. She died in 1880 leaving three children, William D., Mary J. and Florence May Kilpatrick. He married again in 1897 Miss Maria R. Nudles, of Groveport, Ohio, by whom he has one child, Katherine Kilpatrick, aged two years.

SAMUEL ROWLEY KINGSLEY, of Romulus, Wayne County, was born on his father's farm in Newark, Licking County, Ohio, July 10th, 1843. On his father's side he is of French descent and on his mother's side Dutch. He was educated in the public schools of Ohio and Michigan, working meantime on the farm, until 1862, when he enlisted in the Twenty-fourth Michigan Infantry. This regiment was recruited in the County of Wayne, with rendezvous at Detroit. It was in the Army of the Potomac, became part of the Iron Brigade, and was in many battles, including the sanguinary struggle at Gettysburg, where Private Kingsley was wounded, and taken prisoner. He was afterwards released on account of his wounds, and served through the war. After his discharge from the army he returned to Romulus, Wayne County, where he has kept a general store and lumber yard for twenty years.

Mr. Kingsley has been a Republican since 1864 and cast his first vote for Abraham Lincoln. He has been a delegate to numerous State Conventions, and has held several official positions. He was Town Clerk of Romulus from 1882 to 1890; a member of the House in the Michigan Legislature in the sessions of 1893 and 1895 and was elected Register of Deeds of Wayne County in 1898. He is a Director in the Wayne Savings Bank at Wayne, Mich., a member of the Michigan Club, the A. O. U. W., Masonic orders and the G. A. R. He was married at St. Johns, Mich., June 25th, 1868, to Miss Clarissa A. Norris and has had one son, John Morgan Kingsley, who was born October 30th, 1865, and died July 16th, 1872.

EDWARD DEWITT KINNE, of Ann Arbor, who graduated from politics and political offices to the bench and with great credit in each career, was born at Dewitt Center, now East Syracuse, Onondaga County N. Y., February 9th, 1842. His father was Julius C. Kinne, a farmer, and his mother Rachel W. Kinne. The family trace their ancestry back 250 years to Sir Thomas Kinne, of Norfolk, England. His son, Henry Kinne, fled to Holland with the Puritan fathers and thence to Salem, Mass., where he located in 1653. Julius C. Kinne was a member of the New York Legislature several terms.

The subject of the present sketch was educated at the High School in Syracuse; then at Cazenovia Seminary, where he graduated in 1860. He entered Michigan University in 1861, was class orator and graduated in the classical department in 1864, with degree of A. B. He entered the law department of the Columbian University at Washington, D. C., in 1865, graduated as LL. B. in 1867, and was admitted to practice in the Supreme Court of the District of Columbia. During his residence at Washington he was in the Diplomatic Bureau of the Treasury Department. He came to Ann Arbor, Mich., in 1867 and commenced the practice of law, first in partnership with Olney Hawkins; later with Colman & Root, and shortly thereafter preferred to practice alone and enjoyed all the business he could properly attend to.

Commencing with 1869, Mr. Kinne had frequent evidences of the esteem in which he is held by his fellow citizens. In that year he was elected City Recorder of Ann Arbor. He was afterwards elected City Attorney for three terms, commencing in 1871. In 1876 he was chosen Mayor of Ann Arbor and was re-elected in 1877. In 1879 he was elected a member of the State Legislature, where he served as member of the Judiciary Committee and as Chairman of the Committee on Private Corporations, and where he fully sustained the high reputation which Washtenaw County had established for sending able men to that body. In 1887 he was nominated for

E. D. Kinne

Circuit Judge of the Twenty-second Judicial District, comprising the Counties of Washtenaw and Monroe. Both of these Counties were Democratic by at least 2,000 majority, but he ran ahead in Washtenaw County nearly 4,000 votes, carrying the County by nearly 3,000, and was elected by a large majority. His opponent was Hon. George M. Landon. His course on the bench was so satisfactory that he was re-elected in 1893 by a large majority and again elected in 1899 by over 1,200 majority. In 1890 he was a prominent candidate for Supreme Judge, but withdrew early from the contest, by reason of his long and close friendship for Judge Grant.

He cast his first vote for Abraham Lincoln in 1864, and has ever since been identified with the Republican party and has frequently been a delegate to State Conventions. Aside from his law practice and his place on the bench, Judge Kinne's most important business connections are those of President of the First National Bank of Ann Arbor and President of the Ann Arbor Gas Co. His society relations have been numerous. In college he was a member of the Sigma Phi College Fraternity; and he is an honorary member of the Phi Delta Phi Law fraternity. In Masonic matters he is a Knight Templar. He is also a non-resident member of the Detroit Club and a member of the O. L. Club of Monroe. He was married in 1867 to Mary C. Hawkins, of Ann Arbor, who died in 1882. Two children survived her; Samuel Denton Kinne and Mary White Kinne. In 1884 he was again married to Florence S. Jewett.

FRANK EUGENE KIRBY, than whom no one connected with the lake vessel interests is better known, was born at Cleveland, Ohio, July 1st, 1849. His father was Stephen P. Kirby, shipmaster and naval architect, and his mother was Martha A. Kirby. Their descent was from English families who emigrated to America at about the year 1670, and settled in Massachusetts and Connecticut.

Frank E. Kirby was educated in the public schools of Cleveland and Saginaw, supplemented with a scientific course at the Cooper Institute, New York City. He entered the engineering profession by joining the staff on the Allaire Works, New York City in 1866; was afterwards at the Morgan Iron Works and came to Detroit in 1870, and with his elder brother, Mr. F. A. Kirby, superintended the establishment of the iron shipyard at Wyandotte for the late Captain E. B. Ward. He joined the Detroit Dry Dock Co., as a Director and Chief Engineer in 1882, and is now Consulting Engineer and Naval Architect. His work for the Dry Dock Co., and its successor, the Detroit Shipbuilding Company, covers the designing of over 100 vessels, of almost every type that has been in use during the intervening years. The finest side-wheel passenger steamers, and many of the largest freighters came from his drawings. His fame has extended not only around the lakes, but to every shipyard on the

American seaboard. During and after the Spanish War, 1898-9, he was Consulting Engineer for the army transport service of the War Department.

Mr. Kirby's first vote was for James G. Blaine and he always voted the Republican ticket, though too much absorbed in business to pay much attention to politics. He was a Commissioner of the Water Works of Detroit from 1892 to 1896, and President of the Board in 1896. He is a member of the Michigan Club, of the American Society of Naval Architects, American Society of Naval Engineers, American Society of Mechanical Engineers, the Naval Institute, the Institute of Naval Architects, London, England, and the Institute of Naval Architects, Glasgow, Scotland. He was married in 1876 at Wyandotte to Miss Mary F. Thorp and has one son, Russell T. Kirby.

SAMUEL McBIRNEY LEMON comes of good, sturdy Scotch-Irish stock and is one of the men who by honest and well directed efforts, together with his generosity and good influence has helped build up Grand Rapids to its present magnificent proportions, and has been no small factor in the development of Western Michigan.

Mr. Lemon was born November 27th, 1848, at Corneycrew, County of Armagh, Ireland, and was the son of Samuel and Rachel McBirney Lemon, who intended him for the ministry, and gave him the best education the County afforded. But his own inclinations turned toward mercantile life, and at the age of seventeen he was apprenticed to one of the largest grocery merchants in Ireland at Portadown, where he remained five years perfecting a knowledge of the business.

After the completion of his apprenticeship Mr. Lemon, in 1870, came to America and accepted a place with the wholesale grocery firm of Acker, Merrill & Condit, of New York City. Here he commenced at the modest salary of ten dollars a week, out of which he paid eight dollars a week for board and lodging, but within seven months so valuable were his services that his salary was raised again and again.

During the next year he accepted a position with Andrew M. Semple (a wholesale grocer of Rochester, N. Y.), of whose business Mr. Lemon became sole manager for five years, when greater inducements caused a transfer of his services to Lautz Brothers & Company of Buffalo, N. Y., with whom he was connected for the five years following. Although drawing a salary equaled by few in those days, yet his ambition impelled him to embark in business for himself. Accordingly in 1881 Mr. Lemon moved to Grand Rapids and became a member of the wholesale grocery firm of Shields, Bulkley & Lemon, which after years of successful operation was in 1890 succeeded by, and incorporated under, the firm name of the Lemon & Wheeler Company, of which he is President.

Sincerely Yours,

The career of this man has been marked by a steady and undeviating purpose to succeed in his chosen profession. He has aimed to and succeeded in becoming a successful wholesale grocer and has made for himself a place in the business world which does him credit, for his name throughout Michigan is a synonym for honesty and fair dealing.

For many years he has been a Director of the Fourth National Bank and is identified with several other of Grand Rapids' most prominent business institutions.

Mr. Lemon is intensely American, an ardent and influential Republican, but has never sought nor permitted his name to be used for any elective office. November 1st, 1897, he was appointed by President McKinley Collector of Internal Revenue of the Fourth (Grand Rapids) District and still holds the position.

In fraternal society matters Mr. Lemon is a Mason and a member of DeMolai Commandery, Knights Templar. He was married January 17th, 1883, to Miss Mary Peoples (daughter of James and Margaret Peoples, of Rochester, N. Y.) and he and his wife are both members of Westminster Presbyterian Church. Whether in business, politics or social life Mr. Lemon is a hearty, genial and public spirited man and deservedly popular.

HON. WILLIAM LIVINGSTONE was born in Dundas, Ontario, January 21st, 1844, of Scotch parentage. He came with his parents to Detroit shortly after, of which City he has since been a continuous resident. He received an academical education and learned the trade of machinist.

In 1864 he became connected with the shipping interests on the lakes and from year to year increased his interests, and has been and is in a number of other enterprises which have helped contribute to the material growth of the City and State.

As a public man, Mr. Livingstone has been prominent for a number of years and has been a life-long Republican. In 1875 he was elected to represent Detroit in the State Legislature; was Chairman of the Executive Committee of the State Central Committee for a number of years and was twice Acting Chairman of the Committee at National Conventions.

He was appointed by President Arthur, Collector of the Port of Detroit, which position he resigned shortly after the election of President Cleveland.

Mr. Livingstone is at present General Manager of the Michigan Navigation Co. Among vessel men he is held in high estimation for his earnest and effective advocacy of all measures and influences tending to advance and protect their interests. He has been President of the Lake Carriers' Association and is probably one of the best known men in the business on the lakes. He has held quite a number of prominent positions. Among them he has been President

Eng by E. G. Williams & Bro. N.Y.

W. Livingstone

this position afforded a welcome opportunity to supplement his law studies by practical knowledge of the forms of pleadings and methods of court procedure. Following this he was elected Prosecuting Attorney for three terms, from 1874 to 1880. In addition to these local offices he was, in 1880, one of the supervisors for Michigan, of the tenth census; was appointed Judge Advocate by Governor Jerome; was a member of the State Military Board under Governor Alger, and was appointed by Governor Luce one of the Commissioners for Michigan to attend the Centennial celebration of the adoption of the Constitution of the United States. He has for nearly ten years past been President of the Detroit College of Law.

While holding the office of County Clerk Mr. Long was admitted to the bar, formed a law partnership with Mr. George G. Gold, and entered upon a practice which for the next twelve years, was large and varied. It covered almost every kind of civil cause except admiralty practice. This, with the knowledge of criminal law, which his service as Prosecuting Attorney gave, furnished an admirable equipment in general and special law for the higher position to which he was, at a later day, called.

In 1887 the Legislature increased the number of Supreme Court judges from four to five, and extended the term to ten years. Mr. Long was nominated for the position thus created, and was elected by a handsome majority. Notwithstanding his physical disability he has, for the past twelve years, been one of the most industrious members of a very industrious court. He has sat in almost all cases that have come before the court, and his written opinions, scattered through nearly fifty volumes of reports, are fine examples of clear statement, sound principles and logical argument.

Before going upon the Supreme Court bench Mr. Long was very active in Republican politics, serving upon local and Congressional committees, and being a frequent delegate to political conventions. He is still as strongly Republican in sentiment as ever, though no charge of partisanship has ever been made against him or his associates on the bench in the judicial treatment of questions involving political issues.

Justice Long is a popular and honored member of the Grand Army of the Republic, and in 1885 was elected Commander of the Department of Michigan. At the National Encampment, held in Pittsburg, Pa., in 1897, his election as Commander-in-Chief was urged as a rebuke from the veteran soldiers of the treatment of Comrade Long, by the head of the Pension Bureau at Washington in arbitrarily reducing the pension which he had been, for some years, receiving and he would have been elected had he not withdrawn his name rather than have the organization he loved drawn into what might terminate in a disagreeable controversy with the Administration then in power.

Judge Long was married in December, 1863, to Miss Alma A. Franklin, by whom he has had one son and two daughters.

JOHN MUNRO LONGYEAR, of Marquette, one of the prominent business men of the Upper Peninsula, was born at Lansing, Mich., April 15th, 1850. His father was John W. Longyear, a lawyer, Member of Congress, and afterwards Judge of the United States District Court for Eastern Michigan. His mother was Harriett Munro Longyear. The family came from Germany, probably about the year 1700. John M. Longyear had good opportunities for education in the public schools, under private tutors, in Cazenovia, N. Y., Seminary; Olivet College, Mich., and Georgetown College, D. C. His first occupation after leaving college was as inspector of lumber. His main business of late years has been that of dealing in timber and mineral lands, though he has a number of other interests. Mr. Longyear has been a Republican since 1860 and cast his first Presidential vote for Grant in 1872. His career has been business, rather than political, but he was delegate from Marquette County to the Republican State Convention in 1890 and was Mayor of Marquette in 1890 and 1891. He has been one of the Board of Control of the Michigan School of Mines, at Houghton since 1889. He was married January 4th, 1879, at Battle Creek, Mich., to Mary Hawley Beecher. Their children are Abby B., Munro Howard, John Beecher, Helen M., Judith F., Jack M. and Robert D.

JOHN WESLEY LONGYEAR, who gained high reputation, both as Congressman and Judge, was born at Shandaken, Ulster County, New York, October 22d, 1820, and died at Detroit, March 11th, 1875. He had a common school and academic education, and at the age of twenty-four he came west, and settled in Mason, Ingham County, Mich., where he took up the study of law, and where he was admitted to the bar in 1846. The following year he moved to Lansing, which then consisted of a small settlement, a small population and great aspirations, the latter based upon the then recent selection of the place for the State Capital. His brother, Ephraim, was first a student in his office, and then a partner, in a practice which soon became large. Not only did the City itself and the surrounding country grow rapidly, but the location there of the State offices and the sittings of the Supreme Court tended to an increase of law business. Mr. Longyear was one of the leaders at the bar here and had a practice extending into all the State and Federal Courts and into many of the circuits. For three years he was in partnership with S. F. Seager, and the firm was one of the best known and most successful in the State.

Mr. Longyear was a Republican in politics, and his voice was often heard in local and State Conventions. In 1862 he was elected to Congress and was re-elected in 1864, his service covering the last part of the war period, and the first part of reconstruction legislation. He studied the subject of secession and the relations of the States to the Nation from the standpoint of the Constitutional law-

yer, and not from that of the politician. He never took the time of the House, except upon important matters, and then only when he had studied the subject with great care, so that he was always listened to with marked attention. His argument on the first Reconstruction Bill in Congress in 1864, was recognized as one of the most logical discussions of the whole subject that was made during that session.

In 1866 Mr. Longyear was a delegate to the Loyalist Convention in Philadelphia, a Convention called to influence public opinion against the Johnson Reconstruction policy. In 1867 he was one of the most influential members of the Michigan Constitutional Convention. In 1870 he was appointed Judge of the United States Court for the Eastern District of Michigan, and removed to Detroit, where most of the sessions of the Court were required to be held. This court was, at that time, third in the number of admiralty cases in the United States, fifth in the number of bankruptcy proceedings, and second in the amount of judgments rendered. The adaptability of his mind was shown in the readiness with which he laid aside the habit of the advocate, and assumed that of the judge. He devoted to the duties of his new position the same conscientious care that he had to those of other positions, and soon had a wide reputation for the clearness of his decisions, and the force of the considerations upon which they were based. His bankruptcy decisions, especially, were widely quoted as true expressions of law on the subject.

Judge Longyear's arduous labors gradually undermined his health, and he died suddenly while holding court. He was married soon after he moved to Lansing, to Miss Harriett Munro, and left two sons and one daughter. John M. Longyear, one of the sons, is a leading citizen of Marquette. The second, Howard W., is a practicing physician in Detroit, and the daughter, Miss Ida, lives at Lansing.

RALPH LOVELAND, of Saginaw, one of the successful lumbermen of that long-time center of the pine industry, was born in Westport, Essex County, New York, November 23rd, 1863, his father being Ralph A. Loveland. His first education was in the public schools of Chicago and Grand Rapids. He then fitted for college at Beaman Academy, New Haven, Vt., was in Middlebury College in that State in 1882 and in Williams College, Williamstown, Mass., in 1883, and spent two years in Europe. Returning in 1887 he went into the lumber business with his father, in the Saginaw Lumber & Salt Co., and has continued in that business ever since. He is now Vice-President of that company and a director in the Bank of Saginaw.

Mr. Loveland is a member of St. Paul's Episcopal Church in Saginaw, of the East Saginaw Club, the Detroit Club and the Michigan Club. His first vote was cast for Harrison for President, and he has generally been active in campaigns since 1890, when he first began to take a lively interest in politics. He served on the Republican Congressional Committee in the campaigns of 1898 and 1900, was President of the Blaine Club in 1894 and is a member of the State League of Republican Clubs. He was a delegate to the State Conventions in 1896, 1898 and 1900, and to the National Convention in Philadelphia in the latter year.

RALPH A. LOVELAND is another of the men who, after varied employments, have been, for a long time connected with the lumber and salt interests of the Saginaw Valley. He was born in Westport, N. Y., January 17th, 1819, the son of Erastus and Lucy Bradley Loveland, the former a native of New York and the latter of Vermont. His father was a prominent owner and operator of shipping upon Lake Champlain and the Hudson River, and the son thus acquired a double education, spending his summers on the river and lake and his winters in the public schools and later in Essex Academy. He gradually acquired personal interests in the navigation business and in 1845 he consolidated these with those of the Northern Transportation Company, and was for several years connected with that company. In 1857 he formed a partnership with D. L. White and S. W. Barnard and opened a lumber business in Albany under the firm name of White, Loveland & Co., and the firm became the consignees of the Gilmans, then the largest lumber operators in America. He continued in this company, whose operations were very profitable, until 1863, when he was obliged to leave, on account of impaired health, went to Janesville, Wis., and adopted as his business the outdoor work of sheep raising. He went through Southern Michigan, picked up four thousand sheep, which he drove to Iowa, and in a year had the largest flocks of any man east of the Missouri. Having recovered his health he went into the lumber business again in Chicago, and in 1876 he commenced in Michigan, which has since been the scene of most of his operations. He first purchased a small mill in Montcalm County and worked it until the contributary pine gave out when he bought a large tract on the AuGres river in Iosco County, estimated to cut 150,000,000 feet of sawing timber. This was rafted to a mill which he owned on the Saginaw River, near the City of East Saginaw, and lasted until 1893. After that, until the Canadians prohibited the exportation of logs, the mill was supplied mainly from the Georgian Bay district. In 1881 the business was incorporated under the name of the Saginaw Salt and Lumber Co., of which Mr. Loveland has been President since 1893. The company's mill has cut about 25,000,000 feet a year, and it has hired the cutting of from 10,000,000 to 20,000,000 feet annually in other mills. The company also owns a salt block with a capacity of 50,000 barrels annually, and a farm of 1,200 acres north of Saginaw. Mr. Loveland,

R. A. Loveland.

Cyrus G. Luce

with his sons, Daniel K. and Ralph, and his son-in-law, R. H. Roys, are also interested in a large tract of pine land in the Parry Sound district in the Dominion, from which they get their board timber for the Quebec market.

In politics Mr. Loveland was originally a Henry Clay Whig, but cast his lot with the Republican party upon its first organization. He was a member both of the Assembly and Senate while in New York State. but has not held any political office in Michigan. He was married March 25th, 1840, to Miss Harriett M. Kent, daughter of Daniel M. and Mehitabel Goodrich Kent, of Benson, Vt., by whom he had eight children. She died in 1887, and seven years later he was again married, to Miss Helen Crittenden, of San Francisco.

EX-GOVERNOR CYRUS GRAY LUCE, who has had much to do with the agricultural interests of Michigan for more than fifty years, and a good deal to do with its politics for more than half that time, was born in Windsor, Ashtabula County, Ohio, July 2d, 1824. His parents were Walter Luce, a miller and farmer, and Mary M. Luce. His father's ancestors settled at Martha's Vineyard, Mass., at a very early date. In about the year 1720 his grandfather settled in Holland, Conn., where his father was born. His father was a soldier in the War of 1812, and in 1815 settled in the dense woods of Northeastern Ohio. His mother was born near Winchester, Va., her father being of English descent. At an early day he became a Virginia Abolitionist and found his native State an unpleasant abode, and for the enjoyment of freedom emigrated with his wife, four sons and four daughters to Ohio.

Northeastern Ohio was in a pioneer condition in Luce's boyhood days. He attended the district school in the proverbial log school house in the vicinity where he was born until he was twelve years old, when his parents moved with their six boys to Steuben County, Ind., being among the first settlers of the locality. Soon after reaching their destination the citizens erected a tamarack school house, in which young Luce gathered knowledge for two winters, after which he attended an academy located at Ontario, LaGrange County, Ind., for three years. His early occupation was similar to that of other boys of the period. He helped clear up the farm and drove a freight team from his home to Toledo, Ohio. When he was seventeen his father erected a wool-carding and cloth-dressing institution, and the son had charge of the work for seven years, at the end of which time he bought eighty acres of new land in Gilead, Mich., and from that time until the present he has been a farmer, though taking up other occupations as secondary to that.

As a boy and young man Mr. Luce was a Henry Clay Whig and verily thought the world was coming to an end when Clay was defeated in 1844. His first Presidential vote was cast for General Taylor in 1848. In that year without any previous knowledge, his name was placed upon the Whig ticket as a candidate for the Indiana Legislature in the District composed of the Counties of Steuben and DeKalb. While he had no hint of the coming nomination, it was accepted and he made his first political contest and met with the only defeat of his life before the people. In 1852 he was elected Supervisor of the Township of Gilead, and was re-elected for ten years subsequently. In 1854, upon the organization of the Republican party, he was elected to the House of Representatives; in 1858 he was elected Treasurer of Branch County, and re-elected in 1860; in 1864 he was elected to the State Senate, and re-elected in 1866, and in 1867 he was elected to the Constitutional Convention. In 1879 Mr. Luce was appointed State Oil Inspector by Governor Croswell, and was reappointed in 1881 by Governor Jerome. Previous to the time that he assumed the duties of the office, for various reasons the inspectors had met insurmountable difficulties in enforcing the law, but under his administration a complete organization was effected and the difficulties were overcome. With slight changes this organization is still in force. In 1886 and again in 1888, Mr. Luce was nominated, by acclamation, to the highest office in the gift of the people of Michigan, that of Governor. In both of these campaigns the contest was warm, Mr. Luce being opposed by strong candidates, who were placed in the field by a fusion of the Democrats and Greenbackers, or Nationalists. In the speeches which he made on the stump during these campaigns, he not only showed a great familiarity with the affairs of the State, but great skill and resource as a debater, enhancing the reputation he had previously acquired as a forceful and convincing speaker. The election, in each case, by fair majorities, furnished a tribute, not less to his ability than to his popularity among the industrial classes.

As the world goes he has made a success of farming; was from 1868 until 1873 a member of a business firm under the name of Luce, Blass & Co., dealers in dry goods, boots, shoes, groceries and produce. For the last six years he has been associated with Hugh Lyons & Co., Lansing, manufacturers of store furniture. He is now President of the William Coombs Milling Co., of Coldwater, and has for twenty-eight years been a Director in the Southern Michigan National Bank, located at Coldwater, but none of these things have ever diverted him from his original business of farming. His war record is unimportant. He enlisted in the Nineteenth Michigan Infantry in August, 1862, but was thrown out by the examining surgeon. He nevertheless was intensely interested in the success of the Union Army.

Governor Luce was a delegate to the State Convention in 1860, as an ardent supporter of Governor Blair; again in 1864 as a friend of Governor Baldwin; again in 1876 as Governor Croswell's friend, and in 1880 he was a delegate and earnest advocate of the nomination of John T. Rich. He has also been a delegate to several judicial Conventions. He has been a member of the Republican party since the hour of its birth, and has voted for all its Presidential candidates from John C. Fremont to William McKinley.

Mr. Luce has belonged to farmer's clubs, literary clubs and temperance clubs to such an extent that he cannot now remember them all. He has been an active member of the farmer's organization known as the Grange for twenty-six years and has given to it the best efforts of his life. He regards its purposes as high and holy, and while his active life is rapidly drawing to a close, and nearly all the enjoyments must be drawn from the past, there is nothing in his career that he reviews with greater pleasure than the efforts he has made to uplift the American farmers.

Mr. Luce was married August 29th, 1849, in Gilead, to Julia A. Dickinson, a native of Massachusetts, who had come with her parents to Gilead in 1836. To them five children were born; Elmira Jane, August 27th, 1850, married to John G. Parker and now lives at Orland, Ind.; Emery Greeley, a farmer, still living in Gilead; David D., who died when he was two years and seven months old; Florence A., still living at home; Homer D., who lives in Lansing. Governor Luce's wife died August 13th, 1882, and November 8th, 1883, he was again married, to Mrs. Mary E. Thompson.

The most striking characteristic of the administration of Governor Luce was the absolute honesty of the Governor himself. Not assumed honesty, not policy honesty, but stern, rugged, uncompromising adherence to the right thing in every case. He not only lived at the Capital, but he gave up his entire time and energy and mind to the business of the State. He not only found and championed the right in every case brought before him, but he ferreted out and took active measures to settle every case that ought to be brought before him.

While desirous of aiding his party in every way possible he never allowed any amount of political influence to induce him to appoint an unworthy man to any position or even to restrain him from selecting the best man for every office within his gift.

To this remarkable rigidity to principle he added an extraordiary knowledge of men and the world. He took great care to familiarize himself thoroughly with every detail of every institution in the State. He was indefatigable in his efforts to acquaint himself with the inner workings of every part of the State's machinery. He was as well informed as to the number of inmates and the current expenses of each institution as the officers themselves. He knew how, from whom and at what cost they purchased their food supplies. He knew accurately the number of employes and the amount of their respective salaries. Not the slightest thing escaped him.

He was willing and anxious that every department of the Government and every institution should be liberally supplied with what was truly needed, but he firmly insisted upon the most rigid economy everywhere. His entire administration was one of clean, straightforward justice and economy unhampered by personal or political corruption, and was a constant illustration of that ideal philosophy which teaches men that they may always safely accept the peril connected with doing the right thing.

AARON VANCE McALVAY, of Manistee, Ex-Circuit Judge, and one of the leading attorneys in Western Michigan, was born at Ann Arbor, July 19th, 1847, son of Patrick Hamilton and Sarah Drake McAlvay. His father was born in the Northern part of Ireland about six miles from the City of Newry, and was of Scotch parentage. His ancestors were Highland Scotch Covenanters and his mother was a Hamilton. Judge McAlvay's mother was born at or near Elizabeth, N. J., of Puritan stock, which came to this country in the Mayflower.

The son had the advantages of a good education, first in the Ann Arbor High School and afterwards in Michigan University. He received the degree of A. B. from the literary department of the University in 1868, and afterwards that of LL. B. from the law department. He supported himself while studying law, first by work in the office of the Register of Deeds at Ann Arbor, later by work in the law offices of Hiram J. Beakes and Lawrence & Frazer. After that he taught school one year to obtain funds with which to start out in his profession. He went to Manistee in November, 1871, where he has resided continuously ever since, engaged in the practice of law, except when serving a term as Circuit Judge.

Mr. McAlvay's father was one of the few Irish Whigs and Republicans in Southern Michigan in the later days of the former party and the earlier days of the latter. He was a radical, and the son has been, from his earliest days, a Republican. He voted first in the fall of 1868 for U. S. Grant for President. He has been a delegate to nearly every Republican State Convention for the past twenty-five years. Besides doing party work he has held a number of political offices, having been Supervisor, City Attorney several terms, Prosecuting Attorney of Manistee County, and Deputy Collector of Customs at Manistee. He was appointed Circuit Judge in 1878, to fill a vacancy, and was subsequently defeated for election by a Greenback-Democratic combination. He was appointed a member of the State Board of Health in 1895 for a term of six years and has been a very active and useful member. He was appointed by the Regents of the University in June, 1897, a non-resident Professor in the law department, which position he still holds, giving sixty lectures during the second semester of each year. The first year he took Dean Hutchins' work in "Equity Jurisprudence," while Mr. Hutchins was Acting President during President Angell's absence in Turkey. Since that time he has lectured on "Domestic Relations" and "Wills and Administration."

Mr. McAlvay is a Knight Templar, and has been E. C. of Manistee Commandery No. 32 for two years. He was married at Ann

A. V. McAlvay.

Jas C. McCabe

BAY CITY TRIBUNE.

Arbor, Mich., December 9th, 1872, to Barbara Bassler, and they have had six children: Harry Stevenson McAlvay, one year at University of Michigan with class of '96; Carl Emil McAlvay, graduated from University of Michigan, Class of '98, Ph. B.; Bayard Taylor McAlvay; Sarah Drake McAlvay, now Freshman in the University of Michigan; Barbara Rosina McAlvay and Margaretha McAlvay, who died February, 1892, at the age of four.

JAMES CHRISTOPHER McCABE is one of the men whom Grover Cleveland sent from the Democratic to the Republican ranks. He is the son of James McCabe, an insurance agent, and Martha McDowell McCabe, and was born April 30th, 1871, in Allegheny, Pa. His father's people were natives of Ireland, but they left their home in Leitrim County, Province of Connaught, at the time of the famine of 1841, and came to Quebec. A few years later they removed to Port Henry, Essex County, N. Y., where the father of James C. was born. His mother was a daughter of Christopher McDowell, who was born in 1812, in Belfast, Ireland, and came to this country in the early '50's, settling in Cold Springs, N. Y. Thence he went to Bay City in 1862, being one of the earliest settlers there. He married a Miss Warren, descendant of the Warren family of Revolutionary fame.

James C. was educated in the Pittsburg public schools, Bay City public schools, and graduated from Bay City High School in 1889. He was always in the newspaper and printing business, started as an amateur printer and at the age of fifteen was publisher of a monthly, "The Alert," at the same time attending school, and while publishing The Alert attended several conventions of the American and Western Amateur Press Associations. Upon leaving school he went to work for the Bay City Times as collector and afterwards became reporter; remained with the paper until the spring of 1890; then went on the staff of the Bay City Tribune, doing reportorial work. In the spring of 1891 he went to Detroit and for two months was reporter on the Detroit Times, but returned to Bay City to accept the position of City Editor on the Tribune. While on that paper he filled several special assignments, including a voyage from Bay City to Wood's Holl, Mass., on a government lightship, built at Wheeler's shipyard. In order to make the trip it was necessary to ship as watchman, as no passengers were taken. The voyage, which was full of exciting incidents, occupied twenty-eight days. December 1st, 1894, he resigned from the Tribune staff, and started the publication of an illustrated society weekly, "Chat," conducting it with success until March 7th, 1897, when it was discontinued. June 1st, 1896, while still publishing Chat, he was offered the position of Advertising Manager of the Tribune, which had just changed hands, and on October 1st, forming a copartnership with I. W. Snyder, bought out the Tribune, and he has devoted his entire time to this paper, which he and his partner have made one of the principal dailies of Michigan.

Mr. McCabe has been a staunch Republican since 1894. Upon this subject he says: "I was brought up a Democrat, and cast my first vote for Grover Cleveland in 1892, but soon saw the error of my ways, and came over to the right side, and have since been a hard worker for the Republican party." He never sought any political office from either party. In society matters he is a member of Joppa Lodge No. 315, F. & A. M.; the Michigan Club; Valley Tent No. 94, K. O. T. M., and the leading social and political clubs of Bay City. He was married October 20th, 1898, to Frances Cooke and has one child, Warren Lee McCabe, born August 7th, 1899.

JONATHAN NICHOLSON McCALL was born on the 28th of September, 1857, in Nelson, Portage County, Ohio. His father was William Wallace McCall, a farmer, and his mother, Mary A. McCall. His grandfather, Joseph McCall, came from Middletown, Conn., in 1820, and settled in Nelson Township, where he resided until the time of his death. His grandfather on his mother's side, James Knowlton, came with his parents from Blanford, Mass., and settled in the same township. The McCalls were descendants of Scotch ancestry, who came to the New England States in an early day, a branch of the family subsequently settling in New York.

The subject of this sketch obtained his elementary education in the public schools of his native township. Subsequently he attended Nelson Academy and Garretsville High School, and in 1875, entered Mt. Union College at Alliance, Ohio, in which institution, with the exception of the first two terms, he was compelled to bear the entire expense of his own education, which he did by teaching winters and working on the farm in the summer. After four years of Collegiate instruction, he graduated with the class of 1881, of which he was valedictorian. In his senior year, he was managing editor of the class publication, the "Unonian," and during a part of his college course he acted as tutor. Immediately after graduation he was engaged as principal of the Northfield schools; the following year accepted a position as Superintendent of the schools at Windham, Ohio, and the next year was elected Superintendent at Newton Falls, Ohio, which position he held until the spring of 1885, when he was elected Superintendent of the schools at Ithaca, Mich., where he has ever since resided. He continued to hold this position until the spring of 1892, when he resigned to enter the newspaper field, and purchased the Gratiot County Herald. This was a Democratic paper, which he transformed into an Independent paper, and continued it so until September 14th, 1894, when it became a staunch Republican organ, in conformity with the lifelong principles of its editor. Two years later, the Gratiot County Journal, for many years

GRATIOT COUNTY HERALD.

the Republican paper of the County, espoused the cause of Bryan, and renounced its former Republicanism, thus leaving the Herald the only Republican paper in Gratiot County, located at the County Seat. With the field thus opened to him Mr. McCall has, by persistent application to business, wide acquaintance and systematic effort, increased the circulation of the Herald from 1,000 subscribers to 2,800, and has made it one of the recognized leading Republican papers of its section of the State.

Mr. McCall has repeatedly been a delegate to the County and State Republican Conventions, and was elected alternate delegate-at-large from the State of Michigan, to the National Convention at Philadelphia in 1900. He has taken part on the political platform, and as a member of the County Committee, in all the political campaigns in Gratiot County for the past ten years, and is at present Secretary of the County Committee. He was Chairman of the delegation to the Eleventh District Congressional Convention of 1900, and presented to that Convention the name of Hon. A. B. Darragh, the successful candidate. He has for six years been a member of the Republican Newspaper Association of Michigan, of which organization he was elected Vice-President in the spring of 1899 and of which he is now a member of the Executive Committee. Since entering the newspaper profession, he has been a member of the Michigan State Press Association, of which organization he was elected President in the winter of 1900. In the spring of 1900 he was a delegate from the State Press Association to the National Press Association, which held its meeting at New Orleans. Mr. McCall has never sought political preferment, but he has served as a member of the Ithaca Village Council, and as President of the Village, and is very active in all enterprises and undertakings which tend to build up and strengthen the village or his party.

Mr. McCall is a member of Ithaca Lodge No. 123, F. & A. M., in which he has held all the offices save that of Master. He is also a member of Ithaca Chapter No. 70, R. A. M., of which he is the present High Priest. He is Past Chancellor of Ithaca Knights of Pythias Lodge, and a member of the Oddfellows; of Rising Star Lodge, I. O. O. F.; of Ithaca Tent, K. O. T. M.; the Loyal Guards, and the Modern Woodmen of America.

He was first married to Margaret Frances Webb, on the 24th day of August, 1882, at Tallmadge, O. Mrs. McCall died on the 31st day of March, 1893. They had one child, Wallace Webb McCall, who was born August 20th, 1890, and still survives. On the 13th day of November, 1894, he was again married to Harriet Watson Richardson, from which union there have resulted four children: Harriet Irene, born August 22d, 1895; Thelma Margaret, born December 25th, 1896; Jonathan Watson, born September 28th, 1898, and Romayne, born August 8th, 1900.

DANIEL ELSON McCLURE, whose life has been devoted mainly to educational pursuits, was born in Erie County, Pennsylvania, October 25th, 1854. His father was William McClure, a farmer, and his mother was Eliza Taylor McClure. His father was born in Antrim County, Ireland, of Scotch-Irish parents. His mother's ancestors came from England. She was born in New York and was a teacher. Daniel had his education in country schools, in Normal school in Edinboro, Pa., and the Valparaiso Normal, Valparaiso, Ind. He worked on a farm and in the lumber woods of Pennsylvania to get money to enable attendance at school. After completing his studies he taught district and village schools, was Township Superintendent of Shelby Township schools, Secretary of the County Board of Examiners and County Commissioner of Oceana County schools for eight years, from 1880 to December, 1896, when he resigned in order to accept the position of Deputy Superintendent of Public Instruction. He has held this position for four years, having been reappointed by Mr. Hammond in 1899. He cast his first vote for President Hayes and has always been a Republican. He was a delegate to the State Conventions in 1890 and 1892 that nominated James Turner and John T. Rich for Governor, respectively. He also attended as delegate both conventions that nominated Hazen S. Pingree, and was a delegate to the Convention at Jackson that nominated Judge C. B. Grant.

Mr. McClure is a member of Oceana Chapter No. 56, R. A. M., Pentwater; S. W. of No. 33, Lansing Lodge, F. & A. M.; Arbutus Chapter No. 45, O. E. S., Lansing; Capital Lodge No. 45, I. O. O. F., Lansing; Capital Grange, Lansing, No. 40. He was married August 16th, 1876, at Montague, Mich. to Julia E. Rathbone. They have four children· Blanche, Nellie, Floyd and Nyda.

DANIEL McCOY, a leading banker and business man of Grand Rapids, was born in Philadelphia, July 17th, 1845, son of John McCoy, a merchant, and Mary Ann McGowan. His father was a son of John McCoy and Jean Allen, who came to Michigan in 1833, and settled near Oakwood, Oakland County, where they are buried. They were Scotch and all the ancestry on this side were Scotch—Highland Scotch. His mother was born in Bally Castle, County Antrim, Ireland, and all her ancestry was Irish.

The son was educated in the public schools of Philadelphia. His first occupation was in the wholesale hardware house of Shields & Brother, in that City. He left there in 1866 and went into the oil regions of West Virginia at Burning Springs, on the Little Kanawha River; remained a year with but little success; then went West to Kansas City, and being unable to find suitable occupation, came to Michigan in 1868, and finding an opening in Romeo, started in the grain and produce business, finding a good market in the pineries of the neighboring counties. He sold out in 1872 and formed a partner-

Daniel McCoy

W. H. McGregor.

ship with James A. Remick, of Detroit, and John G. Riggs, of Saginaw, and began lumbering on the south branch of the Manistee River; organized the firm of McCoy & Ayer in 1873, for the logging, sawing and marketing of timber and lumber at and near Cadillac. This firm was dissolved in 1883, and he moved his headquarters to Grand Rapids, and continued lumbering until 1893; helped to organize the Edison Light Company of Grand Rapids in 1886, and has been its executive head ever since; assisted in the organization of the State Bank of Michigan in 1893, and has been its active President since that time. Both concerns are very prosperous and their stock closely held. He is a director and stockholder in other important manufacturing enterprises; helped to organize the Village of Clam Lake, in Wexford County, and was chosen its President in March, 1877; assisted in obtaining its charter as a City and changing its name to "Cadillac," and was its Mayor in 1879, 1880 and 1881. He has attended State Conventions from Wexford and Kent Counties, and has been Chairman of the Republican County Committee in both. At the State Convention in June, 1900, he was nominated for State Treasurer and was elected by nearly 100,000 plurality. He has always been a Republican and cast his first Presidential vote for General Grant, and in some campaigns has been a very active worker.

Mr. McCoy belongs to no secret societies; is a member of the Peninsular, Lakeside, Military and Kent County Clubs of Grand Rapids, and the Michigan Club of Detroit. He was married October 19th, 1869, to Gail Lyon Ayer, at Romeo, Mich. Their children are Helen Frances, Ralph, Katherine and Gerald.

WILLIAM HENRY McGREGOR, one of Detroit's shrewd politicians and an active man of affairs, was born in the City of his present residence, August 16th, 1861. His parents, Alexander and Margaret McGregor, came to this country from Paisley, Scotland. The son, William, was educated in the public schools of Detroit and the Detroit College of Law. His occupation, however, since graduating has been in quite another line than that of law, as from 1880 to 1899 he was a pharmacist, and Superintendent of manufacturing with Parke, Davis & Co., of Detroit.

Mr. McGregor, a Republican for thirty-nine years, and casting his first Presidential vote for Garfield, has been quite active in local politics, where he is not only popular, but has the reputation of being long-headed. He has been a number of times a delegate to City and County Conventions, and was a delegate to the State Conventions of 1894 and 1900. He was School Inspector from 1895 to 1900, and was elected President of the Board in 1898. In the latter year he was elected County Clerk and has proved a very efficient officer.

Mr. McGregor is a member of Ashlar Lodge No. 91, F. & A. M.; Peninsular Chapter No. 16, R. A. M.; Monroe Council No. 1, R. & S. M.; Detroit Commandery No. 1, K. T; Michigan Sovereign Consistory, S. R. M.; Knights of Khorassan, Mecca Temple; Majestic Tent, Knights of Maccabees; Fraternal Order of Eagles, Lodge No. 82; Moslem Temple, N. M. S.; Wayne Lodge No. 104, K. of P.; Detroit Lodge, B. P. O. E. No. 34; the Harmonie Society, Concordia Society, and is an associate member of Detroit Post, G. A. R., an honorary member of the Detroit Light Infantry and of the Michigan Yacht Club. He is unmarried.

WILLIAM T. McGRAW, who represented the Fourth District in the State Senate in 1899 and 1900, was born in the Township of Livonia, Wayne County, May 12th, 1860. He received his first education in the public schools of Plymouth, graduated from the High School in that Village, and subsequently took a course in a business university in Detroit. After leaving the latter institution he was Clerk in the First National Bank of Plymouth for two years, and moved thence to Detroit, which has ever since been his residence. He was for a time traveling salesman for the Globe Tobacco Company, and afterwards organized the Detroit Tobacco Company, with which he is still connected. He is also President of the Globe Cash Register Company, and a Director in the Globe Tobacco Co.

Mr. McGraw has always been a Republican and has been active in committee and other party work. In 1898 he was nominated for the State Senate in the District comprising the three Western Detroit Wards, the City of Wyandotte, and the Southern and Western Townships of Wayne County. He was elected by a plurality of nearly 2,000. He served on the Committees on the Asylums for the Insane at Kalamazoo and Traverse City, the College of Mines, Elections, the Liquor Traffic and Public Health, and was Chairman of the Committee on the Reformatory at Ionia, and the Committee on Railroads, the latter of which is one of the most important in the whole list. Senator McGraw was universally recognized by his associates as one of the most industrious and useful members of the Senate.

JAMES BERESFORD McKAY, son of James McKay and Mary McClellan McKay, one of Detroit's leading real estate dealers, was born June 9th, 1848, at Limavady, a beautiful picturesque town in the County of Londonderry, North of Ireland. His father was a storekeeper, mill owner and farmer and his ancestors were from Sutherlandshire, in the Highlands of Scotland. He was educated partly in the public schools, and in private seminaries. He came to Detroit primarily on a visit to relatives in Oakland County, and liked this country so much that he decided to remain, and after returning home came back again and settled permanently. His first occupation upon coming to Detroit, a young man of eighteen, was in keeping books for the old firm of Stephens, Smith & Co., afterwards commencing the real estate business, in which he has been engaged

James C. McLaughlin

for over twenty-five years. In that time he has handled a large amount of property on his own account, and besides that has made many large deals for others, in acreage, business and residence property. He has an abiding confidence in the future of Detroit.

Mr. McKay has been a life-long Republican, and active in campaigns. He has been elected for six consecutive terms a member of the Board of Estimates and twice its President. He is also a Director in the Dime Savings Bank. He is a devotee of field sports, is President of two hunting clubs, and a lover of thoroughbred setters, pointers and spaniels. A lovely wife and one daughter constitute his family.

JAMES CAMPBELL McLAUGHLIN, a leading lawyer and Republican of Muskegon, was born January 26th, 1858, at Beardstown, Cass County, Ill., his parents being David McLaughlin and Isabella Campbell, natives of Edinburgh, Scotland, who had come to this country in 1851. The son graduated from the Muskegon High School in 1876, entered the literary department of Michigan University with the class of 1882, but did not graduate; graduated from University of Michigan law department in 1883. After graduation he immediately began the practice of law in Muskegon with his father, and the partnership lasted until the father died in 1891. He then continued in practice alone till November, 1899, when his cousin, John A. McLaughlin entered into partnership with him. Mr. McLaughlin has, from the outset, been successful in his practice, being a thorough student, familiar with the law, and careful and painstaking in the preparation of his cases. He ranks well up among the leading attorneys in Western Michigan.

Mr. McLaughlin has been very prominent in politics as well as in law. He was a Republican before he became a voter, and cast his first Presidential ballot for James A. Garfield. He has been a hard worker in the local political committees, and has attended, as delegate, a large number of State Conventions. He was elected Prosecuting Attorney of Muskegon County in 1886 and again in 1888, and made a very efficient officer. At the State Convention, held June 27th, 1900, he was a candidate for the nomination for Auditor General, and although he had made but a short canvass, he stood second in the list of those who received votes for that position. The hearty support which he received from his own section in the Convention was very flattering, and certainly places him in the line for future honors. He is known in his home City as a man of sterling integrity and large business ability, and, aside from his law practice has other material interests. He is a Director of the Home Building and Loan Association and its attorney, and also a Director of the Enterprise Foundry Company. He is a member of Lovell Moore Lodge No. 182, F. & A. M., and Muskegon Lodge No. 274, B. P. O. E., which he has served as Exalted Ruler. He is also a Maccabee and Forester. His father, David McLaughlin, now deceased, was one of Muskegon's most venerated citizens; was for twenty-five years a member of the Board of Education and assisted in laying the foundation of the splendid school system the City of Muskegon now enjoys, a system in which the son also has taken great interest.

ALEXANDER I. McLEOD, one of the best known young men in the City of Detroit in newspaper, political and yachting circles, was born in Providence, R. I., August 2d, 1852, the son of Alexander and Janet Reid McLeod. His father was born in the Highlands of Scotland, and at the age of sixteen, worked his passage to America on a sail vessel and settled in Nova Scotia. He learned the trade of ship carpenter and marine draughtsman, which he followed the rest of his life, on land and sea, making voyages to all parts of the world. When the year 1857 opened he was a prosperous shipbuilder of Providence, R. I., but in the financial revulsion of that year he lost most of his fortune. The next year he moved to Michigan, and was for many years Superintendent of the shipyard of Campbell & Owen, predecessors of the Detroit Dry Dock Co., now the Detroit Shipbuilding Company.

The subject of this sketch received his education in the public schools of Detroit, which he attended until the age of eighteen. Inheriting from his father a love of the sea, he shipped before the mast on a lake schooner. Later he returned to Detroit and entered the employ of the Advertiser and Tribune as "printer's devil" for a short time, subsequently serving on the reportorial and editorial staff of the paper. In 1873 he was appointed by Judge George S. Swift, Clerk of the Recorder's Court and retained that position until 1877, when he became one of the incorporators of a stock company for the manufacture of wood chemicals, of which H. M. Pierce was made President, and upon the completion of their plant, he was made Assistant Superintendent, serving in that capacity one year. During the following three years he was associated with Capt. A. C. Donnelly, of Cincinnati, in the running of a line of steamers on the Ohio River, but returned to Detroit in 1882 and entered the employ of the Evening News, where he remained until 1889, being City Editor of that paper the latter four years of his service. From 1890 to 1895 he served as Private Secretary to Mayor Pingree, of Detroit. In 1894 Mr. McLeod was elected Treasurer of Wayne County on the Republican ticket, and was re-elected to that office in 1896. He inaugurated a system in the Treasurer's office which is pronounced by experts to be one of the best methods in use anywhere in the country.

In politics Mr. McLeod has the reputation of being one of the shrewdest men and one of the best organizers in the State. He has attended many conventions, and done much work on party committees, and even when not so engaged, his advice has been much sought. He has planned many successful campaigns, and was probably the best political adviser that Mayor and Governor Pingree had, when that official was making his remarkable runs at the polls. He was one of the very few men that could oppose any of Mr. Pingree's cherished plans, or give him unpalatable advice and criticism, without losing favor with him.

Mr. McLeod has been identified with the shipping and other business interests of the City, and has been quite successful in his enterprises. He is now Secretary and Treasurer of the Ontonagon Silver Land Co., and of the Morgan-Whateley Co., of Detroit. He is an enthusiastic yachtsman; has been partly instrumental in organizing and managing half a dozen yacht clubs; has been Commodore of the Inter-Lake Yachting Association, and has numerous beautiful prizes that attest his own skill as a sailor. He is prominent in Masonic circles; a member of Moslem Temple, Nobles of the Mystic Shrine; Damascus Commandery, Knights Templar; King Cyrus Chapter, R. A. M., and Oriental Lodge, F. & A. M. He is also a member of Michigan Lodge, I. O. O. F.; Myrtle Lodge, K. of P.; the Harmonie Singing Society; the Fellowcraft Club of Detroit; all three of the Yacht Clubs in Detroit, and of various other social and political organizations. In 1876 he married Frances A., daughter of John Millington, of New York City.

HUGH McMILLAN is one of the distinguished family that have done more for the industrial interests of Detroit than any other family that ever resided within its limits. He was the son of William and Grace McMillan, both natives of Scotland, and was born September 8th, 1845, at Hamilton, Ontario, to which point his parents had emigrated in 1834. His father, a sturdy Scotch Presbyterian, in which church he had for a long time been a ruling Elder, was Superintendent of the Fuel Department of the Great Western Railway.

The son, Hugh McMillan, was educated at the Central School and Phillips Academy at Hamilton, and commenced work as a clerk on the Great Western Railway. He came to Detroit in August, 1861, to enter the Superintendent's office of the Detroit, Grand Haven & Milwaukee Railway; was elected Secretary of the Michigan Car Company in 1872, and some years after became Vice-President and General Manager of this company and also the Detroit Car Wheel Co. and Baugh Steam Forge Co. He is now interested as stockholder and in most cases an officer in the following properties: American Car & Foundry Co., American Shipbuilding Co., Michigan Telephone Co., Commercial National Bank, State Savings Bank, Union Trust Company, and Detroit & Cleveland Navigation Company.

In politics Mr. McMillan has always been a Republican and cast his first vote for General Grant, but he has not been especially active in political affairs. He was President of the Detroit Club for four years and is a member of Yondotega Club, and the Country Club. He was married to Ellen Dyar, May 2d, 1867, and to Josephine Warfield, September 4th, 1899. His children are: Gilbert N. McMillan, Mrs. Lewis Warfield, Harold D. McMillan, Maurice B. McMillan and Hugh McMillan.

JAMES McMILLAN, Senior United States Senator from Michigan, was born of Scotch parents in Hamilton, Ontario, May 12, 1838. His father was a Presbyterian Elder, a man of thrift, enterprise, intelligence, which qualities made him influential and prosperous. He gave his son, James, a grammar school education, supplemented by an apprenticeship in a hardware store; and when the lad was seventeen years old started him for Detroit, with excellent letters of introduction to prominent business men. The gift of handling men was born in James McMillan; he has always been able to work with others to accomplish results, in such a way as to have all those associated with him participate in the rewards. He has gone through life helping others at the same time that he helped himself; and in hundreds of instances he has started young men in business or re-established men overtaken by misfortune. He was but a boy when he began to invest his savings, and to borrow capital for enterprises in which he saw a profit. From a clerk in a Detroit hardware store, he became purchasing agent for a railroad, then he handled the work of extending the Detroit & Milwaukee Railroad to Grand Haven, and in the '60's he entered into the business of building freight cars. From small beginnings the manufacture of cars grew to be the largest industry in Detroit; and to this interest Mr. McMillan added the Detroit & Cleveland Navigation Company, the Detroit Dry Dock Company, several lake transportation companies, the building of the international bridge at Sault Ste. Marie and of the Duluth, South Shore & Atlantic Railway across the Upper Peninsula; and various other enterprises.

Engrossing as was his business, he was never at a loss for time to devote to public interests, and his gifts to public and private charities were always proportionate to his means. Besides being a regular supporter of the established charitable and benevolent institutions of his City, his gifts to the State University, the Agricultural College, Albion College, and the establishment of the Grace Hospital have been notably large and effective.

On the death of Zachariah Chandler, Mr. McMillan was called to the leadership of the Republican party in Michigan. His leadership has been one not of the kind that builds up a machine, efficient yet relentless; but has rather been a leadership by the repeated choice and calls of his party, who have recognized in him a man easy to work with, and one who tolerates the largest possible right to individual opinion among those who are striving for a common object. On entering the United States Senate in 1889, Mr. McMillan

James M.

left to his capable sons the more active management of business affairs, although never ceasing to take a keen personal interest in every branch of the numerous activities with which his name had been associated, and even from time to time to enter upon new enterprises. Preferring action rather than speech, and being quick to see the essential features of every plan proposed, Senator McMillan in time has come to be one of the recognized powers of the Senate. This is shown by the fact that for the past six years he has served continuously on those caucus committees that have the adjustment of party matters. When he had been in the Senate but two years he was called to succeed Senator Ingalls as Chairman of the Committee on the District of Columbia, where his business ability, his familiarity with large undertakings, his wide travel and observation, and his infinite tact have enabled him already to accomplish many improvements for the National Capital and to lay the foundations for many others. Although citizens of the District of Columbia have there no vote, it is entirely safe to say that there is no City in this country where the intelligent public opinion has more influence, and where the rights of the individual are so carefully heard and considered. Acting as both a branch of Legislature and of Common Council, the District Committee of the Senate is the busiest continuously of any of the committees of that body.

Less exacting as to time, but not as to the problems presented, are the Committees on Commerce, on Naval Affairs and on Relations with Cuba, of which Senator McMillan is a member also; and with each session of Congress the work increases with knowledge and opportunity.

In social life Senator and Mrs. McMillan occupy the position that cultivation, wealth, and eminent social natures command. Married in 1860 to Miss Mary Wetmore, five married sons and a daughter go to make up a family that has lost but one member.

In his election to the Senate Mr. McMillan has enjoyed the rare distinction of being three times nominated unanimously by acclamation, and once being elected by unanimous vote. His second term expires March 4, 1901. On the 1st of January, the Republican caucus was held, at which he was unanimously renominated by acclamation for the succeeding term.

WILLIAM CHARLES McMILLAN, the son of Senator James McMillan and Mary L. Wetmore, was born in Detroit, March 1st, 1861. His father was born in Hamilton, Canada, and his mother belongs to an old New England family, which has for many years been especially prominent in Eastern Massachusetts and Rhode Island.

W. C. McMillan graduated at Yale College, literary department, in the class of 1884, and at once entered the employ of the Michigan Car Co., of which his father was President. After three years' service, in which he showed marked executive ability, he was appointed General Manager in the company. In 1892 he was instrumental in bringing about the consolidation of that company with the Peninsular Company, and was elected one of the two Managing Directors of the combined corporation. Before he was thirty years of age he was offered a directorship in one of the largest trust companies in New York City, and the same year he was offered the Presidency of one of the Detroit National Banks, both of which places he declined. He is now interested in the following corporations as stockholder and in most cases as Director: First National Bank, Union Trust Company, the Seamless Steel Tubes Company; Detroit & Cleveland Navigation Company, Peninsular Sugar Company, Michigan Malleable Iron Company, State Savings Bank, American Shipbuilding Company, Detroit Railroad Elevator Company and the Detroit Gas Company.

Mr. McMillan is a member of the following social organizations: Union Club, University Club, New York Yacht Club, Calumet Club, New York City; Essex County Club, Manchester, Mass.; Algonquin Club, Boston, Mass.; Detroit Club, Yondotega Club, the Country Club, Detroit; Old Club, St. Clair Flats. He was married July 15th, 1884, at Hanover Square, London, England, to Miss Marie Louise Thayer, of Boston, Mass., and has two children, Thayer McMillan, aged 15, and Doris McMillan, aged 4. In politics Mr. McMillan has been a Republican for thirty years, and first voted for James G. Blaine in 1884.

JAMES MAC NAUGHTON, a mining Manager and Superintendent, was born at Bruce Mines, Province of Ontario, Canada, March 9th, 1864, his parents being Archibald MacNaughton and Catherine MacIntyre. Archibald MacNaughton, as a young man, was a shepherd in the Highlands of Scotland. When he reached his majority, he was married in Scotland, where he lived for about a year after his marriage, and then emigrated to America, settling on a farm in Canada. After five years of farm life, he moved to the mining district on the shore of Georgian Bay, Province of Ontario, where he worked as a miner. James MacNaughton received his education in the public schools of Lake Linden, Mich., and at the University of Michigan. His first occupation was that of water-boy during vacations, attending school in the winter. When fifteen years old he left school and worked on the Calumet & Hecla Railroad. When nineteen years of age he went to school at Oberlin, Ohio, for one year, and the following year entered the University of Michigan and studied engineering. On leaving the University, after his Sophomore year, he entered the mining engineer's office of the Calumet & Hecla Mining Company, where he worked nearly three years. He then became Mining Engineer of the Chapin mine, later Assistant Superintendent, afterwards Superintendent, and then General Man-

Jas. MacNaughton.

ager. He is at present General Manager for the Chapin and Winthrop mines, which are owned by the National Steel Company. He has always been a Republican and cast his first vote for Harrison for President in 1888. He was a delegate to the State Conventions in 1896 and 1900; delegate to the National Republican Convention at St. Louis in 1896, and Presidential Elector in 1900. He was Chairman of the Board of Supervisors of Dickinson County for one year and member of said Board for ten years. The only political club of which he is a member is the Michigan Club. He was married August 27th, 1892, to Mary E. Morrison, of Calumet, Mich. They have one child, Martha Lois, seven years of age.

WILLIAM McPHERSON, JR., a leading banker in the interior of the State, was born near Inverness, Scotland, March 9th, 1834. His father was William McPherson and his mother was Elizabeth Riddle. William McPherson, Sr., left Scotland for America and located in Howell, Livingston County, Mich., in September, 1836, at which time the subject of this sketch was about two and one-half years old. At that time Howell contained only one frame building, a hotel, in which were located the County offices and a store. Wm. McPherson, Sr., at once took up his trade of blacksmithing, which he had followed in Scotland, and continued at that for about six years, after which he entered the mercantile business, which he followed until his death, in 1891.

William McPherson, Jr., received his education in the Village schools of Howell. During his boyhood days he assisted his father in the store during the time that the limited educational advantages of the Village did not claim his attention. There being no railroad through Howell, all produce from the surrounding country had to be drawn by team over the old Grand River road, fifty-two miles, to Detroit, where it was sold and merchandise bought and hauled back to Howell to meet the demands of the little pioneer settlement. Many times while still a boy, in his teens, Mr. McPherson made this trip. Work of this nature and the healthy, hardy life of the early pioneers, gave to him early in life a knowledge of business and a confidence in his ability to perform whatever task was set before him, that has stood him in good stead in his after life. In 1856 he became associated with his father in the mercantile business in Howell, under the firm of William McPherson & Co. In 1861 his brother, M. J. McPherson, was admitted to the firm, the firm name being changed to William McPherson & Sons, under which name it is still continued. In 1867 another brother, E. G. McPherson, was admitted. Mr. McPherson continued an active member in this firm until in 1884, when his outside interests became so extensive that he left the firm in order to give more time to their management. Since that time his attention has been devoted principally to the handling of his real estate, and pine and hardwood lands, both in the North and in Mississippi and Louisiana. In 1890, upon the removal of his brother, Alexander McPherson, to Detroit, where he went to accept the Presidency of the Detroit National Bank, he assumed the management of the Banking House of Alexander McPherson & Co., which his brother had established in 1865. Since 1858 he has been a dealer in wool and interested in general farming.

Mr. McPherson has been a lifelong Republican and cast his first ballot for John C. Fremont. In 1888 he was a delegate from the Sixth District to the Republican National Convention in Chicago; in 1896 delegate from Sixth District, to the Republican Convention at St. Louis, and in 1900, Delegate-at-Large to the Republican National Convention in Philadelphia, and has attended nearly all of the Republican State Conventions for the past fifteen years. He was appointed Commissioner of Railroads by Governor Russell A. Alger in 1885, and served during Alger's administration. In 1896 he was appointed a member of the Board of Control of the State Industrial School for Boys at Lansing, and at the present time is President of the Board. He has always been an active worker in the interests of the Republican party, but has never wished for or sought political preferment at the hands of the party. He has been a member of the Michigan Club since its organization.

Mr. McPherson was married to Jennie M. Ranney in 1859. His oldest son, William Frederick McPherson, died in 1878, at the age of eighteen. The children still living are: Mrs. W. C. Spencer, of Howell, Mrs. J. W. Bigelow, of Detroit, and R. Bruce McPherson, of Howell.

EDWIN CHARLES MADDEN, now Third Assistant Postmaster General at Washington, was born in Montreal, Canada, November 25th, 1855. His father, John B. Madden, was a shoe manufacturer and came from the North of Ireland, and the family of his mother, Anna M. Howell, came from England and settled in Montreal. His great great uncle was Lord Nelson, the hero of Trafalgar. His family came from Canada to Michigan in 1861, and settled in Detroit, where they have since resided.

Edwin C. Madden was educated in the Detroit public schools and Mayhew's Business College. His first occupation was that of bellboy in the Michigan Exchange and later he was clerk in L. S. Freeman's news depot, well known to the old residents of Detroit, located on the north side of Jefferson avenue, near the corner of Brush street. He entered the railroad business at the age of sixteen and continued until January 1st, 1891, serving thirteen years as a locomotive engineer on the D., G. H. & M. R. R. He was then appointed to the position of Registry Clerk in the Detroit postoffice by Postmaster E. T. Hance, and took his position the next day, February 1st; was rapidly promoted in the postal service until he reached

Alexander Maitland

a postoffice superintendency, which he held until appointed to his present position by President McKinley.

Of the improvements made in the postal service by Mr. Madden since he assumed the duties of Third Assistant Postmaster General, "The Fourth Class Postmaster," a paper published at Washington, says: "Probably the most important one instituted by him, and in which he takes greatest pride, is the system of letter carrier registration—by means of which letters can be registered from door to door by letter carriers, thus obviating the necessity for patrons to go to the postoffice for that purpose, as previously. This system is one that was rather discouraged at the outset, because of the fear that the carriers would work overtime in making registrations, thereby increasing the cost of the service, but time has justified the efficacy of Mr. Madden's plan, and the system in now lauded sky high by the beneficiaries of its operations. Another innovation inaugurated by him is the issuing of postage stamps in booklet form for the pocket. These books are an accommodation to the public, and are an additional source of revenue to the Department, in view of the fact that they are manufactured for much less than they cost the retail purchaser. Mr. Madden is the author of a bill, which is likely to pass Congress, the design of which is to facilitate the business interests of the country. It provides that, under certain conditions, letters and postal cards shall be transmitted in the mails without prepayment, the postage being collected of the addressee upon delivery. It will be a new feature of the postal service and will enable merchants and others to solicit orders and information without the loss of postage on that part of the envelopes and cards which they circulate, but which are never returned to them."

Mr. Madden has been a Republican all his life, as his father was before him. He cast his first vote for Garfield for President. He has held no political offices save the appointive one which he now holds, unless his original appointment in the Detroit postoffice be so considered. He has been a Mason since he was twenty-one, and is still a member of Ashlar Lodge No. 91, of Detroit: has been from the date of his eligibility connected with the Brotherhood of Locomotive Engineers and is still a member of that order. He was married on the 26th day of January, 1888, to Kate R. Strong, daughter of William and Esther Strong, of Detroit. His children are Russell Strong, the eldest, and Nelson Reyburn, the youngest.

ALEXANDER MAITLAND, State Senator from the Thirty-first District, comprising the Counties of Alger, Dickinson, Iron and Marquette, has been prominent in the politics and business of the Upper Peninsula for more than a quarter of a century. He was born in Ayrshire, Scotland, June 20th, 1844, where he acquired his early education; moved to America with his parents, locating in Canada in 1856, where his education was supplemented by a High School course. In 1864 he came to Michigan, locating at Negaunee, and entered the employ of the Iron Cliff Mining Company. For thirteen years he held the position of surveyor and engineer for that company. During most of the time he served as Acting Manager, and was formally appointed to that position in the spring of 1880, and the following year was appointed General Manager, which responsible position he held for ten years. He is also Manager of the mines of the Republic Iron & Steel Co. In politics he is a Republican; was Postmaster four years and County Surveyor two terms; was Mayor of the City of Negaunee, and was elected to the Senate of 1897-8, by a vote of 9,403 to 3,511 for Robert Blemhuber, Democratic-People's-Union-Silver candidate. He was elected to the Senate of 1899-1900 by a vote of 6,446 to 2,734 for Henry C. Russell, Democratic-People's-Union-Silver candidate, and 60 for Victor E. Cox, Prohibition In the Senate of 1899-1900 he was Chairman of the Committees on the School for the Blind, and on Geological Survey, and a member of the Committees on Railroads, Taxation, Labor Interests, Cities and Villages and Elections.

**FRANK DAY MEAD**, a prominent attorney at Escanaba, was born at Ann Arbor, January 27th, 1856, his parents being John C. and Caroline W. Mead. His father was a farmer, and from 1856 to 1860, was Sheriff of Washtenaw County. His ancestors on both sides were in this country before the Revolutionary War, those on his father's side having come originally from Ireland, and his mother's from Scotland. He was educated at the University of Michigan, graduating from the literary department in 1879. Immediately after graduating he commenced the study of law in the office of Chandler & Grant, at Houghton. He was admitted to the bar by the Supreme Court in the spring of 1881, and was for a time after that, Assistant Prosecuting Attorney of Marquette County, in the office of John Q. Adams, at Negaunee. In the fall of 1881 he moved to the City of Escanaba, and has since practiced law there. He has held no office except that of Prosecuting Attorney for Delta County, which he held for six years, from 1885 to 1891.

Mr. Mead has been a Republican all his life and voted first for James A. Garfield. He was elected as an alternate delegate to the National Republican Convention at St. Louis in 1896, and in the absence of the delegate, whose alternate he was, served in that Convention. He has attended a number of the Republican State Conventions as a delegate from Delta County during the past fifteen years.

Mr. Mead does not belong to any clubs or societies except the college secret society, Alpha Delta Phi. He was married to Sara F. Myrick, May 14th, 1884, at Milwaukee, Wis. The names of his children are: Helen D. Mead and Myrick D. Mead.

F D Mead

HON. WM. S. MESICK was born in Newark, Wayne County, N. Y., August 26, 1856. His father, Smith Mesick, from whom he derived his second name, was a merchant in Newark. He and his wife, Rebecca Shumway, originally came from Columbia County, N. Y.

It was in the atmosphere of the farm that he received his first training and his first school was the common school, such as all New York villages had at that time. After he had exhausted the possibilities of schooling in his home he entered the Kalamazoo Business College, then the University of Michigan and in 1876 begun the study of the law.

Completing this study he was admitted to the bar in 1881, at once settling in Mancelona. There he began the practice of his chosen avocation. He was first publicly before the people of his home City and County when he accepted the nomination for Prosecuting Attorney on the Republican ticket, with Blaine and Logan as the National candidates. It was nearly a hopeless fight from the start, but he made an active and aggressive campaign, and while he lost, he secured a firm hold upon the voters. He took his defeat easily, but was determined to seek an endorsement and he received it in magnificent shape when, in 1888, he again entered the lists for the same office, and was elected. One term was all he cared for and he declined to make the run another time.

Then he was nominated and elected Circuit Court Commissioner of his circuit, and held that office continuously until the electors called upon him to make the race for Congress in the Eleventh Michigan District, in 1896. He made a gallant campaign and carried the District by over 5,000 plurality. His record was such that despite personal opposition he was renominated and as a result of the canvass increased his majority to nearly 7,000 in 1898.

In Congress Mr. Mesick has been a consistent committee worker and confined himself to that branch and to the needs of his District. His work in this particular led to his appointment to the chairmanship of the Elections Committee and in this he occupied a very prominent position in the contested elections cases which came up in the House. His legal training and familiarty with the worth and weight of evidence made his reports on these committee matters of great merit to his colleagues. As a hard worker in both the pensions legislation and that in favor of free rural delivery he was of value to his District.

Mr. Mesick was married in 1884 to Miss Etta Johnson, of his home City, Mancelona, and two sons were born to them, Richard S., 15, and Harry S., 13.

ALFRED JAMES MILLS is of English origin, his father, Alfred Mills, having been a dry goods merchant at the town of Bedford, in Bedfordshire, where Alfred J. was born. He attended school until his sixteenth year, after which he read law for a year at Cambridge, coming to America in January, 1870, and arriving at Kalamazoo in the spring of that year. He found a position in a drug store, which he left after a few months to enter the law office of Arthur Brown, then a well known attorney of Kalamazoo, where he read law for four years, and was admitted to the bar. Moving to Paw Paw, he formed a copartnersip with Chandler Richards under the firm name of Richards & Mills, the connection continuing until 1882. In 1876 he was elected Judge of Probate for Van Buren County and was renominated by acclamation for the same office in 1880, but declined. In 1881, Judge Mills was elected Circuit Judge of the Ninth Judicial Circuit, then comprising the Counties of Kalamazoo and Van Buren, and in the early part of his term returned to Kalamazoo to reside. Before the close of his term, he publicly announced that he would not be a candidate for renomination, and in January, 1888, formed a copartnership for the practice of his profession at Kalamazoo with James W. Osborn, with whom he is still associated. In 1883, Judge Mills was elected a member of the Board of Education of the City of Kalamazoo, serving in that capacity for six years, and was its President two years. He was appointed a member of the Board of Trustees of the Michigan Asylum for the Insane at Kalamazoo in the spring of 1893, by Governor Rich, serving until the spring of 1899. He was President of the Board during the last two years of his term and was reappointed upon this board by Governor Pingree to succeed Samuel Bickerstaff, who resigned from the Board early in 1900. In the fall of 1899, he was appointed by the Superintendent of Public Instruction, as Chairman of the Board of Visitors to the Medical Colleges of this State. He is now the Clerk to the Board of Trustees of the Michigan Female Seminary of Kalamazoo. He is a stockholder and director in the Puritan Corset Company and the C. H. Dutton Boiler Company of Kalamazoo. His religious relations are Episcopalian and he has been a member of the Vestry of St. Luke's Episcopal Church of Kalamazoo for many years. Politically, he has always been a Republican. In the spring of 1900 he was elected Mayor of the City of Kalamazoo, and is now serving in that capacity. He is a member of the Masonic fraternity, including the Knights Templar. He is also a member of the Knights of Pythias and the Elks. Miss Florence Balch, daughter of Luther Balch, of Porter, Mich., became Mrs. Mills in June, 1874, four children being the fruit of the marriage. Mrs. C. F. Cole, of Kalamazoo, Mabel C., James A. and Helen, residing with their parents.

Judge Mills is a hardworking, enterprising man, conscientious in both opinion and action, a close student and of quick perception. He has taken part in many of the prominent legal contests in Southern Michigan, and is a creditable representative of his profession and the intelligent and cultured community in which his lot is cast. This reference to the people of Kalamazoo recalls an ancedote which was once related in the hearing of the writer by the late Judge Wells, of Kalamazoo, and with which this sketch may be appropriately brought to a close. In the Presidential campaign of 1856, Abraham

A. Milnes

Lincoln, who four years later was elected to the Presidency, was one of the speakers at a Republican mass meeting at Kalamazoo. Remarking upon the character of his audience, which presumably (externally at least) outranked that of the audiences to which Mr. Lincoln had been accustomed to speak, "Why," said he to Judge Wells, "they all had clean shirts on."

ALFRED MILNES, of Coldwater, son of Henry Milnes and Mary A. Milnes, was born at Bradford, England, May 28th, 1844, and came with his parents to the United States in 1854. They came over in a sailing vessel and landed at New Orleans, went up the Mississippi River to St. Louis, thence to Kansas City, Mo., and thence by ox team to Salt Lake City, Utah. They resided there until May, 1859, then moved to Newton, Ia., and in the spring of 1861, to Coldwater. The son, Alfred, had his education in the various public schools in Utah, Iowa and Coldwater, and worked on the farm in the first named localities, and in a brick yard in the latter. June 30th, 1862, he enlisted in Company C, Seventeenth Michigan Infantry and served in the same company and regiment to the close of the war, participating in every march, skirmish and battle of the famous Stone Wall Regiment. At the close of the war he went into mercantile business and continued at the same until June, 1898, being fairly successful, gaining a reasonable competency. He is now President of the National Burial Device Co., of Coldwater, Director of the Branch County Savings Bank, and a large dealer in real estate. He is also Postmaster at Coldwater, having been appointed in March 1898.

Mr. Milnes has been a Republican ever since he was old enough to know politics, and cast his first vote for Abraham Lincoln while in the army in front of Petersburg, Va., in 1864. He has been a delegate to most of the Republican State Conventions for the past twenty years. He was State Senator two terms, elected in 1888 and 1892, was elected Lieutenant Governor in November, 1894, and while serving as such was elected to the Fifty-fourth Congress. He was renominated in 1896, but was defeated. He was also Alderman one term and Mayor of Coldwater two terms. In the Senate he was a pioneer in the reform of the method of taxing railroads. In 1889 he introduced bills for putting all the railroads in the State under the general law for the taxation of railroad property, and in 1891 he succeeded in passing some of them. He thus started the agitation which has been going on ever since.

Mr. Milnes has a fancy for social clubs and secret societies. He is a member of the Bon Ami Club; Grand Army of the Republic; Ancient Order United Workmen; Foresters; Masonic Lodge; Knights Templar and a veteran Oddfellow. He was Grand Patriarch of the Grand Encampment of Michigan, I. O. O. F., in 1884, and Grand Representative to the Sovereign Grand Lodge in 1885 and 1886. He

Yours Truly
C I Metcalfe

Waldron & Co. Mr. Cook withdrew in 1863, when Mitchell and Waldron established the Second National Bank. Mr. Waldron withdrew at the death of his brother in 1877, Mr. Mitchell remaining President and having sole charge of the bank until 1884, when he sold his interest, owing to declining health, having had charge of one of the most successful banks in the State for nearly twenty years. In 1855 he was appointed one of the Commissioners to locate and build the State Reform School for boys at Lansing. In 1864 he was chosen a delegate to the Baltimore Convention which nominated Abraham Lincoln for the second term. In 1870 he was appointed Chairman of the State Board of Charities by Governor Baldwin; in 1873 was appointed one of the Trustees of the Michigan Asylum at Kalamazoo by Governor Bagley, and in 1880 he was elected one of the Presidential Electors. He had largely to do with securing to Hillsdale the headquarters of the several branches of the Lake Shore Railway."

Mr. Mitchell was married in September, 1847, to Miss Harriett S. Wing, of Monroe. She was a daughter of Hon. Austin E. Wing, who became a resident of Detroit in 1816, coming with General Cass and Governor Woodbridge from Marietta, O., on horseback through a dense wilderness. Detroit at that time was a small hamlet. Mr. Wing had graduated the year before from Williams College, and was the first Collector of the Port of Detroit. He was twice elected delegate to Congress from the Territory of Michigan, which then embraced Wisconsin. He was afterwards United States Marshal of the State under President Polk, and died in 1848. Mr. Mitchell's children now living are Will W. and Austin W. Mitchell, of Cadillac, and Mrs. W. H. Sawyer, of Hillsdale.

Mr. Mitchell's benefactions were numerous during his lifetime, and he and his wife determined sometime before his death to leave a memorial to the City in which they had lived for many years. In accordance with this purpose he bequeathed to the City of Hillsdale, subject to the life estate of Mrs. Mitchell, the splendid residence and grounds so long occupied by himself and family to be used as a library building and for City offices if all is not needed for the use of the library. Subject to an estate for life in Mrs. Mitchell he also gave to the City ten thousand dollars, the same to be by his executor expended in the purchase of suitable furnishings and books for such library.

SAMUEL MITCHELL, now of Negaunee, has had a varied experience in copper mining in two countries and in several iron mines in the Upper Peninsula besides. He was born April 11th, 1846, in Bridestowe, Devonshire, England, his father being George Mitchell and his mother Ann Hodge. The occupation of his father and forefathers was farming. When he was twelve years of age his parents moved to Tavistock, Devonshire, England, where he lived until he came to America, in 1864. He was educated at the National or common school in England. His first occupation was general work on the farm, until twelve years of age; then worked in a grocery store, and later in a bakery and delivering goods. He next worked in the copper mines near Tavistock, and followed this occupation until eighteen years of age. In his nineteenth year he came to the United States, and proceeded directly to the Lake Superior mining regions, where his brothers had located. He first worked in the Phoenix copper mine, then the Madison, Delaware, Central and Cliff mines, in Keweenaw County, as a miner; next in the Calumet and Hecla Copper Mine, when it was first being opened. In May, 1867, he left the copper country and went to Marquette County, where he has resided ever since. His first work in the iron country, was at the Washington Mine, at Humboldt, where he remained until the spring of 1870, when he moved to Negaunee, having taken a contract from the late Edward Breitung, to mine iron ore from the South Hematite Range. In 1871, he mined the first ore taken from the South Jackson on contract. In 1872, he took a contract from the old Saginaw Mining Company, mining ore by the ton. From 1872 to May 1st, 1873, he worked what was known as the Lake Superior Iron Company's Section 19, or New Burt property, on contract. In May, 1873, he was engaged by the Cleveland Rolling Mill Company, of Cleveland, Ohio, as Mining Captain at the Saginaw Mine, and on December 31st, 1873, was given the agency for the same company, continuing to act as their representative in all of their mining properties, until they consolidated into the American Steel and Wire Company, in 1899. In 1876, he leased the old Shenango Mine, organized the Mitchell Mining Company, and worked the property until January, 1883, when the company was sold to the St. Clair Brothers. In 1878 he leased, with A. G. Stone, of Cleveland, Ohio, one hundred and sixty acres in sections 16-47-27, from the Lake Superior Iron Company, and opened up what was known as the National Mine. He worked this property until 1884, when the ore became exhausted. In the fall of 1885, he went to the Gogebic Range, purchasing controlling interests in the Montreal and Section Thirty-three explorations, which consisted of a few test-pits. He opened the Montreal Mine, sold it to Cleveland parties in the fall of 1886, and then opened the "Section Thirty-three" Mine, and after working it for several years, sold it to the Montreal Mining Company. In 1887, together with Cleveland parties, he purchased the old Jackson Mine, with all its holdings; was elected President and General Manager of the company at that time, and has held that position ever since. In addition to that position he is also President of the Jackson Transit Company, owner of several ore carrying vessels; President of the Negaunee & Ishpeming Street Railway & Electric Company; Vice-President of the First National Bank, Negaunee; a Director of the First National Bank of Escanaba, and is interested extensively in iron and timber lands.

Samuel Mitchell

With this varied business on hand, it might be imagined that Mr. Mitchell would not have much time for politics. He has never held office, but has managed at different periods to attend numerous County, Congressional and State Conventions as delegate. He has been a Republican ever since he came to America, and cast his first vote for General U. S. Grant. He is a member of a Masonic Lodge in Negaunee, but does not belong to any clubs. He was married at Humboldt, Mich., February 2d, 1868, to Miss Elizabeth Penglase. The names of their children are: Mrs. William E. Saunders, Mrs. Eugene W. Adams, Mrs. Rollin E. Drake, Mrs. L. P. Wilson, Mrs. Alvin H. Greene, Mrs. John M. Perkins, Samuel J. Mitchell, the Misses Florence Pearl, Fannie W. and Myrtle Leal, and Arthur G. Mitchell.

ROBERT M. MONTGOMERY, Justice of the Supreme Court, is a Michigan product, having been born at Eaton Rapids, May 12th, 1849. His father, Johnson Montgomery, was a native of New York and descended from the Irish family that have made the name famous in half a dozen countries and through many generations. His mother, Elvira Dudley, was a native of Vermont and of New England ancestry, the family coming originally from England. They came West with the early tide of immigration and settled in Eaton Rapids in 1837. The son, Robert, received his education at the schools of Eaton Rapids, helping out the course by teaching winters, which he commenced doing at the age of sixteen, and continued until he was twenty-one. He graduated from the Eaton Rapids High School at the age of eighteen, and the next year commenced the study of law in the office of F. J. Russell, of Hart, Oceana County. He was admitted to the bar in July, 1870, and at once commenced the practice of law at Pentwater. In 1872, when but twenty-three years of age, he was elected Prosecuting Attorney of Oceana County, and at the following election in 1876, he was re-elected for another term of two years. Continuing in the practice of law at Pentwater until 1877, he removed to Grand Rapids, where he received the appointment of Assistant United States Attorney, holding this appointment until October, 1881. His legal attainments had in the meantime brought him into notice as an able lawyer having a judicial mind, and at the April election in that year, he was elected Judge of the Seventeenth Judicial Circuit, comprising Kent County. He was re-elected six years later, but resigned in 1888 to resume the more lucrative practice of law, which he did, as a member of the firm of Montgomery & Bundy. Their practice was large and widely extended, covering many of the most important cases in Western Michigan, both in the United States and State courts. In the spring of 1891 he was nominated by the Republicans and elected Justice of the Supreme Court by about 5,000 plurality over Justice John W. Champlin, who was regarded as the strongest candidate the Democrats could nominate.

Of Judge Montgomery's stand when on the Circuit Court Bench, the following estimate is given by "Bench and Bar of Michigan:" "It is not too much to say that he won at once and maintained while on the bench the universal respect of the bar and litigants who had occasion to appear before him. As a judge he was exceedingly painstaking. On any doubtful question he invariably supplemented the briefs and arguments of counsel by the most rigid examination of the law of the case before him, by a thorough search of the authorities and in the light of his own reason. He was prompt in his rulings and almost uniformly correct, while he was careful to see that the merits and justice of the case should neither be obscured nor defeated by objections or irregularities that were closely technical and technical only. His instructions to the jury were usually prepared in writing and with great care. The old files of his law office today disclose hundreds of such charges, many of which are very valuable and useful briefs in cases involving the questions which called out the instructions." The same record speaks thus of his work in the more exalted position to which he has since attained. "His work as a Justice of the Supreme Court must be judged by its expression in the official reports. Those which he has written are marked by directness and perspicuity. There is in them no extra verbiage—no surplusage. He makes his points so clear that a layman can understand them, and the reasoning by which he reaches a conclusion is easily followed. It is sufficient to say that his promotion to the Supreme Bench was fully merited, and the people of the State have not seen cause to regret the elevation to its highest tribunal of so able and so just a Judge, as a successor of Cooley and Campbell."

Judge Montgomery was married in 1873 to Miss Theodosia Wadsworth, of Pentwater, and has two children, 24 and 21 years of age respectively.

GEORGE WILLIAM MOORE, one of St. Clair County's prominent business men, was born in Fort Gratiot Township in that County, April 12th, 1850. His parents were Stephen Moore, a farmer, and Eliza A. Thompson. He is a descendant of the Hon. William Moore, who settled in New Hampshire in 1682, on land granted the family by the King of Great Britain. In 1775 George III. gave the family another large grant of several counties in New Brunswick. He received his early education in the district school, and in 1874 his parents removed to Hersey, Mich., where he attended Village school four terms. In 1877 he commenced work for A. V. Mann & Co., in their saw mill in Muskegon, scaling and rolling logs on log deck. This was a man's work and the others objected saying that there should be a man to do it. He worked eleven and one-half hours per day for $1.75, continuing this two seasons, and scaling logs in lumber camps in the winters. In the summer of 1879, in company with a

partner named Cody, he commenced business on his own account, borrowed enough capital to start in business, and struggled along two years employing from forty to one hundred men. In 1881 he went to Missaukee County and built a steam logging road. In 1885 he bought his partner's interest and the following years were prosperous. In 1888 he sold his logging interest, returned to St. Clair County and purchased a farm on the banks of the St. Clair River, where he now resides. In 1889, with his brother, F. T. Moore, he organized the present Bank at Capac, and in 1890 organized the St. Clair County Savings Bank of Port Huron, of which he is Cashier. In 1898 he opened the private bank of G. W. & F. T. Moore, in Marine City. He is also interested largely in real estate and manufacturing interests of the City.

Mr. Moore is one of the young leaders of the Republican party in the County and is serving his third term as Chairman of the Republican County Committee. He is also a member of the Seventh District Congressional Committee, and enjoys the confidence and support of the younger element of the party, and the regard of the older and more conservative men. He is a member of the Port Huron Club. He was supervisor three years in Missaukee County, being Chairman of the Board, also Chairman of the Republican County Committee. He was born a Republican, did his first hurrahing for Grant and Colfax and cast his first vote for Garfield and Arthur. He was elected Senator from the Eleventh District of Michigan in 1898. In 1885 Mr. Moore was married to Harriet Radcliffe, daughter of J. F. Radcliffe of Hersey. They have five children, Carl, Ralph, Mary, George W., Jr., and John.

JOSEPH B. MOORE, who has gained high reputation as politician, legislator and judge, was born in the Village of Commerce, Oakland County, Mich., November 3rd, 1845. His father was Jacob J. Moore, a furniture manufacturer, farmer and lumberman, and his mother Hapsabeth Gillett Moore. His father's family came from Wales at an early period in the history of the country and settled in New Jersey. His grandfather Moore was a soldier in the War of 1812. His father moved to Michigan in 1833 and settled near Utica, in Macomb County, afterward lived in Lapeer County for a short time and now lives at Walled Lake, Oakland County, in his eighty-seventh year. The son received his education in the district school with four terms at Hillsdale College and one year in the law department of Michigan University. From the age of fourteen to nineteen, he worked in his father's sawmill doing the work of a mill hand, and in the evenings read a copy of Blackstone loaned him by the late James D. Bateman, a country lawyer, then living at Walled Lake. For three succeeding winters he taught district school at Moscow Plains, Hillsdale County; Rough and Ready Corners, Wayne County, and Walled Lake, Oakland County, attending school at Hillsdale during the spring and fall terms. The college afterwards conferred upon him the honorary degree of M. A.

Mr. Moore tried to be a soldier, but didn't succeed. When the war broke out an older brother enlisted. The two boys who were left at home wanted to go to the front, also. The family could spare but one of them, however, and Joseph was the one to take the chance. He went at once to Detroit, where he enlisted in the Thirtieth Michigan Infantry. He was in barracks but ten days, when to his great disappointment, the surgeon in charge refused to accept him and sent him back home. The next day after the surgeon's edict, the other brother went to Detroit, enlisted in the Twenty-second Michigan Infantry, and served faithfully, while Joseph B. looked after the folks at home. Judge Moore is popular with the old soldiers and has made many Memorial Day addresses.

Mr. Moore was admitted to the practice of law at Lapeer in the fall of 1869 and at once obtained a lucrative business. In 1878 he was elected a member of the State Senate, and was a colleague of Senators McElroy, of St. Clair; Stephenson, of Menominee; Farr, of Ottawa; J. Webster Childs, of Washtenaw, and T. W. Palmer, of Detroit. He declined, because of professional work, a renomination to the Senate. He was elected Mayor of Lapeer in the spring of 1874. In the fall of 1872 he was elected Prosecuting Attorney and was re-elected in 1874. In 1884 he was a Republican Presidential Elector-at-Large. Though not an active candidate he came within five votes of being nominated for Congress in 1886. In the spring of 1887 he was elected Circuit Judge, and was re-elected six years later. In 1891, he with Hon. Albert K. Smiley, of New York, and Professor C. C. Painter, of Great Barrington, Mass., was appointed a Commission to select lands for permanent reservations for the Mission Indians of California. This work had the approval of Congress and of President Harrison. In 1895 he was elected Justice of the Supreme Court by a very large majority.

Mr. Moore has been a Republican ever since he became a voter, his first vote being for General Grant. Until he became Supreme Court Justice, for more than twenty years he attended as a delegate every State Republican Convention. He was an intimate friend of Hon. John T. Rich and presented his name in nomination at the Jackson Convention in 1880, at Detroit in 1890, and again at Saginaw in 1892, when Mr. Rich was nominated, and it is generally believed that to Mr. Moore's skillful management, more than to anything else except his own inherent worth, is Mr. Rich indebted for the final attainment of his ambitions.

Mr. Moore is a member of the Michigan Club, Michigan State Bar Association, Michigan Association of Judges, American Bar Association, American Social Science Association; A. K. P. Society of Hillsdale College, Grand River Boat Club, of Lansing, and the U. and I. Club, of Lansing. December 3rd, 1872, he married Miss Ella L. Bentley, but has no children.

J. B. Moore

Although attaining distinction as a politician and legislator, Judge Moore's chief and most enduring fame will be upon his career on the bench. Of his work as a lawyer and afterwards as Circuit Judge, the leading paper in his County said in 1895: "He was a diligent and successful trial lawyer, appearing as the attorney of record in upwards of six hundred cases in Courts of Record, and assisted in the trial of many more, a number of them of more than local importance. In his seven years' experience as Judge, he has heard and disposed of upwards of four hundred and seventy criminal and fifteen hundred civil cases, among them the Young murder case and the celebrated election case of Reynolds vs. May. This work has been so well done that but two criminal cases and thirteen civil cases have been reversed by the Supreme Court." Commenting on these facts, "Bench and Bar" of Michigan, a book which has passed discriminating judgment upon many of the leading attorneys and judges of the State, said: "It proves that Judge Moore is possessed of an analytical mind and acute discrimination; that he is thoroughly versed in the law, and has a keen sense of justice; that his judicial investigations are pursued with the purpose of arriving at truth and justice; that he is guided and determined by an integrity of mind and character which cannot be swerved from a line of rectitude. His worthiness for promotion, both as to legal qualifications and personal qualities, caused his nomination in the spring of 1895 as the Republican candidate for Justice of the Supreme Court, and he was elected by the largest majority ever given a candidate for that office. His record as a judge of the highest nisi prius court forms a substantial basis for the prediction that his career upon the Supreme Bench will be entirely honorable to himself and useful to the State." The prediction has been amply fulfilled. His written opinions while on the Supreme Court Bench have been clear in statement, and have shown a comprehensive grasp of legal principles, while he has been one of the most industrious members of the most industrious Supreme Court in the country.

CHARLES T. NEWKIRK has had an active life, not only in his profession of medicine and surgery, but also in politics. He was born December 10th, 1842, in Norfolk, Ontario. His father, whose name was Moses Newkirk, was of Dutch ancestry, and went to Ontario from New York. His mother, whose maiden name was Catherine Topping, was born in Dublin, Ireland. The son's first occupation in life was school teaching, by means of which he obtained money to attend college, and he graduated from the University of Victoria College, Toronto, Ont., in 1863. He entered the Brazilian Army in 1864, in the war with Paraguay, and served four years with the rank of Surgeon of Division. He also served four months in the United States Army in Cuba, with the rank of Major and Brigade Surgeon.

He is United States Pension Examiner and has been County Physician in Bay County for eight years.

In politics Mr. Newkirk has been an active Republican ever since he cast his first vote for General Grant. He has taken part in every campaign for the past twenty-six years, having spoken and been very active in electing Republican candidates, though never a seeker after political offices for himself. Within the past twenty-four years he has attended ten Republican State Conventions, about the same number of County Conventions and eight Congressional District Conventions. He is a member of the American Medical Association, the State Medical Society and the County Medical Society. He is a Mason, and was for some time an Oddfellow. He was married in Port Dover, Ont., September 13th, 1863, to Mary J. Anderson, whose father took an active part in the Rebellion of 1837. His children are Delores M. Tousey, residence at New York City, and Henry A. Newkirk, M. D., Iron Mountain, Mich.

HENRY WIRT NEWKIRK was born at Dexter, Mich., August 1st, 1854, his parents being Sylvester and Julia V. Newkirk. His father's father was John Newkirk, born, as was his father, in New York State. His mother's mother was a sister of Millard Fillmore, Olive A. Fillmore, afterwards Johnson, born near Sempronious, N. Y. His father's ancestry were Scotch and his mother's English. His father was a small farmer, and his older brother having died in the War of the Rebellion, it became necessary for Wirt to work on the farm, and work out by the day or month when he could, going to school at Dexter winters. When fifteen years old he ran away to become a sailor. He didn't like that, and concluded that there was no place like home, to which he returned. When he was eighteen, he tried blacksmithing, but didn't like that any better, too hard work, and set out to get an education. He attended school at Ann Arbor in 1873 and 1874; taught school in Webster Township in 1876 and 1877; entered the law department of the University in 1877; graduated in 1879 and entered the law office of T. A. E. Weadock, of Bay City, the same spring. He was elected Circuit Court Commissioner in 1880, and December 20th of that year married Miss Eleanor J. Birkett, daughter of Thomas Birkett, of Dexter Township, by whom he has had two children, Nellie E., born October 8th, 1883, and Birkett F., born July 7th, 1894.

In 1884, Mr. Newkirk went to Whitley County, Kentucky, where he started the Williamsburg Times. He and a boy did all the work. He lost $500 by fire, sold out and returned to Michigan, and was City Editor of the Ann Arbor Register for a time. He then went to Luther, Mich., where he started the Luther Enterprise, was appointed deputy postmaster; was appointed and afterwards elected Prosecuting Attorney for the County. In 1892 he was elected to the Legislature from Lake and Osceola Counties; was appointed

H. Clint Newkirk

Geo E Nichols

Chairman of the Ways and Means Committee and a member of the Judiciary and U. P. Committees. He was the author of the first Woman's Suffrage Bill that ever became a law in Michigan, but which was afterwards declared unconstitutional by the Supreme Court. The death of Mrs. Birkett, in December, 1892, necessitated his return to Dexter, where in 1893 he helped organize the Dexter Savings Bank, with Mr. Birkett as President and himself as Cashier. He held this position till January 1st, 1897, when, having been elected Probate Judge of Washtenaw County, in November, 1896, he removed to Ann Arbor.

Mr. Newkirk has always acted with the Republicans and cast his first vote for Hayes. When in Luther he was a member of the Congressional Committee, Chairman of the Senatorial and Representative Committees and a delegate to every Republican Convention, local and State. He was also an alternate delegate from the Ninth District to the National Convention at Minneapolis in 1892. He is a member of Dexter Blue Lodge, F. & A. M.; Ann Arbor Commandery; Moslem Shrine of Detroit; the Oddfellows; Maccabees; Elks and Woodmen.

GEORGE ELLSWORTH NICHOLS, an attorney and active Republican in Ionia, was born August 8th, 1861, in Oneida Township, Eaton County, Mich., his parents being George W. and Sarah L. Nichols, farmers. The family originally emigrated from Wales, but have been in this country for more than one hundred years. Their chief occupation has been that of agriculturists. The son was educated in the public schools at Grand Ledge, Mich., and in the private academy at the same place. He lived on the farm until eighteen years of age; paid his way through private schools by working summers on the farm, by the month, and in this way was able to educate himself. He began the study of law in the office of Hon. A. A. Ellis, at Muir, Ionia County, Mich., and at the age of nineteen taught country school to obtain money to carry on law studies. He was admitted to the bar by the Circuit Court of Ionia County, April, 1883, and opened an office in Grand Ledge in July of the same year, remaining there until November, 1884, when he returned to Ionia City to act as Assistant Prosecuting Attorney for two years under A. A. Ellis, then Prosecuting Attorney. From then until the present time he has been in practice in Ionia, and part of the time in Grand Rapids, in partnership with different individuals and under a number of firm names. He is now in partnership with his brother under the firm name of George E. and M. A. Nichols. He has had a very large practice for a good many years and has been connected with a great deal of important litigation. He was attorney for Parsell at the time proceedings were commenced against him to oust him from the position of Warden of the State House of Correction and Reformatory at Ionia. He is now the Attorney for the City of Detroit in the tax litigation cases against the City Railway, acting with Judge Morse; tried those cases in Detroit before the full bench and won them, and expects to win them in the Supreme Court. He has always been engaged in public affairs in the City of Ionia, and has given a great deal of time and attention to the organization of manufacturing concerns and the promotion of the general interests of the City.

Mr. Nichols cast his first vote for James G. Blaine, and has always voted the Republican ticket. He has been several times a delegate to State Conventions, and has campaigned Ionia and other counties for a good many years. He was elected Chairman of the Republican County Committee in 1898, the County then being Democratic, and in the management and by thorough organization, was able to overturn it by a majority of 600. He was re-elected unanimously as Chairman of the County Committee in 1900, and was unanimously nominated as candidate for Senator in the Eighteenth Senatorial District on September 15th. Under his management as Chairman, this year, 1900, the County of Ionia went Republican by 1,000 majority, a result that has not been in many years, and he was elected State Senator from his District by over 3,000 majority, the largest ever accorded any candidate in the history of the District.

Mr. Nichols stands for equal taxation, and by reason of his speeches throughout the District the Republican majority was notably increased. He without question will make a good record in the Senate, and hereafter unquestionably will be known in State politics as being aggressive, energetic and fearless in his methods. He has been a winner in every battle, and without doubt has a bright future before him.

Mr. Nichols has been President of a Business Men's Club of the City of Ionia, known as the Town Club; was its first President, re-elected, and refused to take the office a third time. He is a member of the Maccabees, Royal Arcanum, Knights of Pythias and Elks. He was married October 10, 1888, to Harriet Moseman Kennedy, at the City of Ionia, and has one son, James G. Nichols, ten years of age.

WILLIAM ABLE NORTON, a practicing attorney at St. Johns, Mich., the son of William R. and Phoebe A. Norton, was born at Farmington, Oakland County, October 21st, 1853. His father is a minister of the gospel, F. B. denomination, who came with his parents from the State of New York in 1825, being but three years of age, settling in the Township of Oakland, Oakland County, this State. His father was John Norton, who was born in Massachusetts in 1793, and was in the War of 1812. The father of John was born in England and was also named John.

William R. Norton was educated in the schools of Canandaigua, East Bloomfield and Rochester, N. Y., commenced preaching in Penfield, N. Y., in 1843; the year following moved to Oakland County,

W. A. Norton

where he continued to preach until the spring of 1854, when he moved to the Township of Bath, Clinton County, this State, settling upon a farm, but continuing to preach in different places until the present time, although on account of old age he has no regular appointment.

William A. Norton was brought up on a farm, his early struggles consisting of "trying to see how little he could do between meals, but did not succeed as well as he desired." He was educated at Hillsdale College and the State Agricultural College; was admitted to the bar in 1878, begun the practice of law in the City of Grand Ledge, Mich.; removed to Charlevoix in 1879 where he practiced his profession for upwards of nine years, when he moved to St. Johns, Clinton County, where he has since remained. He has never pursued any other vocation than the practice of law; is at the present time a member of the firm of Spaulding, Norton & Dooling. He held the office of Prosecuting Attorney for four years in Charlevoix County and the same office for four years in Clinton County, but never held any other office, and has "no legislative or political measures lying at his door." He has been a Republican ever since he was capable of knowing right from wrong, and Rutherford B. Hayes was the first Presidential candidate he voted for; has voted for every Republican Presidential candidate since, and has attended Republican State Conventions for several years past. He has stumped the State for the Republicans in several recent campaigns, and in the campaign of 1900 was in the employ of the National Committee. Mr. Norton is a member of several secret societies, including the Knights of Pythias, Knights Templar, and I. O. O. F. He was married in 1881, to Lillian E. Messinger, daughter of Dr. Messinger, of Grand Ledge, and has two sons, Guy W. and Fane R.

THOMAS J. O'BRIEN, the leading railroad attorney, and one of the most prominent general attorneys in western Michigan, was born in Jackson, in this State, July 30, 1842. His father, Timothy O'Brien, was a native of Dunmanway, County Cork, Ireland, who, in early life, went to London, where he married Elizabeth Lander, of Tipperary, Ireland. They came to this country, fell in with the tide of emigration that was then setting Westward, and settled near what was then the small hamlet of Jackson, Mich., in 1837.

The son Thomas remained on the farm, attending the district schools as opportunity offered, until he was 17 years old, when he left to take a course at the High School at Marshall. He subsequently studied in the law office of J. C. Fitzgerald, after that in the law school of Michigan University, and was admitted to the bar in 1864. He commenced practice at Marshall in partnership with his old preceptor under the firm name of Fitzgerald & O'Brien, a business arrangement which lasted until Mr. O'Brien received a proposition from D. Darwin Hughes, of Grand Rapids, to become associated with him in practice. Mr. Hughes was then accounted the ablest, and was certainly the most noted lawyer in Michigan outside of Detroit, and the opportunity offered Mr. O'Brien was a rare one for a young attorney. A partnership was formed under the firm name of Hughes & O'Brien, in 1871. It subsequently became the firm of Hughes, O'Brien & Smiley, and continued until the death of Mr. Hughes in 1883. The firm was engaged in nearly every case of great importance that came up in Western Michigan and many in other parts of the State. Mr. Hughes was general counsel for the Grand Rapids & Indiana Railroad and Mr. O'Brien was his assistant, but the firm had a large general practice besides. Mr. O'Brien often appeared in court, but when not so appearing his services were highly valued as a counselor in important cases.

Upon the death of Mr. Hughes Mr. O'Brien became general counsel for the Railroad company, a position which he still holds, being also a Director of the company. He has been connected with the road for nearly thirty years and seems to have the rather unusual faculty of keeping clients once they employ him. In addition to attending to the duties of this position he still continues the general practice of law, and has a number of other important interests besides. He has been President of the Antrim Iron Company ever since its organization in 1886, and President of the Grand Rapids Law Library ever since the organization of that institution. He has, ever since their organization, been a Director of the Kent County Savings Bank, the Alabastine Company, the Mackinac Hotel Company, and of the Grand Rapids Gas Light Company since it was reorganized. He is also at present a Director in the National City Bank of Grand Rapids, and is receiver of the Grand Rapids Hydraulic Company.

Mr. O'Brien cast his first vote for McClellan in 1864, but since that time has always voted the Republican ticket. He has been delegate to State Conventions a number of times; was also Delegate-at-Large to the National Republican Convention at St. Louis in 1896, and was one of the committee appointed to give Wm. McKinley formal notification of his nomination. He has never been a candidate for office except in the spring of 1883, when he was nominated for Supreme Court Justice. The whole Republican ticket went down to defeat in that election, for the first time since the party was organized, but Mr. O'Brien led the rest of the ticket by a handsome vote. The plurality against him was only 2,309 in a total vote of 246,969. while the pluralities against the other candidates were from 6,679 to 7,506.

Mr. O'Brien's wife, whom he married in 1873, was the daughter of Wm. A. Howard, one of Michigan's most distinguished statesmen. His children are Howard, aged 25, and Katherine, aged 23.

ARTHUR C. O'CONNOR is one of Detroit's young men who has pushed his own way along into a successful career. He is a son of Arthur O'Connor, and was born in Detroit, July 28th, 1866. His elementary education was obtained in the public schools of his native City, but at the early age of ten he began to shift for himself, beginning as office boy in the law office of James Caplis. In 1881, through the influence of Mr. Caplis, he was appointed Messenger in the State Senate, a position which sharpens the wits, and gives promptness in action to any lad. Following this, for several months, he attended Detroit College, and then re-entered the office of Mr. Caplis as clerk and student, and remained there until 1888. The next year he was appointed Index Clerk in the office of the Register of Deeds and remained there for two years, when he was appointed Clerk in the City Assessor's office, and subsequently Assistant Assessor. The field work which he very industriously followed up in that position, gave him a knowledge of real estate values, which was of great use to him afterwards in the higher position of Assistant Corporation Counsel. He was appointed to this in January, 1896, and held the place till July, 1900. In this position he had entire charge of street opening cases, and the work on these cases was never before so thoroughly performed, nor with such complete protection to the interests of the City. He succeeded in reducing many exorbitant claims made against the City for damages in street opening cases, and those awarded did not often much exceed the amounts conceded in his own schedule.

Mr. O'Connor, after he was admitted to the bar, graduated from the Detroit College of Law, and since the close of his term in the Corporation Counsel's office, he has resumed private practice. He has been active in politics ever since he became a voter, has frequently attended conventions, and was one of the large band of workers who added strength to the Pingree organization during the remarkably successful career of that official.

JAMES O'DONNELL, who has been very prominent in Michigan politics for the past thirty years, was born in Norwalk, Conn., March 25, 1842. John and Anna O'Donnell, his father and mother, were Irish, and his father was a potter by trade. The son received his education in the Village schools, clerked for awhile in a grocery store, and then learned the printer's trade. His pursuit of that occupation was interrupted by the breaking out of the war, when he enlisted in the First Michigan Infantry, taking part in the defense of Washington, the first Battle of Bull Run and other engagements.

In 1865 Mr. O'Donnell purchased the Jackson Citizen, which he has ever since owned and edited. With this purchase commenced a connection with Michigan public life, which has continued ever since, and which in its earlier portion may be briefly summed up as follows: He was four times elected Recorder of the City of Jackson, was a

Presidential Elector in 1872, and took an active part in the campaign that year. In the Centennial year he was elected Mayor of Jackson and his administration of municipal affairs was characterized by vigor and economy. Many permanent improvements were made, the City debt was reduced and taxation lowered. He used the veto power fearlessly for the benefit of the taxpayers. In 1877 he served a second term as Mayor of Jackson, being re-elected by a very large majority, although the City was strongly Democratic. In 1877 he served on Governor Croswell's staff with the rank of Colonel. He also served with the rank of Colonel on the staff of General Warner, Commander of the Grand Army of the Republic, during his term of office. He has been Chairman of the Republican County Committee of Jackson County, a member of the Congressional Committee, a member of the State Central Committee, and a member of the National Congressional Committee, in all of which positions he rendered good service to the party.

In 1884 he entered upon a larger field, receiving a unanimous nomination for Congress in the Third District, composed of Eaton, Calhoun, Barry, Branch and Jackson Counties. The campaign was one of the fiercest political struggles ever witnessed in Michigan and he was elected with 1,200 majority, largely leading the ticket. The House contained a large Democratic preponderance. It was a difficult situation for a new Republican member who desired to serve his constituency and make a creditable record, but he succeeded so admirably that he soon took rank among the leading members of the House and was re-elected with increased majorities again and again for four consecutive terms until overwhelmed by the Democratic gerrymander of 1892, which placed him in a new district, with 2,500 Democratic majority.

Mr. O'Donnell's career in Congress was, throughout, one of great activity. He was a vigilant friend of the private soldier and secured more pensions than any other man in Congress at the time. In the Fifty-first Congress Mr. O'Donnell was Chairman of the Committee on Education and there secured the passage of bills endowing the experimental stations for farmers, and also the bill granting perpetually $25,000 each year to the Michigan and other State agricultural colleges for the scientific education of farmers' sons. He labored to secure the forfeiture of unearned land grants, and to restore the lands to the people instead of leaving them in the hands of corporations. He was the originator of the plan for free mail delivery in the rural districts, was an earnest advocate of the removal of the duty on sugar, originated the act requiring automatic couplers for freight cars, the act protecting innocent purchasers of patented articles from prosecution, and the act putting manila, sisal and binding twine on the free list. The last two acts were of great value to the farming interests. He took a good share also in the debates upon all National questions. Since his retirement from Congress he has been twice a candidate for the Republican nomination for Governor, but has missed the prize. He has been on the stump in every campaign, and has done good work through his paper for the party.

Mr. O'Donnell is a member of the Michigan Club, Masons, Oddfellows, G. A. R., Maccabees and Elks. He was married August 1, 1879, at Jackson, Mich., to Miss Sarah George, and has two daughters, Kenneth and Kathleen. He has been a member of the Protestant Episcopal Church for nearly 40 years; is now, and has been for some years, a vestryman of St. Paul's Church, Jackson, and has often served as a delegate to the Diocesan Convention.

HORACE MANN OREN, who has become quite conspicuous in Michigan public affairs within the past three years, was born on a farm near Oakland, Clinton County, Ohio, February 3rd, 1859. His father, Charles Oren, was educated at Antioch College, Yellow Springs, Ohio, while that institution was under the presidency of Horace Mann. He was a school teacher at the time the Civil War broke out; raised a company of colored troops in 1863; was commissioned as Captain Fifth United States Colored Infantry, and was killed by a sharpshooter in the siege of Petersburg, July 27th, 1864. His mother, Sarah Allen, was also educated at Antioch College. After the death of her husband she taught school, first at Antioch College, and later in the Indianapolis High School. In 1873 she was appointed State Librarian of Indiana by the Legislature of that State, being the first woman to hold that position in Indiana, and held the office for two years. In 1875 she became an instructor at Purdue University at Lafayette, in the same State; in 1879 married again, and is still living at Sault Ste. Marie, Mich.

Horace M. Oren was educated in the Indianapolis public schools; graduated from the High School of that place in 1877; then entered Michigan University and graduated in the classical course in 1881 and in the law department in 1883. During the time his mother was State Librarian at Indianapolis, he was Assistant Librarian, and also was attendant in the Indianapolis Public Library from 1874 to 1877. In a school vacation in 1882 he went to Sault Ste. Marie, Mich., and edited the Chippewa County News, the Republican paper at that point. He returned to the "Soo" after graduation from the law department of the University and continued the editing of the paper until 1885, engaging in the practice of law in the meantime. He has held the office of Village Clerk of Sault Ste. Marie, Justice of the Peace, Circuit Court Commissioner, City Attorney and Prosecuting Attorney of Chippewa County, the latter office for two terms, from 1895 to 1898. In 1898 he was nominated and elected Attorney General and was re-elected in 1900. He is a member of the law firm of Oren & Webster, at Sault Ste. Marie, which has a leading business in that locality, and is attorney for the various leading companies and enterprises in that locality. As Attorney General Mr. Oren has been particularly active and devoted to the interests of the State, and has suggested much useful legislation. The bill creating the State Tax Commission was drawn by him and it became quite generally known as the Oren Bill. It provided the most sweeping scheme for taxation reform ever adopted in Michigan. Mr. Oren has been connected with much important litigation during his term as Attorney General. Probably the most important was the case of Pingree vs. Auditor General, a suit commenced at the suggestion of Mr. Oren to determine the constitutionality of the so-called Atkinson Bill for railroad taxation, then before the Legislature. The case resulted in declaring the bill, which had during the pendency, been enacted, to be unconstitutional. The prompt determination of this fact undoubtedly resulted in saving the State from many vexatious complications. Among other cases of importance might be mentioned the Beet Sugar Bounty case and Inheritance Tax case, each of great importance, and in which Mr. Oren exercised chief control.

Mr. Oren cast his first ballot for Garfield and Arthur in 1880, going from Ann Arbor to Indiana for that purpose, and has been a consistent Republican ever since. He was married January 1st, 1890, to Margaret Jane Wallace, of Grindstone City, Huron County, Mich., and has two children, Robert Allen Oren, aged nine, and Chase Osborn Oren, aged five.

WILLIAM MERRITT OSBAND, of Ypsilanti, was born in Arcadia, Wayne County, New York, June 25th, 1836. His father was Wilson Osband, a minister in the Methodist Episcopal Church, and his mother was Susanna Sherman. The ancestors on both sides came from England very early, the Shermans in 1634 and the Osbands about 1720. They all settled in Rhode Island, whence they subsequently moved to New York. On the mother's side he was a descendant of the Lawtons, who were Quakers, living near Tiverton, Rhode Island. His great grandfather, John Sherman, was one of Barton's men who captured the English General Prescott during the Revolutionary War. This family are descended from the Shermans of Yoxley, Essex County, England. William Osband, the first of the family in this country, married Elizabeth Shrieve, of Portsmouth, R. I. Mr. Osband can also trace descent through the Durfees, another prominent Rhode Island family. He received his preparatory education in the Newark Union School, Newark, N. Y., and in Genesee Wesleyan Seminary, at Lima, N. Y.; and graduated in 1861 from Genesee College, now Syracuse University, receiving the degree of A. B.; later he received the degree of A. M. from the latter institution. He worked his way through college by farm work and teaching district schools.

Mr. Osband held a professorship in Gouverneur Wesleyan Seminary and in Albert University, Belleville, Ont.; came to Michigan in 1865; organized the graded school in Northville; was principal of the Chelsea Schools in 1870-1; held the position of principal of the preparatory department and Associate Professor of Chemistry in Olivet

Horace M. Oren

Chase S. Osborn

SAULT STE. MARIE NEWS.

College, and afterward, the Chair of Natural Science in Albion College for six years. He has since then been in business and newspaper life. He was one of the original stockholders in the Globe Furniture Company of Northville and was for eight years actively engaged in the business of that company. He has been editor of The Ypsilantian twelve years, having purchased the interest of Perry F. Powers in 1887, and that of George C. Smithe in 1893. Aside from the Globe Furniture Co., his principal business connection was as President of the Granville Wood & Son Pipe Organ Co., now the Farrand & Votey Company.

Mr. Osband has been a Republican since 1854 and cast his first vote for Lincoln in 1860. He was too young to vote for Fremont in 1856, but won over several Democrats to vote for him, a favor to their boy friend. He has attended various State Conventions and was Chairman of the Washtenaw County Committee from 1886 to 1890. He has been a member of the Michigan Club since its first organization He was six years a member of the Ypsilanti Board of Education, and four years President of that body. He is a member of the Methodist Episcopal Church. He was married August 7th, 1861, to Lucy Aldrich, of Newark, N. Y. and has one child, Miss Marna Ruth Osband.

CHASE SALMON OSBORN, of Sault Ste. Marie, is not as old as some of us, but he has seen more of the world than most of us. He was born January 22d, 1860, in a log house in the woods of Huntington County, Ind. His father was Dr. George A. Osborn and his mother Dr. Margaret A. Osborn. The family name was originally Danish and was spelled Eisbjerne, which means "polar bear." The family was among the early Norse conquerors of England. Among early ancestors in America were "George, the Settler," Fitzgreene Halleck, the poet, the Osborns of Long Island and the Pardees of Connecticut. Some of the ancestors fought in the Wars of the Revolution and 1812. Chase had his education in the Public Schools and Purdue University in Indiana. His first occupation was as newsboy and his early tussles with the world also involved work on the farm, including the pioneer work of wood-cutting, rail-splitting, clapboard-driving, and afterwards all kinds of labor. Since reaching adult years Mr. Osborn has engaged incidentally in mining and lumbering, but is best known in Michigan for his newspaper and official career. He had a valuable training for the former on the dailies in Chicago and Milwaukee, where he occupied responsible positions. In 1883 he bought the Florence Mining News at Florence, Wis.; made a success of it, and sold it in 1887; established the Miner and Manufacturer in Milwaukee; sold that and purchased the Sault Ste. Marie News in 1887, and along with other work has conducted it ever since. His familiarity with the interests that are centered in Northern Michigan, including the Upper Peninsula, together with his political prominence, have made the "Soo" News a much quoted paper of late years. Mr. Osborn came of a family of Abolitionists, and his first Presidential vote was cast for Blaine, and he was a Republican long before he was old enough to vote. He has attended all of the State Conventions in Michigan for fourteen years and before that had attended State and District Conventions in Wisconsin and was Chairman of the Senatorial Committee of the District that he resided in as well as of the Assembly Committee in that State. He was Postmaster at Sault Ste. Marie during the Harrison Administration, was State Game and Fish Warden of Michigan for one term and part of another, and is now Commissioner of Railroads.

Mr. Osborn has found time for numerous society connections. He is a 32d degree Mason and belongs to the Odd Fellows, Knights of Pythias, Elks, Loyal Guard, American Academy of Political and Social Science, Detroit Club, Fellowcraft Club, Milwaukee Press Club, Michigan Press Association, Michigan Republican Newspaper Association, Upper Peninsula Editorial Association, Michigan Society of Social Science, American Historical Society, American Ornithological Society, Michigan State Ornithological Society, Lake Superior Mining Institute, American Canoe Association, Le Saut de Sainte Marie Club, Lacrosse Club, Curling Club, and Country Club of Sault Ste. Marie. May 7th, 1881, at Milwaukee, he married Lillian Gertrude Jones. Their children are Ethel Louise, George Augustus, Chase Salmon, Emily Fisher and Miriam Gertrude.

Notwithstanding his numerous activities, Mr. Osborn has found time for travel. He has visited every State and Territory in the Union, has been in Mexico several times, has thoroughly explored Canada, and has traveled extensively in Cuba, Europe, Asia and Africa.

Mr. Osborn's official career has been exceedingly creditable. As Game and Fish Warden he not only enforced the laws better than they had ever been done before, but suggested and carried into effect a great deal of game and fish preservative legislation. His work as Commissioner of Railroads has been even more efficient. His friends have pushed him for the Congressional nomination in the Twelfth District, and in the spring of 1900 he was in the field for the Republican nomination for Governor, the first Upper Peninsula candidate of any party for that office. His first vote in the Convention was the fourth highest of six candidates and his adherents were particularly loyal. It fairly places him in the field for future honors, while the commendations he received from his comrades in the newspaper field were exceedingly flattering.

CALVIN ALEXANDER PALMER, of Manistee, was born at Marine City, St. Clair County, Mich., February 25th, 1866. His father was Captain I. T. Palmer, a lake Captain for forty years, and his mother was Mary M. Palmer. His parents resided in St. Clair County, Mich., for fifty years, at Marine City and Port Huron, and previous to that at Buffalo, N. Y. His father was born at Portsmouth, N. H., in 1818, and is still living. His mother was born on the ocean, en route from Germany and is still living. His father's great grandfather, Barnabus Palmer, emigrated with two brothers from Cork, Ireland, to New England, in the latter part of the seventeenth century. The ancestors on his father's mother's side emigrated from Stoneyhurst, England, to New England about 1680. Henry Sherburne, his great great grandfather, represented Portsmouth in the General Assembly of the Province of New Hampshire in 1745.

Calvin A. Palmer was educated at Marine City public schools and Assumption College, Sandwich, Ont., and went to Manistee in 1882, at the age of sixteen. He worked in a saw mill during the summer of that year and in the fall took up land-looking in Minnesota, which he continued for two years. He clerked in a hotel, the Dunham House, Manistee, in the summer of 1884, and in the winter of that year took up the study of stenography. He was Private Secretary to Charles F. Ruggles and Edward Buckley, lumbermen, from the fall of 1885 to the fall of 1888, and was appointed Official Stenographer for Benzie County Circuit Court in 1888. He has followed court reporting and general expert stenography up to the present time, and still continues the practice of his profession. In 1892 he reported the investigation of the Pension Office for a Special Committee of the Fifty-second Congress. The work was done at Washington, D. C., consuming four months, and making a volume of one thousand pages when printed. He also reported the investigation of the Grand Rapids Soldiers' Home for a Special Committee of the Michigan Legislature in 1897. He was admitted to the bar in Benzie County Circuit Court in 1895, and was Chairman of the Republican City Committee in the spring of 1894. The first Republican Mayor of the City was elected at this election. He was elected Secretary of the Republican County Committee in 1894 and again in 1896. The entire Republican County ticket was elected in both campaigns for the first time in thirty years. He was Circuit Court Commissioner from 1896 to 1898, and was appointed Postmaster for the City of Manistee on February 4th, 1898. He has attended as delegate, nearly every State, Congressional and Senatorial Convention for the past twelve years. His first vote was cast for Benjamin Harrison, and his father's first vote was for William Henry Harrison.

Mr. Palmer is a member of the Order of Knights of Pythias and was Chancellor Commander of the local lodge for five terms. He has been a member of Michigan Grand Lodge for the past five years, elected Grand Outer Guard at the session of 1900, and is a member of the Foresters and Royal Arcanum and the Olympian Club, City of Manistee. He was married in 1892 to Miss H. May Shrigley, who was born and raised in Manistee, educated in the Manistee public schools and Northwestern University, daughter and only child of James H. Shrigley, retired lumberman. They have one child, James Shrigley Palmer, four years of age.

LEWIS GILBERT PALMER, of Big Rapids, had the reputation, when practicing law, and when in the State Senate, of being one of the most eloquent and persuasive advocates. He was born September 17th, 1851, in Herkimer County, N. Y. His father was Morgan Lewis Palmer, a carpenter, joiner and stone mason, and his mother was Mary Palmer. The son, Lewis G., received his general education in the public schools of Detroit, and the Michigan Agricultural College at Lansing, but he had previously been educated in the school of war. He enlisted at Detroit in January, 1863, in the Michigan Provost Guard, and was regularly mustered into the United States service as a drummer boy at the age of eleven years and about four months. He served from then until the close of the war; was discharged at Camp Blair, Jackson, Mich.; is without doubt the youngest member of the G. A. R. in the country, and the claim is made for him that he is the youngest Union soldier to be found on the muster rolls of the nation. In this service he partook of the spirit that moved other members of the family, for his father and three brothers served in Michigan regiments, leaving only his mother and one sister at home.

Returning from the army he was employed one year, covering part of 1865 and 1866 as messenger boy and clerk for Isadore Kauffman, merchant and clothier in Detroit; then attended school until 1868; then removed with his family to Big Rapids, Mich., and has resided there ever since. He taught his first school in Meridian, Ingham County in 1869; taught school for three years in Mecosta and Osceola Counties, Mich.; was then elected County Superintendent of Schools for Mecosta County, and served in that capacity until the law providing for such officials was repealed; was elected Prosecuting Attorney of Mecosta County and served three terms. He practiced law in Big Rapids, Mich., and vicinity until 1886 and was then elected to the State Senate, where he served two terms. He was then appointed United States Attorney for the Western District of Michigan, and at the close of the term was reappointed ad interim to try important cases pending. He resumed practice of law in the State and United States Courts until elected Circuit Judge for the Twenty-seventh Judicial Circuit for the unexpired term, succeeding his brother, the late Hon. John H. Palmer. He was next elected for the full term of six years and is now serving in that capacity. In 1888 Mr. Palmer was appointed by Governor Luce to represent the State of Michigan in an address at Marietta, and also at Columbus, Ohio, the occasion being the Centennial celebration of the founding of the Northwest Territory.

Among the measures introduced by Mr. Palmer when he was in the State Senate was the present marriage license law, and the law permitting prosecuting attorneys to appear and argue cases for the people before the Supreme Court. He championed many other important measures which became laws under his leadership and management. In politics he has always been an unswerving Republican,

voted first for U. S. Grant, and has been a delegate to nearly every State Convention since he attained his majority.

Mr. Palmer is a Mason and a Knight of Pythias. He was married at Ravenna, Mich., November 12th, 1874, to Miss Una Rice. His children are Emily Una, aged 22; Mollie, aged 20, and Frank R. Palmer, aged 14.

SENATOR THOMAS WITHERELL PALMER has been for many years among the most distinguished of Detroit's citizens in business, in politics and in social life. He was born in Detroit, January 25th, 1830, his father being Thomas Palmer, and his mother, Mary A. Witherell, daughter of Judge James Witherell, and sister of Judge B. F. H. Witherell. Both families were among the most prominent in Detroit at the time, and both had a long line of New England descent. The first of the Palmer family in this country was Walter, who came over in 1635, and was one of the incorporators of the Town of Cambridge, Mass. The Witherell family settled in Massachusetts about the same time, crossing the sea in the Governor Winthrop party, and both families remained in New England through several generations. Mr. Palmer gains eligibility to membership in the Society of Sons of the American Revolution through ancestors on both sides, his grandfathers, James Witherell and Benjamin Palmer, both serving in that war. Another ancestor, Thomas Barbour, spent two or three years in Eastern Michigan just preceding the forming of the Pontiac conspiracy. He had a profitable trade in furs with the Indians, and the traditions of his success here had something to do with the removal of the Senator's father to Detroit.

Thomas W. Palmer received his early education in such schools as Detroit then afforded, supplemented by training in Bacon's excellent private school and afterwards by a course in Rev. O. C. Thompson's Academy at St. Clair. In the latter he had as a schoolmate his future successful rival in the contest for the Governorship of Michigan, David H. Jerome. From this academy he went to Michigan University, but was obliged to leave in his Sophomore year on account of trouble with his eyesight. Then came a long period of travel, with its educating and broadening influences. He spent several months in going through Spain on foot, then sailed to Rio Janiero, stayed several months more in South America and returned by way of the Southern States in this country. After his return he accepted the agency of a transportation company, was for some time a resident of Green Bay, Wis., and then went into the mercantile business at Appleton, Wis., at that time a rapidly growing town on the edge of the great lumber district of that State. His store there was afterwards burned out, and in 1852 he returned to Detroit, going into the real estate and insurance business with his father. Three years later he was married to Miss Lizzie Merrill, daughter of Charles Merrill, and became connected with the lumber firm of Charles Mer-

T W Palmer

ulation of railroads. In the latter he originated the phrase, since then much used, "Equal rights to all, special privileges to none." He was also selected to make several addresses of eulogy. He might have had the nomination for a second term, but refused to be a candidate.

In the make up of President Harrison's Cabinet he was first slated for Secretary of Agriculture, and subsequently, without any previous knowledge on his part of the President's purpose, he was appointed Minister to Spain. Returning from that country in 1891 he was, equally without his solicitation, appointed a Commissioner on the World's Fair at Chicago. He was subsequently chosen, by his fellow Commissioners, President of the Commission, and performed the arduous duties of that position with admirable tact and good judgment.

Senator Palmer's main diversion is his farm. His grandfather, Judge Witherell, secured a government patent for 160 acres of land in Greenfield, six miles from Detroit City Hall. This descended to Senator Palmer through his mother. He commenced to "play with it" in 1864, and subsequently added to it 480 acres more. He had much of it underdrained, built large barns, and in 1883 began the importation of Percheron horses and Jersey cattle, of which he soon had herds that ranked among the best in the country. The Senator continued to work this farm till 1893, when he sold a portion to a syndicate. It was from the remaining portion that he donated to the City of Detroit between 140 and 150 acres for a park, including a fine approach from Woodward avenue, and the famous Log Cabin, with the surrounding improvements, making a magnificent pleasure ground that already draws many visitors from all parts of the City, and that is every year growing in attractiveness. Aside from this munificent gift he has made others in the City of his residence, including $15,000 to the Detroit Museum of Art, of which he was one of the promoters and first President; a like amount to Mary Palmer Memorial Church; $10,000 to the Society for the Prevention of Cruelty to Animals; $10,000 to the superannuated fund of Detroit Methodist Conference, and $5,000 to the Masonic Temple. He was the first Secretary of the Soldiers' Monument Association, and one of the chief promoters of that enterprise. He has also given $10,000 to Albion College, and he and Captain W. H. Stevens donated to the Methodists the Memorial Church fronting Woodward avenue near the Six-Mile road. At the present time Mrs. Palmer is constructing, in Opera House Park, a beautiful fountain, called the Merrill Humane Fountain, in memory of her father, at a cost exceeding $20,000.

Senator Palmer's society tastes have a literary turn. He is a Mason, but not a very active one. He is a member of the New England Society, of which he was the first President; of the Society of the Sons of the American Revolution, of which he has also been President; of the Unity Club, of which he is Vice-President; of the Michigan University Alumni Association, and of the Michigan Club.

He has presided at several banquets given by the latter, where his ready wit has done much to enliven the proceedings. He is in great demand as toastmaster at banquets, and as presiding officer on more serious occasions. He has a large and well selected library, of which he is a most appreciative reader.

Senator Palmer is a philosopher in thought, and is liberal and progressive in his views. He believes in woman's suffrage, is Vice-President of the State Equal Suffrage Association, and was for many years the chief worker in the Society for the Prevention of Cruelty to Animals. Though he has been liberal in gifts to the Methodist Church, of which his mother was a devoted member, his own religious affiliations are with the Unitarian Church, in which he is a Trustee and Superintendent of the Sunday School. He is eminently social, and one of the best entertainers in the City. He has adopted three children—Mrs. Grace Palmer Rice, Miss Bertha Brown Palmer and Higinio Palmer, all of whom are living.

BURTON PARKER was born April 24th, 1844, in the Township of Dundee, Monroe County, Mich. His father, Morgan Parker, was born in Batavia, N. Y., January 1st, 1820; his mother, Rosetta C., whose maiden name was Breningstall, was born in Batavia, N. Y., September 27th, 1824; his grandfather, Joshua Parker, was born in Connecticut on the 7th of November, 1770, and his great grandfather, also named Joshua, was in the Revolutionary War. His grandfather moved from Connecticut to Oneida County, N. Y., where he resided some years, and in 1825 emigrated to the Western part of Monroe County, Mich., eighteen miles West of Monroe City, and took up 100 acres of Government land, from which he cleared up a very pleasant farm. Burton's father was a farmer up to 1855, at which time he engaged in the lumber, milling and manufacturing business at Petersburg, Monroe County.

In October, 1861, Burton and his father enlisted in Company F, First Regiment of Engineers and Mechanics, the father being First Sergeant of the Company. They were in the campaign of 1861 and 1862 in Kentucky with Generals Buell and Thomas, and at the Battle of Mineral Springs, Ky., on January 19th, 1862, when the Confederate General Zollicoffer, who was in command of the Confederate forces, was killed. Burton's father died while in the service in Kentucky on April 4th, 1862, of typhoid fever. A year later Burton was discharged on account of long and continued sickness.

His paternal grandmother, Sina Parker, of Holland descent, was a practicing physician, and the only one in the Western part of Monroe County for years. The early settlers remember her kindly as administering to the sick, traveling through swamps and over corduroys to reach their new homes. His maternal grandfather and grandmother were also of Holland descent. They emigrated from

New York State to Dundee Township, Monroe County, Mich., in 1840. His Grandfather Parker was a Connecticut Yankee.

Burton attended district school in the country until he moved to the Village of Petersburg, and then attended the Village school. Mornings and evenings he worked in and about the lumber mill during the summer, also during the summer and winter vacations; also worked in lumber woods driving teams and running logs down the river. He is the oldest of five children. His father and mother had both taught school and at odd and leisure times kept their children at their school books. After the death of his father, his discharge from the Army, and recovery from his illness, he was engaged in saw-milling as head sawyer, then became a clerk in a dry goods store, and before he was twenty-two years of age, was elected Justice of the Peace and commenced the study of law. He graduated at the law department of Michigan University in the class of 1870, and entered actively upon the practice of law at Monroe City.

He was always a Republican, casting his first Presidential vote for General Grant in 1868. In 1872 he was elected Circuit Court Commissioner for Monroe County; in 1881 was elected Mayor of Monroe by a majority of 246, and was re-elected the following spring by a majority of 318, and elected President of the School Board of that City. The City at that time, was over 200 Democratic. In 1882 he was elected a member of the Legislature in the Monroe City District by a majority of 240, the District at that time being strongly Democratic. As a member of the Legislature he was Chairman of the Committee on Municipal Corporations and assisted in the election of Thomas W. Palmer as United States Senator. He was appointed Indian Agent by President Arthur in the fall of 1884, at Fort Peck Agency, Montana, and was removed by President Cleveland in the winter of 1885-6. In 1890 he was appointed Special Agent of the U. S. Treasury Department, and was removed twenty days after the inauguration of President Cleveland, but reinstated four years later under President McKinley. In March, 1894, he was appointed Deputy Land Commissioner by Land Commissioner William A. French, held that position for three years and resigned to accept reinstatement as Special Agent of the United States Treasury Department.

For more than twenty-five years Mr. Parker has been active in political matters, and in many campaigns has made a tour of the State under the direction of the State Central Committee, addressing the people upon the political issues of the day.

On the 8th day of September, 1863, he was married to Miss Fanny C. Reynolds, of South Amherst, Lorain County, Ohio. Five children have been born to them, three of whom are now living and are practicing physicians; Dr. Hal M. Parker, who is located at Delta, Fulton County, O.; Dr. Thadd N. Parker, who is located in Boston, Mass., and Dr. Dayton L. Parker, located in Detroit. Dr. Dayton Parker, present Police Surgeon of Detroit, is Burton's brother.

In the boyhood days of Burton Parker the country was new, and people were not as well off as they are now. Upon the death of his father, the support and maintenance of the family fell largely upon his brother and himself, and it is quite difficult to portray the labors performed and the hardships realized in the struggle for bread, education and his profession. When he entered the law department of the Michigan University, he had a wife and two baby boys, and but very little means. During vacations he was employed as a clerk in a dry goods store to obtain money for the next ensuing term, and feels quite largely indebted to the cheerful and encouraging words of a devoted and loving wife for his success.

WILLIAM EDWARD PARNALL, of Calumet, Michigan, was born June 3rd, 1839, in the County of Cornwall, England. His father was Christopher Parnall, a stone mason, and his mother was Mary Parnall. His grandfather on his father's side was a sea captain. His mother's maiden name was Vivian, and she was sister to men who figured prominently in mining, two of whom, Sampson and Henry Vivian, were among the first to explore and develop the noted Bruce Copper Mines in Canada over fifty years ago. A brother and three sisters comprised the family of which William Edward was a member. His brother learned the carpenter's trade in a country shop, went to the City of London, and was raised to positions of trust. Among the noted structures he superintended in erecting are the Midland Hotel at St. Pancras, and also the Midland Railroad Station attached, Knightsbridge Barracks, Brompton Oratory, the Imperial Institute at South Kensington, the Hotel Metropole at Charing Cross, new additions to the Admiralty buildings, with many others of lesser importance.

William Edward Parnall attended a private school until he was twelve years old, when he went to work in the mines, and has been connected with mining ever since. He is now General Manager of the Isle Royal Consolidated Mining Company, Osceola Consolidated Mining Co., and the Tamarack Mining Co.

In politics Mr. Parnall was never anything but a Republican, casting his first vote for Lincoln. He has attended every County and State Convention held in the past twelve years, and was Delegate-at-Large at the National Convention in Philadelphia in 1900. He was for ten years Supervisor of Rockland Township, Ontonagon County, and the same length of time in Osceola Township, Houghton County. He is not a member of any societies except the Masonic, in which he is a Sir Knight and Shriner. He was married at Southfield, Oakland County, in 1864, to Miss Isabella Gregg, who died in 1872. He was again married in 1875 at the same place to Mary Gregg. He has three sons living, Samuel A., W. E., Jr., and Christopher G., aged respectively, 34, 32 and 20 years, and one daughter aged 18 years.

W E Parnall

John Patton.

JOHN PATTON, of Grand Rapids, who is one of the best known of the Republicans of middle age in the State, was born in Curwensville, Clearfield County, Penn., October 30th, 1850. He is one of a succession of John Pattons who have attained distinction in this country. The nationality is Scotch-Irish. The first in the line so far as this country is concerned, the great grandfather of the John Patton of the present generation, was born in Sligo, Ireland, in 1745, came to this country twenty years later, and for a time was one of the four auctioneers of Philadelphia, those officers then being appointed by the Government. He was also a successful merchant, and a zealous patriot, and at one time, when the Colonial Army was in great need, contributed two thousand pounds toward a fund for provisioning it. He also did gallant service as Colonel of the Sixteenth Additional Continental Regiment of Pennsylvania Infantry. At the time of his death, he held the rank of Major General of this division of the Pennsylvania Militia.

The second in the line was born in Philadelphia, February 8th, 1783, and at an early age followed the sea. He was midshipman under Commodore Stephen Decatur and was later a Lieutenant in the United States Navy. The third in the line was born in Tioga County, Penn., January 6th, 1823. He commenced working in a store when eleven years old, and ten years later went into business for himself with borrowed money as a lumberman and merchant. Throughout the next half century he was an important factor in the business, political and financial life of Clearfield and adjoining counties in Pennsylvania. He was one of the leading merchants and most extensive lumber shippers in that region, an organizer of banks and a promoter of railroad building. He was a member of the Thirty-seventh Congress, also of the Fiftieth, each time overcoming a strong Democratic majority; a delegate to the National Convention of the Whig party in 1852; also to the Convention which nominated Abraham Lincoln for the Presidency and a Presidential Elector in 1864. He was noted as a philanthropist; was a trustee of Dickinson College, Williamsport Dickinson Seminary, Drew Theological Seminary, and the American University at Washington.

It was from this vigorous stock that the subject of this sketch came. His mother was Catherine M. Ennis, of Holidaysburg, Penn., who died when he was five years old. The son had good opportunities for education, fitting for College at Philips Academy, Andover, Mass., graduating at Yale College in 1875, and after that taking the regular course at Columbia Law School. In 1878 he went to Grand Rapids in this State, spent a year in the office of Hughes, O'Brien & Smiley, and in 1879 he opened a separate office where he has since practiced his profession.

Senator Patton is perhaps best known in the State through his public addresses and his political activity. He has always acted with the Republicans and cast his first vote for Grant. He is an eloquent and forceful speaker, and has participated on the stump in every National and State campaign since 1879; has been a delegate to many local and State Conventions and was a member of the State Central Committee in 1884. At the National League Convention at Cleveland, 1895. he introduced, and after a long struggle, secured the adoption of a resolution he wrote, which relegated the Silver question to the National Republican Convention of 1896, thus averting a party disaster, as the advocates of free silver had packed the Committee on Resolutions. He addressed the Republican editors of Michigan at Hastings in April, 1895, speaking against the free coinage of silver at 16 to 1, when he was hissed by some of the members, and on May 1st, 1895, wrote a letter for the Kalamazoo Telegraph for sound money, which was one of the first published in the State before that memorable contest. He was President of the State League of Republican Clubs in 1891 and 1892, and perfected such an organization with the co-operation of the Republican Press of the State that great credit was given it for the Michigan Republican victory of 1892. The ideas and plan of organization were afterward adopted by the National League. He declined a re-election on account of business On the death of Senator F. B. Stockbridge he was appointed U. S. Senator by Governor John T. Rich over fourteen candidates, May 5th, 1894, and served until January, 1895, when Hon. J. C. Burrows was elected by the Legislature for the remainder of the unexpired term. His speech on "The Wilson Bill and Michigan" received wide comment from the press of the country. He was appointed December, 1897, a member of the Blair Statue Commission, with General R. A. Alger and General W. H. Withington, and at their request delivered the oration at the unveiling of the statue of Governor Austin Blair, at Lansing, October 12th, 1898. He was named as the first member of the Commission to study the tax question and report to the Legislature, in the bill which passed both branches of the Legislature in 1899, and was vetoed by Governor Pingree.

Senator Patton has delivered many public addresses. That on "The Republic, Its Growth and Dangers," before the Michigan University on February 22d, 1900, in which he attacked corruption in Michigan politics and pointed out the necessity for safeguarding the primaries, and the one at Muskegon, May 30th, 1900, at the unveiling of the statues of Grant, Sherman, Farragut and Lincoln, which were presented to the City by Hon. Charles H. Hackley, have received much favorable comment. He made the address of welcome at the Sixth Anniversary Banquet of the Michigan Club and was toastmaster at the banquet, February 22d, 1900. He also made an address to General Benjamin Harrison, at Indianapolis in October, 1888, when a large delegation from Western Michigan visited the candidate.

He was married October 1st, 1885, to Frances S. Foster, daughter of Ex-Congressman Wilder D. Foster, of Grand Rapids, and is the father of four boys, John, Francis F., Philip Sidney and Lawrence. He is a member of the Peninsular Club of Grand Rapids; Sons of the American Revolution, the Scotch-Irish Society of America, the Friend-

*Russel R. Pealer.*

ly Sons of St. Patrick of Philadelphia, the American Historical Society and the American Economic Association. He helped organize the People's Savings Bank of Grand Rapids, of which he is now Vice-President.

RUSSEL RALPH PEALER, a prominent citizen of St. Joseph County, and Ex-Judge of the Circuit Court, was born January 1st, 1842, on a farm near Rohrsburg, in Greenwood Township, Columbia County, Penn. His father's name was George Pealer, and his mother's name was Rebecca Boyd Hampton. The grandparents on the Pealer side were Pealers and Kooders, both German farmers, and on the mother's side were Hamptons and Hopkins, of English descent. They were mechanics and teachers The great grandfather, Caleb Hopkins, was an Episcopal clergyman and founded the church at Bloomsburg, Pa., and afterwards was the rector of the church of Angelica, N. Y.

Russel R. Pealer was brought up on his father's farm, mingling farm work with study in the public schools till he was seventeen years old, when he went to the New Columbus Normal School in Luzerne County, and afterwards to the Orangeville Normal School, in Columbia County. He often walked five miles to and from these schools daily in good weather, studying on the way. He boarded himself when he did not go home, and paid his own way, teaching school in winter, working on the farm during the summer vacations and attending the Normal School during the spring and fall terms.

It had been his purpose to enter the Albany Law School, in New York, but the call of patriotism appealed to him, and in 1862 he enlisted as a private in Company E, Sixteenth Pennsylvania Cavalry, and served until August 11th, 1865, when he was honorably discharged by reason of the close of the war. He was promoted from time to time through the grades of a non-commissioned officer of his company; was then commissioned Sergeant Major of his regiment "for meritorious conduct as a soldier," and later was commissioned Second Lieutenant and then First Lieutenant of his company; was recommended for a Captain's commission, commanded Companies E and I at the Battle of Hatcher's Run, Va., and led them in a charge on Pegram's Division of Confederates; was wounded and carried from the field to City Point and afterwards to Baltimore, where the ball was extracted. He was carried from there to his father's house in Central Pennsylvania on a stretcher, and was cared for by his mother until he returned on crutches to his regiment, then near Farmville, Va. He remained with his regiment until the close of the war. He was in thirty-five engagements of all kinds, was at Chancellorsville, Gettysburg, Shepardstown, Culpepper, Mine Run, Sulphur Springs, through all the Wilderness campaign, at Todd's tavern, North Anne, Howe's Shop, Cold Harbor, and in several engagements on the left and right of the James River, at Petersburg, Weldon Railroad, Boynton Plank Road, and Hatcher's Run.

While confined to bed by his wound, Mr. Pealer studied surveying, and on his return from the war did land surveying to in part pay his expenses while carrying out his original educational purpose. He commenced reading law at Lynchburg, Va., entered the law office of Robert E. Clark, of Bloomsburg, Pa., September 3rd, 1865, and was admitted to the bar at Bloomsburg, September 3rd, 1867, and soon after came to Three Rivers, St. Joseph County, Mich., where he has had a lucrative practice. He served as Circuit Court Commissioner and Prosecuting Attorney for his County, and as Circuit Judge of the Fifteenth Judicial Circuit for six years, from January 1st, 1882, to January 1st, 1888, and was Representative in the Legislature in 1889. In both of these public positions Mr. Pealer was deservedly held in high esteem. His judicial decisions showed a thorough knowledge of the law and a discriminating judgment, and were very rarely reversed by the Supreme Court. He was a very industrious and prudent legislator. Among other committee assignments he was a member of the important Committee on the Judiciary; introduced and secured the passage of a number of bills, supporting the Anti-Trust Bill which is now a law of the State: assisted in securing the passage of the Arbitration Law relating to labor troubles, the revised Liquor Local Option Law, the Soldiers' Aid Law, the Tax Law of 1889, and many other acts of that session.

Mr. Pealer has been supported in the State Republican Convention for Supreme Court Judge, by his County, Judicial Circuit and Congressional District, and other parts of the State, on three different occasions, and in 1896 was supported by the Republican delegation from his County for the nomination for Congress. He was appointed by Governor Rich one of the Commissioners of the State Compilation of the Laws of 1897. He came of Whig stock and first became interested in politics as a boy in the Fremont campaign, when he was a reader of the New York Tribune; cast his first vote for Abraham Lincoln in the open fields of Virginia, while serving as a volunteer soldier, and from that time to this has been an ardent Republican, and has rendered such service as he could in each campaign. He has been Chairman of the Republican County Committee, and his friends know he did his work well. He has often attended the State Republican Convention as a delegate, is a member of the Michigan Club, now President of the First National Bank of Three Rivers, has held many local offices, has served on school and other boards, and is a member of the Local Improvement Company, of Three Rivers. His investments are mostly in real estate, and the stock on his two farms. He has retained an interest in agriculture and in stock raising, and to some extent has been a peppermint oil producer. He has long been a member of the Methodist Episcopal Church and has held all the official positions which laymen attain to, including delegate to the General Conference; is a member of the Bay View Association at Petoskey, and has served as a Trustee of

Edward W. Pendleton.

the association. He is a Mason, a Knight Templar, a member of the Loyal Legion and an ardent Grand Army man; has been Post Commander and Judge Advocate of the Department, and was the Department Commander of this State for the year 1899.

Judge Pealer was first married December 25th, 1865, in his native State, to Sallie Ann Stevens, who died in September, 1870, and left surviving her, two children, Anna G. and Matie A. Pealer, who are the only living children of the family. They are both married. His present wife was Sue F. Sauntee, of Bradford County, Penn., to whom he was married April 15th, 1875. Her father was a Methodist minister and an earnest Republican supporter of David Wilmot, the author of the "Wilmot Proviso," and in whose strong Republican Congressional District he and his family resided. Mrs. Pealer partook of the loyal spirit of that and the Civil War period, is well informed on the early history of the party, and has ever been an ardent supporter of its cause and a zealous worker in a number of societies for the public good.

EDWARD W. PENDLETON, well known as a practicing attorney in Detroit, was born at Camden, Maine, May 22d, 1849, his father, George Pendleton, having been a native of the same State. George was a son of Captain John Pendleton and a descendant, of the fifth generation, of Major Brian Pendleton, the founder of the Pendleton family in America, who came with his family from the Town of Pendleton, Lancashire, England, in the year 1632, settling in Westport, Mass. While still a young man George became Secretary to Commodore Warrington, on board the United States frigate "Constellation," and while acting in that capacity took part in the reception tendered to General LaFayette upon the occasion of his visit to the United States in 1825. He was a man of conspicuous integrity of character, of broad views, with cultivated and cordial manners. In 1831 he was married to Susan Johnson, of Canterbury, Conn., who was a descendant of Edward Johnson, the principal founder of Woburn, Mass., and author of "The Wonder-Working Providence of Zion's Saviour in New England." She was also a descendant of the historic Huntingtons, of Connecticut. Mr. Pendleton died in Detroit, August 27, 1875, at the home of his son.

Edward W. Pendleton received his preliminary education in the Gorham, Me., Academy, and in Bowdoin College, at Brunswick, Me.; in 1870 he entered the University of Michigan and graduated in the class of 1872, receiving the degree of A. B., and subsequently the degree of A. M. During the years of 1872 and 1873 Mr. Pendleton was Superintendent of the Public Schools at Owosso, and was afterwards instructor of classics in the Detroit High School for two years. For one year he attended the law department of the University of Michigan, and completed his preparation in the office of Hon. C. I. Walker, of Detroit. He was admitted to the bar in 1876, and has since been in the active and successful practice of his profession in Detroit. During his years of practice Mr. Pendleton has handled many cases of importance, among them a famous extradition case, in the conduct of which he was appointed Special Agent by President Harrison to go to England. Aside from being well versed in the law, Mr. Pendleton is a man of wide reading and liberal general education, having traveled extensively. In his law practice he is trustworthy in statement and polite and courteous towards his fellow members of the bar as well as witnesses and litigants, and deservedly popular in his profession and universally respected as a public spirited citizen.

Mr. Pendleton is a strong Republican, believing that many of the important commercial and political problems affecting the interests of the world will be successfully solved by the United States, and that becoming the leading manufacturing nation of the world. this country will also hold the balance of power in the settlement of military supremacy. He has never sought elective or salaried offices, but has served the public as a member and President of the Board of Water Commissioners, being twice appointed both by a Republican and a Democratic Mayor.

HAZEN S. PINGREE is one of the men who entered public life with great reluctance. Previous to 1889 he was chiefly known to the citizens of Detroit as a brave soldier who had survived the horrors of Andersonville prison, and as a pushing and successful manufacturer. For some years previous to the date mentioned Detroit was an uncertain City in politics, neither party very often carrying its entire ticket, though with a slight leaning toward Democracy. But in the fall of 1887 there had been a landslide to the Democracy, its candidate for Mayor receiving nearly five thousand plurality over the Republican candidate, and two thousand one hundred majority over all. It was with the recollection of this campaign in mind that, in the fall of 1889, a number of leading Republicans met, upon invitation of James F. Joy, to consider the nomination for Mayor. There were no aspirants for the honor, and a number of gentlemen whose names were proposed, absolutely declined to make the run. A final attempt was made to secure the consent of Colonel H. M. Duffield, in the belief that his personal popularity would carry the ticket through, but he also positively refused. After an interval of silence, Elder F. A. Blades arose and said: "Mr. President, I can name the next Mayor of Detroit and not go out of this room." Mr. Joy replied: "Please proceed, you can do more than I can." Mr. Blades replied: "His name is H. S. Pingree, and he sits right over there," pointing his finger at Pingree. Pingree replied: "No, no, I was never in the City Hall except to pay my taxes; I will double my subscription, but let me out," and he left the room. A committee was appointed, of whom Clarence A. Black was

H. S. Pingree

one, that followed Mr. Pingree to his factory, and finally wrung from him a reluctant consent, and the consent of his partners, to accept the nomination if it was tendered to him without any effort on his part. The City Convention that followed readily enough endorsed the conclusion reached, and Mr. Pingree was nominated by acclamation, and elected by a comfortable majority, thus commencing a public career, which has since made him known the country over.

Mr. Pingree is one of a large number of Mayors that New England has given to Detroit, and one of eight Governors that the same section has given to Michigan, having been born in Denmark, Me., August 30th, 1840. He was the fourth child of Jasper and Adeline Bryant Pingree. His father, a farmer, was also born in Denmark, remained in the place of his birth until 1871, when he came to Michigan and shared in the comforts of his son's home until he died in 1882. The first American forefather of Governor Pingree was Moses Pingree, who emigrated to this country from England in 1640, just two centuries prior to the year in which the Governor was born.

Residing with his parents, and attending school until fourteen years of age, Hazen S. Pingree then began life on his own account at Saco, Me., where he worked in a cotton mill. In 1860 he began the trade of a shoemaker as a cutter in a factory at Hopkinton, Mass., where he remained until August 1st, 1862, when he enlisted as a private in Company F, First Massachusetts Heavy Artillery, for the unexpired three years' term of that regiment, and afterwards re-enlisted, on the battlefield, for three years, or during the war. With this regiment he took part in the second Battle of Bull Run, the Battles of Fredericksburg Road, Harris Farm, Cold Harbor, Spottsylvania Court House, North Anne and South Anne. On May 25th, 1864, while with an escort guarding a wagon train enroute to Port Royal, the escort was captured by a squad of Mosby's men. As prisoners of war they were brought before General Mosby, who exchanged his entire suit with Private Pingree, who was to become as thoroughly known in politics as Mosby was in war, but the coat was given back with the remark that some of his men might shoot him for a "Yank" if he wore it. Pingree was sent as a prisoner of war to Andersonville, where he was confined for nearly seven months; from there to Salisbury prison, in North Carolina; then to Millen, Ga., where, in November, 1864, he was exchanged, afterwards rejoining his regiment in front of Petersburg. He took part in the expedition to Weldon Railroad, the Battles of Boynton Road, Petersburg, Sailors' Creek, Farmville and Appomattox Court House, and after the close of the war was mustered out of service with his regiment in August, 1865.

Coming to Detroit after the war, Mr. Pingree found employment in the shoe factory of H. P. Baldwin & Co. In December, 1866, the firm of Pingree & Smith was established with a capital of but $1,360, with Hazen S. Pingree and Charles H. Smith as copartners. From this small beginning the business continued to grow from the employment of eight men during the first year, until it now requires the services of eight hundred persons, and has an annual output that has, in some years, considerably exceeded one million dollars.

The acceptance of the nomination for Mayor opened a new career for Mr. Pingree. He put his whole energy into the campaign, and was elected by a majority of 2,338 over the same Democrat who had been 4,937 votes ahead of the Republican candidate two years earlier. In 1891 the Democrats, after a tumultous Convention, amounting almost to a riot, divided, the candidate of one faction polling 5,263 votes, and that of the other 9,015, while Pingree's vote increased to 15,335. In 1893 the Democrats were again united and polled 19,124 votes for Marshall H. Godfrey, a popular candidate, but Pingree's vote reached the figure, unprecedented in a Detroit municipal election, of 24,924. Two years later, the Democrats tried the experiment of nominating a labor agitator, of uncertain political fealty, and their vote fell off to 10,432, while Mr. Pingree's vote was 21,024.

Backed by these repeated manifestations of popular approval, Mayor Pingree put his tremendous energy and fertile and resourceful brain into the devising of plans for the improvement of the City. He made appointments to the Board of Public Works of men who put system and energy into that department. Through the combined efforts of the Mayor and this Board, the cost of sewer building was greatly diminished, while the quality of the work was immensely improved. He insisted, with the strongest tenacity of purpose, on concrete foundations for all pavements, instead of the sand and inch board foundations that had formerly been used, and in seven years Detroit was changed from one of the worst paved, to one of the best paved cities in the country. He was always in a fight with the old street railway company. He did not secure the result which was the height of his ambition, three-cent fares and universal transfers, but he did secure one new line, with tickets eight-for-a-quarter in the daytime, and workingmen's tickets during certain hours at the same price on the other lines, and it was largely through his instrumentality that the grooved rail and the vestibuled car came as soon as they did.

After a taste of public life Mayor Pingree conceived a strong desire for a wider field of political activity, and was a candidate for the Republican nomination for Governor at the Saginaw Convention in 1892, and again at Grand Rapids in 1894. He failed in each case, but in 1896 he obtained the prize, and was elected by a vote of 304,431 to 221,022 for Charles R. Sligh, candidate of a combination of Democrats, Populists and Union Silver party. Mr. Pingree's plurality was 27,331 in excess of that given for William McKinley. In 1898, he was re-elected by 75,097 plurality.

Mr. Pingree's administration as Governor was fully as vigorous as that when he was Mayor. During the progress of the Spanish War there was no State in the Union that sent its quota of volunteers more promptly or better equipped than Michigan, and the Governor made three or four trips to camps in the South for the express purpose of looking after their comfort. His most persistent and long continued work as Governor was in the effort to secure greater equality of taxation in the State. It was almost solely through his influence that the Legislature passed the Atkinson Bill for the local taxation of railroad property, but this was, by inference, declared unconstitutional by the Supreme Court. He did not succeed with his tax measures at the regular session of the Legislature of 1899, but through the excellent work of the State Tax Commission, through the agitation which the Governor started, and through the facts which he presented with great force in his message, an impetus was given to the movement which not even a hostile Senate could resist. At a special session of the Legislature, called early in October, 1900, the Governor announced that he would approve any measure calculated to carry out the purpose of equalizing taxation. Within three days the Legislature passed an act repealing all special charters of railroads so as to bring the roads under the general law, and adopted a resolution for a Constitutional Amendment, giving the Legislature power to assess the property of all corporations, including that of railroad, telegraph, telephone and express companies, upon its actual cash value, the same as all other property, so as to bring about equality in methods of taxation. At the November election following, the Constitutional Amendment was adopted by such an overwhelming majority as to constitute the highest tribute to the Governor's entire accord, in the long contest, with the will of the people.

In home life Governor Pingree finds his greatest enjoyment, and being a man of keen sense of the beautiful, has a home complete in its appointments, and replete with works of art. On February 26th, 1872, he married Frances A. Gilbert, of Mt. Clemens. One daughter having passed away a few years ago, the family now consists of Governor Pingree, wife, daughter, and son.

SAMUEL POST, of Ypsilanti, who in the course of a long business and political career, has become well known throughout the State, was born at Ypsilanti, November 9th, 1834. His parents were William Rollo Post, a hatter, and Mary Ann Pardee. Both parents were born in New York State, came to Michigan in 1830, and located at Ypsilanti, where they continued to reside until death, both dying in the same year at the advanced ages of 86 and 87. When they came westward the methods of travel were very primitive, the Erie Canal furnishing the best means of crossing New York State, and an ox team being used for the journey from Detroit to Ypsilanti. Mrs. Post's father, Israel Platt Pardee, was a Captain in a New York regiment during the Revolutionary War and the more remote ancestors were French Huguenots who fled to this country to escape religious persecution by the Catholics during the reign of Louis

XVI. The Post family are very numerous in this country, all descendants from early immigrants to New England.

Samuel Post received his education in the common schools of Ypsilanti, with the exception of one year at the private seminary conducted by Charles Woodruff, for many years editor of the Ypsilanti Sentinel. He earned his first money as "street merchant," selling apples and chestnuts. At ten years of age, while attending school, he was employed by Charles Stuck, in his general store, to work when not engaged in the school room, at $2.00 per month. Before his school days were ended his salary was increased at intervals until he received $6.00 per month. On leaving school at the age of sixteen, he gave his entire time to mercantile business, received a salary of $10 per month, and was advanced yearly until at the age of twenty-one he was receiving $50 per month. He had accumulated at that time $500, with which, and $500 loaned him for five years without security, by his dear friend, Rev. John A. Wilson, rector of the Episcopal Church at Ypsilanti, he embarked in business, forming a co-partnership with Robert Lambie for four years under the firm name of Lambie & Post. They conducted a successful business, selling dry goods, clothing, groceries, etc. At the end of the partnership he sold the business to his partner, and immediately built the largest and best store in Ypsilanti, and under the firm name of Samuel Post & Co., continued the business of a general store, was successful in business and in 1870 disposed of his stock and rented the store.

Mr. Post was elected to the State Legislature in 1870, served in the sessions of 1871 and 1872 and was Chairman of the Insurance Committee and of the Committee on Federal Relations. As Chairman of the former Committee he framed or reported some very important legislation, including the general law under which the first Insurance Commissioner, Samuel H. Row, was appointed and virtually created the Insurance Department.

Mr. Post was Chairman of the Washtenaw County Republican Committee in 1872, when the Republicans carried the County for the first time in many years, and was a member of the State Central Committee during the Chairmanship of Stephen D. Bingham, and has attended as delegate, many National and State Conventions. He was appointed by President Grant on April 1st, 1873, United States Pension Agent at Detroit for four years, was re-appointed by President Hayes for four years from October 30th, 1877, and by President Arthur for four years from January 30th, 1882, serving in all twelve years and ten months. He was appointed by Governor Pingree a member of the Board of Trustees of the Michigan Asylum for the Insane for six years from February 9th, 1897. He cast his first vote for Kinsley S. Bingham or John C. Fremont and has continued in the good old way.

In 1881, with Digby V. Bell, Mr. Post organized the Detroit Soap Co. At the time of Mr. Bell's death he bought his interest and continued the business, taking in as partners his sons, William R. and

*Perry F. Powers*

CADILLAC NEWS AND EXPRESS.

Samuel, Jr., and at present is actively engaged in the manufacture of soap. He was married in 1857 at Ypsilanti to Amanda S. Flower, of Geneva, N. Y., to whom three children were born, William R. Post, Samuel Post, Jr., and Nellie Post. He is a member of the Protestant Episcopal Church, a Mason, Knight Templar, and belongs to the Ancient Order of Workmen.

PERRY FRANCIS POWERS, one of the forceful young newspaper men and politicians who have helped to keep things lively in the Western lumber district of the Lower Peninsula of Michigan for several years past, was born September 5th, 1859, in Jackson County, Ohio, his father, a furnaceman, bearing the same name, and his mother's name being Sarah C. Powers. They were both natives of Pennsylvania, their ancestors being immigrants from Ireland.

The younger Powers was educated in the public schools at Jackson, Ohio. He commenced labor in the coal mines of Jackson County, in work then known as "tending door," given to very young boys. He was hardly more than twelve years of age. The death of his father, who lost his life as a soldier while the son was yet a child, made the boyhood years of his life full of hard work from morning to night. He learned the printing business in Jackson, and went from there to Davenport, Iowa, where he became compositor in the office of a daily paper in that City. From Davenport, he went to Cambridge, Ill., and became a partner with George C. Smith in the publication of the Cambridge Chronicle in 1884; went to Ypsilanti, Mich., in 1885, and in company with Mr. Smith, bought the Ypsilantian, changing its politics from Independent to Republican; sold his interest in the Ypsilantian in 1887, and purchased the Cadillac News and Express, of which he has since been editor and publisher. While a compositor he had made the best use of his opportunities for reading, observation and study, and became well equipped for the work of conducting a paper.

Mr. Powers has been a Republican since childhood, cast his first Presidential vote for Garfield, and is as well known in Michigan for his political activity and official service, as he is in the newspaper field. His face is a familiar one at State Conventions, many of which he has attended, either as a delegate or in his newspaper capacity. He has also done a good share of committee work, and in the last twelve years has made political speeches in nearly every County in the State. He is an easy, fluent speaker, and conveys the impression of honesty and sincerity in everything he says. In the campaign of 1896, instead of going to the larger cities and towns, where he was in demand, he preferred going into the rural districts, where he felt that he could do more good, and where his work was especially effective in combating the free silver notion. The next year he was sent by the Republican Newspaper Association to Mexico to make a personal investigation of the financial system of that country, showing the effect on business of free silver in actual use. The letters in which he gave the result of his investigations contained much valuable information conveyed in an interesting way, were widely read, and were highly praised by such eminent authorities as J. W. Babcock, Chairman of the Republican Congressional Committee, Senator Julius C. Burrows, Congressman Bishop, of Michigan, and others.

Mr. Powers was elected a member of the State Board of Education in 1888 and again in 1894. His twelve years of service on the Board covered the most prosperous period in the history of the State Normal School, of which that Board has control, and no member of the Board was ever more active than he in looking after the interests of that institution or of the new Normal Schools at Mt. Pleasant and at Marquette. Of his services Professor Putnam says in a recent history of the first named institution: "Mr. Powers has been an active member of the Board from the time of his first election, has devoted his time and energy freely to advance the interests of the Normal School, and has always been ready to support any new measures which promised to increase the efficiency and enlarge the influence and usefulness of the institution. In all his intercourse with the teachers of the school he has been uniformly considerate and courteous, and has had a proper regard for their wishes as far as circumstances would permit." The public appreciation of his services was shown at the State Convention, held in Grand Rapids in June, 1900, when he received, against several competitors, on the first ballot, the nomination for Auditor General, one of the most responsible elective positions in the State. In November following he was elected to this position by a popular vote that was equally flattering.

Largely self-educated as he is, Mr. Powers has been recognized as a leader among the educated newspaper men of the State. He has been President of the State Press Association, the Michigan Republican Newspaper Association and the State League of Republican Clubs. He has a taste for fraternal societies, being a member of the Knights of Pythias, the Maccabees, Ancient Order of United Workmen and others. He was married January 29th, 1889, to Jessie Warren, daughter of Mr. and Mrs. Cyrus Warren, of Whiteford, Mich., and has two boys, Warren F. and Perry F. Powers.

EDWY CAMPBELL REID is one of the newspaper men in Michigan who have been not only successful in their chosen profession, but prominent and useful in other fields of action. His paternal ancestors lived in New Jersey for several generations; his mother was a native of Norfolkshire, England, and he was born in Brantford, Ontario, where his parents resided for a time. They removed to Michigan when Edwy was eighteen months old, and his whole education and business experience have been in the Peninsular State.

ALLEGAN GAZETTE.

He received his education in the schools at Otsego, Allegan County, and at the age of sixteen commenced an apprenticeship in the office of the Otsego Herald. From that time on his work has been mainly in the newspaper field, in which he was successively part owner and publisher of the Otsego Record, compositor on the Kalamazoo Telegraph, foreman in the office of the Allegan Democrat, foreman of the Allegan Journal, and finally partner and publisher, with Don C. Henderson, of the latter paper. Henderson was not the easiest kind of man to get along with, and April 1st, 1882, he settled certain disagreements between himself and his partner by smashing a good part of the material in the office. Mr. Reid considered this a virtual dissolution of partnership and immediately secured the aid of friends and started the Allegan Gazette, which he has since built up into a prosperous and influential journal.

Allegan is near enough the center of the Southern Michigan fruit belt to make that an important interest there, and Mr. Reid has been closely identified with that industry. He has given much attention in his paper to fruit growing and marketing. He was for many years Secretary of the State Horticultural Society and one of the most efficient promoters of the fine exhibits made by that society at the State Fair and the Detroit Exposition.

In politics Mr. Reid has always been Republican. He has been active in committee and convention work in his own vicinity, and has been a frequent attendant at State Conventions, either as a delegate or in his newspaper capacity. He has held local positions of trust and was for eight years a member of the Board of Trustees of the State Asylum for the Insane at Ionia, and was President of the Board a portion of the time. In June, 1898, he was appointed by President McKinley, Postmaster at Allegan, an appointment which gave general satisfaction to the citizens.

Mr. Reid was married in 1876 to Miss M. A. Borradaile, of Sodus, N. Y., and a son and daughter are the fruit of the union. He is a prominent member of the Congregational Church at Allegan, is a member of the Executive Committee of the Michigan Republican Press Association and has society affiliations with the Oddfellows, Foresters, Maccabees and United Workmen.

JOHN T. RICH is another of the men, who, with the farm as a starting point, has achieved distinction in a number of different spheres of activity. He was the son of John W. and Jerusha (Treadway) Rich, and was born at Conneautville, Penn., April 23rd, 1841. His ancestors on both sides were English, though living in New England for three or four generations. In 1846 the family moved to Shoreham, Vt., where a year later his mother died, and in 1848 he went to reside with his uncle on a farm in the town of Elba, Lapeer

County, Mich. That farm, afterwards enlarged by additional purchases of land, is still worked under his direction, and until four years ago was his residence.

Young Rich attended the district school in Elba, then took one term at Clarkston Academy and afterwards attended the public schools at Lapeer. For a dozen years after that he confined his work almost entirely to the farm and to public duties that lay in the immediate vicinity. He was five years Treasurer of the Northeastern Agricultural Society, and afterwards, for one year, President of the State Agricultural Society. He was also for some years President of the Lapeer County Farmers' Mutual Fire Insurance Co. For four years he represented the Township of Elba on the Board of Supervisors, during the last two of which he was Chairman of the Board. He was, during this period and has been since, a frequent attendant upon farmers' gatherings. At the death of his uncle, Mr. Rich purchased the farm, which now comprises 300 acres. He takes especial pride in the standard bred live stock with which he keeps his farm supplied; he has always been particularly fond of sheep and has in his flock some of the direct descendants of the early Spanish Merino sheep, brought to Vermont in 1812. Mr. Rich is a connoisseur of wool, and at one time served, in company with Edward A. Green, of Philadelphia; Nicholas Mauger, of New York, and John Houston, of Connecticut, on the National Commission which selects the samples of wool for the Custom House authorities from all sections of the civilized world.

In addition to his farm life, and his participation in interests associated with it, Mr. Rich has had an extended public career. He was always Republican in politics, and cast his first Presidential vote for Lincoln in 1864. He has been delegate to many local conventions and to several State Conventions, and has twice been Chairman of the latter.

In the autumn of 1872 he was elected to the Legislature and re-elected for three successive terms. While a member of that body Mr. Rich was the last Speaker in the old Capitol and the first one in the new. In 1880 he was elected to the State Senate, taking his seat on January 1st, 1881; in the following March he resigned his office to accept the nomination as Representative to the United States Congress, to which body he was elected by a large majority. He was renominated the following year, but defeated at the polls. In 1887 he was appointed, by Governor Luce, Commissioner of Railroads for the State of Michigan, and was reappointed to that position in 1889. In the fall of 1892 he was nominated by the Republican party and elected Governor by a majority of about sixteen thousand and was re-elected in 1894 by a majority of 106,392, being the largest ever given a Governor of the State.

While in the Legislature Mr. Rich was of the type of member commonly classed as "level headed." He is a clear thinker, and his arguments and suggestions in respect to legislation were always

O M Robinson

direct and to the point. His experience in the Legislature, and the familiarity with the laws and interests of the State there acquired, fitted him admirably for the higher duties of Chief Executive. His administration was a progressive one, especially in respect to the State institutions. During his four years' service additions were made to several of the old institutions, and the following new ones were established: School for the Feeble Minded at Lapeer, Asylum for the Insane at Newberry, and the Normal School at Mt. Pleasant. As Commissioner of Railroads Mr. Rich had a way of getting what he wanted for the public without quarreling with the roads. Though not a regular attorney he, on several occasions, appeared in the Supreme Court, and ably prosecuted cases in which the interests of the State were involved. In his first report as Railroad Commissioner he recommended the repeal of the special charters, under which the Michigan Central and other roads were operated, not from any ill-will to the roads, but because he thought it would be for the interest of the public. The general proposition thus started has recently taken definite form in legislation.

In 1881 Mr. Rich took stock in the Delta Lumber Company of Detroit, one of the largest concerns of its kind in the West. It was prosperous for a time, but afterwards became seriously embarrassed, and in 1896 he was appointed Trustee. He has handled its involved affairs with such skill that the company, now nearly wound up, is able to pay all its debts and have something left over for its stockholders. In 1898 he was appointed Collector of Customs for the Port of Detroit, took office March 1st, of that year, and still holds the position

Mr. Rich has been a member of the Michigan Club from its organization, a member of the Detroit Country Club and of the Royal Arcanum. He was married in 1863 to Lucretia M., daughter of Samuel Winship, of Atlas, Genesee County, Mich.

ORRIN WILLIAMS ROBINSON, pioneer, mining clerk and lumberman, for over forty years identified with the interests of the Upper Peninsula was born at Claremont, N. H., August 12th, 1834. His father, a farmer, was named Deen Williams Robinson, and his mother was Mary Zilphia Robinson, nee Clement. His father's paternal grandfather volunteered as a private in the Revolutionary War, served through the War, and returned a Captain, and his father's maternal grandfather served in the Navy during the same war and retired at the close of the war as a Lieutenant. His ancestors, both paternal and maternal, came from England about the middle of the seventeenth century.

Orrin W. received his education in the district schools in New Hampshire and Vermont; left home at the age of ten, and for five years worked for a farmer for board and clothes; at fifteen packed all his belongings into a handkerchief and started out for himself; for the next four years he worked at odd jobs, farming, in a foundry, gunshop, machine shop, etc., attending a good district school each winter for four months; at nineteen borrowed $50 and went to Ontonagon County, Mich., arriving there in June, 1854, and worked about the mines until February, 1856. At that time, there being a general exodus from the mining regions, because many mines were closed, he started overland to Green Bay, traveling on foot with a dog train to carry blankets and provisions, and camping in the woods nights and was two weeks in making the trip. From Green Bay he went to Dubuque, Iowa, by stage and railroad and from there walked 200 miles West, and settled at Irvington, Kossuth County, Iowa, where he remained six years. The financial crash of 1857 so paralyzed the business on the frontier that it was with difficulty that he secured work enough to keep himself fed and clothed. For example, during the summer of 1857 he worked a month for a cow and then traded the cow to a merchant for a $17 suit of clothes. Later he worked six days for a hog, took him home, a small one room house where a chum and himself were "batching" because they could not get money enough to board. Later his chum and he husked corn for a farmer on the halves; fed part of the corn to the hog and ground part in a large coffee mill. Early in the winter they killed the hog and for a time lived sumptuously on pork and "johnny cake." The next summer he taught school six months at $20 per month, paying $8 for board, and these are only a few of several makeshifts he resorted to to keep going. In May, 1862, he returned to Hancock, in Houghton County, Mich., and was employed as shipping and receiving clerk by the Quincy Mining Co. from 1862 to 1873, when he organized the Sturgeon River Lumber Co. and built the mills at Hancock. In 1887 the mills were moved to Chassell and greatly enlarged. The company is one of the largest in its lumbering operations of any in the Upper Peninsula, and has been managed from its organization to the preset time, by Mr. Robinson, who is still its President.

Mr. Robinson has been a Republican ever since the party was created, casting his first vote for Fremont in 1856. His active political career commenced in 1864, helping to build up a Republican party in Houghton County, which at that time was overwhelmingly Democratic. In 1870, by nominating a mixed ticket, the party succeeded in electing Charles E. Holland to the House and Frank G. White to the Senate, both Republicans. It was not, however, until 1876, that a full Republican victory was gained by nominating and electing a full County ticket. He was the second Chairman of the Republican Central Committee of the County, serving from 1870 to 1882, during which time the County was turned from an overwhelming Democratic one to an equally unanimous Republican County.

Mr. Robinson was delegate to the Republican State Conventions of 1892-4-6, and to the National Convention in Minneapolis in 1892. He was a member of the House in the Legislature of 1895, and of the Senate in that of 1897, and was elected Lieutenant Governor in 1898.

and again by a very large majority in 1900. His only club affiliation is with the Michigan Club. In addition to useful general work as a legislator, Mr. Robinson was especially active in pushing the Upper Peninsula Railroad Bill, which was introduced by him in 1895, and passed by the House. but was defeated in the Senate. Was again introduced in the Senate in 1897 and it was again defeated, this time by only one vote. It was known as the Robinson Railroad Bill, and was to place the roads in the Upper Peninsula on the same schedule of rates as Roads in the Lower Peninsula.

Mr. Robinson was married in Cleveland, O., August 20th, 1865, to Cornelia L. Lombard, of Windsor, Vt. Their children are Mae Ethel and Deen L.

WASHINGTON IRVING ROBINSON, a prominent attorney and active Republican campaigner of Detroit, was born July 11th, 1865, at Ogdensburg, St. Lawrence County, New York, son of Charles Wesley Robinson, a vineyardist, and Elizabeth McMartin. His father was born of English parents and his mother of Scotch parents. He was educated in the common schools and Commercial colleges, and School of Oratory, and the beneficial results of this last training are seen in the polished oratory, which has made his campaign speeches acceptable. He has been a Republican all his life, was the youngest orator on the list of speakers in the employ of the Republican National Committee in 1888, and has been in the service of the National Committee, or of committees of other States, in every campaign since that time. Mr. Robinson is single and not a member of any societies. Aside from his law practice he is a Director in the Michigan & Ohio Electric Railway Co. He came, with his parents, to the suburbs of Detroit, when he was only six months old, and is still living upon the farm, now within the City limits, on which he was raised, and upon which he labored until going into the law.

FORDYCE HUNTINGTON ROGERS, who has virtually created one of the largest and most prosperous manufacturing establishments in Detroit, was born in that City, October 12th, 1840. His father was George Washington Rogers, a merchant, born December 14th, 1799, in the same hour that George Washington died, hence the name. His mother's name was Jane Clark Emmons, a sister of the late U. S. Judge, Halmer H. Emmons. The family can boast of an illustrious line of ancestry, among them Rev. John Rogers, the martyr, and ancestors named Borrowdale and Dennison, who fought under Cromwell. Major Rogers is also a lineal descendant of Governor William Bradford, one of the Pilgrims of the Mayflower, who was second Governor of the Plymouth Colony. His father was related to Governor Slade, of Vermont, Stephen A. Douglas and other notable people. His mother was a daughter of Adonijah

Emmons, an officer of the War of 1812, and her mother was a direct descendant of a Colonel on Washington's staff. His great grandfather, Jabez Rogers, was a soldier in the Revolutionary War. His grandmother, Mary Ripley Rogers, was a daughter of a Revolutionary soldier. This gives him three strains of Revolutionary blood and he is quite sure that his mother's family, the Emmons, were Revolutionary, but has not fully traced it yet.

F. H. Rogers was educated in the common schools at Pontiac, Mich. As his first occupation he rolled press each week to get off the editions of the Oakland County Gazette, Whig, and the Pontiac Jacksonian, Democrat, and folded and delivered their town circulation. While a student at Pontiac he had some experience in clerking in his father's store, also during that time he worked a little in almost every shop or factory in that town, so that he knew something of handling the tools of nearly all vocations known in a country town. In April, 1856, he came to Detroit and took a clerkship in a wholesale drug house. In the spring of 1858 he went to California via New York and Panama; went to the mountains and was agent for a water company in Sierra County, selling water to the miners. In the fall of 1859 he returned to Pontiac, Michigan, on account of the ill health of his father and remained with him until he died on April 9th, 1860.

After the death of his father Mr. Rogers was variously engaged until the breaking out of the war in the spring of 1861, when he was the first man to join Colonel Thornton F. Brodhead in raising the First Regiment of Michigan Cavalry Volunteers for the war. He recruited a company for that regiment at Pontiac, known as the Oakland Rangers. He was not of age at that time and felt himself too young to command one hundred men, so he secured a Captain and First Lieutenant for his company and accepted the position of Second Lieutenant for himself. He was promoted to be First Lieutenant and Adjutant and his last command was a Captain's command. He was tendered two appointments as Major, both of which he declined.

After being mustered out of the Army, Major Rogers, for he is commonly given that title, although he declined the honor, returned to California, where he had a varied experience. In 1865 he became bookkeeper of the Pacific Bank, the oldest incorporated bank on the Coast, with a capital of one million dollars; in 1866 and 1867 was Paying Teller, and in 1868 to 1872 was Cashier; after that he conducted a mining office in San Francisco, being an officer of thirty mining corporations at one time, and his office being headquarters for them all. The years 1879 and 1880 he spent in Chicago and New York, where he disposed of some mining interests, and with the proceeds came to Detroit and bought the Detroit White Lead Works in December, 1880. He incorporated a company with above title on December 22d, 1880, with a nominal capital stock of $50,000, paid in $22,500. The company now has a full paid cash capital of $400,000, and a surplus of about $100,000. The plant today is the finest paint and varnish plant in the world and Major Rogers is Stockholder, Director, President and General Manager of the business.

Major Rogers was always a Republican and cast his first vote for Abraham Lincoln, but has never been a delegate to important conventions, nor held political office. He belongs to the following organizations: First Congregational Church, of Detroit; Union Lodge of Strict Observance, Free and Accepted Masons, Detroit; Michigan Commandery Military Order of the Loyal Legion of the United States; Detroit Post No. 384, G. A. R.; Lake St. Clair Fishing and Shooting Club, North Channel Club, and the Fellowcraft Club. He was married May 7th, 1868, at San Francisco, Cal., to Eva C. Adams. She died January 19th, 1892. He was again married May 7th, 1895, at Rochester, N. Y., to Grace J. Haynes, but has no living children.

MORSE ROHNERT, the youngest judge on the Wayne Circuit Bench, was born in Detroit, February 29th, 1864. He is the son of Franz L. Rohnert, who died January 18th, 1886, and Eleonore Rohnert, who died May 11th, 1900. Both his parents were natives of Wittenberg, Province of Saxony, Prussia. They settled in Detroit, Mich., in 1850, and resided there until the time of their death. His father's father operated woolen mills in Germany. His mother's father was engaged in commercial business and was prominent in municipal affairs in his native City.

Morse Rohnert was educated in the public schools of Detroit, and graduated from the Detroit High School. He continued his education in the University of Michigan, graduating from there in 1883 at the age of nineteen years and four months with the degree of A. B. He was the youngest scholar in his class and finished a four years' course in three years. After graduating from the University of Michigan, he entered the law office of John G. Hawley, of Detroit, with whom he studied law until his admission to the bar on March 13th, 1885. He then began the practice of law and continued the same up to June 1st, 1886. He then entered the Probate Court of Wayne County, as Journal Clerk under Probate Judge Durfee. He remained in the Probate Office, first as Journal Clerk and then as Deputy Register until January 1st, 1896, when he resigned therefrom and resumed the practice of law. He continued the practice of his profession until January 1st, 1900, when, having been elected Circuit Judge, he entered upon the duties of that office.

Judge Rohnert has always been a Republican in politics, his first Presidential vote being for Harrison in 1888. He has always been an active worker on behalf of his party. From January 1st, 1896, to January 1st, 1899, he was Secretary of the Wayne County Republican Committee, and as such, conducted the County campaign of his party to its triumphant victory in 1896.

He is a member of the Harmonie Society of Detroit; Knights of Pythias; Benevolent and Protective Order of Elks; A. I. U.; Concordia; Westphalia Shooting Club and the Detroit Greys.

He was married in Milwaukee, February 20th, 1895, to Emma Uihlein, of that City. They have two children, Eleonore Adele, born May 16th, 1896, and Helen Dorothy, born February 3rd, 1898.

ALFRED RUSSELL, for many years one of the foremost lawyers in the West, was born at Plymouth, Grafton County, N. H., March 18th, 1830. The Russell family came from Bedfordshire, England, to Massachusetts, in 1660. Alfred Russell's father was William Wallace Russell, son of Hon. Moor Russell, an officer in the Revolution, and for many years State Councilor of New Hampshire. The father of Moor, Pelatiah Russell, was an officer in the Colonial Army and lost his life at the siege of Fort William Henry. Alfred's mother, Susan Carleton Webster, was the daughter of Humphrey Webster, whose great grandfather came to America from Ipswich, England, and settled in Ipswich, Mass., in 1648. She was born in Salisbury, N. H., in the house next to that in which her kinsman, Hon. Daniel Webster, was born. Alfred Russell's paternal great grandfather, David Webster, was Colonel of the Fourteenth New Hampshire Regiment in the Battle of Saratoga, the decisive battle of the American Revolution. His mother's brother, Humphrey Webster, left Middlebury College to enter the army in the War of 1812, and fell at Lundy's Lane.

Alfred Russell, with his hereditary traits of intelligence, accentuated by the union of two such families, early gave evidence of great promise. He was carefully educated in the best schools of New Hampshire, attending Holmes Academy in Plymouth, Gilmanton Academy in Gilmanton, Kimball Union Academy, Meridan Village, Plainfield and Dartmouth College, from which he graduated second in the class of 1850, Justice Brooks, of Canada, being first. He had at an early age decided upon the profession of the law as his life calling, and on graduating from Dartmouth he entered the office of William C. Thompson, at Plymouth, a son of the preceptor of Daniel Webster. Later Mr. Russell attended the law department of Harvard University, graduating with the degree of Bachelor of Laws in 1852. He wrote a prize essay on the Law of Landlord and Tenant. He was admitted to the bar at Meredith Bridge, now Laconia, N. H., in October, 1852, when twenty-two years old, and removed to Detroit in November following. James F. Joy was then in active practice, and the young man from New Hampshire found his office a safe harbor. He formed a partnership the following year with Judge C. I. Walker, and his brother, which continued until 1861, at which time, at the age of thirty-one, he was appointed by President Lincoln United States District Attorney for Michigan, which is the only office he ever held. This office, during war time, in a frontier State, was one of great responsibility and labor. Mr. Seward, Secretary of

State, sent him on diplomatic missions to Canada, in connection with the St. Albans Raid and the Lake Erie Raid. The suspension of the Habeas Corpus, the Internal Revenue Laws, and the Draft Laws during that period, required a vast amount of labor and judicious administration.

Mr. Russell imbibed the principles of Republicanism with his earliest breath, and brought with him from New Hampshire's hills that love of freedom, and that sense of justice and equality of all men before the law, which led to the formation of the Republican party in Michigan. He took an active part in its organization, being associated, although much younger, with Governor Austin Blair, Senator Zachariah Chandler, the two Howards, Governor Bingham and others whose names afterwards became identified prominently with the party and the State. He was President of the Michigan Republican Club in the Fremont campaign, and also during the Lincoln campaigns, and spoke during the canvass at mass meetings with Hon. Salmon P. Chase and other leaders. He took part in both the political campaigns of General Grant and those of Hayes, Garfield, Harrison and McKinley; and indeed he has been an active participant in the great battles of the party to which he early gave adherence and to which he loyally clung. He has never sought political office of any kind, although he was strongly supported in 1880, and again in 1889, for a vacancy on the United States Supreme Court Bench. Under one Administration he declined the German mission and under another an offer of membership in the Interstate Commerce Commission. He has uniformly refused judicial as well as political office.

When traveling abroad Mr. Russell met Mr. Bryce, author of the "American Commonwealth," and was the first to call that author's attention to the work of Judge Cooley. His aid is acknowledged by Mr. Bryce in the preface of his third edition. He has instructed many students in the law, and some eminent lawyers have graduated from his office, including Judge Henry B. Brown, Associate Justice of the Supreme Court of the United States.

While he has been a very busy and active practitioner in the profession, Mr. Russell has found time for other and congenial occupation as a member of the Michigan Historical Society, as President of the Detroit Club, Vice-President of the Young Men's Society, President of the Michigan Political Science Association, a member of the Webster Historical Society, the Society of the Sons of the American Revolution, and of the Society of Colonial Wars. The study of history and literature has been his pastime and pleasure. Besides addresses at the University of Michigan, he delivered the commencement address at Dartmouth College, in 1878, his subject being "Some Effects of the Growth of Cities on our Political System," and in August, 1891, he delivered the annual address before the American Bar Association at Boston on "Avoidable Causes of Delay and Uncertainty in Our Courts." His address before so important a body was most favorably noticed and attracted wide attention. He has been a contributor of numerous articles to law journals and other periodicals. Dartmouth conferred upon him in 1891, the degree of LL. D.

Mr. Russell's career as a lawyer has been full of activity. In 1858, at the age of twenty-eight, he was admitted to the bar of the United States Supreme Court, and argued the case of Allen vs. Newberry (21 Howard 244), involving a question of Constitutional law, and Cordes vs. Steamer Niagara (21 Howard 7), being the first discussion in the Supreme Court on the Act of Congress of 1851, limiting the liability of shipowners. Both of these cases have been frequently cited since that time. Of other cases in which he has appeared in the United States Supreme Court, there is not space here to enter into detail, but they include many important ones, some of which are often cited. His name is found in every volume of the Michigan Reports from Volume IV. to Volume CXX. and frequently in the Federal Reporter and other United States Reports. He is a laborious student, preparing his cases thoroughly. His retentive memory, wide experience and long practice makes his ready familiarity with decisions appear almost miraculous.

Mr. Russell has been a close student all his life and very fond of literature, not only that of our own tongue, but also French and German. At the age of ten he wrote a translation of the first half of "Cicero de Senectute." He has been identified with the community interests of Detroit. He was one of the founders and President of the Detroit Club. He was a Director of the Chamber of Commerce at the inception of the enterprise, and was instrumental in procuring legislation for it and selecting a site for the building. He delivered the dedicatory address at the opening of the Detroit City Hall. He was one of the founders and charter members of the Detroit Light Guard, in 1855, which furnished eighty general officers in the Civil War. He was also one of the founders of the Detroit Boat Club. He has prepared and secured the passage of some amendments to the Constitution and many of the general statutes. He is general attorney in Michigan and Canada for the Wabash Railroad.

In religion he has been a consistent and active member of St. Paul's Church, Episcopal. He was married October 28th, 1857, to Mrs. Ellen P. England, born Wells, of St. Albans, Vt., whose family was founded in Connecticut by the first Colonial Governor, Thomas Wells, and who is herself an authoress of repute and a social leader, as well as active in benevolent and patriotic societies. Major Daniel T. Wells, U. S. V., was her brother. She has been on the Board of every organized charity in Detroit, and President of the Daughters of 1812. "London Society," "Christmas Stories," etc., are among her works. Mr. and Mrs. Russell have four daughters, all of whom possess distinct talent. The daughters are Mrs. Richard P. Paulison, daughter of Mrs. Russell, of Jacksonville, Fla.; Mrs. John C. Glenny, of Buffalo, N. Y., who attained high rank at the Julien School of Art, in Paris, and whose productions in oil and water colors have been "hung on the line" in New York and Paris exhibitions; she is the President of the Art League in Buffalo and has given an impetus to art culture there; Mrs. Phoebe Hewitt Roberts, of Detroit, as Phoebe Russell, exhibited dramatic talent of a high order in Daly's Company in New York, London and Paris, receiving the approbation of the most eminent critics of those cities, in Shakesperian characters; Mrs. Louisa Brooks Maugham, of Chicago.

Mr. Russell has recently published a book entitled, "The Police Power of the State, with Decisions Thereon as Illustrating the Development and Value of Case Law." This work is highly commended by the profession.

FREDERICK JOSIAH RUSSELL, of Hart, Oceana County, is not only one of the ablest jurists in Michigan, but has also contributed largely to the material advancement of his portion of the State. He was born at Orion, Oakland County, October 7th, 1841, being the sixth out of ten children born to Josiah and Harriett Russell. His father was a pioneer in Michigan, an energetic, capable man, and a natural leader. He came West when the Erie Canal furnished the best means of travel across New York State, and settled in Oakland County the year after Michigan was admitted to the Union. He was a farmer, but also had some practice in law, although never admitted to the bar. He was County Judge in Ionia and Montcalm Counties, and opened the first Court of Record in Montcalm County. He was afterwards Judge of Probate in Oceana County, drifted to the lumber business at Greenville, and then into farming and surveying in Oceana County. He was County Surveyor in that County and was State Senator from the Montcalm District.

Josiah Russell and his wife were both thrifty, enterprising people and for a time prospered as the country grew, but when the subject of this sketch was still quite young they lost their property, and the lad was put to the necessity of pushing his own way. He had received common school advantages, but was ambitious for something better, and put his whole energies into the work of attaining a superior education. Up to the time when he was sufficiently advanced to begin teaching, he worked on the farm or at any other employment he could find in the summer, and attended school winters, doing chores for his board. He attended school at Cook's Corners, Ionia County, where he had, as a companion, a future Judge of the Supreme Court, Allen B. Morse, and during the summers of 1861-2 he attended the State Normal School at Ypsilanti. In August of the latter year, with patriotic purpose, he enlisted in the Twenty-first and Twenty-sixth Michigan Infantry, but was rejected by the Examining Board on account of his condition, he being then threatened with consumption, which developed the following spring in serious form. He afterwards found time to study law with books borrowed from John Morse, father of Judge Morse, and he was admitted to the bar September 20th, 1866. From this time on his advancement was rapid, for he not only speedily acquired a wide and remunerative practice, but was soon honored by his fellow citizens with their franchises for public positions. He had previously been Deputy County Clerk and Register of Deeds, and in January, 1867, he was appointed Clerk of the Probate Court of Oceana County. At the election in 1868 he was nominated for the office of Circuit Court Commissioner, receiving in the ensuing election 1,061 votes, to his opponent's 3, and in 1870 he was re-elected by 930 votes, his opponent receiving 4. Soon after the expiration of his term in this office, in 1871, he was appointed Judge of Probate, and in the election in November, 1872, he was elected to that office, and was again elected November 7th, 1876. He was, on January 5th, 1881, appointed by Governor Jerome, Judge of the Fourteenth Judicial Circuit, which was then composed of Oceana, Muskegon, Newaygo and Mecosta Counties, to fill a vacancy caused by the resignation of Judge Michael Brown, and at the ensuing election he was nominated and elected to that position without opposition. He served in this capacity until January, 1888, then, at the expiration of his term, he retired to private life, again taking up the practice of the law, and, in addition, looking after his own interests. In 1893 he was again called to the bench, being elected Judge of the same Circuit, then reduced to the Counties of Muskegon and Oceana, and in 1899 he was re-elected.

These repeated elections to a position in which he had already been tried, furnish the highest tribute to Judge Russell's fitness for the judicial office. The Circuit is an important one, including as it does, one of the largest lumbering and manufacturing cities in Michigan. Of his qualifications for the bench a prominent attorney, who has practiced before him, says: "Judge Russell has a thorough knowledge of the law, and a fine discrimination in respect to its nicer points; is very familiar with the decisions of the higher courts, and renders his own decisions in lucid terms. He is impartial, is courteous to attorneys, and is popular both with the profession and with litigants." This estimate of Judge Russell is a fair statement of the esteem in which he is held, and which has led to frequent mention of his name as an eminently worthy candidate for a Supreme Court Judgeship.

Judge Russell has very extensive business interests outside of his law practice and his judicial duties. He commenced farming at Hart in 1865, and to him more than any other person is due the introduction of Shorthorn cattle and Merino sheep into Oceana County. For several years he had 1,500 sheep but, as he says, during the Cleveland Administration the "business went Democratic" and he went out of it. He still keeps up his interest in cattle raising and has, on his fine farm, about 125 head of the best stock. In 1875 he engaged in the banking business, and is now senior member of the Citizens' Exchange Bank at Hart, the pioneer banking institution of that

Fred. J. Russell

place. In 1883 he assisted in organizing the Merchants' National Bank of Muskegon, and went on its Board of Directors. In 1888 he assisted in organizing the Union National Bank of Muskegon, becoming one of its principal stockholders. He was one of the principal organizers and the first President of the Hart Improvement Company, a corporation organized to build a hotel and make other improvements in the town, which has successfully accomplished its objects. He is still President of the company. He was also one of the organizers of the Muskegon Electric Light Company, of which he was Vice-President, and was a liberal subscriber and active worker in inducing the Chicago & West Michigan Railway Company to extend its road to Hart, which was done in the summer of 1880. He assisted in organizing the Oceana County Agricultural Society, and was its President for a number of years, finally declining a re-election. He assisted in organizing the West Michigan Agricultural Society at Grand Rapids and has been one of its Directors ever since. He has taken considerable interest in fruit growing, was a Director of the State Horticultural Society for a term, a Director of the West Michigan Horticultural Society for a term, and President of that society for a term. He now has an orchard of seventy-five acres. He is also President of the Hart Cedar & Lumber Company. These interests alone, aside from his law and judicial duties, would absorb the entire attention of a less capable man.

Mr. Russell has been a Republican from the start, his first vote being cast for Lincoln. He has been a delegate to many State Conventions and has been often heard with good effect on the stump. His society affiliations are with Wyton Lodge No. 251, Hart; Oceana Chapter, Pentwater; Oceana Council, Pentwater; Muskegon Commandery No. 22, Muskegon; Blue Lake Fishing and Hunting Club; Michigan Club, and Lincoln Club, of Grand Rapids. He was married October 10th, 1867, at Ionia, to Miss Ellen C. Gurney. Their children now living are Nellie W. S., now Mrs. William F. Lyon, Jr.; Lucy Hayes and Mamie.

JASON EDGAR ST. JOHN is best known to the people of Michigan from his long connection with the State Institution at Lansing, formerly called the Reform School, but now known as the Industrial School for Boys. He was born at Somerset, Hillsdale County, Michigan, May 30th, 1848, and can boast of as old a New England ancestry as any one in the State. There were three brothers St. John who came over in the Mayflower, and he is descended from one of them, Samuel, who settled in Connecticut. His father, Jason St. John, sailed, in his earlier days, as supercargo, between New York and Mexico, later was a brick mason; came to Michigan in 1836; went to California in 1849; stayed there a few years and then returned to the Peninsular State. His wife's name was Lucy A. St. John.

The son, Jason Edgar, attended the public schools of Jackson County winters, working during the summer. His mother died when he was three years old, and he, with a sister two years older, and the father, constituted the family. His first outside work was selling goods behind a counter, which he commenced to do when he was thirteen years old. He left school finally when he was sixteen, being obliged to take care of himself entirely from that time. He sold goods for ten years at different places, and then in 1871 embarked in mercantile business for himself, at the same time taking to himself, as a partner of his joys and sorrows, Miss Addie Bulen, of Dansville, Ingham County. In 1872 they became connected with the Reform School, a connection which they have retained ever since, with the exception of ten months which they spent in Mason, where Mr. St. John had an interest in a flouring mill, and eighteen months spent on their farm near the Agricultural College. August 1, 1893, Mr. St. John was appointed Superintendent of the Reform School, and no better appointment could have been made. During nineteen years which he had spent there as a subordinate officer, he occupied almost every position in the Institution, became thoroughly acquainted with all its workings and received a training which fitted him well for the more responsible position to which he was appointed. His wife has had equally good training for her position as Matron. Both are fascinated with the work among the half-bad boys that get into the Institution, and are giving the State very valuable service. Mr. St. John has always been a Republican and cast his first vote for Grant. He has never held political office and has been too much absorbed in his institutional duties to devote much time to political work.

WILLIAM SAVIDGE, for the past dozen years connected with one of the large lumber firms of the Michigan west shore, was born at Spring Lake, Mich., September 30th, 1863. His father, Hunter Savidge, was one of the founders of the firm of Cutler & Savidge, and his mother was Sarah C. Patten. The son was educated in the Spring Lake Schools, the Grand Rapids High School, Michigan University, class of 1884, and was in Harvard Law School in 1886 and 1887. After leaving the latter he spent one year in foreign travel, and then became connected with the lumbering firm mentioned above. He is now Vice-President of that company, a Director in the Challenge Corn Planter Company of Grand Haven, the National Bank in the same City and the Grand Rapids Fire Insurance Company.

In politics he is Republican, cast his first vote for James G. Blaine in 1884, and was a member of the Republican State Central Committee in 1894-6. He never was a candidate for office till 1896, when he was elected by the large majority of 3,175 to the State Senate from the Twenty-third District, comprising the Counties of Muskegon and Ottawa. Mr. Savidge is a member of the Detroit Club, Yondo-

A. J. Sawyer

tega Club, Detroit; Country Club, Detroit; Peninsular Club, Grand Rapids; Chicago Yacht Club, Columbia Yacht Club, Chicago, and Spring Lake Yacht Club.

ANDREW JACKSON SAWYER, of Ann Arbor, is well known throughout the State as lawyer, legislator and politician, and has put thorough study, sound judgment and ready speech into all three spheres of influence and action. He was the youngest of seven children and was born November 18th, 1834, in the Town of Caroline, Tompkins County, N. Y. His father, Abraham Sawyer was a business man and was engaged at the same time in farming, keeping a hotel, running a blacksmith shop and carriage shop, and grocery business. His mother's name was Polly Phillips Sawyer. His ancestors, both upon the father's and mother's side, were English. They trace their lineage to Sir Robert Sawyer, the Attorney General of England. His grandfather, Rev. John Sawyer, acquired considerable reputation as "The Blind Preacher," having lost his eyesight at the age of thirty, but continuing to preach until he was past eighty.

When the son was ten years of age, his father's entire property was swept away from him because of his endorsing for others. At the age of fourteen the lad struck out for himself, after the old plan which so many have struggled through of working upon a farm summers and attending school winters. At the age of seventeen he began teaching and attending school alternately. In 1856 he graduated from Starkey Seminary, Yates County, N. Y., and in 1857 came to Michigan, located at Mason and began to study law in the office of H. P. Henderson and afterwards in the office of O. M. Barnes. He was admitted to the bar while principal of the Union School at Mason, in 1860. In December, 1860, he moved to Washtenaw County, formed a copartnership with James T. Honey, and began the practice of the law at Chelsea. In 1861 Mr. Honey moved to Dexter and the partnership was dissolved. In 1873 he moved to Ann Arbor and formed a partnership with the late Judge Edwin Lawrence. At the end of the first year the Judge retired from practice and in 1879 Mr. Sawyer formed a partnership with Jerome C. Knowlton, which continued over a period of about ten years, when Mr. Knowlton was appointed Professor in the law department of the University, and the partnership dissolved. In July, 1900, he formed a partnership with his son, Andrew J. Sawyer, Jr., which partnership still exists, under the title of A. J. Sawyer & Son.

In politics Mr. Sawyer is and has always been a Republican. In 1856 he took an active part in the Fremont campaign and his first vote was cast for the Pathfinder. Since that time he has been a member of the Republican party, has taken an active interest in every campaign, County, State and National, and was a delegate to nearly every State Convention, unless prevented by business or illness, from 1864 until the Pingree influence in the party, with which he was not in accord, became dominant in Washtenaw County.

Mr. Sawyer was a member of the House of Representatives in 1877-79-97 and of the special session of 1898, and took an active and useful part in each session. In the House of 1877 there was an onslaught on the appropriations for the University, the Agricultural College and the State Normal School, and Mr. Sawyer, with his colleague, Captain Allen, of the Ypsilanti District, were recognized by everyone at Lansing as the two staunchest and ablest defenders and protectors of these great educational institutions. Mr. Sawyer was second upon the Judiciary Committee of the session of 1877, Chairman of that committee in 1879, and Chairman of the same committee in 1897 and the special session of 1898. He was the author of a number of measures which passed into law at each of said sessions, none of which have been declared unconstitutional. He introduced the first bill to provide a Home for Little Girls, which, in the session of 1879, was changed somewhat in form and has now ripened into what is known as the Industrial School for Girls at Adrian. Jointly with Hon. E. F. Conely, of Detroit, he was the author of the present system of drawing juries in Michigan, except some minor changes since made. He was also the author of the present law providing that the original files in chancery cases be sent up on appeal to the Supreme Court. He was the author of the law providing for the treatment at the University of Michigan, of the children of indigent people, that are afflicted with curable malady, or deformity at birth, and providing for the expenses to be paid by the State; also of the statute providing for the analysis by the University of Michigan, free of charge, of water in use by the public in certain cases where disease is supposed to have arisen from the use of such water. Jointly with Representative Foote, of Kalamazoo, he was the author of the statute authorizing the Judge of Probate to issue a license and perform the marriage ceremony when necessary for the protection of the reputation and good name of girls under the age of consent in certain cases, and also framed a number of other measures of less importance.

Mr. Sawyer has been very successful in his practice; has been engaged in all the important cases arising in the County for a number of years past, and has been engaged in a large number of cases, both civil and criminal, in many other counties in the State, and in various other states. His greatest success has been in jury trials, and by careful and painstaking efforts he has succeeded in securing from the Supreme Court of Michigan a recognition of standing at the bar of which he has reason to be proud, and notably in the case of North vs. Joslyn, 59 Mich. 624. On page 646, in speaking of his efforts in the case, the Court says: "It is well for this unfortunate woman that she had one child who had both the heart and courage to stand by her old mother in these attacks upon her right to liberty and to her

Walter H. Sawyer

property, and it is a satisfaction for us to know that she has been fortunate enough in the end to secure the aid of counsel whose ability and integrity have not failed her, and knowing their client's rights, will faithfully see that they are not imperiled, but enforced and protected." Perhaps the greatest public notice he ever received in an effort before a jury was in the conviction of Hand, for the murder of Pulver, and in all the publications of which he has been the author, the article upon the treatment of criminals after conviction has attracted the widest attention, having been published both in this and the old country, and exciting extensive criticism in both the secular and religious journals.

Mr. Sawyer's life has been one of constant toil. For thirty years he has rarely gone to bed before twelve o'clock or been in bed after six a. m., except during the months of July and August, when he has aimed to suspend active business.

Mr. Sawyer is a member of the Masonic Fraternity and attends the Methodist Episcopal Church. His family consists of wife, to whom he was married at Mason, Mich., August 7th, 1858, her maiden name being Lucy Skinner, and three children, Fred Sawyer, of Milan; Lorenzo Sawyer and Andrew J. Sawyer, Jr., of Ann Arbor.

WALTER HULME SAWYER, of Hillsdale, Mich., was born August 10th, 1861, in Lyme, Huron County, Ohio, his parents being George Sawyer, a farmer, and Julia A. Sawyer. The grandparents came from England in the early '20's, settled in Lyme Township and were prosperous farmers. Walter worked on his father's farm at Grass Lake, Michigan, and attended the high school, graduating in 1881. The next year he entered the medical department of the State University, graduating in 1884, and for a year subsequent to that was house-surgeon in the Homeopathic hospital He began the practice of regular medicine in Hillsdale in July, 1885, and was married to Harriett B. Mitchell, daughter of Charles T. Mitchell, of that place, in 1888. They have one son, Thomas Mitchell Sawyer, aged eleven years. Mr. Sawyer is a member of the State Central Committee from the Third District, but has held no elective office. He is a trustee of Hillsdale College, and a member of the School Board; also Trustee of Oak Grove Hospital at Flint; of the Buchanan Screen Works at Hillsdale, and the Omega Portland Cement Company at Mosherville, Mich. He is a member of the American Medical Association, the Michigan State Medical Society, the Tri-State Medical Society, and corresponding member of the Detroit Academy of Medicine, and also a member of the Detroit Club.

IRA TERRY SAYRE, State Senator from the Thirteenth District, belongs to a family that were among the early invaders of England, as well as of New England. His paternal ancestors are descended from Roger De Saher, who went to England with the Normans in 1066. The family of Sayre have been residents of Bedfordshire, England, since about 1300, as shown by church and other records. Thomas Sayre came to America in 1634, and in 1638 built a house at Southampton, Long Island, which is still standing and is supposed to be the oldest English house in America. In this house the grandfather of Ira T. Sayre was born. His maternal ancestors are all descendants from Richard Terry, who also came from England and settled at Southold, L. I., in 1637.

The subject of this sketch was the son of Augustus Sayre, a farmer, and of Sarah E. Terry, and was born in the Township of Hector, Schuyler County, N. Y., March 6th, 1858. In his early days he worked on the farm and attended the common schools, and later took courses at the Michigan Agricultural College and Michigan University, having taught school winters in order to earn the funds to pay his way. He commenced the practice of law at the age of 22, and is still engaged in that and in farming in the town of Flushing, Genesee County. He has always taken an interest in politics, and has been a Republican from his birth up. He first voted for James A. Garfield, has voted for every Republican candidate for President since then, and expects to do so as long as he lives, unless the party ceases to exist. He has frequently attended State Conventions, and has held several positions of trust, having been Township Clerk six years, Village Clerk six years, Village President, Justice of the Peace, Member of the Board of Control of the Industrial School for Boys, by appointment of Gov. Rich, for six years, and State Senator during the Legislative sessions of 1899 and 1900. He was a very industrious member of the latter body, and was the author of the Anti-Trust Law as it now stands on the books, the law compelling each taxpayer to be sworn, amendments to the law regulating the descent of personal property and others.

Mr. Sayre is a Mason to the 32d degree, a Knight Templar, a member of the Maccabees, of the Loyal Guard, the Grange and about a dozen other beneficiary organizations. He was married August 5th, 1884, at Charlevoix, Mich., to Julia E. Niles, of Flushing, Mich. Their children are Helen Lorraine Sayre, aged 9; Sidney Estelle Sayre, aged 3, and Frank Niles Sayre, aged 3.

CARL ERNEST SCHMIDT, an active and successful business man of Detroit, was born in the same City, his parents being Traugott Schmidt, a tanner, and Wilhelmina Beck. His father was from Thuringia and his mother from Pennsylvania. He studied at the German-American Seminary in Detroit until fourteen and then, until nineteen, in schools in Germany. He learned the trade of a tanner at his father's tannery in Detroit, and was associated with him in business until he died in 1897. Mr. Schmidt has always voted as a Republican. He served as Police Commissioner two years, from July 13th, 1892, but resigned October 5th, 1894, although he had been appointed

Ira T. Sayre

Carl E. Schmidt

for four years. He served as President of the State Board of Arbitration and Mediation for one year, from June 1st, 1897. He belongs to the Detroit Club, the Fellowcraft Club and Harmonie Society, and is a 32d degree Mason. He was married November 4th, 1880, to Alice M. Candler, in Detroit. Their children are Emma W., Alice May and Ida A.

JOHN ANDREW SCHMID, of Detroit, is one of the men who had to make his own way from boyhood, and who has done it successfully. He is the son of John N. Schmid, a mason contractor, and Magdalena M. Schmid, and was born at Monroe, Mich., March 10th, 1856. His father was born in Germany, but at the breaking out of the war, enlisted in the service of his adopted country and died a short time after the close of the war from sickness contracted in the service, leaving a widow and eight children. John A. was next to the oldest and at the age of twelve was obliged to leave home and hustle for himself. What book education he had was received in the public schools at Monroe, and his first work was as clerk in a store, and he has been continuously in some form of active business ever since. He has been a Republican all his life and of late years has received some substantial recognition of his services to the party. He was elected City Clerk of Detroit, November 5th, 1895, by the largest majority any Clerk ever received; was re-elected November 2d, 1897, and was elected for the third time, November 7th, 1899. He was Deputy City Clerk from 1892 to 1895.

Mr. Schmid is a member of the Michigan Club; No. 6 A. O. U. W., Detroit Yacht Club, Knights of the Golden Eagle, Concordia Singing Society, Marshland Club, Detroit Lodge of Elks No. 34, Riverside Lodge No. 303, I. O. O. F.; Zion No. 1, F. & A. M.; Monroe Chapter No. 1, R. A. M.; Michigan Sovereign Consistory, 32d degree; Moslem Temple; Bennett Tent No. 887, K. O. T. M. In Military circles he was one of the organizers of the Detroit Scott Guards and resigned after years of service, as First Lieutenant. He was married at Detroit, June 22d, 1882, to Rosa Erlenbach, and has one daughter, Gertrude A.

G. HENRY SHEARER, a prominent real estate dealer in Bay City, was born in Detroit, January 3d, 1853, son of James Shearer and Margaret J. Hutchison. His father was a builder, architect, lumberman and banker, who, in the course of a long career held a number of public positions, but whose best service to the State was as one of the Commissioners to superintend the construction of the present State Capitol. He, with his public spirited associates, devoted months of time to this duty, made sure that the work was well done, and completed the structure within the appropriation made for the purpose, a thing very unusual in a public building. James

Shearer and his wife were both born in the State of New York, but their parents were Scotch-Irish.

The son received his education in the schools of Detroit and Bay City and the Pennsylvania Military Academy at Chester, Penn. His first work was in and about the lumber mill of J. Shearer & Co., and he has been identified ever since with one form or another of Bay City's industrial interests. He is at present one of the firm of Shearer Bros., real estate dealers, and has been interested in many land companies and in blocks of stores. He has, for many years been a member of the Fire and Water Commissions in Bay City, and is now President of both Commissions.

Mr. Shearer has always been a Republican; worked at the polls for U. S. Grant, before he was of age, and cast his vote for R. B. Hayes. He has no desire for political office, and although he has been offered many different nominations, he has refused them all. Yet he has always been interested in politics and has taken pleasure in helping his friends to positions of trust. He has been in many State Republican Conventions during the past twenty-five years and was elected Chairman of the Bay County Delegates to the State Convention three times in succession, 1896, 1898 and 1900.

Mr. Shearer is a 32d degree Mason, a Mystic Shriner, Knight Templar, Oddfellow, Knight of the Maccabees, member of the Royal Arcanum, the Bay City Club Social, Trustee and member of the First Presbyterian Church, and Vice-President of the Bay County Savings Bank. He was married August 22d, 1876, to Elva D. Culver, daughter of D. Culver, late of Bay City, Mich., but has no children.

HON. CARLOS D. SHELDEN was born June 10, 1840, at Walworth, Walworth County, Wis. His father, Ransom Shelden, of English parentage, was a farmer in Walworth. His mother, Therissa Marie Shelden, was of sturdy Scotch parentage and a worthy helpmeet of his pioneer father.

After exhausting the educational possibilities of Houghton County, to which his father removed in 1847, he was sent as a youth to Ypsilanti to complete his education. When this education was completed—and it is recorded that Carlos D. Shelden was ever a leader among his fellows not only in the pursuit of learning but especially in the youthful exuberance which leads to exhibitions of strength and boyish pranks—C. D. Shelden returned to his father's home and became clerk in his father's store, the largest in what is now Houghton County. It was in this store and under the tutelage of his father that the dominant traits he had inherited became the more marked.

It is here worthy of comment that his training under his father's eye was of the greatest value. That father, Ransom Shelden, was a Whig until the Republican party was born, beneath the oaks of Jackson, and when the party was born Ransom Shelden became one of its founders and one of its most constant and consistent supporters. He

G. Henry Shearer

C. D. Sheldon

enjoyed the warm personal friendship of such grand men as Zachariah Chandler and Austin Blair. He was called "the best Republican in Michigan," because he ever stood steadfast and showed true blue when Republicanism was in question. At every call he contributed both moral and financial support, and he never asked for anything in return. It was under such a watchful eye that Carlos and his brother George received their early training. Until 1862 Carlos D. Shelden served as clerk and confidential man for his father.

When the gun was fired on Sumter and President Lincoln asked for volunteers to support and maintain the Union both the boys had been so taught that they desired to go to the front at once, but owing to the illness of their father they could not do so. C. D. Shelden enlisted in the Twenty-third Infantry in 1862, and his brother in the Sixteenth Michigan Infantry. Captain C. D. Shelden, for he was commissioned at the head of his company, marched to the front and he served wherever duty called him, without lagging and without any question as to his preference. At the close of the war Captain C. D. Shelden laid aside the equipment of conflict and returned to a peaceful life, engaging in mercantile and mechanical pursuits. From 1865 to 1884 he was engaged in the foundry and machine works of his Town, and for the four years following 1884 was a superintendent of the Shelden & Shafer iron mine. Quitting this employment, as it did not possess the room for growth that he desired, he embarked in real estate ventures and every move was attended with success. His fellow townsmen, and the influential people of his County, selected him as one of the Board of Supervisors, and then the Villagers of Houghton chose him for their President, and he served them in this capacity four years. Then he was nominated and elected as member of the Michigan House of Representatives. So well did he acquit himself in this position that on the election in 1894 he was chosen to represent his District in the Michigan State Senate. Carlos D. Shelden became a candidate for Congress in 1896 and graduated from being a member of the Michigan Senate to a seat in the House of Representatives in the United States Congress. He was elected in 1896, re-elected in 1898 and in 1900 obtained 23,000 majority, the largest majority ever given for a Congressman in the Wolverine State.

When the nation needed supporters Carlos D. Shelden was ever ready to respond and his dash in going to the front as Captain of the Twenty-third Michigan Infantry, has been followed all through his career by like abandonment of personal interest in his desire to serve his country.

His bent did not lead him to seek place honors in any campaign and for this reason his record of Conventions attended as delegate is small. He reached his majority in 1861 and his first vote was cast for the Republican candidate for Governor, Hon. Austin Blair, in 1862. His record in politics has been unique, as he never was a candidate for office when the result did not return him a victor.

His Congressional career has been singularly successful. Not being given to orations or finely spun out talks, he accomplished his purpose by that quiet, efficient canvass of the House members which always resulted in his obtaining that for which he labored. He obtained a Postoffice building for Menominee, succeeded in getting better harbors and deeper channels in the waterways of his District, procured for his constituents places of honor and trust under the general government, and it is his unique record that he never recommended for office a man who was not qualified, in every way, to fulfill the position for which he was selected. He was married June 30, 1864, to Miss Mary A. Skiff, daughter of George and Eliza Skiff, of Willoughby, Ohio. One son of this union, R. Skiff Shelden, still survives. Mrs. Mary Skiff Shelden died in 1868, and twenty years later, June 17, 1888, he married Mrs. Sallie W. Gardner, daughter of John W. and Mary A. Dashiell, of Princess Ann, Md.

His first term in Congress was devoted almost entirely to becoming acquainted with his fellow members and the modes of procedure in the House. He did this simply as a means to establish a starting point for his Congressional career. That he chose wisely is manifest, from the fact that he secured all the legislation for which he labored. He introduced sundry bills for the improvement of the waterways in the Twelfth Michigan District and each one of them he passed through the House and most of them were concurred in by the Senate. He took up the work of his predecessor for the building of a Government building at Menominee, and was able to secure the necessary appropriation for the establishment of the building and the purchase of the site. He labored along the lines of necessary legislation and did not devote himself to oratorical displays. As a result of his course he secured as much for his District as any member of Congress could.

RANSOM SHELDEN, resident at different times of several different places in Wisconsin and Michigan, though for nearly two score years the leading citizen of Houghton, was one of the pioneers in that region, and perhaps the most successful of its merchants and mine operators. His life reads like a romance. Born in Essex, N. Y., July 7th, 1814, he spent his early years on his father's farm, and in attending the district school. When sixteen years of age he spent a winter in an academy at Westport, on Lake Champlain. During the following summer, after cradling a field of oats between sunrise and five o'clock in the afternoon, he burst a blood vessel, and was unable to do physical labor for a year and a half. Upon recovering he entered upon a roving life of great business activity. He commenced with buying goods, loaning money, etc., for several merchants of Essex and Westport, and traveled much of the time in Eastern New York and Vermont. After about a year and a half, he returned home. and assisted his father on the farm for two years. In 1836, impelled by a desire to become acquainted with the Western country,

*Ransom Shelden.*

which was fast being settled by the rising generation of New England and New York farmers, he started on a tour of inspection. At Albany he bought a supply of goods, which he sold as he traveled through the settled portions of Ohio, Michigan, Illinois and Wisconsin. He finally settled in Geneva, Walworth County, Wis., when there was but one house in the place. In 1836 he removed from there to the head of Geneva Lake, where, after procuring three yoke of oxen and a plow, and hiring three or four men, he commenced making claims and building houses on the State line of Illinois. He built twenty houses during the summer, all but one of which he sold as fast as they were completed, netting a good income. August 26th, 1839, he married Miss Therissa M. Douglass, whose father owned a large farm on the Big Foot Prairie. In partnership with his brother-in-law, Mr. Shelden undertook to cultivate his father-in law's farm; but, on account of its great distance from market, and the appearance of the rust, which greatly damaged 260 acres of wheat, they sustained great loss in their first year's labor. In 1842 Mr. Shelden removed to his farm in Illinois; the climate did not agree with him, however, and in a year and a half he sold out and returned to Geneva, Wis. For two years, he operated a butcher, blacksmith and cooper shop at Geneva; and, with a team and plow, broke prairie lands for new farms. About that time, his brother-in-law, C. C. Douglass, who had been connected with Dr. Douglass Houghton in conducting a geological survey of the Upper Peninsula of Michigan, and had settled at Eagle River, urged him to remove to that region as a means of curing his fever and ague. Accordingly, in September, 1846, he sold out his business at Geneva, and started for the Lake Superior country. Being obliged to wait a week at Mackinaw, and ten days at Sault Ste. Marie, for boats, his journey to Copper Harbor occupied nearly a month. From there he traveled on foot to Eagle River, where he was met by his brother-in-law. They soon afterwards formed a partnership in the mercantile business, taking a quantity of goods to the Methodist Mission, near L'Anse. In the spring of 1847, Mr. Shelden went to Portage Entry, where he built a store and house, then moved his family, consisting of wife and two boys, from Wisconsin, and carried on business. At this time he traveled quite extensively, making explorations for mineral lands, and, in 1850, when the Government put its lands into market, he procured twenty eighty-acre lots. In the fall of 1851, Mr. Shelden took charge of the Quincy, which, with a number of other copper mines, had been worked to some extent and abandoned. He put a force of men on the mine; opened two new shafts, and, in the course of a year or two, developed the mine to such an extent as to insure its success. During the succeeding winter, he visited Detroit, and disposed of part of his lands to a copper mining company which was then organized. With the proceeds of this sale, he purchased other mining lands in the vicinity of Portage Lake. He formed a partnership with his brother-in-law, investing in mineral lands which had been explored and were considered of value. The impetus given to the copper-mining interests by the formation of companies and sales of land, brought many miners and operators to Houghton; and Mr. Shelden, having removed his store to that place, furnished the supplies for the Quincy and other mines.

In the few years succeeding 1852 he organized a number of mines, including the Portage, Isle Royale, Mesnard, Ripley, Columbian, Huron, Dodge, Jefferson, Franklin, North Star, Concord and Arcadian, all in the Portage district. He was appointed managing agent for each, being at one time agent for twelve different mines. In 1862 he sold his store at Houghton in order to devote his time to the management of his large property. He reorganized the Quincy mine, increased its capital from $200,000 to $500,000, then the extreme limit allowed by law, installed a new manager, and in two years it was paying dividends, being the first mine in the Portage district to make such a return on the investment. It has since divided more money among its stockholders than any other mine in the whole copper region except the Calumet & Hecla.

An incident is related of one of Mr. Shelden's earliest ventures, which was characteristic of the man. When he first arrived at Copper Harbor his possessions consisted of a wife and two small children, two strong arms, a clear head to discern opportunities and a readiness to avail himself of them. He found a potato famine at Copper Harbor. Without a dollar in the world he chartered a small coasting schooner, went to L'Anse, and secured a cargo of potatoes on credit, returned to Copper Harbor, and sold out at a profit of $300 above all expenses. That $300 was the foundation of one of the largest landed estates in the country.

When Mr. Shelden went to Portage Entry in 1847 his trade was almost entirely with the Indians. The house in which the family lived was built of logs, but the store and warehouse were of framed and sawed lumber, and were the admiration of every Indian within trading distance. The nearest white neighbor was at L'Anse, twelve miles distant across Keweenaw Bay, and twice that far by land. The Shelden boys roamed the forest and lake shore with Indians, hardening their muscles and learning wood-craft and the Chippewa language at the same time.

Mr. Shelden's investments almost all proved profitable to himself as they were of benefit to the region which he explored. He was one of the shrewdest judges of mineral values in the district, and his successes and enterprise did much to bring in outside capital for investment. He was active in politics, as well as in business, and was one of the men who was instrumental in bringing the Upper Peninsula around from its old Democratic faith into the Republican ranks. At his death, in 1878, he left a family of three sons, Carlos D., George C. and Ransom B., the first of whom is now a member of Congress from the Twelfth Michigan District.

JAMES MELVILLE SHEPARD, now United States Consul at Hamilton, Canada, was born November 24th, 1842, in Massachusetts. His parents were Rev. James Shepard, of the New England M. E. Conference, and Lucy Bush, his wife. The ancestors on both sides were English. Rev. Thomas Shepard, founder of Harvard College, and General Shepard, of Revolutionary and Congressional fame, were of the family; also many English and New England clergymen. He had his education in the Boston and Cambridge public schools; Wilbraham Academy, and Wesleyan University, at Middletown, Conn.; and subsequently studied medicine and dentistry in Boston. His first occupations were teaching and commercial traveling, and in the War of the Rebellion he served in both the Union Volunteer Army and Navy. In 1868 he settled at Cassopolis, Mich., and practiced dentistry until 1870, when he purchased the Vigilant, which became a leading Republican paper of the Fourth District. He has continued its publication to the present time.

Mr. Shepard was born an Abolitionist, and carried torches for Fremont and Dayton in 1856. He cast his first vote for General Grant; was in the Naval service in 1864 with no provision for voting. He generally attended State Conventions from 1870 to 1896. He was State Senator in the session of 1879. Here among other measures he introduced and pushed the measure called the "Police Bill," which established the present system of regulating the liquor traffic. He has also filled acceptably the following positions: Clerk of the Committee on Territories in the National House of Representatives during the second session of the Forty-seventh Congress; Private Secretary to Senator Thomas W. Palmer, and Secretary to the Senate Committees on Fisheries and Agriculture in the Forty-eighth, Forty-ninth and Fiftieth Congresses; member of the Executive Committee of the Republican State Central Committee from 1880 to 1886; Secretary to the President of the World's Columbian Exposition, 1890 to 1898, of which he prepared the final reports; member of the State Board of Corrections and Charities, 1895 to 1898. He was commissioned Consul of the United States at Hamilton, Canada, Province of Ontario, July 17th, 1897, and still holds that position.

Mr. Shepard is a member of Chi Psi, the G. A. R., Michigan Club from its inception, and several social clubs and fraternities. He was married November 28th, 1870, at Cassopolis, Mich., to Alice M. Martin. Their children are Melville J. and Blanche, now Mrs. E. W. Porter, of Newark, N. J.

THEODORE F. SHEPARD, of Bay City, one of the most prominent and successful lawyers of Northeastern Michigan, was born in Livingston County, N. Y., June 14th, 1844. His father, Howell Shepard, was a native of Yates County, in the same State, an industrious farmer, highly esteemed by his neighbors, and subsequently a merchant in Alleghany County, where he died in 1860. His mother was

Sarah Rathbun, a native of the State of New York. He was educated in the public schools of his native State and in Alfred University, Allegany County. from which he graduated in 1865. Soon after that he began the study of law at Cuba, N. Y., in the office of Hon. Marshall B. Champlin, who was a distinguished lawyer and for six years Attorney General of the State. After a preliminary course of reading he pursued his studies in the Albany Law School and was admitted to the bar in 1866. He remained with Mr. Champlin another year, then came to Michigan, and opened an office in West Bay City, where he formed a partnership with Hon. C. P. Black. He was not only very successful in his practice, but took an active interest and part in public affairs. In 1872 he was elected Prosecuting Attorney and conducted the business of that office with a vigor and impartiality that soon struck terror to the minds of evil doers. During his term of office law-breaking was reduced to a minimum, and many of the law schools and resorts of crime were closed up. The reputation which he acquired in this office afterwards brought to him many criminal cases, and for years thereafter he had the leading business in the City in that class of cases.

Subsequently to this commencement of public life Mr. Shepard was City Attorney of West Bay City for several terms and a member of the Board of Education for twelve years, serving as its Chairman during the whole period. He was also President of the Board of Water Commissioners for ten years. In 1890 President Harrison appointed him United States District Attorney for the Eastern District of Michigan, a position which he filled with great acceptance for four years.

Mr. Shepard's father was, in early times, a Whig, but was identified with the organization of the Republican party, and the son has never been anything but a Republican. He was Chairman of the Congressional District Committee for several years, has been a member of the State Central Committee, and has done good work on the stump. He was a delegate to the National Convention in Cincinnati that nominated Hayes for President, and has been a delegate to almost every Republican State Convention for the past twenty-five years. He has always been active and interested in everything that concerns the success of the party to which he belongs. The only offices he has held have been in connection with the profession of law and education. At this writing he holds the office of Judge of the Eighteenth Judicial Circuit, which is composed of Bay County.

Mr. Shepard was married at Cuba, N. Y., in January, 1868, to Mary M. Randolph, daughter of S. S. Randolph, a native of the Empire State. The children of the marriage were three; Howell G. Shepard, a young man now thirty-two years of age; Lottie E. and Mamie E., daughters, the first dying at the age of six years, and the latter during the year 1900, in her twenty-sixth year, leaving only the son remaining.

V. R. Shepard

LOREN ALBERT SHERMAN, an active business man and one of the most prominent Republicans of the Seventh Congressional District, first saw the light, March 14th, 1844, at Bennington, Wyoming County, N. Y. His father was Albert Clark Sherman, a farmer and merchant, descended from that branch of the Connecticut family of Shermans who had their residence in Woodbury, Litchfield County. His mother's maiden name was Mary Ann Scotford, descended from an English family who came to this country about 1808. The son was educated at Olivet and Hillsdale Colleges. His first occupation was as clerk in grocery, hat, dry goods and book stores. He enlisted in the First Michigan Infantry, Company G, August, 1861; was afterwards appointed hospital steward, and was discharged July 31st, 1862, for disability incurred during the "Seven Days Battles." He entered the office of the Adrian Expositor in 1864, first as bookkeeper and afterwards became editor; joined the editorial staff of the Detroit Daily Post in April, 1866, holding the position of Night and State Editor three and one-half years, and Managing Editor one year. He became editor and publisher of the Port Huron Weekly Times in October, 1870; started the Tri-Weekly Times in 1871 and the Daily Times in 1872, and the latter has continued without missing an issue since that year. In addition to his newspaper business Mr. Sherman was the organizer and is the principal stockholder of the Riverside Printing Company and the Sherman Company; is Secretary of the White Stone Company; Organizer, President and Manager of the Port Huron Auditorium Company, and Organizer, President and Manager of The Deepspring Co., owning the mineral bath house of that name.

He was Chairman of the Port Huron Republican City Committee eight years, Secretary of the County Committee six years, to 1879; has attended many Republican State Conventions, and has never voted any other than the Republican ticket. He was member of the Board of Education of the City of Port Huron six years and was appointed Postmaster April 1st, 1899. He is a member of the Port Huron and Michigan Clubs and many associations and societies. He was married September 6th, 1865, to Estelle C. Ward, at Adrian. The children living are Frederick W., born February 3rd, 1867; Edith W., born March 20th, 1873.

ELLIOTT TRUAX SLOCUM, one of Detroit's active business men, was born May 15th, 1839, at Trenton, Wayne County, Michigan, son of Giles Bryan Slocum, capitalist, and Sophia Maria Brigham Truax. He is the tenth in descent from Anthony Slocum, one of the forty-six "first and ancient" purchasers of the territory of Cohannet, now Massachusetts. Then came Giles Slocum, the common ancestor of all the Slocums, whose American lineage has been found to date from the seventeenth century. He was born in Somersetshire, England, and settled in Portsmouth Township, Rhode Island, in 1638, where he died in 1682. The mother of Elliott T. Slocum is a native of Wayne County, Mich., and a daughter of Col. Abraham C. Truax, a volunteer in the United States Army at the time of Hull's surrender, and a prominent merchant of Detroit in 1808. In 1817 he moved farther down the river, and located at a place along the river front, where about 1834 he surveyed and laid out the present village of Trenton, which was originally called Truaxton, after him.

Elliott T. Slocum first attended Rev. Moses H. Hunter's Episcopal School for Boys on Grosse Isle, Michigan; then Union College, Schenectady, New York, from which he took the degree of Bachelor of Arts in 1862, and later, in 1869, he took the degree of Master of Arts from the University of Michigan. After leaving college he assisted his father in looking after their large land, lumber and farming interests, and later on he continued in business with his father, enlarging and extending their interests, which have since become widely scattered and valuable. He is largely interested in timbered and other lands in Wayne, Muskegon, Oceana, Newaygo and Kent Counties, Michigan, and is the owner of large tracts of valuable timbered lands in Upper Michigan and Wisconsin. In 1887 he laid out and platted the present village of Slocum's Grove, which is located on Crockery Creek in the midst of one of his large tracts of timber in Muskegon County, and at present a large lumber mill, also a planing mill and charcoal kilns are in operation there. He aided his father in raising men and money and in equipping regiments for the field during the war.

Mr. Slocum has always been a Republican in politics, voted first for Abraham Lincoln and has been a delegate to a great many State Conventions. In 1868 he was elected State Senator from the Third Senatorial District, which was strongly Democratic, and has taken an active part in many other important Senatorial contests.

In 1884 he succeeded his father as trustee to the Saratoga Monument Association of New York, and with George William Curtis, Hon. S. S. Cox, John H. Starin and others took an active part in the erection of one of the finest monuments in the world, on the battlefield of Burgoyne's Surrender at Schuylerville, New York, near the home of his father's family. He was one of the first directors of the Chicago & Canada Southern Railroad, and did much to secure the right of way. It is now a part of the Michigan Central System. He was one of the founders and Vice President of the First National Bank of Whitehall, Michigan, at which place he has still large interests. In 1886 he was appointed Park Commissioner of Detroit, and was in turn Commissioner, Vice President and President of the Board for several years. In 1896 he was appointed by Governor Rich Inspector of the Michigan Military Academy at Orchard Lake. Mr. Slocum is a stockholder in several of the leading banks and corporations in Michigan, and is at present a Director in the Union Trust Company of Detroit. He is a member of the Detroit Club, Michigan Club, Country Club, Fellowcraft Club, Bankers' Club, Church Club, Comedy Club, University Club, etc., and member of the American His-

Elliott T. Slocum

torical Association, Sons of the American Revolution and the University of Michigan Association. He was married July 30th, 1872, to Charlotte Gross, daughter of the late Ransom E. Wood, an old resident and wealthy capitalist of Grand Rapids, Michigan, but has no children. Mrs. Slocum died at Dresden, Germany, June 6th, 1891. Mr. Slocum has two homes, one in Detroit and the other on Slocum's Island, about sixteen miles below Detroit on the Detroit River.

GILES BRYAN SLOCUM, one of Wayne County's most industrious and enterprising pioneers, was born July 11th, 1808, in Saratoga County, New York State, son of Jeremiah Slocum, farmer and lumberman, and Elizabeth Bryan. He was of Rhode Island Quaker antecedents. His grandfather, Giles Slocum, was born in Rhode Island, but at an early date moved to Pennsylvania. He was one of the sixty who escaped at the Wyoming Massacre in 1778, and was also a volunteer in General Sullivan's expedition against the Indians of the Genesee Valley. His great grandfather, Jonathan Slocum, was killed by the Indians on the present site of the City of Wilkesbarre, Pennsylvania, and his great aunt, Frances Slocum, a daughter of said Jonathan Slocum, then a little girl of five years of age, was carried off by the hostile Delawares, and after sixty years of captivity was accidentally discovered by Col. Ewing near Logansport, Indiana.

Young Slocum had a common school education. His boyhood years were spent on a farm and he taught school four winters near Saratoga and Lockport, New York. He came to Michigan in 1831 and landed at Detroit. He prospected extensively in the interior, and then settled for the winter and assisted in laying out the town of Vistula, now Toledo, Ohio. He owned the first store there, and got out timber for the first dock at that place. After his father's death, in 1832, he returned east and bought out the interest in his father's estate from the other heirs and then came back to Michigan. In 1833 he was in the stave business at the head of Swan Creek, now Newport, Monroe County, where he established a store and engaged in general trade, and succeeded in getting the Steamers General Brady, Jackson and Jack Downing to run up Swan Creek from Lake Erie to his place. In 1834 he paddled a canoe from Jackson down Grand River to Grand Rapids, and in the same year he established the first store and dock at Truaxton, now Trenton.

For the next fifteen or twenty years he turned his attention to sheep raising and was the largest wool grower in Michigan. At the same time he continued buying up and extending his landed possessions, among which was the purchase of a frontage of over three miles on the Detroit River, including Slocum's Island, where he resided. He was also engaged in driving piles and building docks at Detroit, Windsor, Springwells, Trenton, Sandwich, Gibraltar and Grosse Isle. About 1848 he made a contract with the County of Wayne to build two bridges across the River Rouge, for which he took wild lands in payment. These he located on Crockery Creek, Muskegon County, where in connection with his son, he built mills and conducted a thriving lumbering business. He also purchased large tracts of land on White River and White Lake, in Muskegon County. and in 1859 he, with Mr. Mears, of Chicago, laid out and platted the present village of Whitehall, Michigan.

In 1861 he was an earnest supporter of the Government and did much to raise men and money and equip regiments for the field. He was a member of the first Republican Convention held at Jackson in 1854, and with the Hon. Jacob M. Howard, took an active part in the organization of the Republican party and was ever after an influential supporter of it. He was a delegate to many important political conventions, and was especially active in the memorable senatorial contest of 1875, which secured the election of Senator Christiancy. In 1856 he took an active interest in the construction of the Detroit, Monroe & Toledo Railroad, and was one of its first directors. He was Trustee of the Saratoga Monument Association, of New York, of which the late ex-Governor Seymour was President.

In 1838 Mr. Slocum married Sophia Maria Brigham Truax, daughter of Major Abraham Caleb Truax, founder of the Village of Trenton. They had three children, two of whom, Hon. Elliott Truax Slocum, and Mrs. J. B. Nichols, are living. He died at his residence on Slocum's Island, January 26th, 1884, and his remains were buried in Elmwood Cemetery, Detroit.

FRED SLOCUM, of the Tuscola County Advertiser, published at Caro, was the first to associate the Slocum name with the newspaper enterprises of the State. He was born in Rose, Oakland County, May 25th, 1858. His father, William W. Slocum, was one of the sturdy farmers of Oakland County, and died in June, 1897, at the age of seventy-three. Fred was educated in the district schools, but found his mission at the age of seventeen, when, with a cash capital of $150 and abundance of pluck, he started the Holly Advertiser, although four different papers had already failed in that town. It was first printed monthly and then weekly and during Mr. Slocum's seven years' ownership he enlarged it seven times. In the spring of 1884 he embarked in a new venture, which has since become the pride of his life, purchasing the Advertiser at Caro. Three months after he took possession the office was burned down, with a heavy loss above the insurance. But not discouraged at this, he purchased the lot on which the old building stood and in three months had, in a new building, one of the best equipped newspaper and job printing offices in the interior of the State. Mr. Slocum is not only a thorough newspaper man, publishing a paper that is up to the times in its news columns, but is a constant and stalwart Republican and his paper takes high rank among the weeklies in the state.

TUSCOLA COUNTY ADVERTISER,
CARO.

FLINT GLOBE.

Besides publishing the Advertiser, Mr. Slocum has found time to attend to a number of other matters. He owns a farm near Caro. For eight years he published a monthly family paper called Home Life, which reached a circulation of 30,000 copies and which he sold in April, 1900, to H. C. Coleman, of the Pontiac Post. He is also owner of the Weekly Gazette, established at Millington, Tuscola County, in December, 1898. During 1890, 1891 and part of 1892 he was manager of the circulation department of the Detroit Journal. He has always taken a very active interest in Michigan Press Association matters. He was Treasurer for two terms, during the years of 1884 and 1885, Secretary in 1890, and arranged the first long excursion ever made by the Association through the Upper Peninsula to St. Paul and Minneapolis, through the Yellowstone National Park, to Helena, Butte, Boise City, Ogden, Salt Lake and Denver, occupying four weeks. He first proposed the Bulletin, in a paper read before the Association at the annual meeting in 1893, since which time no less than half a dozen similar papers have been established in other states. He was President of the Association in 1894.

Mr. Slocum was a member of the Republican State Central Committee two terms of two years each; was nominated for the office of Presidential Elector from the Eighth Congressional District in 1892, and elected by over 1,500 majority; was for three years Secretary of the Tuscola County Republican Lincoln Club, whose annual meetings and banquets are scarcely excelled anywhere in the State; and has been President of that organization for the past two years; was elected alternate delegate from the Eighth Congressional District to the National Republican Convention at Philadelphia in July, and was in 1899 President of the Michigan Republican Newspaper Association. He was appointed Postmaster of Caro on February 21st, 1900, by President McKinley, without opposition, and through his efforts a new postoffice was erected and equipped, conceded to be the finest third-class office in the country. He was Chairman of the Tuscola County Republican Committee from 1898 until appointed Postmaster, and conducted one of the most systematic and vigorous campaigns when the party achieved one of its greatest victories in the history of the County.

Mr. Slocum was married November 22d, 1882, at Linden, Michigan, to Miss Eva Leonard. They have three children, William W., aged eight, who already knows how to make copy and set type; Catherine, aged six; and Dorothy aged three.

JAMES SLOCUM, the present publisher of the Flint Globe, was the son of William W. and Sarah A. Slocum, and was born November 28th, 1862, at Holly, Michigan. His parents moved to Holly sixty years ago, being pioneers in that section. James remained on the farm until eighteen years of age, getting such education as he could from the country district schools. After leaving the farm he found employment as railroad fireman for the Flint & Pere Marquette Railroad, following that occupation four years. He returned to Holly in November, 1888, purchased the Holly Advertiser, and owned the same for twelve years; then went to Flint and engaged in the bicycle business as President and Manager of the American Machine Company, until September, 1899, at which time the Company went out of business, being jobbers in that line and not manufacturers. He purchased the Flint Globe in December, 1899. He has always been a Republican and spent a great deal of time in promoting the success of the party, but has never held office. He is a member of the Genesee Lodge, F. & A. M., Flint; Holly Council No. 139; Holly Chapter No. 80; B. P. O. Elks; Oddfellows; Eastern Star; Royal Arcanum; Knights of the Loyal Guards and Modern Woodmen; also a member of the Flint Business Men's Club and Durant-Dort Carriage Company's Blue Ribbon Line Club. He voted for Blaine in 1884. He was married, June 4th, 1887, to Mary Tindall, and has two children, girls, Joyce, nine years old, and Josephine, six.

CHARLES SMITH, who has represented a portion of the Upper Peninsula in both houses of the Legislature, was born in Livonia Township, Wayne County, Michigan. His father was William Smith, a farmer, commonly called "Uncle Billy," and his mother was Ann Eliza Smith, whose ancestors, named Stark, were among those who settled in Massachusetts about fifty years after the landing of the Pilgrims.

The subject of this sketch attended the Union School at Ypsilanti from 1857 to 1861, with a term in 1862, being absent, however, for a three months' service as a private in Company H, First Regiment, Michigan Infantry. In 1863 he located in Houghton County, where he has since made his home. For the past twenty-three years he has been in the employ of copper smelting companies, and at present is clerk of the smelting department of the Calumet and Hecla Mining Company. He is Vice President of the First National Bank of Lake Linden, and a director of the Northern Michigan Building and Loan Association of Hancock. In politics he is a Republican, and is at present Supervisor of his Township for the tenth consecutive term; was a member of the house of 1895-6, and re-elected to that of 1897-8 by a vote of 3,142 to 994 for the Democratic People's Union Silver candidate. He was elected to the Senate of 1899-1900 from the Thirty-Second District, comprising the counties of Baraga, Gogebic, Houghton, Keweenaw and Ontonagon, by a vote of 7,078 to 1,129 for Worth W. Wendell, Democratic People's Union Silver candidate. He was one of the three members of the House who voted against the Atkinson Bill, voting against it again at the time of its passage. He opposed the submission of an amendment to the Constitution, making possible the enactment of such a law, never believed nor admitted that the party at the convention of 1898 in Detroit honestly and

Charles Smith

understandingly declared for ad valorem taxation on railroads and the other quasi public enterprises. He has constantly believed and does believe that our present plan of specific taxation on gross receipts is far preferable to any ad valorem system managed by a board. On this subject Senator Smith says: "If there is anything that I contemplate with pride, it is that I was one of those senators in the Legislature of 1899 who were dubbed 'the immortal nineteen.' Who named us, or why, I do not know. We felt surer at first of eighteen than nineteen, but wound up with a stalwart twenty. We set for ourselves the task of assisting in weeding the populistic ideas and officeholders out of our party. That belittling collection of reforms consisting for the most part of populism, demagoguery and anarchistic talk, seems now to be rolling away from our State, and the hope revives that old-time feeling of glorious pride may thrill our breasts at the mention of our beloved Michigan."

Mr. Smith was a Republican from the beginning of the party; remembers marching and shouting for Fremont, and cast his first vote for Lincoln in 1864. He has been a delegate to a number of State gubernatorial and judicial conventions. In addition to the Legislative positions which he has held, he has been Supervisor of Torch Lake Township from 1888 to the present time. August 9th, 1900, he was renominated for the State Senate from the Thirty-second District, and was re-elected by a large majority.

Of fraternal orders, etc., he is a member of Masonic Lodge, Chapter, Commandery, Consistory and Shrine; of E. R. Stiles Post, G. A. R., Hancock, at one time commander of the same for several terms; member of the Michigan Club and McKinley League Club of South Lake Linden, and of the Ouiganning Yacht Club. He was married at Pewabic Mine, Houghton County, August 27th, 1867, to Miss Fannie I. Hague. They have one adopted daughter, Ruth E. Smith.

HENRY CASSORTE SMITH, the Republican member of the Fifty-seventh Congress from the Second District of Michigan, was born in Canandaigua, New York, June 2d, 1856, of French-English extraction. Young Smith's family at the time of his birth were well-to-do residents of Canandaigua, Wanton C. Smith, the father, being one of the leading merchants of the town.

In the panic of 1857 Wanton C. Smith met financial reverses and saw nearly all his property wiped away. A little later he moved with his wife, Marie M., and his children to Palmyra, Lenawee County, Michigan, where he bought a farm. Young Smith worked on the farm and attended District School until 1869. From then until 1874 he worked early and late on farm and in factories, his one purpose being to obtain sufficient money with which to pay for an education His inherited taste for knowledge, for his father had been educated at the Canandaigua, New York, Academy, and his mother at the Lockport Seminary, was such that he thought no endeavor too rigorous if it led to the accomplishment of his wishes.

In 1872 the afterward elected congressman was working as a farm laborer on the poorhouse farm in Lenawee County, putting in what spare time he had at his studies. The next year still finds him on a farm, but alternating between farming and dairy work. He spent the whole of 1873 in this work, doing chores for his board for John R. Clark of Adrian. In 1874 he entered Adrian College, and from that until 1878, when he graduated on June 22d, he alternately taught school, worked upon the farm, or did any kind of honorable labor which came to his hand to do. Even in his later school life he began to attract attention, as he was chosen the college orator for the Inter-Collegiate State Contest at Kalamazoo in 1877. The reputation that he made on this occasion brought him in very general public notice and led up to his going into the great Greenback campaign as one of the lieutenants of Zach Chandler, the Chairman of the Republican State Central Committee.

For two years he followed the study of law as assiduously as he had his previous work in school, and in September, 1880, was admitted to the bar. The training which he received in the office of Geddes & Miller, of Adrian, was such as to particularly fit him for active legal work. In fact it was only about two weeks after his admission before he was appointed City Attorney, and only about three months later, January 1st, 1881, he was appointed Assistant Prosecuting Attorney. His first participation in national politics came in 1896 when he was elected an alternate to the Republican Convention in St. Louis, when President William McKinley was nominated.

The campaign of 1896 proved the turning point in the political career of Mr. Smith. As President of the Lenawee County McKinley Club that year he took the boys of the club to Canton, to felicitate Major McKinley upon his nomination. His speech in front of the now famous cottage was a memorable one, and at its close Major McKinley paid his visitor from Adrian a most marked compliment in his response. In the primaries and Congressional Convention of 1898 Henry C. Smith was most prominently before the people, and he was chosen as his party's candidate for congressional honor. He toured the District far and wide, and so potent was his logic and able presentation of the issues that he was elected to Congress, in an ordinarily Democratic District, by a majority of 1,913.

Mr. Smith first attracted attention from his colleagues in the Fifty-sixth Congress by his ready oratorical abilities and the brilliancy of his short addresses. His first speech was on the famous currency bill, and in this he showed that he not only had studied deeply into the subject under consideration, but he had also massed his facts together in epigrammatic sentences which caught and held the attention of the House. His later addresses in the House of Representatives on the rural delivery appropriation in the postoffice

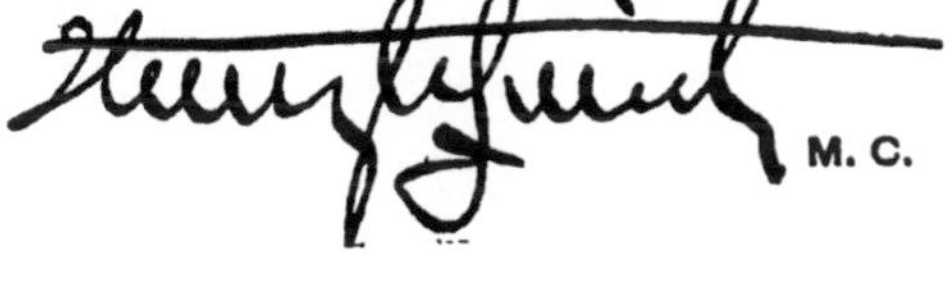 M. C.

budget, and his stand on the so-called Loud Bill, relating to second-class matter, made him especially popular. He was heard to great advantage in his advocacy of some sort of recognition for the struggling patriots, the Boers, in Africa. While the address did not secure the public recognition for the Boers, yet it did secure for Mr. Smith a settled reputation in the House as a convincing master of logic and a rough and ready debater. He was re-elected to the Fifty-seventh Congress in November, 1900, by 3,669 plurality.

Speaker Henderson, recognizing the careful scrutiny which Congressman Smith gave to every bill, appointed him as one of the Committee on Accounts, a most important station, and through his work on this committee he secured a large and powerful acquaintance with the members of the House which was of great value to him, both on the floor of the House and in his committee work. This work also gave him an insight into the needs of reforming the handling of claims against the United States Government and the reforms which he found needed he persistently and successfully contended for from time to time during his congressional career in the Fifty-sixth Congress. Also as member of the Pensions Committee he attracted much public attention and his bill to amend the general pension laws was the most widely discussed measure of its kind in this Congress.

In addition to the political positions which he has held, Mr. Smith has been for some years a trustee of Adrian College. His home life has been most happy. He was married on Dec. 20th, 1887, to Emma, the daughter of Judge R. A. Watt, of Adrian, the city in which he first entered upon his collegiate career, in which he was admitted to the bar, in which he made his reputation as a public official. No children resulted from that union.

HON. SAMUEL W. SMITH was born August 23d, 1852, the son of a farmer in Independence, Oakland County, Michigan. His father was Nicholas B. Smith, who served in the double capacity of a farmer and merchant. Both his parents were born in the Empire State, and came to Michigan as early settlers.

Congressman Samuel W. Smith was educated in the common schools of his home town and later at Clarkston and Detroit. Selecting the study of the law as his avocation for life he fitted himself for the Law Department of the University of Michigan. His endeavors to secure an education were not along the roseate bed of ease, for while at school at Clarkston he served as janitor, in order to eke out his scanty supply of funds, and during the summer vacations he worked on a farm or at any other honest occupation in which he could obtain a livelihood and save a few dollars. At one time he even "carried the hod," and supplied mortar to brick layers. During the whole course of his scholastic training he esteemed no occupation too lowly, so long as it was honest and yielded him the reasonable recompense with which to continue his quest for an education.

He was sixteen years old when he commenced teaching school and at twenty years of age he took charge of the High School in Waterford and for three years remained as its principal. When his scholastic training was completed, he entered the law office of Levi D. Taft, of Pontiac, and was admitted to the bar in Oakland County, in 1877. Then he entered the University of Michigan and graduated in the class of 1878 from the Law Department, and immediately entered active practice. In 1880 he was nominated by his fellow citizens of Oakland County for Prosecuting Attorney and he swept the County by storm, his majority even surpassing that given for Garfield and Arthur by nearly 400. In 1882 he was renominated against a fusion ticket and again won, after a splendid campaign in which he demonstrated his ability as a campaigner and vote getter. Two years later his fellow citizens called upon him to make a campaign for the State Senate, in the Democratic district in which he lived. He was again successful although his companions on the Republican ticket all went down to defeat except one.

In was in the State Senate that he first began to attract general state attention and his famous Oleomargarine Bill, which he introduced and pressed to a passage, became of more than state fame, largely owing to the bitter fight made against it. This fight finally resulted, indeed, in the State Supreme Court declaring the law unconstitutional, although it was nearly identical with the law which the Supreme Court of the State of New York declared constitutional. He was also the moving spirit in the placing upon the statute books of what is known as the "Car-Coupling" Bill which accomplished so much for the preservation of the life of labor employed upon the railroads of the state, and which was really the basis for all state and national legislation upon this subject.

He was first nominated for Congress in the campaign of 1896 by the electors of the Sixth Michigan Congressional District. His campaign was hard-fought and he succeeded in defeating his opponent, Hon. Quincy A. Smith, of Lansing, by 3,415 majority. The record he made during his first congressional term was such that he was renominated without opposition, and in the campaign of 1898 he defeated Hon. Charles Fishbeck, of Howell, by 5,810, and in 1900 he again won by a handsome majority after the sharpest sort of a campaign, in which he was heavily handicapped by the local prejudice against any officer having more than two terms.

His labors during his first and second congressional terms were such as to commend him most heartily to the voters of his district. First as a member of the Committee on Invalid Pensions he proved a hard and untiring worker and a vast benefit to the old soldiers in his State as well as in his district. He was among the first to see the advantages of the rural free delivery system, and was early in getting a large number of routes in his district, by which the farmers and suburban dwellers had many of the advantages of the urbanite. In a national way he attracted attention by his insistent demand that there should be reform in the matter of mail contracts given to the railroad companies. He proved that the charges were exorbitant. The elder members of the Post Office and Post Roads Committee did not want to touch the matter, but Mr. Smith kept up such a persistent fight that it resulted in the appointment of an investigating committee and the result of those hearings proved that he was right. His growth in experience led Speaker Henderson to name him as one of the members of the District of Columbia Committee, which amounts to the same thing as one of the rulers of the affairs of the nation's capital, and there he became most useful.

Going outside the practice of the law, in business investment he was among the pioneers in the building of suburban electric lines. His first venture in this line was the move to connect his home city, Pontiac, with the metropolis of the State and then, with an idea of giving his home city more prominence and making it an electric railway center, he projected the Pontiac & Flint line, which became an assured fact. The possibilities of the road making an all electric line to Bay City were the actuating idealities that led Mr. Smith to push the project.

Mr. Smith was married, November 17, 1880, to Alida D. Deland, the only surviving child of Edwin and Susan M. Deland of Waterford, Oakland County. Previous to their marriage Mrs. Smith was a pupil at the school over which her future husband ruled as principal. As a result of this union four sons—E. Deland, aged nineteen years; Ferris N., aged seventeen years; Wendell, aged fifteen years, and Harlan S., aged ten years, survive. With all his busy life Mr. Smith has found time to ally himself with the fraternal organizations, being a member of the Maccabees, Oddfellows, Knights of the Loyal Guard, Ancient Order of United Workmen, Knights of Pythias, Order of Foresters, Royal Encampment of Oddfellows, a Master Mason and a Knight Templar. Mr. Smith is a member of the Presbyterian Church and an active participant in church affairs at his home city.

TIMOTHY SMITH, the present Postmaster at Howell, Livingston County, Michigan, was born June 17th, 1848, in Howell, and is the son of Henry and Lydia Smith. His father was born near Oxford, England, in 1816; came to America alone at the age of fifteen to seek his fortune in the new world; settled in New York State and worked on a farm by the month. He came to Michigan in 1836, bought eighty acres of wild land five miles from Howell Village, and commenced pioneer life in earnest. He experienced all the hardships of the early pioneer, and by earnest toil and by strict integrity accumulated a competency for his old age. In politics he was a Republican of the Abolitionist school. In 1847 he married Miss Lydia Sutton, who was born in Wayne County, New York, in 1816, whose father and grandfather fought in the Revolutionary War and the War of

1812. To this union were born six children, four of whom are living—Timothy and Robert R. Smith, Mrs. Mary L. Goss and Mrs. Sarah A. Bucknell.

Timothy Smith was born and raised on a farm, receiving his education in the public schools of Howell. He owned and operated a farm up to four years ago, when he moved to the Village of Howell. He was elected Chairman of the Republican County Committee in 1892 and changed a Democratic majority of 500 in 1890 to a Republican majority of 40 in 1892, when the whole Republican County ticket was elected for the first time in years. He held the Chairmanship up to the time of his appointment as Postmaster in 1898. He has been a Republican since his birth, cast his first vote for General Grant. He was elected Supervisor of Howell in 1882 and served one term; was elected Township Treasurer in 1884 and re-elected in 1885 by 196 majority, the largest majority ever received by a Republican in Howell Township. He was married in 1871 to Miss Elizabeth A. Blair, of Almont, Lapeer County, Michigan. They have one daughter, Mrs. Jessie E. Brayton, wife of C. A. Brayton.

WILLIAM ALDEN SMITH, of Grand Rapids, was born in Dowagiac, Michigan, May 12th, 1859. His father, George Richardson Smith, and his mother, Leah Margaret Smith, came from sturdy New England stock, being direct descendants of General James Abercrombie and Israel Putnam, and settled in Michigan when quite young.

Mr. Smith's earliest education was obtained in the public schools of Dowagiac and Grand Rapids, to which city his parents removed when he was about twelve years of age. His broader and better education was obtained in the school of the world and contact with men. Very early in his life he was forced, through the illness of his father, to become a bread winner and assist in the support of his father's family. His first employment was as a newsboy at Grand Rapids, and from there he graduated into a messenger boy for the Western Union Telegraph Company.

In 1879 Hon. John T. Rich, then speaker of the Michigan House of Representatives, appointed young Smith as a page in the House. This gave the youth the opportunity he craved. By serving as special correspondent for the Chicago Times during his term as page he was able to lay by the money he needed and he also had the time to devote to the study of law, which he early resolved to master.

The acquaintances he formed while in the Michigan House of Representatives and the rapid progress he made in the study of law were of the greatest value to him, as out of the one came the demand for his presence on the political stump, and at the rallying places of the Republican party; and out of the other came his admission to the bar, and his whole subsequent legal career where he was associated

Wm Alden Smith

with such able members of the bar as M. J. Smiley, Judge M. C. Burch and Frederick W. Stevens, now general counsel for the consolidated Pere Marquette Railroad System.

He was admitted to the bar of his native state in 1883, and to the bar of the Supreme Court of the United States in 1900. Selecting the City of Grand Rapids as his home, for life, he soon built up a large and lucrative law practice, having for over a dozen years been general counsel of the consolidated railroads known as the Chicago & West Michigan and the Detroit, Grand Rapids & Western System.

His busy life in the law did not permit him the enjoyment of political activity except as an orator in the heat of the campaign, and while he was a member of the State Central Committee in 1888, 1890 and 1892 he did not aspire to hold office. The Fifth District, in which he resides, was represented by a Democrat, when his fellow citizens of the Republican faith unanimously selected him in the campaign of 1894 to make the battle for the place of Representative in Congress. His canvass of the District was a revelation to his opponent and he carried the popular vote with a majority of nearly ten thousand. He entered Congress as a very young man, being only thirty-four years of age, and one of the youngest members of that body. His career as a congressman was along the same lines as the rest of his life work. Waiting until he had grasped the conditions of the House and familiarized himself with the rules, he plunged boldly into debate, and by the force of his logic and clear thinking marked, even during his first term, a place for himself in the membership of the House. Regarded as one of the most promising members, he lived up to the prediction, and Speaker Thomas B. Reed, who recognized the ability of the young man from the Fifth Michigan District, gave him a place on the very important Committee on Foreign Affairs. He has served on that committee with distinction to himself and credit to his District ever since. Going to his people again in the following campaigns he was returned to the Fifty-fifth, Fifty-sixth and Fifty-seventh Congresses.

His ease in handling the weighty matters that the Foreign Affairs Committee have to consider, made him a well-known member of the House, and the power which he wielded by reason of his oratorical ability and force in debate made him a marked figure there. He showed himself a man of more than one line of ability and was heard from with pleasure by the members of the House on all the important measures growing out of the changes in financial conditions and the knotty legal questions which the Spanish war left as a legacy. Among his associates on the committee his services were highly appreciated and his colleagues on his own State delegation made him their Chairman year after year.

But Mr. Smith found time to branch out in a business way and became a man of large affairs in the financial world. In 1897 he promoted, financed and built the Grand Rapids, Kalkaska & Southeastern Railroad, which he now owns, and two years later he purchased the

Lowell & Hastings Railroad. He then built the Grand Rapids, Belding & Saginaw Railroad, and consolidated it with the Lowell & Hastings road. Having thus built up a prosperous system he sold it in 1900 to the Pere Marquette Company which was organized to consolidate several independent lines.

He has also found opportunity to become prominently identified with the interests of Grand Rapids in many ways. He is President of the Grand Rapids Herald, a paper, by the way, which Mr. Smith himself vended on the street as a newsboy, and is the First Vice President of the People's Savings Bank. Mr. Smith, while a self-made man, was not without nature's favors in the battle of life. Gifted with an imposing address and striking personality, he possessed a voice of great power and range and with it a discretion to use it to the best effects With a wit sharpened by experience, but naturally kindly, he is at once at home either at the fireside or in committee room as a companion, on the floor of the House or the stump as a convincing debater and at the post prandial exercises where he perhaps shines the brightest of all. It can be truthfully said that no man who ever met William Alden Smith, in any place, or who ever heard him make an address ever forgot the personality or the face.

The home side of Mr. Smith's life has been most happy. He was married in 1886 to Miss Nana Osterhout, of Grand Rapids, a most gifted and brilliant companion for him. Their life, both in Washington and Grand Rapids, where their society is much sought after, is ideal. Both of the same tastes, liking the same things, the private side of their life has all the things that the newsboy William Alden Smith lacked. A son, William Alden Smith, jr., just fills out the full measure of happiness in the Congressman's career apart from the busy world of affairs and politics.

IRVING WASHINGTON SNYDER, one of the publishers of the Bay City Tribune, was born October 24th, 1858, in the town of Dryden, Tompkins County, New York. His parents were Ira W. Snyder and Sally Ann Snyder, maiden name Manning. His paternal ancestors emigrated from Western Germany in 1747, and settled in the Town ship of Oxford, then Sussex, but now Warren County, New Jersey, on what is known as Scotch Mountain. In the summer of 1802 they started west, and located in what is now the town of Dryden, Tompkins County, New York, taking eighteen days for the journey. It was then a dense wilderness, and they built log houses, commenced clearing, and subsequently turned this wilderness into some of the finest farms in New York State. Several of his ancestors fought in the Revolutionary War, the War of 1812 and subsequent wars up to and including the Civil War.

The son was educated in district schools, in the town of Dryden, and in the High School of Ithaca, New York, and in the preparatory schools for Cornell University. His first occupation was farming,

BAY CITY TRIBUNE.

Stephen F. Snyder

until he went to the Ithaca schools. After finishing school he taught district school in both New York and Illinois, then took a course in a business college at Ithaca, New York, afterwards teaching in the same college. He then kept books in a general store in Ithaca for about a year, then purchased an interest in a grocery store in the same town, continued in business about one year and then sold out to his partner. He came to Michigan in October, 1881, and engaged with T. H. McGraw & Co., they operating the largest sawmill in Michigan, and having very extensive timber and other interests. He started as bookkeeper, and was promoted until he became their confidential man, eventually became general manager of the business, and was with the above firm from 1881 to 1895. In May, 1896, he was asked to look after the affairs of the Bay City Tribune for a short time, and finally acted as general manager for the Tribune Printing Company until October 1st, 1896, when he entered into a co-partnership with J. C. McCabe, under the firm name of Snyder & McCabe, and purchased the Tribune, and he and his partner have raised its standard quite perceptibly.

Mr. Snyder was always a Republican, but has never sought office nor taken a very active personal part in politics till 1900, when he was delegate to the Republican State Convention, held at Grand Rapids in June. He cast his first vote for Garfield. In society affiliations he is a Mason, member of Blanchard Chapter No. 59, Joppa Blue Lodge No. 315. He was married April 30th, 1884, to Mrs. Priscilla Claxton, with two stepdaughters, afterwards adopted, and taking his name, Maude C. Snyder and Nina C. Snyder. The daughter Nina died December 24th, 1898, and the daughter Maude is married to H. W. Garland, of Bay City. Mr. Snyder is an ardent sportsman, extremely fond of shooting, fishing and all outdoor sports.

HON. STEPHEN F. SNYDER, of Marshall, was born in Cayuga County, New York, December 27th, 1829, and is a son of Benjamin and Elizabeth (Fiero) Snyder. The family of Mr. and Mrs. Snyder consisted of five children, Stephen F. being the fourth in order of birth. His father, who was a farmer, was a native of the Empire State, having been born there in 1793, and his father in turn was a native of the same state. The latter, Elias Snyder, was captured by the Indians and taken to Canada, where he was held a prisoner two years and five months. The maternal grandfather of our subject was Stephen Fiero, a native of New York and of German descent, as were the Snyders.

In the district school of his native state Stephen F. acquired a knowledge of the principal branches, and on the home farm he learned industrious habits and good principles. After he had reached his majority he began farming on his own account, and in the spring of 1866 he bade adieu to the Empire State and came to Michigan. He selected a farm in Homer Township, Calhoun County, and here he carried on the vocation in which he had previously been employed. His intelligence and ability were recognized by those about him, who called upon him to serve as Township Supervisor and he held that office for a period of five consecutive years from 1871. In the fall of 1876 he was elected Register of Deeds. The term of the office was for two years and he was twice re-elected. In the fall of 1882 Mr. Snyder was elected to the Legislature on the Republican ticket from the First District of Calhoun County, and in that position did good work for his constituents. He was re-elected to the Legislature and after serving a second term retired to private life, and interested himself actively in the lumber business in the northern part of the State, until 1887, when he sold out. In April, 1890, he received the appointment of Postmaster at Marshall under President Harrison and took charge of the office on May 7th of that year.

The lady whose refined taste is manifest in the appointments of his home was known in her maidenhood as Miss Mary Van Keuren, and she became Mrs. Snyder in 1853. She is a native of Cayuga County, New York, and daughter of Robert and Ann Van Keuren. The only child of the couple is a son, Frank B. Snyder, of Marshall, who is a leading furniture dealer and undertaker. The family attends the Presbyterian Church, and support with their influence various worthy enterprises, contributing to them also substantial aid.

Mr. Snyder has been a life-long Republican and one of the foremost in his section. He cast his first Presidential vote for General Scott and has been a delegate at all the Republican State Conventions for the past twenty years, with the exception of the last one. He does not belong to any secret society, but is a charter member of the Michigan Club. He is an intimate friend of Senator Burrows. He has the only complete abstract books in the County and has had charge of them for the past twenty years with the exception of the period between 1883 and 1889.

EDWARD W. SPARROW, of Lansing, capitalist and manufacturer, the son of Bartholomew and Sarah Sparrow, was born in Wexford, Ireland, December 14th, 1846. His father was the owner of real estate, inherited, having been handed down in the family for several generations. He belonged to the "gentry" class and had no other occupation than that of managing his property. His ancestors emigrated to Ireland from Essex, England, about 250 years ago, obtained a grant of land which they were able to hold through the troublous times that followed. In the rebellion of 1798 the family residence was besieged and partly destroyed, but afterwards rebuilt and occupied. The house is still well preserved and has been frequently visited by Mr. Sparrow.

The subject of this sketch was educated in Ireland and Michigan and engaged as clerk when fourteen years of age, afterwards, in 1873, going into business for himself. His business has been large,

E W Sparrow

growing with the years, and now employs more than 1,000 men, none of whom ever had to wait beyond the appointed time for their wages. He made it a rule from the first that the wage earner should not be delayed or his plans interfered with by not receiving his dues promptly.

In 1886, along with friends, he organized the City National Bank of Lansing, one of the most successful financial institutions in the State. He became its first President and has been annually re-elected since, holding that position now.

In 1895 he organized the Sparrow-Kroll Lumber Co., to manufacture pine lumber at Kenton, Houghton County, where the company has timber to last it for many years.

Inheriting the land hunger attributed to the Anglo-Saxon, he early made an examination of parts of the public domain in the West and became satisfied that Michigan offered the best field for such enterprise. Keeping this steadily in view, he spent months exploring the forests and iron ranges of the Lake Superior region, making long journeys on snowshoes in winter. It was, however, an agreeable occupation, giving an opportunity for the enjoyment of nature in its original wildness.

In Ireland, when nine years of age, his mother read to him that impressive story, "Uncle Tom's Cabin," not even dreaming that they would ever be residents of the land across the sea. However, three years later, the vicissitudes of fortune made it seem necessary that the family should emigrate. The question then was, where to go? Australia, New Zealand or the United States. The latter being selected, Michigan was reached on the first day of August, 1858, by the family, consisting of his mother, five sisters and himself, his father remaining behind trying to save something from the wreck of his affairs, and intending soon to follow. A year after, while engaged in this business, his uncle, Adam Rogers, of Waterford, died, leaving him a bequest of £4,000. He then decided to come to the United States and take his family back to Ireland, but just before embarking he fell ill and died in 1860. His widow, taking into consideration the many troubles of the last year of her residence there, and having now a knowledge of both countries, saw that the "States" offered the better opportunities for a young family and wisely concluded to remain in a land where she had met only kindness on every hand.

Young Sparrow, largely influenced by the story referred to, identified himself, in 1860, with a boys' Republican organization, known as the "Little Giant Killers." The first political speech he heard was by Cassius M. Clay, at Mason, in 1860. Afterwards, in the same year, he heard William H. Seward at Lansing. His first ballot was for Grant; he has always been a Republican, but not especially active in politics, but has attended two State Conventions as a delegate.

Mr. Sparrow's present most active business connections are: President of the City National Bank, Lansing; President of the

Lansing Wheelbarrow Co., Lansing, the largest institution of its kind, sending its wares around the globe; President of the Sparrow-Kroll Lumber Co., Kenton; Director in the Longyear Mesaba Land and Iron Co., in Minnesota. In Masonry he is a Knight Templar.

He was married September 16th, 1897, to Helen T. Grant, daughter of Justice C. B. Grant, of the Supreme Court. He has one son, Edward Grant Sparrow.

GENERAL OLIVER LYMAN SPAULDING has figured in Michigan military, political and official life for more than forty years, and now ranks among the State's most prominent citizens. He is descended from Edward Spaulding, who came to Massachusetts from England about 1632. His parents were Lyman Spaulding, a farmer, and Susan (Marshall) Spaulding, and he was born in Jaffrey, New Hampshire, August 2d, 1833. He was educated at Oberlin College, Oberlin, Ohio, where he graduated in 1855, going thence direct to Michigan. He supported himself in a college, in addition to slight help from his father, by teaching during vacations, and manual labor during the college terms. He taught school for a time after graduation at Hillsdale and Medina, Michigan, removing to St. Johns in 1857, which place has since been his home. While teaching he studied law and was admitted to practice in 1858, and the same year was elected Regent of the University of Michigan.

Mr. Spaulding's law practice and his civil career were interrupted by his response to one of President Lincoln's calls for volunteers. In July, 1862, he recruited a company which was assigned to the Twenty-third Michigan Infantry as Company A, of which he was appointed Captain. The regiment was mustered into service in September, 1862, its muster rolls showing a force of 983 officers and enlisted men, and was mustered out June 28th, 1865. In the intervening period it had, in all, on its muster roll, 1,417 officers and men, of whom 287 were either killed in battle or died of wounds or of disease contracted in the service. It shared in the siege of Knoxville, Tennessee, November 17th to December 5th, 1863; siege of Atlanta, July 22d to August 25th, 1864, in the battles of Franklin, Nashville, the capture of Washington, North Carolina, 1865, and many other engagements and skirmishes besides. During the long service Captain Spaulding was promoted through successive grades to that of Brevet Brigadier General. At the close of the War General Spaulding returned to the practice of his profession at St. Johns. He has since been frequently honored by election or appointment to positions of trust. He was Secretary of the State of Michigan from 1867 to 1871; was a special agent of the United States Treasury Department from 1875 to 1881, when he resigned to take his seat in the Forty-seventh Congress, to which he was elected in 1880. He was defeated for re-election in 1882 by a Democratic and Greenback combination, and declined renomination in 1884. He was Chairman of a special

O. L. Spaulding

O. L. Spaulding

1883 to investigate certain matters
city treaty; was appointed Assist-
resident Harrison; resigned on
stration, and was reappointed
ley in 1897. Concerning his
hns Republican, his home
that this appointment
received by our citi-
paulding has been
y within bounds
of the com-
ing worker,
been the
for him

st.

of the Masonic
Lodge, Grand High Priest of
of the Grand Council of Royal and
Commander of the Grand Commandery of
of the Loyal Legion of the
commissioned of Assistant
rden of the
arried Jennie
Minerva Mead
Maud Spaulding

and the fruit of the union is the subject of this sketch, who was born April 10th, 1845. He received his education in the public schools in that town, supplemented by a course in a commercial college, but commenced at an early age to work on his father's farm, and also to work about the mill. He afterwards accompanied his father to Conneaut, Ohio, where the two were associated in the lumber business. Later he started in business on his own account at Toledo, where he owned a yard and handled hardwood lumber, which he cut at a mill twelve miles out, in the Black Swamp. In 1876 he did what nearly all wide-awake lumbermen of that decade did—headed for Michigan. He commenced with portable saw mills in the woods a few miles from Big Rapids, but striking a season of low prices, lost all he had invested. He then went to Ludington and started over again as clerk in the Catherine L. Ward store, owned by heirs of Captain E. B. Ward. Accumulating a little capital, he again commenced in the lumber business on his own account, but in a modest way, building a small mill at Stearns Station, in Lake County. From this time on his affairs prospered, and he became an expansionist in business matters. He enlarged his plant, added a planing mill, and kept on buying standing pine and hardwood from time to time, until he finally became the only operator in that immediate neighborhood. Since 1882 he has cut most of the pine and much of the hardwood in that section. In connection with the Flint & Pere Marquette Railway Company, he built logging roads through his timber tracts and sends all of his logs to mill by rail, shipping the product east in car lots.

Mr. Stearns is also interested in the Flambeau Lumber Company, established in 1892, and working on the Lac du Flambeau Indian Reservation in Wisconsin. Their mill at that point has a capacity of 200,000 feet a day, has turned out over 40,000,000 feet a season, and employs from 400 to 500 men.

A year later he organized the J. S. Stearns Lumber Company, of which he is President. The plant owned by the company is nearly a duplicate of the one at Flambeau, and is located at Odanah, Wisconsin. Taking his pine interests all together, Mr. Stearns employs from 1,000 to 1,200 men, cuts 125,000,000 feet or more per year, makes money, and has the typical lumberman's liberality in using it.

In addition to his lumber business, Mr. Stearns is a stockholder in the First National Bank of Ludington, and is senior member of the firm of Stearns & Mack, general merchants, at Scottville, Michigan, which firm does a phenomenally large business for a small interior town. He is also owner of what is known as the Ward store and sawmill plant at Ludington, in which store he was employed as a clerk eighteen years ago. In connection with this he has a large planing mill and salt plant, manufacturing from 25,000,000 to 40,000,000 feet of lumber per year, and from 1,000 to 1,200 barrels of salt daily. Mr. Stearns is also an extensive holder of pine and hardwood lands in Tennessee and Arkansas.

Mr. Stearns has always been a Republican, and notwithstanding his large business interests, he has found time to do good work for the party of his choice. He was Chairman of the Republican County Committee for four years, has frequently been a delegate to conventions, and was a Harrison elector in 1888 from the Ninth Congressional District. The State Convention of 1898 nominated him for Secretary of State, and he was elected by a majority of 66,457 over the combination Democratic People's Union Silver candidate. In the State Convention held June 27th, 1900, Mr. Stearns was one of the three leading gubernatorial candidates who commenced with over 200 votes each. The first ballot gave Mr. Stearns 215 votes, Aaron T. Bliss, of Saginaw, 259, and D. M. Ferry, of Detroit, 251. Mr. Stearns' friends in the convention stood by him well until the final break came, keeping him above the 200 mark on every ballot except one up to the fifteenth. The nomination finally went to Colonel Bliss, when Mr. Stearns gracefully accepted the result and heartily supported the successful candidate.

Mr. Stearns married Paulina Lyon, daughter of Robert Lyon, and sister of Thomas R. and J. B. Lyon, of Chicago. They have one son, Robert L. Stearns, a promising young artist, whose drawings are frequently seen in the popular magazines.

GEORGE A. STEEL, for the past four years State Treasurer of Michigan, has had a varied business experience. He is the son of Robert M. and Carrie Hyatt Steel, and was born in St. Johns, Clinton County, Michigan, June 19th, 1862. He is of Scotch descent, his grandfather having come from that country and settled in Vermont in 1830. His father was a contractor for railroad construction and other important work, and his operations extended over large areas of western and southern country. The son received his early education in the schools of St. Johns, but commenced business life when quite young. In July, 1878, he went to Sauk Rapids, Minnesota, to take a position as bookkeeper and paymaster for James McIntire & Co., bridge constructors, later discharging similar duties for the same firm at St. Paul, Minnesota. In 1879 he went to Nevada, becoming paymaster on the Nevada Central Railway during its construction; the following year he became general paymaster and purchasing agent of the Oregon Construction Company, in the construction of about four hundred miles of railroad in Oregon, Washington and Idaho, later combining those duties with that of Secretary of the Corporation, having full charge of the finances of the company. In this capacity he disbursed nearly ten million dollars during a period of five years. In 1885 he returned to Michigan, and became interested in banking, mercantile and manufacturing institutions, and also in real estate. He became Vice President of the St. Johns National Bank at St. Johns, Michigan, upon its organization in 1885. On January 28th, 1885, he was married to Miss Cora Stout, of St.

Johns, and has two sons, aged fourteen and twelve years, and one daughter. He organized and became President of the Ithaca Savings Bank at Ithaca, Michigan, in 1893. In January, 1895, he formed a partnership with F. A. Smith, of Detroit, under the firm name of Steel, Smith & Co., for the purpose of carrying on the business of buying and selling municipal bonds and commercial paper, and still carries on that business with an office in Detroit.

In politics Mr. Steel has been an active Republican. He has attended numerous conventions, and served on local committees, and was a member of the State Central Committee in 1893. He was in the State Senate, session of 1893, and was Chairman of the Committee on Banks and Corporations and Public Improvements, and a member of the Committees on Education and Public Schools, Finance and Appropriations, and Printing. He was elected State Treasurer in 1896 and 1898, a position for which his long financial and business training admirably fitted him.

Mr. Steel's social inclinations have led him into membership of the Detroit Club, the Michigan Club, the Lake St. Clair Fishing and Shooting Club, Huron Fishing and Shooting Club and Detroit Golf Club.

During the fiscal year ending June 30, 1898, covering most of the period of the Spanish War, Treasurer Steel's department handled the enormous amount of $5,906,747 in funds. It was during this period also that the State, for the first time since 1865, became a borrower, and the success of the loans made furnished striking evidence of public confidence in the general credit of the State, and in the existing management of its finances. The first issue of Spanish War bonds bore 3½ per cent. interest, and that part offered to the public was subscribed for six times over. The next issue of bonds bore interest at the rate of 3 per cent., yet with less than ten days' notice subscriptions for more than seven times the amount required were received from people residing within the State.

The successful issue of 3 per cent. bonds at par simultaneously with the offering of the United States Government bonds at the same rate of interest and at the same price, speaks volumes for the credit of the State, especially when a comparison of the two issues is made from an investor's standpoint. Leaving out of consideration the fact that on the one hand the bond is the obligation of but a single State, while on the other hand is pledged the combined faith and credit of all the States of the Union, the United States bonds are further made more attractive to investors, as they have double the period to run, bear interest payable quarterly, are payable in coin, and are specifically exempt from all taxation.

The last issue of Michigan war bonds made even a better showing than the previous ones. It was for $100,000, bearing 3 per cent. interest, was subscribed for many times over, and sold at 1 per cent. premium, making a record of which the State and its Treasurer may well be proud.

JOSEPH HALL STEERE, Judge of the Eleventh Judicial Circuit, which comprises the counties of Alger, Chippewa, Luce and Schoolcraft, in the Upper Peninsula, was born May 19th, 1852, in Addison, Lenawee County, Michigan. His father, who combined the occupations of miller and farmer, was born in Ohio, came to Michigan in 1834, and settled first in Adrian and then moved to Addison, where he lived many years. The family belonged to the Society of Friends, or Quakers, and had been in Virginia since Colonial days, having immigrated from Ireland about the time William Penn settled Pennsylvania. The maiden name of Mr. Steere's mother was Elizabeth Comstock. Her family was of English descent, but settled in New York in Colonial days.

The early days of Joseph H. Steere were spent on the farm, and the schooling which came afterwards was interrupted with school teaching. He studied at Raisin Valley Seminary, a Quaker school near Adrian, the Adrian High School and the University of Michigan, graduating from the latter in 1876, with the degree of A. B. He also took law lectures while in the University and continued his law studies in the office of Geddes & Miller, at Adrian, and was admitted to the Lenawee County Bar in 1878. The same year he moved to Sault Ste. Marie, where he has ever since been engaged in his profession, either at the Bar or on the Bench. He cast his first vote for Rutherford B. Hayes, and has always been a Republican, but has not been active in politics.

Mr. Steere was appointed Prosecuting Attorney of Chippewa County the same year that he went to the Soo, and held the position till 1881, when he was elected Circuit Judge for the term commencing January 1st, 1882. He was re-elected in 1887, 1893 and 1899, and the people in the circuit say he can stay on the bench as long as he chooses. When Judge Steere first went on the bench, traveling an Upper Peninsula Circuit was something like the itinerary of a missionary bishop on the frontier. In addition to the counties named above the Circuit included Mackinac and Manitou, the latter composed of islands in Lake Michigan, since vacated as a county, the islands being attached to Charlevoix and Emmet. There were no court houses in the Circuit except in Chippewa and Mackinac, and court had to be held in hotel offices and stores. In winter snow shoes came into requisition in some parts of that country, and in the summer sail boats furnished the most convenient mode of travel.

Judge Steere has never married. Considering the character of the country around him it was natural that he should become a lover of hunting and fishing, as he has. He is also fond of literature, and has made the best collection of books that can be found anywhere on the history of the Lake Superior region. He is socially inclined, is a Mason, a member of the Detroit Club, the Sault Social Club, and the Sault Country Club.

[illegible]

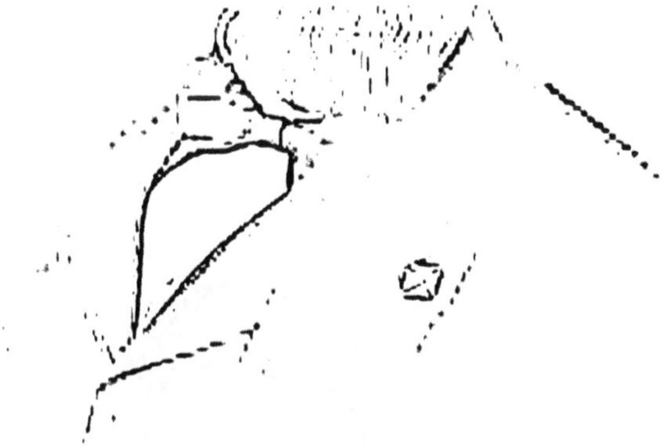

U of M

*Herman W. Stevens*

… practice of law …
… firm name of W… …
… partnership with N. … Thomas, … …
… and this relation continued … several …
… Circuit Court Commissioner from 18… …
… judge of the Sixteenth Circuit …
… Mayor of Port Huron in 1888 and 18… …
… he resumed the practice of law and has …
… enterprises. He is now a director in the … …
… Company, in the Port Huron … …
… Michigan Salt Manufacturing Works, and …
… Trunk Elevator Company, and is a member of …
… In politics he has been a Republican since …
… 1869 to Elizabeth Bishop, of Flint, and has …
… daughters, Mrs. Mary … and Miss … …
… and Walter. His boys … …
… the University.

… STEWART, … …

…e
…'s
…nt-

…Clay
when

he enlisted under Colonel John Atkinson in the Twenty-second Michigan Infantry Volunteers; remained in the service until Lee's surrender, and was mustered out of service July 1st, 1865. After the close of the war, in the spring of 1866, he went to Saginaw and worked on the lumber docks, and in 1867 he clerked in a store in Algonac, Michigan. In 1868 he commenced his career on the lakes, which continued until October, 1898. He sailed as master from 1876, and has been interested in vessels as owner since 1877.

He never sought or held a political office until the fall of 1896, when he was elected to the Michigan House of Representatives and was re-elected in 1898, having served in two regular and three special sessions. He was twice honored by the Republican party with the nomination for Mayor of the City of Detroit and served as Delegate to the State Convention in 1892.

Captain Stewart demonstrated his fighting abilities in the Legislatures of 1897 and 1899. He did not try to make a record in the matter of introducing bills, but devoted most of his energies toward putting through some of the important legislation that was proposed in these two sessions and in fighting other measures, whose enactment he thought would prove detrimental to the interests of the State. He was identified with the determined lot of Republicans who were anxious to see that railroads and other corporations should pay taxes on the value of their property, and he therefore fought strenuously for the passage of the Atkinson Bill, and when that measure was killed in Court, for the amendment of the Constitution, so that the principles of that bill might be put into practice legally. Probably Captain Stewart's best work in both sessions was as a member of the Committee on Ways and Means of the House, in which body he fought all kinds of extravagance, and it was largely due to his efforts that the beet sugar bounty bill, which would have cost the State millions, was killed at the close of the session of 1899. In spite of this Stewart was liked by the farmers of the Legislature, who made him a member of that club, and he was one of their leaders.

Captain Stewart was of Whig lineage, and he has always been a Republican, his first vote being cast for Grant.

The Stewart Transportation Company was the first corporation with which his name was connected, having been Vice President and General Manager since the organization of the company in 1892.

Captain Stewart is a member of Detroit Post G. A. R., Union Lodge, Peninsular Chapter, Monroe Council, Detroit Commandery K. T.; Michigan Sovereign Consistory; Moslem Temple, Mystic Shrine; Concordia Society, and the Fellowcraft Club. He was married in 1873 at Algonac, Michigan, to Elzirene Allen, by whom he had one daughter, Lillian Beers Stewart. His wife died in 1877 and he was married again in 1884 to Minnie E. Tietsort, by whom he has three sons—Herbert Lesher, Garret Dunbar, and Albert Edwin, Jr.

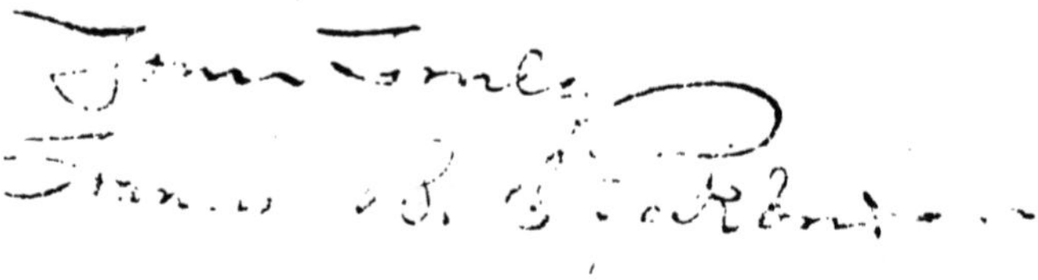

FRANCIS B. STOCKBRIDGE, for many years one of Michigan's leading lumbermen, and twice elected to the Senate of the United States, came of sturdy New England stock and traced his ancestry in this country back to 1635, when a young Englishman named John Stockbridge, well born and prosperous, with his young wife and infant boy settled in Scituate, Massachusetts. He bought a mill and built another, also a mansion house which was used as a garrison during King Phillip's War. Mill building and the milling business seem to have descended in almost regular line from this four times great grandfather down to Senator Stockbridge. From this John Stockbridge have descended some of the most eminent men and women of New England—business men, merchants, lawyers, physicians and scientists. About 1800 Wm. Stockbridge, the grandfather of the Senator, is described as the greatest landholder in Hanover, Massachusetts, and it is of record that he was a man of "ready wit, lively and sociable in his habits;" an "agreeable companion, and an industrious and upright citizen." He was selectman in Hanover in 1812. His son John, father of the Senator, was a physician and settled in Bath, Maine, in 1805, where he practiced his profession for forty-eight years, and was known as a "scientific and successful practitioner, a consistent and devoted friend and an honest and upright man." Here April 9th, 1826, Francis B. Stockbridge was born. His mother, Eliza Isabella Stockbridge, was the daughter of Hon. John Russell, for many years editor and proprietor of the Boston Commercial Gazette. Here Francis B. Stockbridge attended the common schools and academy until he was sixteen years of age, when he accepted a position as clerk in a wholesale dry goods house in Boston.

In 1847 he came West to Chicago, which in those early days showed no prophecy of being the future site of the wonder of the centuries, the World's Fair. In connection with another gentleman, he there opened a lumber yard, under the firm name of Carter & Stockbridge.

In making that move Mr. Stockbridge evinced the rare foresight and sagacity displayed in all the after transactions of his successful career. From a clerk in a dry goods house in Boston he became a lumber merchant in Chicago, and from that time onward his interests rapidly widened until he became one of the most prominent and extensive lumber dealers in the northwest. In 1853 he removed from Chicago to Allegan County, Michigan, where he had a number of sawmills. Locating at Saugatuck he remained there until 1874, when he removed to Kalamazoo, which was afterward his home.

Shortly after his removal to Kalamazoo Mr. Stockbridge became connected with O. R. Johnson & Co., whose mills then turned out about twenty-five million feet of lumber annually. Soon afterward he became a member of the Mackinac Lumber Company, whose mills were of about the same capacity, and in 1875, was elected President of the company. Three years afterward he founded and became President of the Black River Lumber Company. He led a busy life. In 1887 he organized the Kalamazoo Spring and Axle Company, of which he was also President. He was a member of the Fort Bragg Lumber Company, of California, and a large owner of Mississippi pine lands; a leading stockholder in Menominee iron mines and the Menominee River Lumber Company, of the Upper Peninsula of Michigan, and largely interested in the famous S. A. Brown & Co. stock-breeding farm, near Kalamazoo. During the war, though not in active service, he was on the staff of Governor Blair, and gained the rank of Colonel.

In 1869 Mr. Stockbridge was elected to represent Allegan County in the State Legislature, and after completing his term was elected to the State Senate, where he served most acceptably until 1873. In both Houses he was distinguished for his tact as an organizer, his calm insight and prudence as a manager, and his great ability in committee work in every form. He was engaged in several political campaigns, in which his reputation as a statesman and as a man of keen business, as well as political foresight, was clearly demonstrated, thus adding year by year to his reputation and the esteem in which he was held by his colleagues and constituents. His course seems to have been steadily progressive, both politically and in his business. "Confidence is a plant of but slow growth," but the people had tried him and he had their confidence, and in 1887 they elected him to succeed Hon. Omar D. Conger in the Senate of the United States. When his first term closed in 1893 he was renominated on the first ballot, elected and served in the Senate of the United States until his death, April 30th, 1894.

In that time-honored chamber, filled with the sacred memories of departed greatness, where the god-like Webster thundered, where still linger the echoes of the voices of Clay, Sumner, Everett, Conkling, Blaine, and a host of mighty ones, not dead, but living evermore—here, as elsewhere, his practical ability made itself apparent. He served with marked ability on several Senate committees; on the Committee on Fisheries, which was of great importance as affecting the food supply of the people. Of this Committee he was Chairman. He served on the Census Committee, on the Committee on Epidemic Diseases, the Committee on Indian Affairs, the Committee on Railroads and Naval Affairs. Though perhaps less known as a politician, much less as a mere politician, he was a Republican of the most pronounced type, one who ever labored for the interests of his party. As a legislator he had marked ability and discretion in considering and deciding grave questions of national policy and practicality, and preserved his equanimity among the many clashing and discordant elements that beset a man in political life.

The Senator was married in 1863 to Miss Betsy Arnold, of Gun Plain. Allegan County, Michigan, the estimable daughter of Daniel Arnold, Esq., one of the pioneers of the State. Their social and domestic relations were ever most pleasant. At the federal capital they moved in the highest and most select circles, and were noted for the munificence and royalty of their entertainments and receptions, as also at their elegant Michigan home, one of the finest in the State. Here the Senator threw off for a short season the oppressive cares of State and business, enjoying the beauties of his extensive grounds, and giving himself to restfulness and the indulgence of his natural tastes for all that was choice and elegant in literature and art, in the full enjoyment of all that an ample competence could gratify, the sure result of wise and well-directed commercial enterprises. Like the California Croesus, Senator Stanford, he was a great lover of the horse, his keen eye taking in with admiration the points and beauties of a well-bred animal, and in the raising of fine stock he perhaps found one of his greatest sources of pleasure.

Notwithstanding the multiplicity of his business interests, the time and attention devoted to political and Government affairs, and the demands of social life, we find the Senator was not unmindful of the sober and more important duties and promptings of the higher life, for as a member of the Protestant Episcopal Church, he was one of the Vestrymen, and prominently and actively connected with all church and charitable matters. He was President of the Kalamazoo Children's Home, a most worthy charity. He bought and gave the site and paid liberally toward the building of the beautiful edifice of the Young Men's Christian Association, which now stands a monument to his munificence, that donation alone amounting to $10,000. He also subscribed liberally toward the building of the Academy of Music, and was a munificent patron of a hospital in Chicago.

In October, 1887, we find the Senator one of three gentlemen who gave $13,000 toward carrying on the work of Kalamazoo College, and to causes such as these he gave freely of his means, keeping ever in view the prosperity and best interests of the city of his residence. He was a man of majestic and courtly presence, yet affable and easily approached. He was popular with all classes and with none more so than with his own employes. He did much for Kalamazoo, as well as for localities in the lumber districts where he had interests, and later, for the great State in which they formed a part. An open-hearted, free and whole-souled man, doing from day to day some generous deed for others, high rank or station counting little in his eyes, he valued a man for what he was and what he had accomplished, and there was no one more open to the approaches of the poor or humblest. Personal interests never encroached upon his higher duties to the public. Patiently he listened to every argument advanced for or against a measure, which might affect his constituency or the public good, tearing down the web of political sophistries and getting at the true bearing and merits of any bill under discussion; and when at last his decision was reached, his judgment fixed, he stood immovable as a rock, and the persuasions or entreaties of his warmest friends had no effect upon his judicial mind, when he felt that he was in the right. A self-poised, level-headed man, his adopted State was proud of him and he of her, and he stands high ranked among the sons of Michigan. His genial presence and kindly nature are now a loved remembrance.

WILLIAM STOCKING comes as near being a Connecticut Yankee as anyone now living in Michigan. He is a direct descendant of George Stocking, who came from England in 1633, was a freeman in Cambridge, Mass., in 1635, and was one of the original proprietors of the Town of Hartford, Conn., in 1639. On his mother's side he is descended from Thomas Newell, who was one of the first proprietors of the Town of Farmington, Conn., in 1640, and from the Wolcott family, who furnished three governors to the Colony and State of Connecticut. Seven generations of the Stockings and Newells lived in Connecticut before the subject of this sketch got away and came West. His ancestors included one officer in the French and Indian War, two in the War of the Revolution and one in the War of 1812, while almost every male relative between the ages of 18 and 45, took part in the War of the Rebellion.

William Stocking is the son of John M. and Emeline (Newell) Stocking, and was born in Waterbury, Conn., December 11, 1840. He attended the common and High School of the Town, the course being broken by one year as clerk in a hat and fur store. After leaving the High School he was three years clerk in the Waterbury Bank, and then, having a taste for salt water and adventure, shipped before the mast on a sailing packet running between New York and Liverpool. He took a short tour through Scotland and the North of England, and returned on the same vessel. A mention of this adventure at a later period called out the remark from a Detroit afternoon paper that "there were several good deck hands spoiled when the Detroit morning papers were started."

Mr. Stocking took two terms at Williston Seminary, Easthampton, Mass., jumped a year, and entered Yale College in 1861. In the summer of 1864 he enlisted in a Massachusetts hundred-day regiment, which was allowed to work overtime, and which was in service about five months. His discharge paper, however, reads that "William Stocking, private, Company F, Sixtieth Massachusetts Volunteers, enlisted for the period of one hundred years, and was discharged by reason of the expiration of his term of service." He, therefore, awaits with complacency the passage of a service pension act.

Returning from the army, Mr. Stocking graduated with his class, receiving the degree of A. B. in 1865, and M. A. in 1868. In College he was one of the editors of the Yale Literary Magazine, and early decided to go into the newspaper business. His first negotiation was for the editorship of a Presbyterian organ in the West, but this fell through, fortunately for both parties, for Stocking would not have

Wm Stocking

learned anything about modern journalism on a religious weekly, and the paper, under his editorship, would have been speedily tried for heresy and burned at the stake. He finally took the place of Local and State Editor of the Hartford Evening Press, of which General Joseph R. Hawley was the principal owner, and Charles Dudley Warner was editor. He was afterwards City Editor of both the Evening Press and Morning Courant, and in November, 1867, came to Detroit as Managing Editor of the Daily Post. From that time to this, though with occasional incursions into other fields of work, his main occupation has been with the Republican papers of Detroit, upon which he has held the various positions of Legislative Correspondent, Washington Correspondent, Managing Editor, Editor-in-Chief and editorial and special writer.

Mr. Stocking was brought up in an Abolition family, his father's barn being an "underground railway station," and the family reading including the Hartford Charter Oak, the New York Independent and Dr. Bailey's National Era. He was the only boy in town who put up a Hale and Julian flag in 1852, ran away from school and walked nine miles to hear Anson Burlingame speak in 1856, and walked twenty-two miles to cast his first vote, which was in favor of amending the Constitution of Connecticut so as to give suffrage to the negroes. He has been a Republican ever since the party was organized, and has attended nearly every Republican State Convention in Michigan since 1868. Though never on the stump he hopes that his advocacy, in the quiet of the editorial room, of stalwart Republican and sound money principles has been of some service to the party and the State.

His society affiliations have been almost entirely patriotic or literary, including the college fraternities of Alpha Delta Phi, and Phi Beta Kappa, the Loyal Legion during the war, and the first Post of the G. A. R. in Connecticut, of which he was one of the organizers. He was married May 19, 1869, to Elizabeth Lyman, a descendant of one of the founders of Hartford. Their children are Elizabeth Lyman and Frederick Newell Stocking and Mrs. Margaret Van Fleet.

HENRY H. SWAN, of Detroit, Judge of the United States District Court, is the son of Joseph G. Swan, a native of New York, whose ancestors were Scotch and English, and Mary C. Ling, whose parents emigrated from Germany, and settled at Detroit in 1832. Henry H. was born in the latter City October 2d, 1840. His earliest education was in the public schools. This was followed by a course in the excellent private school conducted by S. L. Campbell, where he fitted for college, and where he had, as classmates, Henry M. Duffield, David O. Farrand, Henry B. Ledyard and other young men who have since become prominent in Detroit's history. He entered Michigan University in 1858 and remained through Junior year, when, without completing his course, he left the University and went to California.

Here he remained five years, engaged in steamboating on the Sacramento and San Joaquin Rivers, acquiring a knowledge of inland navigation which was of service to him in later years in his maritime law practice. While in this business he occupied his leisure time in the study of law and was admitted to the bar early in 1867.

Mr. Swan returned to Detroit the same year, entered the law office of D. B. & H. M. Duffield, and in October, 1867, was admitted to practice in the Supreme Court of the State. April 15th, 1870 he was appointed Assistant United States District Attorney at Detroit, and held the position for seven years, when he became associated in partnership with A. B. Maynard, who had been his superior in office during a portion of that period. Their intimate relations in their official positions had given each member of the firm a good knowledge of the qualifications and characteristics of the other, and the partnership was attended with the most satisfactory results. It continued till January 13th, 1891, when the junior partner was appointed United States District Judge.

Judge Swan's career upon the bench has vindicated the wisdom of his appointment. The court is second among the district courts of the whole country in the number of its admiralty cases, and under previous capable judges had done much toward establishing sound principles of maritime law. For this part of the business Judge Swan was admirably fitted at the start, having had, in his private practice some of the largest and most involved cases occurring on the lakes. Aside from this specialty, his decisions in other important civil cases, have maintained the high reputation which the Court had acquired under his predecessors, Judges Longyear and Brown.

No case has occurred in this District for many years which attracted more widespread attention than that of the City of Detroit against the Detroit City Railway Company. Judge Swan's conclusion in that case was afterwards sustained by the United States Circuit Court of Appeals. He has had many other important cases in the Court of Appeals.

Judge Swan's social and family relations are of the pleasantest and best. He was married April 20th, 1873, to Miss Jennie E. Clark, daughter of Rev. W. C. Clark, a retired Presbyterian clergyman, and they have two children, William M. and Mary C. Swan.

ALBERT DELOS THOMPSON, for many years in the office of the Register of Deeds of Livingston County, was born in Howell, in that County, January 22d, 1840. His parents were Edward Thompson, a farmer, and Rocelia Thompson. His father came from Herkimer County, N. Y., in 1836, and settled, with his parents, near Howell. His mother came from Cayuga County, N. Y. He was educated at Hillsdale College and took a course at the Ames Business College in Syracuse, N. Y. His father and mother died when he was but five years old, and he lived with an uncle until seventeen years

W. B. Thompson

old; then worked by the month on a farm except the time spent in school. He continued work at farming until January 1st, 1889, when he moved to Howell, and acted as Deputy Register of Deeds during the years from 1889 to 1894 inclusive. During 1895 and 1896 he was Probate Clerk of the County. In the campaign of 1897 he was elected Register of Deeds, being the only Republican elected on the County ticket. In 1899 he was re-elected by an increased majority and still holds the office. He held the office of Supervisor for three terms in succession and Township Clerk for several years previous to that. He has been a Republican ever since the party was organized, and voted for every Republican candidate for President beginning with 1868. He has been a Knight of the Maccabees since February, 1885. He was married to Emily J. Hammond, January 30th, 1868, in Cohocton, Livingston County, Mich. Their children are Lyman H. Thompson, Mrs. Robert H. Brown, Jr., Lillie J. Thompson, now Mrs. C. E. Garland, and Alvaro G. Thompson.

WILLIAM BAKER THOMPSON, who has done the country good service both in military and official positions, was the son of Israel Thompson, a farmer, and Martha Ann (Baker) Thompson, and was born in Fort Ann, N. Y., August 27, 1838. The Thompsons came of a long line of New England ancestry, the founder of the family in this country being Anthony Thompson, who came from England with Governor Eaton and Rev. John Davenport, and settled in New Haven in 1638.

The subject of this brief sketch received his education in the common schools and at the Academy at Fort Edward, N. Y., and commenced his business career as clerk and bookkeeper in a mercantile establishment. Later the Union cause in the War of the Rebellion claimed his services, and in 1863 he went out as Second Lieutenant of Company D, Eleventh Michigan Cavalry, and was subsequently promoted to First Lieutenant in the same regiment. In July, 1865, he was transferred to the Eighth Cavalry as Quartermaster, and was mustered out with his regiment September 22d, 1865. There were a number of Michigan regiments that saw very active service in the war, but none that was in more engagements in the same period of time than the Eleventh Cavalry. From May 17, 1864, till May 2, 1865, it met the enemy in fifty-nine different engagements in Kentucky, Tennessee, Virginia, North Carolina and South Carolina.

In 1867, with his brother, G. I. Thompson, he engaged in the banking business at Hudson, and is now President of the Thompson Savings Bank. He is also interested with his other brother, R. W. Thompson, in the First National Bank, St. John, Kas.

Mr. Thompson was for many years connected with the United States postal service, having been Superintendent of the Ninth Division, General Superintendent of the Railway Mail Service, and Second Assistant Postmaster General during President Arthur's Administration and it was largely due to his efforts that the first great fast mail between New York and Chicago was established and made a success.

Mr. Thompson has always been active in the Republican party, and cast his first vote for Lincoln, and has attended numerous State Conventions as delegate. He has been Treasurer of the Republican Congressional Campaign Committee for several campaigns, and is now of the firm of Thompson & Slater, attorneys before the Executive Departments in Washington.

He is a member of the Michigan Club of Detroit; Masonic bodies, Cosmos Club, Military Order of the Loyal Legion, Sons of the American Revolution, and Society of Colonial Wars. He was married June 20th, 1883, to Miss Emma Key, daughter of Hon. D. M. Key, who was Postmaster General and later Judge of the United States Court in Tennessee.

CHARLES ELROY TOWNSEND, attorney at Jackson, Mich., was born on a farm in Concord, Jackson County, August 15th, 1850. His parents were James Weeden Townsend, a farmer, and Eunice Salina Townsend. His father's ancestors went with William the Conqueror into England in 1066 and settled there, and his mother's people came originally from Scotland into England. His father was very poor and heavily in debt and he worked on the farm for his father and at times for neighbors, till about nineteen years of age, when he borrowed enough money to carry him through school at Jackson and one year at Ann Arbor. In 1878 he hired out to teach a district school in District No. 6 of Concord, and taught there for fifteen months when he was elected principal of the High School at Parma, Mich., and remained as Principal at Parma from September, 1880, till January 1st, 1887. In November, 1886, he was elected Register of Deeds from Jackson County and was renominated and re-elected four times successively. In 1896 he refused a renomination for Register of Deeds and formed a law partnership with Charles A. Blair and Charles H. Smith, under the firm name of Blair, Smith & Townsend, and on January 1st, 1897, entered into partnership business which has continued since to date. He is attorney for the Cincinnati Northern Railroad Company, attorney and Vice-President of the Jackson State Savings Bank, and Attorney and Director of the Pandora Corset Company.

Mr. Townsend has been a Republican since 1856 and cast his first vote for Garfield; was a delegate from the Third Congressional District of Michigan to the Republican National Convention at Chicago in 1888 and has been a delegate to nearly every State Convention of the party since 1886. He is a member of the Republican State Central Committee, to which position he was elected in 1898. He is a Knight Templar and Shriner in Masonry, and is a member of the Elks and of the Jackson City Club. He was married September 1st, 1880, to Rena Paddock, of Concord, but has no children.

SAMUEL W. VANCE, of Port Huron, for one term and part of another Judge of the Thirty-first Circuit, was born in Durham County, Canada, December 9th, 1852. His father came from County Antrim, Ireland, in 1815, with his parents, who located in Durham County, settled on a farm and raised a family of twelve children, of whom Samuel W. was the youngest. His mother came from County Caven, Ireland, with her parents when she was eleven years old. The father moved in 1857 to Lambton County, where he continued the occupation of farming till his death, in 1860.

Samuel W. had the usual fortune of a farmer's boy, working on the farm summers and attending school winters, but as he approached maturity he decided to use the small patrimony left him in providing himself with a good education, and begun his course at Albert College, Belleville, Canada. He matriculated at the University of that place, and in the fall of 1876 entered the law department of the University of Michigan at Ann Arbor, and graduated in 1878, with the degree of LL. B. He was admitted to the bar at Ann Arbor, March 25th, 1878. He now found himself the possessor of a degree, but no money in his pocket. In his own expressive language, he had "put his capital all into his head." Subsequent events proved that this was a much better investment than putting it in even the very best Canadian soil. He settled at Port Huron, January 2d, 1879, and took a position in the office of Atkinson & Stevenson, where he remained for some time as a clerk; later entering into partnership with William F. Atkinson, which continued from 1879 to 1881. For the next year he was with P. H. Phillips. He then formed a partnership with Judge E. W. Harris, upon the latter's retirement from the bench of the Circuit Court, which was continued until 1885. From that time on he was associated with O'Brien J. Atkinson until he was nominated for Circuit Judge in April, 1892. He was elected to fill a vacancy, and at the expiration of the term was re-elected for a full six-year term, which expired January 1st, 1900. Before attaining the judicial position Judge Vance served two years as City Attorney of Port Huron. He was a Republican and was somewhat active in politics, but never sought office except in the line of his profession. He was married in September, 1887, to Miss Carrie Sines, of Wayne County, Mich., and they have one child, Harold.

While practicing law Mr. Vance had no specialty in his profession, but soon became interested in important cases. both in the State and Supreme Court, and in the United States Circuit and District Courts. When the Congress of Judges was about to convene at the Exposition in Chicago in 1893, he was appointed to represent Michigan in that assembly. As a Judge he looked mainly at established legal principles. and did not give much weight to opinions or decisions which conflicted with his convictions of what those principles were, and the lawyers of the circuit often refer to this trait of his character. On the bench he was always considerate and courteous and was regarded by members of the bar as one of the best of judges.

PHILIP TAYLOR VAN ZILE, who has taken rank among the most prominent men in Michigan in the private practice of law, upon the bench, and in the Government service in a remote territory, was born at Osceola, Tioga County, Pennsylvania, July 20th, 1844, being descended from old Holland stock. He prepared for college in the public schools of Osceola and at Union Academy, Knoxville, Penn., and entered the University at Alfred Center, N. Y., in the classical course. He paid his way through by teaching and other occupations, and graduated in 1862. He was then principal of a private school in Rochester, O., for a time, and while there he was unanimously elected Captain of Company D, Third Ohio Militia, which was organized to resist the Morgan raids in that State. He was recommended by the military committee as an efficient officer, and was offered a commission as Captain, if he would raise a company for the Thirty-second Ohio Infantry, then in the field. He preferred, however, another branch of the service, and enlisted as a private in Battery E, First Ohio Artillery. He was engaged in all the campaigns with the Army of the Cumberland, including the campaign against Hood after the siege of Atlanta, and the important Battle of Nashville.

In 1865 Mr. Van Zile entered the law department of Michigan University, graduated in 1867, was admitted to the bar the same year, and settled in Charlotte, Eaton County. He soon obtained a lucrative practice and in 1875 was elected Judge of the Fifth Judicial Circuit. In 1878, after twice declining the office, he was, at the earnest solicitation of U. S. Senator Isaac P. Christiancy, who represented that President Hayes urgently requested it, persuaded to accept the appointment of United States District Attorney for Utah, and entered upon his duties there in March, 1878, remaining in charge of the office until the spring of 1884, when he resigned and returned to Charlotte. In 1884 he was chosen Chairman of the Republican State Central Committee. In 1890 he removed to Detroit. At its semi-centennial anniversary the degree of Ph. D. was conferred upon him by his Alma Mater, Alfred University, and in 1893, that of LL. D. Soon after settling in Detroit he was engaged as special lecturer in the Detroit College of Law and in 1893 he was elected Dean of the Faculty of the Institution.

Judge Van Zile's career as District Attorney for Utah, was memorable as furnishing the first successful attempt to enforce the United States laws against murder and polygamy. The whole power of the Mormon church was opposed to the enforcement of the laws, and it was generally successful. As one of the first steps toward breaking that power, Mr. Van Zile secured in the famous "Miles Case" a ruling from the District Judge on the ineligibility of polygamists or members of the Mormon Church as jurors in the trial of polygamy cases. The challenge to Mormon jurors, upon the ground that they were biased by their belief that polygamy was a law of God unto that people and therefore right, was sustained by the United States District Judge, a Gentile jury was obtained, and Miles was

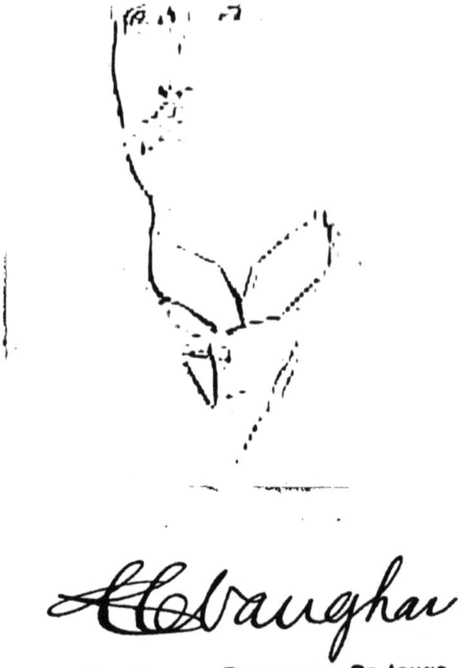

THE CLINTON REPUBLICAN, ST. JOHNS.

convicted and sentenced to five years in the penitentiary. The case, because of this ruling of the District Court, was appealed to the Supreme Court of the Territory, where it was affirmed, and then appealed to the Supreme Court of the United States, where it was again affirmed. This was most important and far reaching in its results as it made possible the securing of unbiased juries.

After settling in Detroit Judge Van Zile easily took a leading position at the bar. In 1893 he was appointed by the Wayne County Circuit Judges, Chairman of a standing committee for the examination of applicants for admission to the bar. Two years later, after the Legislature had provided for a State Board of Examiners for such service, he was, upon recommendation of the Supreme Court Judges, appointed a member of the Board. At the spring Convention of 1895 he was a candidate for the Republican nomination for Justice of the Supreme Court. He had a strong following from other parts of the State, but owing to the factional quarrels in Wayne County, his own home, part of the vote of that County went to others, and he failed of the nomination.

Judge Van Zile has always been a Republican and always active in politics. When in Charlotte he was one of a little circle of workers, with good capacity for organization, who were instrumental in making Eaton County one of the most steadfast Republican Counties in the State. He was for several years a Director, and one year President, of the Michigan Club; has often attended State Conventions as a delegate, and has been both Temporary and Permanent Chairman of such Conventions.

COLEMAN CHAUNCEY VAUGHAN, one of Michigan's wide awake editors, is the son of Chauncey Vaughan, a farmer, and Mary A. Hungerford, and was born August 1st, 1857, in Machias, N. Y. His grandfather Vaughan was born in Vermont and his great grandfather McMaster, on his mother's side, was born in Pennsylvania. There are six or seven generations of the family in this country. The name Vaughan is of Welsh origin.

Coleman C. Vaughan was educated in the common schools and Ten Brook Academy at Franklinville, N. Y., until his sixteenth year, then went into the Clarion office at Lapeer, Mich., and served four years' apprenticeship, and later worked two years at the case on the Free Press. Two years after that he bought the Lapeer Clarion, which he published eighteen months, and then engaged in other business for a couple of years, going to St. Johns in 1889, when he bought the Clinton Republican, which he has since published. He has been a Republican ever since he was born. He served one term as Alderman in Lapeer about 1887 and has been twice elected President of the Village of St. Johns. He is Secretary of the Hicks Lumber Company, and a director in the St. Johns National Bank and Clinton

County Savings Bank, and is a Knight Templar, Knight of Pythias and member of the Royal Arcanum.

Mr. Vaughan was married to Isabel Stilwell, of Franklinville, N. Y, September 30, 1885, who died June 21st, 1888. One son was born to them. September 14, 1892, he was united in marriage with Jennie M. Hicks, at St. Johns. She died in a hospital, at Chicago, March 7. 1895. May 26, 1897, Mr. Vaughan was married to his present wife, who was formerly Miss Nettie L. Davies, of St. Johns.

ALONZO VINCENT, one of the best known hotel men in Southwestern Michigan, was born in the Village of Clayton, Jefferson County, N. Y., January 16th, 1844. His father was Albert Vincent, a farmer, and his mother's maiden name was Harriett Slater. His parents were natives of New York, who came to Michigan in 1845, locating in Marshall, and three years after moved to Berrien County. They settled on a farm, where the father engaged in agricultural pursuits for some time: later removed to Benton Harbor, where he died in 1885. The ancestors came from France before the Revolutionary War.

Alonzo received his education in the public schools of Berrien County, and in 1861, when seventeen years old, enlisted in Company D, Sixty-sixth Illinois Volunteers, the Western Sharpshooters, and participated in a number of the hardest fought battles of the war, including the Battle of Ft. Donelson, Shiloh, Iuka, siege of Corinth, the second battle of Corinth and Atlanta campaign. He was then transferred to the Fifteenth Army Corps, General Logan commanding, and marched with Sherman to the Sea and through the Carolinas and Virginia to Washington, where he took part in the Grand Review. He was mustered out at Springfield, Ill., in July, 1865.

Coming home from the war in 1865, Mr. Vincent engaged in the grocery business. In a short time he was burned out and worked for other men until 1870, when he engaged in the hotel business in Coloma. In 1874 he bought and operated a farm for three years, when he moved to Benton Harbor and engaged in the hotel business, which he has followed ever since, with the exception of a few years when engaged as a hardware merchant. He has always been successful in the hotel business, operating different hotels as new ones were built for the growing City, including the American House, Higbee House and then the Hotel Benton. In 1895 he moved to St. Joseph to the Hotel Whitcomb, and in the spring of 1900 bought the hotel property, where he is actively engaged in the firm of Vincent & Blake.

Mr. Vincent was always a Republican and cast his first vote for Lincoln at Rome, Ga., in 1864, being then in the Army. He has been active in local and State politics and has often been delegate to State Conventions and served three terms on the State Central Committee. He is a member of Lake Shore Lodge No. 298, A. F. & A. M., of the Elks and George H. Thomas Post No. 14, G. A. R. In 1866 he was

Alonzo Vincent

married to Miss Elmira Edith, daughter of Joseph and Luck (Young) Enos, of Bainbridge Township, Berrien County. He has two children, Maud Edith, wife of Clarence E. Blake, and Gertrude Marie.

BYRON SYLVESTER WAITE, late a Judge in the Wayne Circuit Court, was the son of Elihu Waite, a farmer, and Elizabeth Tarbell Waite, and was born September 27th, 1852, at Pennfield, Monroe County, N. Y. His ancestors came from England, the Waites settling at Hatfield, Mass., in 1670. Many descendants live in that section still. The Tarbells settled in Vermont near Braintree at an early date, both branches having representatives in the Revolution. Elihu Waite moved to Michigan in 1855, living in Rose, Oakland County, about one year, when he moved on to a piece of land in Tyrone, Livingston County, where he reared his family of seven children. The old homestead still remains in the family.

Byron S. Waite was educated at the district school in Tyrone, Fenton Seminary, Fenton High School and University of Michigan. He worked on the farm when not in school until eighteen years of age, and then taught district school for two winter terms and went to school and worked on the farm when not teaching or attending school. When attending school he walked four miles, night and morning, to and from school in Fenton, over the hills of Tyrone. In 1874 he commenced teaching the schools at Rochester, Mich.; taught for two years and entered the University in 1876; took a four years' literary course, completing the work for master's degree; completed his college course on what money he had saved, and what credit he had; was admitted to the bar on examination in 1879 in Washtenaw County. After graduation in 1880 he was with the Superintendent of Public Instruction at Lansing one year, then became a member of the law firm of Cramer, Corbin & Waite, with offices at Ann Arbor and Dundee, Monroe County. In 1882 he went to Menominee and formed a partnership with A. L. Sawyer, of that place, for practice of the law, remaining there until 1895. The firm had a large business and a paying one. He was also engaged in the lumber business some, made considerable by purchasing land, and dabbled some in mining. In 1895 he removed to Detroit and was engaged as Assistant Prosecuting Attorney and Circuit Judge till January 1st, 1901.

Judge Waite has been a Republican ever since he could distinguish principles. He has been to eight or ten different State Conventions and had a hand in all the legislation of any importance during the sessions of the Legislature of 1889 and 1895. He was Circuit Court Commissioner in Menominee County 1882 to 1886, and Representative in the Legislature from Menominee County in 1889 and 1895, but resigned when he removed to Detroit in September, 1895.

He is a Knight Templar, member of the Shrine, Knights of the Maccabees, A. O. U. W., Elks, Wheelmen, Harmonie Society, Fellowcraft Club, Country Club and Detroit Athletic Association. He was married January 20th, 1881, to Ismene Cramer, of Ann Arbor, who graduated from the University in the same class, and they have six children, four boys and two girls in the order following: Donald Cramer, Marjory Ismene, Elizabeth Alice, Stanley Byron, Malcolm Ivan and Alan Frederick.

GEORGE PROCTOR WANTY, of Grand Rapids, United States District Judge of the Western District of Michigan, is the son of Samuel Wanty and Elizabeth Proctor Wanty and was born at Ann Arbor, Mich., March 12th, 1856. On his father's side, he is a descendant of an old Huguenot family who went from France early in the seventeenth century and settled at Thorney Abbey, in Cambridgeshire, England. His parents came to the United States in 1853, settling first in Brooklyn, N. Y., thence coming to Detroit and finally to Ann Arbor in 1855. George P. Wanty was educated in the common schools at Ann Arbor and the University of Michigan, and on graduating at the law department of the University in 1878, he moved to Grand Rapids, was admitted to the bar, and practiced law in that City until he was appointed United States District Judge on the 12th of March, 1900. During this long period of active practice he was associated at different times with Col. Thaddeus Foote, Hon. Fred A. Maynard and Niram A. Fletcher.

Mr. Wanty enjoyed the friendship and counsel of Judge Cooley from his youth up. Part of the advice that the Judge pressed upon him was to make the law and not politics his profession. He has heeded this advice and has held no offices except the judicial position which he now occupies. He has nevertheless been a consistent Republican in politics, casting his first ballot for Garfield.

He was married June 22d, 1886, to Miss Emma Nichols and they have two children: Helen, aged 13, and Thomas Cooley, aged 11. In religion he is an Episcopalian. He never belonged to a secret society and has never been connected with large companies or properties. He has held the office of President of the Michigan State Bar Association, and Chairman of the General Counsel of the American Bar Association, and although he never belonged to a secret society he is a member of every club not inconsistent with his religious and political views, that exists in the City where he lives.

FRED MALTBY WARNER, of Farmington, is made out, by the votes he has received, to be about the most popular man in Eastern Michigan. He was born in Hickling, Nottinghamshire, England, July 1st, 1865, and was brought by his parents to this country at the age of two months. His mother died soon afterwards, and he was adopted by P. Dean Warner, who has been a resident of Farmington since 1824 and who has held many offices of prominence, including

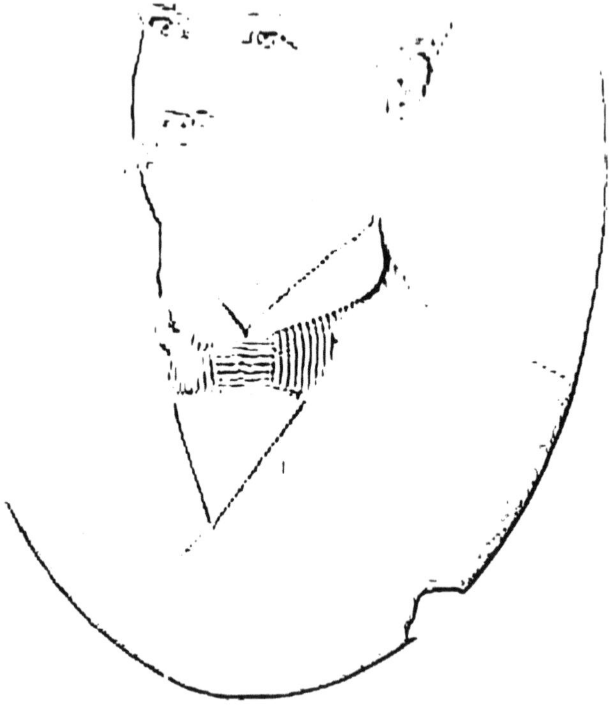

Fred M. Warner

membership in the House of Representatives in 1851, 1865 and 1867, and in the State Senate in 1869. He was Speaker of the House in 1867.

Fred says his own early struggles were chiefly with the old high wheel bicycles, on riding which he held the State championship for one and five miles. He was educated at the Farmington High School and Michigan Agricultural College, began as clerk in his father's store at the age of sixteen, and at the age of twenty-one the mercantile business was turned over to him by his father. Two years later he bought out a hardware store, and united it with other business. The next year he built a cheese factory at Farmington, and from that time the manufacture of cheese has been his leading business, though he still continues the mercantile business, having a large general store at Farmington. He has since established cheese factories at Novi, Franklin and Spring Brook, all in Oakland County. The annual output of the four factories is over a half million pounds of cheese per season. He is also half owner in the large brick manufacturing plant at Farmington, is a Stockholder and Director of the Farmington Exchange Bank, is the owner of a large cold storage plant and handles large quantities of butter and eggs. He takes a hand, also, in matters of public concern, and was the most influential man along the line in securing franchises, right of way and other facilities for the Detroit & Northwestern Electric Railway, connecting Farmington with both Pontiac and Detroit.

Mr. Warner has also been active in politics and always on the Republican side. He cast his first vote in November, 1886, and his first Presidential vote was for Harrison in 1888. He was elected a member of the Farmington Village Council when he was twenty-three years of age and has served on the Council ten years, five of them as President of the Village. He was four times elected without opposition, and the one time when there was an opposing candidate he had a greater majority than his opponent had votes.

In 1894 Mr. Warner was elected to the State Senate from the Twelfth District, comprising the Counties of Oakland and Macomb. He made the most remarkable run ever made by any candidate for a political office. In his own Township of Farmington he received four times as great a majority as his opponent had votes. In both Oakland and Macomb Counties he led the ticket, receiving a much larger vote than the most popular of the men on the County ticket, notwithstanding the fact that it is much more difficult to run ahead of one's ticket for a legislative than for a County office. He was re-elected to the Senate in 1898. Among the important measures in which he was instrumental in passing, was one compelling toll road companies to keep their roads in proper condition. He was a candidate for Secretary of State in 1898, but was defeated by a small majority in the Convention. At the Convention in June, 1900, he was again a candidate, and was nominated by acclamation, receiving every vote in the Convention. He was elected with the rest of the Republican ticket by a large majority.

Mr. Warner is a Knight Templar, a Knight of Pythias, a member of the Maccabees, Loyal Guard and the L. A. W. He was married in September, 1888, to Martha Davis, daughter of Samuel Davis, of Farmington. Their children are Edessa, Howard, Harley and Helen.

HOMER WARREN, who is one of the best known real estate men and Republican politicians in the City, is the son of Rev. S. E. and Ellen Davis Warren, and was born in Shelby, Mich., December 1st, 1855. He attended public schools in several cities, where his father was called to the pastorate of different churches, and at the age of seventeen located permanently in Detroit. For six years he was engaged as clerk in the large book and stationery establishment of J. M. Arnold & Co., resigning his position to accept the appointment as Deputy Collector of Customs at Detroit, and was later made Cashier of the Customs Office. In 1886 Mr. Warren went into the real estate business, in which he has been actively and successfully engaged ever since. He operated alone until 1892, devoting himself to the improvement, subdivision and marketing of several tracts of land which he had purchased previous to resigning from the Customs service. In 1892 the present firm of Homer Warren & Co. was organized, the company members being Messrs. Cullen Brown and Frank C. Andrews. Their business extends over the entire State of Michigan and they also transact business for numerous large estates in other localities.

Within the past few years the firm have negotiated many of the largest real estate transactions that have been made in the City, and have been particularly successful in handling high priced business property. Mr. Warren's judgment upon real estate values and prospects is considered to be of the best. In 1894 Mr. Warren added to his business the Michigan agency for four of the largest fire insurance companies in the world, viz., the English-American Underwriters Co.; Providence, R. I.; German-Alliance Co., and the Mutual Fire Insurance Company. Mr. Warren is prominently identified with the business interests of the City. He is one of the Board of Governors of the Fellowcraft Club and is a member of the Michigan Club, Detroit Club, and St. Clair Flats Fishing and Gun Club of Detroit, and holds high honors in the Masonic fraternity.

Mr. Warren has always been a strong Republican, and a hard working one, often helping other people to office, but not aspiring to office for himself. He has been repeatedly urged to be a candidate for Mayor and other high positions, but has declined on account of the pressing demands of business. But he has found time to do a few weeks' good party service during several recent campaigns. In the spring of 1900 he managed D. M. Ferry's canvass for the Guber-

natorial nomination in Wayne County, and through the summer and fall, acted as Treasurer of the Republican State Central Committee, where he rendered very efficient service. In all the relations of life Mr. Warren is a man of the strictest integrity of character and purpose and is deservedly held in the highest esteem.

WILLIAM WALTER WEDEMEYER, of Ann Arbor, was born March 22d, 1873, on a farm in the Township of Lima, Washtenaw County, Mich., his father being Frederick Wedemeyer, a farmer, and his mother Augusta Wedemeyer, nee Gruner. His father was born at Lilienthal, near Bremen, Germany; received a fine education especially in the languages, and was fitted for a business career. He spent several years in the West Indies, with Havana as his business home, as agent for his brother, a wholesale merchant of Bremen, Germany. He afterwards came to this country to settle, and on account of poor health, went to farming at Lima, Mich., where he remained until his death, in 1885. He had been a great traveler and was an accomplished linguist. His wife was born in Windecken, Hesse Darmstadt, Germany, and came over to the United States with her parents in the '50's.

The subject of this sketch attended district school near home in Lima until 14 years old; then entered Ann Arbor High School and graduated in 1890. He graduated from the literary department of the University of Michigan in 1894 and from the law department in 1895. He was class orator of his literary class, President of the Students' Lecture Association, on the Editorial Boards of the University of Michigan Daily and Castalian in the literary department and of Res Gestae, in the law department. He was also active in oratorical work at the University, and represented the University at the Chicago Union League Club Washington birthday exercises in 1894. He held numerous minor positions in college life. Before entering the University he had worked on the farm at home and taught district school. He worked his way through the University entirely by his own efforts, mainly by newspaper work. His parents died before he finished school.

In the spring of 1895 Mr. Wedemeyer was elected Commissioner of Schools of Washtenaw County. In the spring of 1896 he was elected Chairman of the Washtenaw Republican County Committee and took an active part in the speaking campaign in that year, going out for the State Central Committee. In 1897 he was appointed Deputy Commissioner of Railroads and held the position for two years. In 1898 he was a prominent candidate for the Republican Congressional nomination in the Second District, losing by a narrow margin. He was only twenty-five years old when he made that fight. He took an active part in the campaign that fall throughout the State, under the State Central Committee, under whose direction he spoke throughout the campaign of 1900. He declined appointment

A. O. Wheeler

1880, and was a delegate from the Ninth District of Michigan to the National Convention in Philadelphia in 1900. He was Senator in the State Legislature in 1891 and 1895 and was in the field for the Republican nomination for Governor in 1896. The next year he was appointed United States Marshal for the Western District of Michigan, a position which he still holds. The only society affiliation he has is with the Masons. He was married May 10th, 1870, in Manistee, to Miss Ella M. Barnes, daughter of Russell Barnes, the first hardware merchant of Manistee. They have four children, as follows: Isma L. Wheeler, now Mrs. Rufus C. Thayer; Abram Oren Wheeler, Jr., Morton Barnes Wheeler and Burr Wheeler.

GEORGE WILLARD, of Battle Creek, now in his seventy-seventh year, is one of the veterans of the Republican party, and one of the comparatively small remnant of men now living who voted for Kinsley S. Bingham for Governor in 1854. His parents were Allen Willard, a farmer, and Eliza Barron Willard, and he was born at Bolton, Vt., March 20th, 1824. He is the eighth in descent from Simon Willard, of Horsmonden, Kent County, England, who was one of the founders of Concord, Mass., and was distinguished in early New England history. His father, Allen Willard, was a classmate of Rufus Choate in Dartmouth College.

The subject of this sketch came with his father to Michigan in 1836, and settled at Battle Creek, where he still resides. He was educated at the Kalamazoo branch of the University of Michigan, where he took an academic and classical course, and afterward received the degree of A. M. from Kalamazoo College. In 1845 he became the principal of the Marshall Academy, studied for the ministry of the Protestant Episcopal Church and was subsequently rector of St. Mark's Church, Coldwater, St. Thomas' Church, Battle Creek, and St. Luke's Church, Kalamazoo. He retired from the ministry and in 1867 purchased the Battle Creek Journal, with which he has since been connected as publisher and editor.

Mr. Willard cast his first Republican ballot for Kinsley S. Bingham and the rest of the Republican ticket in 1854, the year the party was formed. He has been a member of several State Conventions, was Chairman of the Committee on Resolutions at the State Convention in 1868; was delegate-at-large from Michigan to the National Republican Convention in 1872, and was a member of the Michigan Constitutional Convention in 1867. Mr. Willard was elected a member of the State Board of Education in 1856, during the Fremont campaign, and served six years. It was while he was a member of this Board that the State Agricultural College was first opened, in the year 1857, that being the first State Institution established by the Republican party. The college was under the direction of the State Board of Education at that time and for some years thereafter.

Mr. Willard was elected to the Board of Regents of the University in 1863 and was re-elected in 1865, serving in all ten years. While on this Board he introduced and earnestly labored for some years for the adoption of the resolution for opening the University of Michigan to women, and this was finally accomplished in 1870.

He was a member of the House in the Michigan Legislature in 1867, and was elected Member of Congress from the Third Michigan District in 1872 and 1874. During his second term he was a member of the Joint Committee of the two Houses which reported the Bill for the Electoral Commission in the disposal of the Hayes-Tilden controversy, an account of whose membership and transactions is given quite in detail in the first volume of this publication. He was also a member in 1876-7, of the United States Monetary Commission which reported on the coinage of gold and silver. The full membership of this Commission was Senators John P. Jones, of Nevada, Chairman; Lewis V. Bogy, of Missouri; George Boutwell, of Massachusetts; Representatives Randall L. Gibson, of Louisiana; George Willard, of Michigan; Richard P. Bland, of Missouri, and Messrs. William S. Groesbeck, of Ohio, and Professor Francis Bowen, of Massachusetts. He was also member of the National Centennial Board of Finance for the World's Fair at Philadelphia.

Mr. Willard was a delegate to the General Convention of the Protestant Episcopal Church in Philadelphia in 1856; Chicago in 1886; New York in 1889; Baltimore in 1892, and Washington in 1898. He is a member of the Athelstan Club, Battle Creek, but no other social organization. He was married in 1844 to Emily Harris, and after her death, to Elizabeth A. Willard. His children are Mrs. C. D. Brewer, Mrs. E. W. Moore, and George B. Willard, all residing in Battle Creek.

FRANK HAWLEY WILLIAMS, of Allegan, is the son of William B. Williams (a sketch of whose life follows this), and of Marietta Osborn Williams. He was born July 12, 1864, at Allegan, and graduated from the High School in that Village in 1881. He spent the summers of 1881, 1882 and 1883 working on his father's farm near Allegan. In the winter of 1881-2 he was a student under H. W. Foster preparing for the University; taught in district schools and also as a substitute in the Grammar and High School at Allegan in the winter of 1882-3, and earned enough money to pay his way for one year at the University, taking an engineering course. Shortage of finances compelled him to leave that institution at the end of the first semester in February, 1885. He then commenced work as a clerk and student in the law office of his father; was admitted to the bar October 21st, 1886, and became partner in the law firm of W. B. Williams & Son, which is still continued. As clerk in the

Frank H. Williams

office he had charge of the business of the Kellogg estate, which at that time amounted to about forty thousand dollars, and retained control of this business until elected Judge of Probate. He made use of his engineering knowledge in his summer vacations, was employed in the summer of 1887 as transit man to survey the extension of the C., J. & M. R. R. to Saugatuck; was appointed Village Surveyor of Allegan, October 3rd, 1887, and was reappointed each year until March, 1891, and made a compilation of Village surveys and a permanent record of the same. In May, 1891, he was appointed City Engineer of Big Rapids, going to that place to do such work as was required, and held the position until May, 1895. In March, 1894, he was appointed Village Attorney of Allegan, Mich., holding office for one year. In March, 1896, he was reappointed and held the office until March, 1898.

September 3rd, 1896, after a vigorous campaign, Mr. Williams was unanimously nominated for the office of Judge of Probate of Allegan County and was elected by a majority of 1972. At a meeting of the Judges of Probate within the District of the Kalamazoo Asylum, he was elected Secretary of a preliminary organization with a view of perfecting a State organization. At Lansing, in Mar. h, 1897, he was unanimously chosen as President of the State Association of Probate Judges and held that office until October, 1899. At the annual meeting in Detroit, in 1898, he recommended that a committee be appointed to revise the probate blanks of the State. The Association adopted the recommendation with the provision that he should appoint the committee and act as Chairman, and Judge Jewell, of Kent, and Judge Maynard, of Eaton, were appointed upon the committee. These committeemen, by the expenditure of much time and money have revised nearly all of the important blanks used in the Probate Court and are now ready to submit them to the State association for adoption. He was unanimously renominated by the Republicans of Allegan County for a second term as Judge of Probate, August 22d, 1900, and re-elected by a majority of 2,436. In addition to his official law business he is a Stockholder and Director in the Allegan Wheel Company, a manufacturing corporation.

Mr. Williams was brought up a Republican, and always stayed with the party, casting his first vote for President for Harrison, in 1888. He was Secretary of the Republican County Committee, 1894 to 1896, and Chairman, 1898 to 1900, and was Delegate-at-Large from Allegan County to the State Convention, held at Grand Rapids in June, 1900. He was made a Master Mason in 1893 and held all of the subordinate offices in Allegan Lodge No. 111; was elected W. M. in December, 1898 and still holds that position. He is Master of the Third Veil, Eureka Chapter No. 50, Allegan; member of Moriah Lodge of Perfection, the Council and Rose Croix Chapter of Grand Rapids; is a Maccabee and member of Camp Elisha Mix, Sons of Veterans.

WILLIAM BREWSTER WILLIAMS, was born July 28th, 1826, at Pittsford, Monroe County, N. Y. His father, who was descended from one of the earliest settlers of Massachusetts, was Deacon Erastus Williams, a farmer, formerly of Stockbridge, Mass., who located at Pittsford about 1822. His mother's maiden name was Elizabeth Lumley, a native of Wales. His father was a Captain of a volunteer company from Stockbridge in the War of 1812.

The subject of this sketch was educated in the common schools of the State of New York, and in the High Schools in existence at that time in Pittsford. His early occupation was that of farming and teaching winter schools. In 1850 he commenced the study of law in Rochester, N. Y., and in 1851 graduated from an institution then known as the "State and National Law School," located at Ballston Spa, of which institution at that time Chancellor Wallworth was President of the Board of Trustees. In the spring of 1852, he became a partner in the law firm in which he was a student, and remained with that firm two years. In January, 1855, he removed to Allegan, Mich., where he still remains, engaged in the practice of law, which has been his principal occupation since that time. In 1856 he was elected Judge of Probate of Allegan County and was again re-elected in 1860. In August, 1862, he enlisted as a private in Company B, Nineteenth Michigan Infantry, of which he was elected First Lieutenant. Before reaching the rendezvous of the regiment he was ordered to bring a company to Detroit, where, as Company I, it was attached to the Fifth Michigan Cavalry. In 1863 he resigned on account of physical disability, caused by serious illness. In 1864, as Commander in Camp he organized the Twenty-eighth Michigan Infantry, of which he was in command until the regiment left for the front, when he was appointed by the Governor to take the vote of that regiment and other Michigan soldiers, at Louisville, Ky. He was also appointed a member of the Board of Visitors of the University of Michigan.

In 1866 he was elected by the Republicans as Senator for the Allegan District. In the Senate he was Chairman of the Committee of Public Instruction and a member of the Railroad and Judiciary Committees. At that time there was a very earnest effort made by the friends of education for putting the Agricultural College on a basis that would properly represent the State of Michigan. The institution was located three miles from Lansing, without any adequate dormitory provision for the students. He was the champion of the cause in behalf of suitable accommodations for students at the college, and a bill passed the Senate for that purpose, but failed in the House, owing to the prejudice then existing on the part of the farmers against that institution. In the spring of 1867, he was elected a member of the State Constitutional Convention, and served in that body as Chairman of the Committee on Miscellaneous Provisions, and was also a member of the Committee on Judiciary. As a member of the latter committee he submitted a proposition for a

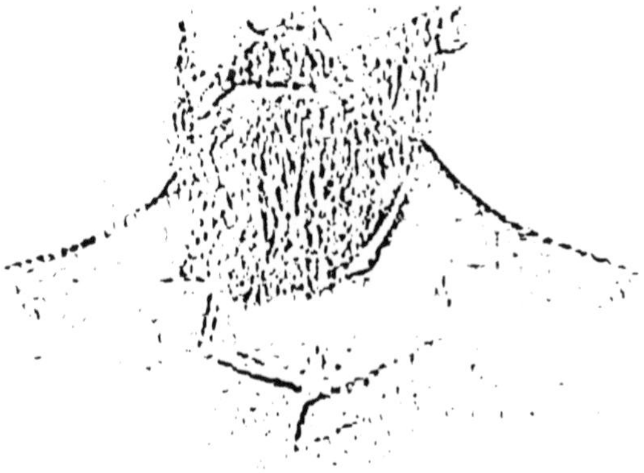

Truly Yours

W. B. Williams

division of the state into judicial circuits for the purpose of providing three judges for each circuit, who should alternate with one another in holding terms of court, and also gave an opportunity for providing by legislation for courts en banc, which would relieve the Supreme Court of a very large amount of business, and at very little expense. After some slight changes of the scheme as submitted by Mr. Williams it was adopted by the committee and became a part of the ill-fated Constitution of 1867. In 1868, he was re-elected a member of the State Senate and served in that body as President pro tem, and Chairman of the Judiciary Committee. As a member of this committee he was called upon to act upon the revision of the tax laws of the state, and among other things secured the taxation of shares of National Bank stock, which before that time had escaped the burden.

An extra session of the Legislature was called in 1870, to provide by Constitutional Amendment for some means of paying railroad aid bonds that had been issued by municipalities to the companies to aid in the construction of railroads, the law of 1869 having been decided unconstitutional. After a number of propositions had been proposed and rejected, Mr. Williams submitted a resolution instructing the Judiciary and Railroad Committees jointly to prepare and submit an article to be entitled "Article 19a" of the Constitution, which finally passed both Houses of the Legislature, was adopted by the people, and now stands as part of the constitution.

In 1868 Mr. Williams was a delegate to the National Convention at Chicago, and in 1872 he was appointed a member of what is now known as the "State Board of Corrections and Charities," a position which he held about two years.

In consequence of the death of Congressman Foster, Mr. Williams was elected to Congress by the Republicans of the Fifth District, and served two terms, expiring on the 4th of March, 1877. In the Forty-third Congress he was a member of the Committee on Pacific Railroads. The most important legislation in that congress with which he was connected particularly was to provide for the collection from these roads aided by the government of what is known as the "Five per cent. of the gross earnings of the companies." He prepared a bill for that purpose, discovering that this amount never had been paid, although provided for in the Charter. The bill became a law and was litigated through the Supreme Court of the United States and sustained, and brought in a large amount of revenue to apply on the sinking fund against the indebtedness of the railroads. Another matter on which he takes some pride was an amendment to a bill that had been handed to him from the Indian Department, providing for the homesteading of what were known as "The Indian Treaty Lands." These were lands that were set apart by treaty in 1855, at the same time as the grant of lands to the State of Michigan for railroad purposes. The Northern part of the lower peninsula had been retarded in its growth, and the treaty of 1855 in regard to the Indians, tied up large tracts of lands in the Northern portion of the Lower Peninsula from settlement. An act had been passed providing for the setting apart of the Indian lands to the Indians in severalty by patents from the Government. but it was found necessary to amend it to provide for certain Indians who had been omitted. and then providing for the sale of the lands at public auction. The bill was prepared at the Department at Mr. Williams' request. He attached a rider to it, giving the homesteaders the first chance over the speculators for one year, which was extended by subsequent legislation. The bill passed, although it was strenuously fought for over a year by speculators. This and an act of which Mr. Williams had secured the passage when he was in the State Senate, settling disputes in reference to Grand Rapids & Indiana Railroad lands, and securing the extension of that road northward from Grand Rapids, aided very largely in the rapid settlement of the Northern portion of the Lower Peninsula.

In May, 1877, Mr. Williams was appointed Commissioner of Railroads of the State of Michigan, and held that office for about six years. He has been a Republican since 1855. Prior to that time he was a Whig, and cast his first ballot for General Scott for President. He is not now connected with any companies or large properties; is not a member of any society except the G. A. R.; is a member of the Protestant Episcopal Church and has been a member of the Vestry of the local Church of Allegan since 1858. He is also a member of the Board of Trustees of the Ackley Institute, located at Grand Haven, being a church school for young ladies, and has been one of the trustees since the organization of the institution.

He was married to Marrietta L. Osborne, in Rochester, N. Y., in September, 1853. She was a niece of Nehemiah Osborne, the builder of the City Hall in Detroit and the State Capitol in Lansing. He has five children: Marion L., now Mrs. Frank L. Rudd, of Detroit; William B. Williams, Jr., of Manitoba; Ella, now Mrs. T. S. Updyke, of Allegan; Theodore O. Williams, of Grand Rapids, and Frank H. Williams, of Allegan.

GENERAL WILLIAM HERBERT WITHINGTON, of Jackson, who rendered to the country distinguished military service, and who has since had an active political and business career in Michigan, was born in Dorchester, Mass., February 1st, 1835. The family are descended from Henry Withington, who came from England in 1635, with Rev. Richard Mather, the first Minister of Dorchester, in whose church Henry Withington was ruling Elder. The subject of the present sketch was the eighth in direct descent from Henry. His father was Rev. William Withington, and his mother's maiden name was Elizabeth W. Ford, also of Dorchester, Mass. That the family were vigorous and sturdy in body, as well as in intellect and character, is shown by the fact that Rev. William Withington lived to be

W. H. Withington

ninety-four years of age, his sister one hundred, while his brother, Dr. Leonard Withington, of Newburyport, Mass., died at the age of ninety-six. The family abounded in professional men, and as was common with the best New England families, placed a high value upon a liberal education.

William H. Withington was educated at the Boston public schools and at Phillips' Andover Academy. His father was a scholar, retiring and unworldly in character, and the home responsibilities were thrust to a large extent upon the young man, turning him toward business channels. On leaving the academy, he gave his attention to practical affairs, first entering a leather store in Boston as a salesman. He soon became bookkeeper for the North Wayne Scythe Company, and in a short time was given full charge of the details of their extensive business. Some idea of his capacity, even at this early age, may be inferred from the fact that when but nineteen years of age we find his employers entrusting him with important missions to New York, Baltimore, Philadelphia and other points at which they had large patronage. While in this connection the young man came into acquaintance with the large agricultural implement manufacturing concern of Pinney & Lamson, who had a contract for prison labor at Jackson, Mich. The death of Mr. Lamson had left the whole control in the hands of Mr. Pinney, who desired Mr. Withington to go to Jackson and give his services towards the righting of a state of affairs that certainly needed straightening out. The engagement was made, and in 1857, when but twenty-two years of age, the young man went to Jackson and assumed graver responsibilities than any he had yet borne. He found matters in chaos. The affairs were nominally in the hands of a son of Mr. Pinney's, but in reality had no head and no management. The bookkeeper had left some months before, and the office was in charge of a traveling man. There was full scope for the energy, enterprise and new life that had been sent to the rescue. It was not long before the effect was seen and felt all through the concern. The business was altogether new to the young bookkeeper from the East, and there was no one on hand to give him direction or even initiation in his duties. The one surviving partner, Mr. Pinney, lived in Columbus, Ohio, and was not in Jackson when Mr. Withington arrived. His first effort was to bring the books up from their arrears and entanglement. The correspondence, the oversight of sales, the purchase of material for manufacture and shop supplies, the control of foremen, the collections and payments, in short all the office work of a manufacturing business, employing one hundred and twenty-five workmen and six traveling salesmen, dropped at once on his young and inexperienced shoulders.

The financial panic of October, 1857, came on in its full force, and, unable to stand before the storm, Mr. Pinney committed suicide, and the burden that he had refused longer to bear had to be taken up by another. The labors that fell upon Mr. Withington were greater than ever. It was directed in Mr. Pinney's will that the business should be continued until the termination of the contracts with the State then in force. An administrator, de bonis non, with the will annexed, was appointed. This official was from Connecticut, unfamiliar with the business, and the chief labor, therefore, remained where it had been previously laid. A year after the death of Mr. Pinney the business was offered for sale, and was promptly purchased by the newly organized firm of Sprague, Withington & Co., composed of men already in the employ of the old company. The company soon took a higher place in the manufacturing world, and has continued to the present day, the firm name for many years past having been Withington, Cooley & Co. Their trade is not only co-extensive with this country, but extends to Australia and South America and through Europe.

But this company has not furnished the only field for General Withington's business activities. The extent of his operations, and the estimate put by his business associates on his administrative ability are shown by the fact that he has been chosen President of the following corporations in addition to the one already mentioned. The Union Bank, Grand River Valley Railroad Company and the Jackson Vehicle Company, all of Jackson, Mich.; the Withington Handle Co., Fort Wayne and Huntington, Ind.; Geneva Tool Co., Geneva, Ohio; Oneida Farm Tool Co., Utica, N. Y.; National Snath Co., Erie, Penn., and the Steel Goods Association, New York, N. Y. He has also been since 1875 an owner and Director in the Iowa Farming Tool Co., of Fort Madison, Iowa.

Mr. Withington's business enterprises were broken into at the opening of the war. He had previously aided in the organization of the Jackson Greys, and the day before Governor Blair's call for volunteers was issued, April 16th, 1861, Captain Withington had called a special meeting of the Greys for this important crisis. The enlistments made included a large portion of the company, which became Company B, First Michigan Infantry, with Mr. Withington as Captain. It was in the first battle of Bull Run, where Captain Withington was taken prisoner, but not until he had performed a service for which he was given one of the Congressional "medals of honor." This in its terms, was "for most distinguished gallantry in voluntarily remaining on the field, under heavy fire, to aid and succor your superior officer in the battle of Bull Run, Va., July 21st, 1861." It was some time after the battle before Captain Withington's whereabouts became known, and he was given up for dead, till three weeks afterwards his wife was informed by a dispatch from a comrade that he was a prisoner, and on his way to Richmond. He was exchanged January 30th, 1862, was made Colonel of the Seventeenth Infantry, August 11th, 1862, and continued in the service till March 21st, 1863. March 13th, 1865, he was breveted Brigadier General U. S. Volunteers, "for conspicuous gallantry at the Battle of South Mountain, Md., September 14th, 1862."

General Withington has been a Republican since the organization of the party, casting his first Presidential vote for Lincoln. In addition to local positions of trust he was a member of the House in the Legislature, session of 1873, and the special session of 1874, and State Senator, session of 1891. The most important single piece of legislation with which he was intimately associated was the law passed by the Legislature of 1873, under which the State troops, now the National Guard, were organized. He drafted this bill, and it was largely through his intelligent and persistent advocacy that it passed. To all matters of general legislation he gave careful attention, and in the discussion of many of them he took part, both in the regular sessions of 1873 and 1891, and the Constitutional revision session of 1874. Gen. Withington has often attended State Conventions as a delegate, and was also delegate to the National Conventions of 1876 and 1892. He has done his share of political committee work in Jackson City, and County, and was for four years a member of the State Central Committee. He has also served the State as a member of the Board of Trustees of the Michigan Asylum for the Insane at Kalamazoo, and of the Board of Managers of the Soldiers' Home at Grand Rapids.

General Withington's society affiliations have generally been military or political. He is a member of the Military Order of the Loyal Legion, of which he has been Department Commander; the G. A. R.; Society of the Army of the Potomac; Michigan Club, Detroit Club and others. He is one of the prominent laymen in the Episcopal Church of Michigan. He was married in 1859 to Miss Julia C. Beebe, daughter of Hon. Joseph E. Beebe, of Michigan. Six children were born to them, of whom three are living, Kate W., Philip H. and Winthrop.

EDWARD TALCOTT WOODRUFF, who, at about thirty years of age, came into the rank of Republican newspaper men, was born in Olean, N. Y., June 30th, 1853. His father was Rev. Jonathan Alden Woodruff, a Presbyterian clergyman, who was largely influential in forming the early history of Lapeer County, one who had been prominent in educational circles and at the head of various institutions in the East, earlier in life. His mother was Aurelia Talcott Woodruff, daughter of Mr. and Mrs. Erastus Talcott, sturdy New England Congregationalists.

Young Woodruff's education was academic, principally at Lapeer and Flint. His first occupations were assisting as farm hand, working in the mills and lumber woods, running a circular saw as head sawyer, foreman in lumber mills, teaching school winters and clerkship in office lines. His early struggles were those of the pioneer in the woods of Michigan, with privations that he cannot now look back upon except with feelings of thankfulness that they were survived, and that he and his family are not called upon to pass through the same at this time. The turning point of his life was the mangling of his hand in a large circular saw, which he was adjusting while same was in motion, in 1873. He came out of it with only the loss of a finger, but before being again able to do manual labor, he secured an office position, his right hand being uninjured, and from that on his business has been in the line of office work. The death of both his parents about the time he attained his majority, left him with some debts of his father's, which he considered it a matter of honor to pay, and he discharged every one of them, although it took a number of years for him to accomplish the cancellation of these obligations.

In 1880 Mr. Woodruff was elected Register of Deeds for Lapeer County, and in 1885 he purchased The Lapeer Clarion, of which he has been editor and publisher ever since. In this business he has been satisfactorily successful, the Clarion being today one of the best properties of its kind in the State. It has steadily improved in standing and in financial returns ever since he became its owner.

Mr. Woodruff cannot remember when he was not a Republican. He first voted in 1874, but his first Presidential vote was in 1880, for Garfield. He has the satisfaction of knowing that, as publisher of the Republican paper of the County, he has been enabled to do as much toward promoting the harmony and interests of the party in his locality, as any one man, at least. Certainly there are few men in the State who have shown greater devotion to the party than Mr. Woodruff did, when two years ago, in the interest of party harmony, he withdrew his candidacy for the Lapeer Postoffice. He has never held any office except Register of Deeds, to which he was elected in 1880, and again in 1882. He has declined several overtures looking toward official positions, believing that he could do better work for himself and the party, by devoting himself mainly to the newspaper end of political campaigns. He has, however, been delegate and Chairman of the delegation at a number of State and Congressional Conventions. He belongs to several clubs and societies, of which the Knights of Pythias is perhaps the most prominent. He was married to Lena M. Van Wormer, of Phelps, N. Y., October 2d, 1873, and they have two children, Blanche A. and Charles H.

CHARLES AUGUSTUS WRIGHT, of Hancock, Mich., was born at Hartford, Conn., December 4th, 1854. His father was Joseph Augustus Wright, and his mother Emily S. Barker, daughter of Samuel Woodbury Barker, of Roxbury, Mass. His father was Treasurer of one of the large insurance companies of Hartford, and afterwards continued the insurance business at Chicago, where he died in 1862. His ancestors on both sides originally came from England, and were among the early settlers of the North American colonies. On the father's side they are traced directly back to Thomas Wright, who lived in Wethersfield, Conn., in 1640, and was a Deputy to the

C. A. Wright.

General Court in 1643. The family afterwards moved to Glastonbury, near Hartford, and lineal descendants have ever since continued to occupy the "old brick homestead" on the main street of that Village, where the house now in existence was built in the early part of the nineteenth century by Joseph Wright, grandfather of Charles A. Wright, who was a graduate of Yale College, and who married Sarah Lockwood, daughter of Rev. William Lockwood, a friend of General Washington and at one time his chaplain during the Revolutionary War, and who was also a member of the celebrated patriotic society, the "Cincinnati."

Charles A. Wright received his early education principally in the schools of Hartford, Conn., though it was frequently interrupted, owing to his mother having married, the second time, an officer in the Army of the United States, Captain J. W. Keller, who was transferred from post to post, and whose wife and her only son and daughter generally accompanied him. Charles A. Wright, in 1873, at the age of eighteen, came west, and accepted a position in the leading banking office of E. H. Towar & Co., at Hancock. A year later this firm organized the First National Bank at Hancock, of which Mr. Wright was at once appointed Teller, and held that position till 1880, when he accepted the office of Secretary and Treasurer of the Mineral Range Railroad. In 1885 he was made General Manager of that company, and in 1887 he was also made General Manager of the Hancock & Calumet Railroad, which positions he continued to hold until October, 1893, when he resigned, intending to enter the practice of law. He was admitted to the bar in April, 1894, and was engaged in active practice until March, 1899, when he became General Manager of the Copper Range Railroad, of which he was the chief promoter. After the completion of this road, from Range Junction to Houghton, Mich., Mr. Wright resigned in March, 1900, to give his attention to other affairs in which he is interested. In 1890 he organized the Superior Savings Bank of Hancock, and in 1896 the State Savings Bank of Laurium, and since their organization has been President of both institutions. He has just completed in Hancock one of the finest office buildings in the Upper Peninsula, known as the "Wright Building," in which are located the offices of the Superior Savings Bank, which for elegance and convenience of appointments, are probably without an equal in Michigan, outside of Detroit. Mr. Wright is President of the Fuel & Supply Co., of Hancock, Vice-President of the Peninsula Electric Light and Power Co., which does the lighting for Houghton County, and a Director in various other corporations.

Mr. Wright has borne an important part in the industrial and business development of the copper mining district of Northern Michigan, and was mainly instrumental in the construction of the Mineral Range Railroad bridge across Portage Lake, between Hancock and Houghton, in 1885, giving the first railroad outlet for the industries and population North of Portage Lake, including the great Calumet and Hecla, Tamarack, Quincy and other famous copper mines; and also in the construction of the Copper Range Railroad in 1899, opening the great South range between Houghton and Ontonagon, where the mineral resources promise to rival in wealth those of the North side of Portage Lake, judging from the rich openings at the Champion, Tri-Mountain and other mines in this territory.

Mr. Wright has always been an active and consistent Republican. He has been for four terms, Chairman of the Houghton County Republican Committee, and is at present serving his second term as member of the State Central Committee. He entered the field as a candidate for Congress in the Twelfth District in the spring of 1900 and had practical control of the Houghton County Convention which was to choose delegates to the Congressional Convention, but in the interest of harmony in County politics, generously withdrew in favor of Carlos D. Shelden, also of Houghton, who desired a re-election. Mr. Wright is a member of Empire State Society of Sons of the American Revolution, New York City; also a member of Oniganning Yacht Club of Houghton, Mich., and Portage Lake Club of Hancock, Mich. He was married in September, 1876, to Lillian Gregory Taylor, daughter of the late Rev. Barton S. Taylor, of Albion, Mich., by whom he has four children: Charles A. Wright, Jr., age 21; Edith Emily Wright, age 18; Rowland Gregory Wright, age 12, and Gerald Lockwood Wright, age 10.

CHARLES WRIGHT, Collector of Internal Revenue for the First District of Michigan, was born in Wolcott, Wayne County, N. Y., in the winter of 1850. His father was Rev. Thomas Wright, a Presbyterian clergyman, and his mother was Ruth Smith Wright. The family came originally from Wrightsbridge, England, in 1642, and settled at Northampton, Mass., at which place Deacon John Wright, one of Charles' great grandfathers, was killed by Indians while with his townsmen he was defending Northampton. Judge Solomon Wright, of Pownal, Vt., was also his great grandfather. Charles Wright, a famous lawyer of his time, was grandfather of the present Charles Wright, who is also great grandson of Moses Robinson, first Governor and first United States Senator from Vermont.

The subject of this sketch was educated at the Normal School, Ypsilanti, Michigan University and Columbian College, New York City. He commenced the study of chemistry at Ann Arbor and has always been a student in that line. The first money he ever made was by organizing a State base ball tournament, but he has always been in the one business of pharmaceutical chemistry. His first work in this line was as prescription clerk, and later an assayer in a Western assay office. Of late years he has been engaged in the manufacture of chemicals and pharmaceutical goods, which he commenced in 1882. He is head of the manufacturing house of Charles

Wright & Co., and is also interested in several tracts of land out North Woodward avenue.

Mr. Wright has been a Republican all his life and cast his first Presidential vote for Hayes. He was first elected a member of the Republican State Central Committee in 1886, and was re-elected four times. He was six times elected Treasurer of that committee, serving in all twelve years. A high mark of appreciation of his services in this connection is the fact that he was three times elected Treasurer when he was not a member of the Committee, though it is very unusual for the committee to go outside its membership for the appointment of its fiscal officer. Mr. Wright was always familiar with the needs of the committee and the drift of the campaign, had the entire confidence of the wealthy members of the party, and was singularly successful in raising campaign funds. He was elected estimator from the Second Ward two terms in the later eighties; was elected member of the Board of Aldermen in 1891, and was re-elected in 1893, and did a good deal toward securing legislation favorable to the development of the City parks and Boulevard. He was appointed Collector of Internal Revenue for the First District of Michigan by President McKinley and assumed the duties of that office in February, 1898.

Mr. Wright is a member of the Detroit Club, Detroit Athletic Club, Detroit Boat Club, Country Club, Knights Templar; Knights of Pythias and Chi Phi College Fraternity. He was married in Brooklyn, N. Y., in 1880, to Miss Louise Kemlo, and has three children, Thomas K. Wright, Charles Wright, Jr., and Louise Helen Wright.

H. OLIN YOUNG, prominent as an attorney and Republican in the Upper Peninsula, is the son of Horace C. Young and Laura P. Walker, both of English descent. His mother's family is a very large one, embracing nearly all the Walkers in this country. Her mother was one of the Olin family of Vermont, a daughter of Gideon Olin, who was a member of the Committee of Safety during the Revolutionary War, and the first State Treasurer of Vermont. Two brothers, John Olin and Abram B. Olin, were each members of Congress, and Judges of the Supreme Court of Vermont. A cousin, Stephen Olin, was quite prominent as a college President and Bishop of the M. E. Church. Horace C. Young, who was a contractor, builder and farmer, removed soon after his marriage, to New Albion, Cattaraugus County, N. Y., where H. Olin Young, the youngest of six children, was born, August 4th, 1850. He lived the ordinary life of a country boy, working on the farm and attending district school. Between his fourteenth and twentieth years he attended school at Chamberlain Institute six terms, alternating this schooling with work upon the farm and teaching district school. The greater part of his real education, however, was obtained outside the schoolroom. His father and mother were people of considerable force of character and enquiring minds. Both were deeply interested in public affairs and entertained a cordial hatred of slavery. The father served in both branches of the State Legislature, and was a strong personal friend and warm supporter of Governor Seward. His little library contained more books than were commonly found in farmer's houses, and among them were such standard works as Plutarch's Lives, Shakespeare, Milton and Pope. The New York Tribune was always the family newspaper. Among these surroundings the subject of this sketch acquired the habit of reading and study and delight therein which has been his constant and steady friend through life. All public questions, and especially the burning subject of slavery were discussed in the family conclave, and he early acquired very positive, if not well-founded opinions on such matters, among which a hatred of slavery and a deep-seated distrust of the Democratic party were the most prominent. It was arranged that he should take a college course in Cornell University, but the asthma, his constant enemy in those days, became so much worse as to render the fulfillment of this plan impossible, and he went West seeking for a more favorable climate. This he found at Ishpeming, Mich., at which place he arrived on April 10th, 1872, and soon after entered the employment of the Lake Superior Iron Company. That fall he obtained a school and taught for one year, and in the fall of 1873 opened a store at the Kloman mine, in Republic, Mich. The mine proving unprofitable, was closed down in the winter of 1875-6, whereupon he disposed of the remains of his stock, and returned to Ishpeming. On March 20th of that year, he was married to Mary J. Marsh, of Randolph, N. Y. He accepted a position as bookkeeper, and continued in that employment till 1878, when he was elected to the Lower House of the Legislature. He warmly supported the election of Zachariah Chandler to the United States Senate, seconding his nomination on behalf of the Upper Peninsula, strongly opposed the enactment of a stringent usury law, but devoted himself mainly to the interests of his own section of the State, assisting the passage of legislation in aid of the construction of the railroad from the Straits of Mackinac to Marquette. In 1880 he was appointed Supervisor of Census for the Fourth District of Michigan; in the meantime he had been appointed Assessor of the City of Ishpeming, an office he held for nine years and in his absence at Lansing was elected a Justice of the Peace. On his return from the session of the Legislature he became a silent partner in a small mercantile establishment and soon afterwards engaged in a mining venture which proved reasonably successful.

He began the study of law about 1878 and in 1882 was admitted to the bar. Soon afterwards he formed a law partnership with George Hayden, which continued till 1898. He is still engaged in the practice of his profession.

In 1886 Mr. Young was elected Prosecuting Attorney of Marquette County and held that office for five terms. A Republican

H O Young

always, his first political speech was made in 1868, when he was but eighteen years old and his first vote was cast for General Grant in 1872. Since that time he has always taken an active part in the politics of his locality and State; was a warm supporter of Jay A. Hubbell, Seth C. Moffatt and S. M. Stephenson in each of the Conventions in which they were nominated for Congress; has attended nearly all the State Conventions of the Republican party held in Michigan since 1876, and has taken an active part in all the political campaigns, speaking frequently in the different counties of the Upper Peninsula. He was for many years Chairman of the Republican City Committee of Ishpeming, for two years Chairman of the County Committee of Marquette County, and for ten years was a member of the Republican State Central Committee. He has always belonged to that wing of the party which is known as stalwart.

RALPH LANE POLK, the best known man in the country in the publication of directories and gazetteers, was born in Bellefontaine, Logan County, O., September 12, 1849. His father, Rev. David Polk, was a prominent Presbyterian minister, a graduate of Jefferson College and of Princeton Theological Seminary. He was born in Baltimore in 1809, and his ancestors removed from Scotland into the North of Ireland and from there emigrated to the United States, and settled in Maryland in 1668.

All Mr. Polk's father's relatives were Scotch, while his mother was English, a native of Trenton, N. J. He received a common school education supplemented by a course in Pennington Seminary. He worked on a farm, after that was clerk in a grocery store in Trenton then had charge of an ice business for Patrick O'Neil, in Trenton. He diversified business by military service, for at the age of fifteen he enlisted in Company G, Fortieth N. Y. Volunteers, as a musician, remained in the service seven months, and was mustered out at Hall's Hill, Va., in August, 1865.

Mr. Polk was brought up a Democrat, all of his relatives being of that faith except his brother and himself, who during their war experience became Republicans, and have remained so ever since.

In 1870 Mr. Polk struck the line of business to which he has since shown himself to be so admirably adapted. He organized the firm of R. L. Polk & Co., of Detroit, which was incorporated in 1885, and which has become known the country over, for the publication of State gazetteers and City and County directories. Of the former about thirty, in as many different States and Territories, have been published within the last three years, while more than that number of City directories have been published within the same period.

Mr. Polk is President of the Association of American Directory Publishers, and is a member of the following social, business and military organizations: Fellowcraft Club, Detroit; Detroit Fishing and

Hunting Association; Chamber of Commerce, Detroit; Merchants and Manufacturers' Exchange, Detroit; National Union, A. O. U. W., Royal Arcanum; Masonic bodies, as follows: Corinthian Lodge, Peninsular Chapter, Detroit Commandery, Michigan Consistory and Moslem Temple; youngest member Detroit Post No. 384, G. A. R.

He was married to Amelia Hopkins in 1877, and their only child is Ralph Lane Polk, Jr., born September 10th, 1882, now attending Shattuck Military School, Faribault, Minn.

## IV.

## REPUBLICAN NEWSPAPER ASSOCIATION.

The Organization of Michigan Republican Newspapers Into a State Body—Useful Work of the Organization—It Gives Unity of Purpose and Promotes Efficiency in Work—An Outline of Its Plans and Purposes—A Brief Sketch of Its History—The Annual Banquets—List of Officers From the Start.

A general recognition of the work of the old Whig and Free Democratic newspapers of the State in bringing about the organization of the Republican party in Michigan has been given in one of the earlier chapters of this book. During the three decades following that organization the work of the Republican press of Michigan was probably not excelled by that of the press of any other State in the West, and during a portion of that time at least, there was a more or less effective organization of Michigan's Republican newspapers, but into its records it is not the province of this chapter to explore. It is, however, only within the last decade that, in the organization of the Michigan Republican Newspaper Association, the Republican press of the State has reached the highest degree of efficiency to which it has yet attained in aiding the work of the party, and it is with this organization that the present chapter has to do.

The statement that the Republican press has reached its highest degree of efficiency in aiding the party in Michigan only in the last decade may be made in perfect fairness to those editors who were staunch supporters of the principles of the party long before the present organization began its career. This organization was the result of the conviction on the part of those very men that something better could be done by the Republican press of the State through such an organization. The men who alone and unaided would have done the most for their party were the first to realize that the press would do its best only if from center to circumference of its territory, the Republican editors of Michigan could feel that they were receiving the sympathy and were being enabled to avail themselves of the experiences of their fellow workers, and that only as they united in demanding some sort of uniform recognition of their services could they ever expect to make those services all that they might become.

The reasons for the organization of the Michigan Republican Newspaper Association were therefore of the most practical sort. On the one hand it was realized by those Republican editors who were also party leaders that the party was not getting the service from the Republican papers of the State which it needed, or which the ability of their editors and the influence which all acknowledged that the papers possessed in other lines would warrant it in expecting. On the other hand it was realized that in many cases the party was receiving loyal and efficient service, both in season and out, from journals which were ably edited by men bearing the brunt of the political labor in their cities and counties and districts—men who were doing and sacrificing much for the party, but who were given scarce anything of the recognition of which they were deserving. The two-fold motive for the organization then becomes apparent. The effort was to be made to so develop and bring out the latent power of the Republican press of the State that its efficiency in aiding the Republican party should be vastly increased—that it should be enabled to do much more effective work in the spreading of information and educating the people concerning the vital principles of the Republican party. And as one means to this end the new Association was to do all in its power to secure the assistance of the Republican State and County Committees in making the individual Republican papers of the State as strong as possible.

Although the securing of the co-operation and assistance of the party organization has just been given as a part of a two-fold object, it can readily be seen that it is but a necessary step in the process of carrying out the first named object of making the Republican press of the State of greater value to the party, for to be of the highest usefulness each of the papers making up the Republican press must be developed to the highest possible state of efficiency. That must necessarily mean that each must receive in some measure at least credit and compensation for the exertions that it puts forth. Any organism that works must be fed, and if a certain work is expected from it, anything that tends to build up its component parts tends to make its work just so much the more effective. All within certain bounds that goes into the organism is found again in the work. On the other hand if the benefits of the work are kept entirely away from the organism which performs a large part of it, both it and the work must suffer. So in the case of the Republican press of Michigan it was felt that in getting the co-operation of the party organization the party would receive the benefit in the end. It was realized that the increased value of the press to the party was the object pre-eminently for which the Association should work. The strengthening of the individual papers and consequent benefiting of the editors of the same would naturally follow as the most effective means to that end. Such then were the objects which in the minds of those who were seeking its organization should be the aims of the Michigan Republican Newspaper Association.

A preliminary meeting was held in Lansing in January, 1891. Hon. Perry F. Powers, of the Cadillac News and Express, was made Temporary President, and Mr. M. L. Cook, of the Hastings Banner, Temporary Secretary. Then on the 27th of March, 1891, another meeting was held in the parlors of the Morton House in Grand Rapids and the Michigan Republican Newspaper Association was organized with Hon. Perry F. Powers as its first President, Mr. F. T. Ward, of the Allegan Journal, as its Vice-President, and Mr. M. L. Cook as its Secretary and Treasurer. An Executive Committee of one Republican editor from each Congressional District, except the First and Eleventh, was chosen at the same meeting, and eight other Republican editors paid the membership fee and were also enrolled as members of the Association. By the provisions of the constitution there adopted the membership was limited to editors and publishers of Republican papers in Michigan, but with the added provision that no representative of any paper that did not at all times support Republican principles and Republican candidates should be eligible to membership. The paper which was Republican only during the continuance of a campaign, and perhaps then only after being urged into line by some candidate, was not encouraged to join until it had changed its practice. Such a paper was first asked to give loyal and intelligent support all the year round to the party whose principles it espoused. The purposes of the Association were further set out along the line above indicated of stimulating and enthusing the Republican editors of Michigan.

Definite plans were also undertaken at this first meeting for effective co-operation with the State Central Committee and with the District and County Committees, along such practical lines as the securing of the political canvass in each County of the State, the securing of lists of possible Republican voters who did not take any Republican paper, but who might be influenced by such papers to support the party, and finally the placing of party papers in the hands of such voters. Considerable encouragement was given the members of the Association by prominent Republicans outside of newspaper circles. At a meeting held in Grand Rapids in October of the same year the President and Secretary of the Association were authorized to co-operate with the officers of the State League of Republican Clubs in whatever work they might deem to be for the best interests of the party. The Secretary of the State Central Committee was also made a member of this joint committee. Plans were adopted for the extending of the circulation of Republican papers. It may be mentioned incidentally that during the next year their circulation was extended in a measure which has been hard to exceed in the years since.

The feature of the work of the Association which has attracted the greatest amount of attention from the public has naturally been its annual meetings. At these times there have been gathered together the best brains which the Michigan press affords, and at some of the assemblages there have been as notable gatherings of statesmen and orators of National fame as have ever been seen and heard at the banquets of the Michigan Club itself or any other political organization in the country. Particularly has this been true of the banquets which have usually attended these meetings. At their business sessions many interesting papers have been read, many valuable points brought out in earnest discussion, but there is little that can be added about them at this time which has not already been told in telling of the reasons which led to the organization of the Association and of its purposes and plans. It was always the same theme; the betterment of the individual newspaper, that it might be of greater service to the party; the strengthening of the bonds between the two. These were the subjects—the objects for which the Association had its creation and still has its existence—which occupied the attention of the editors when they sat behind closed doors, and the public, if it knew of their presence at all, was probably but slightly curious even to know what the meaning of the meeting was. It was at the banquets that the public was given the chance to see the men of the pen and pencil, the scissors and paste, the men at whose dictation the typewriters and the types themselves spoke to it from week to week. It was at the banquets, too, that the editors were, perhaps, after all, best satisfied to see and be seen, for then the men who, for perhaps all their lives, had been held up to public admiration by the papers of the State had a clear opportunity to even old scores by telling the newspaper men, when they could not well reply, what noble, self-sacrificing heroes they really were, and to tell it before the public which both the newspaper man and the statesman served, but a public which sometimes seemed to forget the newspaper man who made the statesman long before the public ceased singing the praises of the statesman he had made. The annual meetings of the Michigan Republican Newspaper Association were always enjoyable affairs, and the banquets were perhaps the most enjoyable parts of all the proceedings of their sessions. Lansing, Owosso, Hastings, Jackson, Port Huron, Alma, Detroit, Owosso again, Charlevoix and Kalamazoo have in turn entertained the Republican editors of the State, and each place acquitted itself well of the task. Many are the Republican newspaper men who have bright spots in their memories for these cities of the State which have opened their hearts and doors to them for their annual meetings. And who can say that the banquets themselves have not done their full share in bringing about and extending the influence of the Association by acquainting both the public and the statesmen, servants of the public, with one another and with the members of the Association at the same time and under such propitious circumstances?

The organization has made its influence felt from the very start. It could scarcely have been otherwise, for when men to the number of two hundred or more, the present approximate membership of the Association, and men of the ability which they undeniably represent, unite firmly on one or two sharply outlined purposes as has this organization, it cannot fail to make its influence felt. The Michigan Republican Newspaper Association has in season and out confined its efforts consistently to the objects for which it was organized. Even in the seeming divergence of securing beneficial modifications in the libel law, which it helped bring about, this purpose was kept in mind. It sought to make itself a greater power for good in the Republican party—to make the Republican party stronger by making itself stronger—and it has done both. One of the first attempts in this line was the effort as has already been noted, to place, so far as possible, a Republican local paper in the hands of every Republican or possible Republican voter in the State. While of course such a purpose will always be impossible of complete fulfillment, the matter was taken in hand to such an extent that the circulation of the Republican papers of the State was greatly increased, even during the first year. As an illustration of what was going on all over the State, one county weekly alone sent in over nineteen hundred subscriptions to one of the big Republican City weeklies of the State, subscriptions which had been taken with a corresponding increase in its own subscription list. Michigan is normally Republican anyway, but there can be no doubt in the minds of those who were acquainted with the kind of work done by this Association that the work which it did in the line of extending the circulation of the Republican papers of the State had more than a little to do with the fact that Michigan did not join the general slump to Democracy into which so many States, always counted on for good Republican majorities, fell in 1892. This was in the face of the fact that the Democracy in this State was already in possession of the State government and felt confidently that it had so entrenched itself that its chances for victory were better than before and certainly better here than in some of the States which assisted in giving the lamentable Democratic majority of that year. Just how much of the credit for saving Michigan to the Republican column that year is due to the work of the Michigan Republican Newspaper Association can of course never be told with any exactness, but that it was commented on at the time and that there were many among the Republican workers of the State outside of the newspaper men who credited the Association with having had a large share in making that record, is a matter of history. Since that time the influence of the Association has been felt more and more. A better feeling has been brought about between party managers and the publishers of the party papers, and the closer association and better understanding that have resulted have had, just as had been expected, the result of strengthening the party and the party papers at the same time. The party managers have come to realize more than ever before the assistance which the party papers can be to them and have at the same time learned to be a little more fair in their treatment of them. They have realized to a greater extent than ever before that, after all, the editor of a Republican newspaper is a human being and more than likely a Republican himself—individually and personally, who by the added reason of his editorial position is enabled to do more for the party than they had often been willing to give him credit for. The Association has not attempted to encourage the idea in the minds of its members that they are the only persons entitled to any of the credit or rewards which the party's success means, but it has made the Republican press of the State more influential as a whole, if for no other reason than that it has taught it to regard itself with a better appreciation of its own worth and to exact a corresponding degree of appreciation from others. Its work is not done, but is still going on. The Republican editor in Michigan is today a more important person because of its influence, but he is becoming still more so through the same influence, for he is learning how to make himself more valuable at each successive meeting of the Association. The old time publishers were often as strong editors as those of today—sometimes stronger it would seem. An occasional editor was also a politician. Without losing sight for one moment of the fact that the Republican editor who wishes to have influence politically must still be an editor, the Michigan Republican Newspaper Association has taught some of the Republican editors of the State and is teaching an increasing number that to be of the greatest use to the party they must be politicians as well. And that is one reason why the influence of the Association is still in the ascendancy.

Much of the success which the Michigan Republican Newspaper Association has attained has been due to the officers whom it has chosen to manage its affairs from the time of one annual meeting to another. Of course nothing could have been accomplished by them had they not been loyally supported by Republican editors all over the State, and there are many who may be recalled as being among the most influential advisers of the Association whose names will not be found among the names of its officers given herewith. In most cases they have made their influence felt on the Executive Committee at some time or other and all have assisted in the work in some way. And the best of it is that the greater part of even the best known of these are still young men of whom much better things may be expected than anything that they have done up to the present time.

The officers who have served the Association since its organization, and the Executive Committee for the present year, are as follows:

1891-2—President, Perry F. Powers, Cadillac News and Express; Vice-President, F. T. Ward, Allegan Journal; Secretary and Treasurer, M. L. Cook, Hastings Banner.

1893—President, Perry F. Powers; Vice-President, E. N. Dingley, Kalamazoo Telegraph; Secretary, Thomas T. Bates, Traverse City Herald; Treasurer, E. O. Dewey, Owosso Times.

1894—President, Chase S. Osborn, Sault Ste. Marie News; Vice-President, F. R. Gilson, Benton Harbor Palladium; Secretary, E. O. Dewey, Owosso Times; Treasurer, W. J. Hunsaker, Detroit Journal.

1895—President, F. R. Gilson, Benton Harbor Palladium; Vice-President, H. O. Fifield, Menominee Herald; Secretary, W. R. Cook, Hastings Banner; Treasurer, C. H. Chase, Ithaca Journal.

1896—President, F. R. Gilson, Benton Harbor Palladium; Vice-President, A. S. Coutant, Mt. Pleasant Enterprise; Secretary, W. R. Cook, Hastings Banner; Treasurer, Mrs. T. S. Applegate, Adrian Times.

1897—President, L. A. Sherman, Port Huron Times; Vice-President, E. M. Moore, Battle Creek Journal; Secretary, L. P. Bissell, Charlotte Republican; Treasurer, Mrs. T. S. Applegate, Adrian Times.

1898—President, Robert Smith, State Republican; Vice-President, James O'Donnell, Jackson Citizen; Secretary, E. O. Dewey, Owosso Times; Treasurer, Mrs. T. S. Applegate, Adrian Times.

1899—President—Fred Slocum, Caro Advertiser; Vice-President, J. N. McCall, Ithaca Herald; Secretary, E. O. Dewey, Owosso Times; Treasurer, Mrs. T. S. Applegate, Adrian Times.

1900—President, E. N. Dingley, Kalamazoo Telegraph; Vice-President, E. J. March, Hillsdale Leader; Secretary, D. H. Bower, Buchanan Record; Treasurer, Mrs. T. S. Applegate, Adrian Times.

THE END.

Lightning Source UK Ltd.
Milton Keynes UK
UKHW020123220119
335965UK00008B/353/P

9 780428 190569